Dictionary of Literary Biography

Documentary Series

Yearbooks

Concise Series

Dictionary of Literary Biography® • Volume One Hundred Eighty-Six

Nineteenth-Century American Western Writers

Nineteenth-Century American Western Writers

Edited by
Robert L. Gale
University of Pittsburgh

A Bruccoli Clark Layman Book
Gale Research
Detroit, Washington, D.C., London

Printed in the United States of America

Published simultaneously in the United Kingdom
by Gale Research International Limited
(An affiliated company of Gale Research)

The paper used in this publication meets the minimum requirements
of American National Standard for Information Sciences–Permanence
Paper for Printed Library Materials, ANSI Z39.48-1984. ∞ ™

Library of Congress Cataloging-in-Publication Data

Nineteenth-century American western writers / edited by Robert L. Gale.
    p. cm.–(Dictionary of literary biography; v. 186)
"A Bruccoli Clark Layman book."
Includes bibliographical references and index.
ISBN 0-7876-1682-6 (alk. paper)
1. American literature–West (U.S.)–Bio-bibliography–Dictionaries. 2. American literature–19th
century–Bio-bibliography–Dictionaries. 3. Authors, American–19th century–Biography–Dictionaries.
4. Authors, American–West (U.S.)–Biography–Dictionaries. 5. Western stories–Bio-bibliography–
Dictionaries. 6. West (U.S.)–In literature–Dictionaries. I. Gale, Robert L., 1919– . II. Series.
PS271.N56 1998
813'.08740903–dc21
                                                                97-40333
                                                                CIP

10 9 8 7 6 5 4 3 2 1

To the members of the Western Literature Association

Contents

Plan of the Series

. . . Almost the most prodigious asset of a country, and perhaps its most precious possession, is its native literary product — when that product is fine and noble and enduring.

Mark Twain*

The advisory board, the editors, and the publisher of the *Dictionary of Literary Biography* are joined in endorsing Mark Twain's declaration. The literature of a nation provides an inexhaustible resource of permanent worth. We intend to make literature and its creators better understood and more accessible to students and the reading public, while satisfying the standards of teachers and scholars.

To meet these requirements, *literary biography* has been construed in terms of the author's achievement. The most important thing about a writer is his writing. Accordingly, the entries in *DLB* are career biographies, tracing the development of the author's canon and the evolution of his reputation.

The purpose of *DLB* is not only to provide reliable information in a convenient format but also to place the figures in the larger perspective of literary history and to offer appraisals of their accomplishments by qualified scholars.

The publication plan for *DLB* resulted from two years of preparation. The project was proposed to Bruccoli Clark by Frederick C. Ruffner, president of the Gale Research Company, in November 1975. After specimen entries were prepared and typeset, an advisory board was formed to refine the entry format and develop the series rationale. In meetings held during 1976, the publisher, series editors, and advisory board approved the scheme for a comprehensive biographical dictionary of persons who contributed to North American literature. Editorial work on the first volume began in January 1977, and it was published in 1978. In order to make *DLB* more than a reference tool and to compile volumes that individually have claim to status as literary history, it was decided to organize volumes by

*From an unpublished section of Mark Twain's autobiography, copyright by the Mark Twain Company

topic, period, or genre. Each of these freestanding volumes provides a biographical-bibliographical guide and overview for a particular area of literature. We are convinced that this organization—as opposed to a single alphabet method—constitutes a valuable innovation in the presentation of reference material. The volume plan necessarily requires many decisions for the placement and treatment of authors who might properly be included in two or three volumes. In some instances a major figure will be included in separate volumes, but with different entries emphasizing the aspect of his career appropriate to each volume. Ernest Hemingway, for example, is represented in *American Writers in Paris, 1920-1939* by an entry focusing on his expatriate apprenticeship; he is also in *American Novelists, 1910-1945* with an entry surveying his entire career, as well as in *American Short-Story Writers, 1910-1945, Second Series* with an entry concentrating on his short stories. Each volume includes a cumulative index of the subject authors and articles. Comprehensive indexes to the entire series are planned.

The series has been further augmented by the *DLB Yearbooks* (since 1981) which update published entries and add new entries to keep the *DLB* current with contemporary activity. There have also been *DLB Documentary Series* volumes which provide biographical and critical source materials for figures whose work is judged to have particular interest for students. One of these companion volumes is entirely devoted to Tennessee Williams.

We define literature as the *intellectual commerce of a nation:* not merely as belles lettres but as that ample and complex process by which ideas are generated, shaped, and transmitted. *DLB* entries are not limited to "creative writers" but extend to other figures who in their time and in their way influenced the mind of a people. Thus the series encompasses historians, journalists, publishers, book collectors, and screenwriters. By this means readers of *DLB* may be aided to perceive literature not as cult scripture in the keeping of intellectual high priests but firmly positioned at the center of a nation's life.

DLB includes the major writers appropriate to each volume and those standing in the ranks behind them. Scholarly and critical counsel has been sought in deciding which minor figures to include and how full their entries should be. Wherever possible, useful references are made to figures who do not warrant separate entries.

Each *DLB* volume has an expert volume editor responsible for planning the volume, selecting the figures for inclusion, and assigning the entries. Volume editors are also responsible for preparing, where appropriate, appendices surveying the major periodicals and literary and intellectual movements for their volumes, as well as lists of further readings. Work on the series as a whole is coordinated at the Bruccoli Clark Layman editorial center in Columbia, South Carolina, where the editorial staff is responsible for accuracy and utility of the published volumes.

One feature that distinguishes *DLB* is the illustration policy—its concern with the iconography of literature. Just as an author is influenced by his surroundings, so is the reader's understanding of the author enhanced by a knowledge of his environment. Therefore *DLB* volumes include not only drawings, paintings, and photographs of authors, often depicting them at various stages in their careers, but also illustrations of their families and places where they lived. Title pages are regularly reproduced in facsimile along with dust jackets for modern authors. The dust jackets are a special feature of *DLB* because they often document better than anything else the way in which an author's work was perceived in its own time. Specimens of the writers' manuscripts and letters are included when feasible.

Samuel Johnson rightly decreed that "The chief glory of every people arises from its authors." The purpose of the *Dictionary of Literary Biography* is to compile literary history in the surest way available to us—by accurate and comprehensive treatment of the lives and work of those who contributed to it.

The *DLB* Advisory Board

Introduction

"An image of the West was formed [by the 1890s] in which at least five elements can be ascertained:

  a. Surprise
  b. Plentitude
  c. Vastness
  d. Melancholy
  e. Incongruity. . . ."

–Howard Mumford Jones and Richard Ludwig, *Guide to American Literature and Its Backgrounds since 1890*

"We need wilderness preserved–as much of it as is still left, and as many kinds–because it was the challenge against which our character as a people was formed. The reminder and the reassurance that it is still there is good for our spiritual health even if we never once in ten years set foot in it. It is good for us when we are young, because of the incomparable sanity it can bring briefly, as vacation and rest, into our insane lives. It is important to us when we are old simply because it is there–important, that is, simply as idea."

–Wallace Stegner, *The Sound of Mountain Water*

It is a commonplace in studies of the nineteenth-century American West that when the first white men and women ventured into it, they found a region–or rather, they found several regions–that struck them over and over again as vast and teeming, full of incongruities, and causing alternate invigorating wonder and inexplicable melancholy. Indeed, as Ivan Doig observes in *Winter Brothers: A Season at the Edge of America* (1980), "there are and always have been many Wests, personal as well as geographical." Many of the regions or subregions lying west of the Mississippi River have little in common geographically. The southwestern deserts do not resemble northwestern rainforests of the Pacific; the Great Plains and the Rocky Mountains have little in common. Nevertheless, much of the West receives little rainfall, and even the rain-drenched subregions share with the arid areas a feature essentially western, that is, wide-open spaces.

The human diversity of the West surpasses its geographical variety. Native Americans still live on lands their ancestors first came to thousands of years ago. Since the early seventeenth century immigrants from around the world, especially the American East, have been arriving in the West, at first in small numbers, in waves in the nineteenth century, and in what seems like a flood in our own time. And as Wallace Stegner points out in *The American West as Living Space* (1987), this immense diversity of peoples remains more mobile than people are in the East. Stegner adds that one difficulty in defining western character and culture is that both "are only half-formed and constantly changing"–largely as a result of western mobility. The other difficulties in defining what is western stem from popular and enduring myths as well as from the rich recorded history of the region, beginning in the sixteenth century and achieving epic dimensions in the nineteenth.

Written records of European explorers, pioneers, colonizers, and settlers appeared soon after such men as Francisco Vásquez de Coronado, Hernando de Soto, and Juan de Oñate first penetrated and began to explore and exploit the great Southwest in the mid and late sixteenth century. The seventeenth century witnessed the creation of the first American "frontiers," first in Virginia, New Mexico, and Massachusetts and then along the Great Lakes and down into the Mississippi Valley. During the eighteenth century activity became more intense, notably in areas opened by Daniel Boone and those whom he inspired to follow him and even farther west once the French and Indian War and the American Revolution ended and more Americans could with greater ease cross the Appalachians and push beyond the Mississippi River. With the Louisiana Purchase of 1803 doubling the area of the United States and the completion in 1806 of Lewis and Clark's twenty-eight-month expedition, the western movement early in the nineteenth century, together with its written records, expanded exponentially.

Western writers and their readers were challenged by the quickened pace of events. Maj. Stephen H. Long explored the Southwest (1819–1820); men looking for new lives began following the tortuous and significant Santa Fe Trail (1821); Jedediah Smith began his brave explorations (1822). Fur trappers and traders, mountain men, and fur company agents flourished grandly (into the 1830s and a little later). The fall of the Alamo, with the deaths of Davy Crockett and Jim Bowie among others (1836), occasioned many later fictionalized treatments of that event and its participants. The Oregon Trail soon beckoned (1843). The year 1846, the well-known watershed "year of decision" in American history, quickly followed. It was the year in which California and the lands of the Southwest were seized, and in which the Oregon question was finally resolved. The American victory (1848) in the Mexican War had tremendous ramifications not only territorially but also politically, socially, and culturally. The Gold Rush began (1848-1849), and California soon became a state (1850). The Fort Laramie Treaty brought a false promise of peace with the Plains Indians (1851). The Utah (Mormon) War (1857-1858) included the Mountain Meadows Massacre (1857). Erastus Beadle, the New York publisher, brought out the first of thousands of "dime novels," which collectively led to the circulation of millions of copies sensationalizing the West for voracious readers (1860).

In the last forty years of the century the West was transformed. The Pony Express dramatically linked East and West (1860-1861), as did the telegraph (beginning 1861). The Homestead Act (1862) encouraged western pioneering settlements. Army massacres of Indians occurred (1864-1867 and later). The first transcontinental railroad lines met in Utah (1869). Yellowstone National Park was established (1872)—the first such park in the world. The defeat of George Armstrong Custer and his Seventh U.S. Calvary command (1876), which occasioned uniquely voluminous literary attention, was followed by the poignant retreat of the Nez Perce (1877). Railroads linked the East with southern California and the Pacific Northwest (1882-1883). Geronimo's capture (1886) and the Battle of Wounded Knee (1891) ended armed "uprisings" by Native Americans. The U.S. Census proclaimed that the frontier was closed (1890), and the Sierra Club was founded soon thereafter (1892). The Spanish-American War (1898) lured many cowboy soldiers to action in Cuba and trumpeted the emergence of the United States as an imperialistic power.

The writers documenting and commenting on the conquest of the West in the nineteenth century were legion. Some, notably the much-publicized John Charles Frémont and John Wesley Powell, were primarily explorers, as were the less well-known Josiah Gregg, Lewis Hector Garrard, and George Frederick Ruxton. Others, such as Adolph Bandelier and Charles Fletcher Lummis, were mainly, though not solely, socioscientific and linguistic in their orientation. Naturalists included John Muir and John C. Van Dyke. Many other writers were principally historians, recording what pathfinders not long before them had accomplished; notable among them are Thomas J. Dimsdale, Timothy Flint, Francis Parkman, and Frederick Jackson Turner. Many authors were journalists who branched into other categories, for example, Bret Harte, Alfred Henry Lewis, and Bill Nye.

Many western writers defy easy categorization. Ambrose Bierce, for example, was a soldier, journalist, poet, and fiction writer. Washington Irving, a famous expatriate author, ventured to tour the prairies and undertake western historical scholarship after achieving international fame. Charles Siringo was a cowboy turned detective and much else; Charles Warren Stoddard, a poet, fiction writer, and travel essayist; Theodore Rossevelt, a rancher, hunter, and historian who became president; and the nonpareil Mark Twain. Among the more strictly literary figures may be listed many novelists and story writers—Hamlin Garland, Frank Norris, Charles Sealsfield (Karl Postl), and Owen Wister, among others—and a few poets, such as Edwin Markham and Joaquin Miller. George Catlin and Frederic Remington were famous artists who were also writers of considerable competence. Conspicuous by their absence are dramatists.

Although western cities and towns often sported theaters shortly after the dust settled on their land offices and saloons, plays put on in them were eastern in origin. Most of the dramas that did hold an artistic mirror up to life in the West dropped into obscurity soon after they were staged. Alonzo Delano's *A Live Woman; or, Pike Country Ahead!* (1857), for example, reached print soon after it was staged, but so few copies survived into the twentieth century that it remained virtually unread until it was reprinted in *California Gold-Rush Plays* (1893), edited by Glenn Meredith Loney. Walter Meserve also includes some rediscovered dramas in his "The American West of the 1870s and 1890s as Viewed from the Stage" in the Winter 1991 *Journal of American Drama and Theatre*. Scholarly rediscoveries of nineteenth-century western dramas have not yet led to an interest in such plays beyond some specialists in American dramas and western literature. Plays concerned with the Old West were overshadowed by William Vaughn Moody's *The Great Divide* (1903), a masterpiece that many critics regard as the drama that signaled the beginning of the modern era in American theater.

Authors who wrote about the Old West found many avenues to publication. Printing presses arrived in the region well before the California Gold Rush. Once the *Overland Monthly* began publication in 1868, it soon rivaled the literary journals of the East. Editors in the East increasingly published books about the West. The most cursory reading of mid- and late-nineteenth-century issues of the *Atlantic Monthly, Harper's Monthly Magazine, Harper's Weekly,* the *North American Review,* and *Scribner's Monthly* reveals works by many of the authors included in *DLB 186: Nineteenth-Century American Western Writers* as well as works by many of their professional and personal friends. Western publishers never achieved the stature of the big eastern firms; all the same, eastern publishers, judging well the appetite of their readers, welcomed books on western subjects.

In *DLB 186* men as subjects outnumber women, although the women writers treated are exceptional talents—the poet Ina Coolbrith, the novelists Gertrude Atherton and Mary Hallock Foote, and Helen Hunt Jackson, who was not only a novelist but also a social historian. Too often the male writers discussed offer abundant evidence that females venturing west in the nineteenth century were generally fated to suffer, as Foote of upstate New York did, and to adapt to their men's macho code, as Molly Wood, the schoolmarm from Vermont, allegedly will do after marrying Owen Wister's Virginian.

The writers included in *DLB 186* are varied in their geographical origins and their time periods, fittingly so since the region and century could not be well represented otherwise. Thirty-three came from sixteen states, only three of them east of the Mississippi River. Of the other five subjects, three—Thomas J. Dimsdale, John Muir, and George Frederick Ruxton—were born in the British Isles, and two—Adolph Bandelier and Charles Sealsfield—hailed from the Continent. Six were born in the late eighteenth century—the earliest being Timothy Flint in 1780. Nineteen were born between 1800 and 1849—the so-called emergence period of western literature. The remaining thirteen were born between 1850 and 1870—the latest being Frank Norris in 1870. Several of the included writers were significantly productive well into the twentieth century.

More important than statistics showing variety is a consideration of the various ways these authors approached and viewed the West. Many, especially the early ones, journeyed westward in the hope of validating extravagant claims they had read about or learned about by word of mouth—that the West was a land of milk, honey, and Garden of Eden scenery. After all, the Far West had been romanticized, often ridiculously, ever since García Ordóñez de

Montalvo identified "California" as an island of cliffs, rocks, black female warriors, wild beasts, and acres of gold in *The Adventures of Esplandian* (1510). In *The Memorial* (1630), one of many glowing seventeenth-century accounts, Fray Alonso de Benavides provides pious exaggerations of the land that would become New Mexico for the purposes of church propaganda. Among the more accurate eighteenth-century treatments of the West, Jonathan Carver's immensely popular *Three Years Travels through the Interior Parts of North America* (1778)—the interior parts being what became Wisconsin and Minnesota—was especially notable. Nineteenth-century writers from the East, whatever their expectations from reading, learned that the trails to the golden West included nearly impassable mountains of numbing cold and lowlands of hellish sand and heat. Such impediments became more real to them than romanticized or even accurately described accounts could ever be.

In addition to the landscapes, often depicted in word and less often on canvas, many of these writers also encountered Native Americans and Hispanics already on the ground; their responses to these indigenous people varied greatly. They adopted attitudes of Anglo-Saxon superiority, provided sociable accommodation, and—later—offered shame-faced apologies for the way most soldiers, traders, and settlers had behaved and were continuing to behave. Rather quickly, many writers came to recognize that America in the West—as had already been seen in the East—was to be less a melting pot than a pressure cooker. Some writers found relief in making western humor—tall tales, bumbled speeches, social satires, pro-animal sketches—out of the congeries of miseries seen.

The styles of the authors treated in *DLB 186* run the same gamut observable in other literary galleries: historical (Flint, Parkman, Turner), scientific (Bandelier, Frémont, Muir, Powell), down-to-earth observant (Meriwether Lewis and William Clark), military (King, Remington), smoothly realistic (Atherton, Foote, Garland, Roosevelt), belletristic (Irving), clumsy (Ned Buntline, Siringo), naturalistic (Norris), sentimental (Coolbrith, Sealsfield), satiric (Bierce), powerful but sometimes bordering on the phony (Markham, Miller), and humorous (Dan De Quille, Nye, Twain). Others, Garrard, Gregg, and Ruxton included, are mainly autobiographical. Many may be properly placed under more than one rubric; the most notable examples are Jackson, Lewis, Lummis, Roosevelt, and Stoddard. The personalities of most shine through, sometimes with a glare, as in the case of Bierce and Roosevelt, and sometimes with a flicker, notably Stoddard. Many readers will inevitably feel that certain omitted figures should have been included. But given not only the range of the topic–excellent and representative nineteenth-century writers about the American West–but also the constraints of space, all such omissions are easily rationalized. The melancholy editor hopes the bibliography at the end of the book will guide the intrepid to strike out elsewhere for themselves.

Scholars and critics have long studied the literature of the American West. By the 1920s a few colleges and universities began including courses on western American literature in their curricula. However, since American literature in general received little more than grudging space in most English departments until after World War II, regional studies were few and far between. With the publication of *Virgin Land: The American West as Symbol and Myth* by Henry Nash Smith in 1950, eager western literature scholars had a seminal work to cite in defense of their field. Focusing on the nineteenth century, Smith discussed not only belles lettres but also popular writing, such as dime novels. Moreover, since several mid-twentieth-century western authors, including Walter Van Tilburg Clark, Bernard DeVoto, and A. B. Guthrie Jr., had been praised and awarded prizes for their work, scholars, critics, and reviewers increasingly realized that the literary West was vast enough for more writers than Max Brand, Zane Grey, and Louis L'Amour.

After the Western Literature Association was founded in 1965 and its journal, *Western American Literature,* began publishing the following year, the amount of critical attention paid to nineteenth-century American western authors increased tremendously. The Steck-Vaughn Southwest Writers Series began publication in 1967, and when Steck-Vaughn announced the demise of its series, Boise State University's Western Writers Series started publishing in 1972. Richard W. Etulain's *A Bibliographical Guide to the Study of Western American Literature,* an important tool for study in the field, was published in 1982. The culmination of more than a decade of work by members of the Western Literature Association and many of their colleagues was *A Literary History of the American West* (1987), edited by J. Golden Taylor, Thomas J. Lyon, and their associates. Etulain and N. Jill Howard coedited a sizable expansion of his bibliography of western American literature in 1995, and Lyon and others edited *Updating the Literary West* (1997), which as a sequel to *A Literary History of the American West* offers reassessments of several nineteenth-century writers. *DLB 186* will both complement and supplement *Updating the Literary West.*

Four of the most engaging characters in the entire sweep of American fiction looked longingly to the West. In *Huck Finn and Tom Sawyer among the Indians,* the last of several stories by Mark Twain about Tom and Huck, the two boys find life in Missouri so dull that they seek adventure in Indian country. During his youth Jay Gatsby of *The Great Gatsby* (1925), hero-victim of F. Scott Fitzgerald's masterpiece, read and reread a book called *Hopalong Cassidy* by Clarence E. Mulford. And close to the end of J. D. Salinger's *The Catcher in the Rye* (1951) the disillusioned Holden Caulfield wants to leave New York, get a job at a filling station in the West where nobody would know him, and pretend to be a deaf-mute. What Huck, Tom, Gatsby, and Holden sought were adventure, freedom, clean behavior, solace, and renewal in an Old West definable in nineteenth-century terms. They all failed. Nor can present-day Americans find enough in their present-day West of what Stegner wanted the wilderness to hold precious–challenge, spiritual health, sanity, and "idea." However, readers of this volume can vicariously experience some of what the best nineteenth-century westward-turning authors saw and recorded.

–*Robert L. Gale*

Acknowledgments

This book was produced by Bruccoli Clark Layman, Inc. Karen L. Rood is senior editor for the *Dictionary of Literary Biography* series. George P. Anderson was the in-house editor. He was aided by Karen Rood, Denis Thomas, Sam Bruce, Tracy S. Bitonti, and Penelope M. Hope.

Administrative support was provided by Ann M. Cheschi and Brenda A. Gillie.

Bookkeeper is Joyce Fowler.

Copyediting supervisor is Jeff Miller. The copyediting staff includes Phyllis A. Avant, Patricia Coate, Christine Copeland, Thom Harman, and William L. Thomas Jr. Freelance copyeditors include Ron Aiken and Rebecca Mayo.

Editorial associate is L. Kay Webster.

Layout and graphics staff includes Marie L. Parker and Janet E. Hill.

Office manager is Kathy Lawler Merlette.

Photography editors are Margaret Meriwether and Paul Talbot. Photographic copy work was performed by Joseph M. Bruccoli.

Production manager is Samuel W. Bruce.

Systems manager is Marie L. Parker.

Typesetting supervisor is Kathleen M. Flanagan. The typesetting staff includes Judith E. McCray, Pamela D. Norton, and Patricia Flanagan Salisbury. Freelance typesetters include Melody W. Clegg and Delores Plastow.

Walter W. Ross, Steven Gross, and Mark McEwan did library research. They were assisted by the following librarians at the Thomas Cooper Library of the University of South Carolina: Linda Holderfield and the interlibrary-loan staff; reference-department head Virginia Weathers; reference librarians Marilee Birchfield, Stefanie Buck, Stefanie DuBose, Rebecca Feind, Karen Joseph, Donna Lehman, Charlene Loope, Anthony McKissick, Jean Rhyne, and Kwamine Simpson; circulation-department head Caroline Taylor; and acquisitions-searching supervisor David Haggard.

The editor expresses his profound thanks to all of the contributors to this volume. It is surely they who give it whatever value it has. In addition special debts of gratitude are owed to Dr. James H. Maguire, who recommended several contributors and also generously helped with the introduction, and to Dr. George Anderson, whose knowledge and editorial skill saved the volume from many errors. Maguire and Anderson are in every sense my coeditors.

Dictionary of Literary Biography® • Volume One Hundred Eighty-Six

Nineteenth-Century American Western Writers

Dictionary of Literary Biography

Gertrude Atherton
(30 October 1857 – 14 June 1948)

Charlotte S. McClure
Georgia State University

See also the Atherton entries in *DLB 9: American Novelists, 1910–1945* and *DLB 78: American Short-Story Writers, 1880–1910.*

BOOKS: *What Dreams May Come, A Romance,* as Frank Lin (Chicago & New York: Belford, Clarke, 1888; London, Glasgow, Manchester & New York: Routledge, 1889);

Hermia Suydam (New York: Current Literature, 1889); republished as *Hermia, An American Woman* (London: Routledge, 1889);

Los Cerritos, A Romance of the Modern Time (New York: Lovell, 1890; London: Heinemann, 1891);

A Question of Time (New York: Lovell, 1891; London: Gay & Bird, 1892);

The Doomswoman (New York: Tait, 1893; London: Hutchinson, 1895);

Before the Gringo Came (New York: Tait, 1894); revised and enlarged as *The Splendid Idle Forties, Stories of Old California* (New York & London: Macmillan, 1902);

A Whirl Asunder (New York & London: Stokes, 1895; London: Cassell, 1895);

Patience Sparhawk and Her Times, A Novel (London & New York: John Lane/Bodley Head, 1897);

His Fortunate Grace (New York: Appleton, 1897; London: Bliss, Sands, 1897);

The Californians (London: John Lane, 1898; New York: Grosset & Dunlap, 1898);

American Wives and English Husbands, A Novel (London: Service & Paton, 1898; New York: Dodd, Mead, 1898);

The Valiant Runaways (New York: Dodd, Mead, 1898; London: Nisbet, 1899);

A Daughter of the Vine (London & New York: John Lane/Bodley Head, 1899);

Gertrude Atherton, circa 1902 (photograph by Arnold Genthe; courtesy of Barbara Jacobsen and Araminta Blackwelder)

Senator North (New York & London: John Lane/Bodley Head, 1900);

The Aristocrats, Being the Impression of the Lady Helen Pole During Her Sojourn in the Great North Woods as Spontaneously Recorded in Her Letters to Her

3

Friend in North Britain, the Countess of Edge and Ross (London & New York: John Lane, 1901);

The Splendid Idle Forties, Stories of Old California (New York & London: Macmillan, 1902);

The Conqueror, Being the True and Romantic Story of Alexander Hamilton (New York & London: Macmillan, 1902); revised as *The Conqueror, A Dramatized Biography of Alexander Hamilton* (New York: Stokes, 1916);

Heart of Hyacinth (New York: Harper, 1903);

Mrs. Pendleton's Four-in-Hand (New York & London: Macmillan, 1903);

Rulers of Kings, A Novel (New York & London: Harper, 1904);

The Bell in the Fog and Other Stories (New York & London: Harper, 1905);

The Traveling Thirds (New York & London: Harper, 1905);

Rezánov (New York & London: Authors and Newspapers Association, 1906; London: John Murray, 1906);

Ancestors, A Novel (New York & London: Harper, 1907; London: John Murray, 1907);

The Gorgeous Isle, A Romance, Scene, Nevis, B.W.I., 1842 (New York: Doubleday, Page, 1908; London: John Murray, 1908);

Tower of Ivory, A Novel (New York: Macmillan, 1910; London: John Murray, 1910);

Julia France and Her Times, A Novel (New York: Macmillan, 1912; London: John Murray, 1912);

Perch of the Devil (New York: Stokes, 1914; London: John Murray, 1914);

California, An Intimate History (New York & London: Harper, 1914);

Mrs. Balfame, A Novel (New York: Stokes, 1916; London: John Murray, 1916);

Life in the War Zone (New York: Systems Printing Company, 1916);

The Living Present (New York: Stokes, 1917; London: John Murray, 1917);

The White Morning, A Novel of the Power of the German Women in Wartime (New York: Stokes, 1918);

The Avalanche, A Mystery Story (New York: Stokes, 1919);

Transplanted, A Novel (New York: Dodd, Mead, 1919);

The Sisters-in-Law, A Novel of Our Time (New York: Stokes, 1921; London: John Murray, 1921);

Sleeping Fires, A Novel (New York: Stokes, 1922); republished as *Dormant Fires* (London: John Murray, 1922);

Black Oxen (New York: Boni & Liveright, 1923; London: John Murray, 1923);

The Crystal Cup (New York: Boni & Liveright, 1925; London: John Murray, 1925);

The Immortal Marriage (New York: Boni & Liveright, 1927; London: John Murray, 1927);

The Jealous Gods, A Processional Novel of the Fifth Century B.C. (Concerning One Alcibiades) (New York: Liveright, 1928); republished as *Vengeful Gods* (London: John Murray, 1928);

Dido, Queen of Hearts (New York: Liveright, 1929; London: Chapman & Hall, 1929);

The Sophisticates (New York: Liveright, 1931; London: Chapman & Hall, 1931);

Adventures of a Novelist (New York: Liveright, 1932; London: Cape, 1932);

The Foghorn, Stories (Boston & New York: Houghton Mifflin, 1934; London: Jarrolds, 1935);

Golden Peacock (Boston & New York: Houghton Mifflin, 1936; London: Butterworth, 1937);

Rezánov and Doña Concha (New York: Stokes, 1937);

Can Women Be Gentlemen? (Boston: Houghton Mifflin, 1938);

The House of Lee (New York & London: Appleton-Century, 1940; London: Eyre & Spottiswooﾠe, 1942);

The Horn of Life (New York: Appleton-Century, 1942);

Golden Gate Country (New York: Duell, Sloan & Pearce, 1945);

My San Francisco, A Wayward Biography (Indianapolis & New York: Bobbs-Merrill, 1946).

PLAY PRODUCTION: *Julia France,* Toronto, 17 January 1912.

MOTION PICTURE: *Don't Neglect Your Wife,* screenplay by Atherton, M-G-M, 2 February 1921.

OTHER: *A Few of Hamilton's Letters, Including His Description of the Great West Indian Hurricane of 1772,* edited by Atherton (New York & London: Macmillan, 1903);

"Concha Arguëllo, Sister Dominica," in *The Spinner's Book of Fiction* (San Francisco & New York: Elder, 1907);

"Wanted: Imagination," in *What Is a Book? Thoughts about Writing,* edited by Dale Warren (Boston: Houghton Mifflin, 1935).

SELECTED PERIODICAL PUBLICATIONS—
UNCOLLECTED:
FICTION
"The Randolphs of Redwoods: A Romance," as Asmodeus, *Argonaut,* 12 (31 March 1883): 1–2; (7 April 1883): 1–2; (14 April 1883): 1–2; (21 April 1883): 1–2; (28 April 1883): 1–2; (5 May 1883): 1–2;

"Mrs. Pendleton's Four-in-Hand," *Cosmopolitan*, 10 (December 1890): 186–204;

"The Doomswoman," *Lippincott's*, 50 (August 1892): 261–365;

"Andreo's Love: The Vengeance of Padre Arroyo," *Current Literature*, 16 (September 1894): 196–197;

"Death," *Anti-Philistine*, 4 (15 September 1897): 220–227;

"Sylvia's Last Story," *Pocket Magazine*, 6 (May 1898): 1–33;

"Modern Primitives," *Good Housekeeping*, 77 (October 1923): 12–16, 214–220;

"Flotsam," *Regionalism and the Female Imagination*, 4 (Winter 1979): 60–91;

"Deep Collar," *New Orleans Review*, 7, no. 1 (1980): 69–81.

NONFICTION

"The Literary Development of California," *Cosmopolitan*, 10 (January 1891): 269–278;

"The Novel and the Short Story," *Bookman* (New York), 17 (March 1903): 36–37;

"Some Truths About American Readers," *Bookman* (New York), 18 (February 1904): 658–660;

"Why Is American Literature Bourgeois?," *North American Review*, 175 (May 1904): 771–781;

"Affinities," *Overland Monthly*, second series 51 (January 1908): 4–7;

"The Woman of Tomorrow," *Yale Review*, new series 2 (April 1913): 412–435.

Gertrude Atherton's ambition to be a writer was fulfilled in the turbulent 1890s, the decade in which she fashioned the theme of the American West as a significant part of an evolving western European civilization. She would elaborate this theme in short stories, romances, and novels through the first half of the twentieth century. From 1889 to 1900 she lived and wrote in Paris and London as well as in her native San Francisco, and her writing was shaped by disparate influences: the idealism and style of Walter Pater, the fin de siècle decadence associated with the figure of the New Woman, the boredom of leisured women and men, and the restless, unruly history of California and San Francisco following the settled life of the Spanish-Californian haciendas of the 1840s. Searching for her literary voice as a westerner while seeking the recognition of the eastern establishment of publishers and critics, Atherton wove these ideas into the novels that became part of her California chronicle.

At the center of Atherton's chronicle of San Francisco and California from the 1840s to the 1940s was the western New Woman, her version of the liberated woman who had fled Henrik Ibsen's *A Doll's House* (1879). Atherton's female protagonist struggled not only with the conflict between nature and civilization but also with the clash between her ambitions and the constraints of society. In *The Doomswoman* (1893)—which Atherton claims is the beginning of her chronicle—Atherton created a heroine, Chonita Moncada y Iturbi, who personifies California, "magnificent, audacious, incomprehensible, a creature of storms and convulsions and impregnable calm: the germ of all good and bad in her." In her biography *California's Daughter: Gertrude Atherton and Her Times* (1991) Emily Wortis Leider declares that Chonita is her creator's idealized self.

Atherton was born Gertrude Horn in San Francisco on 30 October 1857, a little more than seven years after California had become the thirty-first state. She was the daughter of a New England businessman, Thomas Ludovich Horn, and of a southern belle, Gertrude Franklin. She had an unsettled, undisciplined childhood and an adolescence marked by the decline of the family fortune and her parents' divorce. She believed that her mother's passivity was one of the causes of the divorce and later saw it as contributing to the failure of a second marriage. Horn attended public and private schools and was encouraged to become a serious reader by her grandfather Stephen Franklin. She nurtured her aspiration to become a writer in his library of literary classics and histories of Western civilization. On 14 February 1876 eighteen-year-old Horn eloped with George Atherton, a member of a prominent San Francisco family.

For the twelve years of her married life Gertrude Atherton fulfilled the traditional woman's role of wife and mother, bearing two children, one of whom died of diphtheria, and participating in the social life in and around San Francisco. These seemingly fortunate circumstances created tensions that affected Atherton's self-image and her understanding of the world. She suffered the same sense of ennui that she noted in the lives of the leisured women in the Atherton family and in her social set, which she believed was caused by their acceptance of the restricted woman's role and by their lack of a personal aim in life. Although her husband and staunch Catholic mother-in-law objected to her writing, Atherton wrote in secret and sent articles to local periodicals.

Atherton thought that the provincialness of California retarded not only her progress as a writer but also the state's assumption of a leadership role for the nation. She believed that the idyllic climate and the isolation of California from the "bold dynamic energy" of the East fostered a complacency

Atherton in 1886

and indolence among some of the inhabitants that delayed the development of an orderly civilization for the state and the nation. In the 1880s and 1890s San Francisco had not yet wholly outgrown its past of mining camps, vigilantism, and blatant corruption and faced problems of social unrest brought on by economic disparities within a diverse population that along with the descendents of Europe included Chinese, Russian, and people of Spanish and Indian descent. The city, though, did boast of three respectable journals, *The Overland Monthly, The Argonaut,* and *The Wave,* as well as William Randolph Hearst's newspaper, *The San Francisco Examiner.*

In 1883 Atherton published her first work, "The Randolphs of Redwoods: A Romance." The story, a fictionalized version of a scandal of alcoholism in an old San Francisco family, appeared in six parts in *The Argonaut* under the pseudonym Asmodeus. When Atherton revealed herself as the author, she was ostracized by her family and friends as well as by the wider society of the city.

After the sudden death at sea of her husband in June 1887, Atherton moved east to New York to carve out her literary career, leaving her daughter, Muriel, with her grandmother Atherton. She did not turn at first to the West as her subject, for in three of her first four novels the characters and settings are not Californian. Her first novel, *What Dreams May Come, A Romance* (1888), features a reincarnated

heroine, and her second, *Hermia Suydam* (1889), depicts an independent woman who has an illicit affair. The heroine in Atherton's fourth novel, *A Question of Time* (1891), breaks the taboo of an older woman marrying a much younger man.

In these novels Atherton evidently exorcised internal conflicts through her rejection of social customs that in her view restricted the choices of women. The heroines' unconventional behavior was regarded as decadent, and New York critics either derided the novels for their sensationalism or ignored them. After a little over a year in New York, Atherton had published but had not gained literary recognition or financial reward. In 1889 she decided to accept an invitation from her sister-in-law Alejandra Rathbone to visit her in Paris.

After a period of socializing in Paris with Alejandra and her husband, Maj. Lawrence Rathbone, American consul general, Atherton retreated to a nearby convent to continue to work on a book that she had begun in New York and that had a California setting. In *Los Cerritos, A Romance of the Modern Time* (1890), Atherton's heroine is Carmelita, a quick-minded young woman who is the daughter of Joaquín Murieta, a celebrated California bandit. Having lived an isolated life among poor Mexican squatters on a central California ranch, Carmelita, like Atherton, who remembered her alienation on her husband's ranch, yearns for "higher" circumstances. She finds some stimulation in her education by the Cerritos mission padre and in a romance with a wealthy landowner who is bored with civilized cities and who affects an interest in the poor. With him Carmelita can discuss her own growing awareness of the world beyond her ranch.

The preliminary note on the dialect used in *Los Cerritos*—like that of Mark Twain's *Adventures of Huckleberry Finn* (1884)—indicates Atherton's growing knowledge of literary matters and the works of other authors. Most of the characters speak what Atherton calls Spanish-California English, a dialect new to American literature. A critic in the 4 April 1891 *Athenaeum* remarked that it added "a charm of quaintness."

While in Paris in 1889 Atherton received word that G. Routledge and Sons in London had accepted her first two books for publication. William Sharp, a London poet and critic, praised her fiction in *The Spectator* and invited her to stay with him and his wife, Elizabeth, in South Hampstead. In London she had the opportunity through Lady Wilde to meet her son Oscar Wilde, who at the time was celebrated as an aesthete, poet, and witty conversationalist. Atherton recorded in her memoir, *Adventures of a Novelist* (1932), that she made an excuse to avoid the meeting because she found him physically repulsive. Later, in a June 1899 article she wrote for the London *Bookman,* she asserted that Wilde's work represented a precious style that she associated with "the decadence, the loss of virility that must follow over-civilization." Leider argues that during this sojourn in London, Atherton felt a growing conflict between the "aesthetic languors" of style for its own sake and "American dynamism, particularly the dynamism of California and the American West." In London, where Bret Harte's popular California gold mining tales held readers' attention, Atherton devised a plan of life for herself in Europe and America as a Californian and for selling her books on both sides of the Atlantic.

Atherton used her visits to England in the 1890s to observe the social behavior of the middle and upper classes in London. She noted that some well-to-do Britons practiced boredom as a public style and that authors used it as a catalyst for writing: writers write and readers read in order to keep life interesting. She drew from reading Walter Pater's essays on art and style his explanation of how art reveals the creative capacity of the human spirit, deducing from that idea the notion of an individual's ability to create an alternative to a life otherwise lacking in any substantial purpose, interest, or solace. Her reading of Hippolyte-Adolphe Taine helped her build on her insight; she imagined lifting a type of woman and man out of the commonplace conditions to which they are apparently doomed and transferring them to an environment full of opportunity, where they could develop their latent potentialities.

Two deaths in her family necessitated Atherton's return to California in 1890. The loss of her grandfather Franklin and her mother-in-law, Dominga Atherton, led her to resume the responsibility of caring for her daughter, Muriel, and other members of her family. For a short time in 1891 she wrote a column for the *San Francisco Examiner,* where she met Ambrose Bierce, with whom she carried on a taunting, almost love-hate friendship.

Reading journalist Kate Fields's remark about California writers' neglect of the picturesque and romantic old Spanish life of the state was the catalyst for Atherton's plan to study the 1840s era, which she had first learned about through her mother-in-law's stories. Atherton explored the mission towns of Monterey, San Juan Bautista, San Luis Obispo, Santa Barbara, Santa Inez, and Los Angeles. As she visited the historic sites and talked with the descendants of some of the original families, she gathered stories and local color details that helped her create a forceful myth of a paradisiacal early California, a

nostalgic past always sought but never regained. Such a literary rendition of the haciendas and missions of the "splendid idle" fit into the national popularity of local color stories. Her narratives of the customs and festivities of pre-Yankee California life present stories of the state and the West that Harte and Twain did not relate.

The literary trend toward regional writing encouraged Atherton to identify and describe the works of contemporary California authors. In a January 1891 article, "The Literary Development of California," she listed nearly forty California authors, none of whom was a native of California. She named Twain, Harte, Joaquin Miller, and Henry George as the most famous writers of the state. She claimed that Ambrose Bierce was an "overlooked Poe." Bierce, she asserted, topped Poe by his "brutal imagination" and by his "subtile art of construction and dominant power over the minds of his readers." Atherton predicted: "Although the South will howl and the North may hoot, I venture to predict that fifty years from now California will be the literary center of America."

In her works previous to *The Doomswoman,* Atherton had made a sharp distinction between the romance and the novel. She believed that the romance presented a narrative of mental and physical adventure, mystery, and love; her understanding of the term suggests her familiarity with the romances of her times such as those of Edgar Saltus, Helen Hunt Jackson, and Winston Churchill. In *Hermia Suydam* her heroine defines the novel as the "correlative with all that was commonplace . . ." offering "neither change nor excitement, nor recognition, nor power. Nothing of mystery, nothing of adventure." *The Doomswoman,* though, marks a change in her attitude. While not abandoning her former attitude, Atherton becomes more interested in capturing the social history of her time, imaginatively recording in novels both the history and current times of her city and state without diminishing the romance of an individual's discovering and carrying out a life plan. This combination evolves into Atherton's expression of her characters' romantic-realistic pursuit of happiness.

The Doomswoman, the most propitious and successful of Atherton's work with the social history of the 1840s, was first published in *Lippincott's* magazine in 1892 and then in book form in 1893. The novel marked the beginning of a prolific decade in which she published nearly a book a year. In summer 1892 she wrote Joseph Stoddart, editor of *Lippincott's,* that she wanted to do only "quality" fiction in order to earn a living. "I think I shall do nothing but literary work now . . . and if *The Doomswoman*

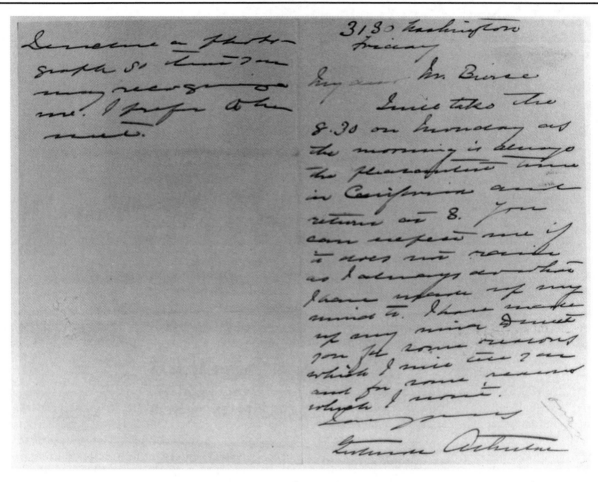

An 1890 letter from Atherton to Ambrose Bierce (Bancroft Library, University of California, Berkeley)

brings me the recognition I hope, literary work would be more profitable than newspaper" writing.

Disclaiming her first four novels, Atherton declared that her career truly began with her tale of the self-conflicted Chonita Moncada y Iturbi, a spirited young woman from an aristocratic family who strives toward an ideal identity and purpose in life. Chonita falls in love with Diego Estenega, a Mexican modeled on Gen. Mariano Vallejo, who dreams of modernizing California, retaining its Mexican character without sacrificing American economic vigor. Chonita's Catholic faith and her loyalty to her Spanish heritage as civilizing values separate her from Diego's political goal. Their private and public conflicts embody the contradictions within California in the 1840s and lead to the dramatic moment when Diego kills Chonita's brother, Reynaldo, and she must decide between her love of Diego and her sibling and cultural loyalty. Their tragic deaths echo the fate of Romeo and Juliet.

To relate this tale, Atherton uses two narrative points of view: Dona Eustaquia knows Chonita well enough to reflect her friend's inner thoughts and feelings, and an omniscient narrator reveals the local color of five days of rituals and festivities that celebrate the wedding of Reynaldo. She combines these points of view ably to tell an insider's story about a place and its community of people, while emphasizing the values held by women. Her use of the female point of view, as discussed by Judith Fetterley and Marjorie Pryse in *American Women Regionalists 1850–1910* (1992), enables Atherton through her narrator to criticize the indolence of the caballeros in a land of great opportunity while she presents them as worthy courters of the senoritas; she knows how women respond to the land, to the men who hold the power, and to each other; her "seeing into others beyond the external facts of history" creates a more complete rendering of the community.

Reviewers praised the "actual vivid reality" of *The Doomswoman* and compared it favorably with Jackson's popular *Ramona* (1884), a compliment that disgruntled Atherton somewhat because Jackson was not a native Californian. Bierce's high praise of *The Doomswoman* as "in its class . . . superior to any that any Californian has done" pleased Atherton immensely. In 1892 Atherton left California for New York, expecting to earn a living through marketing her fiction as well as newspaper writing. In letters to Bierce she confided in him her loneliness, her dismay at the necessity to do freelance writing, especially for the *New York World,* and her inability to enjoy New York's literary groups. The eastern literary establishment, in her opinion, constantly belittled the West and its authors, and because it refused to accept Bierce's strong writing, she wondered whether the East were "effete."

The mission and hacienda life of pre-Yankee California also provided Atherton with subjects for her short stories that were collected as *Before the Gringo Came* (1894). In eleven short stories and sketches she recaptured their history with local color details, but more important, she created individualized women enjoying, and sometimes rebelling against, their pleasurable life. The stories also reveal a realistic dark side of the attitudes and social life of women and men. Atherton believed that human motives such as the drive for love or power were universal and that motives were often manifested differently because of differences in individuals' circumstances and milieu. Her realistic placement of characters in their environment led to a variety of universal themes: the individual's quest for happiness, occurring for most women through marriage; the passions of love, ambition, greed, and revenge among Spanish Californians; and the conflict between old Spanish customs and Americans' pursuit of money and progress. As a result her characters and fictional world express a larger universe than that of the United States and the American West. In her March 1903 article on the novel and the short story in the New York *Bookman* Atherton claimed that her belief in the universal origin of emotion and the uncertainty of the outcome of human choice and diverse motives placed her in the realm of "real creators" of short stories—with Edgar Allan Poe, Mary Wilkins Freeman, Harte, Twain, and Bierce—as distinguished from "intellectually manufactured" writers.

The first three stories of *Before the Gringo Came*—"The Pearls of Loreto," "The Ears of Twenty Americans," and "The Wash-Tub Mail"—relate episodes in Monterey between 1846 and 1847 when the threat of war between the United States and Mexico caused a divided loyalty among Californians. These three romances—each concerned with the consequences of the choice of a mate by a beautiful heroine—contain realistic details of Spanish social events, rituals, and descriptions of the natural beauty of California. Atherton captures the variances in the speech of the Spanish at different social levels and of

Americans trying to speak Spanish. In "The Pearls of Loreto" Vicente de la Vega rides his mustang from Monterey to the Mission of Loreto in Baja to steal the pearls from the mission church for Ysabel Herrera, who had vowed to marry only the man who could bring her a lapful of pearls. Because of his blasphemy in stealing the pearls and killing a priest, both de la Vega and Ysabel jump to their deaths to escape the wrath of the poor people of Monterey.

In "The Ears of Twenty Americans" the struggle of a mother and daughter to choose between loyalty to their Spanish heritage and the American military men they love is told through the viewpoint of the aristocratic mother, Dona Eustaquia, who appeared as a narrator in *The Doomswoman.* Angry at the conquering Americans, widow Dona Eustaquia at first vows she would trade her ranch for a necklace made from the ears of twenty Americans. She ostracizes and lays a curse on her daughter Benicia, who marries the American Lieutenant Russell, while Eustaquia's own new love, Captain Brotherton, tries to persuade her to lift the curse. Her daughter's death by the curse is part of the price of a war that brings cultural change. In a similar tragic atmosphere in "The Wash-Tub Mail," the Indian servants of the hacienda reveal the bittersweet romance of Tulita, *la favorita,* who spurned her Spanish lover in favor of an ambitious American lieutenant who, she learns years later from the "wash-tub mail," will never return to claim her as his bride.

In these and other stories Atherton's use of social history in her fiction predicts the future direction of her writing, which emphasizes the stresses of affinity between women and men and within families. As intermarriage became commonplace among Anglos, Mexicans, and Indians, Atherton experimented with her technique of associating traits with a character's national or regional origin. In the conflicts between husband and wife, parents and children, mother and daughter, motives and choices of action become confused, suggesting the flux of cultural values. "The Conquest of Doña Jacoba," for example, treats the effect of the parental authority of a Scots father and a Spanish mother on their children. Elena, the youngest, most passive daughter, unexpectedly conquers her mother's authority when she insists on marrying a Spanish Indian rancher. In the next story, "A Ramble with Eulogia," the reader learns that Elena, after bearing three children, died of a combination of tuberculosis and the neglect of her husband, Dario. In contrast, Eulogia, aware of romantic perils from reading the novels of Alexandre Dumas, plans to be as independent as men appear to be and waits for the man who

CALIFORNIAN NUMBER.

Portrait of GERTRUDE ATHERTON.

THIS NUMBER CONTAINS

THE DOOMSWOMAN

By GERTRUDE ATHERTON,

Author of " What Dreams May Come," " Hermia Suydam," " Los Cerritos," " Mrs. Pendleton's Four-in-Hand," Etc., Etc.

COMPLETE.

SEPTEMBER, 1892

LIPPINCOTT'S

MONTHLY MAGAZINE

CONTENTS

PRICE TWENTY-FIVE CENTS

PUBLISHED BY

J: B: LIPPINCOTT: CO: PHILADELPHIA:

LONDON: WARD, LOCK, BOWDEN & CO.

PARIS: BRENTANO'S, 17 AVENUE DE L'OPERA.

Copyright, 1892, by J. B. Lippincott Company. Entered at Philadelphia Post-Office as second-class matter.

Cover for the magazine featuring the first publication of Atherton's fifth book, the first novel to show her interest in social history

would never bore her. In Eulogia's characterization as a beautiful, intellectual woman who also wants and needs a man's admiration, her creator forecasts a type that would populate her fictional social world in later novels.

Atherton's experimentation with various points of view in succeeding sketches and vignettes in *Before the Gringo Came* expands her social history of the 1840s. Reviewers generally described the stories as passionate, intense tales that often developed into tragic episodes, particularly in the lives of women. Although the volume did not sell well initially, Atherton was later able to cash in on the critical acclaim for *The Conqueror* (1902), her biographical novel based on the life of Alexander Hamilton, by adding two more California stories and publishing the collection under a new title, *The Splendid Idle Forties, Stories of Old California* (1902). One of the later stories, "The Isle of Skulls," treats the decision of an ambitious Catholic priest to leave the woman he loves in order to further his vocation; the second added story, "The Head of a Priest," deals with the extreme behavior of a mother who believed too strongly in the punishment system of Catholicism.

The next book that Atherton wrote, *Patience Sparhawk and Her Times, A Novel* (1897), proved too controversial to be the next published. The conception of the protagonist came to Atherton unexpectedly, as she reported in her memoir that a "distinctive heroine" walked into her consciousness. She soon linked this figure of a passionate, willful, intellectual California ranch woman with the plot of a sensational murder trial in New York City in 1892. The novel relates the years in young Patience's life on a poor ranch near Monterey in the 1880s and her education and social rise in the environs of New York City in the 1890s. Patience Sparhawk is the first of several distinctive California heroines created by Atherton between 1895 and 1907.

Patience spends a lonely youth on the ranch, inspired only by reading the classics in an old gentleman's library and competing for grades in school, incidents that Atherton drew from her own life. One day her mother's promiscuous and alcohol-induced behavior enrages her sufficiently to cause her to attack and nearly kill her mother. In this characterization Atherton makes concrete her recognition of the duality of human nature in women as well as in men. Patience's willful and anarchic self-assertion stamps her, in Atherton's view, as American and especially Californian. Upon her mother's death Patience is sent into other circumstances: life with her religious spinster "auntie," Miss Tremont, near New York City. She soon marries a wealthy man and experiences a new leisurely but boring upper-

class existence. After she leaves her husband she is accused and convicted of murdering him with an overdose of morphine and sentenced to electrocution at Sing Sing prison. While the plot is melodramatic, Atherton's serious concern is to present a young woman's coming to terms with illusive romantic ideals and the practical realities of sexuality as she searches for an independent purpose in life.

When several major American publishers rejected *Patience Sparhawk and Her Times,* Atherton left New York for England, where her work had sold better. John Lane of the Bodley Hall imprint in London accepted *Patience Sparhawk* in 1895, but he delayed publishing it for nearly two years. On this second journey to London in 1895 to write, Atherton decided to live quietly until she had built up her literary reputation by publishing her Old Spanish California stories and writing book reviews for Oliver Fry's *Vanity Fair*. Staying at Haworth, she rewrote her 1883 serialized romance, "The Randolphs of Redwoods," which was retitled *A Daughter of the Vine* and published in 1899.

When Max Pemberton asked Atherton to write a novelette of ten thousand words for a series he was editing for Cassells Pocket Library, she produced *A Whirl Asunder* (1895), a story of her quintessential California heroine Helena Belmont, who combines a Byronic romantic ego and the intellect of Madame de Staël's Corinne. The self-centered, imperious, beautiful heroine refuses to be chaperoned as she pursues happiness with her idea of an ideal man, an English barrister named Owen Clive, and suffers grandly when he chooses to marry a typical English woman.

Perhaps still smarting from what she saw as the American rejection of her works, Atherton allows Helena to criticize the lack of an authentic love scene in American fiction as her heroine passionately converses with Clive in the redwood forest. Like Patience, Helena has a "mental concept" of companionable love and repeatedly asks: "Who is Man? Who is Woman? What is their part in the universe?" These questions reflect Atherton's concern that an individual have a plan of life in order to avoid boredom. Needing his approval of her concept of self and overlooking social custom, Helena conducts a cerebral courtship in the primeval forest. In the midst of the magnificent natural setting Helena asks, "Has it occurred to you that no American writer has ever written a genuine all-around love scene? They are either thin or sensual, almost invariably the former."

Atherton's criticism of "the littleism" or "thin" realism of the fiction of William Dean Howells—which she made forthrightly in her May 1904 article in the *North American Review,* "Why Is American Literature Bourgeois?"–underlies this scene. Her characterization of Helena as one who achieves a happy union of the physical and the spiritual in this novel and who never marries reflects Atherton's belief that a woman can move from a dependent identity to a separate, idealistic one. She describes this identity as an "intermediate sex" in an April 1913 article in the *Yale Review* "The Woman of Tomorrow." Several of Atherton's western heroines in novels written after 1900 act out this ideal: Ora Stratton of *Perch of the Devil* (1914), Gora Dwight of *The Sisters-in-Law* (1921) and *Black Oxen* (1923), and Mrs. Edington and Mrs. Lee of *The House of Lee* (1940). More a potboiler into which Atherton unloaded many of her incompletely considered notions of the relation of the sexes than a well-organized novella, *A Whirl Asunder* was described as a "disheveled work" in a 15 February 1896 review in *The New York Times* and in the 4 April issue of *The Critic* was criticized as a work weakened by essaylike dialogue.

When *Patience Sparhawk* appeared in 1897 British and American critics gave it mixed reviews. Robertson Nicholl in the 12 April 1897 London *Bookman* called the novel "crude" in its portrayal of a clever young woman with burning interest in life and identified it as a protest against the tame American novel. The reviewer in the 15 May issue of *The New York Times* declared that Atherton had an "uncontestable" ability and a "very original talent" while noting that the book offered a series of "fleshy" episodes in Patience's life that must have scared a sensitive reader.

The reception of *Patience Sparhawk* in California especially rankled Atherton. The book was banned from the Mechanics' Institute Library in San Francisco, and a reviewer in the 8 April *San Francisco Call* asserted that it represented Atherton's departure from her proper literary goal of treating early California themes romantically. Atherton responded to the charge of betrayal of her birth state's romantic heritage by asserting that the East was not interested in California and that Californians did not buy her books. She defended her book as "the most truthful American novel that has been written" and as a realistic portrayal of a romantic aspiring female character that had not been seen in American literature.

Despite the slow buildup of readership of her California fiction, Atherton began to write *The Californians* (1898), her first novel to treat the post-Spanish era. Arguably Atherton's most accomplished novel, *The Californians* features Magdalena Yorba, an inward-looking person, not a New Woman, neither brilliant and beautiful nor articulate like her best friend and foil, Helena Belmont. In contrast to Helena's inherited New England intellect, southern charm, and California individuality (the decadent New Woman), Magdalena is self-conflicted. The legacy of the clash between her mother's Yankee reserve and her father's Spanish passion smothers the potential of her western individuality. In the postarcadian boom in San Francisco of the 1880s, Magdalena, isolated in her parents' gloomy mansion on Nob Hill, struggles to overcome her reticence and her dependence on religion in order to fulfill her desire to write. Happy in her friendship with Helena, she also gains confidence from the sympathetic attention of Jack Trennahan, a bored, "world weary" Adam, who in his own way searches for a purposeful life. Coinciding with the fallen financial fortunes of the three central families of the novel–the Yorbas, the Polks, and the Belmonts–Helena drives a wedge in the developing love between Jack and Magdalena. Magdalena sinks into deep despair following her unsuccessful attempt to kill Helena.

Atherton in the novel takes a closer look than before at her admiration of California's competitive individualism and enterprise. Helena's father, Magdalena's father, and Magdalena's Uncle Polk had amassed fortunes and died unfulfilled. In them Atherton expresses the dark side of California's fortunate gifts in a tale told by a young man at a party: "There is a good deal of tragedy in California. . . . Men came to kiss [her] and stayed to tear away her flesh with their teeth." In *Americans and the California Dream* (1973) Kevin Starr explains that these characters fail "to achieve a harmonious way of life because each denied basic values in his search for wealth."

Atherton does not harshly judge Helena's cruelty to Magdalena and Jack, for her betrayal does not preclude a happy denouement. She enlarges Magdalena's development from dependence to a presentiment of a higher destiny for herself. After walking through the San Francisco streets of prostitution and lawlessness, Magdalena acknowledges that she has to face the problem of her life and to avoid the men's tragedy of unfulfilled lives by vowing to devote her life and her inheritance to aiding the poor. In a melodramatic ending Jack returns from his self-imposed exile, and he and Magdalena plan to be married. Readers learn in *Ancestors* (1907) that Jack and Magdalena became a happy family active in the social life of San Francisco. In her 1914 novel, *Perch of the Devil,* set in Butte, Montana, Atherton creates a similar rivalry between two women for the love of a mining engineer. For this novel Atherton chose Montana as the "new most romantic subdivision of the United States" to replace California as the backdrop for depicting the "modern spirit of America."

Critics in London and New York found more to praise in *The Californians* than in *Patience Sparhawk*. In the 1 October 1898 *Spectator* the reviewer compared the novel to her previous efforts, writing that Atherton "was by far more convincing and attractive in delineating California manners and morals. . . . The novel fairly establishes her claim to be considered as one of the most vivid and entertaining interpreters of the complex characters of emancipated American womanhood." The 15 November London *Bookman* reviewer praised Atherton's "style of her own," her brilliant though profuse language. The reviewer for the 8 November New York *Bookman* called the novel her "most ambitious work," which has "a feeling of surety that only the consciousness of knowing one's ground can convey"; this reviewer praised Atherton's presentation of the city in its sunny and seamy sides and the beauty of the country as well as her characterizations of Helena Belmont and Magdalena.

With such praise in her ears and with an advance for a new novel from a London publishing firm, Atherton traveled to Rouen to write *American Wives and English Husbands* (1898), another novel set in contemporay times, in four months. In this novel she contrasts English and American men, American and English civilizations, and relationships between men and women generally. Aristocratic-born Lee Tarleton, like Patience Sparhawk, spends her early life in less than aristocratic circumstances in San Francisco, but she gains a British titled position in her marriage to Cecil Maundrell, son of the earl of Barnstable. Endowed with southern charm and California individuality, Lee carries out Atherton's observations of how the English and Americans organize their private and public manners.

Atherton divides her heroine's life into its California period (part 1, thirty-two chapters), during which time Lee develops the western American characteristics that contrast with those of the older traditional British civilization, and its British period (part 2, twenty-six chapters), when, married to Cecil, who expects her to become his second self, Lee faces the conflict between the pressure to conform to English ways and her established western individuality. Atherton cleverly pits the conflict between Lee's husband Cecil and Randolph Montgomery, her former American lover and a typical practical American businessman, both of whom act out their inherited and acquired views of civilization and of the relationship between man and woman. Lee frets

Binding for Atherton's 1898 novel contrasting American and English ideas on marriage

at her submission to her husband's expectations and flirts with a return to California and Randolph, who good-humoredly acquiesces to her wishes most of the time.

Atherton uses these conflicts as the basis for a gentle satire of the contrasting American and British views of manners and the marital relationship. Atherton allows an American adaptability to influence both Lee and Cecil to recognize their similarities as much as their differences. She conveys the compromise through an evocative metaphor as both California's primeval redwoods and England's historic beechwoods and ancient monuments are seen as valuable. Acknowledging their respective nations' nature and tradition, Lee and Cecil perceive that their common pursuit of happiness lies in the continuity of the race and civilization.

Henry James, who had commended the satire of the marital relationship in Atherton's first international novel, *His Fortunate Grace* (1897), declared in the 7 May 1898 *Athenaeum* that in *American Wives and English Husbands* she had reduced the "great relation" of the sexes to differences in personality. In the 7 May New York *Bookman* the reviewer remarked on the restrained power of expression and compression in the novel that *Patience Sparhawk* had not promised. Harold Frederic, an American novelist living in London, noted the same growth in Atherton's writing. Atherton reported in *Adventures of a Novelist* that he cautioned her not to write too easily: "You have in extreme degree the talent of lucidity—but melody is an acquired gift with all but the laurel-wreathed few. Do take the pace a little more slowly, and listen with a more solicitous reflective ear." Reflecting on her understanding of Herbert Spencer's and Pater's ideas on style, Atherton turned a deaf ear, declaring "My style is my own."

By 1899 Atherton had lived away from the United States for more than four years. Before deciding to return to New York she wrote *The Valiant Runaways* (1898), an adventure story for boys that is concerned with the early Spanish Mexican attempt to civilize California. In a minor way it displays her ironic and vigorous narrative method as the boys leave home to escape conscription into the army but actually run straight into battle.

Back in America in 1899 Atherton did not write of California again until *Ancestors;* in the following years she produced seven more novels that continued her chronicle up to the eve of World War II: *The Avalanche, A Mystery Story* (1919), *Transplanted* (1919), *The Sisters-in-Law, Sleeping Fires* (1922), *Rezánov and Doña Concha* (1937), *The House of Lee,* and *The Horn of Life* (1942). In these novels she showed the evolution of the western American heroine, weaving characters and families of different decades of San Francisco into a larger narrative. As much a social historian as a writer of novels, Atherton brings her San Francisco heroines into each new decade of the twentieth century, portraying their ambition and individuality in confrontation with the exigencies of an evolving American urban civilization. Her voice, as she suggested in *The Sisters-in-Law,* became that of a "correct historian" writing "a memoir of contemporary life in the form of fiction." Supporting this observation, Starr remarks that Atherton's novelized memoirs precede John Steinbeck's "comparably integrated coverage" of California history. Atherton also wrote nonfiction, including *California: An Intimate History* (1914), to celebrate the Pan-Pacific Exposition in San Francisco in 1915, and two book-length essays on the Bay Area: *Golden Gate Country* (1945) and *My San Francisco, A Wayward Biography* (1946).

The San Francisco protagonists in Atherton's last two novels struggle to find a significant role in their city. In *The House of Lee* widowed Mrs. Eding-

ton leads her woman's club effort to find dignified work for young city women in the decade before World War II, while in *The Horn of Life* Lynn Franklin laments her failure to influence the city fathers' plans for the city's growth and accepts marriage as a last-resort fulfillment of her ambition.

By the end of her life Gertrude Atherton had related the chronicle of her birth city and state in seventeen novels, four short-story collections, and three social histories. Since 1976 when a bibliography of Atherton's works was published in *American Literary Realism,* scholars have examined her whole canon and new readers have discovered her ideas on women's lives. Atherton overcame her early ambivalence to her region, celebrating San Francisco in particular not only in her writing but also in her civic and literary activities for the city. In her California fiction as well as in her work that had other settings Atherton moved beyond region to explore universal motives and emotions of characters. As her career progressed into the twentieth century her ambitious, independent California New Woman lost her early association with decadence; finding few public outlets for their time and energy, they chose marriage to ambitious men or, widowed, found the means to support themselves. The restrictions society placed upon women remained a theme throughout her career. In her last California novel, *The Horn of Life,* Atherton, who utilized her own boredom and discontent as a catalyst for her sixty-year writing career, has her last heroine, Lynn Franklin, cry out, "Why . . . be born at all?" when time, environment, and customs inhibit creative desires. In her ninetieth year, planning a novel on the quicksilver mines in the Almaden area near her grandfather's ranch, Atherton died of a stroke on 14 June 1948.

Interviews:

Gertrude Atherton, as Pendennis, "Novels, Novelists, and Reviewers," *New York Times,* 16 April 1905, III: 3;

"Gertrude Atherton Assails 'The Powers,'" *New York Times,* 29 December 1907, VI: 2;

Atherton, as Pendennis, "My Types—Gertrude Atherton," *Forum,* 58 (November 1917): 585–594;

William E. Harris, "Contemporary Writers, XI, Gertrude Atherton," *Writer,* 39 (1929): 62–64.

Bibliographies:

Charlotte S. McClure, "A Checklist of the Writings of and about Gertrude Atherton," *American Literary Realism,* 9 (Spring 1976): 103–162;

McClure, "Gertrude Franklin Horn Atherton," in *American Women Writers: A Critical Reference*

Guide from Colonial Times to the Present, volume 1, edited by Lina Mainiero (New York: Ungar, 1979).

Biography:

Emily Wortis Leider, *California's Daughter: Gertrude Atherton and Her Times* (Palo Alto, Cal.: Stanford University Press, 1991).

References:

Carolyn Forrey, "Gertrude Atherton and the New Woman," *California Historical Society Quarterly,* 55 (1976): 194–209;

Joseph H. Jackson, *Gertrude Atherton* (New York: Appleton-Century, 1940);

Emily Wortis Leider, "'Your Picture Hangs in My Salon': The Letters of Gertrude Atherton to Ambrose Bierce," *California History,* 60 (Winter 1981/1982): 332–349;

Charlotte S. McClure, *Gertrude Atherton* (Boise, Idaho: Boise State University, 1976);

McClure, *Gertrude Atherton* (Boston: G. K. Hall, 1979);

McClure, "Gertrude Atherton's California Woman: From Love Story to Psychological Drama," in *Itinerary: Criticism: Essays on California Writers,* edited by Charles Crow (Bowling Green, Ohio: Bowling Green University Press, 1978), pp. 1–9;

Kevin Starr, "Gertrude Atherton, Daughter of the Elite," *Americans and the California Dream, 1850–1915* (New York: Oxford University Press, 1973), pp. 345–364;

Sybil Weir, "Gertrude Atherton: The Limits of Feminism in the 1890s," *San Jose Studies,* 1 (1975): 24–31.

Papers:

The Bancroft Library of the University of California, Berkeley; the New York Public Library; the Library of Congress; and the California Historical Society in San Francisco hold the largest collections of Atherton's letters and manuscripts.

Adolph F. Bandelier

(6 August 1840 – 18 March 1914)

James H. Maguire

Boise State University

BOOKS: *Historical Introduction to Studies among the Sedentary Indians of New Mexico and a Visit to the Aboriginal Ruins in the Valley of the Rio Pecos* (Boston: A. Williams, 1881; London: N. Trübner, 1881); republished as *An Archaeological Reconnaissance into Mexico* (Boston: Cupples & Hurd, 1883);

Report of an Archaeological Tour in Mexico, in 1881 (Boston: Cupples, Upham, 1884; London: N. Trübner, 1884);

La découverte du Nouveau-Mexique, par le moine franciscain frère Marcos, de Nice en 1539 (Paris: Leroux, 1886); translated and edited by Madeleine Turrell Rodack as *Adolph F. Bandelier's The Discovery of New Mexico by the Franciscan Monk, Friar Marcos de Niza, in 1539* (Tucson: University of Arizona Press, 1981);

Contributions to the History of the Southwestern Portion of the United States (Cambridge, Mass.: John Wilson, 1890);

The Delight Makers (New York: Dodd, Mead, 1890);

Final Report of Investigations among the Indians of the Southwestern United States, Carried on Mainly in the Years from 1880 to 1885, 2 volumes (Cambridge, Mass.: John Wilson, 1890–1892);

The Gilded Man (El Dorado) and Other Pictures of the Spanish Occupancy of America (New York: Appleton, 1893);

The Islands of Titicaca and Koati (New York: Hispanic Society of America, 1910);

Historical Documents Relating to New Mexico, Nueva Vizcaya, and Approaches Thereto, to 1773, 3 öolumes, collected by Bandelier and Fanny R. Bandelier, edited by Charles Wilson Hackett (Washington, D.C.: Carnegie Institution, 1923, 1926, 1937);

Indians of the Rio Grande Valley, by Bandelier and Edgar L. Hewitt (Albuquerque: University of New Mexico Press, 1937);

The Southwestern Journals of Adolph F. Bandelier, 1880–1882, edited by Charles H. Lange and

Adolph F. Bandelier (Museum of New Mexico)

Carroll L. Riley (Albuquerque: University of New Mexico Press, 1966);

A History of the Southwest: A Study of the Civilization and Conversion of the Indians in Southwestern United States and Northwestern Mexico from the Earliest Times to 1700, 2 volumes, edited by Ernest J. Burrus (Vatican City: Biblioteca Apostolica Vaticana, 1969–1987);

The Southwestern Journals of Adolph F. Bandelier, 1883–1884, edited by Lange and Riley (Albuquerque: University of New Mexico Press, 1970);

The Southwestern Journals of Adolph F. Bandelier, 1885–1888, edited by Charles H. Lange, Riley, and Elizabeth M. Lange (Albuquerque: University of New Mexico Press, 1975);

The Southwestern Journals of Adolph F. Bandelier, 1889–1892, edited by Charles H. Lange, Riley, and Elizabeth M. Lange (Albuquerque: University of New Mexico Press, 1984).

OTHER: *The Journey of Alvar Nuñez Cabeza de Vaca and His Companions from Florida to the Pacific, 1528–1536,* edited by Bandelier (New York: Barnes, 1905).

SELECTED PERIODICAL PUBLICATIONS–
UNCOLLECTED: "On the Art of War and Mode of Warfare of the Ancient Mexicans," *Tenth Annual Report of the Peabody Museum of American Archaeology and Ethnology* (1877): 95–161;

"On the Distribution and Tenure of Lands, and the Customs with Respect to Inheritance, among the Ancient Mexicans," *Eleventh Annual Report of the Peabody Museum of American Archaeology and Ethnology* (1878): 385–448;

"On the Social Organization and Mode of Government of the Ancient Mexicans," *Twelfth Annual Report of the Peabody Museum of American Archaeology and Ethnology* (1879): 557–699;

"Notes on the Bibliography of Yucatan and Central America," *Proceedings of the American Antiquarian Society,* new series 1 (1880–1881): 82–118;

"Reports by A. F. Bandelier on His Investigations in New Mexico during the Years 1883–1884," *Fifth Annual Report of the Executive Committee, Archaeological Institute of America* (1884): 55–98;

"An Outline of the Documentary History of the Zuñi Tribe," *Journal of American Ethnology and Archaeology,* 3, no. 4 (1892): 1–115;

"On the Relative Antiquity of Ancient Peruvian Burials," *Bulletin of the American Museum of Natural History,* no. 20 (1904): 217–226;

"The Cross of Carabuco in Bolivia," *American Anthropologist,* new series 6 (1904): 599–628;

"The Aboriginal Ruins at Stillustani, Peru," *American Anthropologist,* new series 7 (1905): 49–68;

"Traditions of Precolumbian Landings on the Western Coast of South America," *American Anthropologist,* new series 7 (1905): 250–270;

"The Truth about Inca Civilization," *Harper's Monthly,* 110 (March 1905): 632–640;

"Traditions of Pre-columbian Earthquakes and Volcanic Eruptions in Western South America," *American Anthropologist,* new series 8 (1906): 47–81;

"The Ruins of Tiahuanaco," *Proceedings of the American Antiquarian Society,* no. 21 (1911): 218–265.

As a pioneer of historical, archaeological, anthropological, and ethnological studies of the Southwest, Adolph Francis Alphonse Bandelier has a secure place in the intellectual history of late-nineteenth-century America. His one novel earned him even greater eminence, for, as Stefan Jovanovich says, "On publication in 1890, *The Delight Makers* was quickly recognized by anthropologists and archaeologists as a classic of both science and literature." In *Southwest Heritage: A Literary Heritage with Bibliography* (1972) Mabel Major and T. M. Pearce argue that "*The Delight Makers* will remain without rival among the nineteenth-century creative works dealing with the American Indian." "Taken strictly as literature," Jovanovich argues, "*The Delight Makers* can stand comparison with some of the better works of late-nineteenth-century naturalist fiction."

Bandelier was born in Bern, Switzerland, on 6 August 1840, the son of Adolph Eugene Bandelier and Marie Senn Bandelier. Perhaps because of his foreign background, some accounts of Bandelier's early life contain erroneous information. Charles H. Lange, Carroll L. Riley, and Elizabeth M. Lange point out, for example, the error in the statement of author and editor Charles Lummis, who said that Bandelier's mother was a member of the Russian nobility. Although Marie Senn had gone to Russia as a governess and had met her first husband there, she was not a Russian noble by birth or marriage. A professional man who had studied law at Lausanne, Bandelier's father went to Brazil in 1847 and then immigrated to the United States in 1848, settling in the Swiss community of Highland, Illinois, thirty miles east of Saint Louis, in September. A month after the father's arrival in Highland, Marie, their son Adolph, and the family maid joined him there.

Growing up in a highly literate and multilingual community, Bandelier received private tutoring in mineralogy and geology from Dr. J. F. Bernays and was strongly influenced by the career and publications of Baron Alexander von Humboldt, a German naturalist and statesman. In 1854 Bandelier's father entered into a partnership with two other Swiss immigrants, Frederick C. Ryhiner and Morris Huegy, to begin a bank. Bandelier's mother died the next year, and his father's strong influence on him intensified. In the late 1850s Bandelier traveled to Switzerland (although he did not study geol-

Page from Bandelier's journal, 5 September 1880 (Museum of New Mexico)

ogy there, as earlier biographical sketches report). His brief travel account was published in the 23 February 1858 *Saint Louis Republican*. His father served as Highland's school director from 1858 to 1860 and was elected first president of the town's literary society in 1859. Despite the father's strong interest in education, the son apparently never attended college.

On 5 January 1861 Bandelier married the daughter of one of his father's banking partners. His bride, Josephine "Joe" Huegy, was four years older than Bandelier, and she suffered long periods of ill health during their marriage. Bandelier had started working at his father's bank when he was fourteen, and he continued to work there for the first two decades of his marriage to Joe. In 1870 he acquired an interest in the Confidence Coal and Mining Company and, at about the same time, a stake in the Highland Mechanical Works. During this same period Bandelier wrote articles on climatology for local newspapers and gave lectures in the Saint Louis area on archaeological and historical subjects. For his lectures he drew upon the resources of the Mercantile Library, which had been founded by Saint Louis merchants in 1846.

Exploring the collection of Americana of the Mercantile Library, Bandelier began his study of pre-Columbian American Indian society sometime around 1869. As students of his writing have noted, his work falls into three categories, each associated with a particular area: New Mexico, Old Mexico, and Peru. In the 1870s, after spending his days working at the bank and dealing with his other business interests, Bandelier would retire from social entertainments to spend the first part of his nights translating Fernando Alvarado Tezozomoc's *Chronica Mexicana* (1598), which he had found among the nine volumes of Edward King's *Antiquities of Mexico* (1830–1848). Bandelier's translation was not published and has never been located, but his reliance on it for his first articles on the Aztecs is apparent from his many citations of Tezozomoc.

Of even greater importance to his writing and his intellectual development was his friendship with Lewis H. Morgan, "the Father of American Anthropology" and author of *League of the Ho-dé-no-sau-nee, or Iroquois* (1851), *Systems of Consanguinity and Affinity of the Human Family* (1871), and *Ancient Society; or Researches in the Lines of Human Progress* (1877). Bandelier met Morgan in the summer of 1873 in Rochester, New York, and corresponded with him from 20 December 1873 until Morgan's death on 17 December 1881; he then wrote to Mrs. Morgan until her death in 1883. The correspondence was edited by Leslie A. White and published under the title *Pioneers in American Anthropology: The Bandelier-Morgan Letters, 1873–1883* (1940). As White notes, the letters show Bandelier being persuaded by Morgan's argument about the nature of American Indian cultures. Morgan believed that

All forms of government are reducible to two general plans . . . fundamentally distinct. The first, in order of time, is founded upon persons, and upon relations purely personal, and may be distinguished as a society (*societas*). . . . The second is founded upon territory and upon property, and may be distinguished as a state (*civitas*).

White says that Morgan thought no American Indian cultures "had developed beyond the stage of *societas;* monarchy, feudal institutions, aristocracy, and so on, he declared, were wholly absent from the cultures of the New World."

Except for occasional brief mention of personal matters such as his coal mine or his wife's poor health, Bandelier's letters (Morgan's apparently did not survive) discuss the sixteenth-century books he was buying and reading, and his main focus is on Morgan's view that there was no actual monarchy in ancient America. At the beginning of the correspondence, Bandelier tried to refute Morgan; then, after he was won over to Morgan's view, he wrote to share evidence that he thought confirmed Morgan's theory. The fact that Bandelier considered himself to be Morgan's disciple is clear in a letter he wrote to Morgan on 8 October 1878: "The amount of ignorance displayed by me already is astonishing, the only good thing is and has been a more or less faithful adherence to your ethnological principles."

Morgan's views of ancient Indian societies differed from those expressed in the works of his prominent contemporaries. William Hickling Prescott's *History of the Conquest of Mexico* (1843) and *History of the Conquest of Peru* (1847), Lew Wallace's novel *The Fair God* (1873), and Hubert Howe Bancroft's *Native Races* (1874–1875) portrayed Indian societies with rulers resembling pharaohs, sun kings, and other hereditary monarchs of the Old World. Bandelier considered these depictions romanticized and inaccurate. To correct the record he wrote a series of three articles that were published successively in the tenth, eleventh, and twelfth annual reports of the Peabody Museum, in Cambridge, Massachusetts: "On the Art of War and Mode of Warfare of the Ancient Mexicans" (1877), "On the Distribution and Tenure of Lands, and the Customs with Respect to Inheritance, among the Ancient Mexicans" (1878), and "On the Social Organization and Mode of Government of the Ancient Mexicans" (1880).

"In asserting a revolutionary interpretation of the Aztecs," Jovanovich writes, "Bandelier was acting not as Morgan's ideologue but as an iconoclast who was completely on his own." Yet Bandelier restates Morgan's thesis in each of the three articles, and he concludes the last article by saying, "*the social organization and mode of government of the ancient Mexicans was a military democracy, originally based upon com-*

munism in living" (Bandelier's italics). To prove his point Bandelier provides lengthy footnotes for almost every assertion he makes, with the result that the footnotes dominate most of the pages of the three articles. So voluminous were his footnotes and so numerous his citations and quotations that in January 1880 F. W. Putnam, editor of the Peabody Museum reports, declined to publish anything more by Bandelier.

Beginning in 1876 Bandelier had also been serving as archaeological reviewer for *The Nation,* and he continued until 1892, earning modest sums by writing reviews and articles. But by 1879 he had grown increasingly dissatisfied with being only a part-time archaeologist, and in the fall of that year he traveled to New York City to do research at the Lenox and Astor libraries. He returned to Highland, and after receiving the bad news from Putnam in January 1880 he wrote to Morgan, asking for help. Morgan urged the newly founded Archaeological Institute of America (AIA) to send an expedition to the Southwest, and he recommended that Bandelier be appointed a member of the project. Later in the spring Bandelier went to Washington, D.C., where he met with Maj. John Wesley Powell and C. C. Rau to plan an archaeological expedition to the Southwest and Mexico under the auspices of the AIA, the executive committee of which included among its members Francis Parkman, Charles Eliot Norton, and Alexander Agassiz, all of whom Bandelier would eventually visit.

On 23 August 1880 Bandelier arrived in Santa Fe, New Mexico, and began archaeological fieldwork, which would be his occupation intermittently for the next twenty-three years. He kept detailed journals recording his work; the Southwestern journals have been edited and thoroughly annotated by the Langes and Riley and published in four volumes (1966–1984). The editors say that some of the entries "have considerable literary quality," but such entries are few. More typical are passages filled with details about the ruins Bandelier explored, including measurements, descriptions of settings, and listings of potsherds and other fragments. Many entries are filled with ethnological information that Bandelier was given by the Pueblo Indians. When he writes about himself and his family he usually only complains about illness or other discomforts and he rarely shares thoughts and feelings about matters not trivial or mundane.

During his years in the Southwest, Bandelier met and in some cases became friends with many of the region's luminaries, including Lew Wallace, Archbishop John B. Lamy (the model for the principal character in Willa Cather's 1927 novel *Death*

Comes for the Archbishop), Frank Cushing, Lummis, Dr. Washington Mathews, and Walter Gunn Marmon (older brother of Robert G. Marmon, the great-grandfather of contemporary Laguna author Leslie Marmon Silko). Unfortunately, Bandelier seldom includes more about these people than he says about Lummis in the entry for 7 December 1890 (original in Spanish): "No letters. Nothing, nothing. Still I won't despair. In the afternoon, Henry and I went to the plaza. At night Lummis came, well disposed and happy as always." In writing about the Indians, however, Bandelier gives much more information. Moreover, the editors' annotations provide so much detail that the combination of their notes with Bandelier's entries creates a fascinating picture of the intellectual and upper social circles of the late-nineteenth-century Southwest.

At the end of 1880 Bandelier returned to Highland, and in February 1881, with a salary granted by the AIA, he went to Mexico to join the Lorillard de Charnay expedition to the Maya region. When he arrived at Mexico City in early March, however, there was no expedition to join since those involved had given up their plans for exploration upon becoming fever-ridden in Chiapas. After meeting with De Charnay (who soon after left for France), Bandelier began his own explorations in the areas of Oaxaca, Mitla, Mexico City, and the State of Puebla. He sent reports of his travels to a German-language newspaper, the *Highland Union;* these were later translated and published as *A Scientist on the Trail: Travel Letters of A. F. Bandelier, 1880–1881* (1949), edited by George P. Hammond and Edgar F. Goad. The editors state that these letters, "in contrast to the staid and dull phraseology of [Bandelier's] various scientific reports, are often almost poetic in tone." One significant event not mentioned in the letters is Bandelier's conversion to Catholicism in July 1881 while he was in Cholula.

After he returned to the United States in 1881 Bandelier spent the next eleven years in the Southwest, with annual trips to Highland, to eastern states, to Europe, or to Mexico. His scientific reports, which began to appear in the papers of the AIA and in newspapers and magazines as well, are indeed marked by "staid and dull phraseology," but to the nascent fields of American archaeology, anthropology, and ethnology these works contributed the insights of a scholar who had read and re-read the early Spanish reports in the original and who had then studied not only the localities mentioned in the reports but also the descendants of the native peoples. In a 6 July 1877 letter to Morgan, Bandelier describes his diligence in studying the Spanish sources: "It takes years till you get to know an

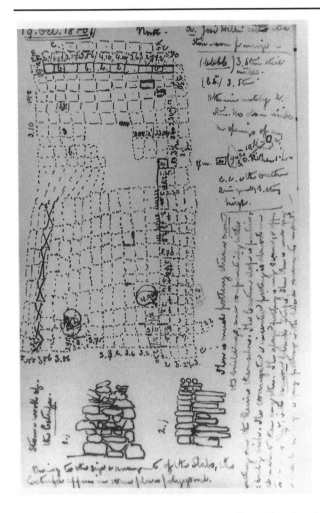 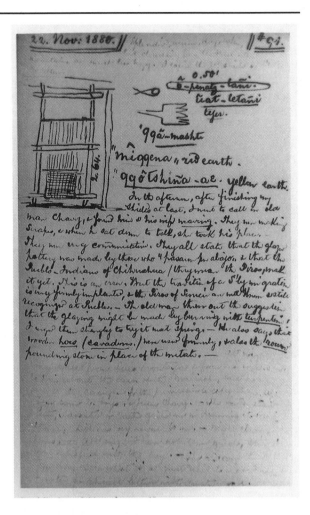

Pages from Bandelier's journal, 19 October and 22 November 1880 (from Charles H. Lange and Carroll L. Riley, Bandelier: The Life and Adventures of Adolph Bandelier, *1996)*

author; and especially such an author, though you should have read him five times over. I am perhaps the only living man in the United States who can say that he has read Herrera *twice* through in the original, still I do not pretend to know him."

Hammond and Goad claim that Bandelier "was a superficial field investigator," but he nevertheless helped to establish the practice of combining historical research with archaeological and ethnological fieldwork. As he puts it in his *Contributions to the History of the Southwestern Portion of the United States* (1890):

We are but on the threshold of American ethnology, and ethnology alone, considered as a "method of research," can supply a key to the maze of material which the Spaniards and their missionaries accumulated, or which they enabled the natives to render intelligible to a public accustomed to methods of commemoration highly in advance of any which the American Indian had ever conceived.

In addition, Bandelier knew many of the leading field investigators of the times; he corresponded with them, read their reports, and mentions their insights and discoveries in his own work. In his *Final Report of Investigations among the Indians of the Southwestern United States . . .* (1890–1892), for example, he refers his readers to the works of Capt. John G. Bourke, Mathews, Albert S. Gatschet, and Cushing.

In 1885 a financial crisis at his father's bank interrupted Bandelier's scientific work. In April he returned to Highland to help out, but a month later the bank failed. Warrants were issued for the arrest of the Bandeliers and other bank officers. Bandelier's father disappeared, and his brother-in-law committed suicide. Although not a partner in the bank, Bandelier was taken to court. Released on a bond, he returned to Santa Fe in June but returned to Highland in October for a hearing on the indictment. The case was dropped, and after he was released from the bond he left in November to make Santa Fe his permanent home. Without his earlier means of financial support, he began to study law in June 1886; in October he began work as historiographer of the Hemenway Southwestern Archaeological Expedition, and he accepted a commission from Archbishop J. B. Salpointe to write a history of the missions of the Southwest and northern Mexico. Written in French and completed in 1888, Bandelier's four-volume, fourteen-hundred-page manuscript was presented to the Vatican and placed in the Vatican Library; portions of it have been translated and published as *A History of the Southwest* (1969–1987), edited by Ernest J. Burrus.

Several years before the bank failure Bandelier had started a fiction project. His first reference to it, in a journal entry dated 24 August 1883, is laconic: "Began to write my novel." He worked on the manuscript sporadically for the next several years. The list of his publications indicates that by the late 1880s he hoped to gain more income from writing. He not only accepted the commission to write the history of the missions but also contributed eighty-six articles to the *Catholic Encyclopedia* (1890). Yet, in spite of his need for money, his primary motive for writing *The Delight Makers* was not financial. He gives his main reason in a 2 September 1888 letter to his friend and fellow writer Thomas A. Janvier:

I consider the "novel" of much greater importance [than scientific articles] in regard to Mexico even. We have, Mr. Morgan, and I under his directions, unsettled the Romantic School in Science, now the same thing must be [done] in literature on the American aborigine. Prescott's Aztec is a myth, it remains to show that Fennimore Cooper's Indian is a fraud. Understand me: I have nothing personal in view. Cooper has no more sincere admirer than I am, but the cigar-store red man and the statuesque Pocahontas of the "vuelta abajo" trade as they are paraded in literature and thus pervert the public conceptions about our Indians, THEY—I want to destroy first if possible. Afterwards the time will come for a republication of the scientific tracts.

He wrote the novel in German, completing it on 12 May 1886; it was initially published in serial form under the title *Die Köshare* in the *Belletristisches Journal* of New York from 1 January to 14 May 1890.

A 31 January 1876 letter to Morgan explains why Bandelier chose German in writing his novel: "the English language, with all my efforts, still remains equally foreign [as Spanish] to me." The editors of his journals discuss his imperfect understanding of some of the languages he used, and Bandelier himself knew the dangers of multilingual scholarship, as he notes in a letter to Morgan on 28 January 1878: "Not a single day passes without my using at least 4 languages in speech, in reading, or in writing.

Sometimes I have to use 5 or 6. This must corrupt the proper use of any single one, unless the greatest care is taken." When he translated *Die Köshare* into English, he took great care, as he explains to Janvier in a letter dated 2 September 1888: "I have here a circle of kind friends who assist me materially by revising the King's English; a very necessary task, for more and more I see how lamentably deficient I am in knowledge of the language." Although Bandelier exaggerates, his uneasiness about the language probably accounts in part for the formality of his English translation, a style well suited to the narrative.

After he finished translating the novel in 1889 he had difficulty finding a publisher for it. He stayed in Santa Fe, relying upon Janvier to see that the manuscript made the round of the publishers, but he suggested that it be sent to Harper's since he knew editor George William Curtis there. For some unknown reason Janvier sent it to Scribners instead, but on 19 March 1889 Scribners rejected it. Then Bandelier asked that it be sent to Charles Eliot Norton and Francis Parkman. On 13 October 1889 Bandelier told Janvier that both of them had "passed judgment upon it in the most favorable manner possible, as something unique in literature." Norton and Parkman suggested "indispensable" revisions for the novel to be published, which Bandelier eventually followed.

After several other rejections Janvier sent the manuscript to Dodd, Mead, and in 1890 the firm published it as *The Delight Makers*. In a 31 January 1891 letter to Mrs. Janvier, Bandelier writes: "Many papers have spoken of the book quite favorably, but the papers are not the public." The *Santa Fe Daily New Mexican* and journals such as *The Critic* and *The Dial* gave the book generally favorable reviews, but it apparently did not sell well enough for the publishers to keep it in print. Because *The Delight Makers* did not gain great popularity he quit writing a second novel he had begun. By 1916, however, Lummis could report in the introduction to a second edition that "During the six years I was Librarian of Los Angeles Public Library, . . . no other out-of-print book on the Southwest was so eagerly sought as *The Delight Makers*."

The novel begins at a time "much anterior to the discovery of America, to the invention of gunpowder and the printing-press in Europe." A community from the Pueblo people called the Queres (Keres) live at Tyuonyi (which the Spaniards, centuries later, would call El Rito de los Frijoles). Tensions build when a divorced couple, Tyope and Shotaye, plot revenge on each other and try to gain control of the community, even resorting to betrayal of the tribe to its enemies. The schemes of the divorced miscreants eventually destroy the community, but their effect is shown on one family in particular. The wife, Say, and her husband, Zashue, have three children; the first part of the novel focuses on the two boys, Shyuote and Okoya.

Zashue is a *koshare,* a delight maker, one of a society responsible for insuring the successful growth and harvesting of plants in the summer and autumn. During dances and other ritual ceremonies, the koshare clown around, obscenely satirizing and poking fun at everyone. In contrast to the riotous koshare, another society, the *cuirana* (kwerena), have the responsibility for the spring season, and their demeanor is dignified. Zashue's brother, Hayoue, is a member of the cuirana.

When Okoya falls in love with Mitsha, the daughter of Tyope and Shotaye, he turns to Hayoue for advice since the adolescent boy knows that his mother despises Tyope, who is not only Mitsha's father but also a koshare. Shotaye had earlier convinced Say to put a ritual curse on the koshare, and Say fears that the koshare will discover what she has done and will retaliate. While the uncle and nephew discuss the boy's Romeo-and-Juliet-like predicament, Tyope betrays the Queres to the Navajo, and Shotaye sells out to their rivals, the Tehuas. As a result of these machinations a Navajo kills one of the leaders of the Queres, but the killing is made to seem the work of the Tehuas. The outraged Queres prepare to revenge the death, but before they launch their attack Shotaye goes over to the Tehuas and warns them. The Queres warriors lose their nerve when they meet the prepared resistance, and they are slaughtered. The few survivors return home to find that their pueblo has been attacked by a Navajo war party, who have killed many of the Queres and forced others to flee. Zashue learns that his daughter was killed and his wife and sons are among those who fled. He and Hayoue search for months until they find the exiles, but within hours after they find them, Say dies. The narrative closes with an indication that Okoya and Mitsha will marry and Hayoue will lead the remnants of the Queres community to a new site where they will build a new pueblo.

Bandelier interweaves a wealth of ethnological information into the narrative. Readers learn not only about the koshare and the cuirana but also about clans and other aspects of Queres social organization. The division of labor within the community is explained as well as methods of education and practices of courtship. Bandelier also describes Queres religious beliefs and superstitions and depicts their governing bodies in action and their warriors preparing for a campaign. The narrator de-

Bandelier and his second wife, Fanny Ritter Bandelier, in Peru (Museum of New Mexico)

scribes life in a pre-Columbian pueblo dwelling not only by telling us about the size and appearance of the rooms but also by explaining how the people occupied themselves while in their domestic environment. This fusion of fiction and ethnological data is what Bandelier referred to when he wrote in the preface to the first edition of "clothing sober facts in the garb of romance."

Although some passages of *The Delight Makers* read like excerpts from an anthropology text, the narrative really is, as Jovanovich puts it, "much more than a fictional tour of primitive New Mexico." The characters do not seem to be textbook examples, for their behavior is sometimes unpredictable, but Bandelier endows them with believable motives and emotions that make them credible. Nor does Bandelier manipulate the plot to fit a formula. Instead of completing the parallel with Romeo and Juliet, Okoya and Mitsha live and will probably marry. The Macbeth-like Tyope dooms the pueblo, but he loses only face, not his life, and his Lady

Macbeth-like ex-wife, Shotaye, suffers not at all after she betrays her own people. Moreover, as Jovanovich points out, Bandelier creates a fictional world, not without humor, consistent with his naturalist vision, "a world of Nature that is disinterested and merciless."

Almost wrenching this tapestry of fact and fiction is a tension created by the contradiction between occasional narrative pronouncements and the rest of the novel. These pronouncements seem to stem from Bandelier's apparent desire to remain faithful to Morgan's belief that American Indian cultures never evolved beyond a primitive level. For Bandelier, "primitive" sometimes meant "inferior." Here, for example, is how the narrator explains Say's response to a rainbow that she believes is a sign from the Shiuana, or spirits:

> This implicit, slavish obedience to signs and tokens of a natural order to which a supernatural origin is assigned, is the Indian's religion. The life of the Indian is therefore merely a succession of religious acts called forth by utterances of what he supposes to be higher powers surrounding him, and accompanying him on every step from the cradle to the grave. The Indian is a child whose life is ruled by a feeling of complete dependence, by a desire to accommodate every action to the wills and decrees of countless supernatural beings.

Since the adult characters in *The Delight Makers* do not seem at all like "The Indian" in that description, the narrator's story undercuts the ideology he expresses.

Another example of this tension occurs after Okoya has learned that his mother approves of Mitsha after all. The narrator comments that Okoya "felt glad, he felt happy, because his mother approved of him. He was fond of his mother at the bottom of his heart, as fond as any Indian can be." The narrator's implication that the primitive Indian was not capable of emotions as intense as those of civilized people is belied by the evident emotional intensity of most of the characters in the novel. The distance between what the narrator says about "the Indian" and what is shown about particular Indian characters throughout the book is so great that the tension ultimately remains unresolved. It may be what led Paul Radin in the introduction to *The Unpublished Letters of Adolphe F. Bandelier Concerning the Writing and Publication of* The Delight Makers (1942) to his conclusion about the author's relation to his work: "That it is more than simply a description of the Indians of the Southwest is clear to anyone who reads it. Manifestly, it contains, in a disguised and symbolical form, some part of that very much agitated and strangely unintegrated self that was Adolphe Bandelier."

Instead of continuing in fiction, Bandelier worked for some months cataloguing and translating the territorial archives of New Mexico. As the Langes and Riley report, "For a brief period [in the early 1890s] he became actively engaged in business matters, but an anticipated commission from a major land sale, which would have made him financially independent and so allowed him to continue his Southwestern research on his own time, failed to materialize." From 1890 to 1892 he traveled throughout the Southwest, often in the company of Lummis, who in his 1916 introduction writes of his friend: "He has always reminded me of John Muir, the only other man I have known intimately who was as insatiate a climber and inspiring a talker. But Bandelier had one advantage. He could find common ground with *anyone*." Lummis added:

> I have known many scholars and some heroes—but they seldom come in the same original package. As I remember Bandelier with smallpox alone in Northern Mexico, with no more weapon than a pen-knife, on the trails of raiding Apaches . . . I deeply wonder at the dual quality of his intellect. Among them all, I have never known such student and such explorer lodged in one tenement.

In 1892, two years after Mary Hemenway had withdrawn the Southwestern Archaeological Expedition's financial support from Bandelier because she had lost confidence in the expedition's director, Frank Cushing, Bandelier and Lummis went to New York City, Baltimore, Washington, and Cincinnati and succeeded in receiving funding from Henry Villard and the American Museum of Natural History for an expedition to Bolivia and Peru.

Bandelier and his wife sailed from San Francisco on 6 June 1892 and arrived in Lima, Peru, on 11 July. His wife became ill in the autumn, and she died on 11 December. While Bandelier watched over her deathbed, the wife of his friend Janvier was helping to see through the press a new book by Bandelier: *The Gilded Man (El Dorado) and Other Pictures of the Spanish Occupancy of America.* Although the book seemed new to most of the public when it appeared in 1893, many of its sections had originally been written in German and had been published in the *New Yorker Staats-Zeitung, Sonntags Blatt* from April 1876 to July 1877 and continued in 1885–1886. The first of the five sections of the book gives a historical summary of European (mainly Spanish) attempts to find the South American indigenous people who coated their leader with gold dust. Bandelier traces the reports of the gilded man, stories that began with Christopher Columbus's first voyage. In 1536 Gonzalo Ximenes de Quesada of Granada led 705 soldiers into the jungle in search of El Dorado. Most of Quesada's men perished, but he managed to return laden with gold and emeralds, although he had not found the fabled country. Other Spanish explorers tried, but none succeeded. Bandelier describes these and other efforts, including the expedition of some Germans, and he closes this section with remarks on the research of Humboldt in the early nineteenth century.

In the next section Bandelier summarizes the history of Spanish attempts to find the Seven Cities of Cibola. He had written before about the adventures of Hernán Cortes, Cabeza de Vaca, Fray Marcos de Niza, and Francisco Vásquez de Coronado, and here he also shares his knowledge of Pueblo life in order to shed light on what he finds in the Spanish journals and reports. In the section titled "The Massacre of Cholula" he corrects the accounts of historians such as Prescott, and in "The Age of the City of Santa Fé" he argues that "Santa Fé was not founded till after the year 1607." The final section, "Jean l'Archévèque," uses Spanish documents to tell the story of a member of the La Salle expedition who, after the murder of La Salle, went to New Mexico and later lost his life while he was a member of the Villasur expedition of 1720. Although Bandelier had written about many of these subjects before, the collection of all the essays into one book gives a more intense effect, one described by D. H. Lawrence in *Phoenix:*

> There is, in reality, a peculiar dread horror about the conquest of America, the story is always dreadful, more or less. Columbus, Pizarro, Cortes, Quesada, De Soto, the Conquistadores seem all like men of doom. Read a man like Adolph Bandelier, who knows the *inside* of his America, read his *Golden Man*—El Dorado—and feel the reverberation within reverberation of horror the Conquistadores left behind them.

After the publication of *The Gilded Man* Bandelier began archaeological collecting for Villard and then for the American Museum of Natural History. At the same time he also began a new domestic life, one described by biographer Edgar F. Goad:

> In December, 1893, Bandelier married Fanny Ritter, in La Paz. She seems to have been the daughter of a Swiss immigrant, her mother, a widow, either living in, or operating the boarding house where the Bandeliers stayed. She was considerably younger than Bandelier, now fifty-three, and an accomplished linguist. This union was peculiarly fortunate. Fanny Bandelier proved herself to be almost as much a scholar as the ethnologist himself. She read Spanish, of course, and in addition, French, Italian, German, and English. Vivacious and

devoted, she was a worthy companion to such a man as Bandelier. Thenceforth they were constantly together, with Adolph leading and Fanny picking up the pieces. Before the death of Bandelier, Fanny translated the narration of Cabeza de Vaca into English, and after his death, while teaching in Fiske University, she translated one volume of Sahagun into English.

During the latter part of 1893 Bandelier traveled into the Amazon drainage. The following year he and Fanny moved to La Paz, where they resided until 1903. Charles H. Lange and Carroll L. Riley in the first volume of *The Southwest Journals* assert that "In the main Bandelier's work in Peru and Bolivia paralleled what he had done in New Mexico." He continued searching in libraries and archives for documents of the conquest, and he traveled to old ruins that he explored and measured. Lange and Riley also say that "he had little to do with the Indians . . . [because he felt that] the Indians of these areas had degenerated through mixture with the lower classes of the conquerors."

When Bandelier and Fanny moved to the United States in 1903 they settled in New York City. For the next three years he continued working for and lecturing at the American Museum of Natural History; in 1904 he was appointed lecturer in Spanish American literature at Columbia University. In 1906 he resigned from his position at the American Museum because of a publishing disagreement, and he accepted another position at the Hispanic Society of America. From 1909 to 1911 he experienced virtual blindness as a result of cataracts, yet during that same period, without leaving New York, he served as a staff member of the Museum of New Mexico and the School of American Archaeology (now the School of American Research).

In 1910 the Hispanic Society published *The Islands of Titicaca and Koati,* a book Bandelier based on his field work in Peru and Bolivia. The six chapter titles indicate its contents: "The Basin of Lake Titicaca," "The Islands of Titicaca and Koati," "The Indians of the Island of Titicaca," "The Ancient Ruins on the Island of Titicaca," "The Ruins on the Island of Koati," and "Aboriginal Myths and Traditions Concerning the Island of Titicaca." Most of the text is factual and descriptive, but occasionally Bandelier expresses his sense of superiority to the primitive natives: "Surrounded by the magnificent water-sheet of the Lake, in full view of the Andes, Titicaca lacks but arborescent vegetation and the presence of civilized man with his resources for comfort, to make it a spot worthy of being counted among the precious sites on the earth's surface." The book also includes Fanny's "List of Indigenous Plants" as well as several photographs.

In late 1911, having sufficiently recovered his sight to begin working again, Bandelier was appointed a research assistant at the Carnegie Institution of Washington. In 1912 he and his wife spent several months in Mexico. They returned to New York City in the spring of 1913, and in the fall of that year they sailed to Spain to undertake research that Bandelier had been wanting to do for years. He wanted to comb Spanish libraries and archives to find ancient documents, reports, letters, and journals written in or about New Mexico. Unfortunately, he fell ill and could not continue the work after December 1913. He died in Seville on 18 March 1914. After his death Fanny stayed in Spain, working in the archives until the end of 1915. When she returned to the United States she gave the documents she and Bandelier had collected to the Carnegie Institution, which published them in three volumes (1923, 1926, and 1937).

Another work by Bandelier was published posthumously. His "Documentary History of the Rio Grande Pueblos" had been written from 1910 to 1912 when he was an associate of the School of American Archaeology. Edgar L. Hewett had suggested the project and had arranged for Bandelier to receive financial support. Modeled on his earlier "An Outline of the Documentary History of the Zuñi Tribe" (1892), the work covers materials that he had written about before—narratives by De Vaca and Castañeda, for example—but he also discussed Gaspar Perez de Villagra's *Historia de la Nueva Mexico* (1610), Fray Juan de Torquemada's *Monarchia Indiana* (1615), Fray Alonso de Benavides's *Memorial* (1630), Carlos de Sigüenza y Góngora's *El Mercurio Volante* (1693), Fray Agustín de Vetancurt's *Teatro Mexicano* (1698), and several other works. Though nearly blind, Bandelier had Fanny's assistance in writing the work. Initially it was published only in fragments. Hewett included the complete study as part 2 of *Indians of the Rio Grande Valley* (1937; part 1 is Hewett's "The Rio Grande Pueblos Today"). Acknowledging "that historical research in the Southwest has been carried much farther since Bandelier's time," Hewett says that the more recent contributions had "been mainly an extension, not a revision, of Southwestern history. The Old Master has been found amazingly accurate."

Even more laudatory are Hewett's comments about Bandelier's overall career:

> The foundation for all ethnological and historical study of the Southwest was laid by Adolph Bandelier. . . . Even yet the magnitude of his work is but faintly realized. He made a stupendous contribution to American history and science during the three and a half decades of his service to science, with financial resources that in these days of vast foundations would be considered beggarly. He lived most of his life in harassing poverty. . . . The works of his brain, could they be assembled and made known to the world, would constitute such a monument as commemorates the lives of very few of the world's scholars.

Almost fifty years after Hewett's praise, the Langes and Riley gave a more qualified assessment of Bandelier's career, noting that "throughout his life Bandelier lived with scholarly contradiction and made little or no effort to reconcile differing points of view." Nevertheless, they also see him as "wonderfully modern. His study of the American Indian past in a setting of the total environment was reinvented with great fanfare in the 1960s and, with mechanistic philosophical underpinnings (which would have been anathema to Bandelier), has come to be known as New Archaeology."

Bandelier the novelist had received little critical attention until Jovanovich's preface to his company's 1971 edition of *The Delight Makers*. In 1981 Russell S. Saxton provided a detailed analysis of the novel's structure; in 1982 Barbara A. Babcock explained some of the anthropological underpinnings of Bandelier's fiction. In 1995 Randall C. Davis argued that "Bandelier was unable to avoid the struggle between 'savagery' (or, in Bandelier's case, 'barbarism') and 'civilization' which had governed most literary representations of American Indians through the twentieth century." Although Jovanovich, Saxton, Babcock, and Davis have not reached consensus about *The Delight Makers,* their work should sustain the reputation of the novel as one of the American West's minor classics.

Letters:

Pioneers in American Anthropology: The Bandelier-Morgan Letters, 1873–1883, 2 volumes, edited by Leslie A. White (Albuquerque: University of New Mexico Press, 1940);

The Unpublished Letters of Adolphe F. Bandelier Concerning the Writing and Publication of The Delight Makers, edited by Paul Radin (New York: Charles P. Everitt, 1942);

A Scientist on the Trail: Travel Letters of A. F. Bandelier, 1880–1881, edited by George P. Hammond and Edgar F. Goad (Berkeley, Cal.: Quivira Society, 1949);

Correspondencia de Adolfo F. Bandelier, edited by White and Ignacio Bernal (Mexico City: Instituto Nacional de Antropología e Historia, 1960).

Biographies:

Frederick W. Hodge, "Biographical Sketch and Bibliography of Adolphe Francis Alphonse Bandelier," *New Mexico Historical Review,* 7, no. 4 (1932): 353–370;

Edgar F. Goad, "A Study of the Life of Adolph Francis Alphonse Bandelier, with an Appraisal of His Contributions to American Anthropology and Related Sciences," dissertation, University of Southern California, Los Angeles, 1939;

Eric Rufener, *Adolphe-François Bandelier, 1840–1914: Un Promoteur de l'Archéologie Américaine* (Tramelan, Switzerland: Editions Intervalles, 1982);

Charles H. Lange and Carroll L. Riley, *Bandelier: The Life and Adventures of Adolph Bandelier* (Salt Lake City: University of Utah Press, 1996).

References:

Barbara A. Babcock, "Ritual Undress and the Comedy of Self and Other: Bandelier's *The Delight Makers,*" in *A Crack in the Mirror: Reflexive Perspectives in Anthropology,* edited by Jay Ruby (Philadelphia: University of Pennsylvania Press, 1982), pp. 187–203;

C. W. Ceram, *The First American: A Story of North American Archaeology* (New York: Harcourt Brace Jovanovich, 1971), pp. 57–67;

Randall C. Davis, "'The Path toward Civilization': Sociocultural Evolution and *The Delight Makers,*" *American Literary Realism,* 27, no. 2 (1995): 37–52;

Stefan Jovanovich, "Adolf Bandelier: An Introduction," in *The Delight Makers* (New York: Harcourt Brace Jovanovich, 1971), pp. v–xix;

Charles H. Lange, Carroll L. Riley, and Elizabeth M. Lange, "Introduction," in *The Southwestern Journals of Adolph F. Bandelier, 1889–1892* (Albuquerque: University of New Mexico Press, 1984), pp. 1–47;

D. H. Lawrence, *Phoenix: The Posthumous Papers of D. H. Lawrence,* edited by Edward D. McDonald (New York: Viking, 1968), pp. 336, 359;

Charles Lummis, "Death of Bandelier an Irreparable Loss," *El Palacio,* 1 (April–May 1914): 1, 3;

Russell S. Saxton, "'The Truth about the Pueblo Indians': Bandelier's *Delight Makers,*" *New Mexico Historical Review,* 56, no. 3 (1981): 261–284;

T. T. Waterman, "Bandelier's Contributions to the Study of Ancient Mexican Social Organization," *University of California Publications in American Archaeology and Ethnology,* 12, no. 7 (1917): 249–282.

Papers:

Bandelier materials are housed at the Southwest Museum (Los Angeles), the University of New Mexico Library, Houghton Library at Harvard University, the Massachusetts Historical Society, the Museum of New Mexico, the Huntington Library at San Marino, California, the John M. Longyear Museum at Colgate University, and the American Museum of Natural History.

Ambrose Bierce

(24 June 1842 – 11 January 1914)

M. E. Grenander
State University of New York at Albany

See also the Bierce entries in *DLB 11: American Humorists, 1800–1950; DLB 12: American Realists and Naturalists; DLB 23: American Newspaper Journalists, 1873–1900; DLB 71: American Literary Critics and Scholars, 1880–1900;* and *DLB 74: American Short-Story Writers Before 1880.*

BOOKS: *The Fiend's Delight,* as Dod Grile (London: John Camden Hotten, 1873; New York: A. L. Luyster, 1873);

Nuggets and Dust Panned Out in California, as Dod Grile (London: Chatto & Windus, 1873);

Cobwebs from an Empty Skull, as Dod Grile (London & New York: Routledge, 1874);

The Dance of Death, by Bierce and Thomas A. Harcourt, as William Herman (San Francisco: Privately printed, 1877; corrected and enlarged edition, San Francisco: Henry Keller, 1877);

Tales of Soldiers and Civilians (San Francisco: E. L. G. Steele, 1891); republished as *In the Midst of Life* (London: Chatto & Windus, 1892; revised and enlarged edition, New York & London: Putnam, 1898);

Black Beetles in Amber (San Francisco & New York: Western Authors Publishing, 1892);

Can Such Things Be? (New York: Cassell, 1893; London: Cape, 1926);

Fantastic Fables (New York & London: Putnam, 1899);

Shapes of Clay (San Francisco: W. E. Wood, 1903);

The Cynic's Word Book (Garden City, N.Y.: Doubleday, Page, 1906); enlarged as *The Devil's Dictionary,* volume 7 of *The Collected Works of Ambrose Bierce* (New York & Washington, D.C.: Neale, 1911);

A Son of the Gods and A Horseman in the Sky (San Francisco: Elder, 1907);

The Shadow on the Dial and Other Essays, edited by S. O. Howes (San Francisco: A. M. Robertson, 1909); revised as *Antepenultimata,* volume 11 of *The Collected Works of Ambrose Bierce* (New York & Washington, D.C.: Neale, 1912);

Ambrose Bierce in his study, 1899

Write It Right: A Blacklist of Literary Faults (New York & Washington, D.C.: Neale, 1909);

The Collected Works of Ambrose Bierce, 12 volumes (New York & Washington, D.C.: Neale, 1909–1912)—comprises 1) *Ashes of the Beacon, The Land Beyond the Blow, For the Ahkoond, John Smith, Liberator, Bits of Autobiography;* 2) *In the Midst of Life;* 3) *Can Such Things Be?, The Ways of Ghosts, Soldier-Folk, Some Haunted Houses;* 4) *Shapes of Clay, Some Antemortem Epitaphs, The Scrap Heap;* 5) *Black Beetles in Amber, The Mummery, On Stone;* 6) *The Monk and the Hangman's Daughter, Fantastic Fables, Aesopus Emendatus, Old Saws with New Teeth, Fables in Rhyme;* 7) *The Devil's Dictionary;* 8) *Negligible Tales, The Parenticide Club, The Fourth Estate, The Ocean Wave, "On with the Dance!," Epigrams;* 9) *Tangential Views;* 10) *The Opinionator, The Reviewer, The Controversialist, The Timorous Reporter, The March Hare;* 11) *Antepenultimata;* 12) *In Motley, Kings of Beasts, Two Administrations, Miscellaneous;*

Battlefields and Ghosts, edited by Hartley E. Jackson and James D. Hart (Palo Alto, Cal.: Harvest Press, 1931);

Selections from Prattle by Ambrose Bierce, edited by Carroll D. Hall (San Francisco: Book Club of California, 1936);

Enlarged Devil's Dictionary, edited by Ernest J. Hopkins (Garden City, N.Y.: Doubleday, 1967);

The Ambrose Bierce Satanic Reader, edited by Hopkins (Garden City, N.Y.: Doubleday, 1968);

Ambrose Bierce: Skepticism and Dissent: Selected Journalism from 1898–1901, edited by Lawrence I. Berkove (Ann Arbor, Mich.: Delmas, 1980);

Poems of Ambrose Bierce, edited by M. E. Grenander (Lincoln: University of Nebraska Press, 1995).

OTHER: "The Robin and the Woodpecker," "The Dog and the Bees," "The Ant and the Grain of Corn," "The Man and the Goose," "The Nobleman and the Oyster," "The Boy and the Tortoise," and "The Camel and the Zebra," in *Mark Twain's Library of Humor,* anonymously edited by William Dean Howells (New York: Webster, 1888), pp. 129–130, 196, 339–340, 348, 425–426, 542, 558;

Richard Voss, *The Monk and the Hangman's Daughter,* translated by Gustav Adolf Danziger, revised by Bierce (Chicago: Schulte, 1892).

Ambrose Bierce is far more than a regional, or western, writer. He has come to be recognized as an outstanding exemplar of literary impressionism, a counterweight to the emphasis on realism and naturalism embodied in the work of most of his important contemporaries at the end of the nineteenth century. Bierce's writing shows the dependence of external reality on the shifting awareness of a perceiver. He often manipulates the epistemological categories of space and time and builds to an individual's sudden flash of insight, or epiphany. Such features have led critics to cite Bierce as an early postmodernist. Although most of Bierce's notable work was written when he lived in northern California, the writing that might best be termed *western* is his poetry, particularly his satiric verses directed at Californian figures, and a few of his stories that have California settings.

Ambrose Gwinnett Bierce was born 24 June 1842 on a small farm in southeastern Ohio; his family moved in 1846 to another farm in northern Indiana, near Warsaw. While they, as he wrote in a July 1906 article in *Cosmopolitan* titled "The Social Unrest," had "to grub out a very difficult living" from the soil, his father was far from being an illiterate rustic. Named after the Stoic philosopher Marcus Aurelius, he had the largest library in the county and a whimsical turn of mind. He gave each of his thirteen children, of whom Ambrose was the tenth and the youngest to live to maturity, a name beginning with "A," so that they all had the initials "AB." Ambrose was named after a melodrama by the English playwright Douglas Jerrold titled *Ambrose Gwinett; or, A Sea-side Story* (1828), popular on both sides of the Atlantic. As an adult, not only informally to friends but also in the 18 March 1894 issue of the *San Francisco Examiner,* Bierce credited wide reading in his scholarly father's extensive library with his having been able to pull himself "out of the life of obscurity, privation, and labor in the fields" to which he had been born.

As he grew up, Bierce found consolation not only in his father's books but also in the beauties of the changing seasons in the countryside of northern Indiana, dotted with lakes and rolling hills. The years of his early adolescence were spent there except for a stint at the Kentucky Military Institute in 1859. When he returned to Indiana in 1860, he worked on the family farm and at various odd jobs. On 19 April 1861, a week after the first shots were fired at Fort Sumter, South Carolina, Bierce, like many other idealistic youths of his generation, enlisted in the Union Army. The following four impressionable years of his young manhood were marked by the blood and gore of America's most ferocious war. Yet this period, like the whale ship for Ishmael in Herman Melville's *Moby-Dick* (1851), was Bierce's Yale College and Harvard. In middle age he returned to scenes of the battles in which he had participated for the background of some of his most compelling stories and essays. The importance of the war for Bierce is clear from his remark in the 13 November 1898 *San Francisco Examiner:*

> In this tiresome tumult of interests and sentiments which we are pleased to call "politics" there has been in my time but one contest of principles in which it seemed worthwhile for a serious man seriously to engage. The struggle between freedom and slavery affected earnest souls with a compelling fervor. Great-hearted and great-minded men felt the stress, marched to the polls, and thence to camp. There was a chance of action consistent with self-respect for even the pessimist and cynic.

After the war, following working briefly as a treasury agent in Alabama and New Orleans, Bierce joined Gen. William B. Hazen, under whom he had served as topographical officer, on a mapping expedition through Indian territory from Omaha to the West Coast. Had he at the conclusion of the expedition received the captaincy in the regular army that he had been promised, he probably would have em-

Bierce as a Union army lieutenant during the Civil War

mained an ardent Anglophile all his life. His two sons, Day and Leigh, were born in England, and his first three books, which appeared under the pseudonym Dod Grile, were published in London. Of them, *The Fiend's Delight* (1873) and *Nuggets and Dust Panned Out in California* (1873) were for the most part collections of clippings from his California writings. Bierce's wife, however, was not as contented in England as he was. When she became pregnant for a third time, she decided to return to her family in California, sailing for San Francisco in April 1875. He followed her in September, and their third child—a daughter, Helen—was born in that city on 30 October.

Bierce, who had been writing satiric pieces for *Fun* and *Figaro,* gave up a successful career in journalism when he left London. On his return to California, having to find a job to support his young family, he became a clerk in the United States Mint. But he also wrote for San Francisco journals, notably the *Argonaut,* in which he began a muckraking and satiric column, "Prattle." When an opportunity in mining opened in 1880, Bierce left for the Dakota Territory to become general agent of the Black Hills Placer Mining Company. Although his involvement with the company lasted only a few months, the episode was one of the most grueling and ruinous of his life.

Bierce's herculean endeavors to make a success of the mine were frustrated at every turn by mismanagement and outright fraud, not only at the local level but also in the board room of the company back east on Wall Street. The legal difficulties in which he became ensnarled dragged on for years, eventually winding up in the United States Supreme Court. The experience left him not only with a settled distrust for the law but also penniless and facing once again the problem of how to earn a living. The only positive outcome for Bierce was that he had material for some of his most biting satires and a brilliant essay, "Some Features of the Law," which he collected in *The Shadow on the Dial and Other Essays* (1909).

When he returned to San Francisco, he became editor of another short-lived periodical, the *Wasp,* in which he continued the "Prattle" column and began writing the acerbic definitions that were to achieve fame first as *The Cynic's Word Book* (1906), which he later enlarged as *The Devil's Dictionary* (1911). He also continued his slashing attacks against the crooked businessmen and corrupt politicians who held northern California in an iron grip. In the process of uncovering and attacking their depredations he wrote some of his most incisive satires. Although he pilloried poetasters and bad writ-

barked on a military career. Since he was offered only a second lieutenancy, however, he resigned in dudgeon and stayed on in San Francisco to pursue literature.

He wrote both poems and prose for such periodicals as the *Californian,* the *Golden Era,* and the *Alta California.* The biggest boost to his literary ambitions occurred in December 1868 when he became editor of the *San Francisco News Letter and California Advertiser* and took over the regular column "The Town Crier," greatly extending its reputation. He also wrote a series of essays, signed "Ursus," that began appearing in the January 1871 issue of Bret Harte's *Overland Monthly;* his first story, "The Haunted Valley," appeared in that journal in July 1871.

Meanwhile, Bierce had been courting a well-to-do miner's daughter, the beautiful and vivacious Mary Ellen "Mollie" Day, whom he married on 25 December 1871. In March the couple sailed for England, where Bierce's "Town Crier" columns had been favorably received. His years in England from 1872 to 1875 were among his happiest, and he re-ers generally, he also initiated his lifelong practice of helping young writers whom he considered promising.

Bierce's career took a great leap forward in spring 1887 when the twenty-four-year-old William Randolph Hearst, who had recently become publisher of the *San Francisco Examiner,* called on him and offered him a job on very favorable terms, both editorially and financially. Bierce's relationship with Hearst was a paradoxical one. He includes a satiric poem about Hearst under the entry for "Diary" in *The Devil's Dictionary.* In his essay "A Mad World," which he included in the eleventh volume of *The Collected Works of Ambrose Bierce* (1909–1912), he plays with the idea that he himself might be a lunatic whose bizarre imagination created the spectacle of "pointing [Hearst's] eyes toward the White House" and endowing him "with a perilous . . . ambition to defile it." The most extended analysis of his long employment with this "strange and complex character" is the essay "A Thumb-Nail Sketch," included in the twelfth volume of *The Collected Works.*

Although Bierce was out of sympathy with nearly all of his employer's aims, he was nevertheless given the freedom to expound his opposition to them in Hearst's own publications and was handsomely rewarded for doing so. From the time he joined the staff of the *Examiner* Bierce had both financial security and a bully pulpit from which he could attack malefactors. Together with his resumption of "Prattle," Bierce published in the *Examiner* some of his most famous work—stories, essays, and poetry—which he eventually included in his *Collected Works.*

Bierce's most famous poem, "Invocation," was written for a Fourth of July celebration in San Francisco in 1888 and read aloud at the Grand Opera House. The poem, twenty-eight quatrains of iambic tetrameter, emphasizes two of Bierce's favorite themes, the importance of the rule of law and the responsibility of freedom. Bierce upheld the advantages of the rule of law, however imperfect it may be, over anarchy, with its threat of violence. Concomitantly, he refused to regard freedom as an end in itself; instead he believed it was a means that could be used to further base purposes as well as noble ones. Lawrence I. Berkove in "Two Impossible Dreams: Ambrose Bierce on Utopia and America" has pointed out Bierce's reservations about republican democracy. Disturbed by the "liberty-drunken rabble" that he felt was responsible for the social turmoil of the 1870s and 1890s, Bierce claimed that "abstract liberty" was unthinkable; when asked whether he favored liberty, he replied, "Liberty for whom to do what?"

The first nine stanzas of "Invocation" are an apostrophe to the remote and tranquil Goddess of Liberty. Both tyrants and anarchists, prophets and wanton Discord, call on her to justify their ends. Hence, the speaker does not invoke her name to justify the "civic rites" of those for whom he speaks. Rather, he turns for compassion to a nearer deity, addressing the God of his country and his race beginning in stanza ten. Alluding to the Revolution and then to the Civil War, the speaker recounts that the love of this God gave Americans a lowercase "liberty" in the "holy war" that split their manacles and later broke them once again by a "stronger stroke" after they had riveted their own chains.

The speaker warns that Liberty is not an end in itself but an Opportunity that may bring either good or ill, depending on whether it serves right or wrong. He warns against the lawless and bloody crimes that may be embraced by passionate majorities as well as—an even "nearer menace"—the spoliations of Greed and corrupt government. If his countrymen should prove unworthy of freedom, the speaker asks God to "replace / the broken throne, repair the chain, / Restore the interrupted reign / and veil again [his] patient face." The poem closes with the hope that those Californians who are addressed will swear that their country be "ruled in right and grace," so that "men shall say: 'O drive afield / the lawless eagle from the shield, / And call an angel to the place!'"

"Invocation," with its warning of the perils facing the United States from her own weaknesses, is vastly different from the usual chauvinistic self-congratulations of most Fourth of July outpourings. It is hard to believe that the enthusiastic audience who applauded this long and complex poem really understood it at a first hearing when it was read to them aloud. Nevertheless, it says something for the inhabitants of late–nineteenth century San Francisco that they took it to their hearts after its appearance in print the next day in the *Examiner.* It was compared to Rudyard Kipling's "Recessional" and repeatedly republished, most notably in a sumptuous edition brought out in 1928 by the Book Club of California.

Bierce chose for his enemies some of the most powerful interests in California and the nation. Some of Bierce's favorite targets for satire were the so-called Big Four of the Southern Pacific railroad octopus: Mark Hopkins, Charles Crocker, Leland Stanford, and Collis P. Huntington, whom Bierce called "railrogues." His attitude was made plain in the 22 July 1888 *Examiner:*

> The worst railroads on the Pacific Coast are those operated by the Southern Pacific Company. The worst

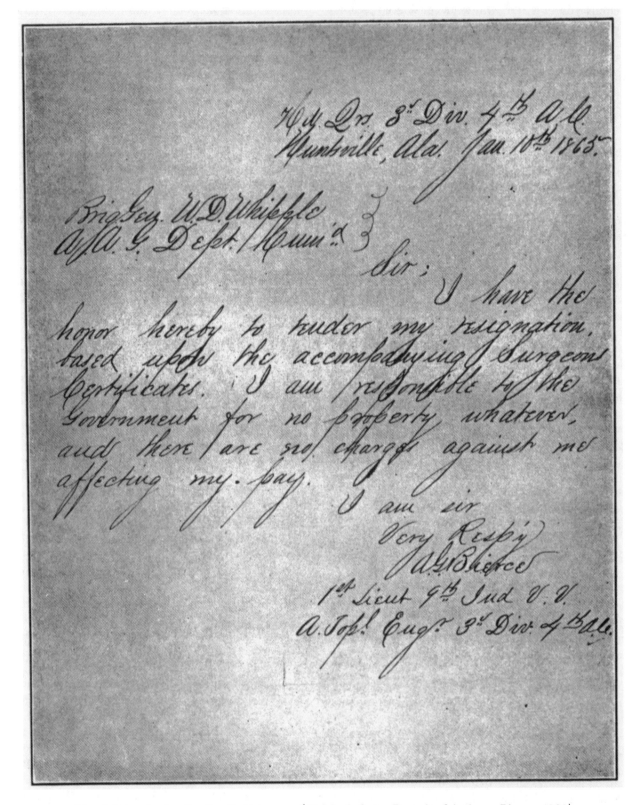

Bierce's letter of resignation from the Union army (Adolphe de Castro, Portrait of Ambrose Bierce, *1929)*

railroad operated by the Southern Pacific Company is the Central Pacific. It owes the government more millions of dollars than Leland Stanford has vanities; it will pay fewer cents than Collis P. Huntington has virtues. It has always been managed by rapacity tempered by incompetence.

Bierce was adamantly opposed to the policy of high tariffs espoused by the Republican Party presidential candidate Benjamin Harrison, who defeated Grover Cleveland's low-tariff bid for the second term in 1888. Bierce wrote in the *Examiner* for 8 October 1888 that it was

the misfortune of the Republican party to have secured the allegiance of most of those men who believe their great wealth to be a creation of the laws–men who believe they would not prosper, and know they would not prosper as well, if the government did not supply them with customers by compelling other men to purchase their wares.

These Republicans regarded the Democratic demand for lower duties as a menace to the sandy and shifting foundations of their fortunes. During the summer of 1888 Bierce often attacked what he regarded as the muddled thinking and hypocrisy of the advocates of protectionism. After Harrison's election, when his triumphal national progress reached San Francisco, Bierce attacked him in the 10 May 1991 *Examiner* for "going about the country in gorgeous state and barbaric splendor as the guest of a thieving corporation, but at our expense" as "the willing servitor of robber corporations and political adventurers."

Two of the greatest tragedies of Bierce's life occurred within a year and a half after he joined the staff of the *Examiner*. One was the split with his wife in the winter of 1888–1889. He apparently discovered a letter or letters sent to her by a secret admirer. Although Mollie had actually done nothing improper, she had certainly not discouraged the writing of these letters. Bierce, who always rejected competition of any kind, left her, and they were never reconciled. Both maintained a dignified reserve about their domestic difficulties, the details of which remain unknown. (Bierce's poem "Oneiromancy" is probably a veiled allusion to them.) The pair were not officially divorced until the spring of 1905, shortly before Mollie died on 27 April. Bierce had loved her deeply, and her death, even though it occurred years after they parted, caused him considerable heartache.

Bierce's separation from his wife was followed by the death on 27 July 1889 of their older son, Day, following a shoot-out over a girl. The impetuous

sixteen-year-old had been working as a journalist in a small town north of Sacramento. He fell ardently in love with the daughter of a boardinghouse keeper in Chico, where he moved to be near her. After she secretly eloped with another suitor and the two returned to her home, the passionate Day exploded in wrath. He and the young husband seized their revolvers and began firing, with Day clipping the ear of the new bride. Although his own death was initially reported as a suicide, its circumstances were ambiguous. What is certain is that both youths were mortally wounded.

In the wake of personal loss Bierce turned to his work and produced some of the most remarkable short stories in the English language. The stories were not in any obvious way about the death of his son, but that death may have led Bierce back to the days of his own youth, when he fought in several of the bloodiest battles of the Civil War. These stories, first collected as *Tales of Soldiers and Civilians* (1891), were published the following year in England under a brilliant title assigned them by their English publisher, Andrew Chatto: *In the Midst of Life,* a phrase taken from the English Book of Common Prayer that resonates with its unspoken completion: "In the midst of life we are in death."

Only one of the tales in this first story collection has a California setting. "An Heiress from Redhorse" (later changed to "The Lady from Redhorse") is unusual among Bierce's tales in that it aims at amusement for its emotional effect. A romantic comedy, it is not one of its author's better efforts, but it is interesting in that, as Berkove has shown in "'A Strange Adventure': The Story Behind a Bierce Tale," it was based on a real-life incident. When Bierce and W. C. Morrow, a younger author he befriended, were taking one of their leisurely strolls through San Francisco, a beautiful female admirer mistook Morrow for Bierce. As Berkove points out, the story reveals a "genial side" of Bierce and shows that he "could enjoy some good-natured public bantering from his friends."

Bierce collected much of his satiric verse–more typical than "Invocation" of what might be called his "western" poems–in *Black Beetles in Amber* (1892). In these poems, which Donald Sidney-Fryer characterizes as "agreeably nasty cast-iron thorns in the Victorian rose garden," Bierce usually throws brickbats at the powerful, but his satiric verses are not uniformly negative. For example, he defends his friend Gertrude Atherton in "A False Alarm." He refers to another friend, Joaquin Miller, in verses parodying Miller's exuberant style in "Arboriculture" and "The Mormon Question" and comments on his long hair in "Borrowed Brains."

Bierce frequently denounces members of the Big Four in satiric poems. The villainies associated with the Central Pacific Railroad are pilloried in "A Spade"; Stanford and Huntington are the objects of "Reconciliation"; and Stanford, Crocker, and Huntington are all satirized in "A Hasty Inference." Crocker is attacked in "The New Dennis," along with Dennis Kearney, an Irish demagogue who early in 1876 had organized a rough and dangerous mob, the powerful Workingmen's Party of California, on an anti-Chinese, antiwealth platform. Bierce was particularly incensed by hate crimes against the Chinese, for which he held his state up to shame in "California," a poem with satiric echoes of the Bible.

Bierce's favorite target of all was "£eland $tanford," a railrogue who had been governor of California from 1861 to 1863. Then, with extensive help from the Southern Pacific, he was elected to the United States Senate in 1885, where he held office until his death. He even aspired to the presidency. Bierce ridicules Stanford's pretensions in a long string of satiric verses: "A Railroad Lackey," "A Political Violet," "A Jack-at-All Views," "Three Candidates for Senator," and "An Election Expense." He is characterized in "Substance or Shadow":

Behold advances in dignity and state—
Grave, smug, serene, indubitably great—
Stanford, philanthropist! One hand bestows
In alms what t'other one to justice owes.

In an amusing antemortem epitaph, Bierce writes:

Here Stanford lies, who thought it odd
That he should go to meet his God.
He looked, until his eyes grew dim,
For God to hasten to meet him.

Stanford's strong supporter, Frank Pixley, a rich Republican and former United States district attorney, is ridiculed in "For President, Leland Stanford." In an effort to run Kearney out of town Pixley had founded a magazine, the *Argonaut,* whose first issue appeared 25 March 1877. Bierce was associate editor of the *Argonaut,* and some of his strongest early work appeared in it. However, he later split with Pixley, whom he holds up to scorn in such poems as "The Transmigrations of a Soul," "The American Party," and "To a Word-Warrior."

Bierce also often satirized Michael H. De Young, the unscrupulous owner of the *San Francisco Chronicle.* Although initially he had supported Dennis Kearney and his Workingmen's Party, De Young turned against them in 1879. Bierce had attacked him as early as his *News Letter* days. What really enraged him, however, were De Young's insinuations that Bierce was a tool of Adolph Spreckels and the Hawaiian sugar interests and that Spreckels was the real owner of the *Wasp.* Bierce rakes De Young over the coals for his vulgar materialism, his indifference to truth, and his vaulting political aspirations both to become minister to France and to be appointed to President Harrison's cabinet, in such poems as "From Top to Bottom," "To an Aspirant," "Valedictory," and "In His Hand."

In their time and place the figures Bierce wrote of were well known, but most of them live on primarily because he attacked them. Their obscurity interfered with plans for the commercial publication of his book by Stone and Kimball, a firm in Cambridge, Massachusetts. A 4 December 1893 letter to these partners from Bierce not only ended his negotiations with them but also illuminates his theory of satire:

> If the obscurity (in the East) of the persons satirized is a fatal objection no considerable selection can be made. It does not appear to be an objection in such works as the "English Bards and Scotch Reviewers," "The Dunciad," and most of the satires which have lived; but of course I am not a Byron nor a Pope. Nevertheless, I cannot see how the quality or interest of a piece is affected by application to a real, though unknown, person instead of presenting it as a general satire, with perhaps a fictitious name. If the verse is good it *makes* the victims known; if not good it is not worth publishing anyhow.

In the preface to the edition published by Western Authors, Bierce concedes that, for readers not of the Pacific Coast, he has "dealt mostly with obscure persons." However, he "begs leave to point out that he has done what he could to lessen the force of the objection by dispelling some part of their obscurity and awarding them such fame as he was able to bestow."

Stanford and Huntington are historically significant figures and exceptions to the general obscurity of the objects of Bierce's satire. Stanford and his wife founded and endowed Stanford University; Huntington's money passed eventually to his nephew, Henry E. Huntington, and was used to establish the Huntington Library, one of the world's great research libraries, in San Marino, California. Ironically, these institutions, named for bitter enemies of Bierce, became major repositories for his papers.

Bierce wrote three more stories with California settings for *Can Such Things Be?* (1893): "The Famous Gilson Bequest," "The Secret of Macarger's Gulch," and "The Death of Halpin Frayser." "The Famous Gilson Bequest," a tale of avarice, corrup-

First page of Bierce's "Town Crier" column in the San Francisco Newsletter and California Advertiser *for 25 September 1869*

tion, and drumhead justice in a mining town, is the very antithesis of Bret Harte's sentimental tales and anticipates Mark Twain's "The Man That Corrupted Hadleyburg" (1900). After a suspected thief, Milton Gilson, is precipitously hanged, a codicil to his will is discovered stipulating that anyone who can prove in a law court during the next five years that he was indeed a thief is to be his heir. If his guilt cannot be proved during this period, however, his estate will go to Henry Brentshaw, his chief accuser. Brentshaw thereupon reverses his former stand and embarks on a feverish campaign to prove Gilson's innocence. Chicanery and perjury characterize the litigation that follows. Although Gilson's innocence is finally established, his entire estate has been eaten up by paid witnesses, bribed judges, and expensive lawyers. Moreover, at the end of the five years Gilson is shown to have been a thief after all, and "the sun went down upon a region in which the moral sense was dead, the social conscience callous, the intellectual capacity dwarfed, enfeebled, and confused!"

"The Secret of Macarger's Gulch" has been of particular importance to one of Bierce's critics, Cathy N. Davidson, because although it is superficially a traditional ghost story, the protagonist tries to explain it in terms of his own perceptual processes. It is thus an excellent example of the postmodern literary theory that Davidson has applied to several of Bierce's stories.

The western story that has attracted the most scholarly and critical interest among serious students of Bierce is "The Death of Halpin Frayser." This uncanny tale of dread concerns a man who goes out hunting one afternoon, gets lost, and lies down to sleep in a forest. He has a horrible dream filled with terrifying symbols. Or are they merely symbols? He is attacked by a dreadful creature of his imagination who takes the form of his mother. Or is this monster imaginary? In any event, his body, strangled to death, is found the next day lying on his murdered mother's grave. Although this story seems to rely on mental telepathy, zombies, and the supernatural, it is widely interpreted by several critics who have wrestled with its powerful and unsettling emotional effect as dealing with terrifying psychological forces that lie at the deepest levels of the human personality.

Bierce's influence on western culture grew enormous in the 1880s and 1890s. His power as a cultural critic has been well described by Vincent Starrett:

> Through the warp and woof . . . of certain California journals, for many years, ran the glittering thread of his genius. . . . he became a mighty censor who made and unmade men and women. . . . It is no exaggeration to say that corrupt politicians, hypocritical philanthropists and clergymen, self-worshipers, notoriety seekers, and pretenders of every description trembled at his name. He wielded an extraordinary power; his pen hung, a Damoclean sword, over the length and breadth of the Pacific coast. Those who had cause to fear his wrath opened their morning papers with something like horror.

Bierce strongly believed that personal identity was to be found not in a narcissistic individualism but in the public arena. As he wrote in "The Stranger" in *Can Such Things Be?:* "A man is like a tree: in a forest of his fellows he will grow as straight as his generic and individual nature permits; alone in the open, he yields to the deforming stresses and tortions that environ him." This focus on man as a social being can be related to the theories of Edmund Burke and Charles Sanders Peirce, whose thought has provided the framework for excellent scholarly studies of Bierce. Jeffrey Raymond Macmillan presents a cogent argument for his filiation from Burkean philosophical conservatism in which sound political judgment is the product of a gradual and continuing collective process. In her perceptive study of his stories in the context of Peirce's philosophy, *The Experimental Fictions of Ambrose Bierce: Structuring the Ineffable* (1984), Davidson also notes Bierce's belief that the self can be meaningful only in terms of its relations to others.

Given Bierce's belief that personhood lay in the social sphere, one can understand why, although his chronic asthma led him often to sojourn in remote villages in the foothills of the San Francisco Bay area, he nevertheless throughout his career was embroiled in the social, artistic, political, and economic controversies swirling around northern California. The paradox between the forced solitude dictated by his efforts to breathe pure mountain air and his avid engagement in the public life lends poignance to the eager invitations he was constantly extending to friends and acquaintances to visit him in his various aeries.

Bierce's theories on political economy, which have never been adequately dealt with, played an important role in his writing. His criticism of the worst excesses of the Gilded Age is well known, but his economic ideas were more subtle than widely acknowledged. To use a term from James M. Buchanan's public-choice theory Bierce was assailing *rent-seeking,* or the attempt to choke off competition in the free market by persuading politicians to grant exclusive privileges to certain contenders. Although bribery was sometimes resorted to, the means used did not have to be illegal. All that was necessary was the control of political power, through votes, campaign funds, or the pressure of special interests.

Bierce wrestled with this problem repeatedly. In "The Game of Politics," an essay collected in *The Shadow on the Dial and Other Essays,* he argues that politicians should not be ruled solely by the desires of constituents:

> A man holding office from and for the people is in conscience and honor bound to do what seems to his judgment best for the general welfare, respectfully regardless of any and all other considerations. This is especially true of legislators, to whom such specific "instructions" as constituents sometimes send are an impertinence and an insult. Pushed to its logical conclusion, the "delegate" policy would remove all necessity of electing men of brains and judgment; one man properly connected with his constituents by telegraph would make as good a legislator as another.

Bierce's insight into political reality in the 9 June 1895 *San Francisco Examiner* foreshadows the analyses of modern economic theorists of public choice: "Make your social machinery what you will, those whom it is designed to protect will not gain control of it; set up such a political system as you can; it is ever the strong that will seize and direct it–mainly to their own advantage." The result, as Bierce wrote in *Ashes of the Beacon,* a historic monograph of the year 4930 included in the first volume of his *Collected Works,* was that "nearly all classes and callings became organized conspiracies, each seeking an unfair advantage through laws which the party in power had not the firmness to withhold, nor the party hoping for power the courage to oppose." The idea of rent-seeking is also evident in a famous definition from *The Devil's Dictionary:*

> POLITICS, n. A strife of interests masquerading as a contest of principles. The conduct of public affairs for private advantage.

Both Harry Lynn Sheller and Macmillan have noted an aspect of rent-seeking that Bierce characterizes in *Ashes of the Beacon* as the "monstrous political practice known as 'Protection to American industries,'" which he believed would eventually destroy the American republic.

Advocates of high tariffs that Bierce opposed included John D. Rockefeller and Andrew Carnegie as well as local magnates such as Claus and Adolph Spreckels and Leland Stanford. The Spreckels brothers, sugar manufacturers made wealthy by rent-seeking, grew grapes in Fresno, California, as did Stanford, who was a viticulturalist as well as a

Caricature of Bierce that appeared in the Wasp *during the 1890s*

railroad baron. This group wanted to keep Greek currants, foreign sugar, and French wines out of the country. In "The Kingdom of Tortirra," one chapter in his Swiftian satire called *The Land Beyond the Blow,* which he included in *Collected Works,* Bierce attacked the McKinley and Wilson-Gorman tariffs of 1890 and 1894:

> For many years [foreign traders] were welcomed in Tortirra with great hospitality and their goods eagerly purchased. They took back with them all manner of Tortirran products and nobody thought of questioning the mutual advantages of the exchange.

However, a Tortirran demagogue (McKinley) persuaded his countrymen that "commerce was piracy–that true prosperity consisted in consumption of domestic products and abstention from foreign."

The flourishing economy of Tortirra was decimated as the people were "deprived of a market for their surplus products and compelled to forego the comforts and luxuries which they had obtained from abroad." Consequently, "the dictum that trade is piracy no longer commands universal acceptance." Nevertheless, "a majority of the populace still hold a modified form" of the "strange delusion" that "importation is theft. . . . The chief expounders and protagonists of this doctrine are all directly or indirectly engaged in making or growing such articles as were formerly" imported:

The articles are generally inferior in quality, but consumers, not having the benefit of foreign competition, are compelled to pay extortionate prices for them, thus maintaining the unscrupulous producers in needless industries and a pernicious existence. But these active and intelligent rogues are too powerful to be driven out. They persuade their followers, among whom are many ignorant consumers, that this . . . policy is all that keeps the nation from being desolated.

Bierce's journalistic career peaked when he led the opposition to Huntington's attempt to get a bill through Congress that would refund a debt the Southern Pacific owed to the government. Under its provisions the company would have been relieved of paying for the privileges it had been granted, thereby saving millions of dollars. Hearst, who strongly opposed the depredations of Huntington, sent Bierce to Washington in 1896 to head up a team that would outmaneuver him. While Bierce was there, telegrams flowed thick and fast from Washington back and forth to New York and San Francisco as Bierce rallied his supporters among the ranks of Hearst's other staff members.

One of the most famous anecdotes of this period in Bierce's life has him meeting the powerful Huntington on the steps of the capitol. The cynical old railrogue, in an effort to ward off the attacks from which he was reeling, is said to have remarked, "Well, name your price; every man has his price." Bierce, refusing to shake his opponent's hand, responded: "My price is about seventy-five million dollars," adding that Huntington could pay it into the United States Treasury.

Successful in his exhaustive—and exhausting—efforts, Bierce returned to California late in 1896. But his taste of the East, where he had lived for almost a year, had whetted his appetite for a change of scene. In December 1899 he left for New York, where his second son, Leigh, was a newspaperman. After a few weeks in New York he continued down to Washington, D.C., this time to settle there permanently. It remained his home until he left it in the autumn of 1913 on a circuitous route covering his old Civil War battlefields that led him eventually to El Paso, Texas. There he crossed the border into Mexico, where he became an observer of the forces of Pancho Villa, a populist rebel against the corrupt government of Gen. Victoriano Huerta. The last communication from Bierce was dated 26 December 1913. Despite the many fanciful conjectures about his death, almost certainly he was killed at the Battle of Ojinaga on 11 January 1914.

Treating Bierce as a western author adds a revealing dimension to his reputation because of his close involvement with the public life of the region in which he spent his most productive years. Bierce wrote for his own time and region as much as he did for posterity. His writing for a western audience thus offers a useful additional perspective on the work of this challenging and influential author.

Letters:

The Letters of Ambrose Bierce, edited by Bertha Clark Pope (San Francisco: Book Club of California, 1922);

M. E. Grenander, "Ambrose Bierce and Charles Warren Stoddard: Some Unpublished Correspondence," *Huntington Library Quarterly,* 23 (May 1960): 261–292.

Bibliographies:

Vincent Starrett, *Ambrose Bierce, A Bibliography* (Philadelphia: Centaur Book Shop, 1929);

M. E. Grenander, "Ambrose Bierce, John Camden Hotten, *The Fiend's Delight,* and *Nuggets and Dust,*" *Huntington Library Quarterly,* 28 (August 1965): 353–371;

Paul Fatout, "Ambrose Bierce (1842–1914)," *American Literary Realism, 1870–1910,* 1 (Fall 1967): 13–19;

Joseph Gaer, ed., *Ambrose Gwinett [sic] Bierce, Bibliography and Biographical Data* (New York: Burt Franklin, 1968);

Grenander, "Ambrose Bierce and *In the Midst of Life,*" *Book Collector,* 20 (Autumn 1971): 321–331;

John C. Stubbs, "Ambrose Bierce's Contributions to *Cosmopolitan:* An Annotated Bibliography," *American Literary Realism,* 4 (Winter 1971): 57–59;

Philip M. Rubens and Robert Jones, "Ambrose Bierce: A Bibliographic Essay and Bibliography," *American Literary Realism,* 16 (Spring 1983): 73–91.

Biographies:

Carey McWilliams, *Ambrose Bierce, A Biography* (New York: A. & C. Boni, 1929); republished with a new introduction by the author (Hamden, Conn.: Archon Books, 1967);

Paul Fatout, *Ambrose Bierce, the Devil's Lexicographer* (Norman: University of Oklahoma Press, 1951);

Fatout, *Ambrose Bierce and the Black Hills* (Norman: University of Oklahoma Press, 1956);

Richard O'Connor, *Ambrose Bierce, A Biography* (Boston: Little, Brown, 1967);

Richard Saunders, *Ambrose Bierce: The Making of a Misanthrope* (San Francisco: Chronicle Books, 1985);

Roy Morris Jr., *Ambrose Bierce: Alone in Bad Company* (New York: Crown Publishers, 1996).

References:

Lawrence I. Berkove, "The Man with the Burning Pen: Ambrose Bierce as Journalist," *Journal of Popular Culture,* 15 (Fall 1981): 34–40;

Berkove, "'A Strange Adventure': The Story Behind a Bierce Tale," *American Literary Realism,* 14 (Spring 1981): 70–76;

Berkove, "Two Impossible Dreams: Ambrose Bierce on Utopia and America," *Huntington Library Quarterly,* 54 (Autumn 1981): 283–292;

Cathy N. Davidson, ed., *Critical Essays on Ambrose Bierce* (Boston: G. K. Hall, 1982);

Davidson, *The Experimental Fictions of Ambrose Bierce: Structuring the Ineffable* (Lincoln: University of Nebraska Press, 1984);

Davidson, "Re-Structuring the Ineffable and Ambrose Bierce's 'The Secret of Macarger's Gulch,'" *Markham Review,* 12 (Fall 1982): 14–19;

Paul Fatout, "Ambrose Bierce Writes about War," *Book Club of California Quarterly News Letter,* 16 (Fall 1951): 75–79;

M. E. Grenander, *Ambrose Bierce* (New York: Twayne, 1971);

Grenander, "California's Albion: Mark Twain, Ambrose Bierce, Tom Hood, John Camden Hotten, and Andrew Chatto," *Papers of the Bibliographical Society of America,* 72 (1978): 455–475;

Grenander, "'Five Blushes, Ten Shudders and a Vomit': Mark Twain on Ambrose Bierce's *Nuggets and Dust,*" *American Literary Realism,* 17 (Autumn 1984): 169–179;

Grenander, "A London Letter of Joaquin Miller to Ambrose Bierce," *Yale University Library Gazette,* 46 (October 1971): 109–116;

Carroll D. Hall, *Bierce and the Poe Hoax* (San Francisco: Book Club of California, 1934);

S. T. Joshi, "Ambrose Bierce: Horror as Satire," in his *The Weird Tale* (Austin: University of Texas Press, 1990), pp. 143–167;

Jeffrey Raymond Macmillan, "Ambrose Bierce: Between Politics and Philosophy," master's thesis, University of Nevada, Las Vegas, 1992;

Carey McWilliams, Introduction to *The Devil's Dictionary* (New York: Sagamore Press, 1957), pp. v–xi;

Lois Rather, *Bittersweet: Ambrose Bierce & Women* (Oakland, Cal.: Rather Press, 1975);

Josiah Royce, *The Feud of Oakfield Creek* (Boston: Houghton, Mifflin, 1887);

Harry Lynn Sheller, "The Satire of Ambrose Bierce: Its Objects, Forms, Devices, and Possible Origins," dissertation, University of Southern California, 1945;

Donald Sidney-Fryer, "A Visionary of Doom," in his *A Vision of Doom: Poems by Ambrose Bierce* (West Kingston, R.I.: Donald M. Grant, 1980), pp. 9–29;

Vincent Starrett, *Ambrose Bierce* (Port Washington, N.Y.: Kennikat, 1920);

Franklin Walker, *San Francisco's Literary Frontier* (New York: Knopf, 1939).

Papers:

The most important holdings of Ambrose Bierce's papers are in the Bancroft Library of the University of California, Berkeley; the Clifton Waller Barrett Collection at the University of Virginia; the University of Cincinnati; the Huntington Library in San Marino, California; the Berg Collection of the New York Public Library; the Division of Special Collections at Stanford University; the George Arents Research Library at Syracuse University; and the Beinecke Library of Yale University.

Ned Buntline
(Edward Zane Carroll Judson)

(20 March 1821 – 16 July 1886)

John O. West
University of Texas at El Paso

BOOKS: *Magdalena, the Beautiful Mexican Maid: A Story of Buena Vista* (New York: Williams Brothers, 1846);

The Black Avenger of the Spanish Main; or, The Fiend of Blood: A Thrilling Tale of the Buccaneer Times (Boston: F. Gleason, 1847);

The Curse! A Tale of Crime and Its Retribution, Founded on Facts of Real Life (Boston: Roberts & Garfield, 1847);

The King of the Sea: A Tale of the Fearless and Free (Boston: Flag of Our Union Office, 1847; London: G. Pierce, 1848);

The Last Days of Callao; or, The Doomed City of Sin! A Historical Romance of Peru (Boston: Jones Publishing, 1847); republished as *Bellamira; or, The Last Days of Callao, an Historical Romance of Peru* (Boston: Jones Publishing, 1849);

Love's Desperation; or, The President's Only Daughter: A Romance of Reality (Boston: F. Gleason, 1847);

The Virgin of the Sun: A Historical Romance of the Last Revolution in Peru (Boston: Hotchkiss & Company, 1847; London: Newman, 1850; Aberdeen: Clark, 1850);

The Volunteer; or, The Maid of Monterrey: A Tale of the Mexican War (Boston: F. Gleason, 1847);

The Red Revenger; or, The Pirate King of the Floridas: A Romance of the Gulf and Its Islands (Boston: F. Gleason, 1847; New York: S. French, 1847);

Cruisings, Afloat and Ashore, from the Private Log of Ned Buntline: Sketches of Land and Sea, Humorous and Pathetic; Tragical and Comical (New York: Edward Z. C. Judson, printed by R. Craighead, 1848; London: H. G. Collins, 1851);

The Ice-King; or, The Fate of the Lost Steamer: A Fanciful Tale of the Far North, bound with *Not in Despair, For I've a Friend: A Lesson of Life* (Boston: G. H. Williams, 1848);

Love's Desperation; or, The President's Only Daughter, and Other Tales, by Buntline and Charles E. Averill (Boston: F. Gleason, 1848);

Ned Buntline (photograph by Sarony)

Matanzas; or, A Brother's Revenge: A Tale of Florida (Boston: G. H. Williams, 1848);

The Mysteries and Miseries of New York: A Story of Real Life (New York: Berford, 1848; Dublin: J. M. M'Glashan, 1849);

Three Years After: A Sequel to the Mysteries and Miseries of New York (New York: W. F Burgess, 1848);

The Queen of the Sea; or, Our Lady of the Ocean: A Tale of Love, Strife & Chivalry (Boston: F. Gleason, 1848); republished as *The Queen of the Sea; or,*

The Female Pirate Captain (Boston: G. W. Studley, 1899);

The B'hoys of New York, A Sequel to The Mysteries & Miseries of New York (New York: Dick & Fitzgerald, 1849?);

Harry Halyard's Ruin: A True Tale for the Intemperate to Read (New York: H. Long, 1849);

Life, Career and Character of Ned Buntline (New York, 1849);

Ned Buntline's Life Yarn, as E. Z. C. Judson (New York: Dick & Fitzgerald, 1849; New York: Garrett, 1849);

Norwood; or, Life on the Prairie (New York: Burgess & Garrett, 1849);

The Romance of Life; or, The Life of Martha E. Miller (Alias Walker) (New York: Edward Z. C. Judson, 1849);

The G'hals of New York; A Novel (New York: Dewitt and Davenport, 1850);

The Convict; or, The Conspirator's Victim (New York: W. F. Burgess, 1851);

The Mysteries and Miseries of New Orleans (New York: Akarman & Ormsby, 1851);

The Wheel of Misfortune; or, The Victims of Lottery and Policy Dealers: A Yarn from the Web of New York Life (New York: Garrett, 1853);

The White Cruiser; or, The Fate of the Unheard-of: A Tale of Land and Sea; of Crime and Mystery (New York: Garrett, 1853);

The Jesuit's Daughter; a Novel for Americans to Read (New York: Burgess & Day, 1854);

The Last of the Buccaneers; A Yarn of the Eighteenth Century (New York: Garrett, 1856);

Secret Circular. To the Know Nothings of Philadelphia (N.p., 1856);

The Red Right Hand; A Tale of Indian Warfare (New York: Dick & Fitzgerald, 1857);

English Tom; or, The Smuggler's Secret: A Tale of Ship and Shore (New York: F. A. Brady, 1858); republished as *The Smuggler; or, The Skipper's Crime: A Tale of Ship and Shore* (New York: F. Starr, 1871);

Luona Prescott; or, the Curse Fulfilled (New York: F. A. Brady, 1858); republished as *Luona's Oath; or, The Curse Fulfilled* (New York: F. Starr, 1870);

The Man-O'War's Man's Grudge: A Romance of the Revolution (New York: F. A. Brady, 1858);

Saul Sabberday; or, The Idiot Spy: A Tale of the Men and Deeds of '76 (New York: F. A. Brady, 1858); republished as *Quaker Saul, The Idiot Spy; or, Luliona, the Seminole: A Tale of Men and Deeds of '76* (New York: Beadle, 1869); republished as *Saul Sabberday, The Idiot Spy; or, Luliona, the Seminole* (New York: F. Starr, 1875);

The Shell-Hunter; or, An Ocean Love-Chase: A Romance of Land and Sea (New York: F. A. Brady, 1858?);

Thayendanegea, The Scourge; or, The War-Eagle of the Mohawks: A Tale of Mystery, Ruth, and Wrong (New York: F. A. Brady, 1858); republished as *Thayendanegea, The Scourge; or, The War-Eagle of the Mohawks: A Romance of New York* (London: Beadle, 1862);

The White Wizard; or, the Great Prophet of the Seminoles: A Tale of Strange Mystery in the South and North (New York: F. A. Brady, 1858; London: Beadle, 1862);

Our Mess; or, the Pirate Hunters of the Gulf: A Tale of Naval Heroism and Wild Adventure in the Tropics (New York: F. A. Brady, 1859);

Seawaif; or, the Terror of the Coast: A Tale of Privateering in 1776 (New York: F. A. Brady, 1859); republished as *Captain Sea Waif, the Privateer* (New York: Beadle & Adams, 1879);

Stella Delorme; or, The Comanche's Dream: A Wild and Fanciful Story of Savage Chivalry (New York: F. A. Brady, 1859); republished as *The Red Warrior; or, Stella Delorme's Comanche Lover* (New York: Beadle & Adams, 1869);

Elfrida, the Red Rover's Daughter, A New Mystery of New York (New York: F. A. Brady, 1860); republished as *Andros, the Free Rover; or, the Pirate's Daughter* (New York: Beadle & Adams, 1883);

Morgan; or, the Knight of the Black Flag: A Strange Story of Bygone Times (New York: F. A. Brady, 1860);

The Death-Mystery: A Crimson Tale of Life in New York (New York: F. A. Brady, 1861); republished as *The Secret Vow; or, The Power of Woman's Hate* (New York: F. Starr, 1871);

Hilliare Henderson; or, The Secret Revealed (New York: F. A. Brady, 1861); republished as *The Planter's Ward; or, A Woman's Love and a Woman's Hate: A Romance of the Shore Plantations* (New York: F. Starr, 1871); republished as *A Fiery Heart; or, A Woman's Love and A Woman's Hate* (New York: Beadle & Adams, 1877);

Ella Adams; or, The Demon of Fire: A Tale of the Charlestown Conflagration (New York: F. A. Brady, 1862);

Grossbeak Mansion, A Mystery of New York (New York: F. A. Brady, 1862);

The Rattlesnake; or, The Rebel Privateer: A Tale of the Present Time (New York: F. A. Brady, 1862);

Life in the Saddle; or, The Cavalry Scout (New York: F. A. Brady, 1864);

Sadia: A Heroine of the Rebellion (New York: F. A. Brady, 1864); republished as *True as Steel; or, the Faithful Sister* (New York: F. Starr, 1871);

Battle of Hate; or, Hearts Are Trumps (New York: F. A. Brady, 1865);

Charley Bray; or, The Fireman's Mission. The Story of a New York Fireman (New York: Hilton, 1865);

Clara St. John (New York: Hilton, 1865);

The Indian Queen's Revenge, as L. Augustus Jones, Beadle's Frontier Series (New York: George Munro, 1865);

Mermet Ben; or, The Astrologer King: A Story of Magic and Wonderful Illusions (New York: Hilton, 1865);

Netta Bride and the Poor of New York, two volumes in one: *Netta Bride; or, the King of the Vultures,* as Captain Cleighmore, and *The Poor of New York,* as Henry Edwards (New York: Hilton, 1865);

The Parricides; or, The Doom of the Assassins: The Authors of a Nation's Loss (New York: Hilton, 1865);

Red Ralph; or, The Daughter of the Night (New York: Hilton, 1865);

Rose Seymour, The Ballet Girl's Revenge: A Tale of the New York Drama (New York: Hilton, 1865);

Agnes; or, The Beautiful Milliner (New York: Hilton, 1866);

Beautiful Nun (Philadelphia: T. B. Peterson, 1866);

The Boot-Maker of Fifth Avenue; or, A Fortune from Petroleum (New York: Hilton, 1866);

Child of the Sun, A Tale of Mexico (New York: Hilton, 1866);

Clarence Rhett; or, The Cruise of a Privateer: An American Sea Story, as Edward Z. C. Judson (New York: F. A. Brady, 1866);

Fanny, the Belle of Central Park (New York: Hilton, 1866);

The Lady Thief (New York: Hilton, 1866);

Lenore; or, The Highwayman's Bride (New York: Hilton, 1866);

Magdalena, the Outcast; or, The Millionaire's Daughter: A Story of Life in the Empire City (New York: Hilton, 1866);

Mark Myrtle, Hilton's Ten-cent Romances (New York: Hilton, 1866);

The Midnight Lamp; or, Life in the Empire City, Hilton's Ten-cent Books (New York: Hilton, 1866);

Rosa, The Indian Captive: A Story of the Last War with England (New York: Hilton, 1866);

Tiger-Eye, Munro's Ten-cent Novels (New York: George Munro, 1866);

Old Nick of the Swamp, Munro's Ten-cent Novels (New York: George Munro, 1867);

The Shadow Scout! or, Screaming Moses of the Fishkill Mountains, Munro's Ten-cent Novels (New York: George Munro, 1869);

War-Eagle; or, Ossiniwa, the Indian Brave, DeWitt's Ten-Cent Romances (New York: R. M. De-Witt, 1869);

The Wronged Daughter; or, A Wife's Intrigue (London: General Publishing, 186-?; New York: Beadle & Adams, n.d.);

Red Ralph, The Ranger; or, The Brother's Revenge (New York: Beadle, 1870); republished as *Red Ralph, the River Rover; or, The Brother's Revenge* (New York: Beadle & Adams, 1884);

The Red Trail; or, The Creek Chief's Captive (New York: Beadle, 1870);

The Sea Bandit; or, The Queen of the Isle: A Tale of the Antilles (New York: Beadle & Adams, 1870; New York: F. Starr, 1870);

Sib Cone, The Mountain Trapper (New York: F. Starr, 1870); republished as *Old Sib Cone, The Mountain Trapper* (New York: Beadle & Adams, 1876);

Mad Anthony's Captain, Munro's Ten-cent Novels (New York: George Munro, 1872);

"The Haze and Her Ocean Cruise," A Story of a Rebel Privateer (New York: R. M. DeWitt, 187-?);

Madeline Desha (New York: R. M. DeWitt, 187-?);

The War Cloud; or, Life for Life (New York: R. M. De-Witt, 187-?);

Buffalo Bill: The King of the Border Men (New York: J. S. Ogilvie, 1881); republished as *Buffalo Bill and His Adventures in the West* (New York: J. S. Ogilvie, 1886); republished as *Buffalo Bill* (New York: International Book, 1886);

Wrestling Joe, the Dandy of the Mines (New York: J. S. Ogilvie, 1881);

Harry Bluff, the Reefer; or, Love and Glory on the Sea (New York: Street & Smith, 1882);

Merciless Ben, The Hair Lifter (New York: Street & Smith, 1882);

Ethelbert, the Shell-Hunter; or, The Ocean Chase (New York: Beadle & Adams, 1884);

Tombstone Dick, The Train Pilot; or, The Traitor's Trail: A Story of the Arizonian Wilds (New York: Beadle & Adams, 1885);

Buffalo Bill's First Trail; or, Will Cody, the Pony Express Rider (New York: Beadle & Adams, 1888);

Bill Tredegar, The Moonshiner of Blue Ridge (New York: Street & Smith, 1889);

Darrow the Floating Detective; or, The Shadowed Buccaneer (New York: Street & Smith, 1889);

The Miner Detective; or, The Ghost of the Gulch (New York: Street & Smith, 1889);

The Naval Detective's Chase; or, Nick, The Steeple-Climber: A Thrilling Tale of Real Life (New York: Street & Smith, 1889);

Shadowed and Trapped; or, Harry the Sport (New York: Street & Smith, 1889);

Buffalo Bill's Best Shot; or, The Heart of Spotted Tail (New York: Street & Smith, 1890);

Buffalo Bill's Last Victory; or, Dove Eye, the Lodge Queen (New York: Street & Smith, 1890);

Dashing Charlie, the Texas Whirlwind (New York: Street & Smith, 1890);

Fire Feather, the Buccaneer King (New York: Beadle & Adams, 1890);

Guiletta the Waif; or, The Girl Wrecker (New York: Street & Smith, 1890);

Hank Cringle, The One-Armed Buccaneer (New York: Street & Smith, 1890);

Hazel Eye, The Girl Trapper (New York: Street & Smith, 1890);

Mountain Tom: A Thrilling Story of the New Diamond Fields (New York: Street & Smith, 1890);

Navigator Ned; or, He Would Be Captain (New York: Street & Smith, 1890);

Orthodox Jeems: A Tale of Wild Adventure in the Black Hills (New York: Street & Smith, 1890);

Rattlesnake Ned, The Terror of the Sea (New York: Street & Smith, 1890);

Red Dick, The Tiger of California (New York: Street & Smith, 1890);

The Red Privateer; or, The Midshipman Rover: A Romance of 1812 (New York: Beadle & Adams, 1890);

Rover Wild, The Jolly Reefer (New York: Street & Smith, 1890);

The Sea Spy; or, Mortimer Monk, The Hunchback Millionaire: A Tale of Sea and Land Fifty Years Ago (New York: Beadle & Adams, 1890);

Sensation Sate; or, The Queen of the Wild Horse Range (New York: Street & Smith, 1890);

Big Foot Wallace; or, The Giant Hero of the Border (New York: Street & Smith, 1891);

Buckskin Sam, The Scalp Taker (New York: Street & Smith, 1891);

Captain Jack; or, The Seven Scouts (New York: Street & Smith, 1891);

Little Buckshot, The White Whirlwind of the Prairie (New York: Street & Smith, 1891);

Long Mike, the Oregon Hustler (New York: Street & Smith, 1891);

Long Tom Dart, The Yankee Privateer: A New Naval Story of the War of 1812 (New York: Beadle & Adams, 1891);

The Revenue Officer's Triumph; or, The Sunken Treasure (New York: Street & Smith, 1891);

Sam Rickety; or, A Well-Planned Plot (New York: Street & Smith, 1891);

"Silver Wing!" The Angel of the Tribes (New York: Street & Smith, 1891);

Texas Jack, The White King of the Pawnees (New York: Street & Smith, 1891);

The Banded Pards of Colorado; or Steel Grip, the Invincible (New York: Hartz & Gray, 1896);

Wild Bill's Last Trail (New York: Street & Smith, 1896);

The Road Agents at Bay; or, Cool Ned, the Cyclone (New York: Dike, 1897);

Barnacle Backstay; or, The Gray Eagle of the Atlantic (New York: Street & Smith, 1899);

The Buccaneer's Daughter (New York: Dick & Fitzgerald, n.d.);

Magic Figure Head (Boston: Jones Publishing, n.d.);

Miriam; or, the Jew's Daughter (New York: Dick & Fitzgerald, n.d.).

PLAY PRODUCTION: *Scouts of the Plains,* Chicago, Chicago Amphitheater, 16 December 1872; renamed *Scouts of the Prairie* and later *Scouts of the Plains; or, Red Deviltry as It Is.*

Ned Buntline, the famous pseudonym of Edward Zane Carroll Judson, was "the patriarch of blood-and-thunder romancers," according to Henry Nash Smith in *Virgin Land: The American West as Symbol and Myth* (1950). He has often been called the originator of the dime novel, and while that is probably an excessive claim, Buntline certainly was an early major dime novelist and one of the most prolific. During a literary career that lasted more than forty years he turned out reams of thrilling tales. In addition to the 130 separately published books listed in the bibliography, he wrote hundreds of short stories and essays for periodicals. In addition to the pseudonym of Buntline, he wrote on occasion as Charlie Bowline, Jack Brace, Captain Cleighmore, Frank Clewline, Henry Edwards, Jiles Edwards, Clew Garner, Edward J. C. Handelboe, Mad Jack, L. Augustus Jones, Edward Minturn, and Harrison Gray Buchanan. A participant in the Seminole War and the Civil War (he also claimed he took part in the Mexican War), rescuer of several persons from drowning, recipient of bullet and other wounds both in line of duty and in less laudatory actions, capturer of two murder suspects, leader of jingoistic political riots, survivor of an attempted lynching and countless other dangers, and husband of at least six wives, Ned Buntline led an eventful life, fully as exciting as that of any of his heroes—and he willingly enlarged upon the facts.

Judson was born 20 March 1821 in Stamford, New York, the son of Levi Carroll Judson, a lawyer, teacher, Mason, and author of *A Biography of the Signers of the Declaration of Independence* and other patriotic works, who wanted his son to follow him into the law. After a bitter confrontation with his father the young Judson—like many fictional characters of the times—ran away to sea. Cruises down the East Coast both in commercial vessels and later in United

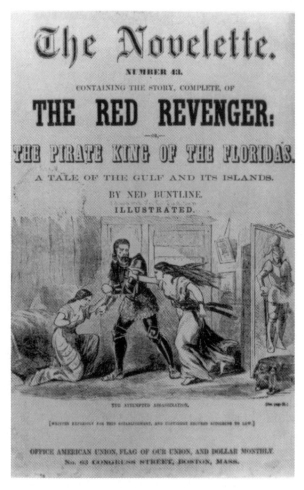

Cover for one of the eight novels published by Buntline in 1847

Ned, with *buntline,* a vital rope supporting billowing sails on a ship. One of Judson's earliest sketches, "Running the Blockade" in the October 1844 *Knickerbocker,* shows his power with words. Ned watches as a Texas ship leaves a Havana harbor to brave the French blockade as well as a hurricane:

> I caught a glimpse of her, struggling through the heavy range of breakers that ran mountain high entirely across the bar, one moment hidden in their tumultuous boilings, the next seeming to leap high above their snowy crests. Oh! it was beautiful, grandly, sublimely, terrifically beautiful! As the lightning flash illuminated the scene, the eye in one hurried glance would cover the high, rolling breakers, tinged with the prismatic hues of the rainbow, that seemed to leap madly up from the quicksand bar; the gallant and beautiful vessel rushing swiftly through the flashing waters, her spars bowing to the full strength of the storm-king's breath; her sails white as the cloud-spot whence the lightning bursts forth; her crew hurriedly flying from one post to another, as their varied duties required, in the dread time of danger.
>
> Again the lightning-cloud closes, and the imagination is left to picture the scene from the wild uproar of warring elements. Once more the jagged rays of lurid light flash forth; the vessel has passed the bar in safety; here she comes, right down in our midst!

All of Judson's Ned Buntline tales were narrated in the first person, as the author's aim was to involve the reader in adventures that seemed real.

Judson's life continued to provide him with material for his fiction. In 1846 he claimed to have captured two murderers for a bounty of $600. While he was awaiting the birth of Seberina's child in Nashville, Tennessee, Judson was accused of luring a married woman away from her husband. He faced three shots from the enraged spouse and then shot him dead. A crowd of the victim's friends pursued him into a building, where he jumped out a third-story window. Although he downplayed the effect of the fall in the May 1846 *Knickerbocker*—"forty-seven feet three inches, (measured,) on hard, rocky ground, and not a bone cracked!"—it crippled him for life. The husband's supporters later hanged him from an awning post, but Judson's friends were able to cut him loose and save his life. His wife died in childbirth soon after.

While serving as correspondent for western papers, Judson tried Boston as an outlet for his stories, with eventual success. With the beginning of the Mexican War in 1846 servicemen needed thrilling tales to read, which he supplied with stories suggested by his adventures at sea and in the Seminole War, as well as Mexican War action gleaned from newspaper dispatches. While the stories were writ-

States Navy ships gave Judson the materials, real and imagined, for future writing. In *The Great Rascal: The Life and Adventures of Ned Buntline* Jay Monaghan stresses the parallels between Judson's life and the adventures of his fictional creations.

After joining the navy Judson was appointed an acting midshipman by President Martin Van Buren on 10 February 1838 after his quick action saved the lives of fellow sailors thrown into the East River in a collision with a ferry. His involvement in the Seminole War gave him even more grist for the fiction mill. His later autobiographical accounts enlarged his part in the action and supplied Indian battles and captured Indians where none existed, but his writing did contain details drawn from life experience.

Judson resigned from the United States Navy in 1842, claiming he needed to care for his wife Seberina, whom he had met first on a voyage to Havana, Cuba. He soon started publishing sea stories and other kinds of fiction. His pen name combined a popular boy's name and nickname for Edward,

ten in his characteristically lurid style and were filled with bountiful realistic detail, Judson's claims that he participated in the Mexican War cannot be confirmed. Monaghan discovered two veterans from the war who remembered having served with him, but others recalled his having been a second in a duel fought by a friend in Quebec during the same time period.

By late 1847 he was in New York, researching vice on the back streets of the city for an exposé, *The Mysteries and Miseries of New York: A Story of Real Life* (1848). The first installment of his book included a glossary of "flash terms"–the jargon of thieves which he maintained were necessary to understand and appreciate the work. He published it at his own expense, trusting that his cliff-hanging conclusion would interest readers and publishers. Berford brought out the subsequent installments.

On the wave of ensuing popularity Judson met and married his second wife, Annie Bennett, moved into her father's home, and saw two popular plays based on his New York serials running simultaneously. He tried his hand as a political reformer in his newspaper, *Ned Buntline's Own,* opposing foreigners and Catholics and leading drives for temperance (although he drank heavily), and lectured on a variety of subjects. In 1848 he also made use of his earlier work by publishing a collection, *Cruisings, Afloat and Ashore, from the Private Log of Ned Buntline: Sketches of Land and Sea, Humorous and Pathetic; Tragical and Comical.*

Judson's reform activities helped begin the American Party and ultimately the "Know Nothings," both of which supplied some of the roots for the Republican Party. His political activism led to trouble with the law. He served a year in prison (1849–1850) for inciting mob violence in New York and was indicted in 1852 in Saint Louis for causing an election day riot. His second wife won a divorce and the custody of their child in 1849. In the ensuing years he married at least four times–to Lovanche Swart (1853), Eva Gardiner (1857?), Kate Myers (1860), and Anna Fuller (1871). Lovanche, especially, did not enjoy competition and frequently plagued Judson with threats and legal charges after he deserted her.

Judson "adjusted" his birth date forward so he would seem young enough to enlist in Union forces, joining the First New York Mounted Rifles on 25 September 1862. Although he quickly became a sergeant, he later was demoted to the ranks. However, upon his return to New York following his discharge in August 1864, he claimed to have been made chief of scouts (and thereafter called himself colonel).

Buntline, "Buffalo Bill" Cody, and "Texas Jack" Omohundro

In late 1869 Judson went to the plains of Nebraska, where he found a subject for further fiction, William F. "Buffalo Bill" Cody. Buntline's play *Scouts of the Plains,* starring Buffalo Bill as himself, was hardly a literary success, but the plainsman/scout/buffalo hunter served as the hero for four of Buntline's imaginative dime novels. Later Prentiss Ingraham and Cody himself wrote scores of similar stories, but Buntline may be said to have made Buffalo Bill the popular figure he became, beginning with a brief article in the *New York Weekly* followed by a twelve-part serial in the same publication called "Buffalo Bill, the King of the Border Men" (23 December 1869–10 March 1870).

The death of an uncle, Samuel Judson, opened a new page in Judson's life: The uncle died in August 1870, leaving his nephew a bequest establishing a memorial library in Stamford, New York, if matching funds were forthcoming from public subscription. Buntline moved to the area where he had been born, successfully raising the required funds and serving as director of the library. In a home he built near Stamford called Eagle's Nest he began to write and publish stories and columns on hunting and especially fishing, at which he was truly adept.

As Buntline he wrote steadily for Street and Smith as well as Beadle and Adams and lectured widely on temperance and politics. Bothered by old wounds he claimed had been received in his various wars and injuries from his many escapades, Judson was made housebound by the winter cold of New York. While his writing was reduced materially in his last years, it did not cease. After a painful and lingering illness and bothered by a faltering heart, he died on 16 July 1886 at Eagle's Nest.

As Ned Buntline, Judson's main line of production—and it was almost factorylike in its volume—was the dime novel, a subliterary genre that the reading public bought by the thousands for more than half a century. He is said once to have written sixty thousand words in six days, and he boasted that the Buffalo Bill play took him only four hours to write. A young Samuel Langhorne Clemens may have been one of Judson's early admirers. He would have been twelve when Ned Buntline's *The Black Avenger of the Spanish Main; or, the Fiend of Blood: A Thrilling Tale of the Buccaneer Times* came out in 1847. Nearly thirty years later, in *The Adventures of Tom Sawyer* (1876), Tom fondly imagines his return to his hometown church, "the whisperings, 'It's Tom Sawyer the Pirate!—the Black Avenger of the Spanish Main!'" In addition to adventure stories Judson wrote sentimental tales and stories of innocent women led astray.

A great literary figure Judson was not, but a fair comparison can be made to modern-day writers of television series and paperback fiction in which little other than setting or character names is changed from one episode or book to the next. If popularity is a test of merit, his work was meritorious. Certainly he wrote with realistic detail and seldom employed the purple prose of other pulp fiction writers. He took pride in the fact that he knew how to seize the reader's attention, with a dramatic, lively action start rather than a lengthy descriptive passage, although, as critic Edmund Pearson points out, he could pack an opening sentence with information, as in *Red Ralph, the Ranger; or, The Brother's Revenge* (1870):

> It was a beautiful place, that of Edgar Rolfe, situated upon the banks of the James river, chosen by his father, when hand in hand he roamed through the forest with the noble-hearted and queenly Pocahontas, whom he married, and who died but too soon after she gave birth to her only son—died a stranger in a foreign land, but not unwept did she perish.

Ordinarily he knew his audience and fulfilled its wants with carefully chosen words in less unwieldy structures. His enlargement and use of his own life story in fiction is understandable in a publishing era when self-advertisement was standard and writers vied vigorously for a share in the market. The popularity of some of his stories endured through many reprintings. The name and contributions of Ned Buntline cannot be ignored in any tracing of the development of American culture via the printed word.

Biographies:

Fred E. Pond, *The Life and Adventures of "Ned Buntline"* (New York, 1919);

Jay Monaghan, *The Great Rascal: The Life and Adventures of Ned Buntline* (Boston: Little, Brown, 1952).

References:

Albert Johannsen, *The House of Beadle and Adams and Its Dime and Nickel Novels* (Norman: University of Oklahoma Press, 1950), pp. 56–62, 167–176;

Daryl E. Jones, *The Dime Novel Western* (Bowling Green, Ohio: Popular Press, 1978);

Edmund Pearson, *Dime Novels; or, Following an Old Trail in Popular Literature* (Boston: Little, Brown, 1929);

Henry Nash Smith, *Virgin Land: The American West as Symbol and Myth* (Cambridge: Harvard University Press, 1950), pp. 90–111.

Papers:

Buntline's papers are widely scattered in the holdings of the Huntington Library, San Marino, California; the Library of Congress; the Knox College Archives in the Henry M. Seymour Library, Galesburg, Illinois; the Boston Public Library; the Houghton Library, Harvard University; the University of Rochester; Haverford College; the Historical Society of Pennsylvania; the John Hay Library, Brown University; the Harold B. Lee Library, Brigham Young University; and the New York Historical Society.

George Catlin

(26 July 1796 – 23 December 1872)

Joseph R. Millichap
Western Kentucky University

BOOKS: *Catalogue of Catlin's Indian Gallery of Portraits, Landscapes, Manners, Customs, Costumes, &c.* (New York: Piercy & Reed, 1837);

A Descriptive Catalogue of Catlin's Indian Collection, Containing Portraits, Landscapes, Costumes, and Representations of the Manners and Customs of the North American Indians (London: C. Adlard, 1840);

Letters and Notes on the Manners, Customs, and Conditions of the North American Indians, 2 volumes (New York: Wiley & Putnam, 1841; London: Printed for the author by Tosswill and Myers, 1841); republished as *The Manners, Customs and Condition of the North American Indians* (London: Published by the author, 1841); republished as *Illustrations of the Manners, Customs, and Condition of the North American Indians,* 2 volumes (London: H. G. Bohn, 1845); republished as *North American Indians* (London: Chatto & Windus, 187?; Philadelphia: Leary, Stuart, 1913); republished as *Catlin's Indians* (Philadelphia: Hubbard Brothers, 1891);

Catlin's North American Indian Portfolio of Hunting Scenes and Amusements (London: Published by the author, 1844; New York: J. Ackerman, 1845);

Catlin's Notes of Eight Years' Travel and Residence in Europe, with his North American Indian Collection. With Anecdotes and Incidents of the Travels and Adventures of Three Different Parties of American Indians whom he Introduced to the Courts of England, France, and Belgium, 2 volumes (London, 1848; New York, 1848); republished as *Adventures of the Ojibbeway and Ioway Indians in England, France, and Belgium: Being Notes of Eight Years' Travels and Residence in Europe with his North American Indian Collection* (London: Published by the author, 1852);

Souvenir of the North American Indians as They Were in the Middle of the Nineteenth Century, 3 volumes (London: Published by the author, 1850; Chicago: C. W. Farrington, 1870);

George Catlin, a self-portrait at age fifty-three
(Smithsonian Institution)

Life Among the Indians: A Book for Youth (New York: D. Appleton, 1857; London: Sampson Low, 1861);

Prairie Scenes (New York: Currier & Ives, 1857);

The Breath of Life or Mal-Respiration. And its Effects upon the Enjoyment & Life of Man (London: Trübner, 1861; New York: J. Wiley, 1861); republished as *Shut Your Mouth* (New York, 1864; London: Trübner, 1869);

An Account of an Annual Religious Ceremony Practised by the Mandan Tribe of North American Indians (London: Printed by Whittingham & Wilkins, 1863–1864);

Last Rambles Among the Indians of the Rocky Mountains and the Andes (New York: D. Appleton, 1867;

London: Gall & Inglis, 1867); republished as
*Rambles Among the Indians of the Rocky Mountains
and the Andes* (London: Gall & Inglis, 1877);

O-Kee-Pa: A Religious Ceremony (London: Trübner,
1867; Philadelphia: Lippincott, 1967);

*The Lifted and Subsided Rocks of America with Their In-
fluences on the Oceanic, Atmospheric, and Land Currents and the Distribution of Races* (London: Trübner, 1870);

*North and South American Indians. Catalogue Descriptive
and Instructive of Catlin's Indian Cartoons* (New
York: Baker & Godwin, 1871).

Although best known as a graphic artist,
George Catlin was also an important writer about
the Native Americans of the frontier West, a fact
that will doubtless be increasingly recognized as the
canon of American literature continues to expand.
Like his striking graphics, Catlin's writing about the
North American Indians combines accurate documentation and romantic vision, creating the artistic
tension that obtains in the best painting and writing
from the so-called American Renaissance of the mid
nineteenth century. His mixture of illustrations and
prose creates a rich intertextuality that makes his
work arresting in form as well as in content. Catlin
is also an intriguing figure in American culture as
much for his persona—the artist as innocent, inspired entrepreneur—as for his artistry.

Born 26 July 1796 in Wilkes-Barre, Pennsylvania, George Catlin grew up in the Susquehanna Valley, then little removed from its frontier existence.
His father, Putnam Catlin, a decorated veteran of
the Revolution originally from Connecticut, found
success as a lawyer and planter in Wilkes-Barre following the war; his mother, Polly Catlin, was born
on the frontier and briefly had been a captive of a
raiding Iroquois war party after British Loyalists
and their Indian allies had massacred settlers in
Pennsylvania's Wyoming Valley on 4 July 1778.
Young Catlin, the fifth of fourteen children, was a
favorite of both parents, who indulged him with a
formal education at the Wilkes-Barre Academy and
later at the Litchfield Law School in Connecticut.

Catlin was always more interested in hunting
and fishing than in school activities, although he enjoyed recording his outdoor experiences in drawings and prose sketches. As Catlin puts it in the
autobiographical introduction to *Letters and Notes on
the Manners, Customs, and Conditions of the North American Indians* (1841), he grew up "with books reluctantly held in one hand, a rifle or fishing pole
grasped firmly in the other." After passing the bar
examination in 1819 he spent a few years as "a sort
of Nimrodical lawyer," but his heart was not in the

work. He then sold his possessions, "save rifle and
fishing tackle," to set himself up as a painter of
miniature portraits, a vocation that caused him to
move to Philadelphia, where his new career soon
earned him a comfortable living. Catlin may have
received informal instruction in the graphic arts at
Charles Wilson Peale's Philadelphia Museum.

The young artist formulated his artistic project
of recording the people already considered "Vanishing Americans" as early as 1823 when he viewed a
party of western Indians traveling to Washington
for treaty negotiations. His first portrait of a Native
American, the celebrated Seneca orator Red Jacket,
was painted in 1826. By this year Catlin had moved
to New York, where he earned his membership in
the National Academy and won the hand of Clara
Gregory, the beautiful, accomplished daughter of a
wealthy family from Albany, New York. The couple
were married in 1828 despite her family's skepticism about the young painter's prospects. They had
four children—a boy and three girls.

Catlin's ambitions extended to the worlds of
society, culture, and commerce as well as art. As a
talented, educated, and well-connected young man,
he had every hope of financial reward as well as artistic acclaim for his bold plan to record the western
tribes in their native country. Catlin can be seen as a
version of Ralph Waldo Emerson's American
Scholar, a transcendental "jack-of-all-trades" who
would immerse himself in Nature to learn the true
meaning of culture. For American Adams such as
Catlin and Emerson no inherent contradiction existed between spiritual and material success; rather,
the latter tended to imply the former, as with their
Puritan forebears. Because the museum or picture
exhibition was the popular culture's main visual entertainment, Catlin planned to create a gallery of
Native American pictures and artifacts and thus become rich and famous.

Catlin's career as a writer and painter is organized around the dichotomy of artistic and entrepreneurial efforts. In 1829 he established his base of operations in New York, the center of the American
arts, which, with the ascendency of the Knickerbocker writers and the painters of the Hudson River
School in the early nineteenth century, had wrested
the artistic and intellectual leadership of America
from Boston and Philadelphia. The 1820s had witnessed the first real stirrings of American art in the
writings of Washington Irving, William Cullen Bryant, and James Fenimore Cooper as well as in the
paintings of Thomas Cole, Asher Durand, and Thomas Doughty. Catlin was beginning his career at the
dawning of a renaissance in American art.

*Sketches from Catlin's notebooks (Thomas Gilcrease Institute of American History and Art,
Tulsa, Oklahoma)*

Catlin longed to begin his artistic mission, and in 1830 he visited Saint Louis with a letter to Gen. William Clark, who with Meriwether Lewis had blazed the trail to the Oregon country in 1804–1806 and now served as superintendent of Indian affairs for the West. General Clark approved of Catlin's project and took him along on treaty-making excursions to visit resettled tribes in Kansas and Wisconsin. The following summer Catlin at last saw the Plains Indians in their natural setting as he visited the villages of the Kansa, Oto, Missouri, and Pawnee tribes on the Platte River in what is now the state of Nebraska. Although Catlin would later claim to have also fol-lowed the Platte to the Rockies, his assertion is contradicted by other accounts.

In the summer of 1832 Catlin made what proved to be his most important trip among the Indians. Traveling up the Missouri River in the first steamboat to navigate it as far as the confluence of the Yellowstone River, he visited Fort Union, the headquarters of John Jacob Astor's American Fur Company and the focus of the fur trade of the high plains and the Rocky Mountains. Catlin encountered the Plains Indians at the height of their glory, and his recording of their images in paint and prose helped establish these peoples as the archetypal American Indians. He met Sioux, Poncas,

Assineboines, Ricarees, Crow, Blackfeet, Hidasta, Gros Ventres, and the mysterious Mandans, who would become his most frequent subjects. At Fort Union he also began a series of colorful letters contracted by the *New York Commercial Advisor* which would become the opening chapters of his most important book, *Letters and Notes on the Manners, Customs, and Conditions of the North American Indians.*

Catlin's lengthy gestation period for this work is explained by his artistic theory and his methodology. As a Romantic, Catlin stressed the immediacy of experience and the importance of impression. In his autobiographical remarks introducing his book he explains his aesthetic:

> Man in the simplicity and loftiness of his nature, unrestrained and unfettered by the disguises of art, is surely the most beautiful model for the painter–and the country from which he hails is undoubtedly the best study or school of the arts in the world: such I am sure, from the models I have seen, is the wilderness of North America.

Catlin felt that the artist must capture nature with a grace beyond the reach of artifice, with the immediacy of impression. To this end Catlin developed a skillful and practical method of doing field sketches and quick watercolors which then could be transported back to his studio for polish and refinement in other media, particularly in oils. His writing practice was analogous: in the field he would make quick notes, often on his sketch pad, which he then expanded in journal entries and letters, both private and public, and finally polished for book publication.

Catlin's superiority as a graphic artist owes something to the process he developed for his work. His field methods pushed him beyond studio art to a vivid style that matches the vitality of his subjects. No one grasped the essence of this style more fully than the French writer Charles Baudelaire, who lauded Catlin in his review, published in the 22 June 1845 issue of *Le Constitutionel,* of the Paris Salon of 1845 for finding an appropriate style for his subjects. Unfortunately, Catlin was not able to achieve the same success in his writing–his measured, neoclassical style is often at odds with his subjects, a situation that also obtains with such contemporaries as James Fenimore Cooper. Such a judgment does not mean that Catlin is an uninteresting writer but rather that he is more successful as a graphic artist, though limited in both forms by the very enthusiasm that creates his strengths.

Another reason Catlin delayed his book was that he was simply too busy with other parts of his career to pursue publication. He had several seasons of travel, gathering impressions, and creation ahead of him even as he reached the high point of the summer of 1832. After his return to Saint Louis in early autumn 1832, Catlin spent the following year finishing and assembling his Indian materials for showing in Pittsburgh, Cincinnati, and Louisville, with one field trip to the Gulf Coast of Florida in the winter of 1832–1833.

In the summer of 1834 he took a steamboat up the Arkansas River as far as Fort Gibson in what was then the newly established Indian Territory and the new home of the Five Civilized Tribes lately removed from the Southeast by President Andrew Jackson. Here he joined a company of dragoons on an expedition to "show the flag" to the southwestern tribes, especially the troublesome Comanches. The company also visited the Osage, the Pawnees, and the Kiowas. However, record heat, bad water, and hard riding soon took their toll on the detachment; Catlin had to recover for several weeks before he returned to "civilization" in Saint Louis. After wintering in Florida, the following summer Catlin ascended the Mississippi River to Fort Snelling in what is now Minnesota, visiting the Sac and Fox, the Ojibways, and the eastern Sioux. In 1836 he returned to explore the great pipestone quarry in the lands occupied by the eastern Sioux though by tradition open to all the tribes who traded this soft red stone throughout the West. The mineral, found only at this spot, was called *catlinite* after the location's first recorded reporter.

As the 1830s progressed, Catlin began to spend less time exploring and creating and more time finishing and marketing his materials. By 1837 he felt ready to open his Indian gallery in New York City. The following year he took his exhibition on tour to Boston, Philadelphia, and Washington. Returning to New York in 1839, Catlin attempted unsuccessfully to sell his collection to the American government as the basis of a national gallery of art and science. The politics of this project were complicated and murky; probably Catlin's general championing of the Native Americans, including a specific proposal to preserve the Great Plains and Rocky Mountains as a vast reservation, cost him the support of Jacksonian Democrats intent on peopling the plains with tax-paying settlers. In reaction, Catlin carried his Indian gallery off to England, where he hoped to play on American chauvinism with the threat of a sale to a foreign power. He would not return to America to stay for three decades. Far from his sources of inspiration in the West, Catlin had entered the entrepreneurial phase of his career.

Book publication became a major part of Catlin's salesmanship. Previously he had published oc-

Catlin's sketch of his gallery in Paris (from George Catlin: Letters and Notes on the North American Indians, *edited by Michael M. Mooney, 1975)*

casionally, most notably the series of newspaper letters chronicling his Missouri River expedition in 1832 and the New York catalogue of the Indian gallery that appeared in 1837. These early efforts inclined to two poles of his talents: the former was prose without pictures, while the latter was prose about pictures. As he was preparing the descriptive catalogue for his London exhibition of 1840, Catlin apparently conceived the idea of a major publication combining pictures and prose, a book he could sell by subscription to support his growing family and his new position as one of London's social lions. *Letters and Notes on the Manners, Customs, and Conditions of the North American Indians* was a signal success, both upon its publication and later. Focused on its subject, the book combines his best writing and his finest illustrations.

Catlin deals organically with the themes of nature much as Henry David Thoreau does in his portrayal of the seasons at Walden Pond or Herman Melville does in his descriptions of voyages across trackless seas. Invariably he employs the journey motif to order his encyclopedic materials. Both volumes of *Letters and Notes* use an epic river voyage as an organizing principle: volume one follows the Missouri River trip of 1832, volume two the Arkan-

sas River expedition of 1834. On both voyages he steamed upriver only to float back down. It is as if Catlin, once immersed in the wilds of nature, leaves as slowly and reluctantly as possible. This is the pattern of his major prose efforts throughout the rest of his career.

Catlin's introductory chapter, which he admits to the reader was more recently written than the other parts of the book, sets forth not only his autobiographical sketch but also a statement of his artistic purposes. Catlin makes two major points about the Native Americans to his white audience: that they are "human beings, with features, thoughts, reasons, and sympathies like our own," and that they face death and destruction "introduced and visited upon them by acquisitive white men." The greater part of his narration attempts an accurate, sympathetic account of Native Americans in their natural state, punctuated by elegies for this race he felt was doomed by the corrupting touch of American culture. At the same time he laments that "black and blue cloth and civilization are destined, not only to veil, but to obliterate the beauty and grace of Nature." Thus the artist must act quickly to preserve "the history and customs of such a people . . . themes worthy of the lifetime of one man."

At the same time he proposes "to perpetuate them in a *Gallerie unique,* for the use and instruction of future ages."

In the initial narrative chapter Catlin's romantic themes and motifs are evident. He celebrates the journey up the Missouri as "a voyage so full of incident, so many scenes of the picturesque and the sublime," that he could not capture them adequately. He describes the rolling country as well as its picturesque inhabitants, both native and white. When he participates in a buffalo hunt, he seems to discover a sublime state through this immersion in nature:

> I have often waked (as it were) out of the delerium of the chase (into which I had fallen, as into an agitated sleep, and through which I had passed as through a delightful dream), where to have died would have been but to remain, riding on, without a struggle or a pang.

In a sense all of Catlin's narrations have a dreamlike quality about them, showing a sort of childlike wonder even in the face of the most extreme dangers. As his picture making was a mystery of the highest order to his Indian audiences, such danger extended to his vocation as well as to his avocations. One of his portraits indirectly caused the death of its subject when a rival chief used it as the occasion for insult. Although he was protected by his hosts in the American Fur Company, Catlin soon learned that life was often dangerous on the western frontier.

Perhaps because his artistic magic had led to the death of one of his subjects, Catlin was particularly fascinated with the magic or medicine practiced by the Indian shamans. When a Blackfoot warrior was mortally wounded by a rival chief, Catlin compared the shaman's ministrations to the last rites of the Catholic Church. He describes the shaman's costume in detail, pointing out that his bearskin robe is festooned with "the skins of many animals, which are anomalies or deformities, which render them in their estimation, *medicine.*" In the rest of letter 6 Catlin presents the whole subject of totemism in a succinct yet sympathetic manner, concluding that the Native American because of his unity with nature represents a naturalness lost to most whites.

In his letters from Fort Union, Catlin carefully conveys the most general aspects of Indian life as he narrates his particular experiences. After three letters discussing his trip from Saint Louis, letter 4 uses the occasion of his first buffalo hunt to analyze the importance of the animal to the culture of the Plains Indians; letter 5 describes Native American dress; 6, religion; 7, housing; 8, physical characteristics; and 9, character. These discussions usually stem from some specific incident, often shown in one of the illustrations which he provides with his text. Overall, in these early chapters Catlin presents a thorough introduction to Native American life on the Plains.

Beginning with letter 10, Catlin looks more carefully at a single tribe, the Mandan Sioux, who had developed a complex culture based on a combination of hunting and farming economies. Catlin was particularly interested in the tribe because frontier folklore connected the Mandan Sioux with lost colonies. Some members of the tribe had lighter eyes, complexions, and hair than their near neighbors, and their more developed culture led to the supposition that they could be lost Welshmen, Israelites, or even descendants of the lost white race of Moundbuilders, as posited by reputable historians in Catlin's day. Perhaps because of his own Welsh ancestry, Catlin convinced himself that the Mandans were the last remnant of Prince Madoc's legendary band of late-medieval colonists, and he spends letter 23 pointing out corroborating details such as the resemblance of the Mandan buffalo hide "bull boat" to the traditional Welsh *corracle.*

Catlin's careful observations in other chapters balance his romantic theories of the Mandan's origins. He describes in detail several aspects of Indian life that he had treated more generally in his opening chapters. In letter 22, the longest in the book, he reports the Mandan's O-Kee-Pa rituals, which celebrated the return of their life-sustaining agriculture in summer. These colorful and often cruel ceremonies climaxed in initiation ceremonies for their young warriors. After four days of fasting, dancing, and praying the initiates were skewered through the pectoral muscles and suspended from the lodge poles until they fainted, thus placing their lives in the hands of the "Great Spirit." Catlin would revisit this ceremony in his later book *O-Kee-Pa: A Religious Ceremony* (1867), which was occasioned by published doubts about the accuracy of his accounts. These attacks on his veracity were made plausible, sadly enough, by the decimation of the Mandans in a smallpox epidemic within a year of Catlin's initial observations. Catlin ends his first volume with his return to Saint Louis and an impassioned plea for a reservation to protect the vanishing buffalo and the native peoples of the Great Plains who depended on the bison for their existence.

In the second volume of *Letters and Notes* Catlin uses his journey up the Arkansas River in 1834 as the structuring device. Catlin's encounters with the colorful horsemen of the southern plains yield adventures and discoveries; yet the second volume proved somewhat less successful, for several reasons, than his first. The 1834 expedition was much more arduous, and illness depleted Catlin's energy so that he could not capture the Osages, the Kiowas, and the Commanches with the vitality of his earlier efforts in either paint or prose. In contrast to the first volume, he did not have a set of published letters to draw on for inspiration, and his haste to get his book into circulation probably caused him to rush through his materials. Also, when the 1834 expedition did not produce a volume as long as that recording the 1832 venture, he padded out the second volume with miscellaneous material from his western trips in 1830 and 1831 as well as his journeys on the Upper Mississippi in 1835 and 1836. The second volume reads more like the writing found in an encyclopedia than the focused, immediate writing of the first volume.

Despite its flaws *Letters and Notes* received positive initial reviews, and its publication marked the zenith of Catlin's career professionally and personally. Brisk book sales buoyed Catlin when attendance fell off at his Indian gallery, but he was soon driven to staging Indian shows, first with himself and friends in costume. Later he staged the shows with traveling groups of Native Americans brought to Britain by missionary groups.

Although the presence of the "savages" brought the crowds back to his exhibition hall, Catlin was still searching for a patron to buy the entire gallery and ensure his fortune. Failing to find one in England despite an audience with the queen, Catlin packed his gallery and his group of Iowas off to France in 1845. His new venue brought renewed interest in his work, including positive reviews of a newly published portfolio of hunting scenes. Yet even in Paris public interest waned, and an attempt to sell the gallery to the French government faltered.

A series of personal disasters soon followed. Shortly after his beloved Clara died of pneumonia in 1845, Catlin's Indian troupe was stricken with smallpox, and several perished despite his efforts to care for them at his own expense. In 1848 he attempted to recover his fortunes with another book, *Catlin's Notes of Eight Years' Travel and Residence in Europe, with his North American Indian Collection,* but its publication proved both a critical and financial failure. Catlin soon was forced to mortgage his gallery, and he would lose it after the illness and death of his only son, Georgie, in the same year. His wealthy in-laws took his three daughters off to America, although they offered him no help. Catlin seemed a broken man and disappeared from sight for several years.

As might be expected from his experiences abroad, *Catlin's Notes of Eight Years' Travel* is in many ways the dark mirror vision of *Letters and Notes,* even

to the eight-year period covered in both books. As in the previous book, Catlin is the central consciousness, something of the innocent abroad, as he journeys by steamer to Europe. The heart of his narrative is Catlin's shepherding of the troupes of Native Americans who performed parts of his shows in England and France. He is thus able to view the putative civilization of Europe through the even more innocent eyes of the "primitives," a device often used in dystopian attacks on the inequities and contradictions of "civilized" life. Many of the remarks of his Indian wards are humorous and incisive, in particular their amazement at the poverty and prostitution discovered in the slums of London and Paris. However, the narrative often abandons its satiric focus while Catlin rails about general or personal injustices, and the tiny groups of primitives seem swallowed by the masses of civilization. The book is more interesting for its biographical data than for its information about either Indians or Europeans.

The story of Catlin's later life and work replays his early career in several curious ways. According to Catlin in *Last Rambles Among the Indians of the Rocky Mountains and the Andes* (1867), he resurrected himself through several expeditions among the remaining "wild" Indians of North and then South America. His adventures included navigating the Amazon to its headwaters, crossing the Andes to Lima, voyaging up the Pacific Coast of North America as far as Alaska, and returning to New York by way of the southern Rockies and the Rio Grande River. Although his biographers have noted contradictions in this incredible itinerary, they have accepted Catlin's accounts of his later travels more or less at face value. However, recent scholarship, in particular the research of Latin American historian Edgardo Carlos Krebs, points out that these later travels are not corroborated by any independent sources. Moreover, all of the materials Catlin presents as the products of these later expeditions would have been available to him in Europe during the years when he assembled and published them. So it is possible that his later efforts are more fiction than fact. At the same time Catlin's romantic insistence on personal experience and the intricate detail of some of this later work would seem to argue for its essential verity. In all probability, truth exists somewhere between these two extremes; Catlin made some of these voyages and lived some of these adventures, though probably not all.

In any case, Catlin's later work proves demonstrably weaker in both his painting and his prose. He hoped to incorporate South American materials in the re-creation of his Indian gallery, but the paintings that treat his early subjects seem imitative, while the new materials seem stiff and caricatured, perhaps influenced by the recent development of photography in ethnographic work, which required subjects to hold poses for good pictures to be made. The same difficulties also obtain in his writing.

In *Life Among the Indians: A Book for Youth* (1857) Catlin retells some of the best incidents from *Letters and Notes* while adding new adventures from the several South American expeditions. Catlin's tone is uneven as he veers from deadly earnest to arch humor and from coy disclaimers to breathless adventures. Although the book may have been appropriate for the youth of his era, his retelling of the earlier material adds nothing to it, while the new descriptions seem rushed and simplistic.

Last Rambles Among the Indians was intended as Catlin's major chronicle of his later expeditions, a complement to his reconstituted gallery much as *Letters and Notes* was to the original London exhibition. Just as the later graphics proved weaker, so too does the later prose. Where he had been excited and observant earlier, Catlin is now garrulous and rambling—half pseudoscientist and half reckless adventurer as in the book for youth. The opening of this book among the Native Americans on the western slope of the Rockies recalls the later parts of the second volume of *Letters and Notes,* where the author crammed in miscellaneous materials from several years' travels. The rest of the book traces the South American journeys with colorful detail but seems to lack the purpose of the earlier volumes.

By contrast, Catlin's *O-Kee-Pa: A Religious Ceremony* ably extends and amplifies his earlier observations of the Mandan initiation rites. Countering the attacks on the accuracy of his earlier descriptions, Catlin writes in a tone of objective observation, creating lucid prose supported by a sheaf of finely executed illustrations. Although the book adds few new details to his description in *Letters and Notes* and seems somewhat less exciting, it has an enduring value as early ethnography.

Catlin's later work did return him to the public eye and finally reunited him with his family. In 1870 he returned to America to live with his daughters and try to sell his new gallery to the Smithsonian Institution, again unsuccessfully. Catlin died on 23 December 1872 at the age of seventy-six, ignored by his countrymen. Yet as the frontier West he depicted closed, his work was rediscovered. His original Indian gallery was found in storage and finally sold to the Smithsonian in 1874, where it began the restoration of Catlin to his rightful place as one of the most important observers of the Native Americans of the West in both paint and print.

Letters:

The Letters of George Catlin and His Family: A Chronicle of the American West, edited by Marjorie Catlin Roehm (Berkeley: University of California Press, 1966).

Biographies:

Loyd Haberly, *Pursuit of the Horizon: A Life of George Catlin* (New York: Macmillan, 1948);

Harold McCracken, *George Catlin and the Old Frontier* (New York: Dial, 1959);

Brian W. Dippie, *Catlin and His Contemporaries: The Politics of Patronage* (Lincoln: University of Nebraska Press, 1990).

References:

Thomas Donaldson, *The George Catlin Indian Gallery in the United States National Museum* (Washington, D.C.: Government Printing Office, 1886);

John C. Ewers, *Artists of the Old West* (Garden City, N.Y.: Doubleday, 1965);

Edgardo Carlos Krebs, "George Catlin and South America: A Look at His 'Lost' Years and His Paintings of Northeastern Argentina," *American Art Journal,* 22 (1990): 5–39;

Joseph R. Millichap, *George Catlin,* Western Writers Series, no. 27 (Boise, Idaho: Boise State University, 1977);

William Truettner, *The Natural Man Observed: A Study of Catlin's Indian Gallery* (Washington, D.C.: Smithsonian Institution Press, 1979).

Papers:

The major holdings of George Catlin's papers include the Bancroft Library; the Newberry Library, Chicago; the California State Library, University of California at Berkeley; the Gilcrease Institute; and the Amon Carter Museum.

Samuel Langhorne Clemens
(Mark Twain)
(30 November 1835 – 21 April 1910)

Hamlin Hill
Texas A&M University

See also the Clemens entries in *DLB 11: American Humorists, 1800–1950; DLB 12: American Realists and Naturalists; DLB 23: American Newspaper Journalists, 1873–1900; DLB 64: American Literary Critics and Scholars, 1850–1880;* and *DLB 74: American Short-Story Writers Before 1880.*

BOOKS: *The Celebrated Jumping Frog of Calaveras County, and Other Sketches* (New York: C. H. Webb, 1867; London: Routledge, 1867);

The Innocents Abroad, or The New Pilgrims' Progress (Hartford, Conn.: American Publishing, 1869); republished in 2 volumes as *The Innocents Abroad* and *The New Pilgrims' Progress* (London: Hotten, 1870);

Mark Twain's (Burlesque) Autobiography and First Romance (New York: Sheldon, 1871; London: Hotten, 1871);

"Roughing It" and The Innocents at Home (London: Routledge, 1872); enlarged as *Roughing It* (Hartford, Conn.: American Publishing, 1872);

A Curious Dream; and Other Sketches (London: Routledge, 1872);

The Gilded Age: A Tale of Today, by Twain and Charles Dudley Warner (1 volume, Hartford, Conn.: American Publishing, 1873; 3 volumes, London: Routledge, 1874);

Mark Twain's Sketches, New and Old (Hartford, Conn.: American Publishing, 1875);

The Adventures of Tom Sawyer (London: Chatto & Windus, 1876; Hartford, Conn.: American Publishing, 1876);

Old Times on the Mississippi (Toronto: Belford, 1876); republished as *The Mississippi Pilot* (London: Ward, Lock & Tyler, 1877); expanded as *Life on the Mississippi* (London: Chatto & Windus, 1883; Boston: Osgood, 1883);

An Idle Excursion (Toronto: Rose-Belford, 1878); expanded as *Punch, Brothers Punch! And Other Sketches* (New York: State, Woodman, 1878);

Samuel Clemens, circa 1864

A Tramp Abroad (London: Chatto & Windus / Hartford, Conn.: American Publishing, 1880);

Conversation, As It Was by the Social Fireside, in the Time of the Tudors (Cleveland, 1880);

The Prince and the Pauper (London: Chatto & Windus, 1881; Boston: Osgood, 1882);

The Stolen White Elephant (London: Chatto & Windus, 1882); republished as *The Stolen White Elephant, Etc.* (Boston: Osgood, 1882);

The Adventures of Huckleberry Finn (London: Chatto & Windus, 1884); republished as *Adventures of Huckleberry Finn* (New York: Webster, 1885);

A Connecticut Yankee in King Arthur's Court (New York: Webster, 1889); republished as *A Yankee at the Court of King Arthur* (London: Chatto & Windus, 1889);

The American Claimant (New York: Webster, 1892; London: Chatto & Windus, 1892);

Merry Tales (New York: Webster, 1892).

The £1,000,000 Bank-Note and Other New Stories (New York: Webster, 1893; London: Chatto & Windus, 1893);

Tom Sawyer Abroad by Huck Finn (New York: Webster, 1894; London: Chatto & Windus, 1894);

Pudd'nhead Wilson, A Tale (London: Chatto & Windus, 1894); expanded as *The Tragedy of Pudd'nhead Wilson and the Comedy of Those Extraordinary Twins* (Hartford, Conn.: American Publishing, 1894);

Personal Recollections of Joan of Arc by the Sieur Louis de Conte (New York: Harper, 1896);

How to Tell a Story and Other Essays (New York: Harper, 1897);

Following the Equator (Hartford, Conn.: American Publishing, 1897); republished as *More Tramps Abroad* (London: Chatto & Windus, 1897);

The Man That Corrupted Hadleyburg and Other Stories and Essays (New York & London: Harper, 1900); enlarged as *The Man That Corrupted Hadleyburg and Other Stories and Sketches* (London: Chatto & Windus, 1900);

A Double Barreled Detective Story (New York & London: Harper, 1902);

A Dog's Tale (New York & London: Harper, 1904);

King Leopold's Soliloquy: A Defense of His Congo Rule (Boston: P. R. Warren, 1905);

Eve's Diary Translated from the Original Ms (London & New York: Harper, 1906);

What Is Man? (New York: De Vinne Press, 1906); expanded as *What Is Man? And Other Essays* (New York & London: Harper, 1917);

The $30,000 Bequest and Other Stories (New York & London: Harper, 1906);

Christian Science with Notes Containing Corrections to Date (New York & London: Harper, 1907);

A Horse's Tale (New York & London: Harper, 1907);

Is Shakespeare Dead? (New York & London: Harper, 1909);

Extract from Captain Stormfield's Visit to Heaven (New York & London: Harper, 1909);

Mark Twain's Speeches, edited by F. A. Nast (New York & London: Harper, 1910);

The Mysterious Stranger, a Romance, edited by Albert Bigelow Paine and Frederick A. Duneka (New York & London: Harper, 1916); expanded as *The Mysterious Stranger and Other Stories,* edited by Paine (New York & London: Harper, 1922);

The Curious Republic of Gondour and Other Whimsical Sketches (New York: Boni & Liveright, 1919);

Mark Twain's Speeches, edited by Paine (New York & London: Harper, 1923);

Europe and Elsewhere, edited by Paine (New York & London: Harper, 1923);

Mark Twain's Autobiography, edited by Paine, 2 volumes (New York & London: Harper, 1924);

Sketches of the Sixties, by Twain and Bret Harte (San Francisco: Howell, 1926);

The Adventures of Thomas Jefferson Snodgrass, edited by Charles Honce (Chicago: Pascal Covici, 1928);

Mark Twain's Notebook, edited by Paine (New York & London: Harper, 1935);

Letters from the Sandwich Islands Written for the Sacramento Union, edited by G. Ezra Dane (San Francisco: Grabhorn Press, 1937);

The Washoe Giant in San Francisco, edited by Franklin Walker (San Francisco: Fields, 1938);

Mark Twain's Travels With Mr. Brown, edited by Walker and Dane (New York: Knopf, 1940);

Mark Twain in Eruption, edited by Bernard DeVoto (New York & London: Harper, 1940);

Mark Twain at Work, edited by DeVoto (Cambridge, Mass.: Harvard University Press, 1942);

Mark Twain, Business Man, edited by Samuel Charles Webster (Boston: Little, Brown, 1946);

Mark Twain of the ENTERPRISE, edited by Henry Nash Smith (Berkeley: University of California Press, 1957);

Traveling with the Innocents Abroad: Mark Twain's Original Reports from Europe and the Holy Land, edited by Daniel Morley McKeithan (Norman: University of Oklahoma Press, 1958);

Mark Twain's "Which Was the Dream" and Other Symbolic Writings of the Later Years, edited by John S. Tuckey (Berkeley: University of California Press, 1966);

Mark Twain's Satires and Burlesques, edited by Franklin R. Rogers (Berkeley: University of California Press, 1967);

Clemens of the "Call": Mark Twain in San Francisco, edited by Edgar M. Branch (Berkeley: University of California Press, 1969);

Mark Twain's "Mysterious Stranger" Manuscripts, edited by William M. Gibson (Berkeley: University of California Press, 1969);

Mark Twain's Fables of Man, edited by Tuckey (Berkeley: University of California Press, 1972);

Mark Twain's Notebooks and Journals, volume 1, 1855–1873, edited by Frederick Anderson, Michael B. Frank, and Kenneth M. Sanderson; volume 2, 1877–1883, edited by Anderson, Lin Salamo, and Bernard L. Stein; volume 3, 1883–1891, edited by Robert Pack Browning, Frank, and Salamo (Berkeley: University of California Press, 1975, 1979);

Mark Twain Speaking, edited by Paul Fatout (West Lafayette, Ind.: Purdue University Press, 1978);

Mark Twain Speaks for Himself, edited by Fatout (West Lafayette, Ind.: Purdue University Press, 1978);

The Devil's Race-Track: Mark Twain's "Great Dark" Writings, edited by Tuckey (Berkeley: University of California Press, 1979).

Collections: *The Writings of Mark Twain, Autograph Edition,* 25 volumes (Hartford, Conn.: American Publishing, 1899–1907);

Writings of Mark Twain, Hillcrest Edition, 25 volumes, edited by Albert Bigelow Paine (New York & London: Harper, 1906);

The Works of Mark Twain, 9 volumes to date (Berkeley: University of California Press, 1972–   )—includes *Roughing It,* edited by Franklin R. Rogers and Paul Baender, (1972); *What is Man? And Other Philosophical Writings,* edited by Baender (1973); *A Connecticut Yankee in King Arthur's Court,* edited by Bernard L. Stein (1979); *The Prince and the Pauper,* edited by Victor Fischer and Lin Salamo (1979); *Early Tales & Sketches, Volume 1 (1851–1864),* edited by Edgar Marquess Branch and Robert H. Hirst (1979); *The Adventures of Tom Sawyer; Tom Sawyer Abroad; Tom Sawyer, Detective,* edited by John C. Gerber, Baender, and Terry Firkins (1980); *Early Tales & Sketches, Volume 2 (1864–1865),* edited by Branch and Hirst (1981); *Adventures of Huckleberry Finn,* edited by Walter Blair and Fischer (1988); *Roughing It,* edited by Harriet Elinor Smith and Edgar M. Branch (1993).

Mark Twain is the best-known and most-beloved American writer in the world, and his stature as the quintessential American writer rests in large part upon his "westernness." Born at the edge of the frontier, schooled along the great divide between East and West—the Mississippi River—and apprenticed in his craft in Nevada and California, Twain's personality was shaped and his art defined by his western experiences, and even when he wrote works not concerned with the American West, attitudes, methods, and comic devices in his writings bore the unmistakable mark of a western mindset.

In the spring of 1835 John Marshall Clemens and Jane Lampton Clemens loaded up their four children in Tennessee and joined the great migration of the westward movement in nineteenth-century America, heading for fortune and affluence in Missouri, at the edge of the jumping-off point for the frontier. Jane was pregnant with a son who was born prematurely on 30 November 1835; he was named Samuel Langhorne Clemens. His birth, he was later to brag, increased the population of his hometown by one whole percent, an accomplishment that few in the world could claim.

Prosperity was as elusive in Florida, Missouri, for the Clemens family as it had been on the eastern seaboard, and in 1839 the family moved to the more prosperous town of Hannibal, on the banks of the Mississippi, where young Sam was to store up the memories that have become an integral part of the American imagination. Although larger and more settled than Florida, Hannibal nevertheless had the flavor of a frontier town. Gamblers and confidence men practiced their trades on the steamboats that stopped there; slave traders with their "wares" in tow held auctions in the center of town; and frontiersmen passed through on their way to Saint Joseph, Missouri, the beginning of the Overland Trail. Violence was common; death was frequent; and authority was unpredictable. Comedy, sentimentality, and individualism were various antidotes to the stark reality of Sam Clemens's world.

John Marshall Clemens died in March 1847, when his son was eleven, and the following year the boy began working for the *Hannibal Gazette,* then for the *Missouri Courier,* and finally for his brother Orion on the *Hannibal Western Union* in 1851 and the *Hannibal Journal* later that year. As a typesetter and assistant editor, Clemens began adding contributions of his own to several eastern newspapers, beginning with "The Dandy Frightening the Squatter" in 1852. From 1852 to 1856 he produced a spate of comic sketches and burlesque travel letters for Orion's newspapers in Hannibal and for periodicals in Muscatine and Keokuk, Iowa. Many of these juvenilia contain facets of what readers now think of as western comic techniques: the frame narrative, the bumpkin in conflict with the eastern establishment, and the use of colloquial, ungrammatical language in the mouths of commonsensical yokels.

In 1857 Clemens became a cub pilot under the tutelage of master pilot Horace Bixby on the Mississippi. He received his own license in 1859 and remained on the river, piloting between Saint Louis and New Orleans, until the blockade by Union

Clemens's brother Orion, whom he accompanied to the West in 1861

forces at the outbreak of the Civil War ended his profession. His memories of characters, incidents, and settings from this period would surface in much of his major fiction.

On 18 July 1861 Clemens left with Orion for the Territory of Washoe (later to become Nevada) on the Overland stage. While Orion served as secretary to Gov. James W. Nye, the younger brother prospected for silver, speculated in wildcat mining stock, and wrote occasional articles of comic journalism for the *Virginia City Territorial Enterprise.* The editor, Joseph T. Goodman, was so impressed with Clemens's talents that he offered the budding humorist a position on the newspaper in 1862. Clemens moved to Virginia City, joined the staff of the *Enterprise,* and—for the first time, on 3 February 1863—signed a contribution with the pen name Mark Twain. Until 29 May 1864 Twain produced a constant stream of both comic and factual material for the *Enterprise,* gaining a fame (or notoriety) that extended as far west as metropolitan San Francisco.

Twain moved to that city in mid 1864 and became a correspondent and contributor to the *San Francisco Morning Call,* the *Golden Era,* the *Alta California,* the *Californian,* and the *Sacramento Union.* He

leaped into national celebrity when "Jim Smiley and His Jumping Frog" was published in the eastern *Saturday Press,* and he made the first of his many trips outside the continental United States (even farther westward) when the *Sacramento Union* commissioned him to write a series of travel letters describing a trip to the Sandwich Islands (now Hawaii). Clemens returned from that trip on 13 August 1866 and delivered more than a dozen lectures on the Sandwich Islands in California and Nevada before leaving the West forever (except for short visits to San Francisco in 1868 and Seattle in 1895) on 15 December 1866.

Twain's five-year sojourn in the West gave him an arsenal of insights and methods that were to impress practically all of his major works. One such device was a frame technique common to writers called the Old Southwestern Humorists that utilized a genteel, literate, "eastern" narrator who permitted a vulgar, semiliterate, commonsensical "western" character to usurp the narrative briefly to provide comic incongruity. In the early use of the device, the eastern character would retrieve the narrative voice and conclude the fiction, frequently with a disavowal of the bumpkin backwoodsman. However, as the form evolved in the first half of the nineteenth century, the values of the common man became more amenable to American readers than those of the eastern egghead. The backwoodsman became the hero of these frame narratives, and the gentleman became the comic foil. Twain experimented with this East/West dichotomy in his letters from the Sandwich Islands, in which a vulgar character named Mr. Brown constantly deflates the sentimental and literate narrator, and in two additional series of travel letters published after Twain left the West. Several of Twain's finest short works, "The Jumping Frog," "Grandfather's Old Ram," and "Baker's Blue Jay Yarn," employ this frame technique with genius. But even when not encased in the traditional frame, characters such as literate Tom Sawyer and vulgar Huck Finn and (paradoxically) literate Huck Finn and vulgar Jim (in episodes on the raft) in *The Adventures of Huckleberry Finn* (1884) utilize the polar character types to produce comic fiction.

Another component of Twain's western heritage is provided by the hoax and tall tale. Although not limited to the West, the form found a receptive audience there, where life was an unpredictable gamble, nature was hostile, and man had to survive on his physical prowess or his guile and cunning. The hoax reduces an unstable and capricious universe to comic proportions; it tests an audience's gullibility and provides its gifted narrator with authority over "fact" and "truth." Likewise, the tall tale establishes its author as a sort of creator who can move his story from realistic accuracy into the fantastic and the absurd without his audience's knowledge until he springs his trap and it is too late for the audience to escape embarrassment—"being sold," as Twain says in "Grandfather's Old Ram." This mode of humor is in effect a duel of wits (rather than a shoot-out) between speaker and listener in which narrative artistry rather than bloodshed determines the winner.

Like many other western and local-color writers in the nineteenth century, Twain rejoiced in colloquial language: slang, vernacular, regionalism, and argot. Such language had an honesty, a virility, and a masculinity lacking in classic eastern American literature; in addition, it permitted some of the boldest uses of language imaginable: the homely comic simile, the burst of wild hyperbole, malapropisms, and terribly mangled quotations. In *Roughing It* (1872) Mark Twain recollects vividly when he "first encountered the vigorous new vernacular of the occidental plains and mountains," and that vernacular became his own most significant contribution to the liberation of American literature from rigid formality.

From the beginning, with "The Dandy Frightening the Squatter," Twain championed the common man, the underdog, the uneducated opponent to the highbrow, college-educated, intellectual easterner. Almost instinctively, he both spoke to and spoke for a national equivalent of the westerner. His concerns with paradoxes inherent in rugged individualism as opposed to a social contract, in common sense and instinctive morality versus law and order, and his championing of a pragmatic morality rather than wisdom and tradition—all are facets of his westernness. The courageous man who faces down a thoughtless mob fascinated him, most notably in Colonel Sherburn in *Huckleberry Finn*. Even in his cynical and misanthropic old age Twain retained a thin sliver of hope in the native intelligence of at least part of mankind, and his egalitarian sympathies for the downtrodden could not be completely smothered by his determinism.

By the same token, Twain's own brashness, his "vulgarity," his willingness to deal with what were considered sordid, grotesque, and distasteful subjects distressed the eastern seaboard literary establishment for all of the author's life. Finally, even in his bitter and pessimistic old age, he continued to rely upon the techniques and methods of western literature to express his contempt for "the damned human race." His audiences often became foils for a cosmic hoax; reality was a solipsistic tall tale; life was a cruel dream; and God was a trickster or confidence man, playing cruel jokes on unsuspecting humanity.

After he left the West, Twain toured Europe and the Near East, producing his first best-seller, *The Innocents Abroad, or The New Pilgrims' Progress* (1869). He continued his career as a newspaper humorist, married Olivia Langdon in 1870, and settled in Buffalo, New York, before moving to Hartford, Connecticut, in 1871. He and Olivia had four children: Langdon, Susan, Clara, and Jean. In Hartford and Elmira, New York, he produced the full-length works that established his reputation. He left Hartford after declaring bankruptcy in 1894 and spent the last fifteen years of his life—during which all of his family except daughter Clara died—in an increasingly pessimistic attitude, when many of the thoughts he put on paper were consigned to a pile not to be published until after his death. In 1907 Oxford awarded him an honorary Litt. D. degree, and he spent his last years as the social gadfly of the American conscience, writing caustic essays against imperialism, royalty, and human cowardice. At his death on 21 April 1910, his position as the quintessential American author was secure.

The two-volume *Early Tales & Sketches* (1979, 1981) has collected all of Twain's known works written between 1851 and 1865. Many of the items are highly topical, factual, repetitious, or strained in their attempts at humor. From his youth and western years only a few pieces stand the tests of durability and permanence. Indeed, if they were not the apprentice works of the writer who later established international fame, there would be little reason to rescue them from oblivion. Of special interest are "The Dandy Frightening the Squatter" (1852), Twain's first known piece of humor; two successful western hoaxes, "Petrified Man" (1862) and "A Bloody Massacre near Carson" (1863); and "Jim Smiley and His Jumping Frog" (1865).

"The Dandy Frightening the Squatter" was written when Clemens was only sixteen years old, and it shows all the marks of juvenilia. But it is interesting in its use of the frame technique and the confrontation between "a spruce young dandy, with a killing moustache, &c., who seemed bent on making an impression upon the hearts of the young ladies on board" and "a tall, brawny woodsman." The dandy confronts the backwoodsman with a phony recognition and threat: "Found you at last, have I? You are the very man I've been looking for these three weeks! Say your prayers! . . . You'll make a capital barn door, and I shall drill the key-hole myself!" The squatter calmly watches the dandy brandish his pistol, "and then, drawing back a step, he planted his huge fist directly between the eyes of his

Cover for Clemens's first book, in which much of the humor derives from the use of western dialect

astonished antagonist, who, in a moment, was floundering in the turbid waters of the Mississippi." As the defeated dandy swims back to the steamboat, the backwoodsman calls out to him, "I say, yeou, next time yeou come around drillin' key-holes, don't forget your old acquaintances!"

Even this early the basic East/West dichotomy is evident. The dandy is well dressed, speaks proper English, and feels an obvious snobbish superiority to the unprepossessing rustic. But surfaces disguise the true capabilities of the two men; the dandy is all bluff, and the squatter is all action. Their polished language and colloquial drawl ("yeou") provide a comic contrast, and the result gives the squatter the victory over pretension, foppishness, and a failed attempt at superiority. Rudimentary as the sketch is, it outlines in miniature the basic tensions which separated an easterner from a westerner.

Once he took up his duties on the *Territorial Enterprise,* Twain honed his skills at western humor, usually satisfying but occasionally mystifying his Nevada audience. Sometimes, however, he was so successful that his readers swallowed a hoax as literal reporting. Twice in his Nevada years Twain succeeded in hoodwinking a major portion of his readership with hoaxes that were taken for literal truth. The earlier of the two hoaxes, "Petrified Man," suggests the formula for a successful hoax: told completely straight-faced ("deadpan" is the comic term), it must recount an increasingly preposterous tale with the intention of persuading a credulous reader or audience to accept it as literal truth. The account must contain clues to its exaggeration and comic intention, however, so that the auditor ultimately realizes that he has been trapped. "Petrified Man" was so successful (or unsuccessful, according to the formula) that it was reprinted as literal truth in at least eight other West Coast newspapers.

The single paragraph opens with the announcement that "a petrified man was found some time ago in the mountains south of Gravelly Ford. Every limb and feature of the stony mummy was perfect." An extended description of the corpse returns frequently to the position of its two hands and its nose between depictions of the rest of the body. Only if an attentive reader accumulates the descriptions of the hands and nose will he realize that the corpse is actually petrified thumbing its nose at the careless reader. In the final sentences Twain explains that the townfolk wished to give the corpse a decent burial but that a judge named "Sewell or Sowell" refused their request because dynamiting the corpse loose from the bedrock on which it sat would be a sacrilege. Twain was ridiculing G. T. Sewall, a judge for whom he had developed an aversion, but the story rises above the specific sarcasm of the occasion to become a hoax upon scientific marvels which were, according to Twain, flooding newspapers at the time.

The other hoax was even more notorious. "A Bloody Massacre near Carson" appeared in the *Territorial Enterprise* on 28 October 1863 and caused an immediate furor. The article tells of a Philip Hopkins, who "dashed into Carson on horseback, with his throat cut from ear to ear, and bearing in his hand a reeking scalp from which the warm, smoking blood was still dripping." The sheriff dashed to the Hopkins house with a group of concerned citizens and discovered that

> the scalpless corpse of Mrs. Hopkins lay across the threshold, with her head split open and her right hand almost severed from the wrist. . . . In one of the bedrooms six of the children were found, one in bed and the others scattered about the floor. They were all dead. Their brains had evidently been dashed out with a club. . . . The eldest girl, Mary, must have taken refuge, in her terror, in the garret, as her body was found there, frightfully mutilated, and the knife with which her wounds had been inflicted still sticking in her side.

Twain continued the story, explaining that Hopkins had become deranged from making unsound investments in mining stocks and a water company, but, as he later pointed out, readers *never got down* to where the satire part of it began" and did not see the piece as an attack on stock speculation. Although he had placed clues in the story to designate it as a hoax, a torrent of criticism poured down on him from gullible readers who read the widely reprinted story. The following day Twain printed "I Take It All Back," but duped newspapers found the retraction "even worse than that published yesterday." As Branch and Hirst point out, "for more than a year negative comments continued to appear in the local press." "A Bloody Massacre near Carson" reveals a significant vein in Twain's writing, the exploitation of the grotesque. He mused in 1868, "To find a petrified man. . . . Or massacre a family at Dutch Nick's, were feats and calamities that *we* never hesitated about devising when the public needed matter of thrilling interest for breakfast. The seemingly tranquil Enterprise office was a ghastly factory of slaughter, mutilation and general destruction in those days."

In late 1863 Twain met Charles Farrar Browne, whose fame as humorous writer "Artemus Ward" far outshone Twain's at the time. Browne encouraged him to contribute something to a forthcoming volume of humorous sketches on several occasions, but Twain moved abruptly from Nevada to San Francisco on 29 May 1864 and wrote extensively for local newspapers and magazines as well as for the *Territorial Enterprise*. In January 1865 he visited Angel's Camp, California, and heard a series of tales told by master yarn spinners, including one about a jumping frog. Later that year, he wrote the first of his several versions of that story and submitted it to Ward. On the next day he wrote to his brother Orion that he had "had a 'call' to literature, of a low order—i.e. Humorous." Although his own verdict on "The Jumping Frog" fluctuated wildly, apparently he realized at the time that the story was the masterpiece which it has since been judged.

Originally written as a letter to Ward, the story shows the skillful combination of most of Twain's favorite techniques—the frame narrative, humanized animals, deadpan narration, and the tall tale and hoax. The author of the letter is a humorless reporter who has been sent to inquire about a Leonidas W. Smiley. Instead, his interviewer, Simon Wheeler, takes over the narration and tells a series of marvelous tales about Jim Smiley and his penchant for gambling. Twain calls the story "as long and tedious as it should be useless to me" and leaves abruptly before Wheeler can continue his narrative about Smiley's "yaller one-eyed cow that didn't have no tail only just a short stump like a bannanner." Wheeler tells his story in complete deadpan: "'He never smiled, he never frowned, he never changed his voice from the quiet, gently-flowing key to which he turned the initial sentence, he never betrayed the slightest suspicion of enthusiasm—but all through the interminable narrative there ran a vein of impressive earnestness and sincerity.'" This apparently humorless narrator tells a humorless auditor a series of increasingly implausible stories about Smiley's compulsive gambling and three animals who become increasingly human in their qualities.

The first animal is the "fifteen minute nag," who could win her horse races "just about a neck ahead" even though she "always had the asthma, or the distemper, or the consumption, or something like that." In spite of her unlikely appearance, "always at the fag-end of the race she'd get excited and desperate-like, and come cavorting and spraddling up, and scattering her legs around limber, sometimes in the air, and sometimes out to one side amongst the fences, and kicking up m-o-r-e dust, and raising m-o-r-e racket with her coughing and sneezing and blowing her nose."

Equally unprepossessing is Smiley's bulldog, Andrew Jackson, and "to look at him you'd think he warn't worth a cent, but to set around and look ornery, and lay for a chance to steal something." In a dogfight, however, Andrew would wait for his chance "and then all a sudden he would grab that other dog just by the joint of his hind legs and freeze to it—not chaw, you understand, but only just grip and hang on till they throwed up the sponge." One day Smiley puts Andrew up against a dog "that didn't have no hind legs, because they'd been sawed off in a circular saw." When Andrew tries to "make a snatch for his pet holt" he fails and gives up the fight. Realizing that Smiley is responsible for his shame, "he limped off a piece, and laid down and died" of a broken heart. Wheeler admires Andrew because he "would have made a name for hisself if he'd lived, for the stuff was in him, and he had genius—I know it, because he hadn't had no opportunities to speak of, and it don't stand to reason that a dog could make such a fight as he could under them circumstances, if he hadn't no talent."

Wheeler admires Smiley's third animal, Daniel Webster the jumping frog, even more: "You never see a frog so modest and straightfor'ard as he was, for all he was so gifted." Daniel's gift was catching flies. Smiley would put Daniel on the floor "and sing out, 'Flies! Dan'l, flies,' and quicker'n you could wink, he'd spring straight up, and snake a fly off'n the counter there, and flop down on the floor

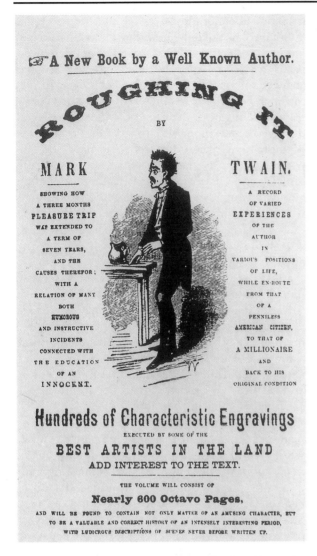

Advertisement for Clemens's 1872 book based on his travels in the West

again as solid as a gob of mud, and fall to scratching the side of his head with his hind foot as indifferent as if he hadn't no idea he'd done any more'n any frog might do." Modesty, genius, and straightforwardness do not help, however, when a stranger arrives in camp. While Smiley searches for another frog for the stranger to bet on, the stranger fills Daniel "full of quail-shot—filled him pretty near up to the chin," so that when Smiley commands him to jump, "the new frog hopped off lively, but Dan'l give a heave, and hysted up his shoulder—so—like a Frenchman, but it wasn't no use—he couldn't budge; he was planted as solid as an anvil."

Wheeler is interrupted in his comic bestiary, and Twain takes the opportunity to flee before Wheeler can tell him about the one-eyed cow with the tail no longer than a banana. There are clues, however, that the narrator has been the victim of a complex hoax. As the tales get taller and taller, he begins to suspect that a trick has been played on him. "I have a lurking suspicion," he tells Ward, "that your Leonidas W. Smiley is a myth—that you never knew such a personage, and that you only conjectured that if I asked old Wheeler about him it would remind him of his infamous *Jim* Smiley, and he would go to work and bore me nearly to death with some infernal reminiscences of him." Indeed, at this level the story is not about Jim Smiley and Daniel Webster at all. It is a confrontation, a comic shoot-out with Wheeler testing the patience of the dull-witted Twain to see how long it will take to vanquish him. Wheeler might have gone on with increasingly absurd anecdotes, and even if readers are left to conjecture what Jim Smiley might have done with a one-eyed, bob-tailed cow, they are also left with the sly, western genius of a storyteller triumphant over a stodgy, humorless narrator.

During his days as a western comic journalist, Twain contemplated several times collecting his sketches to make a book-length publication. But as his career swerved eastward, he delayed those plans in favor of continuing a career as newspaperman. His trip to Europe and the Holy Land, his courtship of and marriage to Olivia Langdon, his duties as columnist for the *Buffalo Express* and *The Galaxy,* and his revision of his overseas letters into his first national success, *The Innocents Abroad,* all intervened before he found time to return to his memories of the Far West and begin work on his major western work, *Roughing It,* published in 1872.

As early as 1869 and 1870 Twain printed sketches and anecdotes—"Baker's Cat," "Pocket Mining, "Silver Land Nabobs," and "The Facts in the Great Land-Slide Case"—that were to become parts of *Roughing It;* on 4 September 1870 he reported to his publisher that he had written the first four chapters of the book, and almost a year later, on 8 August 1871, he delivered 1,830 holograph pages and earlier scissored-and-pasted columns to the American Publishing Company in Hartford, Connecticut. On 30 January 1872 the first copies of the book arrived at the publisher's office, and by the end of the year just over sixty-five thousand copies had been sold.

The composition of the book had been long and arduous, competing for Twain's attention with editorial duties on the *Buffalo Express* and *The Galaxy;* with the birth of his first child, Langdon; with the death of his father-in-law, Jervis Langdon; and most significantly with the entire eastern value system represented dramatically by his wife. Prior to his marriage Twain had been a wandering vagabond for more than a decade; his reputation as a heavy drinker and a vulgar westerner disturbed both his fiancée and his prospective mother-in-law, who acknowledged in a letter that Clemens "seemed to have entered upon a new manner of life, with higher & better purposes actuating his conduct," but she was nevertheless not sure whether "this change, so desirably commenced, make[s] of an immoral man a moral one." His own westernness, in short, was being challenged by the straight-laced, decorous eastern cultural establishment, and *Roughing It* is his response to that criticism.

Although *Roughing It* does not use the frame-narrative technique, it does adapt one of the major strategies of that form. The narrator is deliberately made more naive, more romantic, less world-wise than the author had been in 1861. He announces in the first paragraph, with breathless envy, that his brother was going to travel to the West. His knowledge of the "Noble Red Man" comes from books, the novels of James Fenimore Cooper primarily. As he begins his journey, he does not know what a "thoroughbrace" is, assuming that it is a part of a horse. He carries a six-pound unabridged dictionary with him and "swallow-tail coats and white kid gloves to wear at Pawnee receptions." When Brigham Young meets Twain and his brother Orion, "he put his hand on my head, beamed down on me in an admiring way and said to my brother: Ah—your child, I presume? Boy, or girl?'" Not only is he younger, more innocent, more romantic, and more ignorant of reality than Twain actually was, but also he becomes aware that he is an outsider as well: "we were wretchedly ashamed of being 'emigrants,' and sorry enough that we had white shirts and could not swear in the presence of ladies without looking the other way."

He remains the eastern outsider when he reaches Nevada, buying a Genuine Mexican "plug," unaware of its worthlessness; he finds his first "gold," only to discover that it is "nothing but a lot of granite rubbish and nasty glittering mica"; and his romantic illusions about the Noble Indian are shattered by his confrontation with the Goshoots. Although in one sense he remains an "outsider" throughout the book, the story is also the record of an initiation. Twain becomes a westerner, seeing realistically, and recounting in a relaxed, informal prose, the truth about his original ignorance. Having left home for the first time to seek romance, success, wealth, and fame in the West, the narrator finds instead cold-blooded murders, rigged juries, paper speculation in stocks, and blighted hopes, including his own. After failing to find silver, he announces, "So vanished my dream. So melted my wealth away. So toppled my airy castle to the earth and left me stricken and forlorn." Later he must go to work as a common laborer, and he also relates a story (apparently true) of how he missed becoming a millionaire through bad luck and missed communications.

By chapter 42 the narrator even reinvents his own biography. "I had gone out into the world to shift for myself, at the age of thirteen," he relates, even though he enjoyed "a sumptuous legacy of pride in . . . fine Virginian stock and its national distinction." He catalogues ten different occupations, mostly fictional, at which he had failed and "amounted to less than nothing in each." Finally, at the conclusion of chapter 69, Twain tells his reader, "If you are of any account, stay at home and make your way by faithful diligence; but if you are 'no account,' go away from home, and then you will *have* to work, whether you want to or not."

The admission is more than an act of personal contrition to his wife and the Langdon family. The narrator repeatedly measures the distance between life as he imagined it in the West and its depressing reality. Greeley's injunction to "Go West, young man" turns for Twain into an adventure in poverty, homelessness, and emotional chaos. The geography is usually desolate; democratic institutions are corrupt; the wave of civilization brings, even in the Sandwich Islands chapters, corruption rather than enlightenment. *Roughing It* is, in fact, the announcement of the end of the antebellum myth of the Garden of Eden regained on the American frontier. Chance deaths, chance fortunes, and chance failures permeate its pages. The illusion of freedom, independence, democracy, and self-reliance is splintered over and over by harsh reality.

That subtext of disillusionment is veneered, nevertheless, with some of Twain's finest western humor. Following his usual practice, he alternated factual and historical information with self-contained anecdotes which both he and later editors published separately as short stories. Among the best of these are the description of the coyote in chapter 5, the tale of the Mexican plug in chapter 24, Buck Fanshaw's funeral in chapter 47, and the tale of Grandfather's Old Ram in chapter 53. As Henry Nash Smith notes in *Mark Twain, The Development of a Writer* (1962), the description of the western coyote that confronts a "dog that has a good opinion of himself, and has been brought up to think he knows something about speed," "embodies a view of the relation between vernacular and conventional values." The coyote's appearance is as disreputable as that of any westerner:

The first page of the manuscript for the speech Clemens delivered at a dinner celebrating the seventieth birthday of John Greenleaf Whittier, 17 December 1877 (Beinecke Library, Yale University)

The cayote is a long, slim, sick and sorry-looking skeleton, with a gray wolf-skin stretched over it, a tolerably bushy tail that forever sags down with a despairing expression of forsakenness and misery, a furtive and evil eye, and a long, sharp face, with slightly lifted lip and exposed teeth. . . . He is always poor, out of luck and friendless . . . And he is *so* homely!—so scrawny, and ribby, and coarse-haired, and pitiful.

But when a dog from a wagon train pursues him the coyote's gifts come to the front. Teasing the dog by keeping just a few feet ahead of him, the coyote plays a practical joke on his antagonist. The dog "begins to get aggravated, and it makes him madder and madder to see how gently the cayote glides along and never pants or sweats or ceases to smile." Finally the coyote "turns and smiles blandly upon him once more. . . . And forthwith there is a rushing sound, and the sudden splitting of a long crack through the atmosphere, and behold that dog is solitary and alone in the midst of a vast solitude!" Thoroughly beaten by the vagabond coyote, "for as much as a year after that, whenever there is a great hue and cry after a cayote, that dog will merely glance in that direction without emotion, and apparently observe to himself, 'I believe I do not wish any of the pie.'" In other words, the conventional expectations are turned upside down in the Far West, where external appearances are no indication of merit and skill.

In the same way, the innocent Twain in the story of the Mexican plug yearns "to have a horse to ride. I had never seen such wild, free, magnificent horsemanship outside of a circus as these picturesquely-clad Mexicans, Californians and Mexicanized Americans displayed in Carson streets every day. . . . I had quickly learned to tell a horse from a cow, and was full of anxiety to learn more."

Unfortunately, he does not know enough about horses to know what the Mexican plug actually was and purchases one at auction for twenty-seven dollars. Every attempt to ride him ends in miserable failure: "He placed all his feet in a bunch together, lowered his back, and then suddenly arched it upward, and shot me straight into the air a matter of three or four feet!" Further attempts produce no better results, and Twain finally decides, "I never tried to ride the horse any more. Walking was good enough exercise for a man like me, that had nothing the matter with him except ruptures, internal injuries, and such things."

In "Buck Fanshaw's Funeral" it is not Twain but another newcomer to the Far West who is the outsider to the community, "the minister, a fragile, gentle spirituel [*sic*] new fledgling from an Eastern theological seminary, and as yet unacquainted with the ways of the mines." Scotty Briggs, a miner, volunteer fireman, and gambler, confronts the new minister in order to schedule the last rites for his buddy Fanshaw. Each speaks in the vocabulary of his profession and position, and neither man can understand a word the other says:

"Are you the duck that runs the gospel-mill next door?

"Am I the—pardon me, I believe I do not understand?"

With another sigh and a half-sob, Scotty rejoined:

"Why you see we are in a bit of trouble, and the boys thought maybe you would give us a lift, if we'd tackle you—that is, if I've got the rights of it and you are the head clerk of the doxology-works next door."

"I am the shepherd in charge of the flock whose fold is next door."

"The which?"

"The spiritual adviser of the little company of believers whose sanctuary adjoins these premises."

The conversation continues for pages, with Scotty using the slang and argot of the mines and the minister speaking in literate, dignified English. Finally, the minister guesses that Buck is dead: "Ah—has departed to that mysterious country from whose bourne no traveler returns," he proposes, paraphrasing Hamlet. "Return!," Scotty answers, "I reckon not. Why pard, he's *dead!*" Ultimately, the funeral is arranged and occurs, but the linguistic confrontation between East and West produces a delightful comedy of misunderstanding.

In "Grandfather's Old Ram" Twain employs a more complex frame-narrative technique to produce two different varieties of humor in the one story. The other miners "used to tell me I ought to get one Jim Blaine to tell me the stirring story of his grandfather's old ram . . . They kept this up until my curiosity was on the rack to hear the story." Finally, one evening Blaine is in the proper state of intoxication to narrate his tale. Twain relinquishes narrative control of the anecdote, and Blaine narrates a deadpan, wandering tale that moves by free association from one incident to another with, as in Simon Wheeler's story of the jumping frog, total indifference to economy, coherence, or straightforwardness. Blaine remembers Miss Jefferson, who would lend her glass eye to Miss Wagner, whose eye socket it did not fit so that "it would get twisted around in the socket, and look up, maybe, or out to one side, and every which way, while t'other one was looking as straight ahead as a spy-glass. Grown people didn't mind it, but it most always made the children cry, it was so sort of scary." He moves to the story of Jacops, the gambling undertaker who

Samuel L. Clemens
Hartford
Dec 27, '77

Hartford, Thursday, 27th
To Mr. Emerson, Mr. Longfellow, & Dr. Holmes:

Gentlemen: I come before you, now, with the mien & posture of the guilty—not to excuse, gloss, or extenuate, but only to offer my repentance. If a man with a fine nature had done that thing which I did, it would have been a crime—because all his senses would have warned him against it beforehand; but I did it innocently, & unwarned. I did it as innocently as I ever did anything. You will think it is incredible; but it is true, & Mr. Howells will confirm my words. He does not know how it *can* be true, & neither does any one who is incapable of trespassing as I did; yet he knows it *is* true. But when I perceived what it was that I had done, I felt as real a sorrow & suffered as sharp a mortification as if I had done it with a guilty intent. This continues. That the impulse was innocent brings no abatement. As to my wife's distress, it is not to be measured; for she is of finer stuff than I; & yours were sacred names to her. We do not talk about this misfortune—it scorches; so we only think—and think.

I will end, now. I had to write you, for the easement of it, even though the doing it might maybe be a further offense. But I do not ask you to forgive what I did that night, for it is not forgivable; I simply had it at heart to ask you to believe that I am only heedlessly a savage, not premeditatedly; & that I am under as severe punishment as even you could adjudge to me if you were required to appoint my penalty. I do not ask you to say one word in answer to this; it is not needful, & would of course be distasteful & difficult. I beg you to consider that in letting me unbosom myself you will do me an act of grace that will be sufficient in itself. I wanted to write such a letter as this, that next morning in Boston, but one of wiser judgment advised against it, & said Wait.

With great & sincere respect I am
Truly Yours
Saml. L. Clemens

Clemens's letter to Ralph Waldo Emerson, Henry Wadsworth Longfellow, and Oliver Wendell Holmes apologizing for naming the drunken con men after them in his speech celebrating Whittier's birthday (Emerson Papers, Houghton Library, Harvard University)

loses betting that Robbins will die. Next Blaine tells the story of the Hogadorn family, eaten by cannibals while missionarying. Then comes the story of Uncle Lem and the Irish bricklayer who fell on him from the third story of a construction site. And he concludes with the tale of William Wheeler, who "got nipped by the machinery in a carpet factory and went through in less than a quarter of a minute; his widder bought the piece of carpet that had his remains wove in, and people come a hundred mile to 'tend the funeral. There was fourteen yards in the piece." Wheeler explains, as he gradually goes to sleep, "they didn't bury him—they planted one end, and let him stand up, same as a monument."

These stories of comic mayhem become more outrageous and surreal as Blaine tells them in his humorless, drunken condition. But once Blaine is asleep Twain resumes the narration, and he learns that he has been the victim of a hoax: "The tears were running down the boys' cheeks—they were suffocating with suppressed laughter—and had been from the start, though I had never noticed it. I perceived that I was 'sold.' I learned then that . . . the mention of the ram in the first sentence was as far as any man had ever heard him get, concerning it. He always maundered off, interminably, from one thing to another. . . . What the thing was that happened to him and his grandfather's old ram is a dark mystery to this day."

Although these self-contained tales all favor the disreputable and vulgar westerner over the conventional, uninitiated easterner and suggest Twain's endorsement of the western side of the dichotomy, it is curious that after he left California for the last time on 6 July 1868, he returned infrequently to his western memories and experiences for his fiction. Once *Roughing It* was published he almost literally turned his back on his apprentice days as a source for his humor. Three items deserve mention, however. On 17 December 1877 William Dean Howells invited Twain to deliver one of the after-dinner speeches at the celebration of the seventieth birthday of John Greenleaf Whittier. In his "infamous" narrative—a "hideous mistake," Howells called it—Twain returned to the form of the tall tale, the frame narrative, the setting of the West, and the attitude of scorn toward the eastern establishment. He began the story in his own voice, explaining that fifteen years earlier, when his pen name was beginning to be known in the Far West, he went on an inspection trip in southern California:

> I was callow and conceited, and I resolved to try the virtue of my *nom de plume*. I very soon had an opportunity. I knocked at a miner's lonely log cabin in the foot-

hills of the Sierras just at nightfall. It was snowing at the time. A jaded, melancholy man of fifty, barefooted, opened to me. When he heard my *nom de plume*, he looked more dejected than before. He let me in—pretty reluctantly, I thought—and after the customary bacon and beans, black coffee and a hot whiskey, I took a pipe. This sorrowful man had not said three words up to this time. Now he spoke up and said in the voice of one who is secretly suffering, "you're the fourth—I'm a-going to move." "The fourth what?" said I. "The fourth littery man that's been here in twenty-four hours—I'm a-going to move." "You don't tell me!" said I; "who were the others?" "Mr. Longfellow, Mr. Emerson and Mr. Oliver Wendell Holmes—dad fetch the lot!"

With Henry Wadsworth Longfellow, Ralph Waldo Emerson, and Oliver Wendell Holmes in the audience, Twain narrated the miner's story, in which the three men are drunken, gambling, thieving con artists. His description of the physical characteristics were caricatures of the three poets at the dinner table: "Mr. Holmes was as fat as a balloon—he weighed as much as three hundred, & had double chins all the way down to his stomach." Holmes quotes "The Chambered Nautilus" to criticize the miner's cabin; Emerson quotes "Mithridates" to criticize the food. Each continues quoting famous lines from his own poetry—and that of Whittier, James Russell Lowell, and William Cullen Bryant as well. They get drunk, cheat one another at cards, and start to fight: "Emerson claps his hand on his bowie, Longfellow claps his on his revolver, and I went under a bunk. There was going to be trouble; but that monstrous Holmes rose up, wobbling his double chins, and says he, 'Order, gentlemen; the first man that draws, I'll lay down on him and smother him!'" The trio finally leaves at seven o'clock the next morning, and Longfellow takes the miner's boots with him, reciting about leaving "Footprints on the sands of Time." Twain recaptures the narrative voice to explain to the miner that this trio was a set of impostors, "not the gracious singers to whom we and the world pay loving reverence and homage."

There was an instantaneous outcry from New England newspapers about the vulgar western humorist ridiculing the saintly authors whom he parodied, and Twain wrote letters of abject apology to each of the men he had "insulted." Nevertheless, the rollicking burlesque was a hilarious story, using a perfectly fine premise before the wrong audience. Twain wavered in his own verdict about the speech. But literary historians and critics have used its date to mark a sort of literary declaration of independence of western literature from the control of eastern "umpires of taste," as Emerson himself called literary critics. Irrepressible in his iconoclasm, Twain in the "Whittier Birthday Dinner Speech"—either consciously or semiconsciously—took his stance with western values once more, in spite of all that his wife, Howells, and the literary community of Hartford could do to restrain him.

In April 1878 Twain moved his family to Europe, partly because of his chagrin at having delivered the "Whittier Birthday Dinner Speech." The group lived in Germany and France, and traveled throughout Europe, returning to Hartford in late October 1879. While overseas Twain worked on his travel book later titled *A Tramp Abroad* (1880). Embedded in chapters 2 and 3 of that volume is a western tale embodying all the by now predictable qualities—frame narrative, vernacular language, and humanized animals, but with a twist that suggests Twain's increasing cynicism. Walking in the Neckar woods outside Heidelberg, Twain discovers a raven, and vice versa. For several paragraphs, in his own voice, the humorist muses about how the raven and a friend "sat side by side on the limb and discussed me as freely and offensively as two great naturalists might discuss a new kind of bug."

The event reminds Twain of Jim Baker, "a middle-aged, simple-hearted miner who had lived in a lonely corner of California, among the woods and mountains, a good many years, and had studied the ways of his only neighbors, the beasts and birds, until he believed he could accurately translate any remark which they made." Baker comes onstage and tells the story of "Baker's Blue-Jay Yarn," in which the title bird with an acorn lights on a roof of an empty cabin. "He cocked his head to one side, shut one eye and put the other one to the hole, like a possum looking down a jug." The jay drops his acorn down the hole and then proceeds to try to fill the hole with more acorns. For two hours the jay attempts to fill the hole; other jays come to see the mystery. Finally, one old jay looks in the half-open door: "He flopped his wings and raised a whoop. 'Come here!' he says, 'Come here, everybody; hang'd if this fool hasn't been trying to fill up a house with acorns!'" All of the other jays "fell over backwards, suffocating with laughter," and jays came from all over the United States to see the hole "every summer for three years."

Jays possess not only a sense of humor but also other human qualities as well. Those qualities suggest as much the evils of man as the humanity of jays, however:

A jay hasn't got any more principle than a congressman. A jay will lie, a jay will steal, a jay will deceive, a jay will betray; and four times out of five, a jay will go back on his solemnest promise. The sacredness of an obligation is a thing which you can't cram into no blue-jay's head. . . . Yes, sir, a jay is everything that a man is. . . . If a jay ain't human, he better take in his sign, that's all.

Throughout the early 1880s Twain misspent much of his energy in business speculation, producing *Life on the Mississippi* (1883) and *The Adventures of Huckleberry Finn* before returning for the last time to explicitly western material in an unfinished manuscript, *Huck Finn and Tom Sawyer among the Indians,* written in 1884 but not published until 20 December 1968 in *Life* magazine.

Huck concludes his narration of his adventures with the decision to "light out for the Territory ahead of the rest" after Tom suggests that he, Huck, and Jim "slide out of here, one of these nights, and get an outfit, and go for howling adventures amongst the Injuns, over in the Territory, for a couple of weeks or two." In this abortive sequel the trio indeed heads west, and on the second day of their journey, they join forces with a wagon containing Mr. and Mrs. Mills, their three sons, and two daughters, seventeen-year-old Peggy and seven-year-old Flaxy. After several weeks, they find their first Indians (like the narrator of *Roughing It,* Tom Sawyer has a highly romanticized image of the Noble Red Man). After several days of apparent friendship, the Indians attack, killing most of the party and abducting Peggy.

Peggy's sweetheart, Brace Johnson—"big and fine, and brave, and good, and splendid, and all that"—joins Huck and Tom, and the remainder of the fragment details their futile search for Jim, Peggy, and Flaxy. They discover the Indian camp with "four stakes drove in the ground," implying that the band of Indians had gang-raped Peggy. After another short passage, the manuscript ends in midsentence.

Clearly, by the mid 1880s Twain's attitude toward the Indians had hardened, and his Victorian prudishness could not allow him to continue writing on the subject of rape. Such comedy as the fragment contains derives, however, from the comic juxtaposition of Tom's bookish romanticizing of Indians contrasted with Huck's more suspicious and realistic judgment.

The vein of western materials had played itself out in Twain's creative imagination. Regardless of the extent to which his wife's disapproval of his vagabond years might have contributed, his own increasing misanthropy and his impulse to self-censorship combined to make *Huck Finn and Tom Sawyer among the Indians* an unfinishable book. For the last twenty-five years of his life he wrote increasingly mordant satire such as *A Connecticut Yankee in King Arthur's Court* (1889), *Pudd'nhead Wilson* (1894), and a series of essays expressing his anti-imperialism. His fame and stature grew, but his creative output was increasingly unfinished, increasingly concerned with the paradox of dream and reality, and increasingly shrill about man's incapacity for choice and free will in a deterministic universe.

Nevertheless, Walter Blair has claimed that those few weeks in Angel's Camp in early 1865—when Twain heard the stories of a jumping frog, a curious blue jay, and an almost nonexistent old ram—"brought a crucial turning point in his artistic development. For it enabled him to discover his happiest style of writing, and its yarnspinning sessions were germinal to at least eight of the best stretches of writing in all his books." He learned his craft, made his decision to become a humorist, and adopted all of his major stances (however elusive and contradictory they might have been) during his western days.

Letters:
Mark Twain's Letters, 2 volumes, edited by Albert Bigelow Paine (New York: Harper, 1917);

Mark Twain the Letter Writer, edited by Cyril Clemens (Boston: Meador, 1932);

Mark Twain's Letters to Will Bowen, edited by Theodore Hornberger (Austin: University of Texas Press, 1941);

The Love Letters of Mark Twain, edited by Dixon Wecter (New York: Harper, 1949);

Mark Twain to Mrs. Fairbanks, edited by Wecter (San Marino, Cal.: Huntington Library, 1949);

Mark Twain's Letters to Mary, edited by Lewis Leary (New York: Columbia University Press, 1961);

Mark Twain-Howells Letters, 2 volumes, edited by Henry Nash Smith and William M. Gibson (Cambridge, Mass.: Harvard University Press, 1966);

Mark Twain's Letters to his Publishers, edited by Hamlin Hill (Berkeley: University of California Press, 1967);

Mark Twain's Correspondence with Henry Huttleston Rogers, edited by Leary (Berkeley: University of California Press, 1969);

Mark Twain's Letters, Volume I: 1853–1866, edited by Edgar Marquess Branch, Michael B. Frank, and Kenneth M. Sanderson (Berkeley: University of California Press, 1988);

Mark Twain's Letters Volume II: 1867–1868, edited by Harriet Elinor Smith and Richard Bucci (Berkeley: University of California Press, 1990);

Mark Twain's Letters, Volume III: 1869, edited by Victor Fischer and Frank (Berkeley: University of California Press, 1992);

Mark Twain's Letters, Volume IV: 1870–1871, edited by Fischer, Frank, and Lin Salamo (Berkeley: University of California Press, 1995).

Bibliographies:
Merle Johnson, *A Bibliography of the Works of Mark Twain,* revised and enlarged edition (New York & London: Harper, 1935);

Thomas Asa Tenney, *Mark Twain: A Reference Guide* (Boston: G. K. Hall, 1977);

Alan Gribben, "Removing Mark Twain's Mask: A Decade of Criticism and Scholarship," *ESQ: Journal of the American Renaissance,* 26 (1980): 100–108, 149–171;

Gribben, *Mark Twain's Library: A Reconstruction,* 2 volumes (Boston: G. K. Hall, 1980);

Union Catalog of Clemens' Letters, edited by Paul Machlis (Berkeley: University of California Press, 1986);

Union Catalog of Letters to Clemens, edited by Machlis (Berkeley: University of California Press, 1992);

The Mark Twain Encyclopedia, edited by J. R. LeMaster and James D. Williams (New York: Garland, 1993).

Biographies:
William Dean Howells, *My Mark Twain* (New York & London: Harper, 1910);

Albert Bigelow Paine, *Mark Twain, A Biography,* 3 volumes (New York & London: Harper, 1912);

William R. Gillis, *Goldrush Days with Mark Twain* (New York: Albert & Charles Boni, 1930);

Bernard DeVoto, *Mark Twain's America* (Boston: Little, Brown, 1932);

Minnie M. Brashear, *Mark Twain, Son of Missouri* (Chapel Hill: University of North Carolina Press, 1934);

Ivan Benson, *Mark Twain's Western Years* (Stanford, Cal.: Stanford University Press, 1938);

DeLancey Ferguson, *Mark Twain: Man and Legend* (Indianapolis & New York: Bobbs-Merrill, 1943);

Effie Mona Mack, *Mark Twain in Nevada* (New York: Scribners, 1947);

Kenneth Andrews, *Nook Farm: Mark Twain's Hartford Circle* (Cambridge, Mass.: Harvard University Press, 1950);

Dixon Wecter, *Sam Clemens of Hannibal* (Boston: Houghton Mifflin, 1952);

Paul Fatout, *Mark Twain in Virginia City* (Bloomington: Indiana University Press, 1964);

Margaret Duckett, *Mark Twain and Bret Harte* (Norman: University of Oklahoma Press, 1964);

Justin Kaplan, *Mr. Clemens and Mark Twain* (New York: Simon & Schuster, 1966);

Hamlin Hill, *Mark Twain: God's Fool* (New York: Harper & Row, 1973);

Nigey Lennon, *The Sagebrush Bohemian: Mark Twain in California* (New York: Paragon House, 1990);

Margaret Sanborn, *Mark Twain: The Bachelor Years* (New York: Doubleday, 1990).

References:

Gladys Bellamy, *Mark Twain as a Literary Artist* (Norman: University of Oklahoma Press, 1950);

Walter Blair, *Mark Twain's West* (Chicago: R. R. Donnelley, 1983);

Blair, *Tall Tale America* (New York: Coward-McCann, 1944);

Edgar M. Branch, *The Literary Apprenticeship of Mark Twain* (Urbana: University of Illinois Press, 1950);

Richard Bridgman, *Traveling in Mark Twain* (Berkeley: University of California Press, 1987);

Van Wyck Brooks, *The Ordeal of Mark Twain,* revised edition (New York: Dutton, 1933);

Louis J. Budd, *Interviews with Samuel L. Clemens, 1874–1910* (Arlington: University of Texas at Arlington, 1977);

James M. Cox, *Mark Twain, The Fate of Humor* (Princeton: Princeton University Press, 1966);

Paul Fatout, *Mark Twain on the Lecture Circuit* (Bloomington: Indiana University Press, 1960);

Walter Francis Frear, *Mark Twain and Hawaii* (Chicago: Lakeside Press, 1947);

Robert L. Gale, *Plots and Characters in the Works of Mark Twain,* 2 volumes (Hamden, Conn.: Archon, 1973);

Fred W. Lorch, *The Trouble Begins at Eight* (Ames: Iowa State University Press, 1968);

Kenneth S. Lynn, *Mark Twain and Southwestern Humor* (Boston: Little, Brown, 1959);

Arthur G. Pettit, *Mark Twain and the South* (Lexington: University Press of Kentucky, 1974);

Robert L. Ramsay and Frances G. Emberson, *A Mark Twain Lexicon* (Columbia: University of Missouri Press, 1938);

David E. E. Sloane, *Mark Twain as a Literary Comedian* (Baton Rouge: Louisiana State University Press, 1979);

Henry Nash Smith, *Mark Twain, The Development of a Writer* (Cambridge, Mass.: Harvard University Press, 1962);

Jeffrey Steinbrink, *Getting to be Mark Twain* (Berkeley: University of California Press, 1991);

Albert E. Stone, *The Innocent Eye, Childhood in Mark Twain's Fiction* (New Haven, Conn.: Yale University Press, 1961);

Franklin Walker, *San Francisco's Literary Frontier* (New York: Knopf, 1939);

Henry B. Wonham, *Mark Twain and the Art of the Tall Tale* (New York: Oxford University Press, 1993).

Papers:

The major collection of Mark Twain materials is the Mark Twain papers at the Bancroft Library, University of California, Berkeley. Other major collections are at Yale University Library, the Henry W. and Albert A. Berg Collection of the New York Public Library, Vassar College, and the Alderman Library of the University of Virginia.

Ina Coolbrith
(10 March 1841 – 29 February 1928)

Abe C. Ravitz
California State University, Dominguez Hills

BOOKS: *A Perfect Day and Other Poems* (San Francisco: John H. Carmany, 1881);

The Singer of the Sea (San Francisco: Century Club of California, 1894);

Songs from the Golden Gate (Boston & New York: Houghton, Mifflin, 1895);

California (San Francisco: Book Club of California, 1918);

Wings of Sunset (Boston & New York: Houghton Mifflin, 1929).

OTHER: E. C. Alexander, *A Collection of California Wild Flowers* (San Francisco: The Popular Bookstore, 1894)—includes sonnets by Coolbrith;

Daniel O'Connell, *Songs from Bohemia,* edited by Coolbrith (San Francisco: A. M. Robertson, 1904);

Charles Philip Nettleton, *A Voice from the Silence,* edited by Coolbrith (San Francisco: A. M. Robertson, 1904);

Henry H. Behr, *The Hoot of the Owl,* edited by Coolbrith and Alexander M. Robertson (San Francisco: A. M. Robertson, 1904);

Poems of Charles Warren Stoddard, collected by Coolbrith, edited by Thomas Walsh (New York & London: John Lane, 1917);

Bret Harte, *The Heathen Chinee: Plain Language from Truthful James,* introduction by Coolbrith (San Francisco: J. H. Nash, 1924);

California Writers Club, West Wind: An Anthology of Verse, includes a foreword and poems by Coolbrith (San Francisco: Harr Wagner, 1925).

Ina Coolbrith, 1870 (Oakland Public Library)

Ina Coolbrith, hailed as "the Sappho of the West" in a 1 March 1928 obituary in *The New York Times,* was a friend and adviser to Bret Harte, Joaquin Miller, and Charles Warren Stoddard. She composed technically adept, conventionally styled verses for a newly founded San Francisco periodical, the *Overland Monthly,* and she continued to write poetry until her death, leaving a legacy of more than two hundred uncollected poems and three published volumes that reflect a writer of admirable talent and noteworthy accomplishment.

Coolbrith was popularly identified as the only woman in the Bohemian-styled writers' group that regularly congregated in the editorial offices of the *Overland,* which sought to challenge the *Atlantic Monthly* for a share of American literary eminence; moreover, she brought discipline, intelligence, and sensitivity to critical discussions of the content and

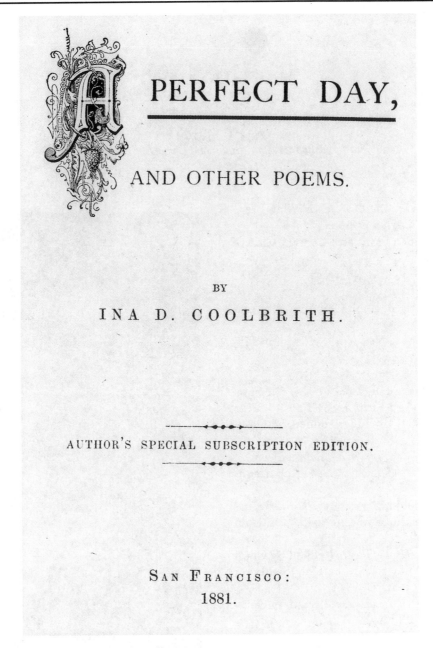

A PERFECT DAY,

AND OTHER POEMS.

BY

INA D. COOLBRITH.

AUTHOR'S SPECIAL SUBSCRIPTION EDITION.

SAN FRANCISCO:
1881.

Title page for Coolbrith's first book, which includes many poems first published in the
Overland Monthly

policy of the journal. Indeed, although she was content to remain in the background, Coolbrith not only published sixty-seven poems in the *Overland* between 1868 and 1875 but also promoted the recognition of aesthetic and literary values in the intellectual circles of San Francisco, then simply part of a rugged boomtown area struggling toward establishing its cultural identity. When the *Overland* circle was prematurely broken by the untimely departures of two key members, Harte and Stoddard, Coolbrith remained in town and became a much-beloved librarian, using her influence to encourage young

talent—most notably Jack London—and to crusade for literature and the arts in her still-unpolished western community.

Beyond her respected presence on this erratic and volatile historical scene, Coolbrith as poet often moved beyond the melodious contrivances evident in "sweet singers" of the genteel tradition, for her own childhood and youth in the American West had oriented her aesthetic concentration toward its wild beauty, with its alternately serene and explosive features. Coolbrith left a body of work that makes vibrant use of the West as metaphor for her own combined reflective and tumultuous experiences. She was able to fuse the meditative with the photographic, capturing the sometimes dangerous nuances inherent in her landscape.

Coolbrith's biography reads like a pulp narrative replete with all the frenzy and romance characteristic of that frequently western genre. Born in Nauvoo, Illinois, in 1841, Josephine (rendered into "Ina") Donna Smith was the second surviving child of Agnes Coolbrith and Don Carlos Smith, the brother of Joseph Smith, who founded the Mormon Church. When Ina was still an infant, the Nauvoo settlement had already become a lightning rod for prejudice and violence against Mormons. Her father, described as a courageous man, died of pneumonia when she was five months old. In 1844 her uncles Joseph and Hyrum Smith, in jail at nearby Carthage, were murdered by an anti-Mormon mob; her uncle Samuel Smith died of exertion and shock after a ride in a fruitless rescue attempt. In 1846 the Mormon faithful, plagued by the everyday abuse directed at them, packed and started west, but Ina's widowed mother remained to marry William Pickett, a non-Mormon lawyer and printer who, denouncing local "gentile" attitudes, had stood with and had spoken out in support of the persecuted sect. The new Pickett family moved to Saint Louis, Agnes Coolbrith Pickett agreeing to conceal her Mormon past to avoid further difficulties.

Although the family grew with the birth of twin boys in 1847, and although Pickett worked steadily as printer, word of the gold rush caught the imagination and interest of this adventurous man. In 1851, therefore, ten-year-old Ina became part of a legendary covered-wagon trek to California, recalling in her poem "The Gold Seekers" the passions driving the adults around her, people virtually crazed by "the metal blood of earth's grim veins," some of whom "a restless tryst forever kept / with Death, beneath the unrecording wave." While the girl felt her first desire to write during this difficult journey, she was mostly scarred by the depressing sights of abandoned wagons, suffering animals, and human deprivation. Nor were the early years in California any kinder. Winter in Marysville found the group awash in swollen streams and flooded-out shacks where Pickett's first gold venture failed. They moved to a bustling San Francisco. Before long, however, more calamity followed: their house was burglarized and, in an attempt to conceal the crime, incinerated. Another move was necessary: in 1855 Pickett took his family to Los Angeles, where, tempo-

rarily cured of gold fever, he opened what would become a successful law practice.

The teenaged Ina became part of the social life of the pueblo. She worked conscientiously at her assigned household chores and began formal education amidst idyllic natural surroundings, which she later described in "The Road to School" as "A meadow greenly carpeted, / A strip of woodland brown and cool" comprising the picturesque trail to the village schoolhouse. The adolescent now became addicted to romantic verse writing, even composing an assigned school theme in rhyme, and by the age of fifteen her work made its way into the Poet's Corner of the Los Angeles *Star,* in which each day's news concerned an essentially lawless town where street murders were frequent and lynch law an accepted fact of life. Surrounded by this threatening environment, Ina composed plaintive lyrics such as "We Miss Thee at Home," "One on Earth and One in Heaven," and "One More Loved One Had Departed." Engaged at sixteen to Robert B. Carsley, part-time actor and iron monger, Ina married at age seventeen. The union was noted in the 24 April 1858 *Star,* which offered "felicities" to "Miss Josephine Smith, whose compositions, over the signature of 'Ina,' have frequently delighted our readers." The marriage proved to have been ill-advised: a disturbed Carsley, jealous of his wife's continued popularity in the community, became an insanely possessive husband whose unfounded rages directed against his young spouse's imagined infidelities ultimately ended in tragedy. Threatening Ina's life, Carsley fired a pistol at her, and although he missed, Pickett, defending his stepdaughter, did not; in a subsequent gun battle Carsley was shot and received a wound that required the amputation of his hand.

By the end of 1861 Coolbrith had obtained a divorce. In the course of the traumatic events in her life, however, she had lost a child, the infant dying shortly after its birth, a loss the poet never spoke of publicly but occasionally mentions in her writing, as in the poem "The Mother's Grief": "Today I call my baby's name, / And hear no lisped replying," for God now holds the innocent "in His keeping." Years later, in the poem "Retrospect (In Los Angeles)," Coolbrith wistfully looks back to a time when her youthful aspirations had seemed easily accessible amidst California's "orange bloom"; with the passage of years, however, the poet reveals in her work an awareness of a sinister force that had threatened her dreams, its menace at the time having been cloaked by the seductive natural beauty of the environment:

Somewhere a stream sings, far away;
　Somewhere from out the hidden groves,
And dreary as the dying day
　Comes the soft coo of mourning doves.

It was again time to move. With mother, stepfather, and twin half brothers, Coolbrith in 1862 returned to San Francisco, in which enterprising young literati were poised to explode in feverish creative activity. Pickett once more took up printing. The former Mrs. Carsley, now officially known as Ina Donna Coolbrith, began to teach school. She had become a pensive woman who lamented, "only twenty, and my world turned to dust."

Coolbrith soon realized the advantages of San Francisco: she went to performances of William Shakespeare's plays; she discovered the Mercantile Library; and she found emotional satisfaction in the antislavery, pro-Union eloquence of Thomas Starr King, "the conscience of the city," whose sermons similarly moved Harte and Stoddard. With such stimulating activities now available to her, Coolbrith expressed dismay in her poem "Longing" at being bound to a teacher's desk and the family kitchen:

O foolish wisdom sought in books!
O aimless fret of household tasks!
O chains that bind the hand and mind–
　A fuller life my spirit asks!

So it was in the spring of 1864 that Harte, assistant editor of the *Californian,* began receiving and publishing verses from an anonymous woman poet; then, between 1865 and 1867 Harte published a dozen of the mysterious lady's poems, first signed "Ina" and at length "Ina D. Coolbrith." Her fellow writer Stoddard observed that her "full throated songs perhaps [were] too often touched with a gentle melancholy."

The first number of the *Overland,* sponsored by Anton Roman, local bookseller and publisher, appeared in July 1868, and alongside Mark Twain's "By Rail through France" it featured poems by Harte and Coolbrith. For the next nine years this ebullient journal was the repository of Coolbrith's poetry, scarcely a month going by without one of her productions, sixty-eight appearing during the halcyon *Overland* era, 1868–1875. The time of Coolbrith's greatest personal pleasure, however, came during the periodical's first three years when she, Harte, and Stoddard "would walk up Russian Hill" to her lodgings "to spend a few quiet hours drinking tea and being lazy." Her influence within this trio was significant: she once persuaded Harte to destroy a print-ready, scathing assessment of Joaquin

Miller's poetry and substitute a positive appraisal she had written, for Coolbrith had come to regard Cincinnatus Hiner Miller as her protégé, even insisting on his name change to Joaquin. When Coolbrith lightly tossed off a limerick that started "There was a young writer named Francis," Francis (Bret) Harte responded:

There is a poetic divinity–
Number One of the Overland Trinity–
　Who Uses the Muses
　Pretty much as she chooses–
This dark-eyed, young Sapphic divinity.

Indeed, Coolbrith's gatherings at her home with Harte, Stoddard, and other area aesthetes underscored the literary prominence of the *Overland* group, but when Miller in 1892 reflected on those creative days, he emphasized Coolbrith's singular importance: "She was the center of a little world, the San Francisco world." Yet, even while Coolbrith thrived during this exciting era in her life as artist, images of darkness and foreboding permeated her work. She wrote of "silence and bitter tears" in "The Years," an *Overland* poem of February 1870:

What do I owe the years, that I should bring
　Green leaves to crown them king?
Blown, barren sands, the thistle, and the brier,
　Dead hope, and mocked desire,
And sorrow, vast and pitiless as the sea:
　These are their gifts to me.

With artistic recognition and pleasing personal relationships filling her life, the twenty-nine-year-old Coolbrith nevertheless projected a somber vision of pessimism and regret, a dismal prophecy soon to become an immediate reality: Stoddard left the city for the South Seas in 1870; Harte went triumphantly east in 1871; and Miller departed for England, hailed there as the "Byron of Oregon." Coolbrith's life, personal and literary, would never be the same. Yet, the departure of her beloved associates aside, family survival suddenly loomed as the single major consideration for the poet, who from this point on was to be controlled by extreme financial exigencies.

From the mid 1870s Coolbrith became a veritable economic prisoner relegated to the status of avocational, occasional poet. Her gold-fevered stepfather disappeared, probably having run off once more to pursue his lifelong dream of the big strike; her widowed sister died and left two children; the twins were earning little money, and Agnes Coolbrith needed support; and in addition, Calle Shasta, Miller's "half-breed" daughter, was charitably taken

Coolbrith's letter to the mayor of Oakland after she was appointed to represent California at the 1927 Women's World's Fair in Chicago (Oakland Public Library)

into the home and became, along with everyone else, Coolbrith's nobly accepted responsibility. By 1874 an entire family was thus dependent on Coolbrith, who could not be content subsisting on irregular payments for her published poems. Her financial pressures were well known locally; in fact, the new Bohemian Club of San Francisco organized a "complimentary testimonial" for her, an event which realized $600 and gave minor, temporary relief. Producing poetry became a secondary consideration, its place in Coolbrith's life symbolized in "Question and Answer":

> Ah, in those dreary walks
> Behold the flowerless stalks
>   The fruitless tree!

Circumstances forced a significant detour in Coolbrith's continued literary ambitions. She needed to find a reliable career.

It was announced on 4 September 1874 that "Miss Ina Coolbrith, the San Francisco poet," was appointed librarian for what would soon be known as the Oakland Free Library at a salary of eighty dollars a month. Conscientious, dedicated, and knowledgeable, Coolbrith quickly became a meticulous professional working twelve-hour days virtually without assistance and maintained her high-profile post until 1892 when, caught in a municipal-political crossfire, she was asked by the trustees to resign. Having taken her librarianship as seriously as she had taken her association with the *Overland,* Coolbrith had perhaps indiscreetly spoken out against insufficient financial support for book acquisition as well as against trustee disinclination to eliminate unsafe features in the library building. Although in happier days of their mutually beneficial association the trustees had allowed Coolbrith to hire her well-qualified niece and nephew as assistants, these same officials eventually began a campaign of harassment against their librarian, whom a newspaper had described as "probably the busiest woman in this city." To help precipitate Coolbrith's resignation the trustees cut the book budget by 25 percent, removed the likes of Emile Zola and other undesirables from library shelves, and sold Coolbrith's files of the *Atlantic Monthly,* the *North American Review,* the *Eclectic Magazine,* and *St. Nicholas.* At last, one member candidly asserted, "We do not care for a poet in the library. We want a librarian."

A saddened Coolbrith's letter of resignation–effective 1 January 1893–stressed that she had "faithfully and diligently" discharged her duties and that she remained ignorant of the causes for her forced and totally unwarranted departure. While outpourings of support from literary friends buoyed her spirits, the poet's career in Oakland was finished; she was succeeded, ironically, by the nephew for whom she had sacrificed her literary aspirations. Indeed, Coolbrith expressed regret that her prioritized choices, motivated by altruism, perhaps, and philanthropy, had ultimately constituted a personal "wickedness," confessing that her "whole life has been forced to be against its truer self." A journalist in the *San Francisco Examiner* for 27 November 1892, describing the contemporary perception of Coolbrith and her well-publicized plight, stated that she "ranks first among California poets" but that "Other duties have stepped between her and the work which would have been most congenial."

At age fifty-two Coolbrith began a new but not particularly different phase of her life in which poetry was a pastime and poverty was always at close proximity. Over the years, however, she occasionally managed to travel: to the Columbian Exposition in 1893 and to New England and New York, where she was lionized at various literary receptions. Having organized her significant materials on western authors and their works, Coolbrith tried the lecture podium, telling audiences about "The Indian of Romance" and offering "Reminiscences of Early California Writers," but she needed to fall back on her experience as a librarian to earn a living. In 1898, therefore, Coolbrith worked at the Mercantile Library of San Francisco; then she accepted a part-time post as librarian at the prestigious Bohemian Club. Novelist Gertrude Atherton, who met Coolbrith at this time, observed that while "she had another ambition, to write a history of California, and had collected a great quantity of valuable material . . . she was old and ill . . . although her eyes were still bright and animated, often sparkling with humor, and she had a fascinating personality."

By 1902 the poet had moved back to Russian Hill, not far from where she, Harte, and Stoddard, the "Trinity," had once gathered to discuss *Overland* business, but the once-hardy woman who had truly been a western pioneer had become bruised by hardship and afflicted with a painful inflammatory rheumatism. Coolbrith, fortunately, found a constant companion who dedicated herself to the poet's care until 1919. Yet, once more unpredictable misfortune struck: Coolbrith's hope to become literary historian of California was obliterated by the San Francisco earthquake and subsequent fires of 1906, which destroyed her library, manuscripts, and papers. It would be four years before the dispirited woman could reestablish a home. She was now approaching seventy and in constant pain. Still, this once-robust poet of the Far West would compose

verse intermittently well into the era of modern poetry with its experimentalism and imagism, its wasteland psychology, and its social protest motifs, although such trends never intruded upon her efforts. Coolbrith began spending winters in New York, where her rheumatism seemed somewhat alleviated and where her energies for writing were revived. In the final decades of her life Coolbrith was heralded as a writer whose visible presence symbolized the link between an illustrious American literary past and its promising, optimistic present, a celebrity honored as the first poet laureate of California—the title bestowed in 1915 and accepted with characteristic self-deprecation. Coolbrith's accomplishment was recognized as transcending the mere friendships and associations that continued to bring her notice.

Three collections of poetry establish the mark of Coolbrith as writer, her first volume, *A Perfect Day and Other Poems* (1881), defining the intense, serious focus that comes to identify her work. Although she wrote in "Summer Past," "Ah, eternal summer-time / Dwells within the poet's rhyme!," the totality of the book reveals a center that lies in themes of dejection and loss delivered in conventional metrics. Powerful autobiographical currents lament the disappointments and frustrations of her personal and professional life: "Youth's sweet May passed quite away / May that never more is May!" ("A Hope") and "For Eden's life within me stirs / And scorns the shackles that I wear" ("Longing") are typical verses that project resignation conflicted with youthful ambition, hopes already vanishing amidst the obstacles suddenly before her. Coolbrith's landscape poems, chants of nature, employ symbols that underscore a melancholy world: a dead summer rose and a slain blossom dominate "In Time of Falling Leaves," while "woods brown and sere" control "My Cloth of Gold." At times the Coolbrith persona appears overwhelmed by the gravity of existence and resonates with a passionate expression of self-pity, as in "The Years":

> Rather thrust
> The wine cup to the dust!
> What have they brought to me, these many years?
> Silence and bitter tears.

Coolbrith's frequent allusions to and invocations of death darken the tone of *A Perfect Day*. In "Forgotten" the mantra of "Death, sweet Death, be nigh, be nigh" occurs near verses in praise of "Oblivion":

> Wherein the poet's brain
> The rapture and the pain

Of song knows not again,
Through all the years.

There are, to be sure, poems of religious exaltation in the volume, exuberant encomia to "the Master" and "the pure of paradise," but Coolbrith's reliance on images of "desolate dawn," "falling tears," and "chains that bind" supersedes her occasional, positive landscape panegyrics to "the far Yosemite," "the slopes of Tamalpais," and "the Saucelito hills." Love, whose blandishments are especially "cheerless" by the "cold, sad river," comes to be treated as a transient, destructive power, even in so frivolously titled a poem as "Cupid Kissed Me":

> Love from whom more pain than bliss
>   Every heart obtaineth,
>   For the joy soon vanished is
> While the pang remaineth.

The mainly oppressive tenor of Coolbrith's life clearly shaped the materials and orchestrated the tone of her initial volumes. The Trinity pleasures were muted; her feelings about thwarted aspirations were keenly expressed, a prophecy, as it were, of imminent foreboding.

Songs from the Golden Gate (1895) is a veritable republication of *A Perfect Day,* fifty-six poems from which were reprinted alongside forty-four new pieces. Yet while the tone is now occasionally mellow and soft, fundamental themes of disappointment and loss are extended in the poet's meditations on her life and her art, as in "Quest":

> The dry leaves fall and fall;
>   The days grow less in the sun:
> I falter, fail, and my soul is weary–
>   The quest unwon.

In "Freedom" Coolbrith even portrays herself as an unfortunate bird sadly freed from song and now relinquishes past hopes for eminence:

> Ah, well! was it so to be,
>   And better so?
> I shall never, never know,
>   It is gone–let it go.

Such rationalized regret, however, is especially painful, for a pious Coolbrith acknowledged that she had stepped away from collaboration with the Almighty: "The Poet" is a sanctified historian of the race, one who "walks with God upon the hills" and "gives her secrets to his hands." Still, the most striking poem in Coolbrith's second collection is "The Captive of the White City," an effort inspired by the presence in the Midway Plaisance at the Chicago

World's Fair of 1893 of Sitting Bull's log cabin. The poet paints a vivid portrait of the alienated Sioux Rain-in-the-Face, a curiosity to "children of every zone" who, paradoxically, walk by gazing "in brotherly love and grace"; the poem, too, captures the emotional violence and moral complexities in the tortuous and ethically suspect relationship between the U.S. government and the Native American tribes. Coolbrith's humanitarian focus evenly divides opprobrium and sympathy, deploring "the wrongs of the White Man's rule," "the hate in the Red Man's veins," and the "blood-stained hands of all": "Alas, for the death-heaped plains! / Alas for slayer and slain." The "ghostly shadow" hovering over the log cabin mirrors as well the solemn shade encroaching into Coolbrith's life and art, a somber reminder of her own loss of freedom and restricted options: the vanishing American and the poet, victims both.

Wings of Sunset (1929), Coolbrith's posthumously published collection of 116 poems, includes selections from her earlier volumes and despite its appearance in the late 1920s confirms the author as distinctly of the nineteenth century, an artist whose poetics are steeped in Victorian rather than modern strategy. The sense of nostalgia and wonder in Coolbrith's autobiographical poems is preserved in its essential sadness. Colorful verses describing California horticulture and topography are presented along with occasional pieces for commencements, dedications, and eulogies, as well as testimonials for Bret Harte, Luther Burbank, and Edmund Clarence Stedman. Most notable, though, in *Wings of Sunset* is "Concha," a ninety-line narrative poem and Coolbrith's most ambitious single effort. Although the work was finished in 1922, it bears no relation to the twentieth century either in materials or in metrics, for "Concha" is a skillful evocation of Old California garrison and mission life. The tale involves young Concha's ultimately successful battle with the church, a ponderous force in this "heathen land," for the love of Ramon, who must choose her or the priesthood. In the course of Concha's determined drive to educate herself she elevates the consciousness of everyone around her by questioning the very structure of their society:

> The White Man makes his laws
>   And executes them. Right!
> Why? *Quien sabe?* . . . Because–
>   Well, just because he's White.

Concha, however, realizes that "'tis a new day." At the age of eighty-one when she wrote these lines, Coolbrith, perhaps, now quietly reflecting on the forces that had ordered her own difficult life, ascribed to her assertive heroine that internal rebellious fire she herself had lacked.

Manifesting a human sympathy and invariably able to unify in her work personal emotion and adept technical skill, Coolbrith provided western writing with poetry that understood the region, its people, and its unique challenges. Scholar Lionel Stevenson has observed that "From her library desk her imagination and emotion winged out freely into the ageless ether." Typical of her unpretentious character, when she was crowned poet laureate of California, Coolbrith modestly dismissed "any special merit" of her own and instead paid tribute to "that wonderful group of early California writers with which it was [her] good fortune to be affiliated." Coolbrith wrote during an era when the West was looking toward literary affirmation in the East as aesthetic validation of its rough efforts. Thus the humble Coolbrith, who had once met John Greenleaf Whittier and had personally received his accolades, would have been delighted as well when she learned of the praise directed her way by America's distinguished household poet, Henry Wadsworth Longfellow. Despite his genteel, Brahmin preferences in literature, Longfellow asserted that "California has at least one poet. Her publisher sent me a book of Ina Coolbrith's poems and I have been reading them with delight." Indeed, beyond its technical virtuosity and emotional power, Coolbrith's poetry captures the essence of California's vigorous ethos, its dilemmas, and its beauty.

Bibliography:
Ivalu Delpha Stevens, "A Bibliography of Ina Coolbrith," *News Notes of California Libraries,* 27 (April 1932): 105–123.

Biography:
Josephine DeWitt Rhodehamel and Raymund Francis Wood, *Ina Coolbrith: Librarian and Laureate of California* (Provo, Utah: Brigham Young University Press, 1973).

References:
Henry Mead Bland, "Sketch of the First Western Literary Period," *Pacific Short Story Club Magazine,* 4 (July 1911): 5–7;

Lannie Haynes Martin, "The Literature of California," *Out West,* 3 (January 1912): 62–64, 98–100;

Edward F. O'Day, "Some Poets of San Francisco," *Society of California Pioneers Quarterly,* 10 (1933): 45–52;

Lionel Stevenson, "The Mind of Ina Coolbrith," *Overland Monthly,* new series 88 (May 1930): 150;

Franklin Walker, *San Francisco's Literary Frontier* (New York: Knopf, 1939).

Papers:
The San Francisco earthquake and fires of 1906 destroyed Ina Coolbrith's personal library, ravaging most of her books and papers. Her extant manuscripts are scattered in California libraries. The Bancroft Library of the University of California at Berkeley, the California Historical Society in San Francisco, the California State Library in Sacramento, the Huntington Library in San Marino, the Mills College Library in Oakland, the Oakland Public Library, and the Southwest Museum and Charles E. Lummis House in Los Angeles are the principal repositories.

Dan De Quille
(William Wright)

(9 May 1829 – 16 March 1898)

Lawrence I. Berkove
University of Michigan-Dearborn

BOOKS: *History of the Big Bonanza: An Authentic Account of the Discovery, History, and Working of the World Renowned Comstock Silver Lode of Nevada* (Hartford, Conn.: American, 1876; San Francisco: A. L. Bancroft, n.d.); republished as *The Big Bonanza: An Authentic Account of the Discovery, History, and Working of the World Renowned Comstock Silver Lode of Nevada* (Hartford, Conn.: American, 1876);

The Wonders of Nevada. Where They Are and How to Get to Them (Virginia City, Nev.: Enterprise Printing House, 1878);

A History of the Comstock Silver Lode & Mines, Nevada and the Great Basin Region; Lake Tahoe and the High Sierras (Virginia City, Nev.: F. Boegle, 1889);

Snow-Shoe Thompson (Los Angeles: Glen Dawson, 1954);

Washoe Rambles, edited by Richard E. Lingenfelter (Los Angeles: Westernlore, 1963);

Dan De Quille of the Big Bonanza, edited by James J. Rawls (San Francisco: Book Club of California, 1980);

Silver Walled Palace, edited by Dave Basso (Sparks, Nev.: Falcon Hill, 1981);

Little Lucy's Papa: A Story of Silverland (Sparks, Nev.: Falcon Hill, 1987);

Dives and Lazarus, edited by Lawrence I. Berkove (Ann Arbor, Mich.: Ardis, 1988);

The Gnomes of the Dead Rivers, edited by Berkove (Sparks, Nev.: Falcon Hill, 1990);

Dan De Quille, the Washoe Giant: A Biography and Anthology, edited by Richard A. Dwyer and Lingenfelter (Reno: University of Nevada Press, 1990);

The Fighting Horse of the Stanislaus: Stories and Essays by Dan De Quille, edited by Berkove (Iowa City: University of Iowa Press, 1990);

The Sorceress of Attu, edited by Berkove (Dearborn: University of Michigan–Dearborn, 1994).

Dan De Quille was the chronicler of the Comstock Lode and one of the most talented authors of the Old West. He lived in the Comstock Lode region of western Nevada and eastern California forty

Dan De Quille

years, from 1857 to 1897, and wrote about it not only with love but also with unequaled firsthand knowledge. Many other authors became better known than he mainly because he neglected in his lifetime to collect and publish in book form the many short stories, essays, and works of humor that made him a famous and much sought-after author by magazines and newspapers across the country.

At the *Territorial Enterprise,* the major newspaper of Virginia City, Nevada, he was a fellow employee, roommate, and friend of Mark Twain. He was both a mentor to Twain and a source of anecdotes that found their way into *Roughing It* (1872), *Life on the Mississippi,* (1883), and *The Adventures of Huckleberry Finn* (1884) as well as other shorter works. De Quille, like Twain, was a skilled hoaxer and in his narrower range wrote some literary hoaxes that were as good as or better than Twain's early ventures. De Quille's talents and views are a valuable reflection of American culture from the epic era of the Old West, as is the unique legacy of anecdotes and tales he contributed to American literature.

De Quille began life on 9 May 1829 as William Wright, the son of Paxson and Lucinda Markley Wright, who farmed near Fredericktown, Ohio. Whatever formal education he received was limited, but his family loved reading, and it is certain that young Wright read widely and deeply on his own and acquired an impressive education by this means. In 1847 his father moved the family to a farm near what is now West Liberty, Iowa; he died soon afterward, leaving William, the oldest of nine children, the responsibility of taking care of the family. William managed well enough so that in 1853 he was able to marry Carolyn Coleman and start a farm of his own. Five children were born in quick succession to the couple, two of whom died in infancy, but two daughters and a son would survive their father.

In 1857 Wright left his wife and children to go to California and seek his fortune prospecting for gold. He was not notably successful at this, but he was highly successful at writing travel letters and humorous sketches for publication in various periodicals. News of the immensely rich Comstock Lode took him to Virginia City in 1860, and in 1861 he joined the staff of the *Enterprise,* soon to become one of the great papers of the West. From then on writing was his sole occupation. He adopted the pen name of Dan De Quille, and it all but replaced his real name in the course of his career. De Quille remained in Virginia City for almost all of the rest of his life, returning to West Liberty for only eight months in 1862 and eight months at the end of his life. Little is known of his relationship with his wife and children. There is evidence that strongly suggests he continued to support his family while he lived in Nevada, and his wife and daughters came separately to live with him for periods of time. However, he essentially lived on his own.

De Quille earned a reputation for expertise and probity as the mining editor of the *Enterprise,* but it was his second career as a writer of short stories, historical sketches of the Comstock, tongue-in-

cheek hoaxes, whimsical tall tales, and moving allegorical novellas that made him beloved in his time and worthy of attention by future generations. Until recently his fame depended on his relationship with Mark Twain, a few works of humor that were occasionally republished, and his *History of the Big Bonanza: An Authentic Account of the Discovery, History, and Working of the World Renowned Comstock Silver Lode of Nevada* (1876), the one important book he published in his lifetime. Now that many of his uncollected works have been recovered and edited—including some pieces that were never before published—a truly representative fraction of his oeuvre is at last accessible.

De Quille was an extraordinarily prolific and varied writer. Those who knew him never ceased to admire his ability to sit down and dash off pieces that required little revision. Even while he was prospecting for gold in California he was capable of writing thousands of words at night and sending off articles in the morning to several different periodicals. He quickly developed and progressively mastered a wide repertoire of styles.

His career may be roughly divided into three stages. The first, lasting from 1860 to around middecade, was his apprentice period, during which time he rapidly learned the trade of journalism and experimented with different modes of fiction and humor. He began by writing travel sketches for the *Cedar Falls Gazette* in Iowa and a San Francisco literary magazine, the *Golden Era*. The travel letters were colorful, newsy, personal, and often laced with narrative and humor. They informed readers not only about little-known geographical features of California and Nevada but also about such interesting topics as Indian affairs, the customs of the local ethnic communities, social and cultural activities, and crime.

Even early in his career De Quille developed a skill for blending fact and fancy so cleverly that readers could not always be sure where one left off and the other began. In 1861, for example, De Quille wrote a series of letters called "Washoe Rambles" for the *Golden Era,* reporting on a prospecting expedition into western Nevada. He peopled the expedition with a variety of characters and embellished factual details with humorous narratives about the adventures of these individuals: their supposed conversations, including some in dialect quoted at length; stories they told; and frictions between them. Twain later used these same techniques in his 1866 series of letters from Hawaii to the *Sacramento Union* and incorporated them into *Roughing It.*

In addition to travel letters De Quille contributed news stories and short stories to the *Cedar Falls*

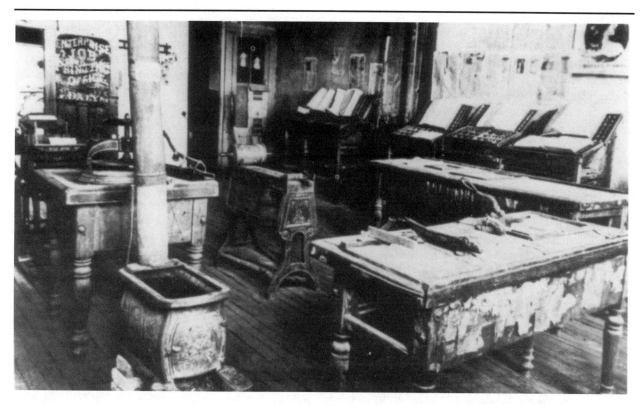

Composing room of the Territorial Enterpise, *Virginia City, Nevada (Nevada State Historical Society)*

Gazette until September 1862 and stories, humorous sketches, and novellas to the *Golden Era* until October 1865. He was famous for his lightness of touch and his gentleness of spirit, but the outbreak of the Civil War stirred him so deeply that he wrote emotionally of it. De Quille sympathized with the Union and despised the Confederate cause. His story for the 6 April 1862 *Golden Era,* "We Gave Our Willie," is a one-sided tearjerker about the goodness of the North and the viciousness of the South. Most of what he wrote, however, was characterized by light humor and wit.

As one of the earliest employees of the *Enterprise* De Quille was given two responsibilities: mining reports and local news. In the first category he soon established himself as an expert and honest reporter. Mining reports were an especially critical feature of all Comstock newspapers as investors from all over the country as well as from international financial centers such as London and Berlin looked to the regional papers for independent evaluations of mining properties. From all accounts De Quille's knowledge of mineral formation and mining was impressive, and miners and investors considered his reports reliable.

While his mining reports established his value to the newspaper and financial community, his role as local news editor gave his literary inclinations an avenue for expression. De Quille was a good journalist when

it came to regular news coverage, but he became creative when there was a dearth of news or unfilled space. In chapter 42 of *Roughing It* Twain acknowledges the importance to his own development as a journalist of De Quille's example of generating news "out of the hay wagons in a dry time when there were no fires or inquests." De Quille inserted short pieces of whimsy or sly hoaxes, which he called "quaints," into his daily list of "local items," thus turning a catchall column into a sort of treasure chest, with humor as the reward for the diligent reader. Occasionally one of his longer quaints would masquerade as a news item on the front page. Unlike the case with most tall tales, there normally would be no obvious indication that the article was a hoax. De Quille characteristically began with an impossible situation but then so convincingly supported it with plausible details that credulous readers were taken in. He soon became a past master of the hoax, a form of humor characteristic of the West.

De Quille took Twain under his wing when the younger man joined the *Enterprise* in 1862. The two men were kindred souls who shared a sense of humor and an especial fondness for hoaxes. Twain and De Quille engaged in friendly insults on the front page, each magnifying the minor mistakes of the other into prodigies of calamity. These mock duels attracted readers to the newspaper and gave both writers valuable literary training.

Several months after he began work on the paper Twain wrote "The Petrified Man," one of his earliest hoaxes of genius, which was published on 4 October 1862. It is a slyly satirical account of how the discovery of a petrified man causes a local coroner to conclude, ridiculously, that the man had died of "protracted exposure." The entire Comstock community was taken in but resented Twain when they realized that he had duped them. Three years later De Quille successfully passed off a similar hoax on much the same audience with his "The Wonder of the Age. A Silver Man," which appeared in the 5 February 1865 *Golden Era*. De Quille's piece, much longer and more detailed than Twain's, was more entertaining and not cutting; readers who fell for it did not feel later that they had been made fools of. Probably the most famous of De Quille's many successful hoaxes concerned a man who invented a rubber suit with a portable air conditioner. He supposedly died crossing Death Valley in the summer not because the device failed but because it worked too well; he froze to death. De Quille first wrote the "Solar Armor" story for the 2 July 1874 issue of the *Enterprise*.

During his apprentice period De Quille occasionally wrote short stories and novellas. A few of his literary pieces were set in the East or even in medieval Europe, or were obviously productions of exuberant fancy. "Petrified! Or the Stewed Chicken Monster," which was first published in the 30 August 1863 *Golden Era,* is such a tale, a humorous account of a nightmare induced by bad food. None of De Quille's early novellas is distinguished, and the few stories that show talent usually feature the people and the parts of the country he knew best.

The second phase of his career took place between the mid 1860s and 1876, the year he published the book usually referred to as *The Big Bonanza*. During these years De Quille enlarged his knowledge of the Comstock while he continued to write quaints and other pieces marked by humorous exaggeration. He produced many sketches and tall tales about mining life and miners and entertaining accounts of the Comstock's heterogeneous ethnic mix of whites of European origin, Indians, Chinese, and Jews. He also wrote on Comstock history. He became more mature and psychologically sensitive and perfected his ability to entertain with so clever a mix of fancy with fact that only the most astute readers could pick up the subtle clues of his hoaxes.

De Quille's association with Twain shaped his life more than he realized. As friends, colleagues, and roommates, the two men challenged, inspired, and complemented each other. No one knows the details of what passed between them—what they told each other of their experiences, what anecdotes and jokes they exchanged, what files of clippings De Quille might have shown Twain, or what comments on their craft they might have shared with each other—but it is clear that they deeply influenced each other. Part of the influence came from being young men with similar values in an exciting place at an exciting time. It was a boom time. Opportunity, money, fun, and adventure were abundant, and they could give their talents full rein. They were the premier journalists in the West, and De Quille could be pleased that he was generally considered the better of the two.

Twain's fortunes began to soar when he left the Comstock. De Quille was aware of it, baffled by it, but although he did not openly admit it, somewhat resentful of it. Without Twain's knowledge or intention the friends became competitors. Twain was soon known as a literary figure while De Quille still longed for that distinction. Twain published book after book while De Quille had yet to publish his first one. Twain traveled widely, prospered, and mingled with the elite of the nation while De Quille stayed at the same job and the same salary in Virginia City. As he grew older, moreover, the hectic and hard-drinking lifestyle that he had shared with Twain became too much for him. De Quille became an alcoholic, somewhat of an occupational hazard for newspapermen of the era. Drunkenness doubtless allowed him to vent pressures and passions that he suppressed when sober.

At first his friends covered for him by assuming his duties for a day or two. Then *Enterprise* owner and friend Joe Goodman sent him to a California clinic to sober up. Next, Goodman tried the shock treatment of firing him but soon relented and rehired him. When De Quille lapsed, Goodman fired him again for a longer period. This happened again before De Quille made a mighty and temporarily successful effort to stay away from liquor. Then a series of events occurred that overwhelmed De Quille.

In 1873 the "big bonanza," the richest part of the Comstock lode, was discovered, and another boom was started. In order to develop the new find, the mining companies needed massive infusions of capital. In 1874 a group of "silver kings," John Mackay, James Fair, Sen. John P. Jones, and William Ralston, urged De Quille to write a book that would increase popular interest in the Comstock and stimulate stock purchases. De Quille resisted the suggestions for several months because he was trying to compile a book of his best work that would establish him as a literary figure. He was not good, however, at standing up to strong personalities or pressures. In 1874 Goodman was forced to sell the *Enterprise* to his enemy William Sharon, a powerful and ruthless financier. De Quille stayed on at his old salary, but with Goodman's departure he lost a trusted friend and stabilizing influence. It would be surprising if Sharon did not add his voice to that of the silver kings to persuade De Quille to write a book that would make Comstock mining companies attractive to potential investors.

In late February 1875, apparently unable to bear the strain of resisting the pressure any longer, De Quille took to heavy drinking again after having abstained for two years. Several weeks later he wrote Twain for advice. Twain replied with enthusiasm. He invited De Quille to visit him in Hartford, strongly urged that he first write a book on the Comstock instead of a pamphlet that would leave him time to prepare the collection he wanted to put together, and offered to help De Quille with the writing of the Comstock book and its publication. Still unsure of what to do, De Quille wrote Goodman for his opinion of Twain's advice. Goodman encouraged De Quille to proceed with his own plan for a pamphlet and literary anthology instead of Twain's more grandiose scheme. De Quille decided to follow Twain's advice.

It was a fateful choice that affected him for the rest of his life and his literary reputation for more than a hundred years afterward. Under Twain's guidance De Quille used many of the pieces he intended for his own anthology and adapted them to the full-sized book he was to title *The History of the Big Bonanza*. After much delay and tribulation the book was published in 1876, just after the excitement of the new mining developments had peaked. As a result, the book did not bring De Quille the income that Twain had led him to believe would result and that he expected. And a major casualty of De Quille's choice to write it was the literary anthology he wanted to publish. He never completed it in his lifetime, and more than one hundred years would pass before his wish was realized by other hands.

The Big Bonanza did, however, ensure that De Quille would not be utterly forgotten. De Quille's encyclopedic knowledge of mining and the region combined with his sprightly writing made it a classic of its kind and easily the best contemporary account of the Comstock. Delightful as well as informative, the book is rich in entertaining anecdotes and includes sly humor where least expected. The phenomenon of the Comstock Lode in nineteenth-century American culture cannot be understood without it.

As good as it is, however, it is not what it could have been: the definitive history of the Comstock. De Quille was torn between writing its history and promoting it, and he compromised mostly on the side of promotion. His temperamental indisposition

to be critical kept him from telling the whole truth. He wrote of the desperadoes of the Comstock but not of its stock scandals, its labor problems, the sickness and accident rate among its miners, the buying of votes and juries and public offices that earned Nevada the sobriquet of "the rotten borough." He invariably praised the good qualities of the silver kings but did not mention their trickeries, deceits, and bullying. His book is lavishly illustrated with woodcuts of men such as the silver king James G. Fair but never indicates why he was locally referred to as "Slippery Jim," and the comments on the "Hon. William Sharon" touch but lightly on the ruthlessness that Goodman exposed fully and fearlessly in a famous 1872 editorial that cost Sharon the election for the U.S. Senate.

De Quille's critical comments are always circumspect. He briefly admits that the Sierra Nevada adjacent to the Comstock was being denuded of its forest cover, with adverse consequences to climate and water supply, but embeds this observation in a chapter on how the Comstock gets its fuel and timber. In a January 1875 letter to his sister De Quille wrote that he was sometimes tempted to show the Comstock millionaires "the terrible damage I could do them in a single paragraph," but in his book he is, instead, their champion. De Quille knew right from wrong, but like every other writer of the Comstock except for one or two heroes and a few recklessly idealistic fools, he temporized.

The third, final, and richest phase of De Quille's career lasted from the mid 1870s until the mid 1890s. It is a surprising, even inspiring, phase because although he was beset by adversity, De Quille responded with resourcefulness and fecundity. The adversity came partly as a continued consequence of his alcoholism and partly as a result of the decline of the Comstock, beginning around 1880, which led to the closing of mines and mills, the loss of jobs, population flight, and finally the closing of the *Enterprise*.

The firings from the newspaper that Goodman had initiated as a means of shocking his friend back into responsibility continued under subsequent managements as punishments for his unreliability. What had started as layoffs lasting weeks and later months grew until De Quille was barred from the paper for years at a time. Instead of breaking him, however, these firings had the reverse effect. He apparently got his drinking under control—at least the diarist Alfred Doten stops recording incidents of his drunkenness—and began to concentrate on freelance work. When the *Enterprise* failed to pay what he wanted, he explored the network of outlets he had already cultivated. A wide variety of periodicals in Nevada and California, including most of the major

San Francisco newspapers, were glad to print his contributions, as were papers in New York, Chicago, Cincinnati, Louisville, and many smaller cities, including his hometown of Fredericktown.

Freelancing induced De Quille to become even more prolific, though he also recycled old material. He sometimes sent pieces he had published years before to new markets in a different part of the country. "Butter-mouth Bill," for example, appeared in the *Enterprise* for the first time on 8 November 1874. It was revised as "Tongue-Oil Timothy Dead" for the 5 December 1886 *New York Sun*. The bodies of the two versions are almost the same except for the latter's changed name and the beginning and ending. Some recycled pieces were left untouched; others had only minor changes; and still others showed significant reworking. Most of what De Quille wrote, however, was new material, sometimes tailor-made for a specific periodical.

He was an associate editor of the *Montana Mining Review* in 1889 and frequently placed articles in other professional mining journals. National magazines such as *Overland Monthly* and *Cosmopolitan* took his stories, and he placed invited articles in the *Encyclopedia Britannica* and *Johnson's Cyclopedia*. He signed up with three national syndicates: S. S. McClure, the Lorborn Company, and the American Press Association. The stories they accepted were widely disseminated. His freelance work eventually brought him the national reputation and demand that his work for the *Enterprise* had not. In 1896, when he was too sick and weak to accept, James Gordon Bennett of the *New York Herald Tribune* telegraphed him an authorization to send copy.

De Quille had always used reminiscences as literary material, but in his fifties and sixties he made even more use of the past. He was a child of the last generation of the American frontier, the end of a remarkable three-century tradition. The epic age of the West was short, and De Quille, like the more perceptive of his contemporaries, sensed in the rapid industrialization and exploitation of the Comstock and then in its equally rapid decline the imminent end of a way of life. Tales set in the Ohio and Iowa of his youth joined his narratives of earlier days in Nevada and California.

Reading these recalled experiences at face value, one would be led to wonder first at the extraordinary range of his adventures and acquaintances and then at his extraordinary memory. His memory was good, but not all of the recalled incidents were ones that he actually experienced. He often used the claim of recollection as a literary device to lead into a story, and he made extensive use of his library and files to supply both ideas and details.

Some of his "recollections" of Ohio, for example, were derived from A. Banning Norton's *History of Knox County* (1862).

Appearing in the *Enterprise* of 24 January 1875, "Pilot Wylie," an unusual blending of fact and fancy, purported to be an account of De Quille's first meeting with Twain when Twain was a pilot on the Mississippi River. The whole work was fiction–such a meeting never occurred–yet most of its parts had a factual basis in hitherto-unrevealed biographical details of Twain's life. The sketch inspired Twain soon afterward, in a curious example of back influence, to use those details in the June 1875 *Atlantic Monthly* installment of his "Old Times on the Mississippi" memoirs. A long, richly detailed article in an October 1894 issue of the newspaper on a "lost seal island" in the Aleutians, supposedly based on an interview, was probably DeQuille's last major hoax. It is the direct antecedent of his 1894 manuscript *The Sorceress of Attu* and was almost certainly made up. Whether the narratives De Quille claimed to be memoirs were literally true or not, they were reflections of the last years of America's frontier age and authentic products of its literary spirit.

A major influence on the last years of De Quille's life was his association with the *Salt Lake City Daily Tribune*. Early in 1885 De Quille informed C. C. "Judge" Goodwin, a former editor of the *Enterprise* who had become the publisher and owner of the flourishing Salt Lake City paper, that he was out of work and asked if he would accept some piecework for pay. A staunch friend, Goodwin expressed strong sympathy for De Quille and wrote him on 23 February to "send as you can and we will pay as we can." The opening quickly grew into a commitment for a weekly article that lasted until 1898.

Goodwin had many good qualities, including loyalty to friends, a sentimental attachment to the Comstock, and editorial fearlessness, but he was also driven by some powerful prejudices. He wasted few opportunities to be critical of the Mormon Church; he was fiercely devoted to free silver; and he opposed emigration from the Orient. It may not be coincidental, therefore, that one of the first De Quille pieces Goodwin published in the *Tribune* was a spoof on Mormons. There is no doubt, though, that De Quille shared Goodwin's view on the issue of free silver, a political movement for the unlimited coinage of silver. A large portion of what De Quille wrote for the newspaper related to the issue, and he was quite impassioned about it. For years encomia for silver alternated in his weekly columns with vituperative diatribes against the gold standard.

The animus behind these pieces, verging upon bigotry, contrasts with almost everything De Quille wrote before and most of what he wrote later. Throughout his long career he had usually spoken up for tolerance. Most of his stories about African Americans–for example, "The Earth Never Dies," which was first published in *The Fighting Horse of the Stanislaus: Stories and Essays by Dan De Quille* (1990)–reflect goodwill, as do his journalistic commentaries on the Chinese people and many of his pieces on Indians. On 7 July 1889 he wrote in the *Tribune* a long philo-Semitic piece titled "America the True Canaan." After an impressive and sympathetic overview of Jewish history he concluded that the United States and Jews had much to offer each other and that America might well be the true Promised Land for Jews. But in June and July 1893 he wrote articles denouncing "President Cleveland and His Partner Levi" and the "Shylock Rule of the Rothschilds." He also justified the killing of Chinese if they continued to come to the United States. This unexpected viciousness probably derived not so much from a total change of heart as from his profound distress and frustration at the drop in world silver prices in 1893, with the consequent shutting down of most Comstock mining operations and the accelerated exodus of population from the area. Seeing the deathblow not only to Comstock industry but to a way of life he loved, De Quille apparently imbibed the extravagant populist rhetoric about Pharisee moneylenders and cheap Chinese labor and struck out in blind passion.

Although the imminent defeat of the free silver movement brought out the worst in De Quille, it did not poison the entire output of this final phase of his career. On the contrary, much of what he wrote shows psychological depth and sophistication, and even an emergent religiosity. The adversities he had endured made him more sensitive to human nature. For example, on the surface "A Strange Monomania," which appeared in the 13 September 1874 *Enterprise,* is a humorous story about a man who believed he had a beef liver in his nose, but it is also a psychologically astute and sympathetic study of someone whose irrational fears reach phobic proportions and of those around him. "A Dietetic Don Quixote," published in the 13 September 1885 issue of the *New York Sun,* is a similarly layered psychological portrait of a man who starved himself to death while rationalizing his every self-deprivation as a health measure. "The Fighting Horse of the Stanislaus," which appeared in the 28 June 1874 *Enterprise,* is one of De Quille's most skillful criticisms of the brutality that was a characteristic of Comstock competition. On the surface it is a retelling of a true story about Jones, an influential Comstocker and someone with whom he was on good terms. But more subtly it is an ethical as well as psychological de-

nunciation of the savagery in men who heartlessly pit animals against each other in fights to the death.

Although De Quille spent the better part of his life promoting and defending the industries and people of the Comstock, he was also critical of their rampant getting and spending. In 1880 he published an antimaterialistic novella, *The Gnomes of the Dead Rivers,* as a serial in the *Nevada Monthly.* He had developed a strong interest in legends and mythology, and this readable work makes use of both to warn against the insidious dangers of wealth to character. His excellent short story "The Eagles' Nest," which was published in the 17 May 1891 issue of *Overland Monthly,* combines a brilliant representation of vertigo and an unflattering contrast of humans with animals, with an antimaterialistic theme: "for gold men will venture all things,–even life."

De Quille's strongest attack on materialism occurs in his unique and impressive novella *Dives and Lazarus,* written around 1893–1894 but not published until a century later. The theme of free silver versus the gold standard is an important but not domineering aspect of the book, which describes the wanderings in an amazing underworld of the souls of two recently deceased men: the poor Comstock miner Lysander P. Lazarus and U.S. senator Magnificus Auriferous Dives. A lifetime of deliberative reading is behind this book. It is inspired by the New Testament accounts of two men, both named Lazarus, in Luke 16 and John 11–12; its structure is based on Dante's *Divine Comedy;* and its chapters are composed of adaptations of mythology and the familiar classics of world literature. To contrast *Dives and Lazarus* with Twain's "Extract from Captain Stormfield's Visit to Heaven" (1907) is to see how far De Quille and Twain ultimately diverged. At the end of his life De Quille found peace in his faith.

Despite the uncharacteristic bursts of passion and prejudice, the last decade of De Quille's life was significantly colored by a mood of retrospection. "Old Times on the Prairies" and "Trailing a Lost Child," both published in the *Tribune* in January 1892, are two beautifully written and vivid recollections of Iowa in the 1850s when it was frontier country. "Lorenzo Dow's Miracle," which appeared in the 12 February 1893 *San Francisco Examiner,* is a delightful anecdote about the famous Methodist circuit rider. Whether De Quille adapted the tale from one of the published anecdotes of Dow that were popular earlier in the century or recalled a local tale from his native Knox County, he gave the story new life. When the *Enterprise* discontinued publication in 1893, De Quille quickly composed two articles that drew on his recollections: "Salad Days of Mark Twain" was published in the 19 March 1893 *San Francisco Examiner,* and "Artemus Ward in Nevada" appeared in the 4 August *Californian Illustrated Magazine.*

De Quille had long been sympathetic to Indians, and in 1890–1891, during the unrest over the spread of the Ghost Dance ritual, he wrote courageous articles defending the local Paiute leader Wovokah against the charge that he was advocating violence. In 1893 and 1894 De Quille came to empathize with Indians as he never had before. "Pahnenit, Prince of the Land of Lakes" and "The Sorceress of Attu" were two legends he concocted and set, respectively, in the West and the Aleutians before they were explored and exploited. In "Pahnenit," especially, he seemed to regret what had happened to the land and its original inhabitants, and it may be read as his appreciation of the Indians' longing for a messiah and redemption. These two novellas were not published in his lifetime. They, along with *Dives and Lazarus,* represent a burst of activity in the final years of his life. Perhaps because he was old and sick and knew that his active years were close to an end, he did not take his usual steps to publish these three novellas, all rooted in his deepest feelings. "An Indian Story of the Sierra Madre" (1895), illustrated by Frederic Remington and published in the *Cosmopolitan* magazine, on the surface appears on the surface to be another cowboy-and-Indian story, but a close reading reveals its elegiac nature. The frontiersmen who are the heroes are also the victims of their own success, for with the end of their Indian opponents also comes the end of their reason for being and their way of life.

Dan De Quille's life and the Golden Age of the West ended at the same time. He was long aware that the Comstock's best days were behind it. For all his passion for free silver, he must have realized that he was fighting a rearguard battle. The retrospective note in so much of the fiction and essays of his final ten or fifteen years clearly expresses his sorrow over the passing of a deeply loved way of life. In 1897 his friend Alfred Doten described him as sick, bent, and "used up." John Mackay, the greatest of the silver kings, learned of his condition, bestowed a pension upon him, and paid his way back to his daughter's house in West Liberty, Iowa. De Quille's fingers were too gnarled to write any more, but he spent the remaining eight months of his life contentedly. Neither he nor his family ever collected his works for publication, but scholars in the last decades of the twentieth century have realized the importance of his writings and have brought them and him back into circulation.

References:

Lawrence I. Berkove, "Dan De Quille and *Roughing It:* Borrowings and Influence," *Nevada Historical Society Quarterly,* 37 (Spring 1994): 52–57;

Berkove, "Dan De Quille's Narratives of Ohio: Four Sketches," *Northwest Ohio Quarterly,* 61 (Winter 1989): 3–12;

Berkove, "Dan De Quille's Narratives of Ohio: 'Odd Sticks,'" *Northwest Ohio Quarterly,* 62 (Summer & Autumn 1990): 54–64;

Berkove, "Dan De Quille and 'Old Times on the Mississippi,'" *Mark Twain Journal,* 24 (Fall 1986): 28–35;

Berkove, "Free Silver and Jews: The Change in Dan De Quille," *American Jewish Archives,* 41 (Spring/Summer 1989): 43–51;

Berkove, Introduction, *Dives and Lazarus* (Ann Arbor, Mich.: Ardis, 1988), pp. 13–47;

Berkove, Introduction, *The Fighting Horse of the Stanislaus* (Iowa City: University of Iowa Press, 1990), pp. xiii–xxiv;

Berkove, "The Literary Journalism of Dan De Quille," *Nevada Historical Society Quarterly,* 28 (Winter 1985): 249–261;

Berkove, "New Information on Dan De Quille and 'Old Times on the Mississippi,'" *Mark Twain Journal,* 26, no. 2 (1988): 15–20;

Berkove, "'Nobody Writes to Anybody Except to Ask a Favor': New Correspondence between Mark Twain and Dan De Quille," *Mark Twain Journal,* 26 (Spring 1988): 2–21;

Berkove, "'Trailing a Lost Child': A Dan De Quille Memoir," *Palimpsest,* 69 (Fall 1988): 120–131;

Alfred Doten, *The Journals of Alfred Doten 1849–1903,* edited by Walter Van Tilburg Clark, 3 volumes (Reno: University of Nevada Press, 1973);

Richard A. Dwyer and Richard E. Lingenfelter, Introduction, *Dan De Quille, the Washoe Giant* (Reno: University of Nevada Press, 1990), pp. 3–53;

Oscar Lewis, Introduction, *The Big Bonanza* (New York: Crowell, 1947), pp. vii–xxv;

Richard G. Lillard, "Dan De Quille, Comstock Reporter and Humorist," *Pacific Historical Review,* 13 (1944): 251–259;

Effie Mona Mack, "Dan De Quille (William Wright): 1829–1898," *Nevada Magazine,* 2 (September 1946): 6–9, 33–34; (October 1946): 6–9, 33; (November 1946): 6–11, 35.

Papers:

The largest collection of De Quille's manuscripts and letters is held in the William Wright Papers and Grant Loomis files of the Bancroft Library at the University of California, Berkeley. Letters, scrapbooks, miscellaneous files, and photographs are held in the Morris Family Collection of Dan De Quille at the State Historical Society of Iowa in Iowa City.

Thomas J. Dimsdale

(1831? – 22 September 1866)

John D. Nesbitt

Eastern Wyoming College

BOOK: *The Vigilantes of Montana, or Popular Justice in the Rocky Mountains. Being a Correct and Impartial Narrative of the Chase, Trial, Capture and Execution of Henry Plummer's Road Agent Band, together with Accounts of the Lives and Crimes of Many of the Robbers and Desperadoes, the Whole being Interspersed with Sketches of Life in the Mining Camps of the "Far West"* (Virginia City, Mont.: M. T., D. W. Tilton, 1866).

Thomas Josiah Dimsdale, frequently referred to as "Prof. Thos. J. Dimsdale" or "Professor Dimsdale," claims a place in nineteenth-century western American literature on the strength of one book, *The Vigilantes of Montana, or Popular Justice in the Rocky Mountains. Being a Correct and Impartial Narrative of the Chase, Trial, Capture and Execution of Henry Plummer's Road Agent Band, together with Accounts of the Lives and Crimes of Many of the Robbers and Desperadoes, the Whole being Interspersed with Sketches of Life in the Mining Camps of the "Far West,"* published in 1866. It gives a detailed account of vigilante justice in the early settlement of Montana, and it has been a direct source for later writers, most notably Mark Twain in *Roughing It* (1872) and Ernest Haycox in *Alder Gulch* (1941). It strongly endorses popular justice and is an important early text in the debate about lynching that figures in later works such as Owen Wister's *The Virginian* (1902) and Walter Van Tilburg Clark's *The Ox-Bow Incident* (1940).

Dimsdale was born in England in the early 1830s and came to this country by way of Canada. Biographical details before his arrival in Montana in 1863 are sketchy, but he is usually portrayed as an educated Englishman. He attended Rugby and then Oxford but did not finish a degree at the latter. He originally went to Montana to take part in the gold rush, but poor health kept him from being a miner. In 1863 he opened a small private school in Virginia City, which he operated into the next year. He also conducted the first Episcopal service in Virginia City. Shortly after the territory of Montana was

formed in 1864, the governor appointed Dimsdale as superintendent of public instruction. Later the same year Dimsdale became editor of the *Montana Post* in Virginia City, the first newspaper in the territory. For the *Post,* beginning in 1865, he wrote a series of articles about the Montana vigilantes and their activities in 1863–1864. The *Post* then published the material in book form in 1866, and *The Vigilantes of Montana* is known as the first book published in Montana. Dimsdale continued working for the *Post* until shortly before he died of tuberculosis, at age thirty-five, on 22 September 1866.

The bulk of *The Vigilantes of Montana* concerns itself with a short period of time in the early history of Virginia City and the nearby towns of Nevada City and Bannack, all of which sprang up as gold-mining towns in the early 1860s. Dimsdale gives many examples of the crime that was rife in that setting, especially organized robberies conducted by a group of road agents allegedly headed by Henry Plummer, the sheriff of both Bannack and Virginia City. The narrative tells of the formation of the Vigilance Committee and its successful efforts at pursuing, capturing, and executing the criminals. This part of the book served as good source material for writers, particularly novelists such as Haycox, who were interested in the Plummer story of corruption, organized crime, and the triumph of popular justice.

When the last of Plummer's gang had been "launched into eternity" (a phrase used with some frequency in the book), the Vigilance Committee continued to protect the social order, as Dimsdale portrays the vigilantes' activities. Among their subsequent executions was that of the renowned desperado J. A. Slade, who has been made famous in Mark Twain's account of meeting Slade in 1861 on the Overland stage route. Twain met the famed bad man a few years before Slade went to Montana and met his end there; years later Twain wrote *Roughing It* and made use of Dimsdale as a source. Twain gives a colorful account of Slade as a coldhearted, vengeful murderer—a more detailed narrative than Dimsdale's cursory account of Slade's celebrated earlier cruelties. Then Twain quotes a long passage from Dimsdale (a little over six pages) to show how Slade came to his punishment.

The Vigilantes of Montana is a veritable treasure of sensational material. It provides detailed narration of fights, shootings, robberies, murders, chases, captures, and executions. The reader learns how the robberies were conducted, how the "malefactors" were apprehended, how the various execution sites were improvised, and how the condemned men met their deaths. Dimsdale's accounts proved to be a rich source for authors less celebrated than Twain and Haycox, such as Will Henry in *Reckoning at Yankee Flat* (1958).

Dimsdale is explicit about his purposes. Toward the end of the eighth chapter he writes, "The account is purposely literal and exact," and he goes on to say that his purpose is to "tell the truth for the instruction of mankind." What he means by "instruction," however, is at least as much opinion as fact. At the end of the previous chapter Dimsdale also cites his intention. After narrating a feud between Plummer and another elected lawman, Dimsdale writes: "The account of the troubles of one man, which we have given above, has been inserted with the object of showing the state of society which could permit such openly planned and persistent outrages, and which necessitated such a method of defense." This comment is part of Dimsdale's overall design, which is to justify vigilante justice as a necessary "method of defense." By portraying the effrontery of the outlaws, he provides his rationale for citizens taking the law into their own hands.

Prior to the narration proper, Dimsdale offers his first chapter as a polemical introduction. He begins by sketching out the general features of life in a mining camp, which he asserts attracts opportunists and brings out evil behavior more than life in an agricultural community does. He shows that in distant territorial locations the law is ineffective. Then he moves into his defense of vigilante justice. In the latter part of the chapter he writes: "Finally, swift and terrible retribution is the only preventive of crime, while society is organizing in the far West." He maintains that "in affairs of single combats, assaults, shootings, stabbings, and highway robberies, the civil law, with its positively awful expense and delay, is worse than useless." Without the cooperation of "good, law-loving, and order-sustaining men," he continues, "society would collapse in the throes of anarchy." While he grants that "self-constituted authority" is unnecessary in "civilized and settled communities," he reinforces his idea of how society

must be preserved in the last sentence of the chapter: "But where justice is powerless as well as blind, the strong arm of the mountaineer must wield her sword; for 'self-preservation is the first law of nature.'"

Dimsdale has a dogmatic tone that frequently borders on propaganda. In chapter 17, for example, he asserts that "for the low, brutal, cruel, lazy, ignorant, insolent, sensual, and blasphemous miscreants that infest the frontiers we entertain but one sentiment—aversion—deep, strong, and unchangeable. For such cases the rope is the only prescription that avails as a remedy." In chapter 20 he cloaks his opinion in the certainty of truth: "The truth is, that the Vigilance Committee simply punished with death men unfit to live in any community, and that death was, usually, almost instantaneous, and only momentarily painful." Dimsdale's narrations of the executions support his contention that the deaths were usually quick, but his personal opinions of the criminals are not always reasonable.

Dimsdale's immoderate judgments are clear in many passages. At the beginning of chapter 30, for example, his indignation crosses the line into invective: "The crimes and punishment of many a daring desperado have been chronicled in these pages; but among them all, none was more worthy of death than the blood-stained miscreant whose well-deserved fate is recorded in this chapter." After detailing Jake Silvie's crimes and punishment, Dimsdale reports that each of the men who pulled on the hangman's rope "felt that his strain on the fatal rope was a righteous duty. . . . Such an incarnate fiend, they knew, was totally unfit to live and unworthy of sympathy. . . . He lived a sordid and red-handed robber, and he died unpitied the death of a dog." Here, Dimsdale self-righteously takes the liberty of omnisciently reporting thoughts and feelings he could not know, which may or may not reflect the attitudes of some of the vigilantes.

Dimsdale often tries to show in his depictions of the "miscreants" that they deserve lynching, but he often intensifies his rhetoric to push his argument. In the opening of chapter 32, titled "Boone Helm," Dimsdale describes Helm as a "savage and defiant marauder, who died with profanity, blasphemy, ribaldry, and treason on his lips." Two pages later he refers to Helm as "all guilt and without a single redeeming feature in his character." With this sort of absolute pronouncement Dimsdale overstates his case: he supports opinion with opinion rather than opinion with fact. In the same chapter, which contains capsule biographies of several of those hanged, Dimsdale writes that James Daniels was executed because he threatened the lives of peo-

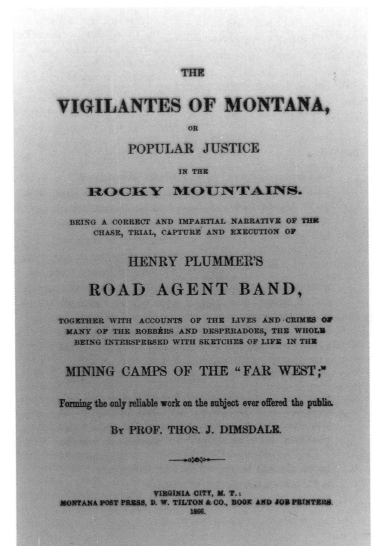

THE

VIGILANTES OF MONTANA,

OR

POPULAR JUSTICE

IN THE

ROCKY MOUNTAINS.

BEING A CORRECT AND IMPARTIAL NARRATIVE OF THE
CHASE, TRIAL, CAPTURE AND EXECUTION OF

HENRY PLUMMER'S

ROAD AGENT BAND,

TOGETHER WITH ACCOUNTS OF THE LIVES AND CRIMES OF
MANY OF THE ROBBERS AND DESPERADOES, THE WHOLE
BEING INTERSPERSED WITH SKETCHES OF LIFE IN THE

MINING CAMPS OF THE "FAR WEST;"

Forming the only reliable work on the subject ever offered the public.

BY PROF. THOS. J. DIMSDALE.

————◦•◦•◦————

VIRGINIA CITY, M. T.:
MONTANA POST PRESS, D. W. TILTON & CO., BOOK AND JOB PRINTERS.
1866.

*Title page for Dimsdale's only book, in which he argues for the justice
of vigilantism*

ple who testified against him, but he later slides into interpretation when he contends that he "was hanged . . . because he was unfit to live in the community." While Dimsdale's narration of the events may be dependable insofar as it is based on eyewitness accounts, his judgment is not necessarily so. He mixes fact, or what he accepts as fact, with bias; as a result, his accounting for the reasoning of the Vigilance Committee is not always reliable.

A reader might well wonder in a case such as Slade's whether the committee's attributed motives were really their motives or Dimsdale's interpretations. In chapter 24 Dimsdale states that the "Vigilance Committee now felt that the question of social order . . . had then and there to be decided." Later in the chapter he writes: "The Vigilantes deplored the sad but imperative necessity for the making of one example," and he concludes the chapter with an interpretation of the event: "The death of Slade was the protest of society on behalf of social order and the rights of man." From the narration it does seem as if the committee chose to hang Slade as an example, for the "most wonderful effect upon society" that Dimsdale says it had. However, it is difficult to tell where Dimsdale as a reliable narrator giving an account of what he believes to be true might leave off and where Dimsdale as an unreliable narrator imposing his own dogma might begin.

Dimsdale's narrowness of mind, evident in small touches in the narrative, together with his absolute pronouncements about criminals and about lynching as a remedy, cumulatively imply an author whose judgments need to be weighed and questioned. In chapter 22 he describes Indians—not a particular tribe or band—as "intent on scalping and other pleasant little amusements, in the line of ravishing, plundering, fire-raising, etc., for the exhibition of which genteel proclivities the Eastern folks recommend a national donation of blankets and supplies to keep the thing up. . . . If the Indians were left to the Vigilantes of Montana they would contract to change their habits at small cost. . . ."

He shows a similar condescension toward women. In chapter 13 he regrets that some women succeeded in stopping a hanging. Writing again in the editorial *we,* he observes:

> We cannot blame the gentle-hearted creatures; but we deprecate the practice of admitting the ladies to such places. They are out of their path. Such sights are unfit for them to behold, and in rough and masculine business of every kind women should bear no part. It unsexes them, and destroys the most lovely parts of their character.

Dimsdale goes on to suggest that a woman should be "a queen in her own home." The "gentle-hearted creatures" are fine as "sisters, mothers, nurses, friends, sweethearts, and wives," but they should not present impediments to the "masculine business" of lynching, which Dimsdale characterizes as imperative and unimpeachable.

Dimsdale is not always gallant in his treatment of women. In chapter 20, after a man called "the Greaser" has been hanged and then burned to ash in a bonfire, Dimsdale reports: "In the morning some women of ill-fame actually panned out the ashes, to see whether the desperado had any gold in his purse. We are glad to say that they were not rewarded for their labors by striking any auriferous deposit." He directs his derision toward the mercenary women, though he had earlier nonchalantly narrated how the crowd had fired more than a hundred shots into the swinging corpse of "the Mexican" before tossing it onto the fire.

Dimsdale's racist and sexist attitudes come together in a curious passage toward the end of the book. At the end of chapter 31, which he devotes to the career of Henry Plummer, Dimsdale notes "one instance of the many little incidents that so often change a man's destiny." While he was still in California and supposedly law-abiding, Plummer sold his assets and was intending to return to the East:

It is supposed that his infatuation for a Mexican courtesan induced him to forego his design and return to Nevada City. But for this trifling interruption, he might never have seen Montana, or died a felon's death. The mission of Delilah is generally the same, whether her abode is the vale of Sorek or the Rocky Mountains.

Thus ends the chapter in which Plummer has been portrayed as a murderer, a philanderer and homewrecker, a whorehouse brawler, and a crook. Although Dimsdale vilifies Plummer at every turn, he pauses here to deliver a stereotype about women, particularly nonwhite women.

Dimsdale's use of irony and understatement is part of his literary style. Most of the chapters have literary epigrams—proverbs, paraphrases from the Bible, quotations from poets such as John Milton; George Gordon, Lord Byron; and John Greenleaf Whittier, and especially from William Shakespeare. By making such allusions, Dimsdale implicitly places himself in a literary tradition. He often aspires to a literary style, as seen in this passage in the chapter on George Ives:

> Some of his ardent counsel shed tears, of which lachrymose effusions it is well to say no more than that they were copious. The vision of a long and scaly creature, inhabiting the Nile, rises before us in connection with this aqueous sympathy for an assassin.

This passage is in the quasi-literary, derivative style of nineteenth-century journalism. Elsewhere, Dimsdale uses wording such as "close proximity" and "swarthy visage," typical contemporary diction—the former showing wordiness and the latter reflecting the conventional portrayal of dark-featured persons as being evil. At times the humor is effective, as in the description of a man who had a fondness for "gold without labor, and horses without purchase," but this touch comes in the same sentence in which the author resorts to calling the criminal a "low-minded villain." The final judgment on Dimsdale's book must be that it is valuable not for its style or its worth as literature but as an account of the events in Montana in 1863–1864 and as a cultural document.

The Vigilantes of Montana has not received much critical attention and has been regarded more as a background book than as a primary text in nineteenth-century American literature. In his last paragraph Dimsdale expresses his hopes for the reception of his book:

> As a literary production he [the author] will be rejoiced to receive the entire silence of critics as his best reward. He knows full well what criticism it deserves, and is only anxious to escape unnoticed.

Regardless of Dimsdale's wishes, the book did receive notice not long after its publication. In *Roughing It* Twain refers to it as "a bloodthirstily interesting little Montana book." When he later quotes a sentence saying that Slade was "feared a great deal more than the Almighty," he compliments the author: "For compactness, simplicity and vigor of expression, I will 'back' that sentence against anything in literature." Twain's use of Dimsdale as a source, along with his praise of the book, has no doubt helped secure the book a place in literary history.

Dimsdale's place, though, is that of a footnote more than a main entry. In a chapter of *A Literary History of the American West* (1987) Levi S. Peterson mentions Dimsdale's book as an example of "historical literature of an informal and polemic nature." He refers to *The Vigilantes of Montana* in the same paragraph with Nathaniel Pitt Langford's *Vigilante Days and Ways* (1890), a book that is often cited by historians as following Dimsdale's lead in its treatment of vigilante justice. In *A Literary History of the American West* (1987), edited by J. Golden Taylor, James H. Maguire cites Dimsdale's book as a source for Twain's *Roughing It*. Dimsdale is conspicuously absent from other standard reference works in American biography, literary biography, and literary history.

In historical writings Dimsdale is frequently mentioned. In Wayne Gard's well-known *Frontier Justice* (1949) Dimsdale is covered in a footnote of thumbnail biography. In other historical works, especially works on the history of Montana, Dimsdale's work is a common topic. James McClellan Hamilton presents the standard biographical information about Dimsdale, referring to him as "a cultured Englishman." He also refers to *The Vigilantes of Montana* as being "brilliantly written," but he does not cite any passages or discuss the book as a piece of writing. In *Montana: A History of Two Centuries* (1976) Michael P. Malone and Richard B. Roeder do make reference to Dimsdale as a writer, but they do not discuss *The Vigilantes of Montana* as a text. They characterize Dimsdale as a "Radical Republican" in his political leanings, and they discuss him as a journalist: "Some of the best known early editors, like Thomas Dimsdale of the *Montana Post* . . . were better known for their prejudices than their talent."

Generally, historians discuss the quality of the book in terms of how accurate or reliable it is as history. Granville Stuart, a well-known settler and community leader in Montana's early days, mentions Dimsdale in *Forty Years on the Frontier* (1925). Stuart refers to *The Vigilantes of Montana* as "an abso-lutely correct narrative of the operations of that society." In *Montana: Images of the Past* (1978) William E. Farr and K. Ross Toole write that Dimsdale's is an "accurate and splendid" account but not complete; they say that the picture derived from Dimsdale in "subsequent writers" is "wildly distorted" in displaying lawlessness as being so prevalent. In "Afterthoughts on the Vigilantes" J. W. Smurr develops this point more thoroughly, asserting that later historians have followed Dimsdale too closely: "The greatest failing has been in making poor use of the older materials." In reference to both Dimsdale and Langford, Smurr says that the subject of vigilantism "has been treated superficially by the popular writers, the ones most people read." From the point of view of a historian, Smurr proposes that Dimsdale is "unreliable," and he cites the "vulgar boastfulness of Dimsdale in dealing with terrorism when applied to Western criminals."

Clyde A. Milner III, in "The Shared Memory of Montana's Pioneers," continues in the vein of skepticism. His analysis is interesting to compare with endorsements by Dimsdale's contemporaries such as Stuart. According to Milner, "Dimsdale's book, because it appeared so quickly after the actual events, became part of people's memories of those events." Pursuing the idea of shared memory, Milner goes on to write, "Although both Dimsdale and Langford relied on the memories of observers from the vigilante days, the accuracy of these books still may be questioned. Each book is an uncritical apology for the vigilantes' action." Both Smurr and Milner relate the ideological excesses to the question of historical accuracy; their skepticism does not constitute a dismissal of Dimsdale's book, but it does provide a point of view to balance against the writers of memoirs and popular history who generally commend the validity of *The Vigilantes of Montana*.

Elizabeth Stevenson in her *Figures in a Western Landscape* (1994) devotes a chapter to Dimsdale and his historical relation to Plummer. Like other scholars in the last forty years, Stevenson is skeptical of Dimsdale's reliability and authenticity. She grants that the "account is instantly vivid and engrossing" but cites as Dimsdale's greatest fault his failure to "document his descriptions and conclusions." In her judgment "He simply states or accepts the guilt of each successive hanged man and goes on with enthusiasm to make the reader see the sudden and violent death." She also writes, "It is as if he cannot see or comprehend the gross exaggeration of a claim for justice." Stevenson portrays Dimsdale as a man enthralled with the burgeoning new society in Virginia City, of which he was a prominent member. Thus, she sees his editorializing as a justification of a society in which he believed.

Stevenson also depicts Dimsdale as a friend of influential Republicans who may have wanted to rub Plummer out because they considered him a Democrat rising in power and therefore a political enemy. She summarizes recent research that suggests that Plummer may not have been as guilty as charged and that possibly Dimsdale's book has promulgated an inaccurate portrait of Plummer as the well-mannered sheriff yet sinister mastermind of an organized band of robbers and murderers. According to Stevenson, the portrayal of "such a striking instance of duplicity" in this "story of the bad man wrapped in the disguise of a good one" has been crucial in keeping the book popular. In Stevenson's interpretation, "the crusading editor let himself be swept beyond justifiable reasoning" because "he loved a new civilization to the point of blindness." As a result "he loaded all his partiality on the side of the better citizens—as it seemed to him."

While the question of Dimsdale's reliability is still open, recent studies no longer accept his accounts at face value. But because his is a contemporary treatment of a controversial topic, *The Vigilantes of Montana* will remain an item of interest. The accounts in the narrative (some of which may be inadvertent fiction) will no doubt continue to fascinate readers. Those scholars who believe Plummer has been unfairly maligned (not to mention unjustly executed) may try to rectify his image, but Dimsdale and others have established his legend. As Joseph Henry Jackson wrote about the status of legendary outlaws, "There are many who prefer to cherish the romantic legend, however much it may be shown to be pure fantasy; and I suppose there is no good reason why they should not do so." Jackson suggests several times in *Bad Company* (1977) that the public will believe what it wants to believe, and that will probably be the case with *The Vigilantes of Montana* and the subsequent works—both historical and fictional—that it has inspired.

References:

E. DeGolyer, Introduction to *The Vigilantes of Montana* (Norman: University of Oklahoma Press, 1953), pp. vii–ix;

William E. Farr and K. Ross Toole, *Montana: Images of the Past* (Boulder, Colo.: Pruett, 1978);

Wayne Gard, *Frontier Justice* (Norman: University of Oklahoma Press, 1949);

James McClellan Hamilton, *From Wilderness to Statehood: A History of Montana 1805–1900* (Portland, Oreg.: Binfords & Mort, 1957);

Michael P. Malone and Richard B. Roeder, *Montana: A History of Two Centuries* (Seattle: University of Washington Press, 1976);

Clyde A. Milner II, "The Shared Memory of Montana's Pioneers," *Montana: The Magazine of Western History,* 37 (Winter 1987): 2–13;

J. W. Smurr, "Afterthoughts on the Vigilantes," *Montana: The Magazine of Western History,* 8 (Spring 1958): 8–20;

Elizabeth Stevenson, "Editor and Outlaw: Thomas Dimsdale and Henry Plummer," *Figures in a Western Landscape* (Baltimore: Johns Hopkins University Press, 1994), pp. 62–77;

Granville Stuart, *Forty Years on the Frontier,* 2 volumes (Cleveland: Arthur C. Clark, 1925).

Timothy Flint
(circa 11 July 1780 – 16 August 1840)

Charles Duncan
Virginia Polytechnic Institute and State University

See also the Flint entry in *DLB 73: American Magazine Journalists, 1741–1850.*

BOOKS: *A Sermon, Preached May 11, 1808, at the Ordination of the Rev. Ebenezer Hubbard, Over the Second Church and Society in Newbury* (Newburyport, Mass.: E. W. Allen, 1808);

A Sermon, Delivered in Leominster, at the Commencement of the Year, Lord's Day, Jan. 1st, 1815 (Leicester, Mass.: Brown, 1815);

An Oration, Delivered at Leominster, July 4, 1815, before the Washington Benevolent Society of Lancaster and Sterling and of Leominster and Fitchburg (Worcester, Mass.: Manning, 1815);

The Columbian Harmonist: In Two Parts, to Which Is Prefixed a Dissertation upon the True Taste in Church Music (Cincinnati: Looker, Palmer & Reynolds, 1816);

Recollections of the Last Ten Years, Passed in Occasional Residences and Journeyings in the Valley of the Mississippi, from Pittsburg [sic] and the Missouri to the Gulf of Mexico, and from Florida to the Spanish Frontier: In a Series of Letters to the Rev. James Flint, of Salem, Massachusetts (Boston: Cummings, Hilliard, 1826);

Francis Berrian; or, The Mexican Patriot (2 volumes, Boston: Cummings, Hilliard, 1826; 3 volumes, London: Newman, 1834);

A Condensed Geography and History of the Western States; or, The Mississippi Valley, 2 volumes (Cincinnati: Flint, 1828); enlarged as *The History and Geography of the Mississippi Valley: To Which Is Appended a Condensed Physical Geography of the Atlantic United States, and the Whole American Continent* and *The United States and the Other Divisions of the American Continent* (Cincinnati: Flint & Lincoln, 1832);

The Life and Adventures of Arthur Clenning, 2 volumes (Philadelphia: Towar & Hogan, 1828);

George Mason, the Young Backwoodsman; or, 'Don't Give Up the Ship': A Story of the Mississippi (Boston: Hilliard, Gray, Little & Wilkins, 1829);

The Lost Child (Boston: Carter, Hendee, Putnam & Hunt, 1830); republished as *Little Henry, the*

Stolen Child: A Narrative of Fact (Boston: Simpkins, 1847);

The Shoshonee Valley: A Romance, 2 volumes (Cincinnati: Flint, 1830);

Lectures upon Natural History, Geology, Chemistry, the Application of Steam, and Interesting Discoveries in the Arts (Boston: Lilly, Wait, Colman & Holden, 1833);

Indian Wars of the West; Containing Biographical Sketches of Those Pioneers Who Headed the Western Settlers in Repelling the Attacks of the Savages, Together with a View of the Character, Manners, Monuments, and Antiquities of the Western Indians (Cincinnati: Flint, 1833);

Biographical Memoir of Daniel Boone, the First Settler of Kentucky: Interspersed with Incidents in the Early Annals of the Country (Cincinnati: Guilford, 1833); republished as *The First White Man of the West; or, The Life and Exploits of Col. Dan'l. Boone, the First Settler of Kentucky: Interspersed with Incidents in the Early Annals of the Country* (Cincinnati: Conclin, 1847); republished as *The Life and Adventures of Daniel Boone . . . New Edition, to Which Is Added an Account of Captain Estill's Defeat* (Cincinnati: James, 1868);

The Bachelor Reclaimed; or, Celibacy Vanquished. From the French (Philadelphia: Key & Biddle, 1834);

Journal of the Rev. Timothy Flint, from the Red River, to the Ouachitta or Washita, in Louisiana, in 1835 (Alexandria, La.?, 1835?).

OTHER: "Oolemba in Cincinnati," in *The Western Souvenir: A Christmas and New Year's Gift for 1829,* edited by James Hall (Cincinnati: Guilford, 1828), pp. 68–101;

"The Indian Fighter," in *The Token; a Christmas and New Year's Present,* edited by S. G. Goodrich (Boston: Carter & Hendee, 1830);

James O. Pattie, *The Personal Narrative of James O. Pattie of Kentucky, during an Expedition from St. Louis, through the Vast Regions between That Place and the Pacific Ocean,* edited by Flint (Cincinnati: Wood, 1831); republished as *Pattie's Personal Narrative of a Voyage to the Pacific and in*

Timothy Flint's home in Alexandria, Louisiana

Mexico, June 20, 1824–August 30, 1830 (Cleveland: Clark, 1905);

Joseph Droz, *The Art of Being Happy: From the French of Droz, 'Sur l'Art d'être Heureux'; in a Series of Letters from a Father to His Children, with Observations and Comments,* translated by Flint (Boston: Carter & Hendee, 1832);

"Nimrod Buckskin, Esq.," in *The Token; a Christmas and New Year's Present,* edited by Goodrich (Boston: Gray & Bowen, 1832);

"The Blind Grandfather," in *The Token and Atlantic Souvenir: A Christmas and New Year's Present,* edited by Goodrich (Boston: Gray & Bowen, 1832);

Pattie, *The Hunters of Kentucky; or, The Trials and Toils of Trappers and Traders during an Expedition in the Rocky Mountains, New Mexico, and California,* edited by Flint (New York: Graham, 1847);

Willard, *Inland Trade with New Mexico–Downfall of the Fredonian Republic,* edited by Flint (Cleveland: Clark, 1905).

Despite his background as New England minister, Timothy Flint became one of the more important men of letters in the American West during the first half of the nineteenth century. Demonstrating a remarkable range of interest and knowledge, he wrote books that classified geographical, historical, and biological features of the West. He also wrote fiction and served as a biographer for Daniel Boone, one of the enduring symbols of the West. Although much of Flint's work seems dated to twentieth-century readers, he was one of the best-known writers of his day and contributed substantially to conceptions of the literary West.

Born on or about 11 July 1780 in North Reading, Massachusetts, Timothy Flint was the fifth of nine children of William and Martha Kimball Flint. Although born into a farming family, Flint apparently did little work on the farm, probably because of ill health that plagued him all his life. His early lack of experience as a farmworker might account in part for Flint's failure when he attempted later in his life to support his own family by farming in Missouri. In any case, instead of doing farmwork as a child, Flint was sent to school, where he apparently flourished. Although biographical details of his early life are sketchy, commentators generally suggest that, after receiving some education from ministerial teachers in North Reading, Flint attended Phillips Academy in Andover, Massachusetts, in 1795.

From 1796 to 1800 Flint attended Harvard College, where both he and his cousin James Flint, who later helped persuade Timothy to write, decided to study for the ministry. After marrying Abigail Hubbard—daughter of the Reverend Ebenezer Hubbard—on 12 July 1802, Flint began his career as a minister for the parish of Lunenburg, forty miles from Boston. His tenure at Lunenburg lasted until 1814 but was apparently unsatisfactory to all. A salary dispute occasioned Flint's resignation, but his biographer emphasizes the coolness that had dominated the relationship between the young minister and his congregation. Some attribute the dissatisfaction with Flint to his failure to endorse strict Calvinist doctrine or to his laxity in performing ministerial duties. Although John Ervin Kirkpatrick suggests that Flint might have suffered from an inability or unwillingness to compromise his rigid principles, James K. Folsom posits a different interpretation of Flint's ties to the ministry:

> One does not get an overwhelming impression from Flint's writing that he was a man with a real call to the saving of souls, but rather that appurtenances of the clerical life attracted him. The satisfactions he wished to gain from the ministry, one feels, were not those of pastoral service, but rather the general satisfactions of the contemplative life—of study, of reflection, of literature.

In short, leading a congregation proved unpleasant for Flint, and his temperament apparently made him incompatible with the requirements of such a calling.

After resigning from the parish of Lunenburg, Flint became a missionary, first for the Massachusetts Society for Promoting Christian Knowledge and later for the Missionary Society of Connecticut. Working for the latter, he immigrated to the West for the first time in 1815, preaching to settlements in Ohio and Kentucky and later in Missouri. In order to perform his missionary duties Flint and his family traveled from Lunenburg to Cincinnati, a journey that included a month-long wagon trip to Pittsburgh. From there Flint, his wife, and their three children traveled by flatboat down the Ohio River. When Flint became seriously ill along the way, the family had to stop at Wheeling, and in November 1815 they finally arrived in Cincinnati.

Flint's missionary work continued in Ohio, Indiana, and Kentucky for much of 1816, and he soon asked to be reassigned to the Mississippi Valley. Although by 1818 Flint had severed all ties to missionary societies—apparently for many of the same reasons that he had failed to succeed as the minister of Lunenburg—he did not attempt to return to New England. Instead, he and his family lived in or near Saint Charles, Missouri, from 1816 through 1822. In 1821–1822 he tried to support his family by farm-

ing, and this venture might have proved disastrous if kindhearted neighbors had not intervened.

By 1823 Flint's fortunes began to change. He and his family moved to Alexandria, Louisiana, a town he had visited during his missionary days. There Flint presided over a small college, a position that paid him, for the first time in several years, enough to support his family in some comfort. Among other benefits of his stay in Alexandria, Flint met Judge Henry Bullard, a fellow Harvard graduate who supplied Flint with much of the background material he eventually used in *Francis Berrian; or, The Mexican Patriot* (1826), his first novel. Amid his newfound comfort, however, Flint again became seriously ill and returned with his family to New England, where he believed he would soon die. But James Flint helped him regain his health, and in late 1825 Flint returned to Alexandria. This was a move that marked a turning point in his life, for thereafter the Harvard-educated New Englander became a permanent resident of the West and a leading chronicler of western lands and people. After an initial period of tepid interest following his return, Flint became an avid promoter of migration to the West.

In addition to deciding to cast his lot in the West, the forty-five-year-old Flint also elected to become a writer. During his recuperation he had drafted what became *Recollections of the Last Ten Years, Passed in Occasional Residences and Journeyings in the Valley of the Mississippi, from Pittsburg and the Missouri to the Gulf of Mexico, and from Florida to the Spanish Frontier: In a Series of Letters to the Rev. James Flint, of Salem, Massachusetts* (1826), and on the trip back to Alexandria he began writing *Francis Berrian*. The first of these two works establishes the tone and range of his career as a writer and man of the West, and it offers a compelling guide to the transformation of both Flint and his country. Initially finding the West and westerners inferior to New England and its inhabitants, the writer gradually comes to respect and indeed embrace the rugged West. Purportedly a series of letters from Flint to his cousin, *Recollections* thoroughly details the history, geography, climate, population, and economic and social development of such venues as Pittsburgh, Cincinnati, New Orleans, and Alexandria—every place that his family visited between 1815 and 1825. The book represents Flint's rather late beginning of a writing career, and it initiated a period of more personal success than his earlier life had accorded him. Between 1826 and 1833 Flint produced the bulk of his writing, including six nonfiction books, five novels, and a translation.

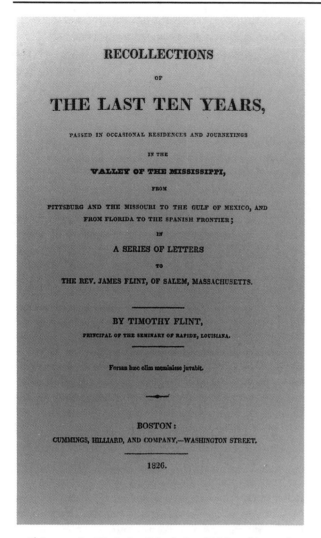

RECOLLECTIONS

OF

THE LAST TEN YEARS,

PASSED IN OCCASIONAL RESIDENCES AND JOURNEYINGS

IN THE

VALLEY OF THE MISSISSIPPI,

FROM

PITTSBURG AND THE MISSOURI TO THE GULF OF MEXICO, AND
FROM FLORIDA TO THE SPANISH FRONTIER;

IN

A SERIES OF LETTERS

TO

THE REV. JAMES FLINT, OF SALEM, MASSACHUSETTS.

BY TIMOTHY FLINT,
PRINCIPAL OF THE SEMINARY OF RAPIDE, LOUISIANA.

Forsan hæc olim meminisse juvabit.

BOSTON:
CUMMINGS, HILLIARD, AND COMPANY,—WASHINGTON STREET.

1826.

*Title page for Flint's fourth book, in which he celebrates the
coming of civilization to the West*

Flint's purpose in writing *Recollections*—and indeed his purpose in writing most of his nonfiction—was to articulate what Folsom calls Flint's belief in "the triumph of progress" and "the victory of civilization over barbarism." Although Flint admired the natural beauty of the West and the hardy spirit of its pioneers, one cannot underestimate how much he regarded the taming of the West as an unqualified good. In *Recollections,* for example, Flint describes the changes—all for the better, in his eyes—that had transformed Cincinnati in the years between his visits:

> Eleven years since, this was the only place that could properly be called a town, on the course of the Ohio and Mississippi, from Steubenville to Natchez, a distance of fifteen hundred miles. It is far otherwise now. But even then you cast your eye upon a large and compact town, and extended your view over the river to the fine buildings rising on the slope of the opposite shore,

and contemplated the steam-manufactories, darting their columns of smoke aloft. All this moving picture of wealth, populousness, and activity, has been won from the wilderness within forty years. . . . While I am writing, it is supposed to contain between sixteen and twenty thousand inhabitants, with the increase of every appendage to city comfort, beauty, and opulence, in more than a commensurate proportion with its increasing population.

This passage typifies Flint's writing in a couple of ways. It presents his attitude, a clear celebration of the many ways in which civilization had come to the West. He envisions the transformation of once sparsely populated lands into centers of commerce as being, for the most part, a happy and progressive development. In addition, the passage demonstrates both Flint's descriptive skills and his readiness to support his claims with raw data.

Flint became such an enthusiastic convert to the West and its people that in much of his nonfiction he consciously aimed to attract immigrants to the West. This purpose recurs often in *Recollections,* and it is evident in Flint's most ambitious taxonomic work, his two-volume *A Condensed Geography and History of the Western States; or, The Mississippi Valley* (1828), perhaps the work for which he is best remembered. Despite wanting his writing to engender westward migration, however, Flint offers a clear-headed admonition about the dangers that inevitably attend such a course. In *Recollections,* for example, he recounts many stories of emigrants who suffer in their attempts to move west:

> They were but too often wretchedly furnished with money, and the comforts almost indispensable to a long journey. It seemed to have been their impression, that if once they could arrive at the land of milk and honey, supplies would come of course. . . . Many suffered, died, and were buried by charity. Numerous instances of unrecorded suffering, of the most exquisite degree, and with every agonizing circumstance, occurred. The parties often were friendless, moneyless, orphans, infants, widows, in a strange land, in a large town, as human as might be expected, but to which, unfortunately, such scenes of suffering had become so frequent and familiar, as to have lost their natural tendency to produce sympathy and commiseration.

Flint encourages migration, but he refuses to minimize the risks and dangers in such a venture. His own travels throughout the Mississippi Valley and his frequent ill health made him a sober salesman, careful to depict the West as accurately as he can.

At the same time he began his career as a historian and geographer by publishing *Recollections* Flint also became a novelist with the publication of *Francis Berrian*. Although both works generated praise for the author, the nonfiction and the fiction branches of his writing diverge sharply thereafter. While *Francis Berrian* was relatively well received, his four other novels—*The Life and Adventures of Arthur Clenning* (1828), *George Mason, the Young Backwoodsman; or, 'Don't Give Up the Ship': A Story of Mississippi* (1829), *The Lost Child* (1830), and *The Shoshonee Valley: A Romance* (1830)—never attracted much attention. To twentieth-century readers Flint's novels seem didactic, and although he weaves his stories with interesting and important historical developments (many of which primarily concern the West), readers today may find it difficult to embrace Flint's scarcely disguised sermons. In *The Lost Child,* for example, he relates the heroic resolve of four-year-old Henry during the two years he spends in captivity after having been kidnapped. In the midst of Henry's woes, the voice of the narrator intervenes to offer this commentary:

> What a blessed thing it is, my dear young friends, amidst all the changes and chances of this vale of mortality and tears, to have a friend that no one can separate us from—a friend, who goes with us, wherever we go; who remains with us, wherever we remain; who is above us, and around us, by land and by sea, in sickness, in sorrow, in death; who watches over our mortal body, when it is consigned to its clay-cold bed; who will not suffer a hair of our head to perish in the grave; but will raise these vile bodies incorruptible and immortal! What an unspeakable privilege, to love, fear and trust such a friend!

One can see the rhetorical power of Flint as a preacher in this passage, but this posture does not serve him well in his career as a novelist.

Francis Berrian, which recounts the story of a soldier of fortune living in Mexico during the Mexican Revolution, was the novel Flint's contemporaries were most likely to read. Throughout its melodramatic plot Berrian serves as an exemplar of principled behavior and religious tolerance: his willingness to attend a Catholic worship sharply contrasts with the intolerance of his Mexican hosts, most of whom are portrayed as selfish and greedy. Thus, like all of Flint's novels, *Francis Berrian* imparts a moral lesson: in this case, Flint attempts to demonstrate the costs of intolerance and the benefits of acting morally and reasonably, two patterns of behavior that Berrian follows throughout the novel. Flint's attacks on intolerance, particularly on religious intolerance, can be traced to his unsuccessful tenures both as a minister of his Lunenburg parish and as a missionary.

Flint gained substantial financial rewards and a literary reputation following publication of *Recollections* in particular, but after 1825 his health, even more than his success as a writer, influenced much of his life. By 1827 he had decided that the climate of Alexandria taxed his constitution too heavily, and he moved the family to Cincinnati, where he established the *Western Monthly Review,* a journal that he edited from May 1827 through June 1830. In addition to his editorial duties he found it necessary to write nearly all the material in the journal during those years. In the first edition he announced that his purpose was to provide a literary resource for the people of the West and that the journal would cover various topics. True to his interest in describing westerners and the West, he published articles such as "The Missouri Trapper" (1827), "Sketches of the Character of the North American Savages" (1827), and "The Hermit of the Prairies" (1828). He also acted as a literary critic, producing pieces such as "To Correspondents" (1827), "Writers of the Western Country" (1828), and "Impediments of American Literature" (1829). In the first of these essays he offers commentary on James Fenimore Cooper, whose work Flint, at this stage of his career, did not praise highly.

This period was the most prolific in Flint's career as a writer: in addition to editing and writing for his new journal he published *A Condensed Geography* and three novels between 1828 and 1830. The first volume of *A Condensed Geography* deserves special attention from readers interested in the American West, which during Flint's lifetime was understood to include almost any part of the nation other than New England. Given the lack of information and resources on which Flint could draw, he thoroughly and accurately describes a huge expanse of territory, and he does so in detail. In his preface to the book Flint anticipates possible objections to his purpose and outlines the main goal he hopes to achieve with this work:

> To those, who have predicted, that he [Flint] would draw too largely upon the language and the coloring of poetry and the imagination, he can only say, that it has been his first aim, to compress the greatest possible amount of useful information into the smallest compass. He has, therefore, rather to apprehend, that the intelligent will find it too statistical and laconic, too much abbreviated, and divested of detail.

Flint offers not only botanical, biological, and other scientific data about the Mississippi Valley but also demographically breaks down the populations of each region under various rubrics. As a handbook of diverse raw data, it has few peers. One can look

THE

WESTERN

MAGAZINE AND REVIEW.

MAY, 1827.

EDITOR'S ADDRESS.

In presenting our readers with the first number of our proposed Journal, they will expect of us our inaugural speech, for in our country no one enters on the duties of a new office without one. We shall not follow the common example of reviewers by making our portico larger than our house, but shall come to our point at once;—Where is the use of a review at Cincinnati? At the census of 1830 the Mississippi valley will contain more than four millions of inhabitants. We are physically, and from our peculiar modes of existence, a scribbling and forth-putting people. Little, as they have dreamed of the fact in the Atlantic country, we have our thousand orators and poets. We have not a solitary journal expressly constituted to be the echo of public literary opinion. The teeming mind wastes its sweetness on the desert air. The exhausted author, after the pains of parturition, is obliged to drop the dear offspring of his brain into the immense abyss of a public, that has little charity for any bantlings, that do not bring money in their hands, and

> 'Where it is gone and how it fares,
> Nobody knows and nobody cares.'

The ornament, the grace, the humanity and even the lesser morals of society, as has been said a thousand times, essentially depend upon the cultivation of literature. A community without it is like a rude family without politeness, amenity and gentleness. It may be a family of wealth and power, and courted, as such, by

VOL. I.—No. 1.   2

Flint's statement of purpose in the first issue of his magazine

to *A Condensed Geography,* for example, to learn how much of the waters in Indiana were navigable, what literature had been produced in Ohio, or what kinds of diseases one might encounter in Alabama.

The book also provides a detailed history of many of those states then regarded as western—such as Florida, Alabama, and Louisiana, as well as Ohio, Indiana, and Missouri. Flint excelled as a collector of information, and one cannot underestimate the role he played in shaping his contemporaries' views of the West. Along with Cooper, Flint was one of the foremost commentators on all things western during the first half of the nineteenth century. Other writers such as William Cullen Bryant and Harriet Beecher Stowe lauded *A Condensed Geography,* and John D. Seelye has argued that in writing *The Confidence-Man: His Masquerade* (1857) Herman Melville relied on the book as a source of his descriptions. In a sense, Melville discovered his West partly through Flint.

After slightly revising the two-volume first edition, Flint republished the two volumes together in 1832 and enlarged them in another two-volume edition as *The History and Geography of the Mississippi Valley: To Which Is Appended a Condensed Physical Geography of the Atlantic United States, and the Whole American Continent* and *The United States and the Other Divisions of the American Continent.* In these volumes Flint again devotes substantial parts of his writing to presenting favorable pictures of the West in order to attract potential emigrants from the East.

The Shoshonee Valley: A Romance, the last of Flint's novels, is a final attempt to exploit his knowledge of the West for fictional purposes. Like his earlier novels, *The Shoshonee Valley* teaches a moral lesson, but it is much less didactic than his earlier novels. Folsom argues that it is Flint's best:

> If *George Mason* and *The Lost Child* are the nadir of Flint's fictional career, *The Shoshonee Valley* (1830), is, if not his best work, very near to it. This novel has always been critically neglected and is now unjustly forgotten. It represents Flint's final attempt to come to philosophical terms with the meaning of the advance of civilization, and in both profundity of conception and quality of execution it is, to my view at least, far superior to all Flint's other treatments of the theme.

The origin of the novel is in "Oolemba in Cincinnati," a short story Flint published in James Hall's *Western Souvenir* in 1828. One remarkable difference between the short story and the novel is in Flint's sympathy toward, which sometimes verges on celebration of, the ways of the Shoshone people.

As a novel about Native American life, *The Shoshonee Valley* inspires comparisons with Cooper's novels, and for the first time in Flint's work one can find similarities in philosophy between the two writers. Early in the first volume of the novel Flint describes his moral purpose in writing *The Shoshonee Valley:*

> This narrative contemplates [the Shoshone people] at the point of the first palpable influence of the introduction of money, and what we call civilization. It cannot fail to present a spectacle of great moral interest. With an apparent accession of new ideas, new comforts, new wants, and new views of things present and to come, these simple people are always seen to forego their simplicity, and become less wise; to change their skins for dresses of cloth, and to begin to suffer from the inclemency of the seasons; and to learn the use of our medicines, and modes of applying them, and to become subject to new and more mortal diseases; in short, to melt away, through the influence of our boasted civilization, like the snow wreath of their hills, when a clear sun arises on their southern exposure.

The complexity of this passage differs profoundly from the didactic messages often encoded in Flint's earlier novels, and it marks this novel as the best fictional work of his career.

When *The Shoshonee Valley* was published in 1830, Flint had already decided to cease publishing the *Western Monthly Review* for various reasons, including his inability to make a profit from the journal. His literary ambitions remained diverse during the next three years: he edited *The Personal Narrative of James O. Pattie of Kentucky, during an Expedition from St. Louis, through the Vast Regions between That Place and the Pacific Ocean* (1831) and translated *The Art of Being Happy: From the French of Droz, 'Sur l'Art d'être Heureux'; in a Series of Letters from a Father to His Children, with Observations and Comments* (1832), among other projects. But until 1833 he did not produce another work by which twentieth-century readers might remember him.

In that year Flint returned to a familiar interest in his attempts to encourage migration to the West, although turning his attention to the life of Daniel Boone in *Indian Wars of the West; Containing Biographical Sketches of Those Pioneers Who Headed the Western Settlers in Repelling the Attacks of the Savages, Together with a View of the Character, Manners, Monuments, and Antiquities of the Western Indians* and *Biographical Memoir of Daniel Boone, the First Settler of Kentucky: Interspersed with Incidents in the Early Annals of the Country* engendered one of the more interesting paradoxes of Flint's career. In both of these works Flint reconciled his unbridled enthusiasm for the cultivation of the West with the earnest desire of westerners such as Boone—whom Flint portrays as both heroic and good—to preserve the spaciousness of the wilderness.

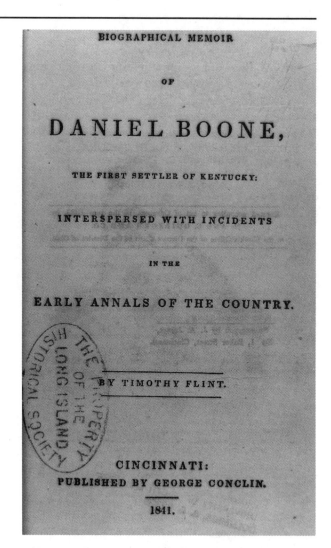

Frontispiece and title page for one of the two books featuring Daniel Boone that Flint published in 1833

When Boone is captured and eventually adopted by a Shawnee tribe, for example, Flint ponders Boone's attraction to the Indian way of life in this passage:

> It is probable, too, that his seeming satisfaction [in living among the Shawnee] is not altogether affected. The Indian way of life is the way of his heart. It is almost one thing to him, so that he wanders in the woods with expert hunters, whether he takes his diversion with the whites, or the Indians.

Flint is thus able to offer an overwhelmingly positive portrait of a man with whom he had considerable differences of opinion.

This ability to convey measured assessments of his subjects makes Flint a valuable recorder of the events and people he describes. He spends much time describing other cultures, including those of various tribes, in his works. Although Flint has generally a dismissive view of Native Americans (mostly because of

what he sees as their refusal to embrace Christianity), he is able to detail many features of Native American cultures with some fairmindedness, especially in *The Shoshonee Valley* and the *Biographical Memoir of Daniel Boone*. In the latter work, in fact, he occasionally manifests a grudging admiration for Native American mores. He devotes most of one chapter to discussing various Shawnee beliefs, including marriage and burial customs, and his commentary features anthropological and sociological information often written in a forceful, entertaining style. For example, Flint describes how the Shawnee's use of torture had evolved into a ritualistic matter of cultural importance:

> If the sufferer in these afflictions be an Indian, during the whole of his agony a strange rivalry passes between them which shall outdo each other, they in inflicting, and he in enduring these tortures. Not a groan, not a sigh, not a distortion of countenance is allowed to es-

cape him. He smokes, and looks even cheerful. . . . He even derides their ignorance in the art of tormenting; assures them that he had inflicted much more ingenious torture upon their people; and indicates more excruciating modes of inflicting pain, and more sensitive parts of the frame to which to apply them.

Although focusing here on one of the more brutal traditions of Native American culture, Flint also attempts to balance his appraisal several pages later:

While we read with indignation and horror, let us not forget that savages have not alone inflicted these detestable cruelties. Let us not forget that the professed followers of Jesus Christ have given examples of a barbarity equally unrelenting and horrible, in the form of religious persecution, and avowedly to glorify God.

Throughout several of Flint's works one finds such broad cultural commentaries on various explorers, settlers, missionaries, and backwoodsmen as well as Native Americans. The *Biographical Memoir of Daniel Boone* best exemplifies this tendency and is one of Flint's most enduring works.

After publishing *Lectures upon Natural History, Geology, Chemistry, the Application of Steam, and Interesting Discoveries in the Arts* (1833), another work that demonstrates the broad range of his interests, Flint moved to New York to coedit *The Knickerbocker; or, New-York Monthly Magazine.* Having already contributed several pieces to that journal, Flint was asked to assume editorial responsibilities of it when Charles Fenno Hoffman, its first editor, resigned following a disagreement with the publishers. Flint's tenure with *The Knickerbocker* was brief; in January 1834 he resigned because of ill health, which the harsh environment of New York had made worse.

Following this brief period in New York, Flint returned to Alexandria to live near his children. For the last six years of his life he traveled extensively in the West and made periodic trips to New England. Poor health curtailed his writing career, and his last publication—a series of letters commenting on the literature of the United States—appeared in the London *Athenaeum* in 1835. During one of his trips to the East a steamboat accident on the Mississippi River broke down his always-fragile health, and when he visited his brother in North Reading, the town in which he had been born sixty years earlier, he lived only a few more days. On 16 August 1840 he died, and he was buried in Salem, Massachusetts.

Few twentieth-century readers are familiar with Timothy Flint's works, but during his lifetime he exerted much influence. Writers such as Frances Trollope, William Cullen Bryant, and Harriet Beecher Stowe generously praised Flint and his works. Both Cooper and Melville may have drawn on Flint's conception of the West in their books. Moreover, Flint remains significant because of his contributions in shaping ideas of the West. In his taxonomic works he described the nature of the West; in his fictional works he explored the sensibilities of the West; and in his biographies he helped engender the national mythology of the West. As an author Flint busily inscribed the West, yet the West reshaped Flint as well. He left Lunenburg as a Harvard-educated minister, but by the end of his life he had become one of the first literary men of the West.

Biography:
John Ervin Kirkpatrick, *Timothy Flint: Pioneer, Missionary, Author, Editor* (Cleveland: Clark, 1911).

References:
James K. Folsom, *Timothy Flint* (New York: Twayne, 1965);
John D. Seelye, "Timothy Flint's 'Wicked River' and *The Confidence-Man,*" *PMLA,* 78 (1963): 75–79;
W. H. Venable, *Beginnings of Literary Culture in the Ohio Valley: Historical and Biographical Sketches* (Cincinnati: Clarke, 1891).

Papers:
Limited collections of Timothy Flint materials are held by the American Antiquarian Society and the Boston Public Library.

Mary Hallock Foote

(19 November 1847 – 25 June 1938)

Christine Hill Smith

BOOKS: *The Led-Horse Claim: A Romance of a Mining Camp* (Boston: James R. Osgood, 1883; London & Edinburgh: Gall & Inglis, 1903);

John Bodewin's Testimony (Boston: Ticknor, 1886; London: F. Warne, 1887);

The Last Assembly Ball, and The Fate of a Voice (Boston & New York: Houghton, Mifflin, 1889);

The Chosen Valley (Boston & New York: Houghton, Mifflin, 1892; London: Osgood & McIlvaine, 1892);

Coeur d'Alene (Boston & New York: Houghton, Mifflin, 1894);

In Exile and Other Stories (Boston & New York: Houghton, Mifflin, 1894);

The Cup of Trembling and Other Stories (Boston & New York: Houghton, Mifflin, 1895; London: Gay & Bird, 1896);

The Little Fig-Tree Stories (Boston & New York: Houghton, Mifflin, 1899);

The Prodigal (Boston: Houghton, Mifflin, 1900);

The Desert and the Sown (Boston: Houghton, Mifflin, 1902);

A Touch of Sun, and Other Stories (Boston & New York: Houghton, Mifflin, 1903);

The Royal Americans (Boston & New York: Houghton Mifflin, 1910; London: Constable, 1910);

A Picked Company (Boston & New York: Houghton Mifflin, 1912);

The Valley Road (Boston & New York: Houghton Mifflin, 1915);

Edith Bonham (Boston & New York: Houghton Mifflin, 1917);

The Ground Swell (Boston & New York: Houghton Mifflin, 1919);

A Victorian Gentlewoman in the Far West: The Reminiscences of Mary Hallock Foote, edited by Rodman W. Paul (San Marino, Cal.: Huntington Library, 1972);

The Idaho Stories and Far West Illustrations of Mary Hallock Foote, edited by Barbara Cragg, Dennis M. Walsh, and Mary Ellen Walsh (Boise: Idaho State University Press, 1988).

Mary Hallock Foote, circa 1874

OTHER: "Gidion's Knock," *The Spinners' Book of Fiction* (San Francisco: Paul Elder, 1907), pp. 77–91.

SELECTED PERIODICAL PUBLICATIONS–UNCOLLECTED:

FICTION

"The Picture in the Fireplace Bedroom," *St. Nicholas Magazine,* 2 (February 1875): 248–250;

"How Mandy Went Rowing with the Cap'n," *St. Nicholas Magazine,* 5 (May 1878): 449–453;

"A Story of the Dry Season," *Scribner's Monthly,* 18 (September 1879): 766–881;

"Menhaden Sketches: Summer at Christmas-Time,"
    St. Nicholas Magazine, 12 (December 1884):
    116–124;

"A Four-Leaved Clover in the Desert," *St. Nicholas
    Magazine,* 21 (May 1894): 644–650;

"How the Pump Stopped at the Morning Watch,"
    Century Magazine, 58 (July 1899): 469–472;

"The Eleventh Hour," *Century Magazine,* 71 (January 1906): 485–493.

NONFICTION

"A California Mining Camp," *Scribner's Monthly,* 15
    (February 1878): 480–493;

"A Seaport on the Pacific," *Scribner's Monthly,* 16
    (August 1878): 449–460;

"A 'Muchacho' of the Mexican Camp," *St. Nicholas
    Magazine,* 6 (December 1878): 79–81;

"A Diligence Journey in Mexico," *Century Magazine,*
    23 (November 1881): 1–14;

"A Provincial Capital of Mexico," *Century Magazine,*
    23 (January 1882): 321–333;

"From Morelia to Mexico City on Horseback," *Century Magazine,* 23 (March 1882): 643–655.

Mary Hallock Foote was one of the first woman regionalists to write about the western part of the United States. Born and raised in New York State, she went west with her mining engineer husband at the age of twenty-nine and did not live permanently in the East again until old age. The first woman to write about the mining camps of the West, she had a significantly different point of view from other woman diarists of her era because unlike most she was well educated and not taken up by the time-consuming tasks of farming or ranching. Her talent as an illustrator and soon her writing gave her a small income that allowed her to avoid most of the household drudgery of raising her growing family. In addition, like Willa Cather a generation later, Foote was able to maintain a detached perspective on the West because she was periodically able to visit the East. In her novels and romances Foote follows the conventions of Victorian novels and poetry, but her setting is the gritty frontier of the American West. The results of this incongruity are twofold: modern readers get a dated but fascinating glimpse into late-nineteenth-century attitudes about literature as well as realistic depictions of the commercial ventures that opened up the West for Anglo settlers and investors.

Born on 19 November 1847, Mary Hallock, the youngest child of Quaker parents Nathaniel and Anne Burling Hallock, grew up on the family farm outside Milton, New York, near the Hudson River. After high school she studied art at Cooper Union in New York City, where she excelled in woodcut illustrations. She made her professional debut in 1867 with four drawings published in A. D. Richardson's *Beyond the Mississippi.* Hallock soon was illustrating selections in *The Century Magazine* as well as books by Bret Harte and Constance Fenimore Woolson. Her biggest artistic honor was being asked to illustrate a gift edition of Henry Wadsworth Longfellow's *The Hanging of the Crane* (1875) and to visit Boston to meet the famous man. During art school she began a lifelong friendship with a fellow student, Helena de Kay. The two corresponded for more than forty years, and much of their correspondence is extant.

Hallock's professional career as an artist was on the rise when in 1873 she met Arthur De Wint Foote, a mining engineer from Yale, whom she married on 9 February 1876. At the time of her wedding, Mary Foote had been illustrating for magazines and books for nine years, and marriage did not slow her down. Armed with book commissions, wooden engraving blocks, and pen and ink, she moved to the West with her husband and lived for most of the next fifty years in small mining towns in Colorado, Idaho, and California. At first Foote continued merely illustrating, but around 1878 her friends in the East encouraged her to write travelogues for publication to accompany her drawings. Conveniently, her best friend Helena de Kay had married Richard Watson Gilder, the influential associate editor of *Scribner's Monthly* and the editor of *The Century Magazine,* which continued the policies of the former in 1881. Foote's short pieces were published in *The Century Magazine* and also in the *Atlantic Monthly.* Soon Foote tried her hand at writing novels. Because her husband, while a brilliant engineer, was not always a practical one and was sometimes unemployed, Mary Foote's work augmented the Footes' usually precarious income. During the course of her career she wrote twelve novels, three collections of short stories, and one collection of stories for children. Almost all of her work first appeared serially in *The Century Magazine* and within the year was published in book form.

Initial reviews of Foote's illustrations and later of her first novels were positive. She was called "the dean of women illustrators" in August 1900 by *The Critic,* which had on 10 June 1893 lauded Foote for dealing with western themes in her fiction, explaining that because of her "big and strong and manly" material, "It is a patriotic duty to extend our felicitations to Mrs. Foote." Reviews of her novels shrunk in size after about 1900, however, and there are only a few articles on her between the review of her last novel in 1919 and a small burst of Foote scholarship in the 1970s and 1980s. Even then there are only a couple of essays to date that cover all of Foote's work and only one full biography.

In her first professional writings—travel sketches of California—Foote is the tourist, giving *Scribner's* readers picturesque pastiches such as "A California Mining Camp," about New Almaden, California, where her husband had his first post as a mining engineer in 1877, and "A Sea-Port in the Pacific," about Santa Cruz, California, where she and their first child, a boy, lived for part of a year. Since the article about New Almaden was pieced together by the Gilders from her letters, it is a little choppy but nonetheless vividly describes the arid, mountainous landscape and the isolated world of mineworks and worker settlements. Foote then turns her attention to the colorful inhabitants of the town, describing the three distinct ethnic "camps": Cornish, Mexican, and Chinese. The remainder of "A California Mining Camp" describes the arid terrain and seasonal changes of the region.

"A Sea-Port on the Pacific" is a more polished piece yet lacks the spontaneity of the New Almaden article. Replete with allusions to British and European culture, it is a tour of the seaside town that includes descriptions of the cliffs and beaches, the ruins of the old mission, New England–style houses, and the profusion of non–New England foliage. Foote, who made few friends in this beautiful but alien environment, obliquely brings up a theme that runs throughout her fiction, that of transplanted easterners who are unhappy in the West, although they have made their lives there. These characters are almost invariably women who because of a father's or husband's job or career must live in the West. Foote's letters to Helena Gilder from this time indicate her yearning for the eastern change of seasons and the congenial company of educated, eastern friends. "A Sea-Port on the Pacific" also touches on a related theme that echoes throughout Foote's nonfiction, fiction, and letters: that of the differences between eastern and western society. From the first, Foote defends the West's promise and energy yet uses the values of the East as touchstones of refinement and culture.

Other short writings from this early period include "A 'Muchacho' of the Mexican Camp" (1878), a sketch about a little local boy in New Almaden; "The Story of a Dry Season" (1879), a heavy-handed, partly autobiographical tale about a young Santa Cruz mother who feels forced to choose between her husband and her baby; and "In Exile," written in 1877–1878, which became the title story of her first collection, *In Exile and Other Stories* (1894). In "In Exile" Foote puts revealing speeches into the mouth of a mining engineer who explains to a comely young schoolteacher that in remote western wastes, men have jobs to absorb them while women pine for the "attachments" of settled communities. "Most women," he says, "require a background of family and friends and congenial surroundings." This sentiment poignantly echoes Foote's own deep loneliness for her friend Helena Gilder and for her family, despite her love and joy in her husband and baby. She was to bring up the theme of what women sacrifice by moving to the West many times in her fiction, often in asides.

The Footes spent the better part of the next two years in Leadville, Colorado, during the silver rush days of 1879 and 1880. Arthur managed a mine, and Mary, ever one of the "protected women of that time"—as she recalled in a 15 October 1922 letter to Thomas Dawson, the curator of the State Historical Society of Colorado—worked on illustrations and stories while doing her best to ignore the rowdy town around her. After the Colorado job ended, Foote was able to accompany her husband when he was hired to assess silver mining possibilities in the interior of Mexico. Her three-part travelogue of the trip for *The Century Magazine,* published in November 1881 and January and March 1882, describes an almost feudal Mexico, as the Footes traveled by armed convoy, often on horseback, and stayed with several aristocratic landowners who lived in the grand European style in the midst of impoverished peons. Foote revels in the charming, centuries-old architecture and makes frequent mention in all three articles of what she considers the medieval condition of Mexican technology and culture. She keeps the tone upbeat, however—perhaps knowing her audience—and focuses attention on the exotic costumes of the people and the beauty of the cities, hamlets, and countryside through which her party passes. Foote's only criticism of the culture comes out as she slowly realizes how little personal freedom women in Mexico have. She is frustrated when she is chaperoned by a retinue of servants even in the smallest towns and not allowed to sketch at will.

After the Mexican trip the family needed money to augment their income when Arthur Foote was jobless; money was tight even after he initiated a large, protracted irrigation project near Boise, Idaho, that would last eleven years, from 1884 to 1895. Mary began writing novels to keep her growing family afloat. She had a second child while staying with her parents after coming back from Mexico but kept to her writing. Elizabeth Townsend Foote was born in Milton on 9 September 1882.

Foote's first three novels are set in Leadville during the silver-boom years. They generally reflect

An illustration by Foote for her three-part Mexican travelogue, published in The Century Magazine *in 1881–1882*

a youthful confidence and a love of the novels of Sir Walter Scott and James Fenimore Cooper. Foote chose the romance form, and at first was liberal with medieval and mythic allusions and parallels for these sentimental mining stories. The Leadville novels were written in Milton, while she was living with her parents, and in Boise after she had rejoined her husband. Mary went back and forth from Milton to Leadville in 1879 and 1880, avoiding the writers in Leadville and caring for her son, who was often ill. After her husband's job as mine manager in Leadville was terminated, she stayed in Milton with her parents and the baby between 1880 and 1884, except for occasional vacations along the northeastern shore with Arthur

and other members of their families. Arthur started visiting and making irrigation plans in Idaho several years before Mary and the two children moved there in 1884.

Foote's first novel, *The Led-Horse Claim: A Romance of a Mining Camp* (1883), has echoes of William Shakespeare's *Romeo and Juliet* (1599). The plot involves the growing affection between Cecil Conrath, the well-brought-up and modest sister of Harry Conrath, an unscrupulous ruffian mine owner, and George Hilgard, the good-looking, earnest manager of a rival mine. Cecil's unsavory brother tries to jump Hilgard's mine; violence ensues; the couple parts; and they are unexpectedly and coincidentally reunited back in the East.

Foote wrote in her 1922 letter to Dawson that she had planned to end the story

> as I believe it would have ended: the young pair would, in the order of things as they were, never have seen each other again. But my publisher wouldn't hear of that! I had to make a happy ending.

In *The Led-Horse Claim* Cecil is the first in an increasingly sophisticated line of heroines. In the early novels Foote's heroines are naive and protected; in the later works they are often worldly, sophisticated, and even occasionally jaded. As Foote notes in her letter to Dawson, Cecil was a "silly sort of heroine . . . Yet girls were like that, 'lots of them!' in my time." Reviewers from eastern magazines such as the *Atlantic, Book-Buyer,* and the *Spectator* lauded her early novelistic efforts. Her friend Helena Gilder later echoed their views in an 1894 issue of *Book Buyer* by stating that Foote's novels represented a point of view "which was a contrast to all that had been written before of the West—more delicate, more sympathetic, and especially more moral."

Foote's heroes in *The Led-Horse Claim* and in her next novel, *John Bodewin's Testimony* (1886), are stalwart, honest types, given to few words, but fiercely loyal to their friends. Foote often compares them to Greek heroes and Arthurian knights. The more interesting characters in Foote's early novels are not the protagonists but those in supporting roles such as the slightly seedy but honorable doctor in *Led-Horse Claim* and the disreputable scoundrel with a weakness for damsels in distress, Col. Billy Harkins in *John Bodewin's Testimony.*

Foote's second novel deals with more claim disputes and another couple who find themselves on opposite sides of a legal battle. The heroine, Josephine Newbold, is a mere pawn between her capitalist father and the honest surveyor John Tristram Bodewin. The plot is based on a case Arthur was involved with in Denver, and the setting, as in the first novel, is a realistic portrait of the bustling, violent mining town Leadville must have been. Yet Foote consciously distances herself from the rough-and-tumble milieu of western fiction by men. The heroine's father notes that Bodewin, while indeed being "one of the types of the place," is "Not the red-flannel shirt and revolver style, but something a little more subtle." Foote also ends the book on as lyric and romantic a note as in any of her fiction.

The last image of Bodewin and his demure bride is of their alighting at a desert train station as they prepare to start a new life in the West. The mistakes they made in Colorado are past. They can begin again, their former lives a dark shadow, with the "Wind of the great Far West, soft, electric, and strong, blowing up through gates of the great mountain ranges. . . . Wind of prophesy and of hope, of tireless energy and desire." In classic American fashion, they are given the chance (or the illusion) of a new life by starting over elsewhere, as Foote and her husband did several times themselves. *The Literature of the American People* (1981) calls *John Bodewin's Testimony* Foote's best book and cites Foote as "the first realist" of the Far West for these Leadville novels.

The most interesting character in the final Leadville novel, *The Last Assembly Ball, and The Fate of a Voice* (1889), is the landlady, Mrs. Fanny Dansken. This upwardly mobile widow manages to beguile one of her well-brought-up young boarders to the extent that he marries her and settles in the West. A more realistically rendered and mature female type, she marks an energetic shift from the conventional, pliant ingenues of the earlier romances. The hero and heroine of the novel, gentlemanly Frank Embury and Millie the maidservant, lack Mrs. Dansken's sparkle.

James H. Maguire asserts that Foote's structure "emphasizes the grimly realistic ending" of *The Last Assembly Ball,* and certainly it is the darkest of the Leadville novels in tone. However, aside from the unlucky Frank getting himself killed in an unnecessary duel, the story has a happy ending for the female characters. Mrs. Dansken gets an eastern husband younger and better educated than herself, and the waiflike Millie develops a short career in nursing and then marries a rich rancher from Montana. The opportunities for resourceful women open up in this novel, and Foote's ostensible hero dies in the duel because he insists on sticking to outmoded, European standards of etiquette.

The Fate of a Voice, a novella, was published in the same volume as *The Last Assembly Ball* and has all the features—autobiographical, geographic, and literary—of Foote's other fiction. An aspiring young singer, Madeline Hendrie, comes west for her health to a lovely river in Idaho. She is aggressively pursued by the engineer, Aldis, who wants her to give up her artistic aspirations to marry him and stay in the West. In a distinct contrast to Willa Cather's Thea Kronborg in *The Song of the Lark* (1915), the talented and professionally trained singer in this tale is ridiculed for wanting a separate professional career and in the end abandons her career to her romantic idea of love. The book includes some revealing arguments between the two lovers, especially in light of Foote's situation, stranded as she was in Boise with three children (another daughter had been born in 1886) and a husband whose irrigation schemes had fallen on hard times. The narrator casually informs the reader at the end of the tale that Madeline "threw away a charming career, just at its outset, and went West with a husband–not anybody in particular. It was altogether a great pity." Although the novella concludes with some uplifting words about "the dawn of a new day of art and beauty" in the West, Foote's resentments are all but transparent.

"Pictures of the Far West," a series of illustrations with accompanying commentary and explanation by Foote, ran in *The Century Magazine* from November 1888 to November 1889 and was collected in *The Idaho Stories and Far West Illustrations of Mary Hallock Foote* (1988). The sketches of daily life in the Foote's Idaho canyon are striking not for the pleasant but prosaic drawings but for the sometimes grim texts that accompany them. While some of the short essays foreground positive attributes of the West–its vast beauty, its restful stillness, and the resilience of the settlers–most of them also allude to the discontent and anxiety of settling a remote region. In "The Coming of Winter" Foote notes that the young wife in the sketch

> is not so sure of the marksman's aim as she would have been a year before she married him. He is one of an uncertain crop of husbandmen that springs up quickly on new soil, but nowhere strikes deep roots.

Foote picks up this theme in other essays, most notably in the last of the series, "The Winter Camp–A Day's Ride From the Mail," in which she explains that to "get left" in an unprofitable western locale is especially frustrating for an educated man with "technical training." She notes that such a life is one of "conspicuous tests, moral and physical," and that "the capable man with his hands tied, in a community where life means nothing if not action, finds there is a bitter difference between the 'something' that takes the place of work . . . and the divine gift of a man's own work."

Biographer Lee Ann Johnson asserts that Foote's near desperation at this point with her life in Idaho accounts for the dramatic strength of these essays. Foote was contending with the effects of undercapitalization for her husband's massive irrigation scheme for the Boise River. His drinking problem, which had surfaced only occasionally in the past, worsened considerably. The editors of *The Idaho Stories and Far West Illustrations* note that Foote presents a realistic West of daily cares and family life, not the "playground for masculine adventure" that men such as Frederic Remington and Theodore Roosevelt portrayed in the pages of *The Century Magazine* and other magazines.

The Chosen Valley (1892) is a more sophisticated novel than those set in Leadville. There is the same kind of Romeo and Juliet romance between the young people from rival claims–this time irrigation claims rather than mining claims–but the family dynamics are drawn more subtly than before. Young Philip Norrison goes to Idaho after finishing his college engineering training to help his opportunistic and selfish father build a dam. Philip becomes enamored of the fresh young daughter of his father's former partner, the stubborn Scotsman named Robert Dunsmuir, and comes to see his father's greed and shortsightedness. Like Foote's husband, Dunsmuir is an excellent engineer but an impractical visionary who cannot find the capital to finance the grand irrigation ideas he has for his small piece of prime river property. He and Norrison are at loggerheads about the project for ten years until fate takes a hand, destroying Dunsmuir but uniting the two lovers. An important theme in *The Chosen Valley* is that of polish and eastern education versus western experience. As Maguire points out, the untutored, westernized children of Dunsmuir feel neglected and inadequate because they lack an eastern education, while young Philip Norrison declines a Grand Tour of Europe to come to the West and get practical knowledge of the New World.

The reviews of *The Chosen Valley* in 1893 were mixed. The reviewer for the 10 June 1893 issue of *The Critic* stated that there was "no plot at all" to the story, and the reviewer for *The Nation* of 16 March argued that the novel was seriously "impeded by insignificant discourse," citing Foote's overuse of the technical details of irrigation. Most reviewers, however, praised the story for its patriotic theme of western settlement, its characterization of greed, and, as the critic for the 16 February *Dial* asserted, its "clear-cut style and vivid phrases." As Foote's fame as a novelist continued to grow, her reputation as an illustrator had remained high, and she was invited to judge etchings at the Chicago World's Fair in 1893.

Foote's next novel, *Coeur d'Alene* (1895), is based on the events that transpired in the Idaho mine of Coeur d'Alene during the summer of 1892. Foote sets a romance plot in a particularly violent episode, in which a mining union blew up a mill and later killed civilians in an ambush. Foote favors the mine owners' point of view in the novel, although she presents a drunken, degenerate mine manager, Frederick Bingham, as one of the villains. She describes in detail the good family that Bingham comes from in the East; his sister, the mild Faith Bingham, is the love interest for the hero. Foote

UNDERGROUND.

Frontispiece for Foote's first book, The Led-Horse Claim: A Romance of a Mining Camp

stresses the worthy antecedents that have given Faith her sweet and moral nature.

Darcie, the affable hero, turns out to be John Darcie Hamilton, a son of a member of the British syndicate board that owns the mine, sent out to do undercover work and expose the union's foul dealings. Almost all of the union characters are portrayed as low-class anarchists and drunkards, bent on destroying what Foote paints as an equitable and, except for the behavior of the manager, humanely run mining concern. Foote creates dramatic scenes between the hero, who has been wounded in a union ambush, and the faithful, distraught heroine, while dynamite explodes and bullets fly around them. In the end the corrupt union men are either killed or rounded up by the federal troops, control of the mine is restored to the owners, and Darcie, installed as the new manager of the mine, marries Faith.

In two unpublished letters she wrote to Clarence Clough Buel, an editor at *The Century Magazine,* in late 1892 and early 1893, Foote explains that she

got her facts for the novel from state testimony at the trial and also from one of the mine managers. The magazine had apparently been worried about Foote's accuracy and potential lawsuits. Foote held her ground, defending the mine managers as reasonable and denouncing the mob of outside agitators that the union brought in to ruin the smooth running of the mine. Historians now tend to view the Coeur d'Alene strike with more sympathy for the union, finding the strike reasonable and rejecting the rumored ambush and massacre. Most period reviews of the novel took an antiunion stance and praised Foote for making a stirring romance out of such violent happenings. The reviewer for *The Nation* of 10 January 1895, however, criticized her for using the same stock lovers: "The serious labor troubles at the Coeur d'Alene mines lose actual and literary value by subordination to a tiresome love story."

In addition to the title story, *In Exile and Other Stories* (1894) includes five stories, three of them set in the West. "A Cloud on the Mountain" deals with a theme similar to that in "In Exile": how easterners, especially women and children, may or may not acclimate to western locales. The story portrays an unlettered Idaho canyon girl, Ruth Mary, who, happy living by her wild river, does not understand her mother's pining for settled places back in the East. The story draws from Alfred Tennyson's "The Lady of Shalott" (1842) in both its imagery and its plot, with Ruth Mary cast as the innocent maiden who floats down the river to her beloved and to her death. This seemingly incongruous pairing of opulent mythic poem and prosaic western American setting works quite well in the story. The other western stories feature conventional romantic plots. The main character of "The Watchman" is a man whose job it is to make sure the costly irrigation ditches built by a large corporation do not break and lose precious water. In "The Rapture of Hetty" a young man Hetty's family does not like rides off with his love during a Christmas dance.

Two other stories in the collection, "The Story of the Alcazar" and "Friend Barton's 'Concern,'" are set in the East. Considered the best story in the volume by several critics, "The Story of Alcazar," set on the Maine coast, tells the tale of the suffering and death of a guilty sea captain who had allowed all aboard a slave ship to starve to death. "Friend Barton's 'Concern'" portrays the plight of the hapless family of an unworldly Quaker man who decides he must travel from his family and farm one summer to attend a Quaker convention.

The four stories in *The Cup of Trembling and Other Stories* (1895) cover a range of disturbing subjects, treating adultery, disfigurement, under-handed courtship, and suicide. The tales were written during the dark days of the Footes' Idaho venture, when funding for Arthur's projects came and went as dramatically as it might have in one of Mary's novels. The title story has a daringly different kind of protagonist for Foote: an adulterous woman. Foote explores the shaky moral ground upon which the fragile, selfish Esmee and her young paramour stand and finds it to be untenable. Esmee herself realizes how useless and even harmful she has been to others and lets a spring avalanche bury her in the lovers' mountain cabin.

Two other stories also deal with suicide. In "Maverick" young Rose Gilroy takes her life because she cannot bear the isolation of living at her father's Idaho stagecoach stop. She does not love Maverick because his face is disfigured, and she rides off to certain death in the lava beds of southern Idaho to avoid him. In "The Trumpeter" the suicide is an attractive but careless young soldier stationed in the wilds of Idaho. Henniker the trumpeter disappoints one woman, deserts his half-Bannock Indian wife, and, several years later, finding himself lame, homeless, and spurned in public by a sturdy little boy who turns out to be his own son, drowns himself in the Snake River. Foote in this story discusses the status and treatment of Native Americans and gives the reader a glimpse of the horse-rich northwestern Indian culture of the region.

One story in the collection, "On a Side-Track," has a conventionally happy ending. It has familiar Foote characters: a naive Quaker maiden, her mild father, and a young westerner, Charles Ludovic. He, too, is a Quaker, but one who has committed manslaughter after being greatly provoked. These characters and others are snowbound on a train trip halfway to Pocatello, Idaho, giving the young man time to woo and win his bride.

The reviewer of *The Cup of Trembling and Other Stories* for *The Nation* of 27 February 1896 extols writers such as Foote who renounce the growing tide of realism, noting with approval that "story-tellers cultivate a gracious intention to entertain, and an amiable desire to give pleasure rather than pain." This remark would have given Foote great pleasure, as she deplored the ugliness she found in the realistic writers of her day. At the end of the review the critic discerningly sums up most of Foote's characters: "At all events, her people have always come from somewhere else, and one feels sure that, if they are permitted to live long enough, they will go home again." Foote's letters and stories make it plain that during the Idaho years she longed for the East and found contentment in the West only after

her husband landed a permanent, well-paying job in 1895 managing a mine in Grass Valley, California.

Foote collected nine of her stories for children in the *The Little Fig-Tree Stories* (1899). These vividly depict a late-nineteenth-century slant on childhood, eastern versus western values, and the frustration she felt at her western exile. Through her child characters Foote explores her own reactions to a life apart from extended family and from cultural and geographic touchstones. The stories are mostly pastiches of ordinary life intended for an eastern juvenile audience, the readers of *St. Nicholas Magazine,* but one can sometimes sense the tension between Foote's impulse to depict the real West and her yearning to create cheerful pioneer tales.

The lead story, "The Flower of the Almond and the Fruit of the Fig," is a playful example of eastern values transplanted to western settings. In the spirit of "The Fir Tree" by Hans Christian Andersen and "The Silver Party" by fellow *St. Nicholas* writer Louisa May Alcott, Foote brings to life the trees in a California fruit orchard. She paints a pretty botanical tableau, all the while using it to depict the class structure and rigid moralizing of her own culture and to some degree her era. From a spirited discussion between the various species of trees in the orchard (some transplanted and therefore exiled, and some native), we learn of Foote's generally conservative views on heredity (blood will always tell), tradition (it's good), and regional differences (the East has high culture and meaningful family history; the West is more progressive and vital, yet a little shallow).

Foote's subsequent tales in *The Little Fig-Tree Stories* fall into one of two less allusive types, each in its own way exploring exile. The Idaho sketches depict the simple days of displaced eastern children, who were "transplanted in their babyhood to the far West" and live with their families in a canyon near Boise. The other, more lyrical sketches lovingly describe aspects of the Hallocks' family farm in New York. In this second group Foote approaches the skill of Sarah Orne Jewett and other local colorists in her delineation and appreciation of detail and nuance. Even the four stories set in New York, however, touch on one kind of exile or another.

In the short novel *The Prodigal* (1900) Foote deals primarily with Clunie Robert, the Prince Hal–like figure of a ne'er-do-well son of British wealth, who is inspired to straighten out his life because of the influence of a good woman. The San Francisco setting of *The Prodigal* is more interesting than the characters in this story, for Foote gives fascinating glimpses of busy docks full of clipper ships and steamers, fashionable streets thronged with

*Foote's drawing of a house in Leadville, the setting for her first three novels (Hague
Collection, Henry E. Huntington Library and Art Gallery)*

gaily dressed urbanites, and romantic footpaths to the hills overlooking misty San Francisco Bay.

Foote continued to write for another twenty years into the twentieth century, though she notes in her letter to Dawson that the vogue for her sort of sentimental story had passed by then. In her next novel, *The Desert and the Sown* (1902), Foote still shows some of the bitterness of the Idaho years in her somber tale of a pioneer couple, who, eloping from disapproving parents, become separated in the West and meet again only many years later after the man has become a recluse in the wilderness. Johnson considers this novel Foote's most realistic and least sentimental.

Most of the stories in *A Touch of Sun, and Other Stories* (1903) had been first published before the turn of the century. "A Touch of Sun" deals with an older couple who get involved with their son's courtship of a woman with an allegedly unsavory past. "The Maid's Progress" depicts a family's strange, repressed journey through rural Idaho in

search of their son's grave. "Pilgrims to Mecca," one of Foote's most memorable stories, is about a snobbish western matron who wants to take her daughter to the East for finishing school. She learns just how shallow and unwanted such training is. "The Harshaw Bride," like "The Maid's Progress," has a woman who is betrothed to one member of a family end up marrying another almost by default. Such situations are common in Foote's fiction.

After *The Royal Americans* (1910)—set during the Revolutionary War, her only novel that does not concern the West—Foote in *A Picked Company* (1912) follows a group of pioneers traveling overland from New England to Oregon. One of the main characters is a morally dubious femme fatale of southern blood, Stella, who ends up a pathetic prostitute and is killed by her husband. Even though Foote abhorred the bleakness of realism, during the course of her career she became more realistic. Perhaps she had taken to heart the words of the reviewer in the 17 November 1894 issue of *The Critic* who complained about "the same exasperatingly lovely virgin and adventuresome youth, in whose love-affair the interest of Mrs. Foote's novels usually culminates."

Foote wrote her last three novels before the beginning of the 1920s. In *The Valley Road* (1915) she explores the complicated, semiautobiographical saga of two families in a mining-irrigation project in California's Sacramento Valley. Foote comments on the extent to which parents can interfere in their children's lives, noting that "the understanding of one generation [does not] fit the needs of the next." *Edith Bonham* (1917) is a tribute to Foote's great friend Helena Gilder, who had died the year before. It is a tale about an educated, cultivated best friend of a dying woman who leaves the East to care for her friend's growing family in an isolated settlement in Idaho. Edith's characteristics are similar to those of Helena, and the widower is a strong, silent type and a poor communicator who resembles Mary's stolid husband, Arthur. In *The Ground Swell* (1919), her last novel, the seventy-one-year-old Foote tells the intricate story of an older couple and their three grown children, who live in and travel to various parts of the country and the world. Foote tackles issues of marital infidelity, alcoholism, and World War I-era alternative lifestyles for women.

In the 1920s Foote wrote an autobiography that was not published until 1972. *A Victorian Gentlewoman in the Far West: The Reminiscences of Mary Hallock Foote* is a fascinating document that details Foote's life and her observations of the settlement of the West. While Foote glosses over some of the painful aspects of her life, she nonetheless relates many of the trials and triumphs of her pioneering, peripatetic existence. She recalls her roles as a professional illustrator, a travel writer in rural Mexico, a successful novelist supporting her family, and the wife of a mining and irrigation engineer. Several years after her husband retired from the mine in Grass Valley, the Footes moved to Massachusetts to live with their daughter, Betty. Arthur died in 1933, and Mary survived him by five years, dying in 1938.

In 1972 Wallace Stegner's *Angle of Repose* (1971), a novel based on Foote's life and writings, won a Pulitzer Prize. Stegner changes only the names of the immediate Foote circle, retaining the names of most other figures, and he quotes liberally from her letters to Gilder, inserting his own additions as he deems necessary for clarification. The complicating factor in Stegner's appropriation of Foote's life is that three-quarters of the way through the novel he has his protagonist, Susan Burling Ward, fall into adultery, and because of her inattention during a dalliance with her lover, allow her child to drown. This in turn results in a deep rift between Susan and her husband and son. In actuality, Foote did not commit adultery; the youngest Foote daughter died from acute appendicitis and not neglect; and the Footes' marriage survived the hard times in Idaho. While *Angle of Repose* has won critical praise and deserves the attention of those interested in Foote's life, readers should be informed not to accept the novel's ending as biographical.

The general assessment of Mary Hallock Foote in standard references is mixed. The *Feminist Companion to Literature in English* (1990) notes that she wrote well of women's frustration and loneliness in the West and blames her focus on romance plots on the demands of the literary marketplace: "Due largely to editorial influence, her novels tended to follow a romance formula." The critic writing for *Notable American Women* (1971) is harsher in her judgment: "No matter how realistically her novels might begin, no matter how bracing their authentic touches of scene and atmosphere, the formulas thrust upon her converted them all into insipid love stories." Stegner may have put the case best in *Selected American Prose: The Realistic Movement 1841–1900* (1958): "Her mining camps in California, Colorado and Idaho are almost the only real ones in local color fiction—very much more real than those of Bret Harte. By no means a major figure, she is too honest to be totally lost." Foote's plots and characters are often stereotyped, but her detailed depictions of western settings and her stronger characters are so appealing that she continues to command the attention of late-twentieth- century readers.

Letters:

Levette Jay Davidson, "Letters from Authors," *Colorado Magazine,* 19, no. 4 (1942): 122–125.

Bibliography:

Richard H. Etulain, "Mary Hallock Foote: A Checklist," *Western American Literature,* 10 (May 1975): 59–65.

References:

Shelley Armitage, "The Illustrator as Writer: Mary Hallock Foote and the Myth of the West," in *Under the Sun: Myth and Realism in Western American Literature,* edited by Barbara Howard Meldrum (Troy, N.Y.: Whitson, 1985), pp. 150–174;

Richard H. Etulain, "Mary Hallock Foote (1847–1938)," *American Literary Realism,* 15, no. 2 (1972): 145–150;

Helena De Kay Gilder, "Author Illustrators," *Book Buyer,* 9, no. 7 (1894): 338–342;

Melody Graulich, "Legacy Profile: Mary Hallock Foote (1847–1938)," *Legacy,* 3, no. 2 (1986): 43–62;

Lee Ann Johnson, *Mary Hallock Foote* (Boston: Twayne, 1980);

James H. Maguire, *Mary Hallock Foote,* Boise State College Western Writers Series 2 (Boise, Idaho: Boise State College Press, 1972);

Rodman W. Paul, "When Culture Came to Boise: Mary Hallock Foote in Idaho," *Idaho Yesterdays,* 20, no. 2 (1976): 2–12;

Paul, Introduction, *A Victorian Gentlewoman in the Far West: The Reminiscences of Mary Hallock Foote,* edited by Paul (San Marino, Cal.: Huntington Library, 1972);

Carroll Smith-Rosenberg, *Disorderly Conduct: Visions of Gender in Victorian America* (New York: Knopf, 1985);

Wallace Stegner, *Angle of Repose* (New York: Fawcett, 1971);

Stegner, *Selected American Prose: The Realistic Movement 1841–1900* (New York: Holt, Rinehart & Winston, 1958;

Mary Ellen Williams Walsh, "Angle of Repose and the Writings of Mary Hallock Foote: A Source Study," in *Critical Essays on Wallace Stegner,* edited by Anthony Arthur (Boston: G. K. Hall, 1982).

Papers:

Approximately 540 of Foote's letters are held at the Stanford University Library. The Huntington Library in San Marino, California, has seventy-five letters, mostly from Foote to James D. Hague and to her editors at *The Century Magazine.* Smaller holdings of letters are at the New York Public Library; Library of Congress; National Portrait Gallery, Washington, D.C.; Houghton Library, Harvard University; State Historical Society of Wisconsin; Beinecke Library, Yale University; and Harry Ransom Humanities Research Center, University of Texas at Austin.

John Charles Frémont

(21 January 1813 – 13 July 1890)

Andrew Rolle
The Huntington Library

See also the entry on John Charles Frémont and Jessie Benton Frémont in *DLB 183: American Travel Writers, 1776–1864.*

BOOKS: *Northern Boundary of Missouri,* 27th Congress, 3rd session, serial 420, House document 38 (Washington: Printed by order of the U.S. Congress, 1842);

A Report on an Exploration of the Country Lying between the Missouri River and the Rocky Mountains on the Line of the Kansas and Great Platte Rivers, 27th Congress, 3rd session, serial 416, Senate document 243 (Washington: Printed by order of the U.S. Senate, 1843);

Report of the Exploring Expedition to the Rocky Mountains in the Year 1842, and to Oregon and North California in the Years 1843–'44, 28th Congress, 2nd session, serial 461, Senate executive document 174 (Washington: Gales & Seaton, 1845); 28th Congress, House executive document 106 (Washington: Blair & Rives, 1845);

Gerographical Memoir upon Upper California, in Illustration of His Map of Oregon and California, 30th Congress, 1st session, serial 511, Senate miscellaneous document 148 (Washington: Wendell & Van Benthuysen, 1848); 30th Congress, 2nd session, House miscellaneous document 5 (Washington: Tippin & Streeper, 1849);

Memoirs of My Life (Chicago & New York: Belford, Clarke, 1887).

Collection: *The Expedition of John Charles Frémont,* 3 volumes, with supplement and map portfolio, edited by Donald Jackson and Mary Lee Spence (Urbana, Chicago & London: University of Illinois Press, 1970, 1973, 1984).

OTHER: "In Command in Missouri," in *Battles and Leaders of the Civil War,* volume 1, edited by Robert U. Johnson and Clarence C. Buel (New York: Century, 1887);

John Charles Frémont in 1856

"The Conquest of California," *Century Magazine,* 61 (April 1890): 917–921.

Frémont, sometimes called "The Pathfinder" and "The West's Greatest Adventurer" as well as "A Man Unafraid," traversed more of the American West than any other explorers, including Meriwether Lewis and William Clark. Although he was not primarily a literary figure, his writings were crucial to the opening up of America's frontier lands. His geographical discoveries became intertwined with controversial decisions made during a long and tempestuous career, giving rise to almost incessant quarrels recorded in the public press and in books and articles by and about him. To this day controversy concerning him seems unending.

John Charles Frémont was born on 21 January 1813 in Savannah, Georgia, the illegitimate son of a

French-Canadian wanderer, Charles Frémon, and a Virginian mother of upper-class origins, Anne Whiting Pryor. His father died or disappeared when the boy was only five years old. With the financial aid of friends, he managed to enter the College of Charleston in South Carolina. There he attracted the attention of an important ally, Joel Poinsett, who later became secretary of war. Before Annapolis was established as the site of a naval academy, Poinsett secured an appointment for the bright and handsome lad as a teacher of mathematics aboard a United States Navy vessel on a training cruise to South America.

When Frémont returned from that assignment, Poinsett obtained a position for him as a lieutenant in the fledging Army Corps of Topographical Engineers. This led to his posting in 1838 as assistant engineer on a railroad survey from Charleston to Cincinnati, in Ohio Territory.

After that assignment was over, for the next three years he assisted the noted French explorer Jean Nicholas Nicollet in charting the upper Mississippi and Missouri river valleys. It cannot be determined how much of the official reports resulting from these expeditions were the work of Frémont. Although an ailing Nicollet relied heavily on his young assistant, Frémont had not yet achieved sufficient status to warrant use of his name on the title page of Nicollet's report.

In 1841 Frémont headed an expedition to survey the upper reaches of the Des Moines River, which led to his first report published by Congress, *Northern Boundary of Missouri* (1842). That same year, on 19 October 1841, Frémont married Jessie Benton, daughter of the powerful nationalist Sen. Thomas Hart Benton of Missouri. Both men yearned to open up America's western expanses, obtained earlier by President Thomas Jefferson. Such ambitions also became a deep concern of the senator's daughter. She would prove to be both an asset and a liability to her husband. Senator Benton's political status became crucial to her husband's future career. However, her repeated meddling in official decision-making would lead to complications with higher authorities that proved to be disadvantageous to Frémont.

In 1842, when immigration to Oregon became an important national issue, Secretary of War Poinsett sent Frémont to survey trails as far west as South Pass in Wyoming—the first of a series of government-sponsored expeditions. On this important expedition the young explorer demonstrated the first signs of an impetuous nature. He insisted upon traversing the swollen Platte River in a flimsy experimental rubber boat, and it capsized. Frémont thus not only imperiled the men in his party but lost valuable scientific instruments and documents as well. Although he was quickly becoming an experienced cartographer, he also became known as unpredictable in his actions. Yet, along with his impulsiveness, there was a courageous sangfroid part of his personality that kept cropping up. Early on he showed a knack for making such personal adversities seem like daring victories.

During his 1842 expedition Frémont also ascended the highest point in the Wind River Range (13,730 feet), since known as Frémont Peak. His exploration of Utah's Great Basin (which he named) and its salty inland sea proved to be significant. Whereas other explorers saw the far western sagebrush and desert as bleak and forbidding, Frémont envisioned future towns and farms in a burgeoning land of lilacs and fruit trees. Later the Mormon leader Brigham Young would acknowledge his debt to Frémont's maps and printed observations in helping him establish the first Mormon settlements near Salt Lake City.

During 1843 he was authorized to attempt yet another government survey as far westward as the mouth of the Columbia River on the Pacific shore. Contrary to army instructions, he decided to take along a twelve-pound cannon, which would cast doubt upon his party's peaceful intentions—the nation was on the verge of a war with Mexico, which claimed disputed territory along the route of the expedition. When Frémont's group made their first camp only four miles away from their point of departure, his wife, Jessie, received a warning dispatch from Washington requesting that her husband explain why he was hauling such a weapon on a nonmilitary survey. As Jessie was a senator's daughter, she well knew that answering this query would delay, if not cancel, her husband's expedition; she thus held the order back. Only upon his return did Frémont learn of this warning dispatch. A lifelong connivance between John Charles and Jessie had begun that would feature repeated difficulties in following orders from superiors.

Yet another impetuous act occurred during this expedition. In today's western Nevada, Frémont, ignoring official instructions, suddenly decided to take his party over the rugged Sierra crest in the dead of winter. There were few passes and no maps then available. Snow-covered peaks soared to fourteen thousand feet. Blinded by snow and lashed by cold winds, his party suffered terribly but finally emerged at Sutter's Fort in today's Sacramento, California. Because several of the men had meanwhile mysteriously disappeared en route, the sur-

A letter from Frémont to Ramsay Crooks, 15 September 1841 (American Fur Company Papers, New York Historical Society Library)

viving members of the expedition were charged with cannibalism. The charges were never proved.

Partly because of Jessie, after the 1842–1843 expedition Frémont produced his first significant writings. With her help he soon completed an official report of his first venture to Oregon and Washington. Trustworthy maps accompanied this publication. Issued under the auspices of the United States Congress, Frémont's *Report of the Exploring Expedition to the Rocky Mountains in the Year 1842, and to Oregon and North California in the Years 1843–'44* (1845) soon became a best seller, read by thousands of persons who planned trips across the continent themselves.

This volume established the explorer's reputation as both naturalist and cartographer. In order to complete accurate astronomical observations he and his scientific assistants had sometimes been up until one or two in the morning, stretched out on their backs upon the barren prairie floor or on mountaintops. Their combined efforts did more than fill in the odd missing blanks of western cartography, as later critics would aver. The report provided a road map of new and remote western trails, including precise descriptions of water holes, geology, fauna, and flora.

Frémont's 1845 volume, accompanied by unique maps and new meteorological details, changed the entire picture of the American West. It represented an important step forward from the earlier crude cartography of Lewis and Clark and an improvement on the army maps of Zebulon Pike and Maj. Stephen Long.

Indeed, Frémont's report demonstrated that the plains between the Missouri and the Rocky Mountains were not entirely arid but were, on the contrary, potentially fertile. This discovery helped dissolve fear of what Major Long had called "the Great American Desert"—no real survey of this area had been published since his 1820 expedition. Prior observations about the future of agriculture in today's great farming states, Nebraska, Kansas, and Oklahoma, had been dourly unfavorable. Frémont's updated findings thus exercised a greater influence on settlement of the West than any other single book.

Once the country's newspapers seized upon his refutation of Long's contentions, Frémont was on his way to becoming a national hero. Readers did not know that his writings had been in large part rewritten by his talented wife. Jessie managed to infuse a charming, knightly quality into the accounts of her husband's exploits. The explorer's work attracted the attention of President John Tyler, who awarded him a double brevet promotion beyond first lieutenant to captain—at the recommendation of the army's most senior officer, Gen. Winfield Scott.

In 1845, on another expedition to California over much the same route, the explorer courted controversy. He stood off several hundred Mexican troops atop Gavilan Peak near the provincial capital of Monterey, against the advice of the American consul there. On the eve of the Mexican War, Frémont hardly acted as though he were at the head of a neutral scientific group. Although actually in foreign territory by sufferance of its authorities, his party next became merged with the Bear Flag Revolt. This episode, staged farther to the north at Sonoma, California, by disgruntled American settlers, might well have led to a second massacre—as

had earlier occurred at the Alamo in San Antonio, Texas.

Frémont's high-handed treatment of important California officials was deeply resented in that Mexican province. After the war ended, he allowed himself to become involved in an unfortunate squabble between the army and the navy over which military branch was in actual command in California. The fact that a junior officer would challenge the authority of senior West Pointers led Brig. Gen. Stephen Watts Kearny to arrest and then march Frémont to Fort Leavenworth, Kansas. After a court-martial trial in Washington, Frémont was cashiered out of the army. Although President James K. Polk offered him reinstatement, Frémont spurned any sort of clemency.

The Pathfinder's actual military contribution to the conquest of California would become a big issue in books written later about the western phase of the Mexican War. Some authors charged that he had falsified accounts of events so as to make himself into a national hero. In fact, as he let Jessie inform their readers, it was the outbreak of war that had forced him to turn his original exploratory party into a military group. Also, he maintained, bungling by officials in Washington had obscured and confused the lines of authority between the army and the navy in the distant Far West. In a strict sense he had indeed fallen victim to the resultant confusion. But because of his officious behavior, he did not further his own cause.

Once the third expedition was finally over, the explorer, with Jessie's help, had to reassume the role of an author—an occupation that he did not relish. Together, however, they managed to prepare another government-sponsored report, this one titled *Geographical Memoir upon Upper California, in Illustration of His Map of Oregon and California* (1848). Early each morning he dictated his recollections while she once more did much of the actual writing. The need to make technical matters clear to Jessie enhanced the readability of their joint product.

His unique contributions to this second report were the many mathematical computations of elevation, temperature, and other physical measurements that went into it. Some of these details had to be verified by renewed astronomical observations far from their original locations. Detailed descriptions of minerals, vegetation, and wild animals that Frémont had encountered en route (including an account of a bear that had charged the party) ensured a wide readership for the report. All these varied aspects of the expedition were described by Jessie with the same verve as in their earlier report.

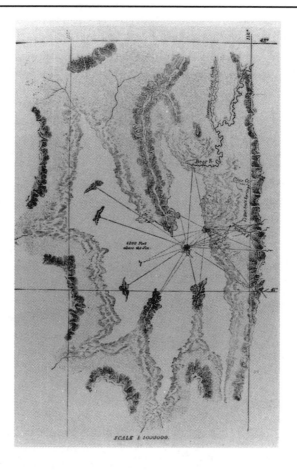

A map of the Great Salt Lake and a sketch of Pyramid Lake, Nevada, drawn by Charles Preuss, who accompanied Frémont on his expeditions, 1843–1844 (Bancroft Library, University of California, Berkeley)

To produce what Frémont called "the cursed manuscript" the government allowed only eight dollars for each day's tedious work. Early in 1848, after he formally presented it to the War Department, the document was transmitted to the United States Senate. Some twenty thousand copies were printed. Senator Benton and his colleagues were particularly interested in Frémont's recommendations regarding the location of forthcoming military posts. Specific suggestions regarding the handling of the Far West's Indian population came in part from the explorer's well-known frontier guide, Kit Carson.

This account was even more useful to future settlers and to the military than his 1845 report. The *Geographical Memoir,* however, did not strike down the myth of a nonexistent Buenaventura River, which was reputed to flow from the interior to the Pacific Coast. More practical were Frémont's descriptions of actual conditions along the Oregon Trail, which had become a virtual highway for covered-wagon pioneers. The *Geographical Memoir* did not gloss over the shortages of grass and water, the rough and rocky ruts of the trail, and its steep ascents and difficult fords to be crossed by tired horses and men. Frémont also contributed data in this report regarding far western climatic conditions, which had previously been portrayed as so hot and dry as to preclude future human habitation.

The explorer proceeded to downplay the dangers of going west, including such risks as those posed by mountain lions and half-ton grizzly bears. Despite the bleakness also of forlorn deserts, many eastern readers, chilled by the ice of winter or sweltering in summer humidity, relished this engaging volume. Inexpensive reprints of it became popular, especially just before and after the 1848 California gold rush attracted an avalanche of settlers anxious for accurate data regarding conditions in the Far West. Newspapers also printed excerpts of the *Geographical Memoir.* Its accompanying maps, although they charted regions previously crossed by others, were little less than magnificent. A modern specialist, Carl Wheat, has called Frémont's cartography, which was actually drawn by his German draftsman, Charles Preuss, superb.

In 1848 Frémont, now an acknowledged authority, decided to head up a fourth expedition. No longer, however, would the government finance his ventures into the wilderness. He and Senator Benton, thus, had to raise the funds privately. Against the advice of experienced local guides, Frémont plunged into the dangerous Sangre de Cristo range of southern Colorado and northern New Mexico, again in the middle of winter. This time he lost a third of his men in the snow-covered mountains. Charges of cannibalism once more surfaced. Despite this tragedy, fortune somehow soon again smiled upon Frémont, for in California gold was about to be discovered on his Mariposas property, and he became an instant millionaire. Subsequently, he was also chosen one of California's first two senators, serving a brief term in Washington.

Eager to return to the wilderness, Frémont planned a fifth and final transcontinental expedition. By the early 1850s Congress, responding to widespread public interest, seemed ready to authorize a series of transcontinental surveys. Frémont was then in England selling shares in his Mariposas mining property, in part to finance a new expedition. He contributed a piece to London's *Sunday Morning Chronicle* for 4 January 1851 that minimized the ill effects of his disastrous fourth expedition.

If he was to implement a transcontinental railroad route of his own, he must overcome public doubts about the treacherous mountain passes he had tried to cross during the fourth expedition. Although the Frémonts were skillful in using the public prints for their own purposes, an old enemy, Jefferson Davis, was now secretary of war. Davis, the future president of the Confederacy, had, like Frémont, fought in the Mexican War. But he was a West Pointer who had also been a senator during Frémont's brief sojourn in the Senate. Well aware of the latter's abolitionist views and his dismissal from the army, he had little use for the Pathfinder. Hence he saw to it that congressional funds were no longer awarded to Frémont.

Frémont's fifth expedition, undertaken during 1853, was again unsuccessful. Once more his men suffered dire hardships on the wintry trail which Frémont insisted upon traversing. The explorer had to disband his expedition in southern Utah, where his men, suffering from frostbite and exhaustion, were lucky to be rescued by the Mormons. The fifth expedition was a pale facsimile of his first three exploits, carried on under government auspices.

Yet only three years later, in 1856, Frémont became the first presidential nominee of the Republican Party. Despite momentary prominence, he was not, however, a completely successful political figure. There were rumors of infidelity to his wife. Furthermore, he remained an ardent abolitionist who had abandoned his native South to follow a career in the North and West, which gave rise to endless accusations in pamphlet form. His political allies replied in kind, publishing several partisan campaign biographies. All these printed missives in favor of Frémont could not, however, elect him president of the United States.

After his defeat the former candidate turned his back on politics, devoting his energies to a variety of businesses, including his Mariposas mining property in California. In 1861, after the Civil War broke out, Abraham Lincoln, who had succeeded as the second Republican presidential candidate, appointed Frémont as one of the four highest-ranking generals in the Union Army. In fact, he became military commander of the western sector of the war, with headquarters in Saint Louis. There he again involved himself in repeated controversies, this time with the War Department in Washington as well as with military and civilian officials in Missouri. When he made the serious mistake of issuing his own emancipation proclamation, Lincoln dismissed him from the Saint Louis command—after only one hundred days.

The War Department next posted Frémont to Virginia's Shenandoah Valley. There he unsuccessfully faced Stonewall Jackson, the versatile Confederate general. Frémont commanded not a real army but a ragtag collection of disgruntled Union volunteers and draftees. And he again irritated Lincoln by persisting in seeking to make strategic policy at the highest level, although he was now only a lesser tactical field commander. Later, Frémont would never mention his subsequent second dismissal from command. But Jessie continued to have harsh words for Secretary of War Edwin M. Stanton as well as for Lincoln and other Washington officials who had brought her husband's military career to an end.

Frémont's last years were far from spectacular. He squandered the wealth which he and Jessie had amassed, and his business speculations involved risky railroad and mining ventures. From 1878 to 1881 the Pathfinder was lucky enough to be appointed governor of Arizona Territory; however, his service there was in no way as noteworthy as that of Gen. Lewis Wallace, administrator of neighboring New Mexico Territory and author of the best-selling novel *Ben-Hur* (1880).

One could say that Jessie had played no minor role in establishing Frémont's self-defeating life pattern. There is little question that she possessed remarkable talents which she used in the service of her often exasperating husband. This created a legend of their compatibility, and of his greatness too. She commissioned his first biographers to perpetuate this roseate imagery. Actually, Jessie made her own aspirations into his by a clever process of transference. She not only colluded with her husband but also instigated, meddled in, and subsequently justified his most controversial blunders. No wonder that a provoked President Lincoln, almost always trustworthy in his judgments, derisively called Jessie "quite a female politician." She also became known as a writer of her own books. These include *The Story of the Guard* (1863), which extolled an elite Civil War unit assembled by Frémont when in command of the armies of the West. Among her other titles are *A Year of American Travel* (1878), *Far West Sketches* (1890), and *Souvenirs of My Time* (1887). Some of her stories appealed especially to children. Others would be too saccharine in tone for today's readers. Yet Jessie's literary efforts provided a vital sustenance for the family. Once he left government service, Frémont demonstrated little business sense, investing in fly-by-night ventures.

Jessie was, however, determined to protect Frémont's reputation at all costs. Indeed, without his wife's constant support, Frémont would have published little or nothing. The governmental reports on which she had collaborated anonymously were, furthermore, of real substance. The *Geographical Memoir* ranked well with those prepared by other explorers, including Frémont's naval rival, Capt. Charles Wilkes. The latter's *Narrative of the United States Exploring Expedition* (1844) contained significant new coastal measurements along the Pacific Ocean. Their altercation first flared up when the *Washington National Intelligencer* for 9 May 1848 blamed a shipwreck on Wilkes's faulty maritime charts. Spurred by Senator Benton, Frémont made some pompous assertions about Wilkes's defective cartography, concerning which he knew very little, for his had all been land-based explorations.

Frémont never wrote full reports of his third, fourth, or fifth expeditions. The 1856 presidential election had gotten in the way, as had his turbulent Civil War years. But his artist-photographer on the fifth expedition, Solomon Nunes Carvalho, did chronicle an account of that venture, *Incidents of Travel and Adventure in the Far West* (1857). It has remained the only available account of the fifth expedition. Carvalho, an admirer of the Pathfinder, prepared his narrative partly to support Frémont's 1856 presidential bid. He extolled his hero's achievements in fulsome, almost adoring, terms.

The first three biographies of Frémont were also written with that political campaign in mind. These books include John Bigelow's *Memoir of the Life and Public Services of John Charles Frémont* (1856), partly written by Jessie herself. Though little more than a campaign tract, it sold more than forty thousand copies. Bigelow was not only Frémont's first biographer but also one of the founders of the new Republican Party. Proud of her collaboration with her husband's biographer, Jessie boasted that the

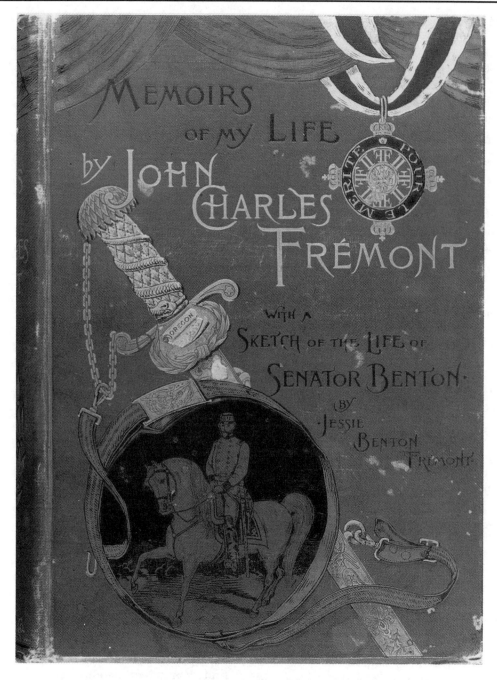

Binding for Frémont's last book, which covers the first thirty-four years of his life

book replaced the family album on half the living-room tables in the United States.

Other campaign biographies had also paraded the Pathfinder's western exploits before a wider audience than he had previously enjoyed. Samuel M. Smucker's *The Life of Col. John Charles Frémont* and Charles W. Upham's *Life, Explorations and Public Service of John Charles Frémont* (both 1856) were totally uncritical. Jessie, too, continued to extol the first Republican presidential candidate by publishing twenty-seven adulatory poems in the work titled *Signal Fires on the Trail of the Pathfinder,* also published in 1856. Some pamphlets and brochures went so far as to compare Frémont to Jesus Christ.

During the 1856 political campaign Frémont had some powerful writers in his corner. They included the Quaker poet John Greenleaf Whittier, an ardent antislavery advocate. Whittier wrote Frémont's main campaign poem, "The Pass of the Sierras." Other adherents included Horace Greeley, whose *New York Herald Tribune* wielded considerable power among voters in the urban North. Its editor,

Charles A. Dana, sought to bury any mention of Frémont's reputation for dueling or marital infidelity. Greeley commissioned a hack writer, W. H. Bartlett, to prepare a thirty-two-page defensive brochure that the *Herald Tribune* sold for twenty-one cents per copy.

Although the Frémont family had once lived in a grand manner, with homes in London, Paris, San Francisco, New York City, and along the upper Hudson River, their later years would be spent in virtual poverty. Frémont was grateful to be offered the territorial governorship of Arizona, although the once-renowned Pathfinder used that office to continue investing in dubious mining and railroad schemes.

Only the benefactions of railroad tycoon Collis P. Huntington made it possible for the Frémonts to go to faraway California in search of a decent retirement. Frémont's last correspondence, in 1889, concerned a petition to the United States Congress requesting a pension as a retired major general. He finally achieved the goal of being placed on the army's retired list, but only a few months before his death.

In 1886, thirty years after he was defeated for the presidency, Jessie succeeded in convincing Frémont to produce a memoir of his entire career. Personal memoirs of prominent figures had become the fashion among former military leaders. Generals Ulysses S. Grant and William Tecumseh Sherman had both written successful reminiscences. By the 1880s, however, they had much greater name recognition. Also, both were West Pointers with solid military reputations. In addition, Grant had become president of the United States. Neither had much use for "political generals" like Frémont. Although Grant and Sherman had nowhere near his cartographic knowledge, their memoirs projected images of a type of leadership that was much more solid, reliable, and composed. Furthermore, Frémont omitted from his memoirs that warm human element which had helped to make his 1845 report so popular.

After the passage of so many years Jessie encountered difficulty finding a publisher for her husband's reminiscences. Finally, a Chicago firm, Belford Clarke and Company, gave the Frémonts a contract for a two-volume work. Although he still hated writing, at Jessie's insistence the couple moved temporarily to Washington, D.C., in order to be near federal records. The *New York Post* for 7 September 1886 described their daily routine:

On the right of the bay-window is placed the General's table. . . . Opposite is Mrs. Frémont's. . . . The General dictates, and Mrs. Frémont writes down each word as it falls from his lips. . . . The rule of the house is to rise at seven, take a cup of tea, work from eight until twelve, when breakfast is taken. From one o'clock to six they forge ahead. . . .

Even in writing his memoirs, Frémont was unable to avoid controversy. A young Harvard professor of philosophy, Josiah Royce, intended to write his own account of California's history. Born of pioneer parents, he closely scrutinized the Pathfinder's controversial record in that province's military acquisition from Mexico. Royce interviewed both of the Frémonts, whom he later called deceitful in answering queries about the conquest era. Ultimately, Royce published *California from the Conquest in 1846 to the Second Vigilance Committee: A Study of American Character* (1886), which excoriated Frémont as a commander who had been out of control, repeatedly disobeying orders from superiors and fully deserving his court-martial trial.

Many of Royce's criticisms would be adopted by subsequent professional scholars who studied the Frémont record. The fiercest of the post-Royce critics was the historian Cardinal Goodwin, whose 1930 biography portrayed the explorer as an upstart who did not deserve the prominence which other scholars had given him. Frederick S. Dellenbaugh, an explorer of sorts, sought to validate the earlier election legendry in his book *Frémont and '49, The Story of a Remarkable Career . . .* (1914). He was followed by Allan Nevins, who perpetuated a fulsome and roseate image of the explorer in *Frémont, Pathfinder of the West* (1929). Nevins was also given to extolling the lives of other public figures, including John D. Rockefeller Sr., and Henry Ford. By 1939, however, Nevins would demote the explorer from "Pathfinder" to "Pathmarker" in a revised edition of his original 1929 biography.

Despite his glowing descriptions, Nevins had provided the first modern and comprehensive biography of the explorer. Other historians, disagreeing with Nevins, perhaps unfairly, called the Pathfinder "a follower of other men's trails." More recent biographies by Ferol Egan (1977) and Andrew Rolle (1991) have sought to present a more balanced picture while also filling out overlooked aspects of Frémont's life based also on new documentation and psychological methodology.

As for the explorer's own autobiographical narrative, it was anything but apologetic, certainly not a life confession, for the author refused to personalize his account. His determination to detach his own persona from the events he narrated thus converted even dramatic episodes into self-righteous justification. Despite Jessie's literary skills, the resulting book was flat and overly technical for most readers.

Titled *Memoirs of My Life* (1887), its 650 pages end with the year 1847. Frémont dodged virtually every controversial aspect of his life. The book does not deal with the court-martial trial, his subsequent dismissal from the army, his blemished career during the Civil War, or his later business failures. Avoidance of any possible criticism is its major characteristic.

Frémont's publishers also overpriced the volume, for which they had, incidentally, advanced no funds. Hence, many months of hard work on the memoirs had produced no income for the Frémonts. The success of Grant's and Sherman's reminiscences had led them to hope that this final statement would rescue their family from a precarious financial condition. But Frémont's recollections proved both an economic and a literary flop.

A projected second volume was never published, although Jessie and their son, Francis, tried to piece one together. They titled the manuscript "Great Events during the Life of Major General John C. Frémont." To this day that voluminous and incomplete work remains unpublished. The manuscript lies dormant in the Bancroft Library of the University of California, Berkeley.

Preparation of his memoirs was Frémont's last creative act. On 13 July 1890 he died of appendicitis, in virtual poverty in a New York boardinghouse, far removed from Jessie and their daughter, Elizabeth (Lily), whom he had left behind in Los Angeles. Though in dire economic circumstances, Jessie, during her last days in California, did what she could to keep alive the memory of the Pathfinder. Frémont's life, though, had been overshadowed by those of his contemporaries.

Jessie lived twelve more years. When she too died, she left her daughter only $500 in cash and a modest wooden bungalow that the ladies of Los Angeles had raised money to buy. Elizabeth, the only surviving female of five children, kept up the family legend of her father's devotion to God and country. In 1912, ten years after her mother's death, she managed to publish *Recollections of Elizabeth Benton Frémont*. That small book was even more lackluster than her father's memoirs. Both she and her mother saw him as a truly great man who had been wronged by his enemies. He had indeed exerted a powerful hold on both women. Even though some of Elizabeth's close friendships had been terminated because of her father's personal feuds, she too never wavered in her loyalty to his memory, even destroying unfavorable correspondence concerning him.

In the end Frémont's confused family origins had contributed to a turbulent pattern of life. Yet, without his personal uncertainties, the world might never have heard of him. Despite his failings, many of his contemporaries considered his life to have been successful, at least outwardly. His ultimate distinction was neither in political nor in economic achievements. It lay in his abilities to coordinate new scientific equipment and to inspire seasoned trail companions. He employed both to describe remote western locales. When not in that outdoor ambience he was uncomfortable. He also lacked the shrewdness required to bring his grandiose plans to fulfillment in an urban setting where he had to deal with bankers and other investors. He was, nevertheless, a remarkably talented human being who has not been forgotten.

In addition to the large volume of written materials about him, more than one hundred places have been named for Frémont. There are counties in Colorado, Idaho, Iowa, and Wyoming as well as many towns and streets all over the country that bear his name. A glacier in Washington's Cascade Range, a grove of redwoods in California's Santa Cruz Mountains, Fremont Peak in Wyoming, Frémont Springs in Nebraska, the Frémont Needle in Arizona, Frémont Pass in Colorado, and the Frémont River in Utah all attest to his lingering fame.

Biographies:

John Bigelow, *Memoir of the Life and Public Services of John Charles Frémont* (New York: Derby & Jackson, 1856);

Samuel M. Smucker, *The Life of Col. John Charles Frémont* (New York: Orton & Mulligan, 1856);

Charles W. Upham, *Life, Explorations and Public Service of John C. Frémont* (Boston: Ticknor & Fields, 1856);

Elizabeth B. Frémont, *Recollections of Elizabeth Benton Frémont,* compiled by I. T. Martin (New York: F. H. Hitchcock, 1912);

Frederick S. Dellenbaugh, *Frémont and '49, The Story of a Remarkable Career . . .* (New York: Putnam, 1914);

Cardinal Goodwin, *John Charles Frémont: An Explanation of His Career* (Palo Alto, Cal.: Stanford University Press, 1930);

Allan Nevins, *Frémont, Pathmarker of the West* (New York: Appleton Century, 1939);

Ferol Egan, *Frémont, Explorer for a Restless Nation* (Garden City, N.Y.: Doubleday, 1977);

Andrew Rolle, *John Charles Frémont: Character as Destiny* (Norman: University of Oklahoma Press, 1991).

References:
William Brandon, *The Men and the Mountain: Frémont's Fourth Expedition* (New York: Morrow, 1955);

Solomon Nunes Carvalho, *Incidents of Travel and Adventure in the Far West, with Col. Frémont's Last Expedition across the Rocky Mountains . . .* (New York: Derby & Jackson, 1857);

Charges and Specifications and Findings and Sentence of a General Court Martial in the Case of Lieutenant Colonel John C. Frémont. General Orders No. 7 (Washington, D.C.: U.S. War Department, 1848);

Jessie B. Frémont, "California and Frémont," *Land of Sunshine* (December 1895): 3–14;

Frémont, "The Origin of the Frémont Expeditions," *Century Illustrated Monthly Magazine,* 41 (March 1891): 766–771;

Andrew Rolle, "Exploring an Explorer: Psychohistory and John Charles Frémont," *Pacific Historical Review,* 51 (May 1982): 131–163.

Papers:
There are collections of John Charles Frémont's papers at the Bancroft Library, University of California, Berkeley; the Huntington Library, San Marino, California; and the Southwest Museum in Los Angeles.

Hamlin Garland
(14 September 1860 – 5 March 1940)

Joseph B. McCullough
University of Nevada, Las Vegas

See also the Garland entries in *DLB 12: American Realists and Naturalists, DLB 71: American Literary Critics and Scholars, 1880–1900,* and *DLB 78: American Short-Story Writers, 1880–1910.*

BOOKS: *Under the Wheel: A Modern Play in Six Scenes* (Boston: Barta, 1890);

Main-Travelled Roads: Six Mississippi Valley Stories (Boston: Arena, 1891; London: Unwin, 1892; enlarged edition, New York & London: Macmillan, 1899; enlarged again, New York & London: Harper, 1922; enlarged again, New York & London: Harper, 1930);

A New Declaration of Rights (Boston: Arena, 1891);

Jason Edwards, An Average Man (Boston: Arena, 1892);

A Member of the Third House (Chicago: Schulte, 1892);

A Little Norsk; or Ol' Pap's Flaxen (New York: Appleton, 1892; London: Unwin, 1892);

A Spoil of Office: A Story of the Modern West (Boston: Arena, 1892; revised edition, New York: Appleton, 1897);

Prairie Songs: Being Chants Rhymed and Unrhymed of the Level Lands of the Great West (Chicago & Cambridge, Mass.: Stone & Kimball, 1893);

Prairie Folks (Chicago: Schulte, 1893; London: Sampson Low, 1893; enlarged edition, New York & London: Macmillan, 1899);

Crumbling Idols: Twelve Essays on Art Dealing Chiefly with Literature, Painting, and the Drama (Chicago & Cambridge, Mass.: Stone & Kimball, 1894);

Impressions on Impressionism: Being a Discussion of the American Art Exhibition at the Art Institute, Chicago, by A Critical Triumvirate, by Garland, Charles Francis Browne, and Lorado Taft (Chicago: Central Art Association, 1894);

Five Hoosier Painters: Being a Discussion of the Holiday Exhibit of the Indianapolis Group, in Chicago, by The Critical Triumvirate, by Garland, Browne, and Taft (Chicago: Central Art Association, 1894);

Rose of Dutcher's Coolly (Chicago: Stone & Kimball, 1895; London: Beeman, 1896; revised edition,

New York & London: Macmillan, 1899);

Wayside Courtships (New York: Appleton, 1897; London: Beeman, 1898);

Ulysses S. Grant: His Life and Character (New York: Doubleday & McClure, 1898);

The Spirit of Sweetwater (Philadelphia: Curtis / New York: Doubleday & McClure, 1898; London: Service & Paton, 1898); revised and enlarged as *Witch's Gold* (New York: Doubleday, Page, 1906);

Boy Life on the Prairie (New York & London: Macmillan, 1899; revised, New York: Macmillan, 1908);

The Trail of the Goldseekers: A Record of Travel in Prose and Verse (New York & London: Macmillan, 1899);

The Eagle's Heart (New York: Appleton, 1900; London: Heinemann, 1900);

Her Mountain Lover (New York: Century, 1901; London: Dollar Library, 1901);

The Captain of the Gray-Horse Troop (New York & London: Harper, 1902; London: Grant Richards, 1902);

Hesper (New York & London: Harper, 1903);

The Light of the Star (New York & London: Harper, 1904);

The Tyranny of the Dark (New York & London: Harper, 1905);

The Long Trail: A Story of the Northwest Wilderness (New York & London: Harper, 1907);

Money Magic (New York & London: Harper, 1907);

The Shadow World (New York & London: Harper, 1908);

The Moccasin Ranch: A Story of Dakota (New York & London: Harper, 1909);

Cavanagh: Forest Ranger (New York & London: Harper, 1910);

Other Main-Travelled Roads (New York & London: Harper, 1910);

Victor Ollnee's Discipline (New York & London: Harper, 1911);

The Forester's Daughter (New York & London: Harper, 1914);

They of the High Trails (New York & London: Harper, 1916);

A Son of the Middle Border (New York: Macmillan, 1917; London: John Lane, 1921);

A Daughter of the Middle Border (New York: Macmillan, 1921);

A Pioneer Mother (Chicago: The Bookfellows, 1922);

The Book of the American Indian (New York & London: Harper, 1923);

Trail-Makers of the Middle Border (New York: Macmillan, 1926; London: John Lane, 1926);

The Westward March of American Settlement (Chicago: American Library Association, 1927);

Prairie Song and Western Story (Boston & New York: Allyn & Bacon, 1928);

Back-Trailers from the Middle Border (New York: Macmillan, 1928);

Roadside Meetings (New York: Macmillan, 1930; London: John Lane, 1931);

Companions on the Trail (New York: Macmillan, 1931);

My Friendly Contemporaries: A Literary Log (New York: Macmillan, 1932);

Afternoon Neighbors (New York: Macmillan, 1934);

Iowa, O Iowa (Iowa City: Clio Press, 1935);

Joys of the Trail (Chicago: Bookfellows, 1935);

Forty Years of Psychic Research (New York: Macmillan, 1936);

The Mystery of the Buried Crosses: A Narrative of Psychic Exploration (New York: Dutton, 1939);

Hamlin Garland's Diaries, edited by Donald Pizer (San Marino, Cal.: Huntington Library, 1968);

Hamlin Garland's Observations on the American Indian, 1895–1905, edited by Lonnie E. Underhill and Daniel F. Littlefield Jr. (Tucson: University of Arizona Press, 1976).

Hamlin Garland is now known almost solely for his short middle-border fiction written before 1895, particularly for his provocative and innovative collection of short stories, *Main-Travelled Roads: Six Mississippi Valley Stories* (1891), and for his autobiographies, *A Son of the Middle Border* (1917) and *A Daughter of the Middle Border* (1921). In these volumes Garland demonstrated that it had at last become possible to deal realistically with the American farmer in literature instead of seeing him simply through the veil of literary convention. By creating new types of characters, Garland hoped not only to inform readers about the realities of midwestern farm life but also to touch the deeper feelings of the nation. As one of America's foremost local-colorists, Garland graphically depicted the countryside of his native Middle West in verse, fiction, and powerful autobiographical narratives in which he portrays the futility of farm life. Less well known are Garland's writings of the Rocky Mountain West—writings that occupied his attention for nearly twenty-two years between his novel *Rose of Dutcher's Coolly* in 1895 and *A Son of the Middle Border* in 1917. However one may judge the merit of these other writings, they are crucial to a full understanding of Garland's development and important to an appreciation of western regional literature as it was developing at the end of the nineteenth century.

The second of three children of Richard and Isabelle McClintock Garland, Hamlin Garland was born on a farm near West Salem, Wisconsin, on 14 September 1860. After spending his formative years on several farms in Wisconsin, Iowa, and South Dakota, he journeyed to Boston in the fall of 1884, where he immersed himself in the evolutionary writings of Charles Darwin and Herbert Spencer, eagerly read Walt Whitman's poetry, and struck up a significant friendship with William Dean Howells. His reading of Henry George's *Progress and Poverty* (1879) in 1884 confirmed his own experiences of farm life and quickly converted him into an advocate of the single tax, which sought to correct the injustice of the unearned increment (profits made from the increased value of land) that favored property owners at the expense of the tenant farmer.

When he returned to the West for a visit in 1887, Garland was more deeply impressed with the harshness of the landscape and farm life than he had been before his sojourn in the East. Encouraged by Benjamin Orange Flower, editor of the radical *Arena,* he vowed to depict his observations in fiction. In addition to *Main-Travelled Roads* he produced several other social and economic documents during the early 1890s. He also lectured frequently on the single-tax theories of George and campaigned for populist candidates.

Although Garland was often appearing in print by 1892, his work was not selling as well as he hoped, and much of his middle-border material was being criticized in both the East and the West. As he later recalled in *Son of the Middle Border,*

> I had the foolish notion that the literary folk of the west would take local pride in the color of my work, and to find myself execrated by nearly every critic as "a bird willing to foul his own nest" was an amazement. Editorials and criticisms poured into the office, all written to prove that my pictures of the middle border were utterly false.

> Statistics were employed to show that pianos and Brussels carpets adorned almost every Iowa farmhouse. Tilling the prairie soil was declared to be "the noblest vocation in the world, not in the least like the pictures this eastern author has drawn of it."

By 1894 Garland was tired of the controversy surrounding his middle-border fiction. In an 18 January letter of that year to his publisher, Herbert S. Stone, he wrote that he was renouncing all controversial literature in favor of purely literary works and planned to look elsewhere for his material. While he continued to treat such controversial themes as woman's rights in marriage, he no longer focused on the economics of the region as he had done in *Jason Edwards, An Average Man* (1892), *A Member of the Third House* (1892), and *A Spoil of Office: A Story of the Modern West* (1892), as well as in much of his earlier short fiction. But while Garland's turn to the mountainous West for his material signaled a change in those subjects with which he had been occupied in his middle-border fiction, the change was not nearly so abrupt as it seemed.

From the beginning of his career Garland considered himself a Western writer and had an emotional, though romantic, attachment to the West. In his November 1892 article in *Arena,* "The West in Literature," Garland extols the region: "And yet for forty years an infinite drama has been going on in those wide spaces of the West—a drama that is as thrilling, as full of heart and hope and battle, as any that ever surrounded any man—a life that was unlike any ever seen on earth, and which should have produced its characteristic literature, its native art chronicle." Drawing upon his own literary theory of "veritism," which he developed in his collection of essays *Crumbling Idols: Twelve Essays on Art Dealing Chiefly with Literature, Painting, and the Drama* (1894), Garland was convinced not only of the need to delineate the West in literature but also that a truthful study of western life must involve the actual speech of the common people. He believed that each character should have his individual accent, just as he has his individual thought.

In assessing the success of contemporary western regionalists and looking to the future development of western writers, Garland concluded in his article:

> That this Americanism, this truth to local conditions, is the certain road to success for young Western writers, is evident already in the success of James Whitcomb Riley, Opie Read, Joseph Kirkland, Octave Thanet, James Lane Allen, and others who have written of Western people. We are certain soon to have a group of Western novelists (Will they be women?) to represent the West, as Mrs. Cooke, Miss Wilkins, and Miss Jewett represent New England. But they must be born of the soil. They must be products of the environment. They must stand among the people, not above them, and then they can be true, and being true they will certainly succeed.

Ironically, when Garland began delineating the region in his own fiction, he was often more interested in mythologizing and romanticizing the West than he was in rendering native dialects and individual thought.

Even while working on *Rose of Dutcher's Coolly* from 1890 until its publication in 1895, Garland felt the lure of the Far West and began to exploit the new region as a source of local-color material. His first western story, "Drifting Crane," published in *Harper's Weekly* in 1890, was the beginning of a long line of stories dealing with Native Americans. He first visited the Southwest and Colorado on a trip to the West Coast in 1892. In the spring of 1893 he spent several weeks in the mountains of Colorado. Finally, two more trips to Colorado in the summers of 1894 and 1895 confirmed his desire to begin a career as a writer of Mountain West fiction. As Garland recalled in *A Daughter of the Middle Border,* "From the plains, which were becoming each year more crowded, more prosaic, I fled in imagination

Garland's recollection of writing Main-Travelled Roads, *twenty-six years after its publication*

as in fact to the looming silver-and-purple summits of the Continental Divide, while in my mind an ambition to embody, as no one at that time had done, the spirit and the purpose of the Rocky Mountain trailer was vaguely forming in my mind."

Rose of Dutcher's Cooly, arguably Garland's best novel, details the stages of Rose Dutcher's growth from her monotonous and stifled farm life, through her university years, to her final achievement of artistic and personal success in Chicago. The novel, which contains mild scenes of Rose's sexual awakening, focuses on two of Garland's concerns: reform of the arts and the difficulties faced by women attempting to maintain freedom and individuality in

marriage. But when the novel was attacked as savagely as *Main-Travelled Roads* had been, Garland became depressed: "With a foolish notion that the Middle West should take a moderate degree of pride in me, I resented this condemnation. . . . Without doubt this persistent antagonism, this almost universal depreciation of my stories of the plains had something to do with intensifying the joy with which I returned to the mountain world and its heroic types, at any rate I spent July and August of that year 1895 in Colorado and New Mexico, making many observations, which turned out to have incalculable value to me in later days." This trip marked what Garland called "a complete 'bout face in my march," for it provided him with material works such as *The Spirit of Sweetwater* (1898), which was revised and enlarged as *Witch's Gold* (1906); *The Eagle's Heart* (1900); and *Money Magic* (1907), as well as a dozen shorter romances.

In *A Daughter of the Middle Border* Garland explained the reasons for his regional shift:

> All my emotional relationships with the "High Country" were pleasant, my sense of responsibility was less keen, hence the notes of resentment, of opposition to unjust social conditions which had made my other books an offense to my readers were almost entirely absent in my studies of the mountaineers. My pity was less challenged in their case. Lonely as their lives were, it was not a sordid loneliness. The cattle rancher was at least not a drudge. Careless, slovenly and wasteful as I knew him to be, he was not mean. He had something of the Centaur in his bearing. Marvelous horsemanship dignified his lean figure and lent a notable grace to his gestures. His speech was picturesque and his observations covered a wide area. Self-reliant, fearless, instant of action in emergency, his character appealed to me with ever-increasing power.
>
> I will not say that I consciously and deliberately cut myself off from my prairie material, the desertion came about naturally. Swiftly, inevitably, the unplowed valleys, the waterless foothills and the high peaks, inspired me, filled me with desire to embody them in some form of prose, of verse.

But although Garland dreamed of "the high country," his biography, *Ulysses S. Grant: His Life and Character* (1898), absorbed most of his time between 1895 and 1897. Garland traveled in the West again in the summer of 1897, this time with his brother Franklin. This trip marks the point that Garland decided to devote himself entirely to western material. His tour began with a study of the Sioux at the Standing Rock Reservation in South Dakota. Although little writing came immediately from his stay at Standing Rock, his observations formed the groundwork for his extensive writings and research on Sioux matters in the next five years. During the next several months he and his brother traveled extensively, living among the Sioux, Crow, and Cheyenne.

Garland attempted to deal with a variety of facets of western life and to create a multiplicity of types, but he usually focused on mountaineers, miners, Native Americans, and foresters. With few exceptions most of his western works contain a sense of the glory of mountain scenery and a conventional love plot. These elements were usually combined with one or more themes that dominate his western writings: the life in the mining camps, the displacement of the American Indian, and the importance of conservation and controlled management of the West. Most of the works were based on his travels: his gold-mining expedition to the Yukon provides the details for *Trail of the Goldseekers: A Record of Travel in Prose and Verse* (1899); his journey to England, for *Her Mountain Lover* (1901); and his many trips to Indian reservations, for *The Captain of the Gray-Horse Troop* (1902) and *The Book of the American Indian* (1923).

Literary critics have consistently disparaged most of Garland's writings of the West, especially his Rocky Mountain romances, considering them as largely failures despite their popular appeal. These critics have particularly regretted Garland's "decline from realism" in his fiction after 1895. Garland associated realism with reform, and many critics have faulted his turning away from realism as a retreat from political idealism. However, the change from realism to romanticism is overemphasized in Garland's later fiction, for a fundamental romantic individualism was at the core of many of his so-called realistic works.

With his marriage in 1899 to Zulime Taft, sister of the noted sculptor Lorado Taft, Garland understandably became concerned about his new financial obligations. In later reflection on his turn to romantic stories, Garland admitted in *My Friendly Contemporaries* (1932) that "some of them were written for the magazines in order that my wife and children might be fed and sheltered and clothed." Nevertheless, although Garland was more concerned with popularity than before, he did not become a hack. Some of his books about the West contained some of Garland's best and most passionate writing.

The Eagle's Heart, Garland's "Colorado novel," was one of the firstfruits of his western travels. Although the work received only mild praise from reviewers, his new novel was not only one of his most ambitious works but also would be the prototype of his romantic novels because he attempted to put everything into it: the scene, the technique, the conventions, and, most of all, the types of characters that were to form the basis of his other western novels. The work illustrates Garland's shifting angle of vision and is significant for being his first attempt to create a genuine hero. The novel also reveals both Garland's strengths and, ultimately, his weaknesses as a writer of romances and an interpreter of the West.

The simple plot of the novel has a single purpose: to trace the adventures, aspirations, and development of its hero, Harold Excell. The action takes place in three sections. In the first section Harold is presented as a boy in the small farming community of Rock River, where his father is a minister.

Garland's Chicago home, where he lived from 1893 to 1916

The boy's wrathful temperament, exhibited even early in his life, makes him a rebel and is a characteristic that he must continually balance with his higher aspirations. As a seventeen-year-old he stabs another man in self-defense when he is unable to hold his temper in check. Found guilty and sentenced to six months in the county jail, he changes his name to Moses N. Hardluck (called "Mose") after his release and sets out for the West alone. The remainder of part 1 follows Harold in a variety of jobs, from cattle driver to sheepherder, always moving westward and adopting the appropriate dress and manners. Losing his temper for the second time, he gets into a fight with some intoxicated cattlemen,

shoots one in self-defense, and is forced to flee to the mountains to avoid further trouble.

The second section occurs four years later in the small town of Marmion, Iowa, where "Black Mose," the legendary name given to him by the newspapers, returns to see Mary Yardwell, a girl with whom he fell in love when she visited the prisoners and sang hymns to them. However, learning that she is engaged to be married, he sets out again for the Rocky Mountains, traveling through New Mexico to the Grand Canyon and on to California, visiting several Indian reservations on the way. During his travels he works at various jobs, including a stint as deputy marshal.

In section three Black Mose is in the famous mining camp of Wagon Wheel when he learns that his mother has died, his father is coming west, and Mary, who has broken off her engagement, wants to see him. Out of money he earns enough in a rodeo to return to Chicago to see Mary. He is unable to find a job in Chicago and becomes ill but is nursed back to health by Mary and other friends. Unable to live in the East because he has had a taste of the "high country," he marries Mary and accepts an appointment as an Indian agent at Sand Lake.

It is not the plot but the portrait of the hero that holds the reader's attention. Garland believed that he had helped to establish the western hero as an archetype. He referred to the origin of Black Mose in *Companions on the Trail* (1931): "I must claim priority over Zane Grey and other authors of 'Westerns,' as they are called in the motion-picture circles. Owen Wister and I were early in the field. Emerson Hough, Harry Leon Wilson, and Stewart Edward White came later. Priority is cold comfort, but that is all I can claim in this contest."

Unfortunately, Garland's character Harold, while intriguing, is not credible. Garland indicates that Harold, even at an early age, became absorbed with an image of the West: "Almost without definable reason the 'Wild West' came to be the land of wonder, lit as by some magical light. Its canons, *arroyos,* and mesquite, its broncos, cowboys, Indians, and scouts filled the boy's mind with thoughts of daring, not much unlike the fancies of a boy in the days of knight errantry." But while readers learn a great deal about Harold's aspirations, he never emerges as a fully realized individual. At times he becomes little more than the typical western hero of the dime novels that he reads while growing up.

The tension between Harold's base instincts and his higher aspirations is not developed, and there is no psychological progression in the character. Except for the two episodes in which Harold loses his temper, Garland makes it clear that his emotions are always held in check by a noble sentiment and higher purpose. Readers are told of but never shown his involvement in a variety of noble social causes, including the improvement of the treatment of the Indians in reservations. Harold is depicted as a romantic individualist, strong, handsome, and self-reliant, who belongs to the class of romantic noblemen who are in quest not of the Holy Grail but of the "mystic mountains of the West." In addition to chivalric images Harold is also associated with animal images. This imagery suggests his baser instincts, acting as a counterpart to higher aspirations represented by the chivalric images, but it also indicates his closeness to nature. Harold's association with the eagle, one of the recurring symbols in the novel, represents his freedom to stand alone and soar to heights unreachable by the common man.

In *The Eagle's Heart,* as in nearly all of Garland's romantic novels, the focus is not on the community but the singular hero. Unlike the minor characters of his middle-border fiction, the minor characters in the western fiction are for the most part wooden. The travels of his characters often provide Garland with an opportunity to render magnificent descriptions of the Far West, but with the exception of his Indian material, the themes are not so compelling.

William Dean Howells felt that Garland's group of short stories, which were written in the same vein as *The Eagle's Heart* and collected under the title *They of the High Trails* in 1916, were well suited to his style. Howells argued in his preface to the collection that Garland's shift of locale had merely broadened his canvas without weakening his techniques. In titling the stories for the volume, Garland attempted to portray the various picturesque types found in the West: "The Grub-Staker," "The Cow-boss," "The Remittance Man," "The Lonesome Man," "The Trail Tramp," "The Prospector," "The Outlaw," "The Leaser," "The Ranger," and "The Tourist." All of the stories in the collection are dominated by a single attitude—a belief in individual freedom and in the abundant possibilities of the West. The deprivation found in his middle-border fiction is absent. Unfortunately, while the stories frequently capture the idiosyncracies of picturesque mountain characters and the scenes are often compelling, the characters seldom emerge from their type.

Part of Garland's difficulties in his western fiction stemmed from his not having so intimate a familiarity with the region as he had with the middle border. To be sure, Garland had spent much time touring the West, and he attempted to transmit his feelings of exhilaration and freedom into his fiction. But Garland was usually not emotionally involved in the social issues that provided the backgrounds for this fiction, and this may have hurt his writing. This was not the case, however, in Garland's treatment of Native Americans.

Garland's interest in the problems facing the American Indian can be found as early as 1890, with his publication of "Drifting Crane" in the 31 May 1890 issue of *Harper's Weekly*. While the work briefly but powerfully indicates the injustices of the whites in their treatment of the Indian and his land, Garland's depiction was not drawn from any personal knowledge of the American Indian. However, he

Garland smoking a peace pipe in a Cheyenne tepee, 1899

had the opportunity to travel extensively and to live for extended periods among the Indians during years subsequent to 1892. He made some fifteen trips among various tribes in the next decade or so.

Garland's firsthand knowledge of American Indians and his awareness of their process of giving up the modified lifestyles of the reservation and adopting those of the dominant white culture resulted in many sensitive portrayals of these painful transitions. From the start his treatment of the Indian was sympathetic, and his moral indignation at their plight was as sincere as his earlier concern for the beaten-down farmer in his middle-border fiction. He not only wrote both fiction and nonfiction about the American Indian but also aided various reform movements to better their living conditions.

Garland's essay "The Red Man's Present Needs" in the April 1902 issue of *North American Re-*

view is perhaps the most explicit statement of his view of the predicament of the Indians. He had little patience with programs that attempted to rehabilitate a defeated race but had little understanding of the Indians' way of life. At the same time he also appreciated the tragedy of Native American attempts to retain their ways of life in modern society. Garland's aim was to encourage the reform of the policy of the United States in regard to Native Americans. He wanted the government to recognize the complexity of Indian needs, to realize that there were diverse peoples under the name "Indian" and that each tribe had its own needs. He wanted to improve the policy of land allotment and ease the assimilation of Native Americans into the dominant European American culture.

Among the suggestions Garland offers to ease the transition of the Indians from their old life to the new are the settlement of Indians on land in family, rather than tribal, groups; the reclamation of the dying arts such as canoe building, weaving, basket making, and pottery baking; and the prevention of the missionaries from regulating the amusements and daily lives of the Indians. He even became involved in a complicated, well-intentioned plan to give the Indians English names in order to establish naming patterns that would end the massacre of their names by inept interpreters. Also, since the laws governing inheritance were based on the Euro-American custom of giving children the surname of their fathers, there was a possibility of confusion, litigation, and fraud in the matter of an Indian's inheritance of land unless some reform in naming practices occurred. The project was ultimately too massive to succeed, but Garland worked out detailed plans and received the official support of his friend President Theodore Roosevelt for the scheme.

Garland reacted strongly against those writers who failed to depict the Indians and their problems as they really existed. In "The Red Man as Material," which appeared in the 2 August 1903 *Booklover's Magazine,* he provides a stinging indictment of writers who shaped public opinion of Native Americans through false and unrealistic presentations, singling out John Smith, James Fenimore Cooper, William Gilmore Simms, Robert Montgomery Bird, Charles Wilkins Webber, and Jack London. In *A Daughter of the Middle Border* he reports telling Maj. George H. Stouch, the Indian agent at Darlington, Oklahoma, of his intention in his own writing: "We have had plenty of the 'wily redskin' kind of thing . . . . I am going to tell of the red man as you and [John] Seger have known him, as a man of the polished stone age trying to adapt himself to steam and electricity."

In his fiction Garland was not concerned with the forces that subjugated the Indian so much as he was with the conflicts that arose when the Indian attempted to come to terms with an alien culture and reservation abuses. His ambitious study of problems affecting Native Americans in *The Captain of the Gray-Horse Troop* was commercially successful (selling nearly one hundred thousand copies) and generally well received by reviewers. The novel, which explicitly exemplifies the views Garland expressed in "The Red Man's Present Needs," was also highly praised by President Roosevelt, who attempted to implement some of Garland's suggestions in the novel.

Partially based on an uprising of the Northern Cheyennes that was instigated by the actions of cattlemen, the story, situated at Fort Smith near Pinion City, Montana, reflects vividly the reservation life and the problems of the Teton Sioux. Capt. George Curtis is on a special assignment to supplant the corrupt Indian agent, Sennett. Arriving at the post with his sister, Jennie, he finds tensions mounting between the Indians and the cattlemen who are determined to drive the Indians from their lands. The cattlemen's cause is aided by the powerful Senator Brisbane, whose attitude toward the Indians reflects those of the cattlemen: "'Human beings!' sneered Brisbane, 'they are nothing but a greasy lot of vermin—worthless from every point of view. Their rights can't stand in the way of civilization.'"

Curtis's situation is additionally complicated when he falls in love with Brisbane's niece, Elsie, and must convert her to his sympathetic point of view, one in which the Indian is regarded as a human being with individual rights. Moreover, Curtis must find a way to prevent the uprising and, at the same time, help the Indians progress. The situation intensifies through a series of violent scenes that culminate in the death of a sheepherder and in the delivery of the accused Indian by Curtis into the hands of justice at Pinion City. Because precautionary measures by the agent to protect the Indian are unsatisfactory, the prisoner is shot and dragged to death by a mob. This outrage, however, produces a reaction: Senator Brisbane is defeated; the settlers withdraw from the reservation; and the federal government, which was previously applying pressure on Curtis, passes a purchase bill to protect the Indians and their land. Curtis and Elsie marry, and they begin helping the Indians change from a hunting to a farming community.

Through the novel Garland stresses the necessity of conversion to modern life for Native Americans and urges the cooperation of sympathetic whites in this process. As in *The Eagle's Heart,* the cattlemen are the villains since their goals and greed make this cooperation difficult. But while the plot is directly and effectively related to the principal themes of the novel and the descriptions of the reservation life of the Indians are evocative, the work suffers from the same problems of characterization that weakened *The Eagle's Heart* and much of his other romantic fiction. Captain Curtis, while clearly sympathetic, serves primarily as a mouthpiece for Garland and as a vehicle for the author's views on reform.

The fifteen stories collected as *The Book of the American Indian* are examples of the best fiction of Garland's western phase. Fourteen of the stories were published in periodicals between 1899 and 1905; one, "The Silent Eaters," was previously unpublished. In these pieces Garland manifests an en-

Garland's wife, Zulime, and their two children, Constance Hamlin and Mary Isabel

gaging and genuine sympathy for Native Americans. In his best stories, such as "Wahiah—Spartan Mother," "Rising Wolf-Ghost Dancer," "The Iron Kiva," and "The Story of Howling Wolf," his treatment has an authenticity unmatched in his other writing of the period. Not only are his innovative and compassionate treatments successful artistically, but in them he effectively presents many of the policies and views that he expressed in "The Red Man's Present Needs." The theme of the necessity of conversion to modern life informs the collection. Garland's heroes are either Indian agents or schoolteachers who show tolerance and compas-

sionate understanding of the Indian. The villains tend to be missionaries who attempt to convert the Indian not by teaching him new ways but by eradicating all of his customs.

Garland combines the theme of the necessity of change with an indignation over the treatment of the Indian on reservations most effectively in "The Silent Eaters." In this fictionalized biography of Sitting Bull, Garland traces the history of the Sioux nation from its long self-sufficiency to the eventual subjugation and decline of the race that culminates with the death of Sitting Bull. The story is told by Iapi, a member of "The Silent Eaters," a band of trusted warriors used by the chief primarily as advisers. Garland's choice of narrator provides him with the opportunity not only to portray Sitting Bull sympathetically but also, through the narrator's development, to indicate the necessity of change if the Indian is to survive.

When Sitting Bull surrenders, Iapi is befriended by Lieutenant Davis, who gives him the opportunity to learn the white man's ways by sending him to the East to study. Almost a spokesman for Darwinian evolution, Davis, who has tremendous respect for the Sioux, convinces Iapi that he will need to advance his education if he wishes to help his people. Although Iapi sympathizes with Sitting Bull, he also senses the futility of attempting to maintain a way of life when the environment is no longer receptive. Iapi becomes a man with divided loyalties caught between his two worlds, incapable in the end of being embraced by either.

Upon Iapi's return from the East, he gives a realistic account of the conditions on the reservations: "They were like poor white farmers, ragged, dirty, and bent. The clothes they wore were shoddy grey and deeply repulsive to me. Their robes of buffalo, their leggings of buckskin, their beaded pouches—all the things I remembered with pride—had been worn out (or sold). Even the proud warriors of my tribe were reduced to the condition of those who are at once prisoners and beggars." As in "Rising Wolf-Ghost Dancer," the Native Americans futilely perform the Ghost Dance, hoping to recapture a lost past. When the dance is unsuccessful, Sitting Bull and "The Silent Eaters" are killed by Indian traitors. The tragic history of Sitting Bull is finally viewed by Iapi in epic terms, as Sitting Bull becomes a metaphor for the entire Sioux nation.

In *Hesper* (1903) and *Money Magic* Garland returns to white culture and shifts scenes from the world of the mountaineer to that of the miner. These novels have much the same strengths and weaknesses as the mountain novels, but Garland employs a woman as a protagonist as he had frequently done in his middle-border fiction. *Hesper,* which Howells in a 3 November 1903 letter to Garland called "a fine book, full of a manly poetry and high ideal," was not only a financial success, selling more than fifty thousand copies, but also a hit with reviewers. A vast majority of the more than eighty reviews of the novel were positive, at times even enthusiastic.

In a handwritten, unpublished preface to the manuscript, dated "West Salem, 1903," Garland discussed the background for the novel:

That *Hesper* is my most romantic novel I must admit, and yet like all my other stories of the mountains, it is based on a careful study of the scenes and issues involved.

The stage for the story was already prepared. For ten years I had been absorbing Colorado life and scenery and the region roundabout Cripple Creek was vividly mapped in my mind. The Bull Hill Miner's War had but lately taken place and I was not only familiar with the conditions which had led to this exciting contest, but I knew some of the chief actors in it. Precisely as the Cheyenne outbreak of 1897 had served me as a sociologic background for *The Captain of the Gray-Horse Troop,* so the Miner's War in Cripple Creek now offered a picturesque and dramatic episode in Western history to my pen.

Although the Bull Hill strike was Garland's inspiration, his treatment of it from both historical and sociological points of view is disappointing. The reader gains only a superficial understanding of the causes of the conflict involving the free miners, the union men, and the mine owners. Unlike Garland's treatment of the poor city workers in the first part of *Jason Edwards, An Average Man* or of the depressing farm conditions depicted in *Main-Travelled Roads,* the miserable economic conditions of the miners are scarcely touched upon. Furthermore, because readers are not shown the miners at work, they are prevented from appreciating their struggles and miseries, even though Garland's sympathies clearly lie with the free miners. Despite Garland's statement in *A Daughter of the Middle Border* that "With a mere lovestory I had never been content. For me a sociological background was necessary in order to make fiction worth while," as was the case with most of his romantic works, the sociological background is not fully integrated into the plot nor is it a significant factor in the development of the main character.

Instead of the mining camp, Garland in *Hesper* is more concerned with the brother-sister relationship of Louis and Ann Rupert as they leave New York for the Rockies and the subsequent transformation of Ann from an easterner to a westerner. Like the Hesperides in Greek mythology, the "daughters of the evening" who dwelt in a garden in the Far West in which there were apples of gold, Ann changes her name to Hesper, the name originally desired by her father, and completes her transformation. With all personal conflicts resolved, Ann travels east in the closing pages of the novel to announce her allegiance to the West and her intention to marry Rob Raymond, a former herder, drifter, and ranch foreman and, eventually, a wealthy mine owner. Although Garland attempts to capture the enthusiasm he felt for the West and therefore describes his western scenery magnificently, he is finally so interested in the demands of his romantic plot Hesper's transformation seems mechanical and lacking in psychological credibility.

Garland had similar difficulties managing his plot and integrating his social materials in *Money Magic*. Set in Colorado Springs, the action of the novel coincides with the second miners' strike at Cripple Creek in 1904. Again the sociological and economic details are thinly sketched, but the theme is well developed.

Garland focuses on the lure and power of money through the situation of a young woman, Bertha, who is torn between desire and duty rather than between the East and the West. When Bertha rejects the proposal of the rich gambler Mark Haney, he abandons his casino to convince her of his sincerity. After an unlucky gambler who does not know that Haney no longer works at the casino provokes a gunfight and wounds him, Bertha is brought to him quickly so that he can marry her and leave her his fortune before he dies. He survives, however, and Bertha remains at his bedside, his devoted wife. Although she eventually falls in love with Ben Fordyce, a young lawyer, she will not forsake her duty to her husband and leave him. Nobly, Mark chooses to give his wife freedom and money: he goes to the mountains, where he knows the altitude will be fatal to his heart.

Although the plot is sentimental, the treatment of Bertha redeems the story as the psychological tension she feels is convincingly rendered. When she comes into her fortune, Bertha feels ennobled by the grace of money, but she cannot find peace by abandoning her husband. Garland effectively captures the lure of money but, unlike other contemporary novelists, did not see this attraction as necessarily destructive. Like Rose Dutcher, the attractive, vivacious Bertha is transformed from an unpolished western girl into a refined woman. Howells wrote in "Mr. Garland's Books" in the October 1912 *North American Review* that it was "the most masterly of the author's books," which demonstrated "that it is our conditioning which determines our characters, even though it does not always determine our actions."

Garland's last western phase was the result of his passion for conservation policy. He had become interested in forestry as early as the 1890s, but his interest was encouraged by a 1902 meeting with Roosevelt and Gifford Pinchot, chief of the Forest Service, on the conservation of the nation's forests. In addition to writing several short stories and two novels on the subject–*Cavanagh: Forest Ranger* (1910) and *The Forester's Daughter* (1914)–his notebooks between 1902 and 1913 are filled with forestry matters. In discussing the background for a lecture on *The Forester's Daughter,* Garland wrote in a 15 April 1913 letter that "As I have done my part in fiction to delineate the heroic side of the cowboys, the miner, and the Indian, so now I indicate the heroic side of 'the man in moss green uniform.'" As guardian of American's natural resources and an example of enlightened government, the forest ranger, the hero of both novels, represented the future of the West for Garland. Garland believed that the pioneer ethic of the exploitation of the western forests was no longer valid and modeled his own conservation ethic on that of Roosevelt's combative forester, Pinchot.

In a letter to Garland included as an introduction to *Cavanagh: Forest Ranger,* Pinchot wrote of the need of conservation in the new West:

> The Western frontier, to the lasting sorrow of all old hunters like yourself, has now practically disappeared. Its people faced life with a manly independence on their own courage and capacity which did them, and still does them, high honor. Some of them were naturally slow to see the advantages of the new order. But now that they have seen it, there is nowhere more intelligent, convinced, and effective support of the Conservation policies than in the West. The establishment of the new order in some places was not child's play. But there is a strain of fairness among the Western people which you can always count on in such a fight as the Forest Service has made.

Unfortunately, despite Garland's passionate interest in the subjects of conservation and forestry, his two novels were obtrusively melodramatic and overall embarrassing failures.

Shortly after the appearance of *Cavanagh: Forest Ranger,* Howells wrote to Garland on 27 March 1910: "One day, I hope you will revert to the temper of your first work, and give us a picture of the wild life you know so well on the lines of *Main-Travelled Roads*. You have in you greater things than you have done, and you owe the world which has welcomed you the best you have in you. Be true to the dream of thy youth–the dream of an absolute and inspiring veritism; the world is yours." In his answering letter written two days later Garland recognized what should be done but also acknowledged his own limitations:

> Your letter came this morning and I gratefully acknowledge and welcome your criticism. I have *not* measured up to my opportunity but perhaps waiting would have been to no avail. The plain truth is I watched the forest service develop for sixteen years and it was only last summer that the motive to use it came. I'm running low on motives. I don't care to write love stories or stories of

adventure and I can not revert to the prairie life without falling into the same reminiscent sadness of the man of fifty.

Discouraged that great artistic success had eluded him but too tired to attempt another major romantic work, Garland again wrote to Howells on 6 April: "I do not see see another book (even of this quality) when I look into my mind. Writing is coming to be a weariness and a plodding. What is the use when all the themes are old and one has grown old with them?"

For the final phase of his career Garland turned to re-creating the past in eight volumes of autobiographies and reminiscences, beginning with *A Son of the Middle Border* in 1917 and continuing until his death in California on 5 March 1940. While Garland's western writings generally lacked the quality of his early middle-border pieces, his western works brought him a small measure of critical approval and a brief popular following. In his grand delineation of the West, Garland imparted an enthusiasm for "the high country" and celebrated an idyllic freedom and romantic individualism that he felt could still exist in American life. Howells was accurate in his assessment in the preface he wrote to *They of the High Trails*: Garland's "rightful place in the sunset" is between Bret Harte and Mark Twain.

Letters:
Selected Letters of Hamlin Garland, edited by Keith Newlin and Joseph McCullough (Lincoln: University of Nebraska Press, 1998).

Biographies:
Eldon C. Hill, "A Biographical Study of Hamlin Garland from 1860 to 1895," dissertation, Ohio State University, 1940;

Jean Holloway, *Hamlin Garland: A Biography* (Austin: University of Texas Press, 1956);

Robert Mane, *Hamlin Garland: L'homme et l'oeuvre (1860–1940)* (Paris: Didier, 1968).

References:
James K. Folsom, *The American Western Novel* (New Haven, Conn.: College and University Press, 1966);

Robert Gish, *Hamlin Garland: The Far West* (Boise, Idaho: Boise State University, 1976);

William Dean Howells, "Mr. Garland's Books," *North American Review,* 19 (October 1912): 523–528;

Albert Keiser, *The Indian in American Literature* (New York: Oxford University Press, 1933);

Daniel F. Littlefield Jr. and Lonnie E. Underhill, "Renaming the American Indian: 1890–1913," *American Studies,* 12 (Fall 1971): 33–45;

Bonney MacDonald, "Eastern Imaginings of the West in Hamlin Garland's 'Up the Coolly' and 'God's Ravens,'" *Western American Literature,* 28 (November 1993): 209–230;

Stanford Marovitz, "'Romance or Realism?' Western Periodical Literature: 1893–1902," *Western American Literature,* 10 (May 1975): 46–58;

Joseph B. McCullough, *Hamlin Garland* (Boston: Twayne, 1978);

McCullough, "Hamlin Garland's Quarrel with *The Dial,*" *American Literary Realism,* 9 (Winter 1976): 77–80;

Roy W. Meyer, "Hamlin Garland and the American Indian," *Western American Literature,* 2 (Summer 1967): 109–125;

James Nagel, ed., *Critical Essays on Hamlin Garland* (Boston: G. K. Hall, 1982);

Donald Pizer, *Hamlin Garland's Early Work and Career* (Berkeley: University of California Press, 1960);

Owen J. Reamer, "Garland and the Indians," *New Mexico Quarterly,* 34 (Autumn 1964): 257–280;

Charles L. P. Silet, Robert E. Welch, and Richard Bourdeau, eds., *The Critical Reception of Hamlin Garland: 1891–1978* (Troy, N.Y.: Whitson, 1985).

Papers:
The chief collection of Garland's papers is in the Doheny Library of the University of Southern California; Garland's diaries and a major collection of correspondence are at the Huntington Library in San Marino, California.

Lewis H. Garrard

(15 June 1829 – 7 July 1887)

Richard H. Cracroft
Brigham Young University

BOOKS: *Wah-to-yah, and the Taos Trail: or Prairie Travel and Scalp Dances, with a Look at Los Rancheros from Muleback and the Rocky Mountain Campfire* (Cincinnati: H. W. Derby, 1850; New York: A. S. Barnes, 1850);

Chambersburg in the Colony and the Revolution (Philadelphia: Lippincott, 1856);

Memoir of Charlotte Chambers (Philadelphia: Collins, 1856).

Edition: *Wah-to-yah and the Taos Trail; or, Prairie Travel and Scalp Dances, with a Look at Los Rancheros from Muleback and the Rocky Mountain Campfire* (Norman: University of Oklahoma Press, 1955).

Lewis H. Garrard's niche in Western American literature is founded on a single book, *Wah-to-yah, and the Taos Trail: or Prairie Travel and Scalp Dances, with a Look at Los Rancheros from Muleback and the Rocky Mountain Campfire* (1850), which recounts the author's ten-month journey (September 1846–July 1847), at age seventeen, along the Santa Fe and Taos Trails of the American Southwest. He presents a vivid and invaluable record of life among the Cheyenne Indians, traders, and mountain men and provides the only eyewitness account of the April 1847 trials and executions of the Taos insurgents. Valued by western scholars as anthropologically accurate, historically authentic, and stylistically refreshing, *Wah-to-yah* has won an enduring place among the several firsthand accounts of the Santa Fe Trail.

Lewis Hector Garrard (he was christened Hector Lewis Garrard but changed the order of his given names in his youth) was born in Cincinnati, Ohio, on 15 June 1829 to a prominent and substantial family. His father, an attorney, died when Lewis was six. His mother, Sarah Bella Ludlow Garrard, was remarried to John McLean, associate justice of the United States Supreme Court, who adopted Lewis and his older brothers, Israel and Kenner, and his younger brother, Jeptha (another younger half brother, Lud, was born to Judge and Mrs. McLean). The McLeans were understanding and in-

Lewis H. Garrard, circa 1846

dulgent parents to Lewis, a restless and bright but sickly youth and an indifferent student whom they schooled, despite his poor eyesight, in the classics of literature and history.

In his introduction to *Wah-to-yah*, Garrard recalls his important first venture from his parental home:

> In February, 1846, being then in my seventeenth year, I tossed away schoolbooks, and glided down the Mississippi River, and along the Mexican Gulf, to Texas, and, shortly after, back to the Louisiana coast, where I stayed until the middle of May, visiting friends, riding horses, and shooting alligators, duck, and rail, from the bow of a long canoe in the cypress swamps.

His wanderlust stirred by this journey, Lewis reluctantly returned to Cincinnati and his schoolbooks. Excited by his recent excursion and "the glowing pages of [John C.] Frémont's tour to the Rocky Mountains in 1842–43," and reminding his protective and concerned mother (as he had in a letter of 24 February 1846) that his body was "weak" and his "eyes . . . precarious," Lewis managed to persuade his parents to allow him to set aside his studies and undertake, for the sake of his health, a longer and surely more perilous journey—this time into the vastnesses of the American West. He would acknowledge late in *Wah-to-yah* that his western journey had been "a trip for fun and health," though by then he had to acknowledge that "it is rather rough fun."

In July 1846 Lewis Garrard embarked for Saint Louis on a low-water steamer bearing an invaluable letter of introduction to the firm of Pierre Chouteau Jr. and Company from his nationally prominent step-father. After securing lodgings in the Planters' Hotel, however, Lewis was soon introduced to Céran St. Vrain (pronounced "San Vrah," Lewis wrote Kenner), of Bent, St. Vrain and Company, foremost traders among the Indians, Mexicans, and settlers of the Southwest. St. Vrain, who was also lodging at the Planters' Hotel and about to lead an outbound freight caravan for Bent's Fort via the Santa Fe and Taos Trails, agreed to take young Lewis along as his guest.

After shipping by steamer up the Missouri River to Westport (present-day Kansas City), the party began their overland journey to Bent's Fort on 12 September 1846. At his elder brothers' urgings, Garrard painstakingly kept a journal of the adventure, taking a few private minutes each evening to "scrawl a few words in a blank book," to read, and to reflect.

On 1 November 1846, after fifty-one days of hard travel, rigorous living, and buffalo hunting, Garrard and party reached Bent's Fort on the Arkansas River. Because Garrard's western adventures would take place along the Taos Trail (a lesser-known westerly fork of the Santa Fe Trail) leading to and from Bent's Fort and always within sight of the imposing, snow-covered, twin Spanish Peaks, called *Wah-to-yah* ("the Breasts of the World") by the Indians, Garrard would name his book after both landmarks. (He supposed, on first view, that the *Wah-to-yah* were fifteen miles from the fort, but soon learned they were actually 120 miles distant.) The notebook jottings of the seventeen-year-old lad later became the loosely structured, often haphazard—with shifting point of view and

frequent dangling modifiers—yet fresh and exciting *Wah-to-yah*.

Garrard's narrative, while not formally a bildungsroman, partakes of many of the traits of the crafted initiation novel. The narrative shows the well-reared and well-behaved but venturesome, fun-loving, and sentimentally inclined tenderfoot startled by what he terms "the fiery ordeal of a year in the Far West" into perceptible change, maturity, and self-confidence arising from a rush of experience and knowledge, and accompanying insight into the complexities, ambiguities, and dark corners of human life.

The dynamics of Garrard's journey to experience are apparent in the "Tarrapins" hoax of chapter 5. After the properly reared Garrard has loudly declared in camp his repugnance at "the very idea" of eating dog meat, John Simpson Smith, mountain man par excellence, takes up the challenge and exclaims, "I bet I'll make you eat dog meat in the [Cheyenne village], and you'll say it's good, and the best you ever hid in your 'meatbag' (stomach)." Before many campfires Garrard's *compañeros* introduce him to "Tarrapins," apparently a tasty meat dish. On partaking, first tentatively and then with gusto, Lewis smacks his lips and lauds the "delicacy of the meat," whereupon Smith informs the shocked Garrard that he has been eating dog. After eating another tasty morsel of boiled pup, the youth recalls his earlier conversation with Smith, and, acknowledging "that 'dog' was next in order to buffalo," he "ever after remained a stanch defender and admirer of dog meat."

After only a few days at Bent's Fort, Garrard accompanied Smith to a Cheyenne village farther down the Arkansas River. Arriving at the Cheyenne camp just as a returning war party is celebrating the taking of Pawnee scalps, Garrard dismounted to join in the Cheyenne scalp dance—beginning two and one-half months of immersion in the strange world of Cheyenne thought, manners, culture, and language. Shunning the white man's condescension and superior airs, the enthusiastic youth recounts how he "danced with the squaws, mixed in the gaieties, and, in every way, improved my time" among the Cheyenne. At night, he relates, "I folded my blanket over my shoulders, *comme les sauvages,* and went out" among the Indian youth, where "often I chasséd up to the scalps and joined in the chorus, much to their gratification and amusement, and no less to my own."

Experiencing the rhythms of Cheyenne life and moving with the band from place to place, Garrard shared their lives as few white men had done. He embraced their customs, lifestyle, and language and reported enthusiastically their games, foods, courtship, dress, courtesies, and ceremonies. For their part the Cheyenne, amused and flattered by the white youth's interest, willingly replied to his repeated inquiries of "*Ten-o-wast?*"–"What is it?"–as he pointed to objects whose names he wished to know and recorded them in a glossary; the youth was soon speaking a halting Cheyenne.

When *O-ne-o* ("Red Dress"), his host's teenage daughter, playfully attempted to elude her friends by crawling into Garrard's buffalo robe and nestling her head familiarly on his arm, the young man was at once flattered and astonished, and records, "I bore the affliction quite heroically, and tucked the clothing . . . snugly . . . around us." Upon being discovered by the others, Red Dress invites the enthralled Garrard to join the "jolting steps and uncertain halts of the grand scalp dance."

Such immersion in Indian life–which Garrard left only reluctantly in order to join the march to Taos–prepared him for his longer schooling among the mountain men, whose rugged lifestyle he quickly adapted, whose adaptation to the wilderness he profoundly admired, whose ways he emulated, and whose language he honored by his genuine rendering of their speech.

By the time Garrard rode west, the fur trade was practically finished, the last fur-trade rendezvous having taken place five years earlier. Still, the mountain men adapted; as western jacks-of-all-trades they became traders, hunters, hide curers, cattle drovers, construction workers, trail guides, lawmen, lumberjacks, miners, and soldiers. Although Garrard was tardy for the brief heyday of the beaver trade, he nevertheless met and rode with some of the best and most notable of "the reckless breed," all of whom had already adapted or were in process of adapting to change: There was St. Vrain, to whom Garrard dedicates his book as "The traverser of the plains–The revered of the Cheyenne Nation"; William Bent and his Cheyenne wife, Owl Woman; Charles Bent, William's brother, the newly appointed and short-lived governor of the New Mexico territory; Lucien B. Maxwell, superintendent of Bent's Fort and owner of the huge "Maxwell Grant"; Jim Beckwith (Beckwourth), the ubiquitous black mountaineer and erstwhile Crow war chief, lately the proprietor of the best-furnished saloon in Santa Fe; and Christopher "Kit" Carson, the renowned scout and guide.

High among these venerated mountaineers was Smith, Garrard's trail companion for most of the journey. Smith's life typifies the heroic journey west, tracing the mountain man's rite de passage from civilized bondage to savage freedom. Fleeing

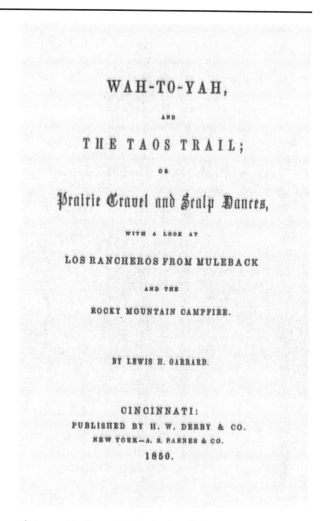

WAH-TO-YAH,

AND

THE TAOS TRAIL;

OR

Prairie Travel and Scalp Dances,

WITH A LOOK AT

LOS RANCHEROS FROM MULEBACK

AND THE

ROCKY MOUNTAIN CAMPFIRE.

BY LEWIS H. GARRARD.

CINCINNATI:
PUBLISHED BY H. W. DERBY & CO.
NEW YORK–A. S. BARNES & CO.
1850.

Title page for Garrard's first book, which records his experiences as a seventeen-year-old in the Southwest

life as a Saint Louis tailor, Smith undertook, via residence with and marriage into several Indian tribes, the geographical and spiritual journey to independence and self-realization since followed by every fictional mountain man. A Cheyenne squaw-man and hymn-singing barbarian, Smith knew something about everything and was an "unaccountable composition of goodness and evil, cleverness and meanness, caution and recklessness!"

It was, however, another well-known mountain man, John L. Hatcher, who personified for Garrard "the beau ideal of a Rocky Mountain man." Trapper, trader, plainsman, guide (for U.S. government expeditions), and Indian fighter, Hatcher was cool, courageous, alert, adept, and a witty teller of yarns couched in colorful mountain lingo.

In "Wah-to-yah," the best-known chapter in the book, Garrard presents the mountaineer at his best when Hatcher recounts a delightful tale of his visit to hell. Meeting the devil, "A kind-lookin' smallish old gentleman," the mountain man defends his old sidekick Jake Beloo against the hot irons of the imps, solemnly proclaims his belief in preachers and the Bible, then straddles a big snake, whereupon, he says, "I waved my old wool hat, an', kickin' him in a fast run, sung out to the little devils to git up behind, an' off we all started, screechin' 'Hooraw fur Hell!'" After a tour of hell Hatcher finally eludes the encroaching devils through repeating "a prayer my mother used to make me say," buying time until his mountain comrades can ride in at the last moment to wrest his soul from the devil.

But Garrard's obvious affinity with the mountain men is demonstrated less in his description of their daily routines and trapping techniques (subjects better reported by Washington Irving and George Frederick Ruxton) than in his uncanny ear for trapper lingo and his natural ability to record the rich metaphors of the trapper's "euphonic language" and capture the trapper-specific vocabulary, idioms, and rhythms of speech, as in this skillful rendering of mountain-man lingo in which Hatcher expounds his love of mountain life:

> This child hates an American what hasn't seen Injuns skulped, or doesn't know a Yute from a Khian mok'sin. Sometimes he thinks of makin' tracks for white settlement, but when he gits to Bent's big lodge, on the Arkansa, and sees the bugheways, an' the fellers from the States, how they roll thar eyes at an Injun yell, worse nor if a village of Camanches was on 'em, an' pick up a beaver trap, to ask what it is—just shows whar the niggurs had thar brungin' up—this child says—"a little bacca, if its a plew [beaver pelt], a plug [pound of tobacco], an' Dupont an' G'lena [powder and lead], a Green River [knife] or so," and he leaves for the Bayou Salade. Durn the white diggins, while thar's buffler in the mountains. "Whoopee!" shouted he to us, "are you for Touse? This hos is thar in one sun, wagh!"

Close examination of Garrard's colorful trapper talk inevitably evokes comparisons with the trapper speech recorded by Ruxton, the English soldier and adventurer. Comparisons suggest that Garrard's renderings were probably influenced and certainly reinforced by Ruxton's standard recordings of mountain-man vernacular, as found in *Adventures in Mexico and the Rocky Mountains* (1847) and, to a greater extent, in *Life in the Far West* (1848), both of which Garrard had read, doubtless with great interest.

Ruxton, who had traveled with Garrard from the Arkansas River to Mann's Fort in the spring of 1847, and whom Garrard describes with admiration in *Wah-to-yah,* would encounter Garrard again in Buffalo, New York, early in August 1848. The former trail companions talked, Garrard recalls in a footnote in *Wah-to-yah,* of "old scenes, [of Ruxton's] book [*Adventures in Mexico and the Rocky Mountains*]" and of the English adventurer's latest book, *Life in the Far West,* then appearing serially in *Blackwood's.* Ruxton, who departed for the West that same afternoon, would die of dysentery in Saint Louis on 29 August 1848 at age twenty-seven. Garrard wrote to his older brother, Kenner: "Never has the death of a relative affected me so much as this one of Mr. Ruxton."

The young man's grief underscores once again the fact that *Wah-to-yah* becomes decidedly more than what Lawrence Clark Powell, echoing others, calls "a lusty poem in prose to youthful freedom and adventure"—although it is that, too. In pleasant weather, enjoying a full stomach and little threat of Indian attack, Garrard's assertion that "better living there could not be" rings sincere. Garrard often hymns the idyllic freedom of western man, insisting that "Here, with mule and gun and a few faithful friends, one experiences . . . a grand sensation of liberty and a total absence of fear."

Garrard soon learned, however, that the fleeting moments of contentment must be bought and paid for with hours of solitude, extremes of physical discomfort, and constant vigilance—caveats that a mountain man takes for granted. While crossing Raton Pass, Garrard writes:

> This is the acme of life. With fat, sleek mules, plenty of provision and tobacco, and the undisturbed possession of our scalps in doubt, we traveled and camped, always on the alert and ready for any emergency, caring little for foe, nor keeping guard; for a mountain man is supposed to always have his ear open to impending danger.

Amid this cherished life of idyllic freedom, then, Garrard identifies the ever-lurking "dark side of prairie life" and observes that sudden death is the high price many must pay for freedom on the trail; it is in the wilderness, confronted by "momentary danger of losing his scalp," that "the mind is stretched to its utmost tension by reason of the continually impending dangers of starvation, thirst, or the wary Camanche, Arapaho, Digger, or Apache."

Observing the variety of humanity in the various throes of western vicissitudes and hardship enabled young Garrard to glimpse humankind's underbelly and probe the dark side of human life. Time after time his essentially optimistic and ebullient nature is tempered by terrible physical hardship—heat, thirst, hunger, exhaustion—and everpresent personal peril from accident, disease, or an Indian surprise attack. *Wah-to-yah* provides vivid glimpses into Garrard's year-long initiation into these hard facts of human life, and, almost as important, the subsequent writing of the book enabled his understanding and thus his articulating of that harsh reality in tight, telling, and honest prose.

Garrard's account of the uprising of the Pueblos of New Mexico, with the ensuing trial and execution of the insurgents, exemplifies his complex emotional responses to those hard but exciting events. After learning about the uprising and killings from a lone Indian who was taking the news to Fort Bent, Garrard left the Cheyenne to join William Bent and his party of twenty-three avengers in their march for Taos. Their martial enthusiasm dulled by the difficult mountain passage in harsh winter weather and by news that the U.S. military had already put down the resistance and arrested the malefactors, the trail-worn party arrived in Taos as the trial was about to begin.

Garrard's vivid descriptions of the attractions and excitement of frontier Taos contrast with his graphic and sobering eyewitness accounts of the trial and executions of the "lousy, greasy, unwashed *pelados*" whose sorry condition evoked at once his revulsion and his sympathy. This stepson of a U.S. Supreme Court justice was outraged by the fact that the judges, jury, and witnesses—all Americans, and most of them related to the victims—had proclaimed the men's guilt before the trials began. He was likewise angered by the "damnable" injustice of the court's finding one of the group guilty of treason—a judgment that required "a great assumption on the part of the Americans to conquer a country and then arraign the revolting inhabitants for treason." He left the trials "sick at heart."

With youthful resilience, however, Garrard and his associates not only loaned their ropes to the hangman, soaping them first for easier slippage, but served as the rear guard for the hanging of the first group of six prisoners. His account of the hangings is conveyed in the terse and controlled prose of a seasoned observer:

> Bidding each other "*adios,*" with a hope of meeting in Heaven, at word from the sheriff the mules were started, and the wagons drawn from under the tree. No fall was given, and their feet remained on the board till the ropes drew taut. The bodies swayed back and forth, and, coming in contact with each other, convulsive shudders shook their frames; the muscles, contracting, would relax, and again contract, and the bodies writhed most horribly.
>
> While thus swinging, the hands of two came together, which they held with a firm grasp till the muscles loosened in death.

After Taos, Garrard returned to Bent's Fort, where he soon bade farewell to his longtime compañeros and joined Captain Enos's eastbound government teamsters. Also joining the caravan was Ruxton, with whom Garrard would experience several buffalo hunts and many hardships.

After bidding farewell to Hatcher at the fort, Garrard notes that "the charm of my backwoods life was broken." His appetite for adventure, however, remained. On 15 May 1847 his homeward-bound party reached Mann's Fort—an outpost being built near the Cimmaron crossing of the Arkansas River, equidistant between Fort Leavenworth and Santa Fe. Garrard and eight other members of the caravan volunteered to guard the newly constructed fort against marauding Pawnees and Comanches. Feeling that destruction of the post was imminent, Smith, the leader of the small unit, soon abandoned the company. His departure left Garrard full of gloomy foreboding. On 15 June, his eighteenth birthday, his grim fears were suddenly relieved by the arrival of Col. William H. "Owl" Russell and his troop of eighty-five men. Russell, an old friend of Garrard's father, virtually commanded the young man to leave his "Prairie Prison" and join the eastward-bound party. Relieved, Garrard obeyed. A few days after his departure from Fort Mann, three members of the garrison were killed by Indians, and the post was abandoned.

Garrard was, however, destined to experience Indian warfare. Not long out of Fort Mann, the wagon train was repeatedly attacked by a large band of Comanches. During one attack Garrard shot and probably killed one of the Comanche warriors. After repelling the Indians, the party trailed homeward, Garrard's joyful anticipations of relaxation from the responsibility of self-preservation and western vicissitudes tempered by "a shade of melancholy" evoked by happy memories of his western compañeros.

The culture shock of the return to civilization provided Garrard's final adventure. Upon arriving at Council Grove the party shed their worn mountain clothing, sheathed their scalp knives for forks and spoons, engaged in an uproarious drinking spree, and said farewell. Garrard returned home to Cincinnati by steamboat.

The great adventure of his life was over. "Abominable chills and fever greeted my return to civilization," he writes in his introduction, and it would be months before he would be well enough to undertake writing his book. Of course, it would have taken some time for Garrard to assess the meaning of his western journey. On 1 November 1846 a homesick and wilderness-stunned Garrard

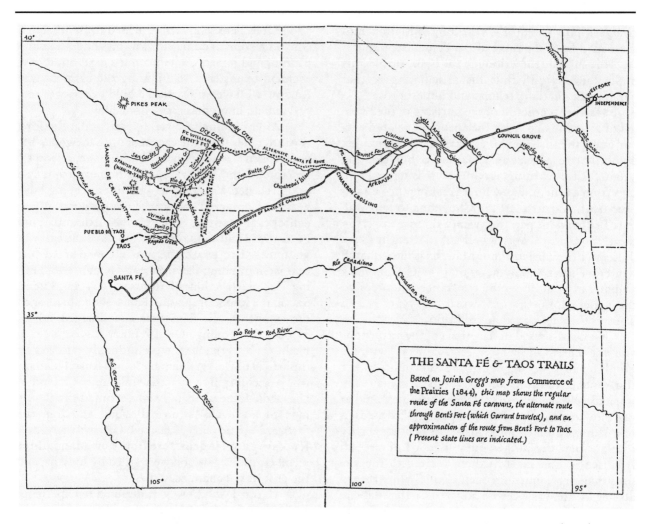

A map of important trails of the Southwest, from the University of Oklahoma Press edition of Wah-to-yah *(1955)*

had advised his mother to tell his brothers "not to think of ever starting out this way & if I knew when I started what I do now I never would have come." Distance and perspective lent enchantment to the view, and on 10 September 1847, the tour now safely behind him, Garrard wrote to his brother, Kenner, then at West Point, about his adventures, relating in several pages of terse and understated prose a few of his thrilling western adventures—doubtless discovering in the process that he had, in fact, a remarkable tale to tell.

Over the next three years Garrard succumbed to his older brothers' and friends' pleas that he write of his experiences. Admitting "a pardonable vanity," he turned to the "scanty pencillings" of his long-missing journal and began to augment and prepare them for publication.

He was sensible of the rudeness of the western life he was describing and expected that some of his readers would recoil from his vivid descriptions of western uncouthness and the honesty of his re-

sponses to the rawness of western life. To such anticipated accusations of grossness or uncalled-for expressions, he notes that "I have naught set down in malice, and it is no more my prerogative to exclude than to add." Pleasing or offending, his little book "has the merit of truthfulness."

Wah-to-yah was published in May 1850 to predominantly favorable reviews but small sales. Ralph P. Bieber, in his 1938 edition of the book, presents samples of generally laudatory reviews from the *Daily Cincinnati Commercial,* the *Daily Cincinnati Gazette,* the New York *Tribune,* and *Harper's Weekly,* but the critic for the New York *Observer* (10 August 1850) concludes, "We do not commend his book to our readers."

Garrard's book failed to reach a wide public and, though occasionally noticed by western historians, soon became a forgotten classic and remained so until 1927 when Walter S. Campbell reprinted a bowdlerized edition "for use in schools and libraries." Subsequent editions introduced the book to a wider public, and in 1955 (and in several printings since) *Wah-to-yah,* with an introduction by novelist A. B. Guthrie Jr., was republished in the University of Oklahoma Press's "Western Frontier Library" series. Garrard's "little book" has since become a well-known and widely read classic of western America, taking its place with at least four other remarkable accounts of life on the Santa Fe and Oregon Trails in 1846–1847: Ruxton's two Western works; Frances Parkman's *The Oregon Trail: Sketches of Prairie and Rocky-Mountain Life* (1849); and *Down the Santa Fe Trail and into Mexico: The Diary of Susan Shelby Magoffin, 1846–1847* (1849). Garrard's narrative, though more in the vein of Richard Henry Dana Jr.'s popular *Two Years Before the Mast* (1840), in most respects compares well with and often excels these companion books. Guthrie, comparing Garrard's book to Parkman's "masterpiece," for example, asserts in his introduction to *Wah-to-yah,* that "in some ways [Garrard] is the better—the fresher, the more revealing, the more engaging, the less labored" because Garrard "not only liked the rude and unfettered life of the frontier, he liked his companions, the traders, the mountain men, the bucks and squaws and papooses."

Garrard would live forty productive years after his momentous western year. Though plagued by illness, he would, on his return to Cincinnati, make at least three attempts at continuing his formal education and devote several months to an unfruitful private study of law before turning, at last, to medicine. Garrard took a medical degree from the University of Pennsylvania in 1853. Although he practiced medicine in Cincinnati for the following year, he was again hindered by ill health, poor eyesight, and a continuing restlessness.

In the late summer of 1854 he and his brother Israel started for the Minnesota frontier but instead dropped down the Mississippi River to the wilderness area at the head of Lake Pepin. After exploring the region, they acquired a tract of land on the lakeshore and founded Frontenac, Minnesota. Garrard soon left the settlement of the community to Israel and to Evert Westervelt and returned to Cincinnati and his medical practice.

In 1856, at the urging of his mother, Garrard published two small books of family history. The first, *Chambersburg in the Colony and the Revolution,* is a fifty-page historical sketch of the life of Garrard's forebear, Benjamin Chambers, founder of Chambersburg, Pennsylvania; the book also presents the Revolutionary War letters of Garrard's great-grandfather, Capt. James Chambers, later a brigadier general of the Pennsylvania Militia. Printed separately but subsequently bound into one vol-

ume, *Chambersburg* is a kind of prefatory sketch to Garrard's second history, the 135-page *Memoir of Charlotte Chambers,* which recounts, in a formal and overwrought prose bearing little resemblance to Garrard's lively style in *Wah-to-yah,* the personal history and selected letters, from 1797 to 1821, of his devout maternal grandmother, Charlotte Chambers Ludlow Riske, and her two husbands, all of whom figured prominently in the establishment of Cincinnati.

Also in 1856, and again in 1857–1858, Garrard traveled to Germany and western Europe. In 1858 he rejoined his brother Israel and settled in Frontenac, where he built a Victorian mansion, which he modestly named "Dakota Cottage," at the end of Garrard Avenue. On the death in 1861 of Justice McLean, Garrard's mother moved to Frontenac to live with her sons. In 1862, at the age of thirty-three, Garrard married Florence Van Vliet, the daughter of a prosperous farmer. The couple had four children, two sons—both of whom died in infancy—and two daughters.

In 1870 Garrard built and moved into a second house in neighboring Lake City. Despite the ill health and poor eyesight that had dogged him since boyhood and prevented his active practice of medicine as well as service in the Civil War (his three brothers were Union Army generals), Garrard became a farmer, a bank founder, and a participant in local and state politics, holding the offices of county supervisor, township chairman, and mayor and serving two terms in the state legislature. He also maintained his interest in history as a lifelong member of the Minnesota, Ohio, and Pennsylvania historical societies. In the early 1880s he began wintering in Cincinnati and in 1884 returned to reside permanently in his hometown. He died on 7 July 1887 at the age of fifty-eight at Lakewood, New York.

It is as a seventeen-year-old adventurer-observer-reporter in the American Southwest of 1846–1847 that Garrard has entered the history, literature, and imaginations of his countrymen; and there, as "the boy traveler," he will remain. His refreshing, boyish, clear-eyed, and honest depictions of life as it was for a fleeting moment along the Santa Fe and Taos Trails in view of the *Wah-to-yah* will continue to incite welcome companions from later centuries to "Durn the white diggins, while thar's buffler in the mountains. 'Whoopee! . . . are you for Touse? This hos is thar in one sun, wagh!'"

References:

Marius Bewley, "*Wah-to-yah and the Taos Trail:* A Minor Classic of the West," in *Masks and Mirrors* (New York: Atheneum, 1970), pp. 221–225;

Bernard DeVoto, *The Year of Decision, 1846* (Boston: Houghton Mifflin, 1943);

Edward Halsey Foster, *Josiah Gregg and Lewis H. Garrard,* Western Writers Series 28 (Boise, Idaho: Boise State University Press, 1977);

Blanche C. Grant, *When Old Trails Were New: The Story of Taos* (New York: Press of the Pioneers, 1934);

George Bird Grinnell, *Beyond the Old Frontier: Adventures of Indian-Fighters, Hunters, and Fur-Traders* (New York: Scribners, 1920);

David Lavender, *Bent's Fort* (Garden City, N.Y.: Doubleday, 1954);

Roy W. Meyer, "New Light on Lewis Garrard," *Western Historical Quarterly,* 6 (July 1975): 261–270;

Lawrence Clark Powell, "*Wah-to-Yah and the Taos Trail:* Lewis H. Garrard," in his *Southwest Classics: The Creative Literature of the Arid Lands: Essays on the Books and Their Writers* (Los Angeles: Ward Ritchie, 1974), pp. 27–35.

Papers:

Garrard Family Papers, located at the Southern Minnesota Historical Center, Mankato State College, Mankato, Minnesota, were donated by Lewis H. Garrard's granddaughter in 1973. They contain several letters written during Garrard's tour and a manuscript draft of nearly one-fifth of his western book.

Josiah Gregg

(19 July 1806 – 25 February 1850)

Richard H. Cracroft
Brigham Young University

See also the Gregg entry in *DLB 183: American Travel Writers, 1776–1864.*

BOOK: *Commerce of the Prairies: or, The Journal of a Santa Fé Trader, during Eight Expeditions across the Great Western Prairies, and a Residence of Nearly Nine Years in Northern Mexico,* 2 volumes (New York: H. G. Langley, 1844; London: Wiley & Putnam, 1844); enlarged, 2 volumes (New York: J. & H. G. Langley, 1845); republished as *Scenes and Incidents in the Western Prairies: During Eight Expeditions, and Including a Residence of Nearly Nine Years in Northern Mexico* (Philadelphia: J. W. Moore, 1856).

Edition: *Commerce of the Prairies,* edited by Max L. Moorhead (Norman: University of Oklahoma Press, 1954).

Josiah Gregg's two-volume *Commerce of the Prairies; or, the Journal of a Santa Fé Trader, during Eight Expeditions across the Great Western Prairies, and a Residence of Nearly Nine Years in Northern Mexico* (1844) has earned him an undisputed place at the forefront of literary historians of the early American West. Called "a classic in the literature of Western history" by Reuben Gold Thwaites, the editor of a 1905 edition, *Commerce of the Prairies* combines Gregg's firsthand account of life along the Santa Fe Trail in the 1830s with his astute and generally accurate observations of the natural history and topology of the region as well as the history and anthropology of its various peoples. *Commerce of the Prairies,* asserts Hiram Martin Chittenden in his own classic, *The American Fur-Trade of the Far West* (1902), is "one of the great works of American history."

Josiah Gregg was born on 19 July 1806 in Elk River, Tennessee, the fifth of seven children (four male, three female) of Harmon and Susannah Schmelzer (or Smelser) Gregg. In 1809 Harmon Gregg, a wheelwright of Scottish-American descent, moved his family to Illinois Territory, twenty miles east of Saint Louis. In 1812, when Josiah was six, the

Josiah Gregg

family moved to Cooper's Fort, Missouri, where they stayed four years, banding with other pioneers for protection against pro-British Indians during the War of 1812. In 1815, after cessation of hostilities, the family removed to a farm in the vicinity and remained there until the fall of 1825 when they moved still farther west to a permanent homestead in Blue township about four miles northeast of what in 1827 would become Independence, Missouri.

A frail and sickly child, Josiah was relieved from performing heavy farm labor and turned early to reading and intellectual pursuits. Always the leading scholar in available schools, Josiah, as his brother John recalled in a letter to Dr. George Engelmann on 24 December 1850, "showed a very early predilection for books, and remarkably mathematical cast of mind." Summarizing his brother's unusual intellectual breadth, John wrote:

> His education was ample—though mainly self taught. . . . He spoke and wrote Spanish with as much facility as his native tongue. He read and translated French and Italian with ease. He professed not to understand Latin—yet his knowledge of it was much better than many who had made a study of it at school. He understood something of the rudiments of the Greek and German. He never professed a knowledge of any thing in literature, except what he understood critically correct.

When Josiah was sixteen he and John undertook to study the science of surveying. John recalls that when it came to understanding Gunter's chain, the sixty-six-foot unit of measurement in surveying, the boys were stumped by an unclear text. Dissatisfied when a neighbor with a reputation as "a learned surveyor" confessed that he, too, did not understand Gunter's chain and had found it unnecessary, Josiah studied the text until he was able to explain the principles and practical use of the chain "as though," wrote John, "he had been familiar with it all his life."

When he was eighteen, Gregg, having exhausted the resources of local education, opened his own school near Liberty, Missouri, and taught there for one year. The next year, not content with teaching as a profession and believing that he might become a medical doctor, he applied to the widely respected physician, John Sappington, of Saline County to become his student and apprentice in medicine. Sappington turned him down. Gregg turned to reading law but found it not to his liking and on the advice of his doctor gave it up after several months. During this period of study the twenty-three-year-old was named the "Speaker of the Day" at the 1829 Fourth of July celebration, an indication of the esteem in which he was held by fellow citizens.

In 1830 Gregg was intellectually unchallenged and restless. Never robust, he became so physically weakened by what he and others variously described as dyspepsia, consumption, and related complications that by winter 1830–1831 he was an invalid. In his preface to *Commerce of the Prairies* Gregg explains how the collapse of his health led him to the Southwest and changed the course of his life:

> For some months preceding the year 1831, my health had been gradually declining under a complication of chronic diseases. . . . The morbid condition of my system . . . had finally reduced me to such a state, that for nearly a twelvemonth, I was . . . so debilitated as rarely to be able to extend my walks beyond the narrow precincts of my chamber. In this hopeless condition, my physicians advised me to take a trip across the Prairies, . . . to seek that health which their science had failed to bestow. I accepted their suggestion, and, without hesitation, . . . [joined] one of those spring Caravans which were annually starting from the United States, for Santa Fé.

Gregg's traders' caravan departed from nearby Independence in May 1831. In traveling to the West to seek his health Gregg was fashionably de rigueur. During the mid and late nineteenth century the western journey, with its rigorous routine, spartan diet, and change of climate became, like the mineral spas of Europe, a popular prescription for curing a variety of ailments. Many saw the West as a vast sanatorium for the ailing and the convalescent as attested to by such western writers as Richard Henry Dana, Frances Parkman Jr., Lewis H. Garrard, George F. Ruxton, and, later in the century, Theodore Roosevelt and Owen Wister.

The immediate effects of this first tour were, he later wrote in *Commerce of the Prairies,* "in the first place to re-establish my health, and, in the second, to beget a passion for Prairie life which I never expect to survive." The journey restored his health almost at once. So ill as to be unable to mount a horse at the beginning of the journey, Gregg was able, after one week on the prairies, to begin leaving his Dearborn carriage and ride his pony for longer and longer periods each day. Three months after his departure from Independence, Gregg was a healthy man, and he remained well as long as he was on the plains; on his return home he would relapse almost at once into chronic illness and psychic malaise.

During the next nine years, from 1831 to 1840, Gregg crossed the prairies eight different times (on four round trips) as a trader based principally in Santa Fe, New Mexico, and later in Satillo and Chihuahua, Mexico. His interest in the trade had been quickened by his brothers, Jacob and John, who had worked in the Santa Fe trade several years earlier. Jacob was a member of the trade caravan of 1824 which reestablished trade with Mexico after the trade expeditions of 1812 had ended disastrously with the Mexicans confiscating goods and imprisoning the American traders as spies.

On his initial trip Gregg used the six weeks of overland travel to Santa Fe for more than recuperation. He served as bookkeeper for Jesse Sutton, one

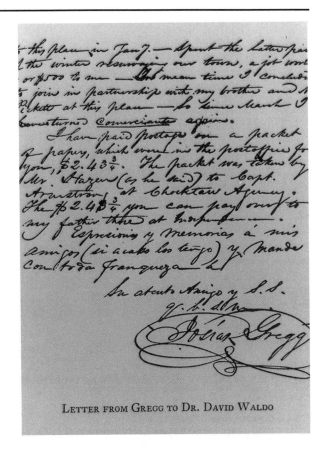

LETTER FROM GREGG TO DR. DAVID WALDO

A 9 June 1842 letter from Gregg to Dr. David Waldo, in which he refers to his travels in Texas during the previous winter (Missouri Historical Society of Saint Louis)

of the merchants; mastered Spanish; and made careful observations of the route, topography, and water courses, meticulously recording a welter of data in his notebooks. His brother John would recall that "It had been his habit from early youth to note down everything he deemed worthy of remembrance. This habit had been well preserved during the time he was engaged in the Santa Fe trade." These notebooks, faithfully filled during his years in the Southwest, became the basis for *Commerce of the Prairies,* which he published four years after leaving the Santa Fe trade.

Interspersed through the two volumes of *Commerce of the Prairies* are what amounts to two major series of nonsequential chapters devoted to distinct aims, with fifteen chapters given over to Gregg's narrative of adventures and eighteen chapters devoted to scientific concerns. In addition, the preface provides a sketch of the early history of the Santa Fe trade, and chapter 6 of the first volume offers the first connected narrative history of New Mexico from the earliest Spanish explorations to 1840. He made his history invaluable by copying information from ancient documents he found in the old Santa

Fe archives, thereby preserving many documents that have since been destroyed or lost.

The most exciting portions of *Commerce of the Prairies* are found in the narrative of Gregg's day-to-day adventures as a Santa Fe trader on the prairies, which comprise chapters 1–5 and 16 in the first volume and chapters 1–9 in the second. These chapters are reminiscent of Washington Irving's *A Tour on the Prairies* (1835) and Charles Fenno Hoffman's *A Winter in the West* (1835), literary works with which Gregg compares his own effort in his preface. He folds into his narrative his subsequent trips along the trail as well as his own and others' exciting accounts of buffalo hunts, Indian attacks, hardships, brushes with death, and sufferings from hunger and thirst. He writes of white cruelties to Indians and reciprocal tortures by Indians, ambushes, skirmishes, scalpings, and imprisonment. These experiences and incidents are all framed by Gregg's four round trips between Independence and Santa Fe.

In the remaining eighteen chapters Gregg undertakes to describe accurately and objectively the landscape, the natural history of the region, and the anthropology of the native peoples between the Missouri River and northern Mexico. The titles reflect Gregg's focus in the chapters given over to such observations. In the first volume the titles of chapters 7 through 15 are "Geography of New Mexico," "Mines of New Mexico," "Domestic Animals," "Arts and Sciences," "Dress and Customs," "Government," "Religious Superstitions and Ceremonies," "The Pueblos," and "Wild Tribes of New Mexico." The second volume continues with similar titles for chapters 10 through 15: "Geography of the Prairies," "Animals of the Prairies," "Aborigines of America," "The Frontier Indians," and two concluding chapters, both titled "Indians of the Prairies." These chapters, replete with scientific observations, anthropological data, legends, and lore, make *Commerce of the Prairies* a valuable compendium of the natural history and geography of the region. Furthermore, Gregg's fondness for statistics, measuring routes, distances, and heights, and tracing watercourses resulted in maps of New Mexico and northern Mexico so nearly accurate that the U.S. Army Topological Survey Corps, traders, and travelers through the region relied on them for years.

Gregg's remarks on several Native American tribes, the Catholic Hispanics of northern Mexico and New Mexico, and the Mormons show that his generally objective observations are occasionally colored not only by personal and cultural biases common in the United States at the time but also by a querulous misanthropy stemming from his chronic ill health and a Calvinist distrust of human nature. He thus describes the various Indian tribes as "thieving," "skulking," and "treacherous," and as evincing that "perverse, restless disposition, which appears ever to have characterized the conduct of half-civilized nations." The New Mexicans he harshly castigates as bigoted, intolerant, and immoral, exhibiting "superstitious blindness" in their Roman Catholic "idolatry" and manifesting "no stability except in artifice; no profundity except for intrigue."

When Gregg returned home in 1840 he found that during his absence the Mormons had settled in and in due time been expelled from Missouri on a decree from the governor. Gregg harshly portrays the Latter Day Saints as lawless, treacherous, and dishonest, a people driven, he wrote, by a "fanatical delusion" and deserving their rejection by good people everywhere because of the "immorality of their lives, and . . . their disregard for the sacred rites of marriage." Still, although Gregg asserts Protestant and American superiority over Spanish, Indian, and Mormon neighbors and sees the U.S. Indian pol-

icy as enlightened and benevolent, he seems equally unhappy with fallen human nature in Protestant America.

Despite his misanthropy and his sense that humankind is degenerate and enslaved, Gregg maintains in *Commerce of the Prairies* that "the wild, unsettled and independent life of the Prairie trader makes perfect freedom from nearly every kind of social dependence an absolute necessity of his being." The self-reliant and free Santa Fe trader and laissez-faire capitalist

> knows no government—no laws, save those of his own creation and adoption. . . . The exchange of . . . this sovereign independence, for a life in civilization, where both his physical and moral freedom are invaded at every turn, by the complicated machinery of social institutions, is certainly likely to commend itself to but few. . . . [Such freedom] is certainly evinced by the frequent instances of men of letters, of refinement and of wealth, voluntarily abandoning society for a life upon the Prairies, or in the still more savage mountain wilds.

In the West, Gregg enjoyed "broad, unembarrassed freedom" from his civilization-based illnesses as well as the physical freedom to explore expansive landscapes that he saw as analogous to the moral freedom he found in a wilderness unsullied by the collective tribal faults that congregate in civilization. Explaining that scarcely a day passes "without my experiencing a pang of regret that I am not now roving at large upon those western plains," he admits that

> this passion for Prairie life . . . will be very apt to lead me upon the plains again, to spread my bed with the mustang and the buffalo, under the broad canopy of heaven,—there to seek to maintain undisturbed my confidence in men, by fraternizing with the little prairie dogs and wild colts, and the still wilder Indians . . . of the Great American Deserts.

Gregg's scientific attention to detail precluded his overuse of inflated rhetoric, and the resulting lack of fashionable embellishment and flourish lends his relatively spare prose an immediacy, authenticity, and honesty that have allowed his literary style to age better than that of many of his contemporaries. Typical of Gregg's narrative style is this description, found at the beginning of chapter 3, of the trader caravan getting under way:

> The familiar note of preparation, "Catch up! catch up!" was now sounded from the captain's camp, and re-echoed from every division and scattered group along the valley. On such occasions, a scene of confusion ensues, which must be seen to be appreciated. The woods and dales resound with the gleeful yells of the light-

hearted wagoners, who, weary of inaction, and filled with joy at the prospect of getting under way, become clamorous in the extreme. . . .

"All's set!" is finally heard from some teamster–"All's set," is directly responded from every quarter. "Stretch out!" immediately vociferates the captain. Then, the "heps!" of drivers–the cracking of whips–the trampling of feet–the occasional creak of wheels–the rumbling of wagons–form a new scene of exquisite confusion. . . . "Fall in!" is heard from headquarters, and the wagons are forthwith strung out upon the long inclined plain.

The Santa Fe trade, Gregg's economic grounds for going west, are at once the focus and wellspring of his book. Following the pattern of the demise of the beaver-fur trade, the Santa Fe trade suffered a steady decline from 1831 until it was shut down by the Mexican government in 1843 following the outbreak of border problems with the Texas Republic, with which the United States sided. The sharp decline in trading profits of the 1839–1840 season apparently convinced Gregg that the time had come for him to drop out of the Santa Fe trade, at least for a time.

In April 1840 Gregg, on completing his last trip on the prairies, returned to Van Buren, Arkansas, where his brother John then resided. Immediately restive and beset once again by several ailments, he undertook another business trip in June 1841, this time to Texas. On returning to Van Buren he gave up farming and merchandising plans for a partnership in Pickett and Gregg, his brother John's firm. Meanwhile, encouraged by his family, he decided to write a book about his prairie adventures, and he noted in his diary on 1 January 1843 that "I commenced preparing notes for the compilation of a work on 'Santa Fé and the Prairies.'" He traveled to Philadelphia in June 1843 in order, he wrote in his diary, "to prepare my work for publication." Disturbed by "the noises of the streets," he moved to Camden, New Jersey, and then, in late November, to Manhattan, in order "to make arrangements about publishing" his still unfinished manuscript.

Turned down by several publishing houses, Gregg eventually signed a contract with D. Appleton and Company and engaged Louis Fitzgerald Tasistro, a minor actor and author, as his manuscript editor. Unhappy with Tasistro's attempts to embellish his spare prose, Gregg turned to John Bigelow, a young attorney recommended by William Cullen Bryant who would later become Bryant's partner on the *New York Evening Post.* Immediately impressed by Bigelow in their first meeting on 23 December 1843, Gregg engaged him as his editor, and the two commenced work on the book. It is probable that Bigelow was behind the dissolving of the Appleton contract and the signing of a new contract with H. G. Langley Company, with whom he had connections. As John Thomas Lee reports in his 1980 article on the authorship of Gregg's book, Bigelow later rejected suggestions that he was the coauthor of *Commerce of the Prairies,* insisting that "My laundry work added no more value to the washing of [the book] than the washing and ironing adds to the value of a new garment."

Bigelow, who remained Gregg's friend and correspondent, has left the only known prose description of Gregg, which reinforces the only extant photograph of Gregg, taken at about the same time:

I found Mr. Gregg to be at that time [1844] a man about forty and about five feet ten inches in height, though from the meagerness of his figure looking somewhat taller; he had a fine head and an intellectual cast of countenance and temperament, though his mouth and the lower part of his face showed that he had enjoyed to but a limited extent the refining influence of civilization. He had fine blue eyes and an honest although not a cheerful expression, due, as I afterward learned, to chronic dyspepsia. He was withal very shy and as modest as a school-girl.

Years later Bigelow described the process of preparing *Commerce of the Prairies* for publication. Through the winter and spring of 1844 Gregg would write a chapter in his Manhattan hotel room, working from his extensive notebooks and memoranda; he would then carry it to Bigelow, who would edit, revise, and polish the manuscript, whereupon Bigelow would personally deliver the text chapter by chapter to Langley for typesetting.

On 22 June 1844 Langley published two thousand copies of *Commerce of the Prairies.* Several favorable reviews of the book, based on prepublication copies, appeared almost simultaneously with its publication and set the tone of its reception. The early critics read Gregg's work as support for United States expansion and the doctrine of Manifest Destiny. One of the reviews, unsigned, was a long and enthusiastic but jingoistic review by Bigelow himself which appeared in the June 1844 issue of the *Democratic Review,* edited by John L. O'Sullivan, an outspoken advocate of American expansionism.

On 30 June, Gregg left New York City for his brother John's new home near Shreveport, Louisiana, with one hundred copies of his book. Unhappy with the political interpretation of *Commerce of the Prairies* but pleased with the brisk sale of his book during that summer, Gregg retraced his steps to

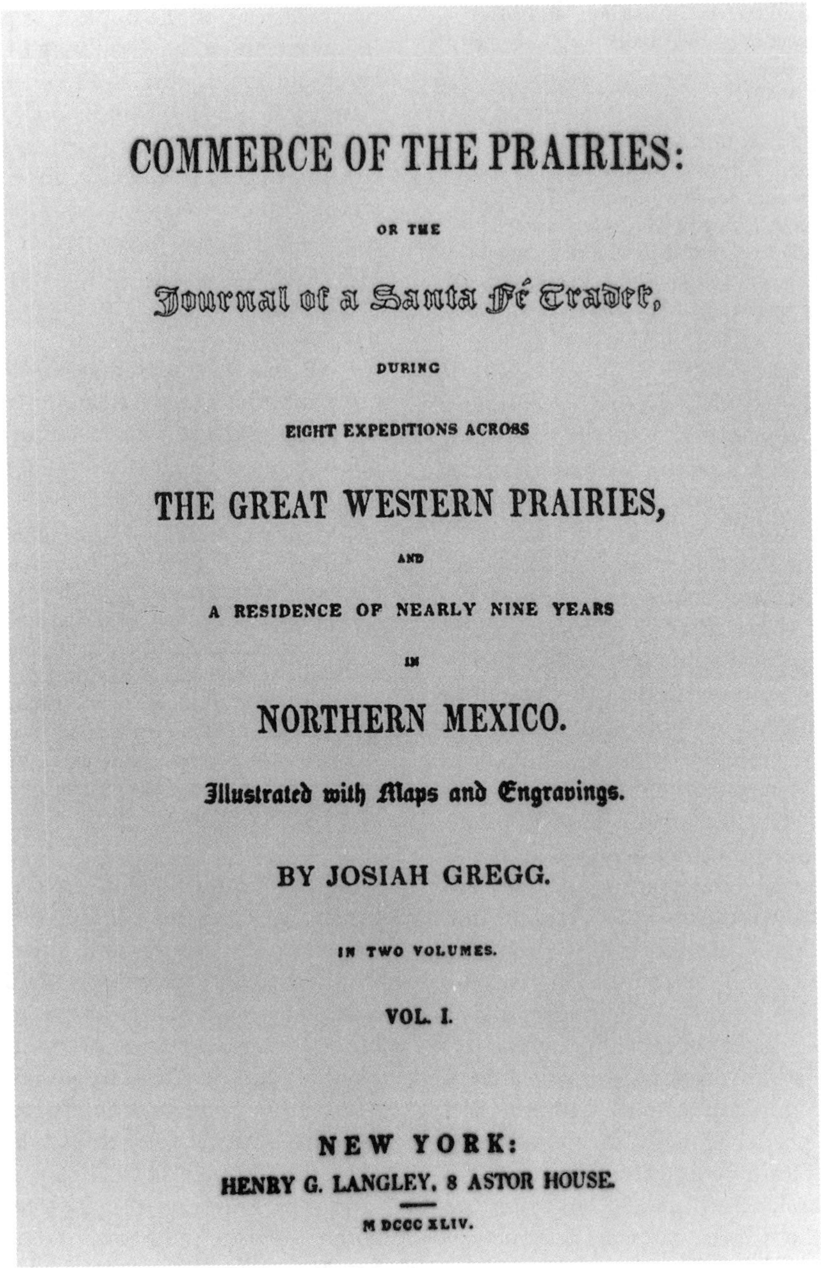

COMMERCE OF THE PRAIRIES:

OR THE

Journal of a Santa Fé Trader,

DURING

EIGHT EXPEDITIONS ACROSS

THE GREAT WESTERN PRAIRIES,

AND

A RESIDENCE OF NEARLY NINE YEARS

IN

NORTHERN MEXICO.

Illustrated with Maps and Engravings.

BY JOSIAH GREGG.

IN TWO VOLUMES.

VOL. I.

NEW YORK:

HENRY G. LANGLEY, 8 ASTOR HOUSE.

M DCCC XLIV.

Title page for Gregg's only book, which mixes personal anecdote and scientific observation

New York City in November to oversee the correction and publication of the second edition. By 1851, a year after Gregg's death, the original American edition of *Commerce of the Prairies* went into its fifth printing and was joined by two editions in German. The book continued to sell moderately well through the Mexican War (1846–1848) and the 1850 ceding of New Mexico to the United States, after which interest in the book fell off, settling into nearly a half-century of neglect.

Not until Reuben Gold Thwaites's republication of the book in the nineteenth and twentieth vol-umes of his *Early Western Travels* (1905) did *Commerce of the Prairies* begin its slow rise to its present prominence among western histories. Since Thwaites's edition the book has been republished in 1926, 1954, 1966, 1967, and 1970 to an increasingly general readership. In 1979 Paul Horgan collected his several articles on Gregg into a literary biography, *Josiah Gregg and His Vision of the Early West.*

Of major significance to the revival of Gregg's book and reputation was the publication of the two-volume *Diary & Letters of Josiah Gregg* (1941–1944), edited by Maurice Garland Fulton. The collection includes Gregg's letters and notebooks as preserved by his brother John as well as his other hitherto uncollected letters and enables scholars to chart Gregg's activities from his retirement from the Santa Fe trade in 1840 through his arrival in the gold fields of northern California in October 1849. The *Diary & Letters* volumes present a documentary biography of Gregg's life and fill longstanding biographical lacunae about his final decade.

The compilation includes Gregg's nine "memoranda books" which he had been shaping into a second book to be titled "Rovings Abroad," but it was left uncompleted at his death. In the projected book Gregg planned to report, firsthand and in much the same format as in *Commerce of the Prairies*, the Mexican War and the Battle of Buena Vista, his several months of medical practice and observations in Saltillo and vicinity, his visit to Mexico City, his abortive expedition to the California coast and subsequent journey to San Francisco, and his expedition to northern California and the discovery of what others later named Humboldt Bay. He planned once more to devote entire chapters to his scientific observations of Mexican flora and fauna as well as to describe the peoples, customs, and institutions as observed during his three-year residence in Mexico from 1846 to 1849.

Gregg's letters clarify the longstanding mystery about his medical studies. Without formal training but after considerable study Gregg had practiced medicine on the Santa Fe Trail and at home and had gained wide respect for medical diagnosis and treatment despite his lack of a diploma. On 1 November 1845 the experienced paramedic entered Louisville Medical College in Louisville, Kentucky, to study for the degree of doctor of medicine. Although apparently not enrolled as a regular student, he stayed just over a year, attending six hour-long lectures daily. Despite being plagued by debilitating headaches throughout the winter of 1845–1846, which almost led him to quit his studies ("I am now in no condition to study," he wrote John on 31 January 1846), he was encouraged by admiring members of the faculty who saw in this brilliant, middle-aged scientist-entrepreneur a superior candidate for the M.D. degree. Still, although he was granted an honorary degree at the March 1846 college commencement, the idea of practicing medicine seemed unimportant to him, and he wrote John that he would certainly never use the "doctor" title unless he actually practiced.

Upon graduation from medical school Gregg, in the face of the Mexican War and the closing of the trade by Mexico, decided to return to the Southwest trade. While en route to join a caravan, how-

ever, Gregg received and eventually accepted invitations from Arkansas congressmen to accompany the Arkansas Volunteers to Texas as a noncombatant expeditionary aide, guide, translator, and "confidential agent." Traveling with eight hundred mounted men under the command of Gen. John Ellis Wool, the forty-year-old Gregg, cantankerous, eccentric, and in ill health, soon felt ridiculed, unappreciated, and neglected by the officers and troops alike. His dispatches to eastern newspapers expressed outrage at military waste, inefficiency, administration, and what he deemed an unseemly hesitation to engage the enemy.

Observing the U.S. victory in the decisive Battle of Buena Vista on horseback from "high and commanding points," Gregg tempered his criticism with admiration for the lately reviled U.S. troops who, he observed in his dispatches, fought bravely in hand-to-hand combat and, the battle over, ministered to the needs of wounded Mexican soldiers. His vivid descriptions of the battle in his journal, letters, and formal dispatches to newspapers at home constitute some of the best war reporting of the Mexican campaign.

Following the battle, Gregg accompanied reinforcement troops to Chihuahua, where he eventually entered into a trading partnership with Samuel Magoffin, the Santa Fe trader and husband of diarist Susan Magoffin, and left Mexico by ship for New York, where he planned to purchase goods for transport to Mexico. He was disappointed to learn while in New York that Magoffin had withdrawn from the venture; Gregg returned almost immediately to Saltillo, Mexico, via the Gulf of Mexico and the Rio Grande, where he opened his first (and last) medical practice. His services became so popular and profitable that the adventurer earned enough money during 1847 and 1848 to enable him to stop practicing medicine and resume his explorations. In autumn 1848 Gregg accompanied a party of prominent residents of Saltillo to Mexico City, which he had not previously visited. While there he determined to take, he wrote Dr. George Engelmann on 30 June 1849, "a tour upon the Pacific Coast as far north as California and perhaps Oregon." He added that the Pacific coast was "an untrodden field for a scientist."

Gregg's scientific, recording eye had made him a keen observer of the largely unexamined plant and animal life of northern Mexico. Encouraged by his botanist friend, Dr. Engelmann of Saint Louis, Gregg sent him and other botanists descriptions and samples of many uncollected plants; these scientists, in turn, honored Gregg by naming some twenty-three species of plants after him, including

*Acacia Greggii, Cereus Greggii, Frazinus Greggii, Sargen-
tia Greggii, Linum Greggii,* and *Porophyllum Greggii.*

In early summer 1849 Gregg undertook to finance, mount, and lead a private scientific and exploring party that would strike out for the Pacific
coast at Mazatlán, cross the Gulf of California, and
travel up the coast to San Diego, Monterey, and San
Francisco. His increasing physical disability prevented the completion of this expedition, however,
and Gregg disbanded it, continuing alone from
Mazatlán to San Francisco, sailing on 16 July 1849
aboard the *Olga.* His journal entries cease with his
arrival at San Francisco, where he left his notebooks
and materials for his second book in the hands of
former business associate Jesse Sutton. Apparently
prompted by awareness of his increasing ill health,
Gregg wrote Sutton from "Trinity River below 3rd
Canon Nov. 1st 1849," giving directions to place his
"effects and memoranda at the disposition of my
brother John."

The rest of Gregg's story and the account of
his final expedition are told by others. In October
1849 Gregg was at Rich Bar, a mining settlement on
the Trinity River, where he mounted an expedition,
apparently at the request of the U.S. government, to
find a westward route through the mountains to a
seaport that could serve as a supply center for the
mines of northern California. With an exploring
party that had dwindled from twenty-four to eight
because of the onset of winter weather, an ailing
Gregg and his small party left Rich Bar on 5 November 1849 to blaze a trail to the ocean. It would be his
last trail.

Among the party was a young Kentuckian
named Lewis Keysor Wood. In 1856 he would publish the only account of the eighty-mile journey to
the sea, titled "The Discovery of Humboldt Bay," in
the *Humboldt Times* of Eureka, California. He called
the expedition an ordeal of "unmitigated toil, hardship, privation and suffering." Told by Indians that
it would take eight days in good weather to reach
the ocean, the party, confronted by rain, snow, and
cold, took more than six weeks. Gregg was ever the
scientist, even under adverse conditions, and Wood
reports that "the old Doctor" (he was forty-four)
measured the giant redwoods and, upon arrival at
the Pacific shore on 17 December, took observations and engraved the latitude and longitude on a
tree at "Gregg's Point," the present-day location of
the city of Trinidad.

Despite the collapse of discipline, the little
company completed their second objective on 20
December 1849, discovering and naming Trinity
Bay. Before they could return to civilization to report their find, however, another party arrived by

sea in April, and, claiming discovery, named it
Humboldt Bay, the site of present-day Eureka. At
Eel River the fractious group decided to divide into
two parties of four each; one party elected to travel
inland, while Gregg's band opted to traverse the
Coast Range southward to San Francisco. The rugged mountains soon defeated Gregg's band, however, and they, too, turned inland, hoping to reach
the Sacramento Valley. Already weakened by the
near-starvation diet and unrelenting exposure,
Gregg's condition steadily worsened until 25 February 1850, when, nearing Clear Lake and not far
from Sacramento Valley, he suddenly "fell from his
horse," and "died in a few hours without speaking."
His companions, reports Wood, who learned the
particulars from Charles C. Southard, one of
Gregg's small party, "dug a hole with sticks and put
him under ground, then carried rock and piled upon
his grave to keep animals from digging him up."

Gregg's meticulous record of the expedition,
including his maps and scientific observations, disappeared at Clear Lake. His family received notifi-
cation of his death in May 1850 but did not learn
any particulars until Wood published his account of
the hapless expedition. As Gregg had instructed,
Sutton sent the Mexican memoranda and Gregg's
belongings to John. The papers later came into the
possession of Gregg's grandnephew, Claude Hard-
wicke, whose widow took them with her when she
moved to Tucson, Arizona. Maurice Garland Fulton of the New Mexico Military Institute in Roswell
tracked down the notebooks.

Gregg's *Commerce of the Prairies,* Fulton's *Diary
& Letters of Josiah Gregg,* and Paul Horgan's several
1940s articles and his subsequent book, *Josiah Gregg
and His Vision of the Early West,* have attracted schol-
arly attention and general interest in Gregg. J. Frank
Dobie, in his *Guide to the Life and Literature of the
Southwest* (1943), called *Commerce of the Prairies* "one
of the classics of bedrock Americana"; Van Wyck
Brooks praised him in *The World of Washington Irving*
(1944) as "a born observer and writer"; Henry Nash
Smith concluded in *The Literary History of the United
States* (1948) that Gregg's book "ranks with the
Lewis and Clark narrative as a literary monument
of the westward movement." Since the mid twentieth century *Commerce of the Prairies* has become, along
with the accounts and narratives of Meriwether
Lewis and William Clark, Irving, Parkman, Ruxton, and Garrard, one of the enduring foundational
texts of western Americana. A major reason for
Gregg's present secure position in American history
and letters was suggested by Harvey Fergusson in
Rio Grande (1933): "In Gregg . . . the American pioneer became articulate," and his important book re-

vealed "an early example of . . . typical American individualism."

Commerce of the Prairies and Gregg's posthumously published writings build an enduring memorial to one prototypical American's "passion for Prairie life." In 1844, as Americans were beginning to look westward, Gregg articulated the allure of wilderness and named and admitted to a personal spiritual bifurcation which continues, at the turn of a new urban century, to tear at city-dwelling but nature-yearning Americans. He wrote:

> I have striven in vain to reconcile myself to the even tenor of civilized life in the United States; and have sought in its amusements and its society a substitute for those high excitements which have attached me so strongly to Prairie life. Yet I am almost ashamed to confess that scarcely a day passes without my experiencing a pang of regret that I am not now roving at large upon those Western plains. Nor do I find my taste peculiar; for I have hardly known a man who has ever become familiar with the kind of life which I have led for so many years, that has not relinquished it with regret.

In *Commerce of the Prairies* Josiah Gregg recovers and preserves for future readers a faithful account of life as it once was along the Santa Fe Trail. His literary legacy continues to reignite in ever-new generations of readers some of that same "passion for Prairie life" as he leads them, for a time, in spirit and in truth, "upon the plains again."

Letters:
New Found Letters of Josiah Gregg, edited by John Thomas Lee (Worcester, Mass.: American Antiquarian Society, 1931);

Josiah Gregg and Dr. George Engelmann, edited by Lee (Worcester, Mass.: American Antiquarian Society, 1932);

Diary & Letters of Josiah Gregg, 2 volumes, edited by Maurice Garland Fulton (Norman: University of Oklahoma Press, 1941–1944).

Biography:
Paul Horgan, *Josiah Gregg and His Vision of the Early West* (New York: Farrar Straus Giroux, 1979).

References:
Owen C. Coy, "The Last Expedition of Josiah Gregg," *Southwestern Historical Quarterly,* 20 (July 1916): 41–49;

Harvey Fergusson, *Rio Grande* (New York: Knopf, 1933);

Edward Halsey Foster, *Josiah Gregg and Lewis H. Garrard,* Western Writers Series, no. 28 (Boise, Idaho: Boise State University, 1977);

John Thomas Lee, "The Authorship of Gregg's *Commerce of the Prairies,*" *Mississippi Valley Historical Review,* 16 (March 1980): 451–466;

Lawrence Clark Powell, *Southwest Classics: The Creative Literature of the Arid Lands: Essays on the Books and Their Writers* (Los Angeles: Ward Ritchie, 1974).

Papers:
Josiah Gregg's eight travel notebooks are housed by the Thomas Gilcrease Institute of American History and Art, Tulsa, Oklahoma.

Bret Harte

(25 August 1836 – 5 May 1902)

Gary Scharnhorst
University of New Mexico

See also the Harte entries in *DLB 12: American Realists and Naturalists, DLB 64: American Literary Critics and Scholars, 1850–1880; DLB 74: American Short-Story Writers Before 1880;* and *DLB 79: American Magazine Journalists, 1850–1900.*

BOOKS: *Condensed Novels, and Other Papers* (New York: Carleton / London: Low, 1867; enlarged edition, Boston: Osgood, 1871);

The Lost Galleon and Other Tales (San Francisco: Towne & Bacon, 1867);

The Luck of Roaring Camp, and Other Sketches (Boston: Fields, Osgood, 1870; London: Routledge, 1870); enlarged edition (Boston: Fields, Osgood, 1871);

Poems (Boston: Fields, Osgood, 1871);

East and West Poems (Boston: Osgood, 1871; London: Hotten, 1871);

Mrs. Skaggs's Husbands, and Other Sketches (Boston: Osgood, 1873);

An Episode of Fiddletown and Other Sketches (London: Routledge, 1873);

Echoes of the Foot-Hills (Boston: Osgood, 1875);

Tales of the Argonauts, and Other Sketches (Boston: Osgood, 1875; London: Low, 1875);

Gabriel Conroy (3 volumes, London: Warne, 1876; 1 volume, Hartford, Conn.: American Publishing, 1876);

Two Men of Sandy Bar: A Drama (Boston: Osgood, 1877);

Thankful Blossom, A Romance of the Jerseys, 1779 (Boston: Osgood; London & New York: Routledge, 1877);

The Story of a Mine (London: Routledge, 1877; Boston: Osgood, 1878);

The Man on the Beach (London: Routledge, 1878);

"Jinny" (London: Routledge, 1878);

Drift from Two Shores (Boston: Houghton, Osgood, 1878);

An Heiress of Red Dog and Other Tales (London: Chatto & Windus, 1879);

Bret Harte

The Twins of Table Mountain (London: Chatto & Windus, 1879); enlarged as *The Twins of Table Mountain and Other Stories* (Boston: Houghton, Osgood, 1879);

Jeff Briggs's Love Story and Other Sketches (London: Chatto & Windus, 1880);

Flip and Other Stories (London: Chatto & Windus, 1882); revised as *Flip and Found at Blazing Star* (Boston & New York: Houghton, Mifflin, 1882);

In the Carquinez Woods (London: Longmans, Green, 1883; Boston & New York: Houghton, Mifflin, 1884);

On the Frontier (London: Longmans, Green, 1884; Boston & New York: Houghton, Mifflin, 1884);

By Shore and Sedge (Boston and New York: Houghton, Mifflin, 1885; London: Longmans, Green, 1885);

Maruja (London: Chatto & Windus, 1885; Boston & New York: Houghton, Mifflin, 1885);

Snowbound at Eagle's (Boston & New York: Houghton, Mifflin, 1886; London: Ward & Downey, 1886);

The Queen of the Pirate Isle (London: Chatto & Windus, 1886; Boston & New York: Houghton, Mifflin, 1886);

Devil's Ford (London: White, 1887);

A Millionaire of Rough-and-Ready (London: White, 1887);

A Millionaire of Rough-and-Ready and *Devil's Ford* (Boston & New York: Houghton, Mifflin, 1887);

The Crusade of the Excelsior (Boston & New York: Houghton, Mifflin; London: White, 1887);

Frontier Stories (Boston & New York: Houghton, Mifflin, 1887);

The Phyllis of the Sierras and A Drift from Redwood Camp (Boston & New York: Houghton, Mifflin, 1888; London: Chatto & Windus, 1888);

The Argonauts of North Liberty (Boston & New York: Houghton, Mifflin; London: Blackett, 1888);

Cressy (2 volumes, London: Macmillan, 1889; 1 volume, Boston & New York: Houghton, Mifflin, 1889);

The Heritage of Dedlow Marsh and Other Tales (1 volume, Boston & New York: Houghton, Mifflin, 1889; 2 volumes, London: Macmillan, 1889);

A Waif of the Plains (London: Chatto & Windus, 1890; Boston & New York: Houghton, Mifflin, 1890);

A Ward of the Golden Gate (Boston & New York: Houghton, Mifflin, 1890; London: Chatto & Windus, 1890);

A Sappho of Green Springs and Other Stories (Boston & New York: Houghton, Mifflin, 1891; London: Chatto & Windus, 1891);

A First Family of Tasajara (2 volumes, London: Macmillan; 1 volume, Boston & New York: Houghton, Mifflin, 1892);

Colonel Starbottle's Client and Some Other People (London: Chatto & Windus, 1892; Boston & New York: Houghton, Mifflin, 1892);

Susy: A Story of the Plains (Boston & New York: Houghton, Mifflin, 1893; London: Chatto & Windus, 1893);

Sally Dows, Etc. (London: Chatto & Windus, 1893); republished as *Sally Dows and Other Stories* (Boston and New York: Houghton, Mifflin, 1893);

A Protégée of Jack Hamlin's and Other Stories (Boston & New York: Houghton, Mifflin, 1894; enlarged edition, London: Chatto & Windus, 1894);

The Bell-Ringer of Angel's and Other Stories (Boston & New York: Houghton, Mifflin, 1894; abridged edition, London: Chatto & Windus, 1894);

Clarence (London: Chatto & Windus, 1895; Boston & New York: Houghton, Mifflin, 1895);

In a Hollow of the Hills (Boston & New York: Houghton, Mifflin, 1895; London: Chapman & Hall, 1895);

Barker's Luck and Other Stories (Boston & New York: Houghton, Mifflin, 1896; London: Chatto & Windus, 1896);

Three Partners or The Big Strike on Heavy Tree Hill (Boston & New York: Houghton, Mifflin, 1897; London: Chatto & Windus, 1897);

Tales of Trail and Town (Boston & New York: Houghton, Mifflin, 1898; London: Chatto & Windus, 1898);

Some Later Verses (London: Chatto & Windus, 1898);

Stories in Light and Shadow (Boston & New York: Houghton, Mifflin, 1898; London: Pearson, 1898);

Mr. Jack Hamlin's Mediation and Other Stories (Boston & New York: Houghton, Mifflin; London: Pearson, 1899);

From Sand Hill to Pine (Boston & New York: Houghton, Mifflin, 1900; London: Pearson, 1900);

The Ancestors of Peter Atherly and Other Tales (Boston & New York: Houghton, Mifflin, 1900);

Under the Redwoods (Boston & New York: Houghton, Mifflin, 1901; London: Pearson, 1901);

On the Old Trail (London: Pearson, 1902); republished as *Openings in the Old Trail* (Boston & New York: Houghton, Mifflin, 1902);

Condensed Novels, Second Series (Boston & New York: Houghton, Mifflin, 1902); republished as *New Burlesques* (London: Chatto & Windus, 1902);

Sue: A Play in Three Acts, by Harte and T. Edgar Pemberton (London: Greening, 1902);

A Niece of Snapshot Harry's and Other Tales (Boston & New York: Houghton, Mifflin, 1903);

Trent's Trust and Other Stories (London: Nash; Boston & New York: Houghton, Mifflin, 1903);

The Lectures of Bret Harte, edited by Charles Meeker Kozlay (Brooklyn: Kozlay, 1909);

Stories and Poems and Other Uncollected Writings, compiled by Kozlay (Boston & New York: Houghton Mifflin, 1914);

Sketches of the Sixties, by Harte and Mark Twain (San Francisco: John Howell, 1926);

Ah Sin, by Harte and Twain, edited by Frederick Anderson (San Francisco: Book Club of California, 1961).

Collection: *The Writings of Bret Harte,* 20 volumes (Boston: Houghton, Mifflin, 1896–1914).

PLAY PRODUCTIONS: *Two Men of Sandy Bar,* Chicago, Hooley's Theater, 17 July 1876;

Ah Sin, by Harte and Mark Twain, Washington, D.C., National Theater, 7 May 1877;

Sue, by Harte and T. Edgar Pemberton, New York, Hoyt's Theater, 15 September 1896;

Held Up, by Harte and Pemberton, Worcester, U.K., Worcester Theater, 24 August 1903.

OTHER: *Outcroppings: Being a Selection of California Verse,* edited by Harte (San Francisco: A. Roman / New York: W. J. Widdleton, 1865);

Charles Warren Stoddard, *Poems,* edited by Harte (San Francisco: A. Roman, 1867);

Titus Fey Cronise, *The Natural Wealth of California,* edited by Harte (San Francisco: H. H. Bancroft, 1867).

SELECTED PERIODICAL PUBLICATIONS–UNCOLLECTED: "Concerning Criticism," *Washington Capital,* 8 July 1877, I, pp. 2–3;

"The Poetry of the Centennial," *New York Sun,* 15 July 1877, II, pp. 2–4;

"The Rise of the 'Short Story,'" *Cornhill,* new series, 7 (July 1899): 1–8.

More than any other American writer, Bret Harte discovered the "literary West," or so Henry Seidel Canby declared in the *Saturday Review of Literature* for 17 April 1926. As founding editor of the *Overland Monthly* in 1868, Harte was instrumental in promoting the careers of an entire generation of western writers. A pioneering western local-colorist, he burst upon the national scene with the publication of a series of popular tales and poems set in the California mining camps and boomtowns of the Gold Rush that crystalized his reputation as a rising western literary star. Lured east by offers of wealth and prestige, he signed in 1871 what was then the most lucrative contract in the history of American letters. A prototype of the man of letters as a man of business, Harte learned through painful experience to gauge his market and trade on his name. Although he never fully realized the promise of his early *Overland Monthly* tales, he was for the rest of his life a steady writer of western fiction that enjoyed wider popularity in England and Europe than in the United States.

Born Francis Brett Hart in Albany, New York, on 25 August 1836 to Henry Hart, a teacher, and Elizabeth Ostrander Hart, young Hart (whose parents later added an *e* to the surname) was called Frank as a child. He was educated in the home and, before the death of his father in 1845, in small academies and ordinary schools located in towns and villages along the Hudson River where his father taught. After his father died, he moved with his mother to New York City, where he continued in school. According to family tradition, he read William Shakespeare at the age of six, Charles Dickens at seven, and Montaigne at eight. At thirteen he quit school to work as a clerk. He later joined a local military company that helped to quell the Astor theater riots.

With his younger sister Margaret he sailed for San Francisco in 1854 to rejoin his mother and her second husband, Andrew Williams, the first mayor of Oakland, whom she had recently married. He soon left for the mining district near Sonora, Tuoloume County, where he opened a school that failed by the spring of 1855 for lack of students. He then spent several weeks as a placer miner but "met with very indifferent success," according to a sketch in the *Chicago Tribune* of 20 November 1870.

During the next five years he worked as an agent and messenger for Wells, Fargo and Company; a druggist's clerk in Oakland; a tutor for ranching families in Humboldt County; a soldier; and a printer's devil for the weekly *Northern Californian* newspaper. "I learned to combine the composition of the editorial with the setting of its type," he wrote George Bainton on 1 November 1888, and so "somewhat condensed my style." Early in 1860, left in charge of the paper, Harte wrote an editorial condemning a massacre of Indians near Eureka. He was apparently threatened by outraged citizens and soon fled to San Francisco.

Harte aspired to a literary career. He had published several verses and sketches in the *Humboldt Times* in 1857, a poem in the *Knickerbocker* in 1858, and after 1857 he wrote irregularly for the *Golden Era,* a weekly San Francisco literary paper, occasionally under the pseudonym "Bret." After "an idle week, spent in listless outlook for employment," as he reminisced forty years later in his essay "Bohemian Days in San Francisco," he went to work as a compositor for the *Golden Era.* During the next several years he contributed dozens of pieces to its pages, including sketches such as "The Man of No Account" and "High-Water Mark," which he would later collect in *The Luck of Roaring Camp, and Other Sketches* (1870).

Front page of the first issue of the literary weekly Harte cofounded and edited. Harte wrote the two articles on the page.

Harte's writings in the *Golden Era* caught the attention of Jessie Benton Frémont, who introduced him to her circle of friends, including the Unitarian minister Thomas Starr King. Frémont and King helped him find employment in the offices of the U.S. surveyor general, the U.S. marshal, and the U.S. branch mint during the years 1861–1869. "If I were to be cast away on a desert island," Harte later wrote in a letter to Frémont that she collected in her *Souvenirs of My Time* (1887), "I should expect a savage to come forward with a three-cornered note from you to tell me that, at your request, I had been appointed governor of the island at a salary of two thousand four hundred dollars."

By 1862 Harte enjoyed local renown as a poet, humorist, and man of letters. Writing from San Francisco, King predicted in the 7 November 1862 *Boston Transcript* that Harte would "yet be known more widely in our literature." He married Anna Griswold, a contralto in the choir at King's church, in August 1862, and with King's help he placed "The Legend of Monte del Diablo" in the *Atlantic Monthly* of October 1863. In the spring of 1864 Harte and Charles H. Webb founded the weekly *Californian,* and his first book, an anthology he edited titled *Outcroppings: Being Selections of California Verse,* was published for the holiday market in December 1865 to decidedly mixed reviews.

Harte began to attract wider attention with a series of so-called condensed novels, brief burlesques of such writers as Charles Dickens, James Fenimore Cooper, Frederick Marryat, and Wilkie Collins. The *North American Review* described him in April 1866 as "a parodist of such genius that he seems a mirror into which novelists may look and be warned." Harte collected these pieces in *Condensed Novels, and Other Papers* (1867), a volume published in New York and designed for sale in the East, although he was outraged by the caricatures with which it was illustrated. He also became the California correspondent to two Massachusetts papers, the *Springfield Republican* and the *Boston Christian Register,* writing thirty-eight short essays for them between January 1866 and November 1867. These essays betray his increasing dissatisfaction with things Californian, especially the "narrow-minded" and "materialistic" values of its residents, its political corruption and restraints on "intellectual life," and even its climate and landscape.

Although Harte as early as 1867 yearned to resettle in the East where he believed his literary ambitions were more likely to be realized, he nevertheless accepted editorial charge of the *Overland Monthly* upon its founding in 1868 by the San Francisco publisher Anton Roman. Harte, according to Roman in a September 1902 *Overland* article on the genesis of the magazine, harbored some reservations, in particular "whether sufficient material of a proper character to interest magazine readers could be secured" from contributors and whether "the field for operating a magazine was large enough." On his part, Roman feared that Harte would "lean too much toward the purely literary articles," while he wanted "a magazine that would help the material development" of the Pacific coast. Harte's aggressive soliciting of the work of prominent local writers such as Mark Twain, Ambrose Bierce, Charles Warren Stoddard, Joaquin Miller, Ina Coolbrith, Prentice Mulford, and Henry George resulted in a magazine that had as wide an appeal as the *Atlantic Monthly,* his model.

The *Overland* was a hit, if not from its first issue in June 1868, then from its second, which contained "The Luck of Roaring Camp." When the printer and a fastidious proofreader objected to Harte's depiction of the prostitute Cherokee Sal, Roman feared the story "might imperil the prospects of the magazine" and agreed to kill it. It ran as written only because Harte threatened to resign as editor over the issue. Although it was hardly mentioned in the local press, the story was hailed in the East. The 30 September 1868 *Springfield Republican* declared it "the best magazine story of the year," and James T. Fields invited the author to contribute similar tales to the pages of the *Atlantic.* Kate Chopin later wrote in the 9 December 1900 *St. Louis Republic* that the story "reached across the continent and startled the Academists on the Atlantic Coast." As Roman had hoped, the *Overland* under Harte's direction attracted a national audience. In July 1870 the magazine sold as many copies in the East as in the states of California, Nevada, and Oregon, and according to Bayard Taylor in the 5 August 1870 *New York Tribune,* it was "more extensively and appreciatively noticed" in the eastern press than in California.

The popularity of "The Luck of Roaring Camp" allowed him to write seven "other stories of a like character" and over twenty poems without further interference from the counting room, as he recalled in his essay "The Rise of the 'Short Story,'" which was published in the July 1899 issue of *Cornhill.* In an 1894 interview he insisted that his characters—the gambler John Oakhurst, the comic Colonel Starbottle, the skalawag Brown of Calaveras, the gruff stage driver Yuba Bill, the inscrutable Ah Sin—"were drawn from life to a greater or less extent." He was no rigorous realist in these works, but a humorist, often a satirist in the Dickensian mode. Harte parodied the gospel account of the Nativity in "The Luck of Roaring Camp" and the parable of the prodigal son in "Mr. Thompson's Prodigal." He satirized traditional gender roles by reversing them in "Miggles," and he laid a trap for the unwary reader of "Tennessee's Partner," a subtle tale of revenge that on the surface seems to celebrate the virtues of selfless friendship. Although his poem "Plain Language from Truthful James," more popularly known as "The Heathen Chinee," seemed to reinforce racial stereotypes and was appropriated by the foes of Chinese immigration, Harte intended the monologue as a satire of the racial prejudices common in the West among Irish day laborers with whom the Chinese competed for jobs. In "The Idyl of Red Gulch" Harte not only introduced the stock character of the eastern schoolmarm but also allegorized his own divided sympathies between the rustic West and the genteel East. Indeed, Miss Mary's escape from the vice and corruption of Red Gulch at the close of the story presages Harte's own imminent departure for "the States."

Despite the critical success of the *Overland,* Harte had a stormy relationship with John H. Carmany, who bought the magazine from Roman for $7,500 a year after it was established. Carmany's derogatory comments about Harte in the *Overland* for August 1915 are revealing: "He was a dandy; a dainty man, too much of a woman to rough it in the mines." Carmany had, he said, "spent $30,000 to make Bret Harte famous." Meanwhile, Harte had received an outpouring of invitations to write for rival publications: Francis Pharcellus Church solicited a series of contributions to the *Galaxy;* Whitelaw Reid wanted him to become California correspondent of the *New York Tribune;* Harper and Brothers offered him between $100 and $150 for every poem he sent them; Parke Godwin tendered the editorship of *Putnam's;* the publishers of the *Lakeside Monthly* wanted him to move to Chicago and take over their magazine. In June 1870 Fields offered him $5,000 to write exclusively for the *Atlantic* for a year.

To entice him to remain in California the new University of California offered Harte a professorship of modern literature at an annual salary of $3,600—a sinecure that would have enabled him to continue his editorial and literary work. He declined the position on the grounds that it would prevent him from making a planned trip to the Atlantic states. Carmany desperately matched Fields's offer—$5,000 annually to remain editor of the *Overland,* plus $100 for each contribution, plus an interest in the magazine. Harte spurned the offer in order to test his wings in the East. He resigned from the *Overland* at the close of 1870, having edited its first five semiannual volumes, and left in early February

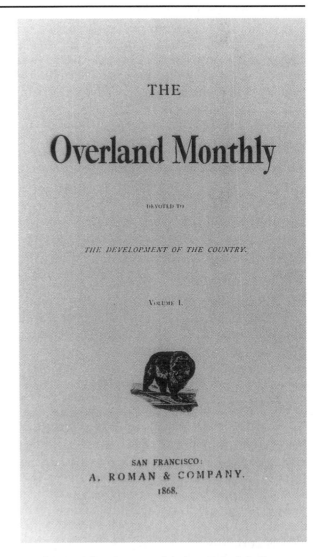

Title page for volume one of the bound set of the literary magazine Harte modeled on The Atlantic Monthly

1871 for New York and Boston with his wife and two young sons in tow. "I go three thousand miles to be found out," he protested facetiously in a 24 January 1871 letter to William Dean Howells, the assistant editor of the *Atlantic.* He wrote more truly than he knew.

So widely reported in the press were his movements across the country that Howells compared the trip in his memoir *Literary Friends and Acquaintance* (1910) to "the progress of a prince" in the "universal attention and interest" it attracted. On 25 February 1871, the day after his arrival in Boston, he was feted at a regular meeting of the Saturday Club. In the next few days he was the guest of honor at dinners hosted by Howells, James Russell Lowell, and Henry Wadsworth Longfellow; driven to Concord to visit Emerson; and taken to the theater by Fields. At the end of a week he concluded an agreement to contribute no fewer than twelve poems and stories exclusively for one year to the *Atlantic Monthly* and *Every Saturday,* both published by the firm of Fields, Osgood and Company, at a salary of $10,000. "I have made some pecuniary sacrifice for the sake of keeping my books in the one house," he bragged in a letter to James R. Osgood on 6 March 1871. Osgood, soon to become the senior partner in the firm, fairly claimed later in the March 1908 *Pacific Monthly* that "never in his business career had he gotten so little out of a contributor, or with such pains."

Harte fulfilled his obligations under the contract, supplying his publishers with fourteen pieces during the year, even giving them two poems gratis two years after the contract had lapsed. The quality of his writing, however, fell off while the contract was in force. The 20 September *New York Evening Post,* for example, reported that Harte's poem "A Newport Romance" in the October 1871 *Atlantic* was "pleasing but not level with his fame, and has the blemish of a grammatical error." Even Harte admitted in a letter to his wife dated 6 September 1871 that it was "poor stuff." From all indications the best story he delivered under the terms of the contract, the sentimental "How Santa Claus Came to Simpson's Bar," was the product of a prolonged gestation. Scheduled for the December 1871 issue of the *Atlantic,* it did not appear until the March 1872 number. Henry James wrote privately that it was "better than anything in his 'second manner'–though not quite so good as his first."

Notoriously improvident, Harte ran up debts soon after the Fields, Osgood contract expired in the spring of 1872. His friend Noah Brooks recalled in the 24 May 1902 edition of *The New York Times* that "he was continually involved in troubles that he might have escaped with a little more financial shrewdness." As his career spiraled downward between late 1872 and mid 1875, Harte capitalized on his waning reputation by lecturing on "The Argonauts of '49" in dozens of cities and towns from New England and Canada to the Deep South and as far west as Omaha, Nebraska, and Atchison, Kansas. Under the best of circumstances, when well rested and temperate, Harte was a passable lecturer, as when he spoke in Boston and New York in December 1872. More often than not, however, his lectures were not delivered under the best of circumstances. He frequently disappointed audiences who expected a deadpan rustic like Twain or Petroleum V. Nasby (David Ross Locke); by comparison, Harte seemed a pompous dandy who dressed in neat suits, sipped champagne from the podium, and spoke in a near whisper.

In the space of barely two years Harte went from being the highest-paid and most popular writer in America to freelancing stories to the Sunday editions of the *New York Sun* and *Times*. In a word, he became the writer the market made him. "My stories have always been *contracted for, accepted* and the *prices fixed* before I had put pen to paper," he bragged to Howells on 8 September 1874. *The New York Times* paid him $600 for "The Rose of Tuolumne" and $500 for "A Passage in the Life of Mr. John Oakhurst," and *Scribner's* paid him $1,000 for "An Episode of Fiddletown" and $500 for "A Monte Flat Pastoral." When Howells offered him $300 to publish "The Fool of Five Forks" in the *Atlantic* in 1874, he withdrew the manuscript and sold it to the *Times* for $400.

After contracting to write a novel in September 1872 for the American Publishing Company of Hartford, a subscription house, and collecting an advance of $1,000, Harte did not begin work on the manuscript until June 1874. Whenever he needed money during the next two years, he submitted brief installments of *Gabriel Conroy* (1876) to Elisha Bliss, president of the company, collecting a total of some $3,600 in advances. Although Bliss sold serialization rights to the completed novel to *Scribner's* for $6,000, divided equally between the author and the publisher, the novel sold so poorly in hardcovers that the advances were never repaid, at least according to the company books. Harte's "breakthrough" novel was a critical and commercial disaster (except in German translation, in which it was exceptionally popular). Horace Elisha Scudder complained in the August 1882 *Atlantic* that "all the dark passages" in the novel lead finally "not into the light, but into the vegetable cellar." Harte's most severe critics joked that he had reversed the path of the sun, rising in the West and setting in darkness in the East.

In the spring of 1875, before he finished his novel, Harte contracted to script a play for the comic actor Stuart Robson in return for $6,000, one half paid in advance and the other half earned at the rate of $50 per performance. In the summer of 1870 Harte had worked on dramatizing some of the main incidents in his stories "Mr. Thompson's Prodigal" and "The Idyl of Red Gulch," and he apparently returned to the unproduced script in writing *Two Men of Sandy Bar: A Drama* (1877) for Robson. In September 1875 Harte estimated that the farce would require more than four hours in performance, and according to Robson in a 14 October 1877 interview in the *San Francisco Chronicle* he "fought against the alteration of a line."

The play was condemned when it was produced in Chicago and New York in the summer and fall of 1876. On 29 August the reviewer for *The New York Times* suggested that Harte had written not a script but a "nondescript," that *Two Men of Sandy Bar* was "the worst failure witnessed on the boards of our theatres for years" and "the most dismal mass of trash that was ever put into dramatic shape before a New York audience." On the same day the *New York Herald* compared the play to "one of Beadle's dime novels struck by lightning."

If only to counter such adverse publicity, Harte questioned the integrity of the New York drama critics, accusing them of soliciting bribes—which he had refused to pay—in exchange for favorable reviews. When the editors of the major New York dailies demanded that he name the offenders, Harte replied that they could sue him and he would testify under oath. In the end he failed to produce any evidence to support his accusations. The cause célebre filled the Union Square Theater in New York during the remainder of the one-month run of the play, but Harte's reputation was indelibly tainted by the scandal. Twain reminisced in 1907 that once Harte had scripted "a play which would have succeeded if anyone else had written it."

Unfortunately, Twain immensely enjoyed *Two Men of Sandy Bar* when he saw it performed in New York, so when Harte proposed they write a script together "& divide the swag," as Twain wrote Howells on 11 October 1876, he agreed with alacrity. The result was perhaps the most disastrous collaboration in the history of American letters. A lame comedy of mistaken identity, its title character a racist caricature, *Ah Sin* opened to modestly favorable notices in Washington, Baltimore, and New York in the spring and summer of 1877, but it closed after a brief tour. It was "a most abject & incurable failure," as Twain wrote Howells on 15 October 1877, and Harte likely received no royalties at all from it.

When Harte approached Twain for a loan, Twain replied with an offer of twenty-five dollars a week and a room in his Hartford house while they wrote another play together. Harte roundly resented this attempt to exploit "my poverty," as he put it in a letter to Twain on 1 March 1877, and the two men never met again. With the passage of time the rift between them grew wider. Harte suspected that Twain, as one of the directors of the American Publishing Company, had conspired with Bliss to defraud him of royalties on sales of *Gabriel Conroy,* and he subtly satirized his former friend in his 1893 story "The Ingenue of the Sierras." For his part Twain slandered Harte on and off the record virtually to the end of his life.

While in Washington in the spring of 1877 to attend the premiere performance of *Ah Sin,* Harte solicited a government appointment, but to no avail—a bitter experience he re-created in his satiric sketch of Expectant Dobbs in "The Office Seeker." Living on loans from such friends as the New York broker Thomas Musgrave, in debt to hostelers, publishers, tailors, and grocers, he agreed to write a summer serial for the *Washington Capital,* a weekly edited by Donn Piatt. Eventually, Piatt offered him a salary of $5,000 or $3,000 and a half interest in the paper to help him edit it—an offer Harte eagerly accepted against the advice of his friend Charles A. Dana, editor of the *New York Sun.* "Washington is the place for a literary man to make money," Harte wrote Anna Harte on 22 July 1877. As so often happened, however, his pipe dream was soon shattered. Although the paper printed installments of Harte's "The Story of a Mine" between July and October, the money Harte was owed was seized by the paper's creditors. He left the city even poorer than he had been when he arrived.

At the nadir of his career, the "awful, terrible" winter of 1877–1878, he begged William Waldorf Astor for a job and he scolded Osgood for failing to rush *The Story of a Mine* (1877) into hardcover so that he might receive an advance on it. His books were no longer popular in the American market, and he wondered in a 6 December 1877 letter to Osgood whether he ought to learn "some honest trade." To the end of his life Harte was haunted by memories of that hardscrabble winter, the last he would spend in the United States. "I could not, and *would not under any circumstances,*" he wrote Anna Harte on 16 October 1886, "again go through what I did in New York the last two years and particularly the last winter I passed there."

At last, partly through the intercession of Howells, whose wife, Elinor, was distantly related to President Rutherford B. Hayes, Harte was offered a diplomatic appointment to the subconsular commercial agency in Crefeld, Germany. "I have a great affection for the man," Howells wrote the president on 9 April 1878; "he has learned a terrible lesson in falling from the highest prosperity to the lowest adversity in literature." With "all my disappointments," Harte wrote his wife from Washington on 19 April 1878, the prospect of the Crefeld post "seemed like a glimpse of Paradise." The appointment, he believed, was "the turning point of my life." To repay a few debts and to raise expense money, he sold Osgood the copyrights to fourteen books and gave him the right of first refusal to all future books—a deal he would sorely regret when Osgood and Company was merged into Houghton, Mifflin.

Harte with his youngest daughter, Ethel Bret Harte (seated left); his daughter-in-law, Mrs. Francis King Bret Harte (standing); and his wife, Anna Bret Harte (seated right)

When he sailed for Europe on 27 June 1878, Harte believed the tide had turned. His family remained in New Jersey because he planned to work in the consular service for no more than a year or two, perhaps only until the next change of administration, and then return to America and resume his literary career. Like many a miner who left behind a family in "the States" to seek a fortune in the West, Harte would never return to his country. Although he would support his wife until his death, he would not see her again for more than twenty years.

Before coming to Germany, Harte wrote on 11 February 1880 to his friend John Hay, the assistant secretary of state, that he had no idea "of my tremendous popularity as a writer here. My books are everywhere." According to Eugene Timpe in the *Jahrbuch für Amerikastudien* for 1965, Harte's fiction was translated into German more often during the 1870s than the work of any other American writer. More than forty German editions of his writings were in print. Still, Harte was never at home in Germany. He disliked the climate, the language, and the customs. He was fortunate to hire an efficient vice consul who handled the affairs of the office, so he was free to write and travel. Early in 1879 he delivered a series of lectures in England, where he cultivated friendships with the historian James Anthony Froude, the Duchess of Saint Albans, and others. He often visited Paris, although he professed disdain for the city, and in company with S. M. H. Byers, the American consul in Zurich, he toured Switzerland in July and August 1879.

At length he prevailed upon Hay for a transfer, and he was reassigned to the Glasgow consulate in July 1880. He complained to his wife on 12 November 1880 that Glasgow was "a hundred times worse than Crefeld—more *depressing,* and poisonous from chemical fumes from the factories." As in Crefeld, he entrusted most of his consular duties to his vice consul, remaining in contact with the office by letter and telegram while living in London with the Belgian diplomat Arthur Van de Velde, his wife, and their nine children. After five years and a change of administration in Washington, Harte was summarily dismissed. James G. Blaine, secretary of state under Benjamin Harrison, remarked to Hay on 31 December 1889 that Harte had been "the worst consul thus far recorded."

Although his literary productivity fell off during his first years of diplomatic service, Harte hired an agent, A. P. Watt of London, in 1884 when he foresaw the loss of his consular salary.

For a small percentage Watt adroitly managed Harte's career during the last eighteen years of his life by selling his stories to the British and American newspaper syndicates that emerged in the 1880s, arranging for favorable publicity, and occasionally advancing him money. After leaving the Glasgow consulate Harte became more prolific, often writing a story at the rate of a thousand words per day. Although his late career is typically relegated to the footnote or regarded in an afterthought, he published at least one volume of new fiction every year from 1883 until his death in 1902, by far the bulk of his collected works. While he often bemoaned the "terrible grind" of literary production, he worked steadily, averaging about one hundred thousand words and about $10,000 per year, his money coming from the magazines and book royalties.

To escape "this perpetual grinding out of literary copy which is exhausting me, and no doubt the public," as he wrote his wife on 17 September 1889, Harte repeatedly tried his hand at playwriting, ever mindful of the mistakes that had spoiled *Two Men of Sandy Bar* and *Ah Sin.* Between 1882 and 1897 he wrote, usually with a collaborator, eleven plays and two librettos, typically adaptations of his own stories. With his hostess Madame Van de Velde, for example, he wrote a dramatic version of "The Luck of Roaring Camp," changing the title character into an ingenue who visits Paris in company with a troop of gold miners. It was never produced or published.

In 1895 Harte and his friend T. Edgar Pemberton, the dramatic editor of the *Birmingham Post,* wrote *Sue: A Play in Three Acts* (1902), based on his story "The Judgment of Bolinas Plain." With the American actress Annie Russell in the title role this play was staged in New York in September and October 1896 and toured the eastern half of the United States throughout the fall and winter of 1896–1897. It was performed in London in June and July 1898 and was staged in Denver as late as August of that year. Although the theatrical producer Charles Frohman claimed that "it never paid" and "financially it was a failure," Harte was more sanguine: "one can hardly call a play 'a failure' which has made the amount of money that 'Sue' has," as he wrote Pemberton on 4 April 1897. Another of Harte's dramatic collaborations with Pemberton, *Held Up,* based on his story "Snowbound at Eagle's," was performed in Worcester, England, after his death.

Many of Harte's late stories such as "The Convalescence of Jack Hamlin" betray both his anxieties about money and his concerns about his failing health. When Hamlin Garland met him in London in May 1899, as Garland confided to his diary, Harte was "affable and polite but looked old and burnt out, his eyes clouded, his skin red and flabby." He regularly visited his wife and their daughter Ethel after they came to England in December 1898, although he worried that they had increased their living expenses even as he was earning less money from writing. "For the last 7 or 8 years I have been warning you of my decreasing income, and my ill health," he complained to his wife on 15 September 1901. "A months illness would stop your income," he concluded. His fears were prescient. He died of throat cancer at Madame Van de Velde's home in Surrey on 5 May 1902.

Though the *Spectator* averred in its obituary that he had "probably exerted a greater influence on English literature than any other American author," the succeeding years have not been kind to Harte's reputation. Bernard De Voto merely voiced a consensus view in dismissing Harte in *Mark Twain's America* (1932) as "a literary charlatan whose tales have greatly pleased the second-rate." While such is a standard judgment of Harte's fiction, it is nevertheless fundamentally unsound. At his best Harte was a preeminent satirist, an astute critic of sham sentiment, and an elegant stylist. His gradual disappearance from American literature anthologies may be attributed to the shifting winds of literary fashion rather than the intrinsic qualities of his best writing.

Letters:

The Letters of Bret Harte, edited by Geoffrey Bret Harte (Boston & New York: Houghton Mifflin, 1926);

Bradford A. Booth, "Unpublished Letters of Bret Harte," *American Literature,* 16 (May 1944): 131–142;

Booth, "Bret Harte Goes East: Some Unpublished Letters," *American Literature,* 19 (January 1948): 318–335;

Brenda Murphy and George Monteiro, "The Unpublished Letters of Bret Harte to John Hay," *American Literary Realism,* 12 (Spring 1979): 77–110;

Bret Harte's California: Letters to the Springfield Republican and Christian Register, 1866–67, edited by Gary Scharnhorst (Albuquerque: University of New Mexico Press, 1990);

Selected Letters of Bret Harte, edited by Gary Scharnhorst (Norman: University of Oklahoma Press, 1997).

Interviews:

"Bret Harte Interviewed," *Washington Capital,* 1 October 1876, I, pp. 3–4;

Henry J. W. Dam, "A Morning with Bret Harte," *McClure's,* 4 (December 1894): 38–50;

"Kate Carew's 12-Minute Interview on 12 Subjects with Bret Harte," *New York World,* 22 December 1901, V, pp. 1–6.

Bibliographies:

Linda Diz Barnett, *Bret Harte: A Reference Guide* (Boston: G. K. Hall, 1980);

Gary Scharnhorst, *Bret Harte: A Bibliography* (Lanham, Md.: Scarecrow Press, 1995).

Biographies:

T. Edgar Pemberton, *The Life of Bret Harte* (London: Pearson, 1903);

Henry Childs Merwin, *The Life of Bret Harte* (Boston & New York: Houghton Mifflin, 1911);

George R. Stewart Jr., *Bret Harte: Argonaut and Exile* (Boston & New York: Houghton Mifflin, 1931);

Margaret Duckett, *Mark Twain and Bret Harte* (Norman: University of Oklahoma Press, 1964).

References:

J. R. Boggan, "The Regeneration of Roaring Camp," *Nineteenth Century Fiction,* 22 (December 1967): 271–280;

William F. Conner, "The Euchring of Tennessee: A Reexamination of Bret Harte's 'Tennessee's Partner,'" *Studies in Short Fiction,* 17 (Spring 1980): 113–120;

Margaret Duckett, "Plain Language from Bret Harte," *Nineteenth Century Fiction,* 11 (March 1957): 241–260;

Harold H. Kolb Jr., "The Outcasts of Literary Flat: Bret Harte as Humorist," *American Literary Realism,* 23 (Winter 1991): 52–63;

Charles E. May, "Bret Harte's 'Tennessee's Partner': The Reader Euchred," *South Dakota Review,* 15 (Spring 1977): 109–117;

Ernest R. May, "Bret Harte and the *Overland Monthly,*" *American Literature,* 22 (November 1950): 260–271;

Patrick D. Morrow, *Bret Harte: Literary Critic* (Bowling Green, Ohio: Bowling Green University Popular Press, 1979);

Morrow, "The Predicament of Bret Harte," *American Literary Realism,* 5 (Summer 1972): 181–188;

Gary Scharnhorst, *Bret Harte* (New York: Twayne, 1992);

Scharnhorst, "The Bret Harte–Mark Twain Feud: An Inside Narrative," *Mark Twain Journal,* 31 (Spring 1993): 29–32;

Scharnhorst, "Bret Harte, Mark Twain, and the Literary Construction of San Francisco," in *San Francisco in Fiction,* edited by David Fine (Albuquerque: University of New Mexico Press, 1995), pp. 21–34;

Scharnhorst, "Whatever Happened to Bret Harte?" in *American Realism and the Canon,* edited by Tom Quirk and Scharnhorst (Newark: University of Delaware Press, 1994): 201–211;

Jack Scherting, "Bret Harte's Civil War Poems: Voice of the Majority," *Western American Literature,* 8 (Fall 1973): 133–142;

Jeffrey F. Thomas, "Bret Harte and the Power of Sex," *Western American Literature,* 8 (Fall 1973): 91–109;

Eugene F. Timpe, "Bret Harte's German Public," *Jahrbuch für Amerikastudien,* 10 (1965): 215–220.

Papers:

The largest archive of Harte manuscripts, including some 670 holograph letters, is located in the Alderman Library, University of Virginia. Both the Research Library at the University of California, Los Angeles and the Bancroft Library, University of California, Berkeley, house substantial collections of letters; the Huntington Library, San Marino, contains more than one hundred manuscripts of Harte's stories and fifty-four letters. Other important collections are those at the San Francisco Public Library; Beinecke Library, Yale; Houghton Library, Harvard; Bobst Library, New York University; Hay Library, Brown University; Humanities Research Center, University of Texas, Austin; Pierpont Morgan Library, New York; the Library of Congress; the National Archives, Washington, D.C.; and the New York Public Library.

Washington Irving

(3 April 1783 – 28 November 1859)

Wayne R. Kime
Fairmont State College

See also the Irving entries in *DLB 3: Antebellum Writers in New York and the South; DLB 11: American Humorists, 1800–1950; DLB 30: American Historians, 1607–1865;* and *DLB 183: American Travel Writers, 1776–1864.*

BOOKS: *Salmagundi; or, the Whim-whams and Opinions of Launcelot Langstaff, Esq. & Others,* by Irving, William Irving, and James Kirke Paulding, 20 parts, republished in 2 volumes (New York: D. Longworth, 1807–1808; London: Printed for J. M. Richardson, 1811; revised edition, New York: D. Longworth, 1814; revised by Irving, Paris: Galignani, 1824; Paris: Baudry, 1824);

A History of New York, from the Beginning of the World to the End of the Dutch Dynasty. Containing Among many Surprising and Curious Matters, the Unutterable Ponderings of Walter the Doubter, the Disastrous Projects of William the Testy, and the Chivalric Achievements of Peter the Headstrong, the three Dutch Governors of New Amsterdam; being the only Authentic History of the Times that ever hath been, or ever will be Published, 2 volumes, as Diedrich Knickerbocker (New York & Philadelphia: Inskeep & Bradford / Boston: M'Ilhenny / Baltimore: Coale & Thomas / Charleston: Morford, Willington, 1809; revised edition, New York & Philadelphia: Inskeep & Bradford, 1812; London: John Murray, 1820); republished as volume 1 of *The Works of Washington Irving* (New York & London: Putnam, 1848); revised edition, 2 volumes (New York: Printed for the Grolier Club, 1886);

The Sketch Book of Geoffrey Crayon, Gent., 7 parts, as Geoffrey Crayon (New York: Printed by C. S. Van Winkle, 1819–1820); revised edition, 2 volumes (volume 1, London: John Miller, 1820; volume 2, London: John Murray, 1820); revised edition (Paris: Baudry & Didot, 1823); republished as volume 2 of *The Works of Washington Irving* (New York & London: Putnam, 1848);

Washington Irving (painting by Henry F. Darby; courtesy of Sleepy Hollow Press, Tarrytown, New York)

Bracebridge Hall, or the Humourists. A Medley, 2 volumes, as Geoffrey Crayon (New York: Printed by C. S. Van Winkle, 1822; London: John Murray, 1822); republished as volume 6 of *The Works of Washington Irving* (New York & London: Putnam, 1849);

Letters of Jonathan Oldstyle, Gent., as The Author of *The Sketch Book* (New York: Clayton, 1824; London: Wilson, 1824);

Tales of a Traveller, 2 volumes, as Geoffrey Crayon (London: John Murray, 1824; abridged edition, Philadelphia: Carey & Lea, 1824; unabridged edition, New York: Printed by C. S. Van Winkle, 1825); republished as volume 7 of *The Works of Washington Irving* (New York & London: Putnam, 1849);

The Miscellaneous Works of Oliver Goldsmith, with an Account of His Life and Writings, 4 volumes (Paris: Galignani/Didot, 1825); biography revised in *The Life of Oliver Goldsmith, with Selections from His Writings,* 2 volumes (New York: Harper, 1840); biography revised and enlarged as *Oliver Goldsmith: A Biography,* volume 11 of *The Works of Washington Irving* (New York: Putnam / London: John Murray, 1849);

A History of the Life and Voyages of Christopher Columbus (4 volumes, London: John Murray, 1828; 3 volumes, New York: G & C. Carvill, 1828); republished in *The Life and Voyages of Christopher Columbus; to Which Are Added Those of His Companions,* volumes 3–5 of *The Works of Washington Irving* (New York & London: Putnam, 1848–1849);

A Chronicle of the Conquest of Granada, 2 volumes, as Fray Antonio Agapida (Philadelphia: Carey, Lea & Carey, 1829; London: John Murray, 1829); republished as volume 14 of *The Works of Washington Irving* (New York: Putnam / London: John Murray, 1850);

Voyages and Discoveries of the Companions of Columbus (London: John Murray, 1831; Philadelphia: Carey & Lea, 1831); republished in *The Life and Voyages of Christopher Columbus; to Which Are Added Those of His Companions,* volumes 3–5 of *The Works of Washington Irving* (New York & London: Putnam, 1848–1849);

The Alhambra, 2 volumes, as Geoffrey Crayon (London: Colburn & Bentley, 1832); as The Author of *The Sketch Book,* 2 volumes (Philadelphia: Carey & Lea, 1832); revised as *The Alhambra: A Series of Sketches of the Moors and Spaniards by the Author of "The Sketch Book"* (Philadelphia: Carey, Lea & Blanchard, 1836); revised as volume 15 of *The Works of Washington Irving* (New York: Putnam, 1851);

A Tour on the Prairies, number 1 of *Miscellanies,* as The Author of *The Sketch Book* (London: John Murray, 1835); republished as number 1 of *The Crayon Miscellany* (Philadelphia: Carey, Lea & Blanchard, 1835); republished in volume 9 of *The Works of Washington Irving* (New York & London: Putnam, 1849);

Abbotsford and Newstead Abbey, number 2 of *Miscellanies,* as The Author of *The Sketch Book* (London: John Murray, 1835); republished as number 2 of *The Crayon Miscellany* (Philadelphia: Carey, Lea & Blanchard, 1835); republished in *The Crayon Miscellany,* volume 9 of *The*

Works of Washington Irving (New York & London: Putnam, 1849);

Legends of the Conquest of Spain, number 3 of *Miscellanies,* as The Author of *The Sketch Book* (London: John Murray, 1835); republished as number 3 of *The Crayon Miscellany* (Philadelphia: Carey, Lea & Blanchard, 1835); republished in *The Crayon Miscellany,* volume 9 of *The Works of Washington Irving* (New York & London: Putnam, 1849);

Astoria, or, Enterprise Beyond the Rocky Mountains, 3 volumes (London: Bentley, 1836); republished as *Astoria, or Anecdotes of an Enterprise Beyond the Rocky Mountains,* 2 volumes (Philadelphia: Carey, Lea & Blanchard, 1836); revised as volume 8 of *The Works of Washington Irving* (New York: Putnam, 1849);

The Rocky Mountains: Or, Scenes, Incidents, and Adventures in the Far West; Digested from the Journal of Captain B. L. E. Bonneville, of the Army of the United States, and Illustrated from Various Other Sources, 2 volumes (Philadelphia: Carey, Lea & Blanchard, 1837); republished as *Adventures of Captain Bonneville, or, Scenes beyond the Rocky Mountains of the Far West,* 3 volumes (London: Bentley, 1837); republished as *The Adventures of Captain Bonneville, U.S.A., in the Rocky Mountains and the Far West,* volume 10 of *The Works of Washington Irving* (New York & London: Putnam, 1849);

Biography and Poetical Remains of the Late Margaret Miller Davidson (Philadelphia: Lea & Blanchard, 1841; London: Tilt & Bogue, 1843);

Mahomet and His Successors, volumes 12 and 13 of *The Works of Washington Irving* (New York: Putnam, 1850); republished as *Lives of Mahomet and His Successors,* 2 volumes (London: John Murray, 1850);

Chronicles of Wolfert's Roost and Other Papers (Edinburgh: Constable, Low / London: Hamilton, Adams / Dublin: M'Glashan, 1855); republished as *Wolfert's Roost and Other Papers,* volume 16 of *The Works of Washington Irving* (New York: Putnam, 1855);

Life of George Washington, 5 volumes (New York: Putnam, 1855–1859; London: Bohn, 1855–1859);

Spanish Papers and Other Miscellanies, Hitherto Unpublished or Uncollected, 2 volumes, edited by Pierre M. Irving (New York: Putnam/Hurd & Houghton, 1866; London: Low, 1866); republished as *Biographies and Miscellaneous Papers by Washington Irving* (London: Bell & Daldy, 1867).

Journals and Notebooks, 5 volumes, edited by Nathalia Wright, Walter A. Reichart, Lillian Schlissel, Wayne R. Kime, and Andrew B. Myers (Madison: University of Wisconsin Press / Boston: Twayne, 1969–1985).

Collection: *The Complete Works of Washington Irving*, 30 volumes, edited by Richard Dilworth Rust and others (Madison: University of Wisconsin Press / Boston: Twayne, 1969–1988).

OTHER: "The Catskill Mountains," in the *Home Book of the Picturesque* (New York: Putnam, 1852), pp. 71–78.

Washington Irving, America's first professional man of letters, won his international reputation in the 1820s as a literary cosmopolitan, an interpreter especially of English and Spanish character, customs, and scenes. During the decade that followed, however, Irving wrote almost exclusively of native subject matter, enriching the indigenous literature of the United States with his three "Western" books–*A Tour on the Prairies* (1835), *Astoria, or, Enterprise Beyond the Rocky Mountains* (1836), and *The Rocky Mountains: Or, Scenes, Incidents, and Adventures in the Far West* (1837), which was better known by its 1849 title, *The Adventures of Captain Bonneville, U.S.A., in the Rocky Mountains and the Far West*. These works, the productions of a leading author who was working at the height of his powers, were widely read and generally admired at the time of their issue. They became watershed writings for the literature of the American West, demonstrating some of the possibilities for portrayal of regions, populations, and modes of life that were as yet but little known.

Born on 3 April 1783 in New York City, Washington Irving was the youngest of twelve children born to William and Sarah Sanders Irving. Early on he revealed a propensity for authorship and a disinclination to participate in the family business–hardware imports and wholesale. Amid rather desultory studies in the law–he was admitted to the New York bar in 1807 but never practiced–Irving amused himself with writing, chiefly satiric prose pieces modeled on the familiar essay form made popular by Joseph Addison and Richard Steele. The Salmagundi papers (1807–1808), written anonymously in collaboration with friends, were in this witty mode, as was their successor *A History of New York* (1809), a burlesque narrative supposedly by an old Dutch antiquarian named Diedrich Knickerbocker.

The youthful Irving was well acquainted with the literature then available describing the American frontier, the Indians, and the fur trade–works such as Jonathan Carver's *Travels* (1778), Thomas Campbell's *Gertrude of Wyoming* (1809), and the journals of Meriwether Lewis and William Clark

(1814). Before his departure for Europe in 1815, however, Irving published only two short pieces whose subject matter had affinities with these works: "Traits of Indian Character" and "Philip of Pokanoket: An Indian Memoir," essays that first appeared in the February and June 1814 issues of the *Analectic Magazine* and were reprinted in *The Sketch Book of Geoffrey Crayon, Gent.* (1819–1820). The latter production, a medley of short prose pieces variously sentimental, reflective, and quietly playful in tone, continued Irving's work within the tradition of the familiar essay. Together with its successors *Bracebridge Hall, or the Humourists. A Medley* (1822) and *Tales of a Traveller* (1824), *The Sketch Book* won for Irving–or "Geoffrey Crayon," the pseudonym he had adopted–a respected position among contemporary European authors.

Committed to the pursuit of literature as a livelihood, in 1826 Irving took up residence in Spain, where he began work on *A History of the Life and Voyages of Christopher Columbus* (1828), a detailed study based largely on unpublished sources. He hoped the work would add to his reputation, entitling him to consideration as a writer not merely of light literature. Irving was fascinated by Spain, both for its eventful, chivalric past and for its colorful present. Before his return to the United States in 1832, after a seventeen-year sojourn abroad, he produced three more works about the country: *A Chronicle of the Conquest of Granada* (1829), an experiment in narrative history that featured a comically biased fictional narrator, Fray Antonio Agapida; *Voyages and Discoveries of the Companions of Columbus* (1831), a suite of biographical narratives; and *The Alhambra* (1832), a collection of essays and sketches based on his three-month residence in that old Moorish fortress.

By May 1832, when he arrived back in New York to a tumultuous welcome by his countrymen, Irving had become a versatile prose writer, adept in the short essay, short fiction, and historical narratives. He knew his own tastes and abilities, and, sensitive to the preferences of the reading public, he was confident that his next book would receive a friendly reception in the United States–especially if, as was urged upon him, he should write about something specifically American.

During his residence in Europe, Irving's interest in the American West had been kept keen through reading in works by Maj. Stephen H. Long, John Neal, James Athearn Jones, and James Hall, and in the summer of 1832 an opportunity was presented him of experiencing a part of that extensive region firsthand. In the course of a tour through the New England states he met Henry L. Ellsworth, who had been named a United States commissioner

Irving's birthplace, as it looked in 1800

to inspect lands in present-day Oklahoma that had been set aside for occupation by immigrating Indian tribes. Ellsworth invited him to accompany the official party as an observer, and the prospect of visiting the distant Osage and Pawnee prairies was too good to be refused.

The Ellsworth party proceeded south and then west via the Ohio River, and following his custom Irving recorded in a series of notebooks his impressions of scenes and personages encountered along the way. He stopped in Cincinnati, comparing the bustling city he saw to the vitriolic contemporary portrayal of it by Frances Trollope in her *Domestic Manners of the Americans* (1832), and thence he continued on to Saint Louis. Near there he observed the celebrated Indian agitator Black Hawk in a military prison. He then traveled to Independence, Missouri, from there setting out with his party across the near-wilderness toward Fort Gibson, an army post that had been designated as the place of rendezvous for the full official party under Ellsworth.

On 9 October 1832 that delegation, with its military escort, began its errand westward from the fort into open country. During the thirty-one days that ensued, the group followed an elliptical route

that extended about 135 miles west, then south, and finally back again to Fort Gibson. "How exciting," Irving wrote in his journal on 16 October, "to think that we are breaking thro a country hitherto untrodden by whiteman, except perchance the solitary trapper. A glorious world spread around us without an inhabitant." A few days later he participated in a breakneck buffalo hunt, an adventure the more intense for its taking place in known proximity to a band of fierce Pawnees. Irving's instincts for usable literary material were clearly aroused, and the persons around him sensed the likelihood of some published result of these experiences. Ellsworth wrote to his wife that Irving would "sketch in a little book every occurrence worthy of remembrance & especially *dates* & *facts*– These he says are his foundations–he makes additional rooms when he builds his fabric and adds the rest which he terms his 'filigree work.'" As yet, however, Irving had no definite project of authorship in mind. Departing from Fort Gibson on 11 November, he boarded a steamboat for New Orleans, and in mid December, after a four-thousand-mile journey of reorientation and personal discovery, he arrived at Washington, D.C. He had amassed a rich store of anecdotes and other data all along the way, but the month's journey into Indian country seems to have captured his fancy.

Throughout his career Irving was subject to moods and distractions that impeded steady progress in his efforts at authorship. These moods, combined with impatience at what he termed the "fancied necessity" of producing a book on an American topic, caused the first of his western works to appear only after considerable delay. The volume was beginning to take shape in his mind by the fall of 1833, but it did not reach the draft stage until late the following year when he learned that a fellow traveler on the Ellsworth expedition, Charles Joseph Latrobe, was about to publish an account of that excursion in his *The Rambler in North America* (1835). Alarmed by the prospect of competition, he completed his own book, and *A Tour on the Prairies* was published in April 1835.

The book was the first of three slim volumes issued serially that year by Irving under the collective title *The Crayon Miscellany*. Each installment developed a topic with which the author had come to be identified or which he knew from personal experience. *A Tour on the Prairies* was followed by *Abbotsford and Newstead Abbey* (1835), a record of visits to the homes of Sir Walter Scott and Lord Byron, and by *Legends of the Conquest of Spain* (1835), recounting passages in the long history of conflict between the Spaniards and the Moors. Because *A Tour on the Prairies* was Irving's first publication since his return to the United States, he wrote a special preface for the American edition in which he characterized the work in much the same modest manner he had used in his preface to *The Sketch Book*. In the earlier work, contrasting himself to travelers whose portfolios recorded visits to all the chief landmarks of a standard Continental itinerary, he confessed the whimsical miscellaneousness of the out-of-the-way sketches he was offering to view. Similarly, he proposed to recount in *A Tour on the Prairies* "nothing wonderful and adventurous," but merely "a simple narrative of every day occurrences; such as happen to every one who travels the prairies."

Notwithstanding this modest introduction, Irving's narrative of the expedition from Fort Gibson in 1832 was surely more wonderful to contemporary readers than he claimed. After all, "a month's foray beyond the outposts of human habitation, into the wilderness of the Far West" was no everyday occurrence. Fording a swollen stream aboard a makeshift raft of buffalo hides, finding oneself lost and alone on the empty prairie, sitting in solemn council with a band of Pawnees—these were memorable experiences and scenes, rich with curious interest. The intrinsic appeal of the book's basic subject matter was complemented by a second object of attention, the author's portrayal of himself as a participant in the adventure. *A Tour on the Prairies* presents Geoffrey Crayon, a man of the eastern states and of Europe, with civilized habits and tastes, as he comes into contact with the characters and customs peculiar to this untamed region, and thereby it records a journey of initiation. Drawing extensively upon the original journal entries, Irving deftly traces the development of his own attitudes and opinions as, from day to day, he comes to know something of the West firsthand, and his initial prejudices and expectations gradually give way to better informed responses. Thus, witnessing the animated behavior of Indians when among themselves, he comes to question the stereotyped conception of them as always taciturn and reserved in demeanor. Watching a settler make malicious threats against the unoffending Indians in his vicinity leads him to suspect that barbarous acts by American citizens often precipitate hostilities that are then publicized and blamed on the Indians alone.

Irving devised an order of climax that roughly parallels the progress of his familiarity with the West. The rising action of the narrative culminates in the exhilarating, half-chaotic buffalo hunt. Once that stirring experience is over, logistics dictate that the work of the official party must presently be concluded; the stress of travel and want of adequate forage have weakened the horses. The young rangers who make up the military escort are themselves new to the prairies; their early enthusiasm has disappeared, and they long for the return to civilized amenities. Likewise, Crayon is well content to begin the return journey toward the fort. When, on the eastward march, the party reaches a frontier farmhouse whose occupant serves them a modest meal of boiled beef and turnips, Crayon is delighted at this approximation of civilized fare. "Head of Apicius," he exults, "what a banquet!" With a characteristic blend of seriousness and humor he thus brings to a close his narrative of personal discovery, with its involvement between East and West, the civilized and the wild. Having experienced something of the West for more than a month, Crayon understands and appreciates it more fully than before; yet he has also confirmed his own identity as no westerner but simply himself, a middle-aged visitor from the East.

Although Irving developed in *A Tour on the Prairies* the twin themes of initiation and self-discovery, those threads of continuity do not stand out insistently. Instead, the work gives the impression of easy miscellaneousness, as of material being introduced just as it had presented itself amid the events of a particular day. Heterogeneity of content

Rip Van Winkle.

a posthumous writing of Diedrich Knickerbocker

By Woden, God of Saxons,
From whence comes wensday, that is Wodensday,
Truth is a thing that ever I will keep
Unto thylke day in which I creep into
My sepulchre ———
                                    Cartwright.

Whoever has made a voyage up the
Hudson must remember the Kaal
Kaalskill mountains. They are a dis-
membered branch of the great appala-
chian family, and are seen away to the
west of the river swelling up to a noble
height and lording it over the surrounding country. Every change of season
every change of weather, indeed every hour
of the day, produces some change in the
magical hues and shapes of these mountains, and they are regarded by all the

First page from the manuscript for "Rip Van Winkle," which was included in The Sketch Book *of Geoffrey Crayon, Gent. (Clifton Waller Barrett Library, Alderian Library, University of Virginia)* is in fact a keynote of the book. The author allows himself little space for elaboration. Confining himself to chapters that average only two thousand words, he slides from topic to topic with easy grace. Within chapter 20, for instance, he recounts anecdotes of famous wild horses of the prairies; notes the speculations that these animals may derive from Arabian or Andalusian stock; comments on the impact the accessibility of horses has had upon Indians; portrays with appreciation a handsome young stallion brought into camp one night by Beatte, a veteran hunter; relates byplay between the rangers and the sullen Beatte as the latter "breaks" his captive horse; details the manner of its capture; represents it the next morning, when thoroughly subjected to the will of its master; and concludes with rueful humor that the stallion's fate has its parallel in human affairs: "one day, a prince of the prairies—the next day a pack horse!" Anecdotes, dialogue, prose panoramas, genre studies, recounted bits of folklore—Irving offers to readers a little of everything. Written in part to satisfy the desire of the reading public for a book about the West by "Geoffrey Crayon," it was well calculated to whet the appetite for another.

The critical reception of *A Tour on the Prairies* was cordial on both sides of the Atlantic but especially in the United States. Irving's New York friend Philip Hone echoed a prevailing view when in his diary for 14 April 1835 he characterized the work as "the very best kind of light reading." Edward Everett, writing in the *North American Review,* praised it as a source of national satisfaction. "We are proud of Mr. Irving's sketches of English life," he wrote; "but we glow with rapture as we see him coming back from the Prairies, laden with the poetical treasures of the primitive wilderness,—rich with spoil from the uninhabited desert." Irving was gratified at the success of his little book, but like Hone he considered it a "light" production. During the century that followed its publication, the popularity and critical status of *A Tour on the Prairies* gradually declined. In recent decades the work has enjoyed renewed regard; and according to its most recent editor, Dahlia Terrell, its status as a "minor classic" of western American literature now seems assured.

During the summer of 1834 Irving was repeatedly urged to begin work on a more challenging project of authorship, one relating to the recent history of the far Northwest. His old acquaintance John Jacob Astor, a wealthy New York merchant, wished him to prepare for publication a narrative of a bold commercial venture in which that old gentleman had played a central role and still took pride. Between 1809 and 1813, only a few years after the

splendid explorations of Lewis and Clark, Astor had conceived and underwritten an effort to establish an American fur-trading depot on the Pacific coast near the mouth of the Columbia River. The outpost, as he envisioned it, would obtain its supplies by ships sent from New York around Cape Horn; it would communicate with settlements in the interior of the United States by an overland trail; it would serve as an exit point for shipment of furs to the lucrative markets of China; and gradually it would become a focal point for fur trappers along the coast and inland, challenging British interests for domination of the trade in that productive region. Though finally unsuccessful, Astor's experiment in empire building had been grandly conceived and was, he believed, too little known.

Irving found the proposal of his old friend attractive in several respects. He knew the Astor topic would be congenial to him, for the personnel and customs of the fur trade had interested him since 1803, when on a memorable visit to Montreal he had been entertained in princely style at the headquarters of the North West Company. What was more, Astor undertook to set before him a wealth of material for research that he would be able to digest amid almost ideal facilities for study and writing. At his handsome estate near New York, Astor had at hand journals compiled by members of overland expeditions to and from the infant trading establishment, diaries and letters written by persons who had reached the post by ship, account books, and inventories—in short, an archive of just such information as would make possible an authoritative account of the enterprise. Several narratives by participants in the venture were already in print, and further collateral lights were to be had from other veterans of the undertaking. In fact, the sheer bulk of the documentation within reach was almost daunting. Still, Irving's difficulties when in Spain of even gaining admittance to the several archives whose contents supported *The Life and Voyages of Christopher Columbus* and *A Chronicle of the Conquest of Granada* had taught him the value of a centralized, readily accessible research collection.

Occupied as he was with other concerns, including *The Crayon Miscellany,* Irving could not consider performing by himself the careful analysis and collation of the Astor materials that would be necessary to set the subject in preliminary order. Still, once the foundation for the projected book had been laid, he was confident of his capacity "to dress it up advantageously, and with little labor, for the press." Astor's offer to pay him a generous author's fee was out of the question, of course. He valued his good name, and he could not permit himself to seem a flattering hack writer who was being rewarded for services rendered to a wealthy patron. He made clear to Astor that, should he decide to take up the project, he would look for remuneration solely for the arrangements he might make with publishers in the United States and England. He proposed only that he be allowed to engage a research assistant to facilitate the initial stages of study; and Astor assented at once. Not long afterward Irving secured the agreement of Pierre Munro Irving, a nephew then living in Toledo, Ohio, to sift through Astor's documents.

On 29 August 1834 Irving addressed a letter to Pierre setting forth his early conception of the Astor book and defining more precisely the contribution his young relative would make. This summary of the work's yet unwritten contents, organization, and popular appeal demonstrates strikingly Irving's experienced ability to assess the latent possibilities of a literary undertaking. He proposed

> to give not merely a history of his [Astor's] great colonial and commercial enterprise, and of the fortunes of his colony, but a body of information concerning the whole region beyond the Rocky Mountains, on the borders of Columbia River, comprising the adventures, by sea and land, of traders, trappers, Indian warriors, hunters, &c.; their habits, characters, persons, costumes, &c.; descriptions of natural scenery, animals, plants, &c., &c. I think, in this way, a rich and varied work may be formed, both entertaining and instructive, and laying open scenes in the wild life of that adventurous region which would possess the charm of freshness and novelty.

Two years ensued before *Astoria* was published in October 1836, but during that period the author's conception of his work in progress remained unchanged.

Whereas in *A Tour on the Prairies* Irving was serving up a suggestive miscellany, he foresaw in *Astoria* a book rich with lore of all sorts. The encyclopedic range of his planned coverage actually suggests the comprehensive instructions addressed by Thomas Jefferson to Lewis and Clark as they prepared to explore and report upon the far Northwest. Perhaps the repeated ampersands in Irving's early statement to his nephew mark most clearly his intention to fashion in *Astoria* a gathering of diverse material about the frontier.

Above all, however, Irving conceived the book as a narrative of the "great colonial and commercial enterprise" set in motion by Astor. Unlike *A Tour on the Prairies* but like *The Life and Voyages of Christopher Columbus,* it purported to make a substantial contribution to knowledge, and Irving hoped it would

strengthen his mature reputation. Accordingly, the narrator of the published *Astoria* is businesslike and serious, as befits one who recounts events that carry national import. The name that appears on the title page is Washington Irving–not, as in *A Tour on the Prairies* and several earlier volumes, "The Author of *The Sketch Book.*" Although the speaker indulges in humor at many points, he is primarily a magisterial presence, coordinating the progress of his complex account and at key points rendering considered judgments. Solicitous to ensure the reader's comprehension of the relationship between simultaneous occurrences at locations sometimes thousands of miles apart, he ranges backward and forward in time as necessary, reminds the reader upon returning to take up an old strand of the action, and in general visibly organizes the work.

The narrative scheme of *Astoria* follows the "grand scheme" of John Jacob Astor, suggesting through its organization the boldness of the projector's initial vision but also the forces that doomed its enactment to failure. Irving first portrays in succession the activities of two groups of men, all partners or employees of Astor's Pacific Fur Company. The first contingent, aboard the ship *Tonquin,* sails from New York to the mouth of the Columbia River and sets up a trading establishment. The second party journeys across the plains and Rocky Mountains toward the same destination. The account of events in these two widely diverging and then converging itineraries continues through chapter 40 (of sixty-one). The daring of the project is manifest from its sheer hemispheric scope, but by portraying the two small parties so far removed from each other, and from any other friendly assistance, the book suggests the numberless possibilities for miscalculation and misfortune that exist.

The final twenty-one chapters depart strikingly from the earlier simple pattern, portraying through accelerating shifts of scene the lack of communication, cross purposes, bad faith, and simple bad fortune that together brought down the undertaking. Once the sea and land parties met at Astoria and passed together the winter of 1811–1812, they attempted to strengthen their foothold and also to communicate with Astor in New York. Meanwhile the projector, who had received no information about either expedition, dispatched in October 1811 a second ship, the *Beaver,* with supplies for the new settlement. From that point the coordination of effort between the various parties broke down. A packet of messages being forwarded to Astor by land was lost, and the returning Astorians required ten months to reach Saint Louis, where they arrived

A sketch drawn by Irving during his western travels in 1832 (New York Public Library; Astor, Lenox and Tilden Foundations)

in May 1813. Astor learned of their safety only by chancing to read of it in a Missouri newspaper.

Following the account of this temporarily inspiriting development, in chapter 51 Irving narrates the disintegration of Astor's cherished project. The action shifts from place to place—Canton, the coast of Alaska, the Sandwich Islands (now called the Hawaiian Islands), New York, the fort at Astoria, and locations between. Timely communication across thousands of miles was impossible, so the persons responsible for various components of the venture directed their respective courses according to what limited information they had. The first ship dispatched by Astor, the *Tonquin,* was destroyed and its crew massacred by perfidious Indians. Meanwhile, following the outbreak of war with Great Britain, Astoria was easy prey for capture by enemy forces, the more so since the port of New York was about to be blockaded by His Majesty's navy. The second ship, the *Beaver,* reached Astoria but, sailing northward on a trading voyage, was diverted from its expected return. A third ship, the *Lark,* sailed from New York in March 1813, but it capsized near the Sandwich Islands and several of its crew were lost. Amid these difficulties the persons in charge at Astoria determined to abandon the fort and dispose of its contents, including valuable furs, to representatives of a rival British company. When H.M.S. *Raccoon* eventually arrived at Astoria to take possession, its

commander was informed that the fort was already in British hands through a commercial arrangement. The place was thereupon renamed Fort George, and the ill-fated undertaking of John Jacob Astor was at an end.

In order to make clear the adverse circumstances that beset Astor's grand scheme, Irving recounts these developments in detail. His careful narration brings into relief the seemingly perverse multiplication of misfortunes and cross purposes so that the far-flung enterprise appears to take on an anarchic, self-destructive life of its own.

The overall structure Irving devised for *Astoria* entailed one awkward constraint: that his chronological organization of events, among several groups of characters in various parts of the world, precluded sustained attention to Astor. Only at points where the scene could naturally shift back to New York could the protagonist receive more than passing attention, and these occasions were few. However, Irving managed to turn the infrequency of Astor's appearances to his advantage. In the early chapters he enlists sympathy for this central figure, showing that the motive behind the ambitious scheme was not merely to secure profit. Already a wealthy man, Astor hoped also to win "honorable fame" as one who had made a contribution to the United States, his adopted country. Having established the worthy aims of the projector, Irving then sets his narrative in motion. He does not permit the reader to lose sight of the capitalist, whom he introduces from time to time as correspondent, issuer of instructions or warnings, or recipient of news. As various partners and employees encounter perils on land and at sea, the reader remains aware of Astor's more than financial involvement with them. However, the scene shifts back to New York only four times in the course of the book.

Irving thus represents the absence of his protagonist from the scenes of activity that concerned him so deeply as contributing to the failure of the enterprise. Although the projector "battled resolutely against every difficulty and pursued his course in defiance of every loss," clearly he could not carry out his plans single-handedly. He had to rely on the sagacity and good faith of his subordinate partners, not all of whom shared his zeal or even his orientation in favor of American interests. Through the design of his narrative Irving points up the almost inevitable failure of a project that required for success not only good fortune but also good faith and steady good judgment. The shape he imposed on *Astoria* reflected his understanding of the forces that combined to shape the events he portrayed so that, as he writes in the introduction, "the work, without any labored attempt at artificial construction, actually possesses much of that unity so much sought after in works of fiction, and considered so important to the interest of every history."

Of course, the apparent inevitability in the design of *Astoria* is the result of analysis and arrangement that yielded the very "artificial construction" Irving seems here to deprecate. Upon beginning the book he had surveyed the material before him, identified the major themes implicit in it, devised an approach that would embody them, and engaged his nephew to trace a thread of continuity along which he could introduce the miscellaneous material that would add "richness." Like *A Tour on the Prairies, Astoria* exhibits a double structure: a narrative line with its exposition, complication, climax, and resolution; and along that line a variety of information related more or less closely to the setting, characters, and action being portrayed. Aside from the far greater complexity of *Astoria,* the differences of effect between it and its predecessor derive primarily from Irving's intention to create a work of authentic history. Like no other of his historical writings, *Astoria* conjoins without confusion or disharmony features of his earlier volumes wherein the tastes and sensibility of the author are implicitly on display and those of the graver, more weighty works in which the narrator is impersonal, an impartial judge and commentator.

Astoria is unique among Irving's writings, which are on the whole apolitical, in one other respect: its vigorous advocacy of a specific federal policy. In his introduction the author explains that a sense of the "national character and importance" of the original undertaking had led Astor to urge upon him the writing of the book; and early in the work proper he places the entire action in an international context of exploration, commerce, and competition for empire. He draws a contrast between "the keen activity of private enterprise," as embodied by Astor, and "the dull patronage of government," which, in failing to support the initiatives of its progressive citizens, frustrates its own interests. He points out that Astor had communicated his plans to the United States government and received encouragement and assurance of "every facility and protection which the Government could properly afford." In the event, however, federal assistance was too little and came too late to prevent the capture of the American outpost. Irving therefore deplores "in a national point of view" the loss of an American presence on the shores of the Pacific. At the close of the work he looks to the future, foreseeing the possibility of renewed tension between the United States and Great Britain over the question of sovereignty in that region. American pioneers consider the West "a grand outlet of our empire," he warns, and they will be impatient with British claims to the contrary. The lesson of history and the implication of *Astoria* for contemporary policy makers are plain: having once let slip the opportunity to assert control over the far Northwest, the United States government should now aggressively assert its territorial claim.

Irving completed his first draft of *Astoria* in October 1835, but a full year passed before the book was offered for sale. During that time he devoted close attention to the swelling manuscript and made his financial arrangements with publishers. The firm of Carey, Lea and Blanchard of Philadelphia paid him the considerable sum of $4,000 for the right to publish an American edition of five thousand copies, and through an intermediary Irving sold the English copyright for £500. The critical reception of *Astoria* was favorable on both sides of the Atlantic, especially in the United States, where its wealth of detail, air of verisimilitude, graphic descriptions, dramatic interest, and little known subject matter all received comment. Writing in the *Southern Literary Messenger* for January 1837, Edgar Allan Poe praised its masterly yet unobtrusive grace of form, "the modesty of the title affording no indication of the fulness, comprehensiveness, and beauty, with which a long and entangled series of detail, collected, necessarily, from a mass of vague and imperfect data, has been wrought into completeness and unity." In England *Astoria* was on occasion faulted for prolixity, but not for its political implications. On the whole it won praise as a worthy product of Irving's talent and a significant contribution to transatlantic literature.

From this level of almost universal admiration the reputation of *Astoria* declined somewhat during the author's lifetime, probably owing in part to the popularity of more contemporaneous accounts of the West. Gradually the opinion gained currency that the book was unreliable as history, being the product of a lively imagination rather than of scrupulous respect for factual detail. To this view was added the notion that, along with Irving's other western writings, *Astoria* was merely a calculated attempt to capitalize on the West as a marketable commodity for authorship. An especially ungenerous variation on both notions came from Hubert Howe Bancroft, who in his *History of the Northwest Coast* (1884) accused Irving of sentimentality, sycophancy, plagiarism, and dishonesty in presenting "pure fiction" as if it were genuine history. The virulent attack by Bancroft provoked a series of rejoinders and corrections that, after several decades, eventually rescued Irving's achievement from such irresponsible misrepresentation. The meticulously annotated edition of the work by Edgeley W. Todd (1964) established the authenticity of Irving's account. In recent years *Astoria* has received increased critical attention. It is now generally recognized as having been written, in the words of a reviewer for the *London Spectator* in December 1836, "with all the art of fiction, yet without any apparent sacrifice of truth or exactness."

The contribution by Washington Irving to the early literature of the American West included one more volume, an outgrowth of his work on *Astoria*. During several months in 1835 and 1836 he busied himself gathering supplementary information from persons whose familiarity with the Rocky Mountain region and points westward dated from the period after the termination of the Astor venture in 1813. Among these individuals was a military man of wide experience, Capt. Benjamin L. E. Bonneville. An officer in the United States Army, Bonneville had been granted leave from duty in 1831 in order to fulfill a long-standing wish to explore the Rocky Mountain region while pursuing a campaign of fur trapping and trading there. He had badly overstayed the eighteen months' leave that had been granted him, and despite his efforts to communicate with Washington so as to explain the situation, he had been given up for lost and his name dropped from the army rolls. Now, having reported to head-

quarters and turned over the journals and maps he had accumulated, he awaited reinstatement. The information he shared with Irving in New York during the summer of 1835 led the author to write Bonneville's commanding officer, Gen. Alexander Macomb, requesting copies of maps the captain had drawn.

Within the next few months Irving met Bonneville two more times, once in Washington, D.C., where Bonneville was preparing for publication an account of his adventures, and later again in New York. At the time of the latter meeting, March 1836, Bonneville was in vain search of a publisher for his book manuscript. Irving's attentions to *Astoria* were now nearing completion, and in the already drafted production of his acquaintance he saw potential for a sequel. Whatever its present deficiencies from the publishers' point of view, the work was a detailed account of Bonneville's peregrinations and observations. If enriched by information from additional sources, a rewritten narrative of the captain's adventures might prove a creditable offering under Irving's own name.

Other considerations suggested the prudence of taking the manuscript off Bonneville's hands. By this time Irving was well acquainted with the character and recent history of the distant territory the captain had traversed; so no extensive background study would be necessary. Much curious material relating to those western scenes remained to be placed before the public, and the likelihood of its appeal seemed strong. Even yet, for example, the customs and colorful employees of the great fur trading companies that had long vied for dominance in the Rocky Mountains were little known. Finally, the continuing international competition for control of the fur trade repeated in contemporary terms the question to be posed in *Astoria,* whether the United States or Great Britain would ultimately reap the benefits of possession in the Northwest. With these inducements in mind, Irving purchased the manuscript from Bonneville for $1,000.

As he composed *The Adventures of Captain Bonneville,* which first appeared in May 1837, Irving naturally revised the manuscript into something stylistically his own. Nevertheless, he drew attention throughout the work to the tastes, enthusiasms, and opinions of its principal source and central character on many topics. Irving represents Bonneville less as a practical man of business than as a person of ardent temperament to whom the Rocky Mountains are a "region of romance." Although the captain had secured financial backing from New York investors and did engage–unsuccessfully–in fur trapping and trading for profit, Irving uses this mercantile activ-

Irving's self-portrait at his home on the Hudson River (Berg Collection, the New York Public Library; Astor, Lenox and Tilden Foundations)

ity as occasion to portray the more narrow business types—independent trappers and representatives of the fur companies—whom Bonneville met. He emphasizes the pleasant personality of his protagonist—his bonhomie, his sense of humor, his curiosity, his admiration of natural beauty, his eye for the eccentric. In fact, Bonneville faintly resembles Irving's representation of himself in *A Tour on the Prairies*. Like *A Tour on the Prairies*, *The Adventures of*

Captain Bonneville details the initiation of a newcomer into a part of the western wilderness, here with the genial soldier in the central role.

The Rocky Mountain exploits of Bonneville and his party afforded Irving a rich fund of adventures to recount—explorations, skirmishes with Indians, and maneuvers against rival traders. Beyond these, Bonneville's sense of humor as expressed in his manuscript underlies entire scenes. The accounts of a drinking bout improvised—in the absence of other liquor—by combining raw alcohol with honey and of the trappers' convivial potations at a fabled, nonalcoholic "beer spring" in the mountains; the parley in which an Indian chief adroitly wheedles the captain and his men into reciprocating again and again for the single gift of a horse; the quasi-judicial proceedings in which an unoffending Indian dog is found guilty of absconding with a valuable fur and summarily executed—all these incidents derive from the pen of Bonneville. Nor did the captain exempt himself from comic treatment: the sobriquet given him by the Indians, "The Bald-Headed Chief," is occasion for amusement at several points. In all, the purchased manuscript yielded a considerably larger proportion of comedy in *The Adventures of Captain Bonneville* than had appeared in its two predecessors. However, Bonneville's lively imagination was also attuned to moods other than the playful. Almost a full chapter is devoted to an autobiographical tale of love, elopement, and revenge related to him by Kosato, a renegade Blackfoot Indian. Commenting on this story, Irving likens its characters to the "heroes and heroines of sentimental civilization."

Like *A Tour on the Prairies* and *Astoria*, *The Adventures of Captain Bonneville* is diverse in its contents. The catholicity of his central character's interests would in effect have dictated this feature to Irving had he not embraced it himself as a point for emphasis. Thus, when Bonneville chances upon a colony of beaver, several pages of observations ensue detailing the habits of that species. When he and his party come across a natural wonder such as the Great Tar Spring, of supposedly medicinal powers, a speculative discussion of its properties is introduced. An overall pattern of expository or descriptive discussions interpolated at the first mention of the persons, peoples, scenes, or phenomena they illustrate characterizes this book, as it had the earlier two.

In striking contrast to the simple main lines of action in the earlier works, *The Adventures of Captain Bonneville* lacks a clear narrative framework. At the time Bonneville entered the Rocky Mountain trading region he had formed only the most rudimentary plans. Thereafter he guided and changed his party's course as events dictated, dividing his followers into subgroups, losing some, later reuniting with others, crossing the same territory until, after more than two years had passed, he made his way back to civilization. As a result, even if Irving's book recounted the travels only of Bonneville and his men, it would not have lent itself to the shaping he had given the two other narratives.

In fact, while preparing the work Irving secured information about the contemporary fur trade from several persons besides Bonneville. The supplementary knowledge he obtained from conversations with such veterans or from study of their journals and correspondence greatly enhanced his presentation; for only by drawing on a variety of sources could he have fashioned a work that continues to sustain its reputation as the premier early account of the Rocky Mountain fur trade during that period. Nevertheless, the presence in *The Adventures of Captain Bonneville* of narrative material, sometimes several chapters in length, describing the activities of parties other than those of the captain exacerbated the difficulty Irving faced in achieving continuity. Realizing that multiple sets of personnel, sequences of action unrelated to each other, and events occurring years before or after the ones nominally being described would pose formidable difficulties for the reader, Irving addressed the problem as well as he could. He devised a sort of splicing technique, piecing together accounts of various parties, all of which he portrayed as representing aspects of the western fur trade: when he reintroduces certain groups of trappers or explorers who have not been mentioned for some time, he summarizes their earlier activities and whereabouts, and when leaving one party to follow another he assures the reader that the group being left behind will indeed be heard from again. In view of the book's amorphousness, Irving titled the first American edition *The Rocky Mountains: Or, Scenes, Incidents, and Adventures in the Far West; Digested from the Journal of Captain B. L. E. Bonneville, of the Army of the United States, and Illustrated from Various Other Sources,* although it has always been popularly known as *The Adventures of Captain Bonneville, U.S.A.*

Despite the problems he encountered in attempting to shape it, Irving enjoyed writing *The Adventures of Captain Bonneville* even more than he had the earlier two books. In *A Tour on the Prairies* he had been constrained by his plan to produce a deft, suggestive work rather than a more exhaustive one and by the limited sphere of the events he was describing. In *Astoria,* enriched by miscellaneous information though it was, his performance as narrator was governed by the primary role he chose as judicious historian and by the extent and complexity of the story he told. By contrast, in writing *The Adventures of Captain Bonneville* Irving felt free to work up his material to whatever length he wished, adopting whatever tone his topics seemed to dictate and shaping passages with regard to their effectiveness in themselves rather than as interlinked segments of some developing whole. Though possessing solid credentials as a historical source, the work was written with verve and attention to literary effect.

Despite its merits, *The Adventures of Captain Bonneville* was only a modest popular success at the time of its publication, being regarded as merely a sequel to *Astoria*. Reviewers in the United States often confined their commentary to statements of opinion about the desirability or otherwise of American expansion in the far West. Those in England likewise saw the work in a political light, reacting with irritation to Irving's sympathetic representation of Bonneville and others who posed a threat to British interests. In later years the reputation of *The Adventures of Captain Bonneville* has been more for its merit as an account of the early fur trade than for its skill as a literary performance.

Washington Irving wrote *A Tour on the Prairies, Astoria,* and *The Adventures of Captain Bonneville* when he was between the ages of fifty and fifty-three and in a state of physical and mental vigor he never again felt so fully. His long experience as an essayist, sketch writer, fictionist, historian, and author of semihistorical legends and chronicles guided his professional judgment as he evaluated the possibilities for these books and then set out to realize them. His authorship of the three western books was remarkably sure-handed. The works are all distinctively his own, yet as differing achievements they manifest his versatility. Deft, evocative, and pleasant, *A Tour on the Prairies* suggests an elegant personal essay in narrative form. Consciously architectonic, predominantly sober, and historiographically orthodox, *Astoria* presents its wide-ranging subject matter in a manner calculated to emphasize its continuing national significance. Various, unhurried, and humorous, *The Adventures of Captain Bonneville* resembles a portfolio of piquant sketches assembled to illustrate a common theme. Each book draws upon skills Irving had developed earlier in his career so that together they constitute a reprise or recombination of styles he had adopted in prior years.

Irving never wrote so much or so well as when he produced his contributions to the literature of the American West. Once dismissed as apocryphal romanticized history or uninspired hackwork, in recent years *A Tour on the Prairies, Astoria,* and *The Adventures of Captain Bonneville* have begun to receive renewed recognition as among the most artistically satisfying of his extensive writings. The current of opinion is thus returning these works to the status they held at the time they first appeared. Irving, critics now recognize, was not only America's first professional man of letters, he was also one of the earliest major literary interpreters of the American West.

Letters:

Washington Irving: Letters, edited by Ralph M. Aderman (Boston: G. K. Hall, 1978–1982), volumes 23–26 in *The Complete Works of Washington Irving.*

Bibliographies:

William R. Langfeld and Philip C. Blackburn, *Washington Irving: A Bibliography* (New York: New York Public Library, 1933);

Edwin T. Bowden, *Washington Irving: Bibliography* (Boston: Twayne, 1989), volume 30 in *The Complete Works of Washington Irving.*

Biographies:

Pierre M. Irving, *The Life and Letters of Washington Irving,* 4 volumes (New York: Putnam, 1862–1864);

Stanley T. Williams, *The Life of Washington Irving,* 2 volumes (New York & London: Oxford University Press, 1935).

References:

Ralph Aderman, ed., *Critical Essays on Washington Irving* (Boston: G. K. Hall, 1990);

Aderman, ed., *Washington Irving Reconsidered* (Hartford, Conn.: Transcendental Books, 1969);

Peter Antelyes, *Tales of Adventurous Enterprise: Washington Irving and the Poetics of Western Expansion* (New York: Columbia University Press, 1990);

Mary Weatherspoon Bowden, *Washington Irving* (Boston: Twayne, 1981);

Stanley Browdin, ed., *The Old World and New World Romanticism of Washington Irving* (Westport, Conn.: Greenwood Press, 1986);

William Bedford Clark, "How the West Won: Irving's Comic Inversion of the Westering Myth in *A Tour on the Prairies,*" *American Literature,* 50 (1978): 335–347;

Martha Dula, "Audience Response to *A Tour on the Prairies* in 1835," *Western American Literature,* 8 (1973): 67–74;

M. H. Dunlop, *Sixty Miles from Contentment: Traveling the Nineteenth-Century American Interior* (New York: Basic Books, 1995);

Hugh Egan, "The Second-Hand Wilderness: History and Art in Irving's *Astoria,*" *American Transcendental Quarterly,* 2 (1988): 253–270;

Henry Leavitt Ellsworth, *Washington Irving on the Prairie or A Narrative of a Tour of the Southwest in the Year 1832,* edited by Stanley T. Williams and Barbara D. Simison (New York: American Book Company, 1937);

Wayne Franklin, "The Misadventures of Irving's Bonneville: Trapping and Being Trapped in the Rocky Mountains," in *The Westering Experience in American Literature: Bicentennial Essays,* edited by Merrill Lewis and L. L. Lee (Bellingham: Bureau for Faculty Research, Western Washington University, 1977), pp. 122–128;

Bruce Greenfield, "Washington Irving: Historian of American Discovery," in his *Narrating Discovery: The American Explorer in American Literature, 1790–1855* (New York: Columbia University Press, 1992), pp. 113–163;

William L. Hedges, *Washington Irving: An American Study, 1802–1832* (Baltimore: Johns Hopkins University Press, 1965);

Hedges, "Washington Irving: Nonsense, the Fat of the Land and the Dream of Indolence," in *The Chief Glory of Every People,* edited by Matthew J. Bruccoli (Carbondale: Southern Illinois University Press, 1973), pp. 141–160;

Wayne R. Kime, "The Completeness of Washington Irving's *A Tour on the Prairies,*" *Western American Literature,* 8 (1973): 55–65;

Kime, "Washington Irving and The Empire of the West," *Western American Literature,* 5 (1971): 277–285;

Thomas J. Lyon, "Washington Irving's Wilderness," *Western American Literature,* 1 (Fall 1966): 167–174;

Jeffrey Rubin-Dorsky, *Adrift in the Old World: The Psychological Pilgrimage of Washington Irving* (Chicago: University of Chicago Press, 1988);

J. A. Russell, "Irving: Recorder of Indian Life," *Journal of American History,* 25 (1931): 185–195;

Edgeley W. Todd, "Washington Irving Discovers the Frontier," *Western Humanities Review,* 11 (1957): 29–39;

James W. Tuttleton, ed., *Washington Irving: The Critical Reaction* (New York: AMS Press, 1993).

Papers:

The New York Public Library holds the most substantial collection of Irving's papers. Other collections are in Historic Hudson Valley, the Carl H. Pforzheimer Library, the Huntington Library, and the university libraries of Virginia, Columbia, Yale, and Harvard.

Helen Hunt Jackson

(14 October 1830 – 12 August 1885)

Mary Louise Briscoe
University of Pittsburgh

See also the Jackson entries in *DLB 42: American Writers for Children Before 1900* and *DLB 47: American Historians, 1866–1912.*

BOOKS: *Verses,* as H. H. (Boston: Fields, Osgood, 1870; enlarged, Boston: Roberts, 1874; London: Roberts, 1877);

Bits of Travel, as H. H. (Boston: Osgood, 1872);

Bits of Talk about Home Matters, as H. H. (Boston: Roberts, 1873; London: Low, 1873);

Saxe Holm's Stories, as Saxe Holm (New York: Scribner, Armstrong, 1874);

The Story of Boon, as H. H. (Boston: Roberts, 1874);

Bits of Talk, in Verse and Prose, for Young Folks, as H. H. (Boston: Roberts, 1876);

Mercy Philbrick's Choice, anonymous (Boston: Roberts, 1876; London: Low, 1876);

Hetty's Strange History, anonymous (Boston: Roberts, 1877);

Bits of Travel at Home, as H. H. (Boston: Roberts, 1878);

Nelly's Silver Mine: A Story of Colorado Life, as H. H. (Boston: Roberts, 1878);

Saxe Holm's Stories, second series, as Saxe Holm (New York: Scribners, 1878);

Letters from a Cat: Published by Her Mistress for the Benefit of All Cats and the Amusement of Little Children, as H. H. (Boston: Roberts, 1879);

A Century of Dishonor: A Sketch of the United States Government's Dealings with Some of the Indian Tribes, as H. H. (New York: Harper, 1881); republished as *A Century of Dishonour: A Sketch of the United States Government's Dealings with Some of the North American Tribes* (London: Chatto & Windus, 1881); enlarged edition (Boston: Roberts, 1885)—includes *Report on the Condition and Needs of the Mission Indians of California;*

Mammy Tittleback and Her Family: A True Story of Seventeen Cats, as H. H. (Boston: Roberts, 1881);

The Training of Children, as H. H. (New York: New York & Brooklyn Publishing, 1882);

Report on the Condition and Needs of the Mission Indians of California, by Jackson and Abbot Kinney

(Washington, D.C.: Government Printing Office, 1883); republished as *Report of Mrs. Helen Hunt Jackson and Abbot Kinney on the Mission Indians in 1883* (Boston: Stanley & Usher, 1887); republished as *Father Junipero and the Mission Indians of California* (Boston: Little, Brown, 1902);

Ramona: A Story, as Helen Jackson (H. H.) (Boston: Roberts, 1884; London: Macmillan, 1884);

The Hunter Cats of Connorloa, as Helen Jackson (H. H.) (Boston: Roberts, 1884);

Cat Stories (Boston: Roberts, 1884);

Easter Bells: An Original Poem, as H. H. (New York: White, Stokes & Allen, 1884);

The Procession of Flowers in Colorado (Colorado Springs, Colo.: Gazette, 1885);

A Calendar of Sonnets (Boston: Roberts, 1886);

Zeph: A Posthumous Story, as Helen Jackson (H. H.) (Boston: Roberts, 1885; Edinburgh: Douglas, 1886);

Glimpses of Three Coasts (Boston: Roberts, 1886);

Poems (Boston: Roberts, 1886–1888);

Sonnets and Lyrics (Boston: Roberts, 1886);

Between Whiles (Boston: Roberts, 1887);

My Legacy (Boston: Carter & Karrick, 1888);

Pansy Billings and Popsy: Two Stories of Girl Life (Boston: Lothrop, 1898).

Westward to a High Mountain: The Colorado Writings of Helen Hunt Jackson, edited by Mark I. West (Denver: Colorado Historical Society, 1994).

TRANSLATION: Jean Pierre Claris de Florian, *Bathmendi: A Persian Tale* (Boston: Loring, 1867).

One of the most prolific women writers of her time, Helen Hunt Jackson hoped to be remembered mainly for *A Century of Dishonor: A Sketch of the United States Government's Dealings with Some of the Indian Tribes* (1881) and *Ramona: A Story* (1884). Before Jackson's death more than fifteen thousand copies were sold of *Ramona,* the novel with which she intended to arouse public outrage at the plight of Native Americans in the California missions, just as Harriet Beecher Stowe's *Uncle Tom's Cabin* (1852) had called attention to the plight of African Americans. While the success of the novel in fulfilling that objective is still debated, the story and its leading characters have continued to attract audiences for more than one hundred years. Since its first publication *Ramona* has been reprinted more than three hundred times; the story has been represented in many pageants and plays for stage, motion pictures, and television; and its main characters and settings have been blended into the legendary past of southern California.

Helen Maria Fiske Hunt Jackson–the first child of Nathan Welby Fiske, a minister and professor of Latin and Greek at Amherst College, and Deborah Vinal Fiske of Boston–was born on 14 October 1830 in Amherst, Massachusetts. Raised in a circle of educated, intelligent family members and friends steeped in the Calvinistic traditions of New England, she was a somewhat rebellious child whom her mother described as "wild–jumping rope, dressing up in odd things, and jumping out behind doors." Helen Fiske was unpredictable and inquisitive and often suffered punishment for disobedience, in contrast with Ann Scholfield Fiske, her younger sister, whom their mother described as a happier child, "honest, artless, and af-

fectionate." Both of her parents died by the time Fiske was seventeen years old. Having been educated at a series of boarding schools in Charlestown, Pittsfield, Falmouth, Hadley, and the Ipswich Female Academy, she was sent to New York City where she attended the school of John and Jacob Abbott, who had been family friends since the latter and Nathan Fiske had been students at Andover. Throughout her life she remained a close friend of the Abbotts, both of whom became popular writers.

After Helen married Edward Bisell Hunt, a lieutenant and eventually a major in the United States Army Corps of Engineers, on 28 October 1852 at the Mount Vernon Church in Boston, the young couple lived in Washington, D. C.; New Haven, Connecticut; and Newport, Rhode Island. She adapted with apparent ease to the transient life of the military, perhaps because she had become accustomed to moving from place to place since childhood, and for the rest of her life she was something of a restless traveler, never residing in a single place for very long. The Hunts' first child, born a year after their marriage, died in infancy of a brain tumor. After serving in several important Civil War battles, Major Hunt died in 1863 while testing one of his military inventions, a submarine explosive device. Two years later their second son died of diphtheria. Devastated and alone while recovering from these losses, Helen Hunt began to write. It was 1865, the end of the Civil War and the beginning of the Gilded Age. Industrialization was transforming American culture, and women writing of children, home, and family values were reaching vast audiences in newspapers and magazines.

The favorable response to her first published poems about the loss of her son surprised Hunt, for she had never considered becoming a writer. Encouraged by that response, she published several more poems and a travel sketch on Bethlehem, New Hampshire, during the next six months. In 1866 she moved back to Newport, Rhode Island, where she became reacquainted with Thomas Wentworth Higginson, a resident at the same boardinghouse, and met other well-known figures in the circle of artists who summered in Newport. Higginson, who had become an important editor, became Hunt's literary mentor and personal editor for the rest of her life. During the next ten years she published hundreds of poems, travel articles, editorials, book reviews, and short stories in magazines and newspapers. The *New York Independent* alone published 371 of her poems and articles. In the fashion of the day she maintained anonymity by signing her work as Marah, Rip Van Winkle, Saxe Holm, and, most frequently, H. H. Many of her prose pieces were unsigned, and although some have been identified through references in surviving correspondence, many pieces remain unidentified. Because of her extraordinary popularity, her poetry was published in book form as *Verses* (1870), and by January 1872 she was being paid from thirty-five dollars to forty dollars per poem.

The death of her second son provided the early subject matter of Hunt's poetry, and although she often returned to themes of death, grief, solitude, and religious doubt, she also wrote extensively about nature—flowers, birds, sunsets, mountains, and seasons. Her love lyrics inspired contemporary critics to compare her favorably to Elizabeth Barrett Browning and Christina Georgina Rossetti. Ralph Waldo Emerson, an early admirer of her work, carried a copy of one of her sonnets in his pocket for a time. Higginson wrote in his *Contemporaries* (1899) that Helen Hunt Jackson was rivaled only by her friend, Emily Dickinson, as the finest American woman poet. Soon after her death a selection of her western poetry was published as *The Procession of Flowers in Colorado* (1885), illustrated with water-colors by Alice A. Stewart, whose work had interested Jackson. While much of her poetry was written early in her career and most is now forgotten, many of her poems—such as "October's Bright Blue Weather," "Poppies on the Wheat," and "Cheyenne Mountain"—have been published regularly in textbooks and anthologies.

In May 1872 Hunt made her first trip to the West, traveling on the recently completed transcontinental railroad from New York to San Francisco with Sarah Woolsey, a friend who became "Susan Coolidge," a popular children's writer. This trip was expensive, costing between $700 and $800 at a time when a restaurant lunch in Philadelphia cost only fifty cents, but the success of *Bits of Travel* (1872), Hunt's collected sketches of Europe, enabled her to negotiate a contract with the *New York Independent* for a series on the West to subsidize her journey. Although writing about a European grand tour had become a familiar tradition among literati (one that Twain would burlesque in his *The Innocents Abroad* in 1869), Hunt seemed to have developed a knack for the form in her early articles on New England, and her European travel sketches were widely praised for their vivid descriptions that avoided the musty flavor of a guidebook. In writing her western sketches for the *New York Independent* and *Scribner's*

Jackson's second husband, William Sharpless Jackson

Monthly Magazine she joined a popular new industry for authors. During the early 1870s *Scribner's*, for example, was running lead articles on the West and the South in nearly every issue and began to replace its serials from English writers with articles, poetry, and fiction by Hunt, Bret Harte, Joaquin Miller, and John Muir.

Initially unimpressed by California, Hunt wrote that the Chinese Theater, distressingly noisy, provided the best experience San Francisco had to offer other than leaving it. Once she began trips outside the city, however, she became enthusiastic about her travels by boat, train, stage, mule, and horseback. She toured the Napa Valley and later marveled at the geysers in Callistoga Springs, the beauty of Lake Tahoe, and the redwood trees and wilderness country of Yosemite Valley. Published individually, her sketches reflect her sense of adventure in the western wilderness, the extraordinary difficulties of primitive travel, and her delight in newly discovered flora and fauna. Before leaving California, Hunt told Woolsey that she wanted to return the following year to study the old missions of the state.

Hunt's next trip west was to Colorado in 1873. Plagued by respiratory illnesses for much of her life, she suffered three bouts of diphtheria within seven months after returning to Massachusetts from California. Her homeopathic doctor in Amherst advised her to spend several months in Colorado Springs, a town that was near the base of Pikes Peak and, although only three years old, had already begun to attract tourists for the curative powers of its clear mountain air and nearby springs. While boarding at the Colorado Springs Hotel, Hunt became acquainted with another resident six years her junior—William Sharpless Jackson, a Colorado banker and Quaker from Pennsylvania. She and Jackson enjoyed long carriage drives in the mountains, traveling to Manitou Springs, Ute Pass, the Cheyenne Canyons, and Central City, and later to more remote parts of the state. In less than a year Jackson proposed marriage; although Helen declined his proposal for several months, they were married in October 1875 at her sister's home in Wolfeboro, New Hampshire. After returning to Colorado Springs, Helen Hunt Jackson took pleasure in decorating their new home and in writing to friends of her great happiness in being settled at last. She was writing furiously, earning an independent income by incorporating her western experiences in poetry and sketches for eastern readers of the *New York Independent,* the *Christian Union, Scribner's Monthly Magazine,* and the *Atlantic.*

Colorado was good for her health and good for her writing. Yet she was still a New Englander at heart, and, sometimes accompanied by her husband and sometimes alone, either by choice or because his business affairs prevented him from being with her, she often traveled back to Amherst, Boston, or New York. By the time of her second marriage Jackson had lived independently for ten years, launched a successful career as a writer, and enjoyed long-term friendships with various men and women, many of whom also had literary careers. In addition to Higginson, she maintained friendships with Moncure Daniel Conway, Emily Dickinson, Charlotte Cushman, Charles Dudley Warner, Josiah G. H., William Dean Howells, Richard Watson Gilder, and her closest friends, Sarah Woolsey and Anne C. Lynch Botta, whose New York literary salon was the most famous of its time. Jackson's contemporaries describe her as a short woman who was not traditionally beautiful but always fashionably dressed and well known for her intelligence, wit, and lively opinions. A phrenologist she visited in 1859 reported that few persons had such intense feelings or clarity of intellect, that she inclined more to thought than most women, and that she was often sarcastic in the sharp, witty conversation she so much enjoyed. These were characteristics also noted in the memoirs of Woolsey, Conway, and Higginson, who described her as "a person quite unique and utterly inexhaustible."

In Colorado, Jackson continued her jaunts by carriage and on foot into mountain country with her husband and with new friends such as Rose Kingsley, daughter of British novelist Charles Kingsley, and Mrs. William Jackson Palmer ("Queen"), whose husband had founded Colorado Springs and was a close friend and colleague of Will Jackson. Colorado Springs and the warm hospitality of the Jackson home attracted many other visitors, such as author Sara Jane Clarke Lippincott ("Grace Greenwood"), who summered in Manitou Springs; Carlyle Channing Davis; and her old friends, the Bottas and the Conways.

In 1878 Jackson published a novel for children, *Nelly's Silver Mine: A Story of Colorado Life,* and *Bits of Travel at Home. Nelly's Silver Mine* tells of Nelly March, a young girl whose father, an eastern clergyman much like Hunt's father, has moved his family to Colorado in the hope of recovering from asthma. As the March family struggles to make a success of their new ranch in high mountain country, Nelly and her twin brother, Rob, try to come up with a means of helping their parents. While selling eggs and butter in the nearby mining town of Rosita, they become acquainted with an assayer, who shows them how he tests ore samples.

In a mountain ravine Nelly finds rocks that she believes to be like those in the assayer's shop, and after she leads her father and two friends to the site, the family dreams of making a strike that will change their lives. No such strike occurs, but the events present simple moral truths, as Nelly learns about the possible disaster that could befall her family if a desire for easy money were to dominate their lives, a common experience of other mountain settlers. A reviewer in the *Atlantic Monthly* (December 1878) regarded the novel highly for introducing young readers to realistic and respectable Colorado characters who were notably absent in much popular fiction about frontier western life. The reviewer praised "H. H." as a highly skilled writer and commended the book

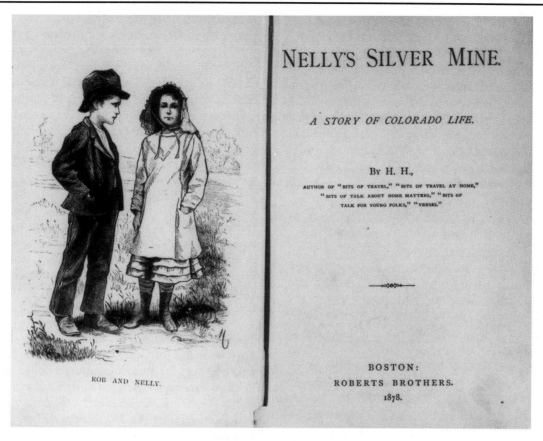

NELLY'S SILVER MINE.

A STORY OF COLORADO LIFE.

By H. H.,

AUTHOR OF "BITS OF TRAVEL," "BITS OF TRAVEL AT HOME,"
"BITS OF TALK ABOUT HOME MATTERS," "BITS OF
TALK FOR YOUNG FOLKS," "VERSES."

BOSTON:
ROBERTS BROTHERS.
1878.

ROB AND NELLY.

Frontispiece and title page for Jackson's 1878 novel for children, in which Nelly learns not to value easy money

for "its lively narrative of adventure, and its freedom from most of the faults of books for children." *Nelly's Silver Mine* became a staple in children's literature and was reprinted at least a dozen times through the 1930s.

Bits of Travel at Home, a collection of Jackson's sketches about New England, Colorado, and California, was not so well regarded, even by the same reviewer who praised *Nelly's Silver Mine.* Although the selections compiled in *Bits of Travel at Home* had been popular when published as individual pieces, the collection was criticized for its repetitious descriptions of flowers, sunsets, and mountains as well as for its overenthusiastic prose style, which seemed too intense and rapturous for the reviewer. Jackson had been influenced by J. G. Holland, her editor at *Scribner's Monthly Magazine,* in an excessive use of dashes, exclamation points, and cheery enthusiasm, and she had fallen into the habit—common among other prominent women writers—of paraphrasing Scripture extensively. The reviewer noted that the books of H. H. "read very much like the talk or the letters of a bright woman, [and] lack at times the qualities that make real literature."

Jackson's first two novels, *Mercy Philbrick's Choice* (1876) and *Hetty's Strange History* (1877), had been published anonymously in Roberts Brothers' "No Name" series and had also received controversial reviews. At the same time the *Saxe Holm's Stories* (1874, 1878), which she always denied having written, created as much commentary on the mystery of authorship as on the quality of the work. Because of the flagging popularity of these stories, *Scribner's,* which had paid Jackson as much as $500 for each of them, decided to publish no more. Depressed by the negative criticism of her work, she decided to turn to literature for children and wrote *Letters from a Cat: Published by Her Mistress for the Benefit of All Cats and the Amusement of Little Children* (1879), a book based on letters that her mother had written to Jackson during her childhood.

During 1878 and 1879 she also published two dozen poems, including "September," "October," and "Cheyenne Mountain," and several new sketches describing trips that she and Will took on the new narrow-gauge railroad, the Denver and Rio Grande, and other explorations that they made into the recently opened southwestern slopes of Colorado. The sketches are somewhat perfunctory, lacking her previous zest and enthusiasm for her home in the West. Letters to friends during this period reveal that she was tired, depressed, and feeling isolated in Colorado with her husband gone on business again that summer, and by August 1879 she was on her way to Mount Desert, Maine, with Sarah Woolsey for several weeks of rest. She also gathered material there for three more travel sketches that were published in October by the *New York Independent*.

Another reason for which she traveled east that summer was to attend a celebration in honor of Oliver Wendell Holmes's seventieth birthday at Boston's Hotel Brunswick. This celebration was postponed from August until December 3, and she sat between John Greenleaf Whittier and Charles Dudley Warner, who read a poem she had written to the guest of honor. Hosted by H. O. Houghton, this august group of literary Brahmans included such well-known figures as Elizabeth Stuart Phelps, Harriet Beecher Stowe, Julia Ward Howe, William Dean Howells, and Thomas Bailey Aldrich.

Jackson spent the fall visiting her sister-in-law, Molly Hunt, in Boston while Will Jackson was in Washington, D.C., where he was representing some political interests of the state of Colorado. In late October she attended a lecture by Standing Bear, a Ponca chief whose address became an event that changed the course of her life and writing. Standing Bear, Bright Eyes (his young interpreter), and Thomas Henry Tibbles, assistant editor of the *Omaha Daily Herald,* were on an organized tour of the East to call attention to the plight of the Poncas, an agricultural Plains tribe that the U.S. government had mistakenly moved from the Dakota homelands of the tribe to a section of the Sioux Reservation and then farther south onto barren land that was depressingly uninhabitable. Through years of broken treaties resulting in hardship, suffering, starvation, and death the Poncas appealed unsuccessfully to agents of the Bureau of Indian Affairs and other government officials, including President Rutherford B. Hayes and Secretary of the Interior Carl Schurz, for the right to return to their lands. In their eastern tour they hoped to raise public awareness and financial support for their situation. After two weeks in Boston they raised considerable money and strong support from Massachusetts governor John D. Long, Sen. Henry Dawes, Boston mayor Frederick O. Prince, Henry Wadsworth Longfellow, and Helen Hunt Jackson,

who submitted her first article on the Native American cause to the *New York Independent*.

Although Jackson grew up in an environment and class that bred reformers, she had shown no interest in any social cause until this time in her life. She cared deeply for her friend Conway, who had been an active abolitionist before his literary career, but she openly disapproved of women with a "cause" and had declared early in her career that she would never become a woman with a "hobby." Yet within weeks of meeting Standing Bear she began to research and write about the Indian cause, and she visited the national office of the Women's National Indian Association in Philadelphia, an organization she later joined. As many friends, critics, and biographers noted, no one could have predicted that the Native American cause would dominate the last five years of her life.

Tibbles, who led the eastern tour of the Poncas, noted that without Jackson's keen interest, energy, wit, and influence in dealing with politicians and editors, the Ponca campaign could not have been so successful. After writing about the Poncas in the *New York Independent,* for example, Jackson called on friends such as Warner of the *Hartford Courant* and Whitelaw Reid of the *New York Daily Tribune* to reprint her articles, challenged Conway to work for Indians, and wrote angry articles for the *New York Daily Tribune*. In these last articles she attacked Schurz for having betrayed the public trust in his recently published annual report, which claimed that the Poncas were happy and content with their current settlement. At the Astor Library in New York, Jackson also began daily research on the plight of other tribes, such as the Utes and Cheyennes in Colorado, that were affected by orders of removal, and she wrote articles for *The New York Times*, the *New York Independent,* and the *New York Daily Tribune* to publicize her findings.

Early that winter she decided that she would incorporate this material in a larger study, *A Century of Dishonor: A Sketch of the United States Government's Dealings with Some of the Indian Tribes* (1881). This work begins with a brief on the original right of Indian occupancy and includes seven tribal histories illustrating her thesis: that in its relations with Indians since the American Revolution, the U.S. government has violated principles of justice that are the bases of international law. The last section is a series of appendices documenting massacres of Indians by whites, excerpts from reports of the Bureau of Indian Affairs, and reprints of her heated exchanges with Carl Schurz and William N. Byers, a former editor of the *Rocky Mountain Times*.

Although Jackson viewed the book as the best work she had done, it suffers from hurried writing and poor editing. Never a best-seller, the book nonetheless attracted attention from humanitarian reformers and many others who for the first time read of the horrible living conditions of Indians. In April 1881 Francis Parkman wrote Jackson that her book was "an honest and valuable record of a scandalous and shameful page in the history of the American people—for the blame lies with them in the last resort." At her own expense Jackson sent every member of Congress a copy of her book, the cover embossed with the words of Benjamin Franklin: "Look upon your hands! They are stained with the blood of your relations."

In September 1881 Richard Watson Gilder commissioned Jackson to write several articles on the California mission Indians for *Century Magazine*. These pieces were to be illustrated by Henry Sandham, and Gilder paid her $1,150 for the series. The Jacksons were in New York by late September, presumably so that Helen could complete some research before her trip, and by early December she was on a train for Los Angeles. She spent the next four months traveling with Sandham throughout southern California, where she recorded historical notes and sketches of the Spanish colonials, the missions, and the surviving Indians who had been driven from their lands, first by the Spanish and then by other whites.

When Jackson and Sandham returned to Los Angeles in late April, she met Abbot Kinney, a well-read, experienced traveler who was also interested in Indians, spoke Spanish, and was well acquainted with California land laws. In the following year Jackson and Kinney were appointed as special commissioners by the Department of the Interior to collaborate on an official investigation that would include the possibility of finding suitable land for Indians who were in California missions and were not on current subsidies. Jackson and Kinney's *Report on the Condition and Needs of the Mission Indians of California* (1883) recommended that white settlers living on Indian reservations be removed and that Native American land rights formerly protected by Mexican agreements be defended by the government. It also urged many improvements in the living conditions of Indians, for whom it recommended better access to physicians, legal assistance, schools, farm equipment, and funding for the sick and elderly. Although Jackson requested that the report

be distributed to more than two hundred people, including every member of Congress, her early hopes that it could have an immediate impact faded within months. President Chester Arthur attached it to a congressional bill on behalf of California mission Indians on 11 January 1884. On 3 July 1884 this bill was passed by the Senate but turned down by the House. It was sent to Congress again every year until it finally was passed on 12 January 1891, six years after Jackson's death.

If the immediate consequences of Jackson's work for Native American interests were disappointing, her research on the Poncas and the California mission Indians prepared her to write *Ramona*, the work for which she is best remembered. In February 1881 Jackson was asked by J. B. Gilder, editor of *The Critic*, to review *Ploughed Under*, a novel about Native Americans by William Justin Harsha, whose father was a member of the Omaha Ponca Committee. After Jackson wrote Gilder and expressed her disappointment that his work, the first realistic novel about Indians, was too weak to do for their cause what *Uncle Tom's Cabin* had done for African Americans, Gilder responded by urging her to write that novel herself.

She declined, but having just completed her report with Kinney, in the summer of 1883 she received reports from friends working with California mission Indians that their conditions were becoming distressingly worse. Restless from inactivity, ill health, and her husband's frequent absences on business trips, she began to reconsider the possibility of writing a novel that might accomplish what her investigative reports about Indians had not. She told friends that the plot for *Ramona* came to her in a flash early one October morning in Colorado, and within weeks she checked into the Berkeley Hotel in New York, where she furiously began writing between two thousand and three thousand words each day for the next four months. The novel was serialized in the *Christian Union* in May 1884 and published in book form by Roberts Brothers in November.

Ramona is essentially a nineteenth-century version of Cinderella with a twist. The life of its central character, Ramona, a foster child half Indian and half Scots, is governed by a cold, cruel stepmother who barely tolerates her presence on her wealthy estate in southern California. Senora Moreno, the widow of a once-famous military man, is an aggressive, deceitful woman who dotes only on her son, Felipe, and the declining family heritage. Felipe, like virtually everyone on the estate except his mother, adores the "blessed" Ra-

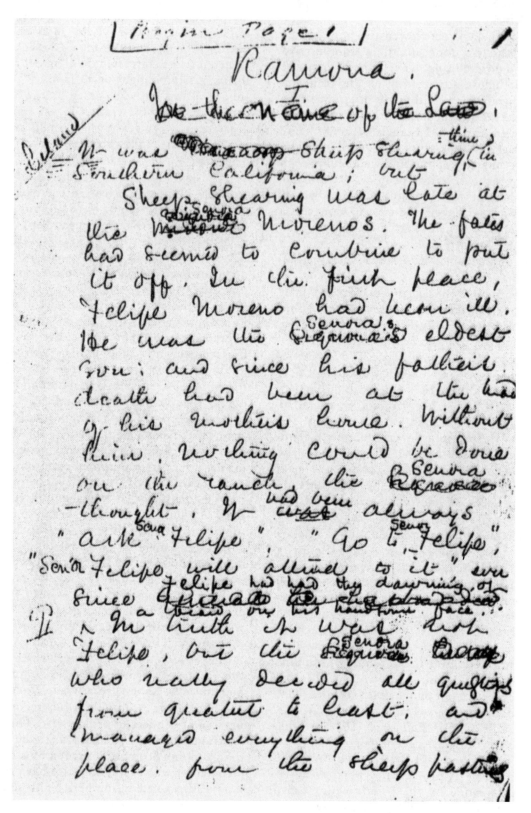

First page of the manuscript for Ramona *(Charles Leaming Tutt Library, Colorado College)*

mona from childhood, but he is as ineffectual in protecting Ramona from his mother's wrath as he is in managing the family ranch. Alessandro Assis, the young, articulate Native American laborer who manages a group of sheepshearers hired to work on the ranch in the spring, so impresses everyone with his well-mannered, quiet authority that Señora Moreno considers hiring him to replace her aging foreman.

When Ramona and Alessandro fall in love the senora threatens to send Ramona to a convent and only then tells the young woman about the cache of jewels that she is holding for Ramona in trust, an inheritance that she says Ramona will lose if she marries an Indian. The two young lovers elope anyway, leaving behind the lush, beautiful life of the ranch to start a new life together. Although their travels west take them through dangerously arid canyon trails, Ramona is enchanted by a new sense of freedom. Having learned from the senora that she is half Indian, Ramona begins to recognize her innate affinities with nature and Indian ways.

The pristine yet passionate bliss of their first days together does not last long, however. As portrayed in the second half of the novel, their life in Indian communities becomes a series of tragedies that illustrate the oppression of their people by white settlers. The village of Temucla, once home to Alessandro's tribe and governed by his father, has been taken over by whites who had driven the tribe off the land that they held through unwritten agreements with the Spanish. When the couple arrives at the first village where they hope to live, it too has been destroyed, and the villagers have been driven into the hills with only meager personal belongings. Ramona's older child dies when the doctor at the government agency refuses to leave his office to treat the child, an episode shaped by an actual incident about which Jackson had learned in California. When Alessandro moves his wife and remaining daughter to a hideaway even higher in the mountains, he begins to lose his mind and eventually is killed for mistakenly taking a horse that belongs to a white man.

Although melodramatic and sentimental to twentieth-century readers, *Ramona* succeeded in having both political and literary consequences, as Jackson intended. Her Native American characters are just as imaginary as those of James Fenimore Cooper, but by refusing to confirm cultural stereotypes in her depictions of Ramona and Alessandro and describing communities of Indians who were hardworking, law-abiding citizens, Jackson stirred popular sympathy for them as victims

during the century of dishonor that she had attacked in her nonfictional reports. In addition to the love story that readers found appealing, Jackson also vividly portrays the twilight of the old Spanish civilization in California, and her novel is rich in picturesque descriptions of the landscape.

The immediate success of the novel was followed by its steady popularity for more than one hundred years. A survey of public libraries in the United States in 1893 indicated that *Ramona* was one of only three contemporary novels read by more than 50 percent of the patrons; Jackson's novel was read by 68 percent. By 1940 six hundred thousand copies of it had been sold. Most contemporary critics praised the work highly and often cited it as the best work Jackson had done, although she was disappointed that some were more impressed by the tragic love story than by the suffering of the Indians. Other critics valued the literary merit of the novel more than its message. A reviewer in the *Atlantic Monthly,* however, noted that the narrative worked extremely well because although readers became indignant about the plight of the Indians, they never lost interest in the unfolding story. A year after Jackson's death Albion W. Tourgée, in reviewing *Ramona* for the *American Scholar,* wrote that it was the best novel yet produced by an American woman.

While twentieth-century assessments have had to acknowledge changes in literary taste, several have recognized the merit of Jackson's achievement. Howard Mumford Jones, in a review for the *Boston Evening Transcript* (22 April 1939), argued that *Ramona* has the strength of Longfellow's *Evangeline* (1847) in depicting the spectacle of human suffering. Allan Nevins lauds the eloquence, vitality, and fiery truth of *Ramona,* which he calls a tour de force in its field. Michael Dorris, in his introduction to a 1988 edition of the novel, commends Jackson for writing descriptive passages of great beauty and originality and depicting Indian characters who, though highly idealized, were appealing to a broad and sympathetic audience.

Back in Colorado Springs to recover from the exhaustion caused by her feverish writing on *Ramona,* Jackson worked on *The Hunter Cats of Connorloa* (1884), her third cat book for children. Connorloa resembles Abbot Kinney's estate, Kinneyloa, where Jackson stayed many times during her visits to southern California. George Connor, an intelligent, well-read world traveler resembling Kinney, lives on a ranch high in the hills of the San Gabriel Valley with eighteen Chinese workers, seventeen cats, and Connor's niece and nephew, whose mother has just died. The children's fascination with the cats brought to the ranch to hunt gophers and other pests is at the center of the book, but Jackson's main interests are in the countryside and in the poverty of the Indians living near the Connor ranch after their property has been taken by white men. The book had at least two printings after Jackson's death but has not continued to interest critics or young readers.

During this period she also continued to write poetry and occasional prose pieces, although her doctor had warned her that she should neither read nor write if she hoped to recover her strength. On 28 June 1884 she fell down the stairs in her home and sustained a compound fracture of the hip, from which she never recovered. Bedridden and immobilized for weeks, she finally arranged to hire three men to carry her on a stretcher to a flatbed wagon so that she could enjoy a drive into the Cheyenne mountains again. By fall her hip had not mended, and she began to dread wintering as an invalid in Colorado Springs. She arranged to spend the next months in Los Angeles on the pretense that the weather would improve her health while she gathered material for another children's story about Indians. Traveling only with her maid, Jackson stayed in Los Angeles from November through March when, her health still failing, she moved to San Francisco in the hope that the northern climate would offer her some relief.

During this period she worked on her last novel, *Zeph: A Posthumous Story* (1885), which, like *Nelly's Silver Mine,* is set in the mining country of Colorado. The story concerns a frontiersman named Zeph who has fallen on hard times, lost the tools of his trade and his job as a carpenter, and lost his wife to another man. He is befriended by Sophy Burr, a woman who has also had a disappointing life on the frontier but has managed to save enough from her boardinghouse income to buy a farm in high mountain country, where she persuades Zeph to work. As he recovers his spirits and self-respect, the two fall in love and begin planning to marry and move to California. In the meantime Sophy works on a plan to regain custody of Zeph's children from his former wife. Like Jackson's other western stories, *Zeph* includes picturesque descriptions of mountain country and frontier life, but the depictions of Zeph and Sophy, a woman who sees innate goodness in the man and whose generosity of spirit eventually help him save himself, have a strong moral cast. Although this novel lacks the literary strength of *Ramona* and is more comparable to Jackson's fic-

tion for children in its simplicity of plot and character, it is remarkable that she wrote *Zeph* during the last months of her life. She sent *Zeph* to her publisher a week before she died. The novel was included in a series of works written by American authors and published in Edinburgh, a series including fiction by Howells, Holmes, Mary E. Wilkins, and Joel Chandler Harris.

With her husband by her side, Jackson died of stomach cancer in San Francisco on 12 August 1885. In her last weeks she had hoped to tour the northern California mountains with John Muir, with whom she had corresponded, but her illness made that trip impossible. She had also written to Higginson again of her pride in her work for Indians: "My *Century of Dishonor* and *Ramona* are the only things I have done for which I am glad now. The rest is of no moment. They will live on and they will bear fruit. They already have." In the last letter she wrote, to President Grover Cleveland on 8 August, she asked him to read *A Century of Dishonor:* "I am dying happier in the belief I have that it is your hand that is destined to strike the first steady blow toward lifting the burden of infamy from our country and righting the wrongs of the Indian race."

Jackson's interest in the West began as an accident of personal history when respiratory illness forced her to move to Colorado, although her affinity for the land and culture of the West evolved from her earlier love of the New England landscape. Her career as a writer was born from her personal grief, but her best writing emerged from her shared grief for others and a sense of outrage that Indians had been legally persecuted by her government. Helen Hunt Jackson was a skilled, prolific, and popular writer during the first ten years of her career, but her deep passion for Native Americans enabled her to rise above other contemporaries regarded merely as "scribbling women" by writing literature that would last beyond her time.

Bibliography:

John R. Byers Jr. and Elizabeth S. Byers, "Helen Hunt Jackson (1830–1885): Critical Bibliography of Secondary Comment," *American Literary Realism, 1870–1910,* 6 (1973): 197–241.

Biographies:

Ruth Odell, *Helen Hunt Jackson (H. H.)* (New York: Appleton Century, 1939);

Evelyn I. Banning, *Helen Hunt Jackson* (New York: Vanguard, 1973).

References:

J. Frank Dobie, "Helen Hunt Jackson and *Ramona*," *Southwest Review,* 44 (1959): 93–98;

Michael Dorris, Introduction to *Ramona* (New York: Signet, 1988);

Thomas Wentworth Higginson, "Helen Jackson ('H. H.')," in his *Contemporaries* (Boston & New York: Houghton, Mifflin, 1899), pp. 142–167;

Valerie Sherer Mathes, *Helen Hunt Jackson and Her Indian Reform Legacy* (Austin: University of Texas Press, 1990);

Antoinette May, *Helen Hunt Jackson: A Lonely Voice of Conscience* (San Francisco: Chronicle Books, 1987);

May, Introduction to *The Annotated Ramona* (San Carlos, Cal.: Wide World Publishing/Tetra, 1989);

Allan Nevins, "Helen Hunt Jackson: Sentimentalist vs. Realist," *American Scholar,* 10 (1941): 169–185;

Frederick W. Turner III, "A Century after *A Century of Dishonor:* American Conscience and Consciousness," *Massachusetts Review,* 16 (1975): 715–731.

Papers:
The major Jackson family archive is in the Charles Leaming Tutt Library at Colorado College in Colorado Springs. Other important collections are in the Huntington Library in San Marino, California; the Jones Library in Amherst, Massachusetts; the Matkinson Library, Trinity College; the Houghton Library, Harvard University; University of Virginia in Charlottesville; and the Boston Public Library.

Charles King

(12 October 1844 – 17 March 1933)

Peter Wild
University of Arizona

BOOKS: *Campaigning with Crook: The Fifth Cavalry in the Sioux War of 1876* (Milwaukee: Sentinel, 1880);

The Colonel's Daughter; or, Winning His Spurs (Philadelphia: Lippincott, 1882);

Famous and Decisive Battles of the World; or, History from the Battle-field (Philadelphia: McCurdy, 1882); republished as *From Marathon to Santiago. Famous and Decisive Battles of the World; the Essence of History* (London & New York: Neely, 1899); republished as *Famous and Decisive Battles of the World; the Essence of History* (Philadelphia: Ziegler, 1905);

Between the Lines: A Story of the War (New York: Harper, 1883);

Kitty's Conquest (Philadelphia: Lippincott, 1884);

Marion's Faith: A Sequel to The Colonel's Daughter (Philadelphia: Lippincott, 1886);

The Deserter (Philadelphia: Lippincott, 1887);

From the Ranks: A Novel (Philadelphia: Lippincott, 1887);

Dunraven Ranch (Philadelphia: Lippincott, 1888; London: F. Warne, 1889);

A War-Time Wooing: A Story (New York & London: Harper, 1888);

"Laramie"; or, The Queen of Bedlam: A Story of the Sioux War of 1876 (Philadelphia: Lippincott, 1889); republished as *The Queen of Bedlam: A Story of Frontier Army Life* (London: Warne, 1889);

An Army Portia, bound with *Two Soldiers* (Philadelphia: Lippincott, 1890);

Campaigning with Crook and Stories of Army Life (New York: Harper, 1890);

Starlight Ranch and Other Stories of Army Life on the Frontier (Philadelphia: Lippincott, 1890);

Sunset Pass; or, Running the Gauntlet through Apache Land (New York: Lovell, 1890; New York: Street & Smith, 1890; London: Gay & Bird, 1892);

Captain Blake (Philadelphia: Lippincott, 1891);

Trials of a Staff-Officer (Philadelphia: Hamersly, 1891);

Charles King, 1879

A Soldier's Secret: A Story of the Sioux War of 1890 (Philadelphia: Lippincott, 1892);

Foes in Ambush (Philadelphia: Lippincott, 1893; London: McClure, 1893);

Sergeant Croesus (Philadelphia: Lippincott, 1893);

Waring's Peril (Philadelphia: Lippincott, 1893);

Cadet Days: A Story of West Point (New York: Harper, 1894);

Captain Close and Sergeant Croesus: Two Novels (Philadelphia: Lippincott, 1895);

The Story of Fort Frayne (Chicago & New York: Neely, 1895; London: Ward, Lock, 1895); also published as *Fort Frayne* (Chicago & New York: Neely, 1895; London: Ward, Lock, 1895);

Trooper Ross and Signal Butte (Philadelphia: Lippincott, 1895);

Under Fire (Philadelphia: Lippincott, 1895; London: Warne, 1895);

An Army Wife (New York: Neely, 1896);

A Garrison Tangle (New York: Neely, 1896);

A Tame Surrender: A Story of the Chicago Strike (Philadelphia: Lippincott, 1896);

Trumpeter Fred: A Story of the Plains (New York & Chicago: Neely, 1896);

Warrior Gap: A Story of the Sioux Outbreak of '68 (London & New York: Neely, 1897);

The General's Double: A Story of the Army of the Potomac (Philadelphia: Lippincott, 1898);

Ray's Recruit (Philadelphia: Lippincott, 1898);

A Wounded Name (London: Neely, 1898);

Found in the Philippines: The Story of a Woman's Letters (London & New York: Neely, 1899);

From School to Battle-field: A Story of the War Days (Philadelphia: Lippincott, 1899);

A Trooper Galahad (Philadelphia: Lippincott, 1899);

Ray's Daughter: A Story of Manila (Philadelphia & London: Lippincott, 1900);

In Spite of Foes: or, Ten Years' Trial (Philadelphia & London: Lippincott, 1901);

Norman Holt: A Story of the Army of the Cumberland (New York: Dillingham, 1901);

A Conquering Corps Badge and Other Stories of the Philippines (Milwaukee: Rhoades, 1902);

A Daughter of the Sioux: A Tale of the Indian Frontier (New York: Grosset & Dunlap, 1902);

The Iron Brigade: A Story of the Army of the Potomac (New York: Dillingham, 1902);

The Way of the West (Chicago: Rand, McNally, 1902);

An Apache Princess: A Tale of the Indian Frontier (New York: Hobart, 1903);

Gainesville, August 20th, 1862 (Milwaukee: Burdick & Allen, 1903);

Comrades in Arms: A Tale of Two Hemispheres (New York: Hobart, 1904);

A Knight of Columbia: A Story of the War (New York: Hobart, 1904);

A Broken Sword: A Tale of the Civil War (New York: Hobart, 1905);

Great Battles of History: From Marathon, B.C. 490 to Auerstadt, A.D. 1806, volume 1 (Philadelphia: Ziegler, 1905);

Great Battles of History: From Waterloo, A.D. 1815 to Port Arthur and Mukden, 1905, volume 2 (Philadelphia: Ziegler, 1905);

The Medal of Honor: A Story of Peace and War (New York: Hobart, 1905; New York: Clafin, 1905);

A Soldier's Trial: An Episode of the Canteen Crusade (New York: Hobart, 1905; New York: Grosset & Dunlap, 1905);

Captured: The Story of Sandy Ray (New York: Fenno, 1906; New York: Grosset & Dunlap, 1906);

The Further Story of Lieutenant Sandy Ray (New York: Fenno, 1906);

Lieutenant Sandy Ray (New York: Fenno, 1906);

Tonio, Son of the Sierras: A Story of the Apache War (New York: Dillingham, 1906; London: Unwin, 1906);

The Rock of Chickamauga (New York: Dillingham, 1907; London: Unwin, 1907);

To the Front: A Sequel to Cadet Days (New York & London: Harper, 1908);

Lanier of the Cavalry; or, A Week's Arrest (Philadelphia: Lippincott, 1909);

The True Ulysses S. Grant (Philadelphia & London: Lippincott, 1914);

Memories of a Busy Life (Madison: Wisconsin Historical Society, 1922);

The Forbidden Hour, by King and Maude Crossley (1925);

The Crimson Feather, by King and Crossley (1926);

Indian Campaigns: Sketches of Cavalry Service in Arizona and on the Northern Plains, edited by Harry H. Anderson (Fort Collins: Old Army Press, 1984).

OTHER: *The Colonel's Christmas Dinner,* edited by King (Philadelphia: Hamersly, 1890);

By Land and Sea, edited by King (Philadelphia: Hamersly, 1891);

An Initial Experience, and Other Stories, edited by King (Philadelphia: Lippincott, 1894);

Captain Dreams and Other Stories, edited by King (Philadelphia: Lippincott, 1895);

Rancho del Muerto, by Capt. Charles King, and Other Stories from Outing (New York: Outing, 1895);

Noble Blood: A Prussian Cadet Story, Translated from the German of Ernst Von Wildenbruch of the German Army by Charles King, U.S. Army, and Anne Williston Ward, and A West Point Parallel: An American Cadet Story (New York: Neely, 1896);

Stories of the Colleges; Being Tales of Life at the Great American Universities Told by Noted Graduates, edited by King (Philadelphia & London: Lippincott, 1901);

Adventures of Uncle Sam's Soldiers, by King, John Habberton, Charles A. Curtis, Charles D. Rhodes, and others (New York: Harper, 1907);

Boy's Book of the Army, by King, Habberton, and others (New York: Harper, 1907).

King's inscription in a copy of A Wounded Name *(National Library of Australia, Canberra)*

In the late nineteenth century Charles King brought the exploits of the United States Army on the far frontier into the nation's literature and thereby helped shape the public's image of military exploits in the West. A soldier who lived the arduous experiences he depicted, King resisted the temptation to inflate the romance of daily army life and achieved popularity while accurately rendering the details of the frontier. When King's novels made their way by wagon to army posts isolated in the deserts of the West, officers and soldiers alike rushed to read them, eager to see if they could identify the real-life people and events King had turned into popular fiction. During a military career that spanned an unprecedented seventy years he was able to lay aside his rifle to turn out more than sixty books—sometimes writing four or five a year.

Intelligent and attuned to his surroundings, King lived through the transition from the nineteenth century to the twentieth century. A friend of Buffalo Bill as well as of other frontier notables, he was surely one of the few Americans to survive being wounded by an Indian arrow and to die after being hit by an automobile. But although he wrote into the twentieth century, King remained a nineteenth-century writer whose novels celebrate such virtues as loyalty, duty, and honor. As his biographer Don Russell cautions in *Campaigning with King* (1991), King's writing, for all its influence and basic accuracy, was not great literature, but while King's western novels contain the impossible plots and oversentimentalized emotions of popular fiction, they often reveal a keen mind and literary skill.

King was born on 12 October 1844 in Albany, New York, the son of Rufus and Susan King. Influential soldiers and citizens studded the King family line tracing back to colonial times. Charles's grandfather was president of Columbia College (now University), an officer in the War of 1812, and the owner of a New York City newspaper. A graduate of West Point, Charles's father served in the Civil War; owned a Milwaukee newspaper, the *Sentinel;* and was a general in the Wisconsin militia.

Young King, slightly built, scrappy, and at times capable of devilish schoolboy mischief, grew up in Milwaukee. At the age of fifteen he was a drummer in Wisconsin's militia. King attended Columbia College, but when the Civil War broke out, he joined his father's brigade in Washington, D.C., serving as a civilian orderly. In 1862 he entered West Point, and upon graduation in 1865 he served as a lieutenant of artillery. Turmoil often broke out in southern cities during the period of Reconstruction, and Lieutenant King commanded the mobile, rapid-fire Gatling guns during the riots in New Orleans in 1868. He then, however, moved to quieter duties at other posts. During one stint his duties as a recruiting officer were so light that he filled his idle time by playing with the Cincinnati Red Stockings, America's first professional baseball team. In 1871 King made the pivotal decision of his military career and transferred to the cavalry. He wed Adelaide Levander on 20 November 1872; they would raise four children.

His various assignments as a cavalry officer included duty in the Apache campaign in Arizona in 1874 and against the Sioux of the Great Plains in 1876. King's assignment to Camp Verde in 1874 in the Arizona Territory fulfilled his hopes for a challenge. During the Civil War the government had thinned its western forces, withdrawing men for battle against the South. In reaction the restive Apaches, perhaps the nation's most efficient and aggressive fighters, went on the rampage against the unfortunate settlers. Excellent horsemen, able to live off the land, and by nature fierce even against other tribes, the Apaches traveled in small bands. Appearing in one spot to kill and burn, they dissolved into desert and forested mountains, slipping through the army's fingers only to reappear suddenly in a distant, unexpected place to raid again.

When Lieutenant King arrived at Camp Verde, his first time in the West, he was in for a shock. Not yet served by the railroad, Arizona was one of the most remote postings a military man could get in the continental United States. Added to that, soldiers found the landscape bare and bleak, a jolting change from the greenery familiar to easterners. No doubt fellow officers had told King about the country and about the hit-and-run guerrilla tactics of the nomadic Apaches. King quickly adjusted to the conditions, and he was soon leading his cavalrymen out of the fort to confront the Apaches in the mountains.

One of the biggest surprises for this West Pointer, who had measured the degree of a soldier's virtue by the snap of his salute and the brightness of his brass, was the careless dress of his men. When he first went out to review them, King strapped on his sword and the other accoutrements of a proper officer only to stand aghast at the ragtag assembly, men in moccasins and buckskins and sporting sweat-stained slouch hats. Their holsters were sewn in a hodgepodge of designs—none of them of the type specified by the regulations—and he spied only two men with the designated slings for their carbines.

At first King thought his men had turned insolent and were playing a joke on their new commander. However, his fellow officers, quipping within earshot that King's long sword would make a rather clumsy scalping knife, soon disabused him. The dress was normal; the men simply were following the example of their cavalry's leader, Gen. George Crook. A veteran of the Civil War, Crook had been so successful in subduing the Indians of the Pacific Northwest that he had been sent to quell the uproar of the Apaches in Arizona, and his eccentric ways were overlooked as long as he got the job done. Reticent and rigidly honest, the general often could be seen in his casual dress riding off alone on his mule and armed with his double-barreled shotgun. An excellent shot, Crook despised liquor, coffee, and tobacco—anything that would impair his mind or body.

Crook's lack of concern for his men's dress was but part of his larger philosophy. An expedient man in the field, he adopted the best means to accomplish his ends. For their part, the Apaches respected Crook as a wily rival who could be trusted to keep his word. It speaks well of King that he could rise above his spit-and-polish training to appreciate his superior's genius.

By the time King arrived in Arizona, the conflict with the Apaches had cooled down, but he was involved in one incident that would have important consequences for his life. When word arrived at Camp Verde that Apaches had stolen a herd of gov-

A cartoon about King's participation in the Spanish-American War. The caption read, "Great Material for My New Military Novel" (State Historical Society of Wisconsin).

ernment cattle, Lieutenant King hastily assembled a force and rode off into the nearby mountains. Recovering the cattle, King pressed the thieves, who fled to a peak. While making his way along the cliffs below King took an arrow in the flesh near his left eye. Next an Apache bullet shattered his upper right arm. Only the bravery of a sergeant, who carried King back to safety as arrows and bullets whizzed around them, saved him. The wounded arm did not heal properly and pained King for the rest of his life.

In 1875, when trouble was brewing among the Sioux, the army transferred Crook to the Great Plains. After a sick leave because of the wound to his arm, King joined his admired general in Fort Hays, Kansas. Spurred by the 25 June 1876 Battle of the Little Bighorn in which Lt. Col. George Armstrong Custer and his 263 men were massacred, the Crook expedition eventfully broke the might of the Sioux, but at the price of grueling weeks in the field during which horses and men alike fell from exhaustion. The next year King was chasing the Nez Perce Indians in the government's determination to subdue native hostiles.

In the spring of 1879 an army surgeon examined King's arm and declared him unfit for duty.

Forced to retire at the rank of captain, he returned to his hometown of Milwaukee. That was blow enough to a man devoted to his army career. Worse, his retirement pay was meager, and he was left without means to support his growing family. Although he cast about here and there, employment eluded him.

Russell relates the story of the encounter that launched King's writing career. Observing King at loose ends in a downtown gentleman's club, a member remarked that Captain King must be well accustomed to idleness, suggesting "that an Army officer has little to do except play cards and drink whiskey." When King responded by recounting one of his experiences with the Fifth Cavalry, an editor of the *Sentinel*, formerly owned by King's father, sat listening nearby. The editor urged King to submit a piece on the subject to the newspaper.

The *Sentinel* took the piece and then ran one King story after another about army life. These formed the chapters of King's *Campaigning with Crook: The Fifth Cavalry in the Sioux War of 1876* (1880), his first book, a factual account of the Sioux war. Its success spurred King to begin writing short stories, novels, and additional historical accounts. His later use of a dictating machine emabled King to spin off thousands of words at a session while his secretary labored nearby transcribing them on her typewriter. It is a tribute to King's disciplined mind that his dictation rarely faltered in bright detail and that he was able to keep in his head the intricate plots of his fiction.

King's journalistic account of the protracted campaign against the Sioux begins at Fort Hays. Gen. Philip Sheridan, the overall commander, ordered Crook and several other generals, each leading his own expedition, to converge on the triangular no-man's-land between the Yellowstone River in southwestern Montana and the Powder River in northwestern Wyoming. This is a cut-up landscape of sandy wastes, a few high peaks, and streams with bad water, a hostile place for outsiders. King records the efforts of the Crook contingent in accomplishing their mission of either driving the renegade Indians back to their reservations or defeating them in battle.

In retrospect, the popularity of the book is something of a surprise. Books of the time using military material were regularly colored by the dramatic recitations of grand battles of the Civil War, offering readers panoramic sweeps of mighty armies clashing to settle great moral issues. By contrast, Crook's men, while they experienced a few sharp clashes, fought no great encounters. King's record, largely one of daily sloggings through dismal country, includes few exchanges of gunfire to pique the adrenaline of either soldier or reader.

King had no love theme to spice up his prose and divert the reader, and as a lowly lieutenant foraging with the men for the few blades of grass that would keep their foundering horses alive in the bleak land, he was not privy to the power struggles and psychological battles among generals and politicians that inevitably form the larger context of warfare. He had not yet arrived in the area at the time of the annihilation of Custer and his five companies, by far the most dramatic moment of the conflict.

While remaining true to his subject, King was able to draw on the drama of his experience, made all the more intense because it was not panoramic but personal. His skill as a storyteller is evident in the opening scene. He begins by describing peaceful Fort Hays, a comfortable post where wives live with their husbands on officers' row, spending their evenings in singing, dancing, and other entertainments. The sun is going down, and the band is playing as the flag slides down its pole; a few children are romping on the lawn, while up at his house the general chats with a few gathered officers and their wives. When a horseman rides up with a message, the conversation stops while the general reads the dispatch. The surrounding officers try to look unconcerned, but their wives huddle about him. The general confirms the worst–there has been an outbreak–and turning from his role as a gracious host into his role as military commander, he orders his regiment into the field. In an instant the fort bustles with activity. On 24 June–an ominous date for readers well aware of the disaster that will happen the next day–the soldiers head off in high spirits into the Powder River country. Thereafter King recounts the drudgery of unrelieved weeks on the trail, of cold and heat, thirst and near starvation, of both men and horses giving out and falling in their tracks from the trek through the rough country.

When a dramatic moment does arise, King, as he would do in his later books, shows a novelist's eye for building a scene. He gives a prominent role to William Cody, the scout known as "Buffalo Bill," a figure known in the East both for his real-life daring and for his Wild West shows. After Cody spots a band of thirty or forty Indians preparing to waylay an unsuspecting wagon train led by two army couriers, King and his men lay plans to ambush the ambushers. With his men deployed in the ravines to surprise the Indians on their flank, King remains on his hill, watching, ready to give the signal for his men to begin firing on the enemy now riding down hard on the wagon train:

Oh, what a stirring picture you make as once more I fix my glasses on you! Here, nearly four years after, my pulses bound as I recall the sight. Savage warfare was never more beautiful than in you. On you come, your swift, agile ponies springing down the winding ravine, the rising sun gleaming on your trailing war bonnets, on silver armlets, necklace, gorget; on brilliant painted shield and beaded legging; on naked body and beardless face, stained most vivid vermilion. . . . And on, too, all unsuspecting, come your helpless prey. I hold vengeance in my hand, but not yet to let it go. Five seconds too soon, and you can wheel about and escape us; one second too late, and my blue-coated couriers are dead men.

When King gives the sign, the soldiers surprise the Indians and carry the battle in which Cody's golden locks and flashing pistol play a prominent role.

In another King encounter with the Sioux, King gives a hint of the sarcasm that could flash out in his writing. While he had no love for Indians, he also had no hate and admired their skill as warriors in battle. Their so-called defenders in the East, however, were another matter. King believed that their stupidities, based on easy sentiment rather than knowledge of the facts, often led to the loss of life on both sides. Giving a larger perspective, King notes that the Indians are intelligent people, knowing enough to catch political factions at cross purposes. He explains how year after year renegades would go on the warpath during the summer, then meekly surrender as winter approached to live on government rations through the cold months. The pattern was all the more destructive, according to King, because misinformed easterners saw to it that the Indians were equipped with repeating rifles, supposedly so that they could better hunt buffalo but often used against soldiers armed with inferior, single-shot weapons. The Indians, snarled King, slap Uncle Sam's "face every spring and shake hands in the fall." The unnecessary suffering of loyal troops because of warring politicians provides heat to the work, as it would to King's following books.

King's talent as a writer went beyond his ability to depict the military engagements and army routines. Blessed with social grace and a sense of humor, he knew the social side of the military as well. From the onset of his career he was a special favorite with the ladies, both because of his charm and because of his smooth dancing. Such characteristics are not incidental to understanding King and his books. Both as a gentleman and as a writer King was sensitive to the subtleties and psychological nuances of his surroundings, and if he could create a gripping scene, with a ragged band of the Fifth Cavalry firing at the gallop while escaping a Sioux ambush,

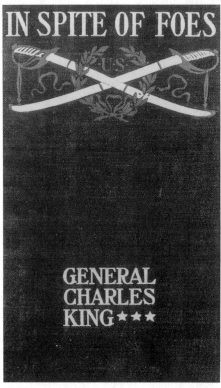

Bindings for three of King's novels

he also could paint pastel evenings back at the fort at day's end. Readers of his novels heard not just bullets but the crack of the mallet as officers played croquet with the young ladies; they were also privy to the murmurs of the general and his staff officers seated up on the verandah, bent over serious games of checkers.

The Colonel's Daughter; or, Winning His Spurs (1882), his first novel, provides a good example of how King combines realism with romance. Among his most popular novels, it serves as a model for his later fiction, whether for a well-known novel such as *"Laramie"; or, The Queen of Bedlam: A Story of the Sioux War of 1876* (1889) or for his many collections of short stories. While his locations and characters change, King in his books repeatedly weaves an appealing romantic web around the realities of military life. His novels also typically treat a military conflict, and the characters experience their measure of agony in both the martial arena and the realm of amour. Time after time readers will feel that their heroes have plunged into black situations beyond possible rescue, but King always manages a happy resolution.

In *The Colonel's Daughter* King goes back before the Sioux wars, drawing on material from his earlier days in Arizona. The story opens at Camp Sandy, a remote outpost in the Arizona desert, much like Camp Verde. The boredom experienced by Lt. John Truscott, the handsome and affable adjutant of the post, is broken when Colonel Pelham's daughter Grace arrives and the Indians go on a rampage. Truscott's courtship of Grace is complicated by the scheming opposition of her mother, who prefers that she marry another man. The various twists of the plot involve a dropped handkerchief, furtive letters, stolen property, and subtle gestures freighted with a significance easily misconstrued. The upshot, however, is that after three hundred pages of successful ploys, Mrs. Pelham's machinations backfire. Virtue prevails, and Truscott becomes engaged to Grace, who is filled with "inexpressible content and joy."

From a modern perspective *The Colonel's Daughter* has many faults. It is certainly melodramatic, and at times King becomes too enamored of romantic rhetoric. Although he held Indian warriors in high regard for their cunning and endurance, he never goes beyond the soldier's view to present an Apache or a Sioux as an individualized human being. While his plot is as intricate as the workings of a watch, it is also highly improbable. It should be noted, though, that King was writing to the demands of a popular audience and that beyond the purloined letters and the breathless rescues of maidens on runaway horses lies solid and innovative writing. Russell asserts that *The Colonel's Daughter,* for all its sentimentalism, "was the height of realism in its own day."

In his preface King frets that his novel is too realistic, that his dialogue lacks the histrionic gauziness then fashionable. The artificiality of words exchanged by courting couples aside, King is right. His conversations ring true to everyday army life, as do many of the characters and events. Underlying the romance there is the hard reality of men sweating in the field. King also manages to capture some psychological complexities in the petty viciousness of Mrs. Pelham, the earnest gossip mongering of the post wives, and the everyday feuds boiling up among soldiers forced to live together in trying circumstances.

King was not content to write novels that mined the exciting materials of his youth. An army man to the core, he angled his way back into the military, though through the back door. First he taught military science at the University of Wisconsin; then as a colonel in the state national guard he commanded the troops in the Milwaukee labor riots of 1886. He then concentrated on whipping the Wisconsin guard into a first-rate unit. King was a stickler for details when he inspected troops because he believed that well-trained troops would be good soldiers under fire. He made his intentions clear and won his men's respect. A fellow officer praised King's demeanor:

> General King's temperament was peculiarly suited to his task of commanding a brigade of raw volunteer troops, and directing their training. His keen eye took in every defect and noted every improvement. In the former case the needed correction or admonition was made in a way that left no sting, he never being either brutal or sarcastic. His readiness to encourage or to praise stirred all to put forth their best efforts.

His success in Wisconsin gained the attention of regular army officers in Washington, D.C.

When the Spanish-American War broke out in 1898, King was promoted to general and sent to the Philippine Islands. There he led his troops into battle, routing the better-equipped insurgents. King led by example, charging out to the front with such verve that at the Battle of the Pasig River in the Philippines a private lamented to a correspondent: "That man will never see America again." Then the soldier added, reflecting dual admiration for King's twin careers, "He is as fine an officer as he is a story-teller, and that's the best compliment I can pay him."

Writer and soldier, King had two parallel careers, captured for the public imagination by a cartoon about the Philippine adventure. It showed the general striding along the battle line, sword tucked under one arm, breezily writing his impressions in a notebook while rebel bullets fly around him. The caption reads: "Great Material for My New Military Novel." At about the same time the *Saturday Evening Post* featured Gen. Charles King as a national war hero, standing erect in immaculate uniform and peering into the swirling smoke of battle.

Because King sometimes revised books long after their original printings, rewriting passages and changing titles, experts continue to puzzle to bring order to his immense production. It can be said with certainty, however, that he published about seventy books, both fiction and nonfiction. Although to one degree or another they all concern the military, within those bounds the volumes deal with a great variety of subjects. In addition to his many novels, King wrote a biography of President Ulysses S. Grant, *The True Ulysses S. Grant* (1914), several books for juvenile readers, collections of short stories, military histories, and a play. These range geographically from the Indian Wars of the Arizona Territory and the Great Plains to West Point to the Philippines. His works also differ widely in quality, ranging from solid analysis of military affairs, still invaluable to scholars, to unabashed sentiment. The sappiness to which he could descend is evident in his synopsis of his single play, which he turned into the novel *The Story of Fort Frayne* (1895): "Act I. A cloud rises over Fort Frayne. Act II. The storm gathers. Act III. The storm breaks. Act IV. Love and sunshine."

King is an important transitional figure in western letters, moving from the near obligatory romanticism of his day toward the realism that during the latter half of his career was coming into vogue. His significance lies in the insight he gives into the military of his time. Russell observes that even his romances "were so realistic that a young lieutenant wrote (in 1896), 'When we joined our regiments later at the remote frontier posts, we found there pretty nearly the things he had taught us to expect.'" It was a feature much appreciated by the small army of the day–underfunded and often ill-equipped–which was asked to perform Herculean tasks in the tumultuous West while being criticized by the far-off public and politicians. King's works educated the nation about its army and brought the military to the fore as a fit subject for literature.

Bibliography:

Charles E. Dornbusch, *Charles King, American Army Novelist: A Bibliography from the Collection of the National Library of Australia, Canberra* (Cornwallville: Hope Farm Press, 1963).

Biography:

Don Russell, *Campaigning with King: Charles King, Chronicler of the Old Army,* edited by Paul L. Hedren (Lincoln: University of Nebraska Press, 1991).

References:

Harry H. Anderson, Introduction to King's *Indian Campaigns: Sketches of Cavalry Service in Arizona and on the Northern Plains* (Fort Collins: Old Army Press, 1984), pp. 9–17;

Hazel M. Flock, *Frontier Army Life: Revealed by Charles King, 1844–1933* (Hays: Fort Hays Kansas State College, 1964);

Russell, Introduction to King's *Campaigning with Crook* (Norman: University of Oklahoma Press, 1964), pp. vii–xx.

Papers:

King's papers are located in the Carroll College Library, Waukesha, Wisconsin, and in the Milwaukee County Historical Society, Milwaukee, Wisconsin.

Alfred Henry Lewis

(20 January 1857 – 23 December 1914)

Abe C. Ravitz
California State University, Dominguez Hills

See also the Lewis entry in *DLB 25: American Newspaper Journalists, 1901–1925.*

BOOKS: *Wolfville* (New York: Stokes, 1897);
Sandburrs (New York: Stokes, 1900);
Richard Croker (New York: Life, 1901);
Wolfville Days (New York: Stokes, 1902);
Wolfville Nights (New York: Stokes, 1902);
Peggy O'Neal (Philadelphia: Drexel Biddle, 1903);
The Boss and How He Came to Rule New York (New York: A. S. Barnes, 1903);
The Black Lion Inn (New York: R. H. Russell, 1903);
The President (New York: A. S. Barnes, 1904);
The Sunset Trail (New York: A. S. Barnes, 1905);
Confessions of a Detective (New York: A. S. Barnes, 1906);
The Throwback: A Romance of the Southwest (New York: Outing, 1906);
The Story of Paul Jones (New York: G. W. Dillingham, 1906);
When Men Grew Tall: The Story of Andrew Jackson (New York: Appleton, 1907);
An American Patrician: The Story of Aaron Burr (New York: Appleton, 1908);
Wolfville Folks (New York: Appleton, 1908);
The Apaches of New York (New York: G. W. Dillingham, 1912);
Faro Nell and Her Friends: Wolfville Stories (New York: G. W. Dillingham, 1913);
Nation-Famous New York Murders (New York: G. W. Dillingham, 1914).

SELECTED PERIODICAL PUBLICATIONS–
UNCOLLECTED: "Confessions of a Newspaperman," *Human Life* (November 1905–December 1906);
"Owners of America," *Cosmopolitan* (June, August–November 1908).

Between 1889 and 1913 Alfred Henry Lewis–short-term cowboy, occasional lawyer, and career journalist–wrote a series of stories about a

Alfred Henry Lewis

fictional frontier community modeled after Tombstone, Arizona, which collectively might be described as the Wolfville chronicles. The stories were published first in newspapers or in popular periodicals such as *Collier's, Everybody's,* and *Munsey's* and then collected into books. The prolific Lewis turned out much more than stories about the West: he was also a skilled big-city reporter and muckraking journalist who shined a public light on presumed malefactors in the heyday of sensational tabloid and magazine exposés. During the most conspicuous portion of his career Lewis was employed by William Randolph Hearst, to whom his first book, *Wolfville* (1897), was dedicated.

The narrator of Lewis's western stories is the Old Cattleman, a grizzled and garrulous septuagenarian. His dialect tale-spinning and social perspectives brought a semblance of the Wild West to eastern readers, who frequently approached the tales as sociological texts. Historian Howard Mumford Jones has ascribed to The Old Cattleman a legendary position on the American landscape, one as prominent as that belonging to Captain John Smith or to Daniel Boone.

Lewis was born on 20 January 1857 in Cleveland, Ohio, the second son of Isaac J. Lewis, a carpenter, and his wife, Harriet Tracy Lewis. Educated in the local public schools and showing no inclination to follow in his father's footsteps, young Lewis read law and at age nineteen was admitted to the bar. Four years later he was serving as city prosecuting attorney in the Police Court of Cleveland. When his father relocated to Kansas City in 1881, Lewis decided to move with the family. Then, giving in to his wanderlust, Lewis left the law for a time and became a hobo cowboy, traveling throughout the West.

In various published sources Lewis alludes to spending much of his next few years in camp, on the range, and behind six-mule teams, learning the ways of saddle and trail. Lewis recalls working on ranches in Meade County, Kansas, and driving cattle to Dodge City. He roamed through the Texas Panhandle and New Mexico to Tombstone, Arizona, at the time of the silver boom. In the "Confessions of a Newspaperman" article that appeared in the May 1906 issue of *Human Life,* Lewis looks back with great nostalgia at what he called his "pampas years" when he roved "for many moons" between "the Canadian in the Panhandle and the Gila in Arizona."

Lewis was not so enamored of cowboy life that he chose to follow it full time. During these vaguely accounted-for years he made abortive passes at newspaper work, for a short time editing and writing in its entirety the *Mora County Pioneer* in Watrous, New Mexico, where he enjoyed passing the time of day with drifters congregating in front of Melinda's House of Call. He moved on in that sparsely populated state to edit the *Las Vegas Optic.* After four years of roaming he returned to Kansas City and planned to resume his career as a lawyer. With his marriage to Alice Ewing in 1885, Lewis realized the need to begin earning a responsible living and leading a stable life.

Lewis was a frequent visitor to the offices of the *Kansas City Times,* where his brother worked. One evening, according to an anecdote repeated in his *New York Times* obituary, Lewis "told one of the picturesque incidents" from his travels. An editor immediately suggested that he type it up, and the result was the creation of "The Old Cattleman" and the birth of fictional Wolfville. It was published anonymously in the newspaper in 1889. Newspapers began to clamor for more, and when Lewis was paid $360 for his second Wolfville tale he recognized that writing would be far more lucrative than either cowpunching or the law. After a year with the *Kansas City Star* Lewis became a correspondent for the *Chicago Times* and moved to Washington, D.C. In 1894 he became the Washington bureau chief for Hearst's *New York Journal.*

This publicized affiliation with Hearst catapulted Lewis into the forefront of American yellow journalism, where he soon gained the reputation as Hearst's hatchet man. Lewis and the publisher became fast friends, often working together on special, sensitive projects. According to W. A. Swanberg in *Citizen Hearst* (1961), during the presidential campaign of 1897 Hearst wanted to smear William McKinley, and Lewis "was assigned to write articles of maximum injury." Later, when Hearst sought to discredit the future political hopes of Woodrow Wilson, Lewis was again given the job of character assassination.

More important than Hearst for Lewis's future as a western author was the friendship he developed in Washington with Col. Theodore Roosevelt, who at the time was a member of the Civil Service Commission. It was Roosevelt who prevailed upon Lewis to gather his Wolfville tales. The pair thought much alike: journalist Lewis admired and subscribed to the strenuous life; the future president, according to Rolfe Humphries in his 28 August 1967 article "Tall Tale Americana" in *The Nation,* recognized in the writer "a crude but fascinating combination of Post-Populist, [and] Bull Moose Progressive elements."

In 1898 Lewis moved to New York to devote himself completely to freelance writing. He soon became immersed in cutthroat metropolitan journalism. He was recognized in the 13 August 1905 *New York Times* as "the most vigorous and vitriolic pen" in the city. He was also regarded, according to John K. Winkler in *William Randolph Hearst* (1955), as "one of the busiest and most versatile of the literary craftsmen" of the day, famous for holding "impromptu receptions one or two afternoons each week in the big cafe of the Hoffman House," where he was surrounded by editors, lawyers, and politicians.

While he was called "one of the most interesting conversationalists of the time" in the 1905 *New York Times* article, Lewis was a tireless worker whose pen was in constant motion. In the early

1900s he edited *Human Life,* a Boston-based humor journal, by long-distance telegraph and also edited *The Verdict,* a political sheet sponsored by Oliver Hazard Belmont Perry. Lewis turned out articles on the "owners" of America–Andrew Carnegie, J. P. Morgan, and John D. Rockefeller–and wrote eastern fiction featuring Gotham detectives and local characters such as Crazy Butch, Ike the Blood, Indian Louie, and Mollie Squint. He used his knowledge of New York's Tammany Hall and the nation's capital in the novels *The Boss and How He Came to Rule New York* (1903) and *The President* (1904).

As his life in New York seethed with activity, Lewis from time to time sought momentary escape by writing of the West he had known as a young wanderer. He had little desire to produce so-called literature and denigrated critics, considering their opinion of "stewed prunes" as valuable as their assessment of a book. He opposed the style of Henry James, whose "spun-glass sensibilities" he excoriated. He called James's *The Golden Bowl* (1904) "a word shambles, an abattoir of the mother tongue . . . to a degree that makes one fear the book was written by a Dutchman!"

Lewis's Wolfville is a town divested of any sophistication: the legal and moral parameters of life are plain; psychological dilemmas are readily identified and confronted; crime–even the appearance of criminal intent–is exposed immediately, and criminals are treated with uncompromising justice. The town and its citizens remain fixed, predictable, and stable throughout the seven books of the chronicle: *Wolfville, Sandburrs* (1900), *Wolfville Days* (1902), *Wolfville Nights* (1902), *The Black Lion Inn* (1903), *Wolfville Folks* (1908), and *Faro Nell and Her Friends* (1913). Lewis's first collection, illustrated by Frederic Remington, includes a brief introduction describing the main fictional strategy carried through all the books: "I shall permit the Old Cattleman to tell his stories in his own fashion" in a style that will be "crude, abrupt, [and] meagre." The Old Cattleman gives the dialogue of all the characters in his own words, which are recorded faithfully by scribe Dan Quin–only one *n*–who is responsible for preserving his sober "jedgements."

With Tom, his "black satellite," nearby to replenish his glass, the Old Cattleman, telling tales "joobilant" and "straight," unifies Lewis's seven volumes. He describes action and dispenses philosophy consistent with frontier fatalism: "Life is like a dance hall; and we'll nacherly keep on dancin; and dyin'; ontil the floor manager. . . orders on the last walse."

The Old Cattleman appears intent throughout the chronicle to challenge gullible eastern "tower-ists" who examine the West through the window of a Pullman car and then naively believe they have seen the entire picture. Such readers he will calculatedly move from sentimentality to horror. On the one hand he shows the compassion of Wolfville by reciting the testimonials for Whiskey Billy, a notorious sot from hated Red Dog, whose mother from Missouri witnesses a funeral ceremony worthy of the brightest and bravest gentleman in Arizona. But on the other hand he tells how the Stranglers save the community the time and expense of a trial. After the attorney Aaron Green agrees to defend a handful of alleged murderers, he ambles into the street only to see "his entire docket hangin' to a windmill." Lewis worked diligently at his combination of pity and horror, infusing these elements with the humor of understated dialect and offhand references to remote incidents of presumedly justifiable violence.

In Wolfville the passage of time is calculated by the drinking hour, all citizens acquiring their "nose-paint" daily at the Red Light Bar. The reappearing cast of American westerners includes Doc Peets, a physician whose "speshulty is shootin' a derringer"; Cherokee Hall, a morbidly quiet, knife-wielding card dealer who loves the beautiful "yearling" Faro Nell; Jack Moore, marshal and "execyootive" officer of the Stranglers, Wolfville's vigilante committee; Colonel Sterett, publisher of the *Coyote* and expert in local politics; Sam Enright, "the Lycurgus of Wolfville," whose "piercin' eye" shines with venerated wisdom; Dan Boggs, who has the "muscles of a cinnamon b'ar"; Old Monte, the stage driver who fears most the interruption of liquor traffic; Texas Thompson, whose nagging wife back in Laredo agitates constantly for a divorce; Mrs. Rucker, who both henpecks her husband and runs the "O.K. Restauraw"; and Dave Tutt, a dignified gentleman who marries Tucson Jennie, their child to be christened Enright Peets.

From time to time Wolfville meets eastern visitors, faces violent invaders from hostile, nearby Red Dog, and confronts an assortment of transient troublemakers such as Silver Phil, Curly Ben, Toothpick Johnson, Dead-Shot Baker, and The Stinging Lizard. An active Committee of Vigilance enforces discipline, as had the Law and Order League of Tombstone and its fifty heavily armed men. Chinese, Mexicans, and African Americans, though necessary to the maintenance of the town, are looked upon with suspicion and scorn as inferior people.

In his first book Lewis establishes the shared values and the structure of the Wolfville community. In "Wolfville's First Funeral" the whole of the town accepts the philosophy emblazoned on the

THE
BLACK LION
INN

BY
ALFRED HENRY LEWIS

Illustrated by FREDERIC REMINGTON

NEW YORK
R. H. RUSSELL
1903

Frontispiece and title page for Lewis's fifth book about the the fictional western town Wolfville (courtesy of Special Collections, Thomas Cooper Library, University of South Carolina)

tombstone that commemorates Wolfville's first funeral: "LifE Ai'N'T in Holding a Good Hand / But In Playing a Pore Hand Well." When in "The Man from Red Dog" an aggressive visitor from the hated rival town spews venomous insults at the "onregenerate set" and threatens to "distribute this yere hamlet round in the landscape," he is in the name of law and order efficiently shot to death and scalped. In "Texas Thompson's 'Election'" the Old Cattleman underscores Wolfville's simple theory on the treatment of crime: "Let any outfit take a bale of rope an' a week off"—soon the camp will be "weeded down to right principles."

All of the major inhabitants and their daily lives of drinking, gambling, and gossiping are introduced in no particular sequence. The town's "hives" of commerce, catering to both business and social activity, also emerge, and the Red Light and the O.K. in particular form the background for future

episodes. The first collection also includes "The Stinging Lizard," a portrayal of the good-hearted gambler who is secretly rearing the child of a man he had killed; "A Wolfville Thanksgiving," which relates a tall-tale contest betweeen two rival settlements; "Jaybird Bob's Joke," which shows the persecution of outsiders; and "A Wolfville Foundling," in which the rough town becomes involved with a temporarily motherless child.

The reviewer for the 12 September 1897 issue of *The New York Times Illustrated Magazine* likened Lewis's Wolfville tales to a collective mock epic of "wondrous deeds" and compared the Wolfville and Red Dog communities to Rome and Carthage, noting of the westerners that "eccentric people were they, having guns and knives handy, clever too in strangling with the lariat," most having died "with their boots on." The reviewer called the Old Cattleman "the Munchausen of the West" who perpetuates "certain remarkable turns of phrases peculiar once to the Wildest West." The reviewer recognized an "atavism" of a "most pronounced type" in the behavior and words of Lewis's characters that carried readers back to dime-novel days. *Wolfville* rapidly went through fourteen printings. According to Joe B. Frantz and Julian Ernest Choate Jr. in *The American Cowboy: The Myth and the Reality* (1955), from its publication until his death, Lewis "was considered a front rank practitioner operating only a plane below Harte and Twain, but operating from such a wide plane that his advertising of western frontier humor represented a contribution of continuing significance."

Lewis's second volume, *Sandburrs,* begins with a preface that defines a "sandburr" as a "foolish, small vegetable, irritating and grievously useless." Most of the fifty-one tales are about the big-city East and are narrated by The Office Boy and Chucky d'Turk, whose slum-ghetto accent—"Nixie! I ain't did nothin,' but all de same I'm feelin' like a mut, see!"—enthralls listeners in a dingy bar on Baxter Street. There are four non-Wolfville sketches of western life, two dealing with hunting experiences, one with a cowboy gun duel over a visiting woman, and one with a cruel joke on a well-meaning tenderfoot who is tricked into believing he is about to be killed in a mine-shaft explosion. The five Wolfville tales include "Wagon Mound Sal," which treats a shotgun wedding arranged by the Stranglers, and "Mistress Killifer" in which Wolfville rejects the morally uplifting presence of an upright woman who seeks to reform the town.

In *Wolfville Days* the Old Cattleman delivers an "onbosomin' of himse'f" in nineteen tales. While he believes that "It's deeds that counts with Omnipotence, same as with a vig'lance committee," he finds life unpredictable: "Life is like stud-poker, an' Destiny's got an ace buried every time." He advises anyone coming to Arizona from "home camp" to make his "deboo" with a spirit of calm and "silent se'f reliance." The collection contains what is probably Lewis's single best western story, "Death; And the Donna Anna," a moving tale of doomed love between a romantically inclined Mexican lady and a "lootenant" of the Pine Knot Cavaliers. The relationship is poignant and touching, reminiscent of Bret Harte's successful fictions depicting mission and hacienda life.

Lewis's humor occasionally seems contrived or trivializing. For the amusement of his eastern readers, for example, he refers to two antagonistic groups within the Osage tribe as the Astor Injins and the Vanderbilt Injins in "Johnny Florer's Axel Grease." Malignant ridicule, albeit within the tall-

tale frontier tradition, surfaces when a storekeeper accidentally discovers a solution to the "Indian problem": selling "hostiles" axle grease as a nutritive food "soothes the savage breast" and brings them to abandon the warpath. In "The Great Wolfville Strike" Lewis lampoons labor problems, a serious phenomenon of the era, through the disgruntled workers at Colonel Sterett's *Coyote.* After a vengeful cowpuncher, an outsider, stirs up the "obtoose printers," the imagined differences are rapidly settled. All go back to working and drinking as "nose-paint" is shown to be the most effective labor arbitrator.

In "Some Cowboy Facts," an introductory essay to *Wolfville Nights,* Lewis describes the code of his fictional community. The "etiquette" of Wolfville is summed up in four specific rules of public behavior: the cowboy must never "insult a woman"; he must not "shoot his pistol in a store or bar-room"; "he must not ride his pony into those places of resort"; and "he must not ride his pony onto the sidewalks." The "taunting defiance" of these rules could quickly result in "an explosive rattle of six-shooters."

Lewis explains the cowboy character, emphasizing its different nature on the range and in the town. These noble westerners are "quiet, just, and peaceable" on the range, but they will "fight and die and storm a jail and shoot a sheriff . . . to rescue a comrade." Although while in town the cowboy is addicted to "women, cards, and whiskey," he is at other times "a youth of sober quiet dignity." Indeed, in an environment where everybody wears a gun, he stoically maintains "deep politeness" to avoid "insult or horseplay." Sober in camp, occasionally drunk in town, involved now and then in feud and gun-play, the cowboy follows a "religion of fatalism," realizing that unpredictable violence and sudden death stalked the everyday streets of Wolfville and other towns like it. The simple, fresh vitality of the untamed western frontier is contrasted to the dark, brooding, conspiratorial violence of the eastern city.

In *Wolfville Nights* Lewis minimally employs a second narrator, Sioux Sam, in addition to the Old Cattleman. Sioux Sam's account of Indians and their traditions in such stories as "How the Raven Died" stands in marked contrast to the prejudice against Native Americans that is frequently evident in Wolfville. "With the Apache's Compliments" and "The Mills of Savage Gods," complete Cattleman narratives, go well beyond the depiction in local talk of "benighted savages," and deal with Indian admiration for man's courage as well as for personal integrity.

The Old Cattleman is the sole narrator for twenty of the twenty-one stories of the collection. His notable tales include "Bill Connors of the Osages," a satire on "philanthrofists" who meddle in the lives of Noble Savages, mistakenly "dragging" Indians off to formal schools for civilized education. A warning against gringo-Mexican romance, "Long Ago on the Rio Grande" shows a soldier choosing suicide over returning home in disgrace after having been placed under arrest by a stern commander for a "dalliance" with a senorita. The most unusual story is "The Dismissal of Silver Phil," in which the protagonist-villain is apparently a homosexual. Described as "evil-seemin' as a Mexican" but "no Greaser," Phil is a "degen'rate" with "a quick, hyster'cal way like a woman or a bird"; he is an "ondersized miscreant" like an "anamile," a "lean an' slim" killer with a temper forever raging. According to the Old Cattleman, Phil's "mind as well as his moral nacher is onbalanced congenital." He meets a grisly end, for he is seemingly not worthy of the violent death from gunplay accorded a "natural" bandit.

In *The Black Lion Inn* Lewis employs three narrators in addition to The Old Cattleman–Sioux Sam, The Jolly Doctor, and The Red-Nosed Gentleman. The Old Cattleman leaves his familiar Wolfville characters and setting to render western narratives such as "The Great Stewart Campaign" and "When the Capitol Was Moved," quasi-historical tales which validate the sage-storyteller's credentials as historian. The Old Cattleman's bloody account in "The Wiping Out of McCandlas," however, falls directly into the familiar tradition that both exaggerates and deifies the Western gunfighter and his exploits. In the story, "Wild Bill Hickox" eliminates the predatory Jake McCandlas gang by six-shooter, shotgun, and bowie knife, putting eleven "fightin' men into the misty beyond."

In addition to writing stories of the West, Lewis also wrote a pair of dismal cowboy novels, neither of which was narrated by the engaging Old Cattleman. *The Sunset Trail* (1905) was a shameless panegyric to Lewis's friend Bat Masterson, whose gunplay in the story, directed mainly against Indians, eventually wins him the love of a beautiful Boston woman. *The Throwback: A Romance of the Southwest* (1906), which was suggested to Lewis by the early adventures of Roosevelt, presents an account of a "sickly, melancholy" young man "full of book-cleverness" who travels to the West to become rejuvenated and is soon the scourge of the Panhandle. The critic for the 21 April 1906 *New York Times* notes Lewis's abdication of his "usual picturesque Wolfville language." In the August 1906 issue of *The Critic* the reviewer asserts that in these works Lewis

descends into "silliness." Without the voice of the Old Cattleman who "approves onreserved of both lies an' liars," Lewis's efforts disappoint his audience.

In 1908, when Lewis brought out *Wolfville Folks,* the repetitious nature of his tales was accentuated by his feeble attempt to unify the work as a novel. This strategy, though, reduced the impact of single, focused episodes and encouraged the Cattleman's recollections to trail languidly from chapter to chapter. Thus, while such characters as Jaybird Horne, Talky Jones, and Cottonwood Wasson contribute to the amiable humor permeating Wolfville life, the critic for the 30 May *New York Times Book Review* noted that "they are preposterous" as "veracious" western types. The familiar Cattleman was becoming predictable in his subjects as well as his delivery.

Lewis published *Faro Nell and Her Friends,* the final volume of the Wolfville chronicle, in 1913. The twelve tales spun by the Old Cattleman contain little new. The most interesting story is "Cynthiana, Pet-Named Original Sin," the tale of a heroine who opens the Votes for Women Saloon in Wolfville. While her preaching of suffrage is "incessant," she retains her feminine sensibilities, shooting a "Greaser" because he was "roode." After using a shotgun in acquiring an unwary tenderfoot husband, Cynthiana leaves town to live in a proper home back east. Despite the woman's frontier brashness and her unladylike western ways, what she truly desires is not the vote but refined domesticity. Lewis's story is a satire on the strident feminist, supporting the conventional posture of his day.

Reading through Lewis's Wolfville volumes, one encounters virtually every device known to local colorists of western Americana, each fully and shrewdly exploited. Gun duels and lynchings are recounted as humorous anecdote. Brutes are tamed by the love of a good woman while outsiders are teased, taunted, and abused. Women, whether dance hostesses, homemakers, or laundresses, are idealized or deified, and abandoned children are solicitously tended by otherwise careless roughnecks. All behaviors are codified: there are even "rooles" for "stage-robbin'" as there are with respect to faro-bank and poker.

Although only one of the Wolfville chronicles was published before 1900, Lewis remains attached to the nineteenth-century literary aesthetic. In his local colorist, dialect presentations of the western ethos he is close in strategy and style to the regionalist American writers who flourished immediately after the Civil War. Despite those who fault Lewis for what they see as his burlesque of the West, his repetition, and his stereotypical humor, the western community that emerged from his stories momentarily unified intuition and art. The emotional tenor of the Old West, with its innocence and its violence, touched a critical eastern audience. In the noteworthy character of the Old Cattleman, Lewis developed a voice whose pragmatic perceptions of life in the West illuminated for many of the uninitiated that segment of the American Dream unfolding across the plains and touching the imagination of the national psyche.

References:
Louis Filler, "Wolfville," *New Mexico Quarterly,* 13 (Spring 1943): 35–47;

Rolfe Humphries, Introduction to *Wolfville Yarns of Alfred Henry Lewis* (Kent, Ohio: Kent State University Press, 1968), pp. v–xviii;

F. D. Manzo, "Alfred Henry Lewis: Western Storyteller," *Arizona and the West,* 10 (Spring 1968): 5–24;

R. F. Mehl, "Jack London, Alfred Henry Lewis, and the Primitive Woman," *Jack London Newsletter,* 6 (1973): 66–70;

Abe C. Ravitz, *Alfred Henry Lewis,* no. 32, Western Writers Series (Boise, Idaho: Boise State University Press, 1978);

John Seymour Wood, "Alfred Henry Lewis," *Bookman,* 18 (January 1904): 486–493.

Papers:
Some of Alfred Henry Lewis's letters are at the Huntington Library, San Marino, California. Correspondence and a manuscript are at the Alderman Library, University of Virginia.

Meriwether Lewis
(18 August 1774 – 11 October 1809)

and

William Clark
(1 August 1770 – 1 September 1838)

Thomas W. Dunlay
University of Nebraska–Lincoln

Meriwether Lewis and William Clark, portraits by Charles Willson Peale (Independence National Historical Park Collection, Philadelphia)

See also the Lewis and Clark entry in *DLB 183: American Travel Writers, 1776–1864.*

BOOKS: *History of the Expedition under the Command of Captains Lewis and Clark, to the Sources of the Missouri, thence Across the Rocky Mountains and down the River Columbia to the Pacific Ocean. Performed during the years 1804–5–6. By Order of the Govern-* ment of the United States, 2 volumes, by Nicholas Biddle, edited by Paul Allen (Philadelphia: Bradford & Inskeep; New York: Abm. H. Inskeep, J. Maxwell, printer, 1814); published as *Travels to the Source of the Missouri River and Across the American Continent to the Pacific Ocean. Performed by Order of the Government of the United States, in the Years 1804, 1805, and 1806,* edited by Thomas Rees (London: Longman, Hurst, Rees, Orme & Brown, 1814);

The Original Journals of the Lewis and Clark Expedition, 1804–1806; Printed from the Original Manuscripts in the Library of the American Philosophical Society and by Direction of its Committee on Historical Documents, together with Manuscript Material of Lewis and Clark from Other Sources, including Note-Books, Letters, Maps, etc., and the Journals of Charles Floyd and Joseph Whitehouse, Now for the First Time Published in Full and Exactly as Written, 8 volumes, edited by Reuben Gold Thwaites (New York: Dodd, Mead, 1904–1905);

The Journals of Captain Meriwether Lewis and Sergeant John Ordway, Kept on the Expedition of Western Exploration, 1803–1806, edited by Milo M. Quaife (Madison, Wis.: The Society, 1916);

Westward with Dragoons; the Journal of William Clark on his Expedition to Establish Fort Osage, August 25 to September 22, 1808; a Description of the Wilderness, an Account of the Building of the Fort, Treaty-Making with the Osages and Clark's Return to St. Louis, edited by Kate L. Gregg (Fulton, Mo.: Ovid Bell, 1937).

Editions: *History of the Expedition under the Command of Lewis and Clark, to the Sources of the Missouri River, thence Across the Rocky Mountains and down the Columbia River to the Pacific Ocean, Performed during the years 1804–5–6, by Order of the Government of the United States,* 4 volumes, edited by Elliott Coues (New York: Harper, 1893);

Lewis and Clark in North Dakota; the Original Manuscript Journals and the Text of the Biddle Edition during the Time the Expedition Remained in North Dakota (Bismarck: State Historical Society of North Dakota, 1947–1948);

The Journals of Lewis and Clark, edited by Bernard De Voto (Boston: Houghton Mifflin, 1953);

The Lewis and Clark Expedition, facsimile of 1814 edition, edited by Archibald Hanna (Philadelphia: Lippincott, 1961);

The Journals of the Lewis and Clark Expedition, 11 volumes to date, edited by Gary Moulton (Lincoln: University of Nebraska Press, 1983–   ).

Meriwether Lewis and William Clark led the first American scientific expedition that the United States government sponsored, the first to cross the North American continent within the present United States. Much of the territory they traversed had never been seen by anyone other than native North Americans, and the expedition of the two explorers provided a thoroughly detailed map of the land. Yet their exploration was more than a heroic feat of geographical discovery because in following the instructions of their sponsor, President Thomas Jefferson, they attempted to provide a comprehensive view of the vast territory they crossed, including anthropological, zoological, botanical, and meteorological information in addition to providing a detailed account of the day-to-day events of the expedition.

Not counting the journals of four of the enlisted men, the two captains wrote more than a million words during their preliminary travels to Saint Louis and the twenty-eight months of the expedition. The Lewis and Clark journals constitute one of the major travel and exploration accounts of American history, and for this achievement the two are inseparably linked in history. Their journals, never published in their own lifetimes, constitute their principal literary accomplishment.

Both men were born in Virginia, Clark on 1 August 1770 and Lewis on 18 August 1774, of families who owned land and slaves but were by no means great planters in the Tidewater tradition. Little is known about the childhood of either, and neither seems to have received any extensive formal education. Both grew up during the Revolutionary War, and older members of both their families were involved in the fighting. Clark's older brother, George Rogers Clark, gained fame for his wartime accomplishments on the Ohio River frontier. Lewis's father, an officer in the Continental Army, died from an illness related to his military service when the boy was about five years old. Clark's parents moved to Kentucky when he was fourteen years old, and Lewis's mother and stepfather went to Georgia when he was ten years old. At age thirteen Lewis returned to Virginia, where private tutors educated him in Latin, mathematics, and some science. Limited as it was, his education was more extensive than Clark's, and this is evident to anyone who reads their journals.

Both young men found their way into the small regular army of the United States. While still a teenager, Clark seems to have participated in militia expeditions against the Native Americans north of the Ohio River, and in 1792 he was commissioned as a second lieutenant in the regular infantry. Lewis joined the Virginia militia during the Whiskey Rebellion of 1794 and was commissioned as a lieutenant of infantry in 1795. Service in the regular army almost invariably meant frontier duty, and this gave servicemen extensive acquaintance with wilderness travel and Native Americans in times of both peace and war. Clark participated in various frontier battles, including the battle of Fallen Timbers in 1794; Lewis apparently did not see combat, but for a time he served under Clark, and the two became friends.

Letter to Clark in which Lewis acknowledged Clark's decision to join the western expedition (Missouri Historical Society)

Clark left the army in 1796 to attend to family business, principally the affairs of his brother George, who was deeply in debt. Lewis remained in the army, but in 1801 he was called, while retaining his military rank, to become the private secretary of President Jefferson. Like Lewis, Jefferson was a native of Albemarle County, Virginia, and undoubtedly knew the Lewis family and, probably, Lewis himself. Jefferson told Lewis that his "knowledge of the Western country, of the army and all its interests and relations" was a primary reason that he had picked Lewis as his secretary.

Having read everything he could get and having collected the latest maps on the West, Jefferson was a president whose own secondhand knowledge of the subject made him one of the nation's leading experts on the territory. When he had taken office, the United States extended only to the Mississippi River, but he already had his eyes on regions as far beyond as the Pacific Coast. He had tried several times to organize a privately funded expedition up the Missouri River and on to the sea; once he had even asked George Rogers Clark to lead such a party, but the elder Clark had declined. Jefferson's regard for Lewis's knowledge of the West has naturally led to speculation that he intended from the first to send Lewis to explore westward along the Missouri River route, an idea strengthened by the fact that Lewis, not yet twenty years old, had volunteered in 1793 for one of Jefferson's unsuccessful attempts to launch such an expedition. In fact, the "Western country" with which Lewis was acquainted was the territory north of the Ohio River; Louisiana, as the land beyond the Mississippi River was called, was territory known only to a few French-speaking fur traders operating from Saint Louis. Nevertheless, Lewis seems to have been interested in such a project, for in a 7 April 1805 journal entry he wrote of the transcontinental exploration as "a darling project of mine for the last ten years."

Having read Alexander Mackenzie's account of his transcontinental journey of 1792–1793 in Canada and fearing that the British would follow up and seize control of the western part of the continent, Jefferson by the end of 1802 had definitely decided to send Lewis on this western expedition. Preparations were well under way before the Louisiana Purchase gave the United States title to the western drainage of the Mississippi River as far as the Continental Divide. In a 28 February 1803 letter Jefferson wrote that the man to head the expedition should be "a person who to courage, prudence, habits & health adapted to the woods, & some familiarity with the Indian character, joins a perfect knoledge [sic] of botany, natural history, mineralogy & astronomy." In Jefferson's mind Lewis apparently was as close to being such a paragon as one was likely to find. He was young and healthy, had experience of wilderness travel and military command, had met Native Americans of the Ohio and Great Lakes regions, and had genuine interests in natural history and, especially, botany.

Jefferson's choice of Clark as a second in command seems to have been an afterthought, an attempt to provide someone who could take charge if Lewis were to die or become incapacitated. Jefferson had met Clark when the latter visited Lewis in Washington in 1802, and Lewis undoubtedly recommended his old friend. When Clark, then living in Clarksville, Indiana, accepted the job in a letter to Lewis on 18 July 1803, he wrote, "The enterprise &c. is Such as I have long anticipated," and this suggests that the president had already given him some hint as to his plans.

Lewis and Clark have become so inseparable in the history of the United States that historians have emphasized their differences in order to distinguish the two. Lewis has been characterized as a moody, sensitive intellectual and Clark as the barely literate frontiersman, perfectly adapted to the wilderness. Both men, however, belonged to landowning, slaveholding families and might have considered themselves gentlemen. Lewis undoubtedly had more education than Clark, and the literary style of his journals—more verbose and literary than that of Clark—reflects this difference. Jefferson noted in his sketch that Lewis suffered from "hypochondriac affections," which apparently refers to periodic depressions. Yet Lewis was able to write detailed, technical descriptions of new plant and animal species, while Clark proved to be a skilled cartographer whose detailed maps of the route of the expedition make it possible to locate the position of the party on any given day with some precision.

In spring 1803 Lewis received instruction and advice from some leading scientists in Philadelphia, all friends and acquaintances of Jefferson, and then set out for the West. He left Pittsburgh on 31 August 1803, headed down the Ohio River with a small party in canoes and a keelboat, picked up Clark at Clarksville, and then went on to Saint Louis. The group set up a winter camp across the Mississippi River in Illinois and gathered a mixed party of Anglo-American frontiersmen, regular army enlisted men, and French boatmen with experience on the Missouri River. On 14 May 1804 they set out up the Missouri.

Their planned route was essentially the one that the president had developed. Jefferson, like most other Americans, regarded water as the preferred means of wilderness travel, if such a means were at all possible. The party planned to journey up the Missouri to its headwaters, then unknown but presumed to be near the Continental Divide. There they planned to make a portage for what they presumed would be a relatively short distance to some stream that flowed into the Columbia River, and then they could resume their journey downriver to the sea. Virtually the whole expedition was through country over which only Native Americans exercised any control, so it was essential that they maintain relations that were as friendly as possible with the natives. White traders had been as far up the Missouri as the Mandan and Hidatsa villages in present North Dakota, and the tribes they met on that portion of the trip had some slight acquaintance with white men. Beyond the Mandans the country was unknown for hundreds of miles until the party could expect to come within one hundred miles or so of the mouth of the Columbia River. Through all this territory they were to be the first white men to see the land, its peoples, and its wildlife.

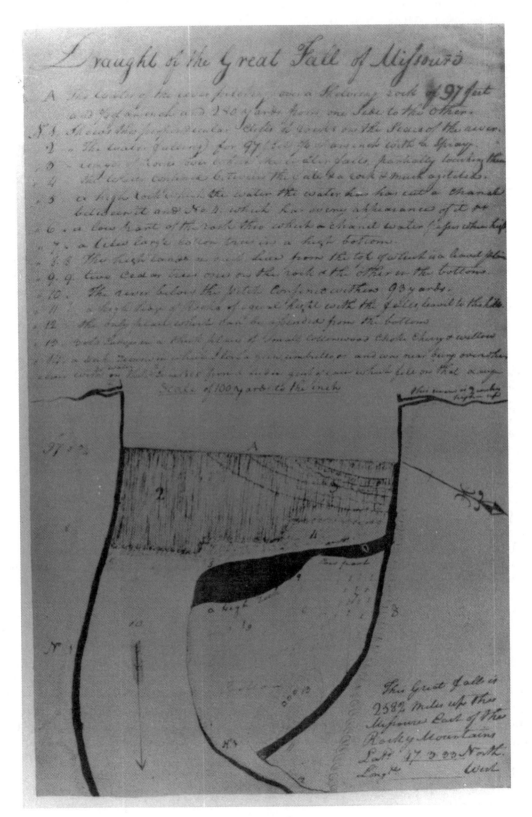

Clark's sketch of the Great Fall of the Missouri River (Library of the American Philosophical Society, Philadelphia)

Keeping journals was not just an extra chore for the two captains; it was one of the most essential tasks of the enterprise. Jefferson's instructions to Lewis include a formidable list of things that the two were to record: a virtually complete picture of the culture of the different tribes; a complete survey of the animal life, plant life, fossil remains, minerals, and climate of the country; and as much geographical information of the territory away from their route as they could gather. This information was in addition to the records of daily events they were to log during their trip. It was a large order for two infantry officers, but within the limits of time, language, and their own knowledge they did their best to fulfill it.

Lewis kept a journal for brief periods of the expedition from Pittsburgh to Saint Louis, and Clark kept one intermittently during their winter camp on the Mississippi and then throughout the rest of the trip. The journals of the expedition proper begin on 14 May 1804 and end on 26 September 1806. Lewis's journals include substantial gaps in time, but Clark's cover all but about ten days, although he may have copied Lewis's entries for some months in early 1806. Their notebooks and loose sheets also contain undated materials such as weather diaries, zoological and botanical notes, and digests of information about various tribes.

The gaps in Lewis's journals appear during all but a few days of the first eleven months of the expedition, until April 1805, and again during all but a few days from late August 1805 to the end of the year. After suffering an accidental gunshot wound Lewis also ceased keeping a journal for the last six weeks of the trip. These gaps have naturally prompted considerable speculation about whether he simply failed to keep a daily journal during those periods and left the task to Clark or whether Lewis kept journals that have been lost. These questions are tied to others about whether the existing notebook journals are the ones that the captains kept on the expedition or whether these journals are copies made from field notes, most of which have been lost.

Donald Jackson, one of the leading authorities on Lewis and Clark, suggests that Lewis kept some daily journal during the first year of the expedition but that this journal was lost or damaged on 14 May 1805 in a canoe accident in which much of the baggage of the party suffered water damage. Such an event does not explain other gaps in Lewis's journal keeping in the latter part of 1805. Other suggestions have been made that parts of Lewis's journals were lost after his death in Tennessee in 1809, but if this were so, one might expect to find some state-ment or letter from Clark or Jefferson bemoaning this loss. In fact, Lewis is known to have done much writing of notes on regional plant and animal life, geological phenomena, astronomical observations, and Native American vocabularies during the first year of the expedition in addition to preparing plant and animal specimens and performing his duties as expedition leader and negotiator with native tribes. With no evidence that extensive material by Lewis has been lost, to assume that such a loss occurred is mere speculation.

Questions about whether the journals that remain are those that were kept on the journey or are later productions concern the sense of immediacy that one feels in reading them. Are they really the records of events and emotions taken down at the time or records made shortly afterward when the writers still did not know the final outcomes? Or are they an elaborated and perhaps laundered version of events written at leisure when the authors were safe in camp or had returned from the wilderness? Editors Elliott Coues and Reuben Gold Thwaites, both intimately acquainted with the manuscript journals, believe that the condition of most of the notebook journals is too good for them to have been taken back and forth across the continent: they believe that the captains kept rough field notes and then copied these notes in compiling an improved version after the two men returned to Saint Louis. This theory is somewhat bolstered by the survival of Clark's actual field notes covering the first year of the expedition and paralleling his more polished notebook journals for the same period. If Coues and Thwaites's theory is true, then the actual journals kept on the trip and written around the campfires day by day are apparently lost.

However, a few years after the expedition Jefferson remembered and stated that when Lewis returned to Washington at the end of 1806 he turned over to the president a complete series of journals that, from Jefferson's description, must be the surviving notebook journals. This leaves Lewis and Clark only three months, during which time they were frequently traveling, to have copied into journals more than two years' worth of entries. Much internal evidence also suggests that the notebook journals were written within a short time of the events they record, if not necessarily on the same day.

Jefferson said that these books were kept "cemented" in tin boxes for protection, and this could explain their relatively pristine condition. There are certain fragments, loose sheets covering a few days, and one of Clark's journals (from 11 September 1805 to 13 December 1805) that is bound in elk skin and seems clearly to merit acknowledgment as a field journal. But none of the fragments contain portions of incomplete entries or give other indications of being parts of a larger whole. The journal bound in elk skin begins as a record of course and distance notes accompanied by sketch maps like those Clark kept to assist him in mapmaking, and it includes extensive additional records of daily events. Other fragments were kept by one of the officers scouting ahead of the main party, a time when keeping a notebook would have risked its loss. There is no reason to assume that the two captains followed a uniform procedure in keeping journals for the entire expedition, nor is the evidence convincing that the notebook journals are products of a massive copying job done after Lewis and Clark returned to Saint Louis.

As the journals exist, they thus have a fair claim to being immediate records of events, writing completed close in time to the events narrated. This does not mean that they record everything: they are not intimate personal records, like the diaries of Samuel Pepys. They are public documents, and their first purpose was to record valuable information. They were also scientific records of discoveries made in the pursuit of knowledge and records of events that occurred during that pursuit. They were to be the bases for a history of those discoveries that Lewis was to write after the expedition, and the technical material was to be analyzed and presented by Benjamin Smith Barton, a Philadelphia naturalist and friend of Jefferson who was, like him, a member of the American Philosophical Society. No one originally intended the journals to be published in their rough original form. Neither of the captains regarded them as opportunities to record or analyze their emotions or their philosophies of life. Lewis is more a self-conscious literary artist than Clark, and he sometimes adds his own thoughts, doubts, and fears, but even his personal asides are most often reflections on the scenes and people he observes, not on his inner world.

Although it would be difficult to write a psychological profile of Lewis or Clark from the journals alone, this does not deter some writers from trying. Many have found the journals to be works of lasting fascination. They are probably most interesting to readers with an abiding curiosity about Western history and with some knowledge of the country through which the expedition passed.

Although Lewis was by no means a perfect speller and his mastery of rules of capitalization and punctuation was a bit weak, his style is essentially that of an eighteenth-century gentleman and echoes that of great Augustan authors. In fact, he is often verbose and drops occasional classical allusions. His

attempts at humor usually illustrate rather strained wit. Some of his descriptions of scenery, notably his depictions of the White Cliffs and the Great Falls of the Missouri, reflect clearly the romanticism of the times. For instance, he writes of "seens of visionary enchantment," and continues that "so perfect indeed are those walls that I should have thought that nature had attempted here to rival the human art of masonry had I not recollected that she had first began her work." He then adds an objective, detailed description of the geological formations he saw. In describing the Great Falls he is unhappy with his inability to present what he sees in accord with the great literary models, and of two of the more impressive falls he writes that "I determined between these two great rivals for glory that this was *pleasingly beautiful,* while the other was *sublimely grand.*" On his thirty-first birthday Lewis records, "I reflected that I had as yet done but little, very little indeed, to further the hapiness of the human race, or to advance the information of the succeeding generation," and resolves "to live for *mankind,* as I have heretofore lived *for myself.*" What is most evident in such prose is the influence of the Enlightenment and especially the personal philosophy and example of Jefferson.

Clark's journals reveal little of this. Besides being far less polished as a writer, Clark is more terse and strictly factual than is Lewis. Clark, who may have been a bit troubled by his lack of formal education, was inclined to emphasize the importance of practical knowledge. If one compares his entries with those of Lewis on the same days, Clark's are almost invariably much shorter, except where he copies Lewis's entries verbatim. Clark's punctuation and grammar are rough, and his capitalization and spelling erratic. It has often been noted that in the first published edition of the journals he spells *Sioux* twenty-seven different ways. He could indeed spell a word two different ways in the same sentence. It may be worth pointing out that rules of spelling at the time were much less rigid than they have become, and the writing of Jefferson, one of the most widely read men in America, was well below twentieth-century standards in all but grammar. Yet Clark gets to his point, is able to say what he wants to say, and only occasionally is a reader in any doubt about what Clark intends to convey.

Clark seldom gives readers much insight into his emotions. On 25 September 1804 he says, about a very tense encounter with the Teton Sioux on the Missouri, "i felt my Self warm & Spoke in very positive terms." Sgt. Patrick Gass reports that Clark told the Indians that he had "more medicine on board his boat than would kill twenty such nations in one

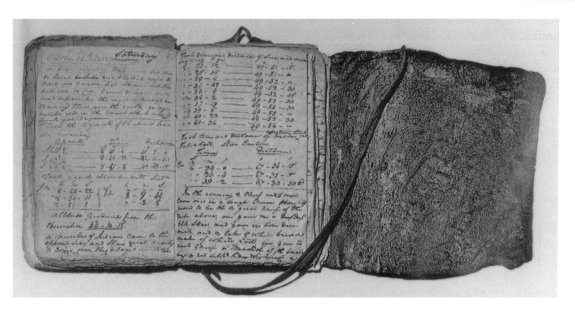

One of Lewis and Clark's original journals, bound in elk skin (Missouri Historical Society)

day." Clark, the rugged frontiersman, frequently complains about the state of his health; Lewis either was remarkably healthy or did not deem his physical condition as worthy of being written about. Yet Clark gives the single most eloquent statement in all the journals when the expedition nears the Pacific Ocean on 7 November 1805: "Ocian in view! O! the joy." And Clark, immobilized along the Columbia estuary a little later by storms, bursts out on 22 November: "O! how horriable is the day."

The journals of four enlisted men supplement the primary recounting that Clark gives of the first year of the expedition since Lewis records so little daily material during this period. This narrative tells of a long haul upstream on the Missouri, a winding and sometimes treacherous river, and a stay of more than five months near the Mandan and Hidatsa villages. The country was at least slightly known to Saint Louis fur traders, and the Native Americans had some experience dealing with whites. The captains informed the inhabitants that they had a new "Great Father" in Washington and admonished them to cease making war on each other. Lewis and Clark seem to have taken their peacemaking efforts seriously, but the natives may have been only polite in their agreement.

The winter with the Mandans and Hidatsas afforded the captains the opportunity to study native culture in some depth. Lewis and Clark were not anthropologists—the discipline did not even exist at the time—and they were better at recording the facts of culture and behavior than at discerning underlying

reasons for actions. They did not understand, for example, that Native American husbands offered their women to the white men in order to absorb some of the supernatural power, or "medicine," of the newcomers. Lewis and Clark could not help judging those whom they met by ethnocentric criteria, but they did not display the contempt or the tendency to make glib generalizations that later white travelers frequently did. They readily discerned the differences in culture and attitudes between different tribes, and they recognized fully their need for native advice and assistance. From the Mandans and Hidatsas they spent much time during the winter of 1804–1805 gleaning information about the country as far away as the Rocky Mountains, information that was of great value to them.

At the Hidatsa villages Lewis and Clark met Sacagawea, the Shoshone woman who became the most famous member of their party after the two leaders themselves. She was a captive among the Hidatsas and the wife of Toussaint Charbonneau, a Canadian trader. Although the journals never give a physical description of her (other than to hint that she was probably quite short) and offer little insight into her character, she is prominent in all subsequent accounts of the expedition and in virtually all illustrations of it. The captains seldom even use her name, which they may have had trouble rendering phonetically; they simply call her "the Indian woman," or "the squaw"—*squar* in Clark's spelling—a word that they probably did not intend to be as offensive as it has become. In fact, Clark seems to have become quite fond of her and her infant son, Jean Baptiste Charbonneau, although the evidence for this is largely outside the journals. Those records provide little support for romantic legends about Clark and Sacagawea. Her greatest service to the party was not as a guide but as an interpreter and as a means of establishing friendly relations between the party and her own people, the Lemhi Shoshones living along the Continental Divide at the headwaters of the Missouri.

The meeting with the Shoshones in August 1805 was one of the explorers' greatest pieces of good fortune because they had with great labor, including a monthlong portage of the Great Falls, reached the limit of navigable transportation in southwest Montana and were realizing that any easy portage to the waters of the Columbia River was not apparent. Lewis, scouting ahead, rejoiced as he stood at the rivulet at the head of "the mighty & heretofore deemed endless Missouri" on 12 August 1805, but from the ridge beyond he saw "immence ranges of high mountains still to the West of us with their tops partially covered with snow." Friendly relations with the Shoshones enabled the party to buy horses and secure the services of a guide whom they called Old Toby and who got them across the mountains to navigable waters that led to the Columbia. Lewis describes in detail the culture and customs of the people, who lived a hard life with scant food in the mountains: "I viewed these poor starved divils with pity and compassion," he writes on 16 August, yet when they secured game, their eating habits made these people seem "nearly allyed to the brute creation."

After traveling in canoes down the Clearwater, Snake, and Columbia Rivers, the party reached the Pacific Ocean in November 1805. There they had to spend a few months in winter quarters, amid the almost constant seasonal rain and storms of the Pacific Northwest coast. While there Lewis recorded some of his most extensive ethnographic and natural history information, and Clark apparently copied this verbatim at least a few months later. The climate and bad food wearied everyone, and the culture of the Chinookan peoples at the mouth of the Columbia—people who were shrewd traders with long experience in dealing with seagoing white traders—seems to have irritated the explorers more than the cultures of other tribes had. Members of the party had always taken precautions when they were among natives, and they fortified their winter quarters, but here on 20 February 1806 Lewis wrote of "the treachery of the aborigines of America" and "the

well known treachery of the natives," a diatribe unprecedented in the journals.

The return journey of the expedition was much quicker than the westward trip had been. Barely six months elapsed from their departure from Fort Clatsop at the mouth of the Columbia until their arrival in Saint Louis in September 1806. This period included a stay of some six weeks among the Nez Perce in Idaho, where they waited for the snow to melt in the mountains. During this period, Nez Perce tradition asserts, Clark fathered a child by a Nez Perce woman. The enlisted men established intimate relations with native women often on the journey, but this Nez Perce report is the only occasion in which either of the captains is alleged to have done so, and the claim is not verifiable.

After crossing the mountains the party split into two groups so that Clark could explore the Yellowstone River while Lewis explored the Marias River in northwest Montana. On this latter trip occurred the only violent confrontation of the whole expedition when Lewis and three of his men encountered a small group of Piegan Blackfoot natives who attempted to steal their guns and horses on 27 July 1806. Lewis and his men killed two of them and then fled to avoid a larger party that might seek revenge. As if wishing to acknowledge responsibility, Lewis left a medal he had given one of the dead men, "that they might be informed who we were."

The only other violent event of the expedition occurred when Lewis was accidentally wounded by one of his men on 11 August. Neither he nor the two enlisted men who recorded the event had any doubt that this was an accident, for it happened while he was hunting in thick brush. The two captains reunited in North Dakota and hurried down the Missouri to Saint Louis, which they reached on 23 September 1806.

After their exploration was completed, the lives of both Lewis and Clark seem rather anticlimactic, although this is more true of Lewis than of Clark. Jefferson appointed Lewis governor of the Louisiana Territory, with its capital in Saint Louis, and Clark became superintendent of Indian affairs for the same territory. Lewis was also charged with formally writing the history of the expedition. He seems never to have started on this literary task, and his administrative appointment proved disastrous. He encountered mounting political opposition in the territory, and after Jefferson left the presidency, the federal government refused to approve some of his expenditures. The evidence is scanty, but it appears that he became depressed and perhaps began drinking heavily. In the fall of 1809, traveling overland from Natchez, Mississippi, to Tennessee on the Natchez Trace, he set out for Washington, D.C., to attempt to get his account approved. On the night of 11 October 1809 he stopped at a lonely cabin in Tennessee, and he died there of apparently self-inflicted gunshot wounds.

Various historians have claimed that Lewis did not commit suicide but was murdered, and they suggest motives ranging from some dark political conspiracy to robbery by the supposedly ill-reputed people with whom he stayed that night. The truth about Lewis's death seems unlikely to be firmly established, but Clark (who had been working with Lewis in Saint Louis until he had left for Washington, D.C.) and Jefferson, who must have known him as well as anyone, seem to have had no doubts that he had killed himself.

Clark, by contrast, lived a long and full life. After his return from the expedition he married Julia Hancock, a young Virginia woman for whom he had named a river in Montana. He served as governor of the Missouri Territory and militia general, and he became a prominent figure in the region. Left with the responsibility for completing the written report on the mission he had shared with Lewis, he commissioned Nicholas Biddle, a lawyer in Philadelphia, to write the official history of the expedition, and this was finally published in 1814. Apparently not trusting his abilities as a writer, Clark never considered trying to write it himself. For many years he was in charge of Native American affairs throughout the vast area west of the Mississippi and was thus saddled with the frustrating task of trying to protect the interests of these people while at the same time promoting the fur trade and the security of the frontier. Reconciling these aims was probably beyond the abilities of any man. For the Native Americans of this era Saint Louis was "Red Head's Town," for there Clark, the redheaded superintendent, greeted the delegations of various tribes.

The Lewis and Clark expedition, the first scientific undertaking sponsored by the federal government, was an outstanding feat of exploration. The two captains, working as a remarkably harmonious team, not only contributed much to geographic knowledge but also produced a well-rounded picture of the people and the natural environment. Because the full scientific results were not published for a century, they have never received proper credit for their many discoveries about animal and plant life. Nonetheless, the published history of their expedition was for many years a primary source of knowledge about the land west of the Mississippi River and was not superseded until the series of expeditions sponsored by the government in the mid nineteenth century.

Few records of exploration surpass the journals of Lewis and Clark in overall detail and interest. As the expedition was the prime achievement of their lives, the journals are their principal literary monument. There is a certain irony in this because Jefferson's original intention was that the formal, polished history he expected Lewis to write would be the record that the world would see. This was the history that Clark arranged for Biddle to write, a work that both Lewis and Clark would have considered as the definitive account of their achievement. The raw journals—with all their repetitions, occasional obscurities, and errors of spelling, grammar, and punctuation—were never intended to be seen by the public, much less to be pored over by scholars and interested readers nearly two centuries after they were written.

Clark would probably have been particularly unhappy to know that, long after his death, readers would find amusement in his spelling errors and colloquial turns of phrase. Yet it seems only fair to note that neither his vocabulary nor his thoughts are those of an illiterate. The taste of a generation following Clark's may value the rawness and immediacy of the original journals more than the polished literary product that Jefferson and Lewis intended.

Letters:

Letters of the Lewis and Clark Expedition with Related Documents, 1783–1854, 2 volumes, edited by Donald Jackson (Urbana: University of Illinois Press, 1978).

Biographies:

Richard Dillon, *Meriwether Lewis: A Biography* (New York: Coward-McCann, 1965);

Jerome O. Steffen, *William Clark: Jeffersonian Man on the Frontier* (Norman: University of Oklahoma Press, 1977);

Stephen E. Ambrose, *Undaunted Courage: Meriwether Lewis, Thomas Jefferson, and the Opening of the American West* (New York: Simon & Schuster, 1996).

References:

Paul Russell Cutright, *A History of the Lewis and Clark Journals* (Norman: University of Oklahoma Press, 1976);

Cutright, *Lewis and Clark: Pioneering Naturalists* (Urbana: University of Illinois Press, 1969);

Thomas W. Dunlay, "'Battery of Venus': A Clue to the Journal-Keeping Methods of Lewis and Clark," *We Proceeded On,* 9 (1983): 6–8;

Albert Furtwangler, *Acts of Discovery: Visions of America in the Lewis and Clark Journals* (Urbana: University of Illinois Press, 1981);

Donald Jackson, *Thomas Jefferson and the Stony Mountains: Exploring the West from Monticello* (Urbana: University of Illinois Press, 1981);

David Lavender, *The Way to the Western Sea: Lewis and Clark Across the Continent* (New York: Harper & Row, 1988);

James P. Ronda, *Lewis and Clark among the Indians* (Lincoln: University of Nebraska Press, 1984).

Papers:
The largest portion of the manuscript journals are in the keeping of the American Philosophical Society in Philadelphia, where Jefferson placed them. Several of Clark's notebook journals and some loose-leaf fragments that he kept during his lifetime are in the Eleanor Glasgow Voorhis Memorial Collection at the Missouri Historical Society in Saint Louis, along with many of his other papers. The expedition maps and field notes that Clark kept before the expedition proper and during its first year are in the Frederick W. and Carrie S. Beinecke Collection of Western Americana at Yale University. Many Lewis papers are in the Lewis-Marks Papers at the Alderman Library, University of Virginia.

Charles F. Lummis
(1 March 1859 – 25 November 1928)

Robert E. Fleming
University of New Mexico

BOOKS: *Birch Bark Poems* (Chillicothe, Ohio: Lummis, 1882);

A New Mexico David and Other Stories and Sketches of the Southwest (New York: Scribners, 1891);

A Tramp across the Continent (New York: Scribners, 1892); republished as *A Tramp across the Continent, from Ohio to California on Foot, 3507 Miles* (London: Sampson Low, Marston, 1892);

Some Strange Corners of Our Country: The Wonderland of the Southwest (New York: Century, 1892); revised and expanded as *Mesa, Cañon and Pueblo: Our Wonderland of the Southwest, Its Marvels of Nature, Its Pageant of the Earth Building, Its Strange Peoples, Its Centuried Romance* (New York & London: Century, 1925);

The Land of Poco Tiempo (New York: Scribners, 1893; London: Sampson Low, Marston, 1893);

The Spanish Pioneers (Chicago: McClurg, 1893); revised and enlarged as *The Spanish Pioneers and the California Missions* (Chicago: McClurg, 1929);

The Man Who Married the Moon, and Other Pueblo Indian Folk-Stories (New York: Century, 1894); republished as *Pueblo Indian Folk-Stories* (New York: Century, 1910);

The Gold Fish of Gran Chimú (Boston & New York: Lamson, Wolffe, 1896);

The Enchanted Burro: Stories of New Mexico and South America (Chicago: Way & Williams, 1897); enlarged as *The Enchanted Burro, and Other Stories As I Have Known Them from Maine to Chile and California* (Chicago: McClurg, 1912);

The King of the Broncos, and Other Stories of New Mexico (New York: Scribners, 1897);

The Awakening of a Nation: Mexico To-day (New York & London: Harper, 1898);

Some Aspects of Indian Education (Los Angeles, 1902);

My Friend Will, Including "The Little Boy That Was" (Chicago: McClurg, 1911);

In Memory of Juan Rodriguez Cabrillo, Who Gave the World California, 1542 (Chula Vista, Cal.: Denrich, 1913);

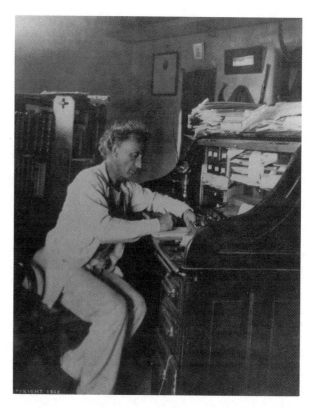

Charles F. Lummis, 1902

Southern California (New York: Mentor Association, 1916);

Stand Fast, Santa Barbara! (Santa Barbara, Cal.: Plans and Planting Committee of the Community Arts Association, 1927);

A Bronco Pegasus (Boston & New York: Houghton Mifflin, 1928);

Flowers of Our Lost Romance (Boston & New York: Houghton Mifflin, 1929);

General Crook and the Apache Wars, edited by Turbesé Lummis Fiske (Flagstaff, Ariz.: Northland, 1966);

Bullying the Moqui, edited by Robert Easton and Mackenzie Brown (Prescott, Ariz.: Prescott College Press, 1968);

219

Dateline Fort Bowie: Charles Fletcher Lummis Reports on an Apache War, edited by Dan L. Thrapp (Norman: University of Oklahoma Press, 1979).

OTHER: Alonso de Benavides, *The Memorial of Fray Alonso de Benavides, 1630,* edited by Lummis and Frederick Webb Hodge, translated by Mrs. Edward E. Ayer (Chicago: Donnelly, 1916);

Spanish Songs of Old California, compiled and translated by Lummis (Los Angeles: Lummis, 1923).

Charles F. Lummis was a multifaceted Southwestern writer. Although he wrote fiction and poetry, more important than his own creative works were his efforts as journalist, editor, photographer, amateur folklorist, and spokesman for Native American rights. His major contribution to the literature of the West consists of four volumes of nonfiction that might loosely be called journalism: *A Tramp across the Continent* (1892), *Some Strange Corners of Our Country: The Wonderland of the Southwest* (1892), *The Land of Poco Tiempo* (1893), and the revised and enlarged edition of *Some Strange Corners* as a work that he considered his masterpiece, *Mesa, Cañon and Pueblo: Our Wonderland of the Southwest, Its Marvels of Nature, Its Pageant of the Earth Building, Its Strange Peoples, Its Centuried Romance* (1925).

Born in Lynn, Massachusetts, Lummis as a boy was ill so often that he was extensively tutored at home before attending Harvard from 1877 to 1881. Although he was an indifferent student and failed to graduate, he considered himself a Harvard man all his life. Perhaps the most important experience of his college years was that of meeting future president Theodore Roosevelt, from whom Lummis learned the doctrine that the strenuous life was the best response to bodily infirmities. In pursuit of that strenuous life Lummis became acquainted with the region that became the focus of his writing from 1884 through 1928.

After leaving Harvard in 1881, Lummis moved to Chillicothe, Ohio, the home of his first wife, Mary Dorothea Rhodes, whom he married in 1880. There he became a reporter for and later the editor of the weekly *Scioto Gazette.* An attack of malaria—and perhaps a touch of marital discord—left Lummis dissatisfied with Ohio. Seeking employment elsewhere, he was offered a job as city editor of the *Los Angeles Daily Times.* Rather than taking the train west, the flamboyant Lummis decided to "tramp" the thirty-five hundred miles to his new job, and he sent newspaper accounts of his experiences back to the *Scioto Gazette* and ahead to the *Daily Times.* In 1892 Lummis turned these newspaper columns into a book, *A Tramp across the Continent.* This walk provided exactly the experience and the stimulus he needed to show him how to develop his talents as a writer.

Lummis threw himself into his work on the *Daily Times* so vigorously that after two years he suffered an apparent stroke that paralyzed him on the left side. Early in 1888 he moved to New Mexico for a long period of convalescence, first at the ranch of a man he had met on his walk through the territory and later at Isleta Pueblo, south of Albuquerque. He again attempted to recover his health by living the strenuous life—hunting, fishing, and exploring archaeological sites with anthropologist Adolph Bandelier. He also courted Eva Douglas, who became his second wife in 1891, a year after his divorce from Dorothea. While he gained strength, the enforced leisure from his journalistic routine allowed Lummis to develop his skills as a freelance writer. He attempted to support himself by writing short filler items for popular magazines, then began writing full-length stories and essays for journals such as *Harper's Weekly* and *Scribner's Magazine,* and finally published *A New Mexico David and Other Stories and Sketches of the Southwest* (1891), a book of stories for young readers.

The nature of *A New Mexico David* can be inferred from the title story. In 1840 Lucario Montoya joins a military expedition against the Utes of western New Mexico. When the soldiers encounter Native American warriors, the two sides form battle lines and the chief of the Utes, a giant figure mounted on a white horse, issues a challenge to engage in single combat. Lucario persuades his uncle, the leader of the Hispanic forces, to allow him to represent the army. The Utes ridicule the young soldier, who expertly exchanges arrows with the Ute chief; when neither combatant seriously wounds the other they attempt to lasso each other, but again fail to do so. Lucario finally kills the Ute warrior by throwing his heavy sheath knife at the same time that the chieftain throws his lance at the soldier. Lucario is wounded, but his enemy is killed.

Lummis found his true vocation when he began to prepare the book manuscript for *A Tramp across the Continent,* a work that he then followed with a second book, *Some Strange Corners of Our Country.* These two volumes marked the beginning of his most productive period as a writer.

A Tramp across the Continent is the relatively routine story of a hike until Lummis arrives in Colorado, where he hunts antelope, climbs Pikes Peak, explores the Garden of the Gods, and wards off an attack by a convict near the penitentiary at Cañon

City. The West, with its distinctive topography and the different cultures of Native and Mexican Americans, appeals to him in a way that he could not have anticipated when he left Ohio. Lummis adopts the persona of a naive, somewhat suspicious traveler and often exaggerates both the sights he encounters and his reactions to them, much in the manner of a teller of tall tales. In other instances the heroic qualities of the persona are highlighted. For example, when he first reaches the Rio Grande pueblos of Tesuque and San Ildefonso, he professes to have arrived with the belief that all Native Americans are primitive warriors in order to heighten his response to the "excellent houses," "pretty farms," and Christian churches that he finds among the pueblos. His response to other exotica of the Southwest—from green chili stew, the first taste of which convinces him that his host has poisoned him, to processions of *penitentes*—becomes the hallmark of Lummis's writing about the region. He is a controversial figure among New Mexican penitentes, a New Mexican religious sect derived from the Third Order of Saint Francis, who regard his writings about their people as little better than libelous. The narrative exaggerates Lummis's heroic qualities in relating some of his feats of marksmanship and in telling how he set his own broken arm in the wilds of northern Arizona.

An excellent example of Lummis's tendency to exaggerate occurs in his story of killing Shadow, a stray dog that has followed him for many miles on his tramp. While crossing the desert between Arizona and California, both man and dog suffer terribly from thirst. Maddened by the heat and thirst, Shadow attacks Lummis, who attempts to fight off the animal without hurting him. Unsuccessful at that, Lummis hastily fires a shot from his frontier revolver at the charging dog, but this only wounds Shadow, and the dog tries to flee across the desert. Dropping to one knee, Lummis aims deliberately and fires again at the dog, now running "like the wind" and 150 yards away. Just as in a Zane Grey novel, "the merciful lead outstripped and caught him and threw him in a wild somersault."

Some Strange Corners of Our Country supports Lummis's claim to be inventor of the phrase "See America first." His "strange corners" include southwestern areas and customs well outside the experience of the average American during the 1890s: scenic wonders such as the Grand Canyon and the Petrified Forest, archaeological sites such as Montezuma's Castle north of Phoenix and Inscription Rock near the Arizona–New Mexico border, and folkways such as the famous snake dances held in the

Lummis at the beginning of his trek from Chillicothe, Ohio, to Los Angeles

villages of Hopi or the practice of witchcraft in Native American pueblos and small Hispanic villages.

These chapters vary in scope and treatment. Those that concern the natural landscape are explicit guidebooks. After presenting brief but sensational descriptive details (for example, that the tallest eastern mountain could be transported to the Grand Canyon and thrown into the abyss without filling it to the top, or that the Statue of Liberty would appear to be the smallest of dolls if it were placed at the base of the canyon), Lummis tells prospective travelers the best way to get to the site, including current fares for stage transportation from the nearest railhead and the price of hotels in the area. Except for some purple prose these chapters might be entries in an early version of an American Automobile Association tourbook.

The chapters that treat folkways, on the other hand, bear the stamp of Lummis's style. "The Rattlesnake Dance," one of the most impressive of these chapters, tells about the annual ceremonies practiced by the villagers of the Hopi nation, or the "Moqui," as Lummis calls them. He begins by comparing them to the Oriental snake charmers that the world travelers describe with so much fascination, and he points out that in the Arizona Territory the traveler can see a sight that is just as impressive. He stresses the exotic qualities of the Hopis, whose distance from the Rio Grande Valley kept them from contact with Spanish explorers who brought their Christian religion to inhabitants of the pueblos to the east in New Mexico. In remote northern Arizona the sacred rattlesnake was therefore not supplanted by the Christian deity of the Europeans, and each August, at an exact date determined by the holy men of Hopi, the men of the villages go out to collect poisonous snakes from each quadrant of the surrounding territory. Snakes are no strangers to the Hopi, Lummis assures his readers, because most homes in a Hopi village include a resident nonpoisonous snake that catches mice for the family.

Once the snakes are collected they are taken to the kiva, or sacred chamber, of one of the Hopi clans and allowed to crawl at large until their ceremonial cleansing. The next day the members of the snake clan dance with the snakes, which the dancers hold in their bare hands or in their mouths. They tame unaccommodating snakes by stroking them with "snake whips" to cause them to uncoil from their striking positions. In 1891 Lummis was present at a ceremony that featured more than one hundred rattlesnakes, and while the dancers were not often bitten, they did not prevent the snakes from biting. Those who were bitten during the ceremony ignored the bites, and Lummis claims that none of the dancers suffered ill effects.

Another entrancing chapter is "The Witches' Corner," in which Lummis describes the prevalence of witchcraft in late-nineteenth-century New Mexico. He recounts that in his experience all of the Native Americans and 90 percent of the Mexican Americans of the territory are firm believers in witchcraft. So firm is their belief that, while nobody seeks to bring a witch to trial, villagers frequently take the law into their own hands and execute witches as a means of self-defense. He cites a "poor old Mexican woman" who was beaten to death in 1887 by two men. The killers were never brought to trial because the community believed that they had been bewitched by the old woman.

If Lummis is at his best when he treats the customs of contemporary natives of the Southwest, he does nearly as well with the relics of past cultures. He explores Montezuma's Well and Montezuma's Castle north of Phoenix, and he debunks the myth that these places have anything to do with the historical Montezuma. While Montezuma's Castle is not the castle of the Mexican leader, he writes that it was an impressive fortress of the Native Americans who lived there, and he presents a primer on the cliff-dwelling Native Americans of the Southwest. Contrary to legend, the inhabitants of the cliff dwellings were not a mysterious, lost race but the ancestors of the contemporary pueblo Native Americans. Lummis describes the scene inside the ruins and invites readers to admire the ingenuity of the architects who constructed this citadel against the Apache warriors and to appreciate the sophistication of the civilization betokened by such a structure.

Water—Montezuma's Well, or waterhole—was the basis for the location of that ancient city, and water was the raison d'être for Inscription Rock, near Zuni Pueblo in western New Mexico. "The Stone Autograph-Album" tells of the generations of Native Americans, Spanish adventurers, and American soldiers, explorers, and settlers who have annotated this site. Early natives who came to the waterhole rested in the shade and tapped petroglyphs—drawings of animals and abstract symbols—into the sandstone. Later Spanish travelers carved names and dates into the rock. Lummis values the historic inscriptions and laments the fact that modern Smiths and Joneses have continued the custom, and his attitude has been adopted by the federal government, which now protects the site as a national monument.

The Land of Poco Tiempo (1893) focuses more narrowly on Lummis's adopted home, the New Mexico Territory. In contrast to the rest of the United States during the Gilded Age and the era of the robber barons, in the 1880s and 1890s inhabitants of New Mexico were content to take life as it came, to put off decisions and actions until mañana. Lummis attributes this relaxed attitude to the history of New Mexico, where European settlements antedate those of most of the United States. Even more impressive to Lummis than the living remains of an earlier culture are the physical reminders of past glory, ruins of Native American walled cities that recall the ruins of ancient Europe. New Mexicans—and Lummis considers only the pueblo Native Americans, the Navajos, and the Mexican Americans to be authentic representatives of the territory—regard time with a different perspective from that of urban American residents. In providing a tour of the territory Lummis recounts experiences that range from exploring the ruins of ancient pueblos to visiting inhabited Native American villages, from meeting peaceful Native American farmers to encountering Apache warriors, from reproducing quaint folk songs that he collected to spying on a group of hostile *penitentes* who resist his attempts to intrude on their observances of Holy Week.

Lummis's photograph of the crucifixion ceremony of the penitentes *in New Mexico Territory, 1888*

One highlight of the book is "The City in the Sky," Lummis's account of the history, geography, and religion of Acoma Pueblo. Acoma is a city built on the seventy acres atop a 350-foot mesa in central New Mexico. The approaches to the pueblo are steep, and the village was considered impregnable to attack until the advent of Spanish conquistadores in the sixteenth century. Lummis retells as fact one of the most cherished stories of the territory, that of the Enchanted Mesa, which Acoma legend identifies as the ancestral home of the pueblo, which had been abandoned centuries ago after a storm had washed out the trail leading to the top of the mesa. After this tragedy the people moved to the mesa top, where the Spanish first encountered them.

The Spanish gained a cultural foothold on the mesa when Juan de Oñate visited the village in 1598 and convinced the native elders to swear submission to the Spanish, but the Acomas repudiated the treaty soon afterward and attempted to kill the next party of Spanish explorers who came to the village. Four of the Spaniards survived a jump from the edge of the mesa and told how the Acomas had treated them. Retaliation was swift, and in January 1599 Vicente de Zaldivar successfully captured the town after three days of fighting. Nearly a century later after the Pueblo Revolt of 1680, Diego de Vargas failed in attempting to take the village again. Through diplomacy the Spanish succeeded in convincing the Acomas to accept Spanish rule peacefully.

Lummis relates this history and describes the mesa top minutely. He also describes a typical pueblo home decorated with animal pelts, Navajo blankets, and the distinctive pottery of the pueblo. He delves into the religion of the people, from their pre-Christian beliefs to their nineteenth-century Catholicism, by recounting a burial in the churchyard on the mesa. The ceremony invokes San Esteban, patron saint of the village, and follows the older burial customs designed to ensure the safety of the departing soul from evil spirits that might prevent it from reaching the afterlife. Catholic prayers mingle with the burial of artifacts with the body. To Lummis the Acoma people seem to have the best of two worlds, the ancient and the modern.

In contrast to contemporary life in the Acoma Pueblo, "The Wanderings of Cochiti" focuses on the ruins of Tyu-on-yi in the Rito de los Frijoles northwest of Santa Fe. Known today as Bandelier National Monument, this collection of cliff dwellings was explored and excavated by Lummis and Bandelier in the early 1890s, as Lummis documented their work with his unwieldy camera. Like many prehistoric ruins in the Southwest, the village had been abandoned for unknown reasons, and the people had disappeared. Lummis fills the blanks in the history of this abandoned pueblo by drawing on the legends of the Cochiti Pueblo, which lies immediately south of the ruins.

These stories maintain that the pueblo was destroyed by tribal warfare and that the survivors settled in a new location to the south, where they built a second pueblo on a mesa top and lived for several generations. Driven from that home, they moved where Cochiti Pueblo now remains, even farther south. Lummis's attempt to draw attention to the archaeological site was almost too successful. Having become a national monument, the village receives busloads of visitors who walk its trails and sometimes have to stand in line to view the rooms carved into the face of the soft rock.

The most exciting and controversial essay in *The Land of Poco Tiempo* is "The Penitent Brothers," a sensational and imaginative account of Lummis's observation of penitente rituals during Holy Week in 1891. Although he despised tourists who fail to respect native cultures, Lummis himself intruded on worshipers from San Mateo, a small town west of Albuquerque. According to Lummis, no one had ever photographed the Good Friday observance of the penitentes, and he became the first to do so only when one of his Hispanic friends held his own neighbors at gunpoint while Lummis set up his camera on its tripod. With Lummis photographing the proceedings, members of the local *morada* (congregation)–three of whom carried heavy crosses as the others whipped themselves–made their way to the top of a hill on Holy Thursday.

The final act on the following day was a crucifixion, when Lummis saw a brother, representing Christ, being tied to the cross while lamenting that his *compadres* refused to use actual nails–as Lummis assures his readers that the ceremonies had always included in past years. Lummis emphasizes the primitive and barbaric nature of the ritual; he also writes that the secret society frequently metes out harsh punishments, including death, to members who disobey rules and that those who betray secrets of the order are buried alive. Lummis claimed to have been ambushed by angry members of the sect, who fired a shotgun at him at close range. Although his treatment of the penitentes makes him appear arrogant, Lummis's relationship with Hispanic New Mexicans was generally positive.

The book that Lummis considered his best was a revision and enlargement of *Some Strange Corners of Our Country. Mesa, Cañon and Pueblo* differs from that 1892 volume in the addition of several new chapters, the expansion of some chapters, and the inclusion of Lummis's photographs in place of the sketches that illustrated *Some Strange Corners of Our Country.* As a result of such changes *Mesa, Cañon and Pueblo* is less a travelogue than an examination of the country and the people Lummis loved best.

Comparing the beginnings of the two works reveals Lummis's technique in expanding his earlier book. The first chapter of *Some Strange Corners* is expanded into three chapters in *Mesa.* The three paragraphs comprising the beginning of "The Grandest Gorge in the World," a general introduction on the attractions that the United States affords travelers, have been expanded into "See America First," a seventeen-page chapter in which Lummis exhaustively compares America's most scenic area with foreign attractions. In place of the short chapter describing what tourists to the Grand Canyon might expect to see and then describing means of transportation and lodging, *Mesa,* includes one chapter on the aesthetics, geology, and wildlife of the canyon and on the early history of its exploration as well as a second chapter about explorations of and notable visitors to the site, from the expedition by Joseph Ives in 1857 through the four-day visit by Theodore Roosevelt in 1903.

In revising his 1892 volume Lummis was not afraid to cut material. "Montezuma's Well" and "Montezuma's Castle" were combined and cut, perhaps because after Lummis had spent an additional twenty-seven years viewing archaeological sites and helping to excavate them, he found the ruins north of Phoenix to be less impressive than they had appeared to him, as a relative neophyte, in the early 1890s. In revising these two pieces and presenting them in a single chapter in *Mesa* Lummis also cut the "how-to" tourist directions given on these two sites in *Some Strange Corners.* In *Mesa* he strengthens his earlier caveat about the legend of Montezuma's connection to the site, and he attributes the name of the site to the press agentry of Mexican politicians during the early nineteenth century. He also updates his earlier treatment by mentioning that the ruins have become a state monument.

Perhaps the best additions to *Mesa, Cañon and Pueblo* are two chapters treating the Acoma Pueblo and its former location, Katzímo, the legendary Enchanted Mesa. In the first of these chapters, "Acoma, the City in the Sky," Lummis refers to his account of the village in *The Land of Poco Tiempo* and briefly recapitulates its history. He then presents a careful ethnographic description of the people of Acoma as they live in the early twentieth century–their dress, customs, and handicrafts–and he closes with a description of the celebration of the feast day of San Juan in the pueblo, beginning with mass at the village church and a stately religious procession and culminating in horse races and games of *gallo.* In these last events live chickens are suspended high above the head of a horseman, and each of the village youths, riding beneath these at full speed, tries to catch a chicken while the other youths cause the birds to bob wildly.

In "The Enchanted Mesa" Lummis recounts the legend that the Acomas consider to be the history of their people, a story that Lummis suggests should not be dismissed as a mere fairy tale. According to oral tradition at Acoma, the top of the Enchanted Mesa was the original site of the pueblo, standing 431 feet above the floor of the surrounding land, at least 50 feet higher than the present area. Although the mesa top covered some 40 to 50 acres, this area was reserved for houses, and all crops had to be grown on the valley floor below. Access was by a single precipitous trail, the steepness and narrowness of which provided defense for the cliff dwellers. One summer during the harvest season all of the residents, except three women who were ill, were at work in their fields. When a series of storms washed out the trail, the Acoma workers could never return to their pueblo, and the three women who had been left at the top died. Lummis had written the story in 1885, and he speculated about what lay at the top of the mesa, which he unsuccessfully attempted to scale.

Lummis's combative nature was awakened in July 1897 when Professor William Libbey of Princeton University beat him to the top of the mesa by shooting a line onto it and having himself hoisted up in a bosun's chair. Taking photographs to prove that no signs of human habitation, which he defined as ruins of houses, existed there, Libbey explored the mesa top for part of a day. When he and a newspaper reporter who had accompanied him to the summit debunked the story of the Enchanted Mesa in the press, Libbey claimed that he was the first person ever to have set foot on there. His story received wide circulation in "The Disenchanted Mesa," an essay he published in the 28 August 1897 issue of *Harper's Weekly.*

Within four months Lummis mounted a campaign to reclaim the legend of the Enchanted Mesa. He reported in *The Land of Sunshine,* a magazine he had begun to edit in January 1894, that Frederick Webb Hodge of the Bureau of Ethnology–quite possibly encouraged by Lummis–had climbed to the mesa top on 3 September 1897, spent twenty hours there with a skilled survey party and a photographer, and found "indisputable proof" that the mesa had been inhabited. This party mapped the mesa top and collected many potsherds, arrowheads, stone axes, and other artifacts that Libbey had overlooked during his brief exploration. Lummis declared victory, but the controversy did not end, as Libbey continued to defend his conclusions.

In June 1898 Lummis made his own expedition to the top of Katzímo. Using the same ladders that the Hodge expedition had used, Lummis scaled the mesa and took his six-year-old daughter with him, as if to show that Libbey's feat had been an easy one. David Starr Jordan, the president of Stanford University, also accompanied Lummis and served as an impeccable witness. The Lummis expedition, like that led by Hodge, found remnants of pottery, arrowheads, and a stone axe head as well as turquoise beads and a pendant. In recounting his exploration in 1925, Lummis had the last word: the legend of Acoma was secure.

Lummis was correct in considering *Mesa, Cañon and Pueblo* to be his best work: it capitalizes on his strengths and diminishes his weaknesses as a writer. He is an accurate recorder of the facts, his camera eye and sharp ear catching each nuance of the places and events that he observes. He is remarkably free of the ethnic prejudices of his time, and he appreciates cultures other than his own. If he is occasionally subject to fits of self-promotion and sometimes exaggerates in order to improve the story he tells, the amusing and interesting qualities of his highly seasoned accounts may merit the forbearance of readers. *Mesa, Cañon and Pueblo* is a fitting capstone to a fascinating body of work.

In addition to these four major studies of the Southwest, Lummis wrote in other genres. Before he ever saw the Southwest, Lummis published *Birch Bark Poems* (1882), a twelve-page volume that was most unusual for having been printed on real birch bark. He continued to write poetry and collected his poems in *A Bronco Pegasus* (1928) shortly before his death. Although poets such as Ezra Pound and T. S. Eliot were among Lummis's contemporaries, his poetry remains firmly attached to nineteenth-century moorings. None of his poetry would startle contemporary readers of the work of Henry Wadsworth Longfellow and Edgar Allan Poe. The subject matter if not the form of some of Lummis's poems, especially "Man-Who-Yawns," a 256-line ballad about Geronimo, is striking. Lummis generally had great admiration for Apache warriors, and he makes Geronimo a mythic figure. In presenting the passing of the Apache and of his wild way of life, the end of Lummis's poem incorporates an *ubi sunt* theme with his lament:

> But here an Epoch petered out,
>   An era ended flat;
> The Apache was the Last Frontier–
>   The Tragedy is *that!*

A Bronco Pegasus was published by Scribners, which brought his work before a national audience, but by 1928 Lummis's poems resembled museum pieces

Lummis's second wife, Eve, and their daughter Turbesé

beside the rich new poetic forms that were supplanting the traditions of the nineteenth century.

Lummis failed also in his one attempt at writing book-length fiction. *The Gold Fish of Gran Chimú* (1896) was a novel loosely based on his archaeological explorations with Bandelier in Peru in July 1892. Despite his friendship with Bandelier, Lummis exhibits a curious sympathy for archaeological vandals who loot ancient tombs for their own profit. The victims in the story are Peruvian peasants, Don Beltran and Gonzalo, his son, and the villains include not only robbers but representatives of the Peruvian government, which appropriates many artifacts in order to display them in a national museum. The heroes are "the Maestro," a heroic archaeologist closely modeled on Bandelier, and Don Carlos, an expert with a revolver and a boxer who repels the bandits plaguing Don Beltran and his son, based on Lummis himself. The peasants' major find, a valuable fish made of gold, is saved from the government by a plot device rather than by the fists and guns of Don Carlos: the fish is discovered on Don Beltran's own land and thus escapes being appropriated by the government.

The plot and characterization of *The Gold Fish of Gran Chimú,* published during the height of the realistic movement in American literature, violate every principle of theorists such as William Dean Howells. Yet the sharp eye that Lummis had as a photographer contributed in one way to the realism of the novel. The excavation of the tombs and descriptions of the mummies and artifacts that are unearthed are as precise as if Bandelier had written them. Lummis was also a talented amateur folklorist, and his rendering of the daily lives and the idiom of the Peruvians shows his ability to observe and depict people accurately. These talents were not sufficient to carry the novel, however, and Lummis never attempted another. Near the end of his life he accurately assessed his strengths and weaknesses when he wrote to his former wife that he lacked the imagination and creative ability that would have made him a good poet or novelist but that he knew he had a talent for allowing others to see sights that he had seen. According to Turbesé Lummis Fiske and Keith Lummis, Charles Lummis acknowledged that "My pen is very little good without my legs."

Lummis also had considerable talent as an editor. After losing his health while serving as editor of the *Los Angeles Daily Times* he was ready for a less arduous post when in 1894 he returned to California from his convalescence in New Mexico. He was probably also looking for an editorial position that would give him a freer hand than he had had as the editor of a major daily newspaper. He found such a position when he became editor of *The Land of Sunshine,* a magazine that had been founded several months before Lummis assumed control and had been envisioned as a recruiting tool to stimulate the growth of business in southern California. Although at first it continued to fill that role under Lummis's editorship, its contents gradually began to include more fiction and poetry, while Lummis wrote a column reviewing books. The nonfiction of the magazine also began to treat California history more fully than it covered business conditions. During the late 1890s Lummis gradually widened the geographical focus of the magazine to include more of the West, a change signaled in 1902 when he changed its masthead to *Out West.*

As editor of this journal Lummis assumed responsibility for nurturing the careers of local writers and for seeking out and developing new talent. Among the successful writers whose works he brought to his journal were poets Edwin Markham, Joaquin Miller, and Robinson Jeffers; ethnologist Washington Matthews; and Jack London, who contributed two stories just as he was about to begin attracting national attention. Beginning a relationship that lasted for seven years, Mary Austin moved to Los Angeles and sought out Lummis in 1899. He published her poems and stories in *The Land of Sunshine* and *Out West* and encouraged her as she began the longer works that she later published in book form. For Eugene Manlove Rhodes, a cowboy writer from New Mexico, Lummis published several early efforts, including Rhodes's first published poem in 1899 and his first published story in 1902. Sharlot Hall, an Arizona poet, writer of short stories, and historian, benefited from Lummis's advice early in her career, and she repaid him by serving as associate editor of his magazine before she became the official historian of Arizona.

Lummis also used his editorial talent in collecting and recording native literature, from pueblo folktales to Hispanic songs. During his stay at Isleta Pueblo, New Mexico, in the 1890s, Lummis began to collect stories. In 1894 he published thirty-two of these in *The Man Who Married the Moon, and Other Pueblo Indian Folk-Stories* (republished as *Pueblo Indian Folk-Stories,* 1910). Although Lummis could not have followed the techniques of twentieth-century anthropologists in transcribing these materials, F. W. Hodge gave his work a strong, positive review in the *Journal of American Folklore* in 1895. By the time he published *Spanish Songs of Old California* (1923) Lummis was able to use new technology, and he recorded singers as they performed so that he could ensure the authenticity of his book by transcribing both their words and music more accurately than he had been able to do in 1894.

Lummis was also an enthusiastic, if opinionated, historian. In *The Spanish Pioneers* (1893) and the subsequently revised and expanded republication of that work as *The Spanish Pioneers and the California Missions* (1929), he traced the history of Spain in the New World. He treated events of more recent history, events that anticipated the administration of Porfirio Díaz, in *The Awakening of a Nation: Mexico of To-day* (1898). Several posthumous books have also

extended the list of his historical works: twentieth-century editors have mined his articles of the 1880s and 1890s to compile works such as *General Crook and the Apache Wars* (1966), *Bullying the Moqui* (1968), and *Dateline Fort Bowie: Charles Fletcher Lummis Reports on an Apache War* (1979).

Charles F. Lummis wrote as a journalist with short deadlines imposed by the demands of editors or by economic necessity. His fiction and poetry, works conventionally regarded as bases for assessing a writer's claim for recognition, are not of the first rank. Nevertheless, Lummis contributed substantially to the literature of the American West. The vivid word-pictures in his best nonfiction preserve sights and customs that have vanished or are in the process of disappearing. Readers still get from his books a sense of discovery that distinguishes the best literature.

Letters:

Letters from the Southwest: September 20, 1884, to March 15, 1885, edited by James W. Byrkit (Tucson: University of Arizona Press, 1989).

References:

Edwin R. Bingham, *Charles F. Lummis: Editor of the Southwest* (Westport, Conn.: Greenwood Press, 1955);

Turbesé Lummis Fiske and Keith Lummis, *Charles F. Lummis: The Man and His West* (Norman: University of Oklahoma Press, 1975);

Robert E. Fleming, *Charles F. Lummis* (Boise, Idaho: Boise State University Press, 1981);

Dudley Gordon, *Charles F. Lummis: Crusader in Corduroy* (Los Angeles: Cultural Assets, 1972).

Papers:

Lummis's papers are scattered. The largest collections are at the University of Arizona, Tucson; the California Historical Society, San Francisco; and the Mary Norton Clapp Library, Occidental College and the Southwest Museum Library, both in Los Angeles.

Edwin Markham

(23 April 1852 – 7 March 1940)

Charles Duncan
Virginia Polytechnic Institute and State University

See also the Markham entry in *DLB 54: American Poets, 1880–1945, Third Series.*

BOOKS: *The Man with the Hoe and Other Poems* (New York: Doubleday & McClure, 1899);

Lincoln and Other Poems (New York: McClure, Phillips, 1901);

The Burt-Markham Primer: The Nature Method, by Markham and Mary E. Burt (Boston: Ginn, 1907);

Children in Bondage, by Markham, Benjamin B. Lindsey, and George Creel (New York: Hearst's, 1914);

California the Wonderful: Her Romantic History, Her Picturesque People, Her Wild Shores, Her Desert Mystery, Her Valley Loveliness, Her Mountain Glory (New York: Hearst's, 1915);

The Shoes of Happiness and Other Poems (Garden City, N.Y.: Doubleday, Page, 1915; London: Curtis Brown, 1915);

Gates of Paradise and Other Poems (Garden City, N.Y.: Doubleday, Page, 1920);

Campbell Meeker (New York: Harold Vinal, 1925);

New Poems: Eighty Songs at Eighty (Garden City, N.Y.: Doubleday, Doran, 1932);

The Star of Araby (Stapleton, N.Y.: John Willig Press, 1937);

Poems of Edwin Markham, selected and arranged by Charles L. Wallis (New York: Harper, 1950);

The Ballad of the Gallows Bird (Yellow Springs, Ohio: Antioch Press, 1967).

OTHER: Edgar Allan Poe, *The Works of Edgar Allan Poe,* 10 volumes, edited, with an introduction, by Markham (New York: Funk & Wagnalls, 1904);

John R. Musick, *The Real America in Romance,* Art Edition, 14 volumes, edited by Markham (New York & Chicago: W. H. Wise, 1909–1927);

The Younger Choir, edited, with an introduction, by Markham (New York: Moods, 1910);

The Book of Poetry, 3 volumes, edited by Markham (New York: W. H. Wise, 1926); enlarged as

Edwin Markham

The Book of American Poetry, The Book of Classic English Poetry: 600–1830, and *The Book of Modern English Poetry: 1830–1934* (New York: W. H. Wise, 1934);

Songs and Stories, edited by Markham (Los Angeles: Powell, 1931);

Poetry of Youth: Selected from The Book of Poetry, edited by Markham (New York: W. H. Wise, 1935).

SELECTED PERIODICAL PUBLICATIONS–
UNCOLLECTED: "The Social Conscience," *San Francisco Chronicle,* 23 May 1898, p. 6;

"How and Why I Wrote 'The Man with the Hoe,'"
Saturday Evening Post, 172 (16 December 1899):
497–499;

"Christ and the Social State," *Twentieth Century,* 1
(January 1910): 345–347;

"Swedenborg: The Eye of the Age," *New Church Review,* 32 (April 1925): 129–148;

"How I Wrote 'Lincoln, the Man of the People,'"
Dearborn Independent, 26 (6 February 1926):
3–4, 19–20;

"Poetry: Defining the Indefinable," *Poetry Review,* 20
(September–October 1929): 349–258.

From the end of the nineteenth century until
his death in 1940 Edwin Markham did much to revitalize American poetry, especially in the eyes of the
reading public. Although his critical reputation
plunged after his early successes, he became a poetic
spokesman for the United States, particularly the
West. He served as poet laureate of Oregon, but he
was also counted as a native son in California, the
state with which he is most often associated. As a
transitional figure in American poetry Markham attained fame with the masses despite his occasionally
"radical" verses, which critics dismissed as socialistic. In fact, the poem that engendered Markham's
meteoric rise to national acclaim, "The Man with
the Hoe" (1899), sparked a national controversy because of its implied criticism of the social system.
Nevertheless, the nation embraced him thereafter as
"The Dean of American Poetry."

Charles Edward Anson Markham was born on
23 April 1852 in Oregon City, Oregon Territory.
His mother, Elizabeth Winchell Markham, was already separated from her husband, Samuel Barzillai
Markham, by the time of Markham's birth, and
there is some question about the identity of his biological father. In 1856 Elizabeth Markham and her
three youngest children moved to a large ranch at
Suisun, California, a rich valley located northeast of
San Francisco. The youngest Markham, then called
Charley, exulted in the natural beauty of the area,
and he learned farmwork. His experiences herding
sheep and cattle, as well as doing the manual labor a
working farm requires, supplied him with poetic images and subjects throughout his career. Although
his life on the ranch provided materials for his poetry, it lacked personal contact. Markham's closest
friend during this time was his brother Columbia,
whose deafness prompted the future poet to learn
sign language. Eventually Columbia ran away from
the ranch, presumably to escape the tyranny of
Elizabeth Markham.

The poet's mother pervades and sometimes
dominates most of the biographical commentaries

*Markham at about the time he enrolled at California College
in Vacaville*

on her son. Something of a poet herself, she exercised an enormous amount of influence throughout
her son's life and career. Described as miserly,
cruel, and loveless by many commentators, Elizabeth Markham affected the poet's life both personally and professionally. Because of her stinginess
Markham was forced to make several concessions in
his education and career, and a wistful yearning for
idealized, loving women recurs throughout his poetry. Some biographers convincingly argue that
Elizabeth abused both Columbia and Charley. Later
in his life–perhaps partly as a result of his relationship with his mother–Markham produced *Children
in Bondage* (1914), a tract that calls for child-labor
legislation.

At fifteen Markham ran away from home, apparently because his mother had refused to let him
continue his schooling. During his several months
of adventuring he came into contact with a highwayman who attempted to lure the hardy young Markham into a partnership of crime. Although the de-

Elizabeth Winchell Markham, the poet's mother

and although his experiences at Christian College fell somewhat short of exploitation, Markham nevertheless drew on his time there for future inspiration.

At the end of Markham's stint at Christian College he and several of his schoolmates decided to begin a newspaper, *The Garden City Times*. The young men apparently believed that the spirited battle going on in San Jose between temperance supporters and those who favored more liberal drinking laws would make the newspaper venture profitable. Markham served as literary editor. The paper was supported financially by a wealthy local farmer until the young newspapermen printed an advertisement for a saloon. When their financial sponsor objected, the new journalists decided to take their chances with freedom of the press as well as the popularity of the temperance issue. The newspaper folded after eleven days.

In September 1874, at twenty-two, Markham accepted a teaching post at Coloma, a town near the Nevada border. At Coloma, Markham also met Annie Cox, whom he married on 1 August 1875. Throughout his life Markham had curious and unfortunate experiences with women, and he quickly discovered that Annie Markham's temperament did not combine with his own into a successful union. They were divorced in 1884. Markham's difficulties with her, and indeed with women after her, can be partially traced to his tempestuous relationship with his mother.

During this period of his life Markham met another major influence on his work, Thomas Lake Harris, whose tenets concerning relationships between men and women were particularly compelling for the young poet. Markham found the socialist-utopian writings of this poet and spiritualist—whom many considered a charlatan as well—compatible with his own developing philosophy, and he embraced Harris as a mentor for the rest of his life. Markham's attraction to Harris's work can partly be traced to their similar romantic visions of their own lives. In his biography of Markham, Louis Filler stresses "Markham's sympathy with Harris' cerebrations respecting divine man-woman relations," explaining that the unhappily married Markham found justification for marital infidelity in Harris's "peculiar doctrine of 'counterparts'—which distinguished between divine male-female unity, and mundane, legal commitments." Markham considered Harris's work so important that he served as the philosopher's official biographer, but he never completed the work, which he began after his subject's death in 1906.

tails surrounding the incident remain vague, Markham often described the event—occasionally changing major elements of the story—in his later life, once even calling himself the "Poet Highwayman." Whether or not Markham actually robbed stagecoaches, he somehow managed to come up with a bag of gold pieces that helped to fund his education at California College in Vacaville in 1868. After earning a teacher's certificate at that school in January 1870 Markham moved to Los Berros in San Luis Obispo County, where he built the college building in which he taught briefly.

Following this first teaching stint, Markham became something of a student-teacher at Christian College, a Campbellite school in Santa Rosa, in 1873 and 1874. At Christian he studied a wide variety of subjects and taught grammar and mathematics. Because of the extreme demands on his time and his continuing struggle to find money on which to live, Markham began during this period to develop his sympathies for the working-class masses. Those overworked and underpaid by an uncaring social system figure prominently in the poet's later works,

By the end of the 1870s Markham had made a modest beginning to his literary career. He had already published "Shut the Door Softly" (circa 1872) and "Fatal Love" (circa 1873) in newspapers. After he and Annie moved to Placerville in 1879 he won an election to become county superintendent of schools. He was a respected citizen who, for the first time in his life, had no money troubles. He also began devoting far more of his energies to his poetry.

By 1880 Markham began to sell his poetry to newspapers. Much of his early work is modeled on the romantic lyrics of poets he admired, including Edgar Allan Poe; George Gordon, Lord Byron; and Percy Bysshe Shelley. One of his early nature poems, "In Earth's Shadow," was published in the July 1880 issue of *California Magazine*. He retitled this poem "On the Gulf of Night" when he included it in *The Man with the Hoe and Other Poems* (1899). The publication of this poem initiated in earnest Markham's career as a poet and anticipated the themes and tones of his later works:

The world's sad petrels dwell for evermore
On windy headland or on ocean floor,
Or pierce the violent skies with perilous flights
That fret men in their palaces o' nights,
Breaking enchanted slumber's easeful boat,
With shudderings of their wild and dolorous note;
They blow about the black and barren skies,
They fill the night with ineffectual cries.

In a letter to his mother the poet commented on his intentions for "In Earth's Shadow," explaining that he had tried "to represent the sad spirits of the world, the poor, the broken-hearted,—all the children of defeat, the dwellers in earth's shadow, under the figures of sad petrels that are forevermore dwelling in the waste place of the seas or piercing tempestuous skies on wind-wearied wings." Markham had written a poem far superior to any of his previous works.

Just as Markham's literary and social standing had begun to rise, however, the poet became involved in a series of entanglements that seemed to feed his poetic career at the expense of his personal reputation. In 1883 he began an unusual, perhaps unconsummated, affair with Dr. Elizabeth Senter, a woman five years his senior who practiced medicine in San Jose and had contracted tuberculosis. Markham was granted a divorce from Annie in 1884, presumably so that he could become more deeply involved with Dr. Senter, but the couple did not have much time together. She died on 27 February 1885.

By 1886 Markham had taken up with a second mistress, Caroline Bailey. When the liaison sparked public controversy Markham resigned his school position. The two married on 10 April 1887, and soon after the wedding Markham's mother moved in with them. One of Markham's biographers suggests that the poet was forced at this point to choose between wife and mother. Caroline Markham left her husband; she died in 1894.

Despite—or perhaps because of—his unsettled personal life, Markham's poetic career began to flourish during this period. In the 11 September 1886 issue of *Commonweal*, a British journal edited by William Morris, Markham published "Song of the Workers." His poems were also published in the *Overland Monthly, Scribner's*, and *The Century*, which in June 1887 printed Markham's "After Reading Shakespeare." With the exception of "Song of the Workers," most of Markham's poetry still tended to be romantic lyrics or traditional odes. Markham apparently felt that the change of fortune heralded a shift in his identity. At one point during the mid 1880s he changed his name from Charles Edward Markham to Charles Edwin Markham.

During the late 1880s, as he began to enjoy the fruits of selling his poems to journals and newspapers, he developed an affinity for Jean François Millet's painting *The Man with the Hoe*. Identifying with a painter who could so sympathetically render the plight of overburdened peasants, Markham nurtured his empathy for Millet's work for more than ten years before borrowing the title and sensibilities of the painting for his most popular poem.

By 1890 Markham had accepted a post as the principal of the Tompkins School of Oakland, then a laboratory school for the University of California. His tenure in this position was apparently quite successful, and he enjoyed a privileged status. As the dispenser of justice at the school, however, Markham was once cited by the Society for the Prevention of Cruelty to Children for what they believed was a particularly harsh beating: such a charge seems out of character for a man who would later champion children's rights. Despite this one event Markham is generally believed to have been a good and diligent principal.

While Markham found himself secure at work, he began to confront a fundamental dichotomy in his own thinking and writing. Most of the early poetic successes he had sold to eastern journals had been conventional verses, celebrating nature or the role of the poet, espousing a philosophy of social optimism, and describing a worldview that closely parallels Harris's. Simultaneously, though, Markham counted among his influences Byron, Shelley, Walt Whitman, and Poe. All these figures attracted Markham because of what he envisioned

Opening stanzas of Markham's best-known poem in the 15 January 1899 issue of the San Francisco
Examiner *(American Art Association/Anderson Galleries auction catalogue, sale number 4175,
24–25 April 1935)*

as their rebelliousness and their social consciousness.

During the early 1890s Markham publicly embraced these "radical" figures, taking something of a risk for a poet whose career had begun to flourish because of his conventional verse. In 1893 Markham traveled east for the first time, visiting Chicago, Montreal, New York, and Boston. During this trip he met many of the leading figures of the literary world, the most important of whom for Markham was Hamlin Garland, who had recently published *Main-Travelled Roads* (1891). The two men found a mutual affinity. A few years younger than Markham, Garland had also been raised on hard work in the West, and like Markham he sought to express the plight of the people of the land. Garland even suggested starting a magazine of the West–to be called "The Great West" or "The Wildwest"–and Markham offered suggestions for the venture. Although Garland and others–including Ambrose Bierce–influenced Markham's literary development to some extent, Markham's marriage to Anna Catherine Murphy on 9 June 1898 provided him with more intimate guidance. Like her husband, Anna Markham had been raised near Placerville and had worked hard to become a teacher. Seven years younger than Markham, she became his editor and collaborator, encouraging him to finish "The Man with the Hoe."

Markham completed the poem by the end of 1898, and because he did not consider it one of his "radical" efforts, he contemplated submitting it to *Scribner's.* On 31 December 1898 Markham read the poem at a New Year's party, impressing the guests–including Bailey Millard, the editor of William Randolph Hearst's *San Francisco Examiner.* Millard found the poem so affecting that he published "The Man with the Hoe" in the *Examiner* on 15 January 1899. As Mark Sullivan wrote later, the poem was soon reprinted in newspapers nationwide and in Canada: "Within a week phrases and couplets from it were on every lip. Newspaper editions containing it were exhausted and publishers reprinted it, together with editorials about it." Like most of Markham's poems, "The Man with the Hoe" centers on a striking physical image, in this case a farmer:

> Bowed by the weight of centuries he leans
> Upon his hoe and gazes on the ground,
> The emptiness of ages in his face,
> And on his back the burden of the world.
> Who made him dead to rapture and despair,
> A thing that grieves not and that never hopes,
> Stolid and stunned, a brother to the ox?
> Who loosened and let down this brutal jaw?
> Whose was the hand that slanted back this brow?

Whose breath blew out the light within this brain?

This powerful image dominates the relatively brief poem in which Markham implicitly comments on the social conditions of the day, another common element in his thought and poetry:

> What gulfs between him and the seraphim!
> Slave of the wheel of labor, what to him
> Are Plato and the swing of Pleiades?
> What the long reaches of the peaks of song,
> The rift of dawn, the reddening of the rose?
> Through this dread shape the suffering ages look;
> Time's tragedy is in that aching stoop;
> Through this dread shape humanity betrayed,
> Cries protest to the Judges of the World,
> A protest that is also prophecy.
> O masters, lords and rulers in all lands,
> Is this the handiwork you give to God,
> This monstrous thing distorted and soul-quenched?

The poem made Markham a celebrity and revealed the extent to which he harbored reformist impulses, changing his life in dramatic fashion.

"The Man with the Hoe" became the first of a handful of Markham poems to generate public interest in poetry; in effect, the poem democratized poetry in the United States, if only briefly. It also established Markham as the artistic voice of progressive politics in the United States for many years. Filler compares its impact to that of Harriet Beecher Stowe's best-selling antislavery novel, *Uncle Tom's Cabin* (1852). Bierce was not alone in the judgment that "The Man with the Hoe " is not Markham's best, but it nevertheless defined him for the rest of his life. The work also became the title poem for Markham's first book, *The Man with the Hoe and Other Poems,* one of the most successful volumes of American poetry of the nineteenth century.

An immediate result of Markham's meteoric rise in stature was his decision to move east to New York, where he would make his home for the rest of his life. During this period he wrote articles on a variety of topics for syndication by Hearst. He also began lecturing, which took up enormous amounts of his time and energy–and kept him traveling–for the next forty years.

Markham's fame was enhanced further in 1900 when he wrote the poem "Lincoln, the Man of the People" on commission for the Republican Club of New York. He was chosen by a committee headed by former president William Howard Taft to read his Lincoln poem at the dedication of the Lincoln Memorial in 1922, and in a 1926 article, "How I Wrote 'Lincoln, the Man of the People,'" Markham reminisced in grand romantic style about the events leading to his writing the poem. "Lincoln,

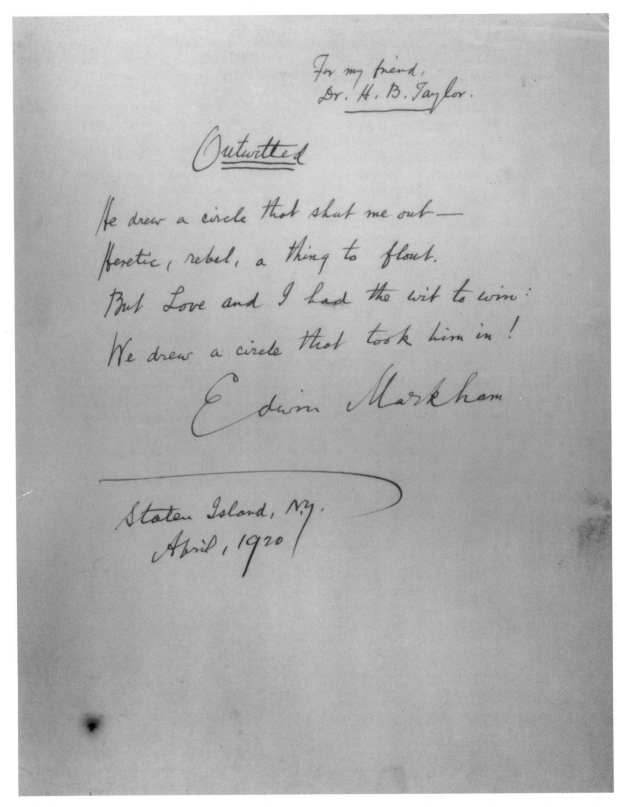

Fair copy of a poem Markham included in his 1915 collection of verse, The Shoes of Happiness and Other Poems *(Lilly Library, Indiana University)*

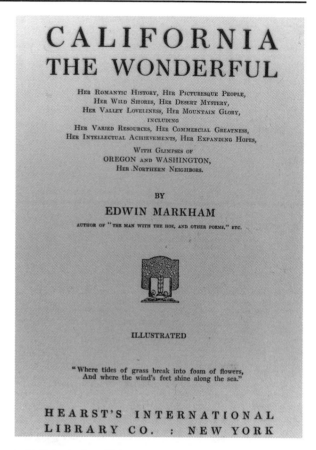

Frontispiece and title page for Markham's 1915 book about his home state

the Man of the People" was the title poem in Markham's second book, *Lincoln and Other Poems* (1901), which was brought out the year after its initial publication in newspapers. The collection also features songs of protest, such as "The Sower" and "The Muse of Labor," but, excepting the title poem, the poems in this book lack the power of those in his first.

Although Markham was immensely popular with the public at the turn of the century—with his opinions sought on a wide range of topical as well as artistic issues—he continued to struggle with the dual impulses of his poetic ambitions. At times the epitome of a genteel writer who conversed easily with establishment figures such as William Dean Howells, Markham also envisioned his poetry as an agent for social reform. Frank Norris, a California literary acquaintance, noted Markham's inner conflict and used the poet as the model for the philosophically mutable protagonist in his 1901 novel *The Octopus.*

For the rest of his long life Markham explored other interests in addition to poetry. *Cosmopolitan* editor Bailey Millard, a friend from Markham's California days, recruited the poet to write a series

of muckraking articles on child labor. With titles such as "The Smoke of Sacrifice," "The Sweat-Shop Inferno," and "Spinners in the Dark," the series revealed Markham to be a compassionate researcher, and he afterward became president of the Child Labor Federation. The culmination of his efforts on the behalf of children was *Children in Bondage,* a book he co-authored with Benjamin B. Lindsey and George Creel.

While Markham continued to produce some poetry—including the popular "Virgilia" (1905), which he later considered one of his best works—he did not publish another volume of poetry until *The Shoes of Happiness and Other Poems* (1915). Despite the lapse of fourteen years between appearances of his book-length collections of poetry and the extent to which his 1915 book signaled his passing from the ranks of serious poets, Markham was probably at the peak of his fame in 1915. He toured almost the entire year, beginning in California, where he had been commissioned to deliver an ode at the Panama-Pacific Exposition. Embraced by audiences as "California's Beloved Poet," Markham began to rewrite his own past, suppressing unpleasant family details while apparently romanticizing his youth.

Edwin and Anna Markham at their home in the West Brighton section of Staten Island, New York

His attempts to mythologize himself culminated in a 1933 biography of the poet by William L. Stidger.

In addition to his own verses Markham made other tangible contributions to poetry. He edited *The Book of Poetry* (1926), a collection later expanded as *The Book of American Poetry, The Book of Classic English Poetry: 600–1830,* and *The Book of Modern English Poetry: 1830–1934* (1934). This editorial effort served in many ways to mark a transition between poetic eras in the United States. Although Markham's editorial skills did not rival his poetic talents, he had the vision to include such figures as Edgar Lee Masters, Vachel Lindsay, and Langston Hughes, among others. Throughout the work one can feel Markham's passion for poetry and his generosity toward a younger generation that would all but ignore him.

Markham continued to write poetry until the end of his life, leaving thousands of unpublished verses at his death. Most commentators agree that his later work lacks the energy of his earlier productions. In 1920, for example, he wrote the less-than-inspiring *Gates of Paradise and Other Poems,* dedicated to Howells. One startling exception is "The Ballad

of the Gallows-Bird," published in the August 1926 issue of H. L. Mencken's *American Mercury.* The poem, which incorporates much of Markham's philosophy as it evolved throughout his life, owes few debts to those who influenced him: "The Ballad of the Gallows-Bird" draws on the poet's vision of the universe, in which life and death are interwoven, to offer what for Markham is a rare grim commentary on the human condition. Tracing a murderer's growing awareness that he has descended to hell, the poem, in typical Markham fashion, uses a striking image to convey the intensity of this realization:

> And now my nearing steps disturbed
>   The ravens at their feast,
> There where the dead man swung in the wind
>   With sound that never ceast.
>
> For they drew their heads from out his brain
>   (Still did the swung rope creak)
> And little crumbs of carrion
>   Clung to each happy beak.
>
> And now they whetter their beads with care
>   Upon the gallows-beam;
> Then slowly turned their knowing eyes
>   Upon me with a gleam.
> A sudden gust, and the strangled shape,
>   That humped and dangling thing,
> Wheeled round its face, with holes for eyes. . . .
>   'Twas I that hung against the skies:
> 'Twas I on the rope a swing!
>
> It was my own, own body I saw
>   A-swing in the spectral night:
> It was my own, own body I saw
>   Fade slowly from my sight.
> And with it faded the hills of home
>   And all my life's delight!
>
> Then a sudden shout crasht into my brain,
>   The truth on my spirit fell. . . .
> God of my soul! I was dead . . . And damned. . . .
>   And trampt the roads of hell!

Markham ultimately thought "The Ballad of the Gallows-Bird" his finest work, even superior to his "Virgilia," and critics generally agree, some even comparing it favorably to Samuel Taylor Coleridge's "The Rime of the Ancient Mariner" (1798). Oddly enough, Markham did not include it in his last collection of poetry, *New Poems: Eighty Songs at Eighty* (1932). Markham read from this last book at a celebration of his eightieth birthday before a crowd that filled Carnegie Hall in his honor.

Markham spent the remaining years of his life traveling and lecturing. He became perilously ill on an extended tour to Mexico in 1938 and never fully recovered. Anna Markham died that same year.

The two events combined to rob Markham of his robust energy. Physically devastated and emotionally exhausted, he finally succumbed on 7 March 1940. He was nearly eighty-eight.

Although Markham's critical reputation has consistently deteriorated since the early twentieth century, no one can doubt that he had a tremendous influence on American poetry. Hailed as "The Dean of American Poetry" for much of his career, Markham made poetry popular and accessible to a wide range of readers, and he left behind a handful of first-rate poems, including "The Ballad of the Gallows-Bird," "Lincoln, the Man of the People," and "The Man with the Hoe." He also served throughout his life as a voice of compassionate reason, and his poems can be credited with infusing some humanity into a culture that periodically needs such a lesson.

Bibliography:

Sophie K. Shields, *Edwin Markham: A Bibliography*, 3 volumes (Staten Island, N.Y.: Wagner College, 1952-1955).

Biographies:

William L. Stidger, *Edwin Markham* (New York: Abingdon Press, 1933);

Louis Filler, *The Unknown Edwin Markham: His Mystery and Its Significance* (Yellow Springs, Ohio: Antioch Press, 1966);

Joseph W. Slade, "Edwin Markham: A Critical Biography," dissertation, New York University, 1971;

George Truman Carl, *Edwin Markham: The Poet for Preachers* (New York: Vantage Press, 1977).

References:

Leonard D. Abbott, "Edwin Markham: Laureate of Labor," *Comrade, An Illustrated Socialist Monthly*, 1 (January 1902): 74-75;

Benjamin De Casseres, "Five Portraits on Galvanized Iron: I," *American Mercury*, 9 (December 1926): 398-399;

B. O. Flower, "Edwin Markham: The Poet-Prophet of Democracy," *Arena*, 35 (February 1906): 143-146;

Jesse Sidney Goldstein, "Two Literary Radicals in 1893," *American Literature*, 17 (May 1945): 152-160;

Virgil Markham, "Literary Tradition on Staten Island," *Staten Island Historian*, 18 (October-December 1956): 33-36; 18 (January-March 1957): 1-5; 18 (April-June 1957): 13-16;

Joseph R. McElrath Jr., "Edwin Markham in Frank Norris's *The Octopus*," *Frank Norris Studies*, 13 (Spring 1992): 10-11;

Joseph W. Slade, "Putting You in the Papers: Ambrose Bierce's Letters to Edwin Markham," *Prospects: An Annual Journal of American Studies*, 1 (1975): 335-368;

Mark Sullivan, "A Picture, A Poem, and the Times," in his *Our Times*, 6 volumes (New York: Scribners, 1926-1935), II: 236-253;

David R. Weimer, "The Man with the Hoe and the Good Machine," in *Studies in American Culture: Dominant Ideas and Images*, edited by Joseph J. Kwiat and Mary C. Turpie (Minneapolis: University of Minnesota Press, 1960), pp. 63-73.

Papers:

Edwin Markham left all of his papers, including unpublished manuscripts, copies of virtually all his work, and his correspondence, to Wagner College, where they are housed in the Markham Archives of Horrmann Library.

Joaquin Miller

(8 September 1839 – 17 February 1913)

Benjamin S. Lawson
Albany State College

BOOKS: *Specimens* (Portland, Oreg.: Carter Hines, 1868);

Joaquin et al. (Portland, Oreg.: S. J. McCormick, 1869; London: J. Camden Hotten, 1872);

Pacific Poems (London: Whittingham & Wilkins, 1871);

Songs of the Sierras (London: Longmans, Green, Reader & Dyer, 1871; Boston: Roberts, 1871);

Songs of the Sun-lands (London: Longmans, Green, Reader & Dyer, 1873; Boston: Roberts, 1873);

Life Amongst the Modocs: Unwritten History (London: Bentley, 1873); republished as *Unwritten History* (Hartford: American Publishing Company, 1874) and *Paquita, The Indian Heroine* (Hartford: American Publishing Company, 1881); revised as *My Own Story* (Chicago: Belford-Clarke, 1890); *My Life Among the Indians* (Chicago: Morrill, Higgins, 1892); and *Joaquin Miller's Romantic Life Amongst the Red Indians* (London: Saxon, 1898);

First Fam'lies in the Sierras (London: Routledge, 1875; revised edition, Chicago: Jansen, McClurg, 1876); revised as *The Danites in the Sierras* (Chicago: Jansen, McClurg, 1881);

The Ship in the Desert (London: Chapman & Hall, 1875; Boston: Roberts, 1875);

The One Fair Woman (3 volumes, London: Chapman & Hall, 1876; 1 volume, New York: Dillingham, 1886);

The Baroness of New York (New York: G. W. Carleton, 1877);

Songs of Italy (Boston: Roberts, 1878);

Songs of Far-away Lands (London: Longmans, Green, Reader & Dyer, 1878);

Shadows of Shasta (Chicago: Jansen, McClurg, 1881);

Forty-Nine: A California Drama [and] *Danites in the Sierras: A Drama in Four Acts* (San Francisco: California Publishing Company, 1882);

Memorie and Rime (New York: Funk & Wagnalls, 1884);

'49: The Gold-Seekers of the Sierras (New York & London: Funk & Wagnalls, 1884);

Joaquin Miller

The Destruction of Gotham (New York & London: Funk & Wagnalls, 1886);

Songs of the Mexican Seas (Boston: Roberts, 1887);

In Classic Shades and Other Poems (Chicago: Belford-Clarke, 1890);

The Building of the City Beautiful (Cambridge & Chicago: Stone & Kimball, 1893; London: Elkin Mathew & John Lane, 1894; revised edition, Trenton, N.J.: Albert Brandt, 1905);

An Illustrated History of the State of Montana, 2 volumes (Chicago: Lewis Publishing Company, 1894);

Songs of the Soul (San Francisco: Whitaker & Ray, 1896);

The Complete Poetical Works of Joaquin Miller (San Francisco: Whitaker & Ray, 1897; London: Routledge, 1897; revised edition, San Francisco: Whitaker & Ray, 1902);

True Bear Stories, edited by David Starr Jordan (Chicago & New York: Rand, McNally, 1900);

As It Was in the Beginning: A Poem (San Francisco: A. M. Robertson, 1903);

Japan of Sword and Love, by Miller and Yone Noguchi (Tokyo: Kanso Runyendo, 1905);

Light: A Narrative Poem (Boston: H. B. Turner, 1907);

Joaquin Miller's Poems, 6 volumes (San Francisco: Whitaker & Ray, 1909–1910);

The Poetical Works of Joaquin Miller, edited by Stuart P. Sherman (New York & London: Putnam, 1923);

Overland in a Covered Wagon: An Autobiography, edited by Sidney G. Firman (New York & London: Appleton, 1930);

Joaquin Miller: His California Diary, edited by John S. Richards (Seattle: Frank McCaffrey at his Dogwood Press, 1936).

SELECTED PERIODICAL PUBLICATIONS–
UNCOLLECTED: "Scenes in Central England," *Overland Monthly,* 6 (May 1871): 409–418;

"Pit River Massacre," *San Francisco Chronicle,* 25 March 1883, p. 1; 1 April 1883, p. 1;

"How I Came to Be a Writer of Books," *Lippincott's,* 38 (1886): 106–110;

"London on the Surface," *San Francisco Call,* 5 February 1893, p. 13;

"Klondike Gold, 1897," *Alaska Review,* 2 (Spring–Summer 1967): 20–39.

The images of the West in Joaquin Miller's immensely popular poetry and prose constitute a major example of late-nineteenth-century American mythmaking. Especially for readers in the East and Europe, Miller's works evoked an exotic and romantic land notable for its escapist appeal if not its verisimilitude. Miller's posturing, his often amateurish versifying of the simple, sentimental, and superficial, his portraying faults of the region such as its tendency to violence and mistreatment of the Native Americans—none of these things undermined the basis for Miller's contemporary fame and influence. He is significant largely because of his reputation as man and as writer rather than for his work. His celebrity status as wild westerner and creator of a fanciful fictive world outweighs the intrinsic aesthetic demerits of his writings. Miller's life and works merge and reveal much of the values and tastes of his audience, just as his diminished reputation in the late twentieth century tells much about this time. In the preface to *The Ship in the Desert* (1875) Miller parallels his role as writer with the exploits of his pioneering parents: "Others will come after us. Possibly I have blazed out the trail for great minds over this field, as you did across the deserts and plains for great men of a quarter century ago."

The son of Hulings and Margaret DeWitt Miller, Cincinnatus Hiner Miller was born near Liberty, Indiana, on 8 September 1839–the year is disputed, but courthouse records list his birth year as 1839. For the first fifteen or so years of his life he moved with his parents from place to place in semi-frontier north-central Indiana, where his father worked variously as shopkeeper, schoolteacher, and farmer. The family lived for a time on land that had been part of the Miami Indian Reserve and then briefly in other small towns before striking out for the Far West via the Oregon Trail in 1852. Young Miller, who had already become intrigued by stories of western heroes and explorers such as John C. Frémont, was given to envisioning a legendary West that seemed to beckon with grandeur and future promise, a land exciting for being anticipated as possibility rather than known as dreary present. During the months of the trek to the Oregon Territory, Miller nurtured a vision of the West as imperfect reality but also as longed-for and deferred ideal.

Because of sketchy evidence and Miller's later self-promoting tales it is possible to provide only an outline of his early years in the West. The Millers initially settled in the Willamette Valley, but they soon took up a claim on the McKenzie River, where in 1853 the last of the five Miller children was born. Among the family's rare respites from labor were the exciting stories told them by "Mountain Joe" De Bloney, a former miner, horse tamer, and scout with Frémont. Miller's journal for 1854 includes his earliest literary attempts, but these few poetic musings seem unimportant in the career of a young man who soon began a life of action, running away from home and joining De Bloney in northern California. There Miller learned the uncertain chances of mining and fell under the influence of De Bloney, whose scheme to found a Native American republic appealed to the future poet, and he spent the winter of 1856–1857 among the Indians of Squaw Valley. Miller sometimes fought along with whites against other tribes, and he reported later that he had been injured in a battle at Castle Crags in 1855 and the Pit River Massacre in 1857. Although he perceived misdeeds and brutality on both sides, his sympathies seemed to lie with the Native Americans. After spending a few months at Columbia College in Eugene City, Oregon, and teaching and prospecting

Self-caricature in a diary Miller kept in 1855–1857 (Willard Morse Collection, Honnold Library, The Claremont Colleges)

in the Washington Territory, he returned to Shasta County, California, to live with Indian friends, including a young woman named Paquita, who by his account became the mother of his daughter, Calli Shasta. In July 1859 these friends may have helped him escape the Shasta City jail just before his trial for stealing a mule or a horse.

Exploits such as these may lie behind Miller's choice of the pseudonym Joaquin, perhaps after bandit Joaquin Murietta, who had become a sort of Mexican folk hero. Exactly when Miller started using this pseudonym is not clear, and poet Ina Coolbrith claimed that she had furnished him the pen name somewhat later. In any case Miller returned to Oregon around 1860, working as a surveyor and schoolteacher before taking up the study of law in the office of George Williams, later U.S. attorney general under President Ulysses S. Grant. After failing to establish a law practice in Idaho he turned briefly to mining again and to riding for a pony-express service. With his modest profits he was able to buy his parents a home in the Willamette Valley, where he also invested in, edited, and wrote for the *Eugene City Democratic Register.* Miller's verse and prose pieces for this newspaper include some quite

controversial pro-southern editorials, written even as his brother John was fighting in Gen. Ulysses S. Grant's army. Miller's was a minority view in Oregon, but it is consistent with his typically siding with the underdog, whether Mexican, Native American, Chinese, or southern American. In the *Eugene City Review,* a literary paper he undertook for a few months in 1862 and 1863, Miller continued to insist on the value of regional autonomy.

On 12 September 1862 Miller married Theresa Dyer, an Oregon poet who under the pen name Minnie Myrtle had made literary contributions to area newspapers. The following spring, seeking to find a milder climate—and no doubt to fulfill literary aspirations—the couple moved to San Francisco, where the *Overland Monthly* and *The Golden Era* (which had earlier accepted pieces from the couple) were helping to create a significant western "school" that included Samuel Langhorne Clemens (Mark Twain), Ina Coolbrith, Bret Harte, and Charles Warren Stoddard. But the Millers found neither literary fame nor fortune there, and they soon returned to Oregon, settling in Canyon City. Miller opened a legal practice, while Minnie Myrtle cared for a daughter, Eveline Maud, and a son, George Brick. For about three years Miller prospered as judge of Grant County, but he often chafed under the routines of family and community life; his letters of the period report that he found little refinement and sentiment in eastern Oregon and apparently in his wife as well. Contentious proceedings, during which accusations of child neglect and moral turpitude were exchanged, resulted in the granting of a divorce on 19 April 1870. Theresa Miller gained custody of a son named Henry Mark, who was born after Eveline and George and whom Miller doubted he had sired. Minnie Myrtle's mother was assigned custody of the older two children for whose support Miller paid $200 a year. His ties with Canyon City broken by scandal, Judge Miller became legally and psychologically free to leave a place in which he had felt culturally isolated.

Late in the 1860s Miller published two thin volumes of verse in Portland. Encouraged by getting these books into print and by the few but generally positive reviews, he took it upon himself to attempt the improbable—to succeed in a true literary capital of the world. After a brief stay in San Francisco, where Stoddard introduced him to Harte, he went on to New York. On 19 August 1870 he took second-class passage on the *Europa* for Glasgow, later visiting London. This eastward movement seems to have been common among writers who mined the West for subject matter but knew that literary fame and the standards of literary culture were created in the centers of publishing in the eastern United States and Europe. Like Harte and Twain, Miller traveled eastward with his literary treasures to cash in on riches and fame. And cash in they did. Twain, Harte, and Miller achieved immense fame and high literary renown. As surely as the cultured easterner Henry James, Miller can be said to have conquered London. During his first days in London, Miller's few dollars went into the printing of a hundred copies of *Pacific Poems* (1871). But favorable notices led to an expanded edition of Miller's verse, *Songs of the Sierras* (1871), published by the established firm of Longmans, Green, Reader and Dyer. In London, Miller became a sensation, "The Poet of the Sierras."

The reasons for Miller's fame are not difficult to find. In style and sentiment his poems were part of an established and easily comprehended tradition of belated Euro-American romanticism, yet he and his subject matter had the appeal of the new and the exotic. While Miller's literary pilgrimage to London included traditional stops at the graves of George Gordon, Lord Byron, and Robert Burns, he appeared in London flamboyantly and untraditionally attired in boots, sombrero, and bearskin cape. To many he was "The Byron of Oregon." Dante Gabriel Rossetti, Robert Browning, and Richard Monckton Milnes, Lord Houghton, were among the many people who wanted to meet the poet who seemed a great and original American and westerner and one of the finest poets the country had produced. Actress Lily Langtry, whom he considered an embodiment of ideal beauty, became one of his favorites. *Songs of the Sierras* and his other works of the early and mid 1870s were met with many and laudatory reviews. Miller became something of a celebrity and literary lion, his provincialisms treated as innovations. Thought of as an authentic if eccentric denizen of the West, he profited from writing about a little-known region that the British considered the most purely American.

Most of Miller's many readers were not prepared to compare his escapist fictive worlds with knowledge of an actual place, but as the nineteenth century wore on, their knowledge of the American West grew, and in the end they came to discover something of the inadequacy of Miller's "pictures" (as he often called them). Miller's novelty could only lessen as he continued to mine the same "exotic" vein in book after book, while other, perhaps more perceptive, western writers appeared as literary rivals. The sentiment and simplicity of his romantic verses began to seem out of date; his obvious, forced rhymes and sing-song, mechanical rhythms seemed increasingly cloyed. Finally, the

popularity of his early western books led to a literary typecasting, so his later books set outside the West were often dismissed and underrated. In other words Miller suffered a fate common to many "regional" writers, and his genius was not of the universal sort to sustain a reputation in the twentieth century—as, for one example, Twain's did. Neither could he be rescued from an antiquarian and regional stereotype on the basis of ethnicity or gender, as Charles Waddell Chesnutt and Kate Chopin have been.

Yet in 1871 *Songs of the Sierras* was widely read and highly praised. When reviewers of this and Miller's other western books did turn to literary considerations they were increasingly prone to mitigate praise with reservations about Miller's characterization, plotting, verse technique, and themes. Early enthusiasm, however, overrode notice of weaknesses in conception and execution. The titles of his works evoked emotion, the allure of strange places and meaningful incident in an Old West already fading into the past. The romantic style of the poems heightened the reader's sense of nostalgia. In fact, *Songs of the Sierras* includes only two poems set in or near those mountains, but all of them share a tone and a tendency to the fantastic. From the start Miller theorized that writing in verse necessitated the choice of melodrama and high passion. As he explained in *Overland in a Covered Wagon* (1930), "there are things that are sacred from severe prose"—presumably even in a California mining camp.

Songs of the Sierras opens with "The Arizonian," a tale of adventure, lost love, and romantic miscalculation. The title character compulsively and sadly reminisces about abandoning a dark-skinned western woman for the eastern woman he left behind in his youth but promised to wed. He returns to the East only to discover that the fair Annette Macleod has long before married and that his western gold serves no purpose. The location of the Arizonian's canyon cabin inspires Miller to vague sentiments and sonorous metric effects:

> And this is the land where the sun goes down,
> And gold is gather'd by tide and by stream,
> And maidens are brown as the cocoa brown,
> And a life is a love and a love is a dream.

At times in Miller's verse too-obvious and forced rhymes dictate and skew meaning and distort natural word order. If the idyllic canyon of love and dreams, not to mention a maiden "brown as the cocoa brown," is so satisfying, why does the central character both abandon this Eden and bemoan the unavailability of his eastern bride? The western

The earliest known photograph of Miller (Herman and Eliza Oliver Historical Museum)

gold he gathers cannot gain for him what he says he wants, whereas for Miller literary proceeds from the region were converted to desired renown in the East and in Europe. The Arizonian's gesture to the East—although he subsequently finds himself adrift, established in neither region—parallels Miller's negotiation of an artistic career by committing himself to the aesthetic terms of the East while employing his colorful western subjects and persona in a place where he was perceived as unique. Unlike his hero, however, Miller was able to return to the West and produce further western myths, eventually becoming something of a self-appointed Pacific Coast prophet.

Several other poems in *Songs of the Sierras* may be taken as characteristic of Miller's western verse. In "The Last Taschastas" Miller voices Indian protest against the depredations of whites and lament for the "vanishing [Native] American." In one imaginative line Miller's Indian narrator reverses the familiar phrase about "beating swords into plowshares" by referring to "the savage white man's plowshare." "The Tale of the Tall Alcalde" describes a miscegenational relationship between an

alcalde, or Spanish judicial officer, and a Native American woman. Heavy casualties do not lessen the Spaniard's sympathy for the dispossessed or his love for Winnema, who in turn nurses him back to health and sacrifices her virtue (followed by a melodramatic suicide) to gain him his freedom from those who consider him a renegade and traitor. But the forlorn alcalde defies those who would detain him, tells his melancholy tale, and disappears into the night, haunted—like many another western hero—by his past. *Songs of the Sierras* also includes "With Walker in Nicaragua," a romantically embellished account of William Walker's actual attempt to take control of that Central American government through military incursion and revolution. (The colorful and mercurial Walker finally succeeded in Nicaragua but failed and was executed when he tried to gain control of Honduras.) "Californian" is replete with typical and tropical exoticism, mountains, and sea; "Kit Carson's Ride" is characterized by fast-paced action and galloping rhythms. "Ina" is a conventional love story set at a Mexican hacienda, while "Myrrh" and "Even So" are about failed love affairs. The volume also includes commemorative encomiums on Burns and Byron. Yet the poems that are in fact "songs" of the Sierras—or at least the West—struck the note that Miller's contemporaries wanted to hear.

Miller's success in England is suggested by an unlikely pairing in his next volume of verse: although the tone, subjects, diction, and far-flung, generally New World settings of *Songs of the Sun-lands* (1873) make it even more extravagantly exotic than *Songs of the Sierras,* Miller dedicated his new book to the Rossettis. The long opening poem, "Isles of the Amazons," and many others are set outside the American West—even outside the Western Hemisphere, as in the case of "Olive Leaves," a series of poems set in the Holy Land. "From Sea to Sea," however, celebrates the desirability and potential of the West, employing it as a symbol of what all America once represented and in this fashion anticipating Miller's most popular poem, "Columbus."

More western than *Songs of the Sun-lands* is Miller's first important prose work, *Life Amongst the Modocs* (1873), dedicated "to the Red Men of America." In date and content this quasi-autobiography falls between Herman Melville's *Typee* (1846) and westerner Helen Hunt Jackson's *A Century of Dishonor* (1881) and *Ramona* (1884). All four works present and, in part, praise native cultures while criticizing many ways and values of Western civilization. Miller's rendition combines the adventures of white protagonists, portrayals of Modoc village life, and protests against injustices in government Indian

Frontispiece and title page for the first collected edition of Miller's verse

policies as well as the public's misunderstandings and indifference. Scenes in mining camps balance those in Indian camps, and acquisitive miners suffer in comparison with Native Americans unaffected by the greed that leads to the violation of their homeland by whites. Yet the Indians are far from perfect, and even a mining camp possesses "history, romance, tragedy, poetry."

While leading a caravan into the wilds of northern California, the first-person narrator is injured in a skirmish with some Indians and taken to their camp. He gradually grows healthier—and more knowledgeable about the ways of the Native Americans, who treat him well. He visits several Indian villages before being allowed to return to white civilization—a small city in which he feels more alone than in the mountains. Turning to mining, he and a man called the Prince pack their gear—"blankets, picks, shovels, frying-pans, beans, bacon, and coffee"—and head off into the high ranges and a camp known as the Forks. Miller's portrait of the Wild

West anticipates later images presented in popular fiction, motion pictures, television, and the graphic arts, including gamblers and prostitutes, and brawling at a saloon called the Howling Wilderness, where a man literally dies with his boots on. The book is filled with descriptions of wildlife, forests, and other mountain scenery. Numbing cold, ice, and snow become backdrops for brutal massacres in which whites are typically the greater offenders. The narrator and the Prince take up with two young Indians: Klamat, a future warrior, and Paquita, a woman "tall, and lithe, and graceful as a mountain lily swayed by the breath of morning."

An old mountaineer, Mountain Joe, becomes the narrator's partner shortly before a full-blown battle during which the narrator's jaw and neck are pierced by an arrow. Recuperating in San Francisco, he soon tires of city life and returns to the mountains, where they witness another melee and the death of Paquita. The narrator constructs and burns a funeral pyre for her and in honor of her people.

Klamat (whose name, appropriately, is also that of a tribe), prophesies his own death in battle, a prophecy soon fulfilled. "The last of the children of Shasta" is now Calli Shasta, apparently the narrator's daughter by Paquita. The note of pathos and valediction continues as he reports a visit to San Francisco twelve years later to see his daughter. She seems muted and out of place in a city school, out of touch with her land and her people. Miller earnestly and poetically evokes sorrow and outrage at the dislocating, if not the passing, of a people. "Shadows of Shasta" (title of the first chapter) darken a significant segment of American history.

Shadows of Shasta (1881)—Miller was given to repeating favorite phrases—carries forward Miller's concerns, this time in fictional form. A young Indian flees ill-intentioned government agents who attempt to capture him and confiscate his home. Protected for a time by two young Indians and their guardian, a lonely maverick miner named Forty-Nine, John Logan nonetheless is captured and forced to live on a reservation, where he and the two children melodramatically and sentimentally pass away. Like the narrator of *Life Amongst the Modocs*, the sympathetic white man is left to mourn the dead and to protest on behalf of Native Americans.

The Ship in the Desert (1875) is quite different, a vaguely wandering long narrative poem treating improbable adventures across the West. Miller's tendency to romantic abstraction and mellifluous musing gets the better of him in this work, in which a regal old husband and his beautiful young bride are pursued across plain and mountain and finally slain by Vasques, a shadowy figure whose precise purposes mystify the reader throughout the poem. Miller's final message seems to be that only in some supernal realm is idealized love possible. Idealization of love and the beloved marks several of Miller's works, especially nonwestern books such as *The One Fair Woman* (1876). This novel, however, does include the memorable young Mollie Wopsus and her western clan traveling in Europe, an entourage that bears comparison with the American tourists in Twain's *Innocents Abroad* (1869) and the American family in James's later *Daisy Miller* (1878) in their confronting European sophistication.

First Fam'lies in the Sierras (1875) is Miller's earliest and most significant work of long fiction. Like Harte's "The Luck of Roaring Camp" (1868), *First Fam'lies in the Sierras* posits a rough-hewn West humanized by "feminine" influences. As in much of *Life Amongst the Modocs*, the setting is an isolated little mining camp in the High Sierra, where crude and uneducated men predominate; not one "respectable" woman is to be seen. Miller's use of the term "first families" as a designation for these poor, unrefined, ordinary folk suggests his democratic view that the common can be worthy in itself and as subject. The saloon, again called the Howlin' Wilderness, serves as courthouse and chapel as well as gambling hall. (Considering the uncouth townsfolk, it seems appropriate not only that their town is in the wilderness but also that there is a wilderness in the town.) The first cultivated lady to arrive is a widow. The "Widder" is "purtier nur a spotted dog." (Miller's use of dialect does not always rise above the ludicrous.) The diminutive and dreamy Little Billie Piper seems to be the only man in camp to become the widow's confidant. Yet under her civilizing influence the town grows gradually better and gentler, never more so than after she gives birth—tended by two prostitutes with proverbial hearts of gold—to Little Half-a-pint scarcely nine months after her marriage to the unsophisticated Sandy. The new family settles down at "the Parsonage," a property left to Sandy by an envious but defeated rival.

Several years pass and the small mining camp grows and changes somewhat, although the "First Fam'lies in the Sierras" remain. After the death of Billie the name Nancy Williams is carved on Billie's tombstone. This disclosure is less shocking to the reader than it might have been if Miller had not earlier digressed to report rumors that the widow was Nancy Williams, the last surviving relative of one of the assassins of Mormon leader Joseph Smith. The widow has helped Nancy remain incognito and thus escape the wrath of the Latter-Day Saints.

Along with essays, poetry, autobiography, and fiction Miller wrote several plays. *Danites in the Sierras* (1882) is a dramatization of *First Fam'lies in the Sierras*, emphasizing in its title and content its vision of the polygamous Mormons as pursuers and persecuters of the virtuous. Anti-Mormon sentiment was not rare in this period and may be found in works from Twain's *Roughing It* (1872) to Zane Grey's *Riders of the Purple Sage* (1912). The rapid action, earthy humor, sentiment, and suspense earned Miller's play long runs on stages in the United States and England. *Forty-Nine: A California Drama* (1882) reprises a title character from Miller's earlier fiction. Conventional sentimentality and melodramatic coincidence mark this story of mistaken identity and conflict between the claims of love and money. Forty-Nine, an old prospector, adrift at times in a haze of nostalgia, optimistically continues to work his old claim long after the glory days of the Gold Rush have come and gone. At first the greedy villain seems the worldly victor, but the girl to whom he becomes engaged turns out not to be an heiress after all. The

Miller writing in a mountain camp, 1903

young hero, Charles Devine, refuses to compete for the hand of the so-called heiress, follows his heart, and courts a spritely girl called Carrots—who, of course, turns out to be the real heiress. Then the audience discovers that Charles is actually the son of Forty-Nine, who finally strikes it rich, as rewards continue to fall to the selfless and sincere.

Miller's heyday as public personality and acclaimed western writer lasted from the early 1870s until the early 1880s. Most of his later writings are set outside the West and sometimes outside the recognizable world altogether; for example, *The Destruction of Gotham* (1886) focuses on life in the streets of New York City, and the poems in *Songs of the Soul* (1896) portray the placeless spirit. As his contemporary following dwindled, Miller found himself repeating some of his old formulas. After his time in England he traveled for several months, visiting Europe, the Near East, Hawaii, and South America. He married Abigail Leland in 1879 and settled in the East. By 1883 the Millers had separated, and Miller went to Oakland, California, where in 1887 he bought land in the hills overlooking the Pacific and built a home with gardens and monuments to John C. Frémont, Moses, and Robert Browning. In 1897 he interrupted his routine of work, receiving visitors, and caring for his mother to join the gold rush-

ers to Alaska and the Yukon, a strenuous undertaking for him. Reports of his trek in California newspapers led to his appearing in fictional form in Frank Norris's novel *The Octopus* (1901).

His last great adventure over, Miller settled again in Oakland, where he fancied himself both western and cosmic guru and where he lived until his death in 1913. During his final decades Miller continued to produce verses, some memorable and some even memorized: a few of his poems voice meaningful thought in powerful images, and others were employed in the American classroom, thus prolonging his reputation at least among the young, who often had to recite "Kit Carson's Ride" or "Columbus." Yet even the worthy late verse was sometimes a re-presentation of earlier themes and phrasing. Oregon and California are again transformed as romantic images in the predictable repetitions and alliteration of Miller's sweet-sounding "songs." Occasionally a poem portrays old western subjects with the freshness of new insight, thereby reminding the reader that apparent freshness itself—the novelty of Miller and of his subjects—was at one time the basis for his reputation.

Collected editions of Miller's poetry in 1909–1910 and 1923 and editions of autobiographical writings in 1930 and 1936 reminded former readers of Miller's work and brought it to the attention of new readers. Yet Miller was largely forgotten in the twentieth century, and what remained of his literary reputation still rested on his early work–and even that work struck sophisticated critics as minor and quaint. The superficial optimism of Miller's depictions of the West as a place of future possibility is balanced by his nostalgia for a mythic Old West. Even in early works Miller expressed a sense of belatedness and eulogized his parents' generation. The romantic hero or the unglamorous miner senses loss and is often alone and melancholy in the present. In his forward-looking mode Miller figured a popular myth of the West that finally turned mystical and merged with the myth of America; his parents blazed a trail across actual deserts for men and women, he wrote, whereas he prepared the way for their minds. As though reality could not support his visions, Miller late in his career wrote of the past or the soul or the city beautiful. In "Columbus," the poem for which Miller is known more widely than any other, he must turn to the past even to discover a future. The poem appears in *Songs of the Soul,* and the voyager's answer to every challenge is the reiterated "Sail On!" The message seemed to support easy American and western and Progressive Era notions, but soon it became the subject of parody. For, if the West is a beginning, on a more profound level discernible in some of his works, it is also the end. It is the end, for example, of the original communal lives of the Native Americans whom he championed. His pilgrims pushing toward the sunset turn ghostly and people the ultimate West, as he phrased it in *Overland in a Covered Wagon.* The impress of the westerly migration antedates and evokes a meditation on human destiny. First and last, the rampart of the High Sierra serves as backdrop to the coastal experience and reminder of the eternal. Most especially, cold and distant and magical Mount Shasta, described in *Life Amongst the Modocs,* becomes a holy monument marking rest: "As lone as God, and white as a winter moon."

Biographies:

Harr Wagner, *Joaquin Miller and His Other Self* (San Francisco: Harr Wagner, 1929);

M. Marion Marberry, *Splendid Poseur: Joaquin Miller–American Poet* (New York: Crowell, 1953).

References:

O. W. Frost, *Joaquin Miller* (New York: Twayne, 1967);

Benjamin S. Lawson, *Joaquin Miller* (Boise, Idaho: Boise State University Press, 1980);

Lawson, "The Presence of Joaquin Miller in *The Octopus,*" *Frank Norris Studies,* 6 (Autumn 1988): 1–3;

Martin S. Peterson, *Joaquin Miller: Literary Frontiersman* (Palo Alto, Cal.: Stanford University Press, 1937);

Kevin Starr, *Americans and the California Dream, 1850–1915* (New York: Oxford University Press, 1973);

Franklin Walker, *San Francisco's Literary Frontier* (New York: Knopf, 1939);

Bruce A. White, "The Liberal Stances of Joaquin Miller," *Rendez-vous: A Journal of Arts and Letters,* 19 (Fall 1983): 86–94.

Papers:

The largest collections of Miller's letters are held by the Huntington Library, San Marino, California, and by the Bancroft Library at the University of California, Berkeley.

John Muir

(21 April 1838 – 24 December 1914)

John P. O'Grady
Boise State University

BOOKS: *The Sierras,* by Muir and others (San Francisco, 1872–1881);

Alaska (Chicago: Northern Pacific Railroad, 1891?);

The Mountains of California (New York: Century, 1894; London: T. Fisher Unwin, 1894; enlarged edition, New York: Century, 1911);

List of the Published Writings of John Muir, Nearly Complete to Date (Martinez, Cal., 1894);

Our National Parks (Boston & New York: Houghton, Mifflin, 1901; London: Gay & Bird, 1902?; enlarged edition, Boston & New York: Houghton Mifflin, 1909);

Let All the People Speak and Prevent the Destruction of the Yosemite Park (San Francisco, 1908);

Stickeen (Boston & New York: Houghton Mifflin, 1909); republished as *Stickeen: The Story of a Dog* (Boston & New York: Houghton Mifflin, 1909);

Mr. John Muir's Reply to a Letter Received from Hon. James R. Garfield in Relation to the Destructive Hetch-Hetchy Scheme (N.p., 1909);

Let Everyone Help to Save the Famous Hetch-Hetchy Valley and Stop the Commercial Destruction Which Threatens Our National Parks (N.p., 1909?);

My First Summer in the Sierra (Boston & New York: Houghton Mifflin, 1911; London: Constable, 1911);

Edward Henry Harriman (Garden City, N.Y.: Doubleday, Page, 1911);

The Yosemite (New York: Century, 1912);

The Story of My Boyhood and Youth (Boston & New York: Houghton Mifflin, 1913);

Travels in Alaska, edited by Marion Randall Parsons (Boston & New York: Houghton Mifflin, 1915);

A Thousand-Mile Walk to the Gulf (Boston & New York: Houghton Mifflin, 1916);

The Cruise of the Corwin: Journal of the Arctic Expedition of 1881 in Search of De Long and the Jeanette (Boston & New York: Houghton Mifflin, 1917);

Steep Trails, edited by William F. Badè (Boston & New York: Houghton Mifflin, 1918);

John Muir, 1872

John of the Mountains: The Unpublished Journals of John Muir, edited by Linnie Marsh Wolfe (Boston: Houghton Mifflin, 1938);

Studies in the Sierra, edited by William E. Colby (San Francisco: Sierra Club, 1950);

The Wilderness World of John Muir, edited by Edwin Way Teale (Boston: Houghton Mifflin, 1954);

To Yosemite and Beyond: Writings from the Years 1863 to 1875, edited by Robert Engberg and Donald Wesling (Madison: University of Wisconsin Press, 1980);

Wilderness Essays, edited by Frank E. Buske (Salt Lake City, Peregrine Smith, 1980);

Mountaineering Essays, edited by Richard Fleck (Salt Lake City, Peregrine Smith, 1984);

Summering in the Sierra, edited by Engberg (Madison: University of Wisconsin Press, 1984);

Letters from Alaska, edited by Engberg and Bruce Merrell (Madison: University of Wisconsin Press, 1993).

Edition: *The Writings of John Muir, Sierra Edition,* 10 volumes, edited by William Frederick Badè (Boston & New York: Houghton Mifflin, 1915–1924).

OTHER: *Picturesque California and the Region West of the Rocky Mountains, from Alaska to Mexico* and *Picturesque California: The Rocky Mountains and the Pacific Slope,* 2 volumes, edited, with seven articles contributed, by Muir (San Francisco & New York: Dewing, 1888);

"Notes on the Pacific Coast Glaciers," in *Harriman Alaska Expedition,* edited by C. H. Merriam (New York, 1901).

John Muir is one of the most important figures in the history of the American conservation movement. A self-styled "poetico-trampo-geologist-bot. and ornith-natural, etc!-!-!," he remains a strong influence on environmentalists, and except for the influence of literary figures such as Henry David Thoreau and poet Gary Snyder, the regard of environmentalists for Muir is unrivaled. He is most often associated with the Yosemite Valley and the mountains of California; Muir joyfully describes these places and his adventures in them. In a passage that bestows on the Sierra Nevada a nickname still widely used, Muir writes with an enthusiasm for the natural world that is as luminous as the mountains he describes: "After ten years spent in the heart of it, rejoicing and wondering, bathing in its glorious floods of light, seeing the sunbursts of morning among the icy peaks, the noonday radiance on the trees and rocks and snow, the flush of the alpenglow, and a thousand dashing waterfalls with their marvelous abundance of irised spray, it still seems to me above all others the Range of Light, the most divinely beautiful of all the mountain-chains I have seen."

At other times, especially later in his career when he directed his energies toward preserving large blocks of American wilderness in the form of national parks, Muir's tone can reach the prophetic pitch of a raging Jeremiah. Of the politicians and engineers who had planned to construct a vast reservoir in the Hetch Hetchy Valley, Muir wrote:

"These temple destroyers, devotees of a ravaging commercialism, seem to have a perfect contempt for Nature, and, instead of lifting their eyes to the God of the mountains, lift them to the Almighty Dollar. Dam Hetch Hetchy! As well dam for water-tanks the people's cathedrals and churches, for no holier temple has ever been consecrated by the heart of man." Although all but one of Muir's books were published in the twentieth century, by the end of the nineteenth century his periodical articles—beginning with "Yosemite Valley in Flood," which appeared in April 1872 in the *Overland Monthly*—had established his literary voice as one of the most remarkable in the American West.

Yet Muir was more than fifty years old before he began actually to assemble his books, the first of which he did not publish until 1894. One explanation for this serotinous debut might be a Calvinist skepticism of secular words, a disposition Muir inherited from his father. Another might be his temperamental aversion to long spells of indoor activity: Muir took his greatest joy in being out in the world, which is the great theme of his writing. The labor of composing lengthy prose came neither naturally nor easily to him; in the early 1870s he confessed in his journal:

> I have a low opinion of books; they are but piles of stones set up to show coming travelers where other minds have been, or at best signal smokes to call attention. . . . No amount of word-making will ever make a single soul to *know* these mountains. . . . One day's exposure to mountains is better than cartloads of books.

The development of Muir's career as a writer is best traced not by following the chronology of his book publication but by turning to his journals, letters, magazine articles, and newspaper pieces that became the trove from which he could draw in writing his books. Muir the writer is best understood as Muir the reviser.

The third of eight children, Muir was born in the seaside town of Dunbar, Scotland, on 21 April 1838. His father, Daniel Muir, adhered to an especially dour form of evangelical Presbyterianism, the influence of which was enormous and regrettable on all of his children, particularly on John, who spent his early years rebelling against his stern authoritarianism. John Muir's mother, Anne Gilrye Muir, is said to have had a more "poetical" nature, and she tempered Daniel's negative effect on the family. At the grammar school in Dunbar young Muir received his first formal education. During these years he was happiest when he escaped his father's uncom-

Muir's 10 May 1882 letter expressing interest in founding an alpine club (from Holway R. Jones, John Muir and the Sierra Club, *1965)*

promising gaze and reveled in the Scottish landscape surrounding his hometown.

In 1849 Daniel Muir decided to emigrate to America, so he sold his grain and feed store and transplanted his family to a pioneer farm near Madison, Wisconsin. John Muir's memoir of his childhood, *The Story of My Boyhood and Youth* (1913), is notable less for describing life on a frontier family farm than for documenting the cruel life he and the rest of the family suffered under his father. It was said around the town that "Old Man Muir works his children like cattle," and in fact Daniel Muir worked his son so hard that the boy's growth was stunted. After John finally left the farm in his early twenties he added one inch to his height and reached his full adult stature of five feet ten inches.

During his Wisconsin years Muir experienced the first of several encounters with death. This first occurred as he was digging an extremely deep well, which his father had ordered him to do. As he resumed his excavations at the bottom of the eighty-foot shaft Muir was overcome by carbon dioxide poisoning; only by a tremendous act of will—a trait that later served him well in his extraordinary feats of solo mountaineering—was he able to crawl back into the bucket that his father had used to lower him. Daniel Muir hauled the bucket up just in time. After begrudging his son a couple days to recover from this experience the elder Muir ordered his son back to the bottom of the well to complete the work, although this time he took precautions to ensure adequate ventilation. Years later when people criticized Muir for publishing such accounts of his father's abusiveness, he defended himself by saying, "There is one thing I hate with a perfect hatred—cruelty for anything or anybody!"

In 1860 Daniel Muir's influence over his son began to wane when the young man displayed some of his inventions at the state agricultural fair. One of these was an ingenious "early rising machine," a device that served as a crude alarm clock: it tilted the bed and tossed the sleeper onto the floor. In Madison the young man also attracted the attention of Jeanne Carr, whose husband, Ezra, was a professor of science at the University of Wisconsin, and in the following year the twenty-three-year-old Muir enrolled at the university. Ezra Carr awakened Muir's interest in the systematic study of geology and botany, and Jeanne Carr, in nurturing the young man's literary talents and his love for nature, profoundly influenced Muir's life, first in Wisconsin and later in California. He left the university after two years, in the middle of the Civil War, and spent the next two years wandering about Canada to botanize.

By 1867 his skill in mechanics led him into a partnership in a carriage-manufacturing company at Indianapolis, but a serious eye injury left him temporarily blinded. Upon recovering his sight he resolved to forsake the pursuit of business and manufacturing for the wilderness. "This affliction has driven me to sweet fields," he commented. "God has to nearly kill us sometimes," he concluded, "to teach us lessons." A few months later Muir set forth on a long walking trip through the South, the account of which makes up his first journal. In a lively hand he inscribed the inside cover of the notebook with words that heralded his destiny as one of the most lyrical American writers on the natural world: "John Muir, Earth-planet, Universe." This journal, *A Thousand-Mile Walk to the Gulf,* was published in 1916, two years after Muir's death. The opening words of this book are vintage Muir, barely able to contain his youthful enthusiasm for stepping into unfamiliar but promising territory: "I had long been looking from the wild woods and gardens of the Northern States to those of the warm South, and at last, all drawbacks overcome, I set forth on the first day of September, 1867, joyful and free, on a thousand-mile walk to the Gulf of Mexico." Although the book can be read as Muir's conversion narrative, a story of his awakening to the spiritual life, the events recounted in this narrative present a culture that was also undergoing a conversion. Following the Civil War the United States was changing rapidly, becoming an urban, industrialized society that embraced increasingly scientific and positivistic views—as well as the milieu of the robber bar-

ons and their wanton exploitation of western lands. As Michael P. Cohen explains, "Muir's tense and excited state of mind during this period reflects not just a personal crisis, but a crisis in world-view of the kind experienced particularly by scientists and philosophers during historical epochs when, suddenly, nobody is sure exactly what the world is like."

One of the central events in *A Thousand-Mile Walk to the Gulf* occurs when Muir, having run out of cash and being wary of the superstitious local people, makes camp in "Bonaventure," an old graveyard near Savannah, Georgia, where he reckons that the locals will be too fearful to come. During the days while he anxiously waits for money from his brother to arrive by post, Muir manages to avoid the morbid brooding of someone forced to bivouac with the dead, and in reflecting on the linkage between human beings and nature, between life and death, he undergoes an epiphany. The old graveyard is deep in a wild wood, and he quickly discovers that this place, rather than being the haunt of dead humans, is the home of many living plants and wild animals:

> I gazed awe-stricken as one new-arrived from another world. Bonaventure is called a graveyard, a town of the dead, but the few graves are powerless in such a depth of life. The rippling of living waters, the song of birds, the joyous confidence of flowers, the calm, undisturbable grandeur of the oaks, mark this place of graves as one of the Lord's most favored abodes of life and light.

Muir reaches a conclusion that allows him all at once to throw off the vestiges of his father's puritanical religion: "On no subject are our ideas more warped and pitiable than on death. Instead of the sympathy, the friendly union, of life and death so apparent in Nature, we are taught that death is an accident, a deplorable punishment for the oldest sin, the arch-enemy of life, etc."

In recognizing that the wilderness was not a howling waste but a companionable home, Muir was presaging a change in the cultural attitudes toward wild places, a change that environmental historian Roderick Nash has documented in *Wilderness and the American Mind* (1967). By 1867 Muir had begun to think on a track very different from that of the utilitarianism that Gifford Pinchot came to espouse in arguing for the formation of an agency to manage the vast forest reserves of the United States. As if to anticipate the debate he had with Pinchot three decades later, Muir writes: "The world, we are told, was made especially for man—a presumption not supported by all the facts." Language such as this—typical of his eloquence and passion—has transformed Muir into an icon for contemporary environmentalists.

Upon reaching Florida at the end of his thousand-mile walk, Muir was overcome with malarial fever that nearly killed him. After recovering, he made his way by ship to California, where he arrived on 28 March 1868. A six-week walk across the state brought him at last to the Yosemite Valley, which he took great delight in exploring. In the nearby Central Valley he found ranch employment that led him to a sheepherding job in the Sierras the following summer. His experience during summer 1869 provided the basis for *My First Summer in the Sierra* (1911), another book that, like *A Thousand-Mile Walk to the Gulf,* was first drafted in a journal. Because many years intervened between Muir's composing and the publication of *My First Summer in the Sierra,* scholars have disagreed about how extensively Muir may have revised his original journal manuscript, but in any event the book remains a key text in American nature writing. In her introduction to a Penguin edition of *My First Summer in the Sierra* Gretel Ehrlich has called this work "the most purely refreshing, savory, and lyrical of all John Muir's books." William F. Kimes and Maymie B. Kimes, Muir's bibliographers, regard the book as Muir's best.

Although written in a journal format, *My First Summer in the Sierra* provides a sustained narrative of both exploration and conversion. During summer 1869 Muir was hired by Pat Delaney, ostensibly to help tend sheep, but Muir writes that Delaney's real interest was "to have a man about the camp whom he could trust to see that the shepherd did his duty." The job proved undemanding, and this gave Muir ample time to explore the high peaks of the upper Tuolumne region. The narrative progresses with the season and with the geographical shifts of the agricultural season, beginning in the lower foothills in June and reaching the High Sierra by July. Muir enthusiastically describes the plants, animals, and terrain he encounters along the way, and with each increase in the elevation of his camp the intensity of his prose increases. "Exhilarated with the mountain air," he writes on 9 July, "I feel like shouting this morning with excess of wild animal joy." Ten days later he adds: "From form to form, beauty to beauty, ever changing, never resting, all are speeding on with love's enthusiasm, singing with the stars the eternal song of creation." The entry for 25 July is one of the more famous passages in all of Muir's writing:

No Sierra landscape that I have seen holds anything truly dead or dull, or any trace of what in manufactories is called rubbish or waste; everything is perfectly clean and pure and full of divine lessons. This quick, inevitable interest attaching to everything seems marvelous until the hand of God becomes visible; then it seems reasonable that what interests Him may well interest us. When we try to pick out anything by itself, we find it hitched to everything else in the universe.

After his first summer in the Sierra, Muir spent much of his next ten years living in and exploring the range. During the early 1870s he devoted his time to firsthand study of Sierra geology, and from this he developed a theory of the glacial origin of the Yosemite Valley and incorporated his findings in a series of magazine articles, his earliest published writings. Muir intended these separate essays to constitute a volume, but other projects attracted his attention, and the essays were never published in book form until the Sierra Club collected them as *Studies in the Sierra* (1950).

The major reason Muir turned from writing geological articles for specialists was his desire to attract a popular audience; he was beginning to think that he could make a living by writing. With the encouragement of Carr—who was now living in Berkeley, where her husband had taken a position at the new University of California—Muir submitted his work to literary journals such as the *Overland Monthly,* which began publishing his articles in 1872. Perhaps the most engaging of Muir's articles written in the early 1870s is "A Geologist's Winter Walk," which appeared in April 1873 in this journal.

Actually an excerpt from a letter that he wrote to Carr (who submitted it for publication without Muir's knowledge), the essay has the refreshing spontaneity that Muir must have experienced during his risky scramble up Tenaya Canyon, one of the more inaccessible of Sierra landscapes. Having just returned to the Yosemite country after a lengthy stay in San Francisco, Muir plunged into the wildest country he could find, as if to purge himself of all the city poisons that had accrued in his soul. In his efforts to heal his spiritual malaise, Muir sounds like an ascetic, writing that "a fast storm and a difficult cañon are just the medicine I require." Soon into this hike and its spiritual cleansing he slips and falls, knocking himself unconscious among the boulders. When he regains consciousness, he is "confident that the last town-fog had been shaken from both head and feet." Tenaya Canyon has restored him to his mountain mind: "Not one of all the assembled rocks or trees seemed remote. How impressively their faces shone with responsive love." The most significant consequence of this purgation, however, is the new resolve with which Muir pursues his writing: he promises Carr that he will "cast away my let-

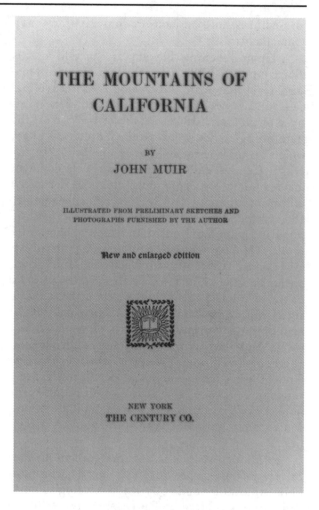

Frontispiece and title page for Muir's third book, which includes his account of climbing Mount Ritter

ter pen, and begin 'Articles,' rigid as granite and slow as glaciers."

Muir's tumble in Tenaya Canyon could well have been fatal, but in rendering his account of it to Carr he passes over it quickly. Brushing off these near-death encounters and focusing on the illumination that comes in their wake became a trademark of Muir's work. He was an inveterate risk-taker when exploring alpine terrain, and more often than not—especially during the 1870s—he traveled alone. In *My First Summer in the Sierra* he established a narrative pattern that he used repeatedly in his mountaineering accounts: ignoring the urgings of common sense and putting himself into exceedingly dangerous positions. Muir may have resorted to this technique as a form of spiritual practice, which he used repeatedly to heighten his awareness of being in the world. "After withdrawing from such places," he writes in *My First Summer in the Sierra* regarding the precipitous rim of the Yosemite Valley, "excited with the view I had got, I would say to myself, 'Now don't go out

on the verge again.' But in the face of Yosemite scenery cautious remonstrance is vain; under its spell one's body seems to go where it likes with a will over which we seem to have scarce any control."

This type of experience recurs in one of Muir's more thrilling pieces of writing, an account of his 1872 ascent of Mount Ritter. Having originally titled the essay "In the Heart of the California Alps" (1880), Muir later revised and retitled it "A Near View of the High Sierra," which he includes as the fourth chapter of *The Mountains of California* (1894). Cohen hails it as "the seminal text" in the Muir canon because the essay "explores the process of awakening and enlightenment" and without it "much of what Muir thought in the seventies would lack true and immediate significance to the modern reader." Muir begins his narrative by recounting how in October, despite the threat of early Sierra snowstorms, he guided into the Tuolumne region two artists who were seeking to paint a "typical alpine landscape." After finding a view that pleases the artists Muir leaves them to their work for a few days and sets off to explore the yet unclimbed massif of Mount Ritter, a strenuous two-day hike from Tuolumne.

As he approaches the peak he keeps reminding himself that it is too late in the season to be attempting any major climb, especially that of the 13,157-foot Mount Ritter. "No," he writes, "I must wait till next summer. I would only approach the mountain now, and inspect it, creep about its flanks, learn what I could of its history, holding myself ready to flee on the approach of the first storm-cloud." Yet, in a moment recalling his excursions to the verge of the Yosemite cliffs, Muir suddenly reverses himself: "But we little know until tried how much of the uncontrollable there is in us, urging across glaciers and torrents, and up dangerous heights, let the judgment forbid as it may." He proceeds to climb the peak–by an extremely hazardous route.

Still trying to convince himself and his reader that he will climb only as far as it is necessary to "obtain some fine wild views for my pains," he ascends the mountain via a formidable avalanche gully. But as is always the case for John Muir, one step leads to another, and he finds himself high on the side of the mountain at the foot of a sheer drop "which seemed absolutely to bar further progress." There is, however, no turning back; it would be even more dangerous to attempt to descend. What follows is one of the most significant passages in the annals of American mountaineering literature:

> After gaining a point about half-way to the top, I was suddenly brought to a dead stop, with arms outspread, clinging close to the face of the rock, unable to move hand or foot either up or down. My doom appeared fixed. I *must* fall. There would be a moment of bewilderment, and then a lifeless rumble down the one general precipice to the glacier below.
>
> When this final danger flashed upon me, I became nerve-shaken for the first time since setting foot on the mountains, and my mind seemed to fill with a stifling smoke. But this terrible eclipse lasted only for a moment, when life blazed forth with preternatural clearness. I seemed suddenly to become possessed of a new sense. The other self, bygone experiences, Instinct, or Guardian Angel,–call it what you will,–came forward and assumed control. Then my trembling muscles became firm again, every rift and flaw in the rock was seen as through a microscope, and my limbs moved with a positiveness and precision with which I seemed to have nothing at all to do. Had I been born aloft upon wings, my deliverance could not have been more complete.

If in writing *The Pilgrim's Progress* (1678) John Bunyan had rendered his character Christian as a mountaineer, that allegorical figure would seem much like the John Muir who ascended Mount Ritter. *The Pilgrim's Progress* was in fact one of Muir's favorite books, and he was known to carry it, along with the New Testament and a copy of Robert Burns's poetry, with him on his Sierra explorations. Like Bunyan's spiritual classic, Muir's "Near View of the High Sierra," *A Thousand-Mile Walk to the Gulf,* and *My First Summer in the Sierra* can all be read as conversion narratives. The protagonist in each case undergoes a spiritual transformation, an "awakening" that brings him to joyous rapture.

Although some interpreters of Muir's work have suggested that his attitude is that of a proto-Taoist or Zen Buddhist, Muir's spiritual background is strongly Christian, as the language of his writing consistently suggests. For instance, this passage from *My First Summer in the Sierra* has its heritage in the tradition of Cotton Mather and Jonathan Edwards:

> Perched like a fly on this Yosemite dome, I gaze and sketch and bask, oftentimes settling down into dumb admiration without definite hope of ever learning much, yet with the longing, unresting effort that lies at the door of hope, humbly prostrate before the vast display of God's power, and eager to offer self-denial and renunciation with eternal toil to learn any lesson in the divine manuscript.

To compare the philosophical orientation of Muir with that of Saint Francis of Assisi would be more illuminating than with that of Lao-Tzu. The writings of geologist Clarence King, author of "The Ascent of Mount Tyndall" in his *Mountaineering in the Sierra Nevada* (1872), provide a contrast to Muir's work. King's prose is informed–indeed, at times torn asunder–by the rhetoric of nineteenth-century science; his account of climbing Mount Tyndall is one of the triumph of man over nature rather than a conversion narrative. Between the works of Muir and King lies a spectrum of American attitudes toward the wild.

The best expression of Muir's philosophy on the importance of wild places and animals is in his essay "Wild Wool," collected in his *Wilderness Essays* (1980). There Muir refutes "the barbarous notion . . . almost universally entertained by civilized men, that there is in all manufactures of nature something essentially coarse which can and must be eradicated by human culture," and he strongly attacks notions that human beings are at the center of the universe and that nature was made merely to be exploited by those human beings. "Wild wool is finer than tame!" Muir exclaims, and he demonstrates this by comparing the quality of wool found in domestic sheep to that in the wild bighorns of the western mountains. In this critique of domestic sheep Muir is critiquing his society. His praise of wild sheep is an exhortation, and his voice is that of a Jeremiah urging his readers to recover a lost virtue by restoring their appreciation for the primal, which the wilderness embodies. "Would it not be well," he asks rhetorically, "for someone to go back as far as possible and take a fresh start?" In later years when Muir argued vehemently for the creation of national parks, the jeremiad became his signature genre. His influence has remained evident in the popular use of this rhetoric by members of the environmental movement.

Muir spent much of the 1870s living in the mountains of California and from time to time making excursions to other ranges along the Pacific Slope and into the Great Basin. In 1879 he made his first trip to Alaska, where he explored Glacier Bay with the Reverend S. Hall Young, a missionary. During the 1870s Muir also wrote prolifically: he published nearly one hundred pieces in magazines and newspapers. In 1880 he married Louie Wanda Strentzel, the daughter of a successful fruit rancher of Martinez, California, and for the next decade Muir devoted much of his time to managing his father-in-law's ranch, which he eventually inherited. He also assumed the responsibilities of fatherhood. His wife gave birth to Wanda in 1881 and to Helen in 1886. Muir did not give up writing during this period, but especially after his daughters were born, his productivity greatly diminished.

The first work to bear Muir's name on the title page was *Picturesque California and the Region West of the Rocky Mountains, from Alaska to Mexico* and *Picturesque California: The Rocky Mountains and the Pacific Slope* (1888), a two-volume collection of nature studies that he edited. He also contributed seven articles, most of them revisions and collations of previous pieces. A coffee-table travel book, this collection is most notable for Muir's essay on Mount Shasta, a revision of what he had originally written in two essays, "Shasta in Winter" (1874) and "Snow Storm on Mt. Shasta" (1877). His work on this project was slow and tedious, and Linnie Marsh Wolfe recounts the emotional difficulties Muir was having during this period, with his father having recently died and his father-in-law nearing death. Wolfe writes that managing the Strentzel ranch had also taken its toll on Muir's good humor, a fact most evident to Muir's wife:

> Louie by this time almost hated the ranch for what it had done to her husband. Nobody knew better than she that he had come to a parting of the ways. His labored, uninspired efforts on the first *Picturesque California* arti-

cles told her that whatever divine fire he had once possessed was all but gone. He must get out into the wilderness once more to recapture it.

Wolfe perhaps overstates the case, as Muir was far from housebound during the 1880s. He made three trips to Alaska during this time, and he made several more during the remainder of his life—all of which provided material for three of his late works: *Stickeen* (1909), *Travels in Alaska* (1915), and *The Cruise of the Corwin: Journal of the Arctic Expedition of 1881 in Search of De Long and the Jeanette* (1917). Although each of these works is charming and certainly enjoys a strong following among fans of Muir's writing, they lack the power of his earlier pieces about his Sierra experiences. This might be because Muir wrote about Alaska as a tourist; he never settled there for an extended period, and he certainly never *lived* in the wilds of Alaska as he had in the Yosemite Sierra. Weaknesses in *Travels in Alaska* can also be attributed to the fact that Muir himself never completed the manuscript. He was engaged in writing this work at the time of his death, and although he left it unfinished, his secretary, Marion Randall Parsons, shaped the manuscript into publishable form. Regardless of its weaknesses, the book remains one of Muir's more popular works.

As an artist Muir must have felt, after he had edited *Picturesque California,* that he was in danger of becoming a hack writer for tourists, but such doubts disappeared in 1889 when he met Robert Underwood Johnson, editor of *The Century Magazine,* a popular and influential journal. On a camping trip to Tuolumne Meadows the two men began to formulate a campaign to make Yosemite into a national park. Wolfe records that Johnson said, "Muir loved this region as a mother loves a child," and he urged Muir to write two articles for *The Century*—to describe the beauty of Yosemite, the threats that unbridled use of the area posed to the mountains, and the need to designate it all as a national park. Muir accepted the offer and thus embarked on the final stage of his career, that of a political activist. From then on he directed his literary talents to developing a political constituency for wilderness. Much of his later writing—including his revisions of earlier essays that he incorporated into his books—should be understood in this light.

With the editorial expertise and encouragement of Johnson, Muir cobbled together from earlier pieces the first book that he could truly call his own. Although only the first chapter of *The Mountains of California* was entirely new material, the book was an immediate and resounding success. Muir

Three of Muir's illustrations for My First Summer in the Sierra: *"Junipers in Tenaya Cañon" (top), "Approach of Dome Creek to Yosemite" (bottom left), and "View of Upper Tuolumne Valley" (lower right)*

A cartoon published in the San Francisco Call *(circa 1909) ridiculing Muir and his opposition to the Hetch Hetchy water project*

and Johnson had hoped that the volume would galvanize public sentiment around issues of conservation, and it did exactly that. Muir became the spokesman for wilderness, a position that he held for the rest of his life, and the reputation he established during these years abides.

The Mountains of California consists of sixteen chapters of rapturous descriptions of plants, animals, mountains, and Muir's adventures among them. The book conveys Muir's profound love for wild places, a love haunted by loss, since human beings, by rapidly expanding urban territory into those wild places, were eradicating them. "When California was wild," Muir writes in the concluding chapter, "it was one sweet bee-garden throughout its entire length, north and south, and all the way across from the snowy Sierra to the ocean." He laments the "deterioration and destruction" of the natural landscape and cites the "sheep evil" (the sheep-ranching operations that made Muir disapprovingly refer to sheep as "hooved locusts") as the reason that so much of the state's grasslands was being denuded. Muir portrays pristine California—before Americans arrived in great numbers—as a lost Eden.

Included in *The Mountains of California* is Muir's revised account of his ascent of Mount Ritter as well as his account of another well-known episode in his life: the time he climbed a Douglas fir in the forests of the Yuba watershed and rode out a fierce storm. "A Wind-Storm in the Forests"—originally published as "A Wind Storm in the Forests of the Yuba" in *Scribner's Monthly* in 1878—is the tenth chapter of *The Mountains of California*. Muir opens this narrative with typical exuberance: "The mountain winds, like the dew and rain, sunshine and snow, are measured and bestowed with love on the forests to develop their strength and beauty." Yet a lingering Calvinist belief that adversity builds character, a belief seared into Muir by his father's cruelty, is implicit. What is good for trees must also be good for humans, Muir insists; thus, at the height of one of "the most bracing wind-storms conceivable," he heads for the summit of the highest ridge and climbs a tree that is one hundred feet high and that "fairly flapped and swished in the passionate torrent, bending and swirling backward and forward, round and round, tracing indescribable combinations of vertical and horizontal curves, while I clung with muscles firm braced, like a bobolink on a reed."

The moral of this experience, as it so often is in Muir's writing, is that human beings are not separate from nature and that they simply delude themselves or indulge in arrogance if they believe otherwise. The chapter concludes with one of his most eloquent expressions of the oneness of all:

> We all travel the milky way together, trees and men; but it never occurred to me until this storm-day, while swinging in the wind, that trees are travelers in the ordinary sense. They make many journeys, not extensive ones, it is true; but our own little journeys, away and back again, are only little more than tree-wavings—many of them not so much.

This passage is not unusual in Muir's writing. Compare it to his reflections on a dead bear that his Yosemite journal records he came upon in 1871:

> There are not square-edged inflexible lines in nature. We seek to establish a narrow lane between ourselves and the feathery zeros we dare to call angels, but ask a partition barrier of infinite width to show the rest of creation its proper place. . . .

> Bears are made of the same dust as we, and breathe the same winds and drink of the same waters. A bear's days are warmed by the same sun, his dwellings are overdomed by the same blue sky, and his life turns and ebbs with heart-pulsings like ours, and was poured from the same First Fountain. And whether he at last goes to our stingy heaven or no, he has terrestrial immortality. His life not long, not short, knows no beginning, no ending. To him life unstinted, unplanned, is above the accidents of time, and his years, markless and boundless, equal Eternity.

Much of Muir's significance as a writer and thinker lies in the counterpoise he presents to the growing strength of utilitarianism and positivism in late-nineteenth-century American thought and social life.

This countercultural resistance that Muir exerted is best exemplified in his dispute with Gifford Pinchot, founder of the United States Forest Service. After an initial period of alliance the two men in 1897 suffered a profound disagreement that split the early members of the conservation movement into two camps—the utilitarians, who followed Pinchot, and the "preservationists," who stood behind Muir. Muir redoubled his efforts to have large segments of public land closed to additional resource exploitation—including the grazing of sheep—by designating such lands as national parks. Two of his books, *Our National Parks* (1901) and *The Yosemite* (1912), demonstrate the extent to which he redirected his efforts toward politics.

Our National Parks includes ten articles he originally had published in the *Atlantic Monthly,* and all of these were designed to rouse public support for protecting western wild lands. "Any fool can destroy trees," he inveighs in "The American Forests," his final chapter. "They cannot run away; and if they could, they would still be destroyed,—chased and hunted down as long as fun or a dollar could be got out of their bark hides, branching thorns, or magnificent bole backbones."

The Kimeses have described *The Yosemite* as "the least appealing of Muir's books since much of it is either a re-write or reprint of previously published material." Nevertheless, this tourist guidebook is important, because it concludes with Muir's plea to save the Hetch Hetchy Valley from officials representing the water interests of San Franciscans who wished to dam the valley canyon for a reservoir, a canyon that was comparable in magnificence to that of the Yosemite Valley. Although he lost his battle to save Hetch Hetchy Valley, Muir contributed significantly to the conservation movement. "In his plea for Hetch Hetchy," Cohen explains in his foreword to a 1986 edition of *The Yosemite,* "Muir established the modern argument for wilderness." In formulating his case for preserving Hetch Hetchy, Muir comes across like an old-time preacher:

> That anyone would try to destroy such a place seems incredible; but sad experience shows that there are people good enough and bad enough for anything. The proponents of the dam scheme bring forward a lot of bad arguments to prove that the only righteous thing to do with the people's parks is to destroy them bit by bit as they are able. Their arguments are curiously like those of the devil, devised for the destruction of the first garden—so much of the very best Eden fruit going to waste; so much of the best Tuolumne water and Tuolumne scenery going to waste. Few of their statements are even partly true, and all are misleading.

The decision to dam Hetch Hetchy was made in December 1913, one year before Muir's death. He was buried in the Strentzel family graveyard, now in suburban Martinez, California. The big Victorian house that he inherited from his wife after her death in 1905 is administered by the National Park Service. Muir's work has never fallen into obscurity; in fact, his reputation began to soar during the wave of environmentalism that began to sweep the United States during the 1960s. During the 1980s he became the patron saint of radical environmentalists who called themselves Earth First!, and each year Muir is honored by the celebration of Earth Day on his birthday. His life and work remain strong influences on all who struggle to preserve the integrity of wildlands.

Muir's greatest influence on western writers is in his vision of a harmonious relationship between human beings and their environment. The tradition of sympathetic writing about the western lands is strong; one can see it in the works of writers such as Gary Snyder, Terry Tempest Williams, Ann Zwinger, Edward Abbey, Lew Welch, Gary Paul Nabhan, Gretel Ehrlich, and others.

Muir concludes his first Sierra journal: "Here ends my forever memorable first High Sierra excursion. I have crossed the Range of Light, surely the brightest and best of all the Lord has built; and rejoicing in its glory, I gladly, gratefully, hopefully pray I may see it again." To judge from the writing that has continued to appear about the American West, Muir's vision remains powerful. For this, too, he would be grateful.

Letters:

Letters to a Friend: Written to Mrs. Ezra S. Carr, 1866–1879 (Boston & New York: Houghton Mifflin, 1915);

Dear Papa: Letters between John Muir and His Daughter Wanda, edited by Jean Hanna Clark and Shirley

Sargent (Fresno, Cal.: Panorama Books West, 1985).

Bibliography:

William F. Kimes and Maymie B. Kimes, *John Muir: A Reading Bibliography* (Fresno, Cal.: Panorama West Books, 1986).

Biographies:

William Frederic Badè, *The Life and Letters of John Muir,* 2 volumes (Boston: Houghton Mifflin, 1924);

Linnie Marsh Wolfe, *Son of the Wilderness: The Life of John Muir* (Madison: University of Wisconsin Press, 1945);

James Mitchell Clarke, *The Life and Adventures of John Muir* (San Diego: Word Shop, 1979).

References:

Michael P. Branch, "'Angel guiding gently': The Yosemite Meeting of Ralph Waldo Emerson and John Muir, 1871," *Western American Literature,* 32, no. 2 (1997): 126–149;

Michael P. Cohen, *The Pathless Way: John Muir and the American Wilderness* (Madison: University of Wisconsin Press, 1984);

John C. Elder, "John Muir and the Literature of Wilderness," *Massachusetts Review,* 22 (1981): 375–386;

George Emanuels, *John Muir, Inventor* (Fresno, Cal.: Panorama Books West, 1985);

Richard F. Fleck, *Henry Thoreau and John Muir among the Indians* (Hamden, Conn.: Archon, 1985);

Stephen R. Fox, *The American Conservation Movement: John Muir and His Legacy* (Madison: University of Wisconsin Press, 1985);

Arlen J. Hansen, "Right Men in the Right Places: The Meeting of Ralph Waldo Emerson and John Muir," *Western Humanities Review,* 39 (1985): 165–172;

Lawrence Hott and Diane Garey, *The Wilderness Idea: A Film* (Santa Monica, Cal.: Direct Cinema, 1989);

Thomas J. Lyon, *John Muir* (Boise, Idaho: Boise State College, 1972);

Lyon, "Nature Writing as a Subversive Activity," *North Dakota Quarterly,* 59 (1991): 6–16;

Sally M. Miller, ed., *John Muir, Life and Work* (Albuquerque: University of New Mexico Press, 1993);

Roderick Nash, *Wilderness and the American Mind* (New Haven: Yale University Press, 1982);

John P. O'Grady, "John Muir's Parables of Desire," in his *Pilgrims to the Wild* (Salt Lake City: University of Utah Press, 1993), pp. 47–85;

Christine Oravec, "John Muir, Yosemite, and the Sublime Response: A Study in the Rhetoric of Preservationism," *Quarterly Journal of Speech,* 67 (1981): 245–258;

Michael L. Smith, *Pacific Visions: California Scientists and the Environment, 1850–1915* (New Haven: Yale University Press, 1987);

Gary Snyder, *Myths and Texts* (New York: New Directions, 1978);

John Tallmadge, "John Muir and the Poetics of Natural Conversion," *North Dakota Quarterly,* 59 (1991): 62–79;

Frederick Turner, *Rediscovering America: John Muir in His Time and Ours* (San Francisco: Sierra Club, 1985).

Papers:

The major collection of Muir materials, including half of Muir's personal library, is housed in the Stuart Library at the University of the Pacific, Stockton, California. The bulk of this material is available on microfilm and catalogued by Ronald H. Limbaugh and Kirsten E. Lewis's *The John Muir Papers, 1858–1957* (Alexandria, Va.: Chadwyck-Healey, 1985) and *The Guide and Index to the Microform Edition of the John Muir Papers* (Alexandria, Va.: Chadwyck-Healey, 1986). The other half of Muir's personal library is held in the Henry E. Huntington Library in San Marino, California. Additional materials are archived with the Robert Underwood Johnson Papers in the Bancroft Library at the University of California, Berkeley.

Frank Norris
(5 March 1870 – 25 October 1902)

Joseph R. McElrath Jr.
Florida State University

See also the Norris entries in *DLB 12: American Realists and Naturalists* and *DLB 71: American Literary Critics and Scholars, 1880–1900.*

BOOKS: *Yvernelle: A Legend of Feudal France* (Philadelphia: Lippincott, 1892);

Moran of the Lady Letty: *A Story of Adventure off the California Coast* (New York: Doubleday & McClure, 1898); republished as *Shanghaied: A Story of Adventure off the California Coast* (London: Richards, 1900);

McTeague: A Story of San Francisco (New York: Doubleday & McClure, 1899; London: Richards, 1899);

Blix (New York: Doubleday & McClure, 1899); republished as *Blix: A Love Idyll* (London: Richards, 1899);

A Man's Woman (New York: Doubleday & McClure, 1900; London: Richards, 1900);

The Octopus: A Story of California (New York: Doubleday, Page, 1901; London: Richards, 1901);

The Pit: A Story of Chicago (New York: Doubleday, Page, 1903; London: Richards, 1903);

A Deal in Wheat and Other Stories of the New and Old West (New York: Doubleday, Page, 1903; London: Richards, 1903);

The Responsibilities of the Novelist and Other Literary Essays (New York: Doubleday, Page, 1903; London: Richards, 1903);

The Joyous Miracle (New York: Doubleday, Page, 1906; London: Harper, 1906);

The Third Circle (New York & London: John Lane, 1909);

Vandover and the Brute (Garden City, N.Y.: Doubleday, Page, 1914; London: Heinemann, 1914);

The Surrender of Santiago (San Francisco: Paul Elder, 1917);

Collected Writings Hitherto Unpublished in Book Form, volume 10 of *The Argonaut Manuscript Limited Edition of Frank Norris's Works* (Garden City, N.Y.: Doubleday, Doran, 1928);

Frank Norris of "The Wave": Stories and Sketches from the San Francisco Weekly, 1893–1897, edited by Os-

Frank Norris

car Lewis (San Francisco: Westgate Press, 1931);

The Literary Criticism of Frank Norris, edited by Donald Pizer (Austin: University of Texas Press, 1964);

A Novelist in the Making: A Collection of Student Themes and the Novels Blix *and* Vandover and the Brute, edited by James D. Hart (Cambridge: Harvard University Press, 1970);

A Student Theme by Frank Norris (Berkeley, Calif.: The Frank Norris Society, 1987);

The Apprenticeship Writings of Frank Norris, 1896–1898, edited by Joseph R. McElrath Jr. and Douglas K. Burgess (Philadelphia: American Philosophical Society, 1996).

Collections: *Complete Edition of Frank Norris,* 10 volumes (Garden City, N.Y.: Doubleday, Doran, 1928);

The Works of Frank Norris, 12 volumes, edited by Kenji Inoue (Tokyo: Meicho Fukyu Kai, 1983–1984).

Frank Norris is known principally as an American novelist rather than a western one. He was perceived as a national artist by the majority of his contemporaries, and at the time of his early death in 1902 his sobriquet, "the American Zola," even indicated a transnational identity. His best-known work then, *The Octopus: A Story of California* (1901), was viewed not so much as a western but as an attempt to produce the Great American Novel. Further, his posthumous best-seller, *The Pit: A Story of Chicago* (1903), was seen by many as the accomplishment of that aim, and its subtitle made it clear that Norris could be as eclectic in his regionalism as he was in his prose style and narrative technique.

On the other hand, Norris in his essay titled "The Great American Novel," collected with others in *The Responsibilities of the Novelist and Other Literary Essays* in 1903, insists that a significant American novelist could not, strictly speaking, claim to have written a national work because of the extraordinary sectional diversity in the United States. Every noteworthy American author he cited when arguing the point was known for a regional sensibility and a local-color focus in his fiction, and Norris was, of course, implying the same about himself. Five of his seven novels are situated in California, and his canon of approximately three hundred works repeatedly demonstrates how appropriate it is to view him as a self-conscious and deliberate regional writer. It was not until Norris was in his mid twenties that he focused on the American West as a subject matter he could develop as his own.

Frank Norris was born in Chicago on 5 March 1870, and whether there were any early indications of the course his life would take is moot because of a dearth of information about his youth. He produced no memoirs; after his death his mother and his younger brother, the novelist Charles G. Norris, offered few recollections of his childhood; even the fact that he attended the prestigious Harvard School shortly before the family moved to the San Francisco Bay area in 1884 was not mentioned by any of his contemporaries. What is clear, though, is that he was born to the manor, the son of a well-to-do wholesale jeweler, Benjamin Franklin Norris Sr., and the one-time promising actress Gertrude Doggett.

Norris's family life in both Chicago and San Francisco was a tumultuous one eventuating in his parents' divorce in 1894, principally because of Gertrude's "artistic temperament": histrionic, self-centered, and given to exercising in public her acknowledged talents as an indefatigable elocutionist, especially her fascination with William Shake-speare, Sir Walter Scott, and Robert Browning ensured that Norris's home environment was neither midwestern nor western but continental. By 1886 he enrolled at the San Francisco Art Association's school, where he received instruction in drawing and painting under the direction of the French-trained Emil Carlsen—never formally completing high school so far as can be determined.

After a brief sojourn in London in 1887, Norris came to adulthood in Paris, where he remained to study in the studio of Guillaume Bouguereau at the Académie Julian. He returned in 1889 to San Francisco a cosmopolitan young gentleman with pronounced Eurocentric cultural interests. Admitted to the University of California in 1890, the sophomore saw the publication of his first book in 1892. *Yvernelle: A Legend of Feudal France* provides an accurate measure of just how unlikely it then was that he would ever figure in the history of western American literature.

Norris's early literary experience had been especially conservative in nature. Writers of the early nineteenth century provided the models that he would eventually transcend, but in *Yvernelle* it was clear that romances such as Edward Bulwer-Lytton's *Harold: The Last of the Saxon Kings* (1848) and Scott's *Quentin Durward* (1823) were as potent influences as the chronicles of Jean Froissart. Following Scott's lead and in imitation of other poets infatuated with things medieval, Norris fashioned a metrical verse romance in which a knight named Sir Caverlaye violates the chivalric moral code, luxuriating in the illicit love of one Guhaldrada. She curses him when his "better self" reasserts itself and he decides to return to his virtuous lover, the fair maiden Yvernelle. The curse is that the next woman he kisses will become a loathsome hag; when he refrains from kissing Yvernelle, his apparent rejection motivates her to become a nun. Sir Caverlaye finally eliminates the impediment to true love by kissing Guhaldrada. At the last minute he prevents Yvernelle from taking her vows and is able to look forward to nuptial bliss. Norris, in short, was not following the paths blazed by Bret Harte and Ambrose Bierce.

Within a decade, however, he had made his adjustments. "As young Felipe Arillaga guided his pony out of the last intricacies of Pachecho Pass, he was thinking of Rubia Ytuerate. . . . [He] was forced to admit that she was as handsome a woman as could be found through all California." Thus begins "The Riding of Felipe," one of the stories collected in *A Deal in Wheat and Other Stories of the New and Old West* (1903), in which Sir Caverlaye becomes Felipe; Guhaldrada is renamed Rubia; and Yvernelle is given Spanish-California ancestry as Buelna Matiarena. Further clarifying the degree to which Norris's focus had become more distinctly western by 1901 is his inclusion of a hair-raising "Mexican duel" in the short story: in *Yvernelle* Sir Caverlaye slays Guhaldrada's brother in a chivalric encounter; in "The Riding of Felipe" the protagonist and Rubia's sibling strap together their left wrists and, each with a knife in his right hand, begin their fight to the death.

Norris did not show any inclination to use traditional fictional materials of the West during his Berkeley years, 1890–1894. It was not until he was at Harvard in 1894–1895, writing under the direction of Lewis E. Gates, that he revealed to what extent his reading experience included dime-novels—which would eventually make their contribution to *McTeague: A Story of San Francisco* (1899) as well as to *The Octopus.* Among the "student themes" first published in *A Novelist in the Making: A Collection of Student Themes and the novels* Blix *and* Vandover and the Brute (1970) is the 8 March 1895 outline of the finale of *McTeague:* "McTeague goes from bad to worse . . . killing his wife. . . . His way is across an arm of an Arizona desert, here he is ridden down by a deputy sheriff. . . . [He] kills the sheriff and is about to go on when he discovers that . . . the sheriff has managed to hand-cuff their wrists together. He is chained to the body sixty miles from help." Harte seems tame by comparison, and Bierce's penchant for stunning ironies appears acknowledged. Yet the completion of *McTeague* was more than three years in the future. It was not until Norris finished his year at Harvard, returned from a journalistic jaunt to South Africa in the winter of 1895–1896, and in April became a staff writer for the San Francisco weekly, *The Wave,* that he began to give sustained attention in print to the sensational literary possibilities of the West.

These possibilities were of two broad kinds. First, like Twain, Dan De Quille, and writers of his own generation such as Frank Bailey Millard, Norris focused on the melodramatic resources of a locale that stood in marked contrast with the "tamed" environments of the Midwest and East. When Millard created a female stage robber in *A Pretty Bandit,* which Norris reviewed for *The Wave* in the summer of 1897, he anticipated by only a few years Norris's casting of Dyke, a disgruntled railroad engineer and failed farmer, in a similar role in *The Octopus*–a novel that is not set in the legendary past.

Second, unlike Harte, Norris had the "painter's eye," and he appropriated the landscape per se to render striking verbal portraits of the West, California, and San Francisco–the turn-of-the-century equivalents of which one can find only in the visual arts and on occasion in the poetry of Joaquin Miller. Indeed, one of Norris's most distinctive accomplishments is to be seen in his frequent and sometimes quite lengthy representations of landscapes. He renders the startling peculiarities of the canyon-ridden Sierra Nevadas, the perspective-defying immensity of the San Joaquin Valley, and the long-ranging coastal mountains defiling southward. He also describes San Francisco, the city that boasts Telegraph Hill and the "cliff-dwellers" living there, and in a little-noted comic piece of 1897 titled "'Boom,'" the still-undeveloped desert that was the San Diego area.

Only occasionally performing as a news reporter for *The Wave,* Norris was for almost two years a peripatetic observer of "local color" at Roberts Island near Sacramento, Santa Cruz, the Mission San Juan at Hollister, Coronado Beach, and many points between them as he crisscrossed California. His distinctive contributions to *The Wave* were those of a fiction writer and an impressionistic essayist with a studiously cultivated Zolaesque flair for sensational description of the spectacles afforded by the ever-varying landscape and its equally eccentric inhabitants. The years 1896 to 1898 stand as the most experimental phase of Norris's brief career as well as the period in which he was deliberately exploiting for the first time a regional subject matter for a regional readership. Most important, he repeatedly redefined what was "western" as he set his stories in his present and strove for originality.

"A Reversion to Type" (1897), for example, introduces the reader to modern western life in the figure of Paul Schuster, who is a floor clerk in a smart San Francisco department store. This most conventional of salaried urbanites suddenly has a distinctly modern experience made popular by the vogue of evolutionary theory and particularly Max Nordau's speculations on predispositions to degeneracy that were then receiving attention in the press. Suddenly violating all of the middle-class habits acquired over a lifetime, he revels in dissipation and runs afoul of the law, whereupon–as McTeague would–he flees to the mountains and ends up near the Big Dipper Mine. Like the Reno Kid in "The Wife of Chino," he decides to intercept a gold shipment, armed with a sawed-off shotgun he has stolen from some Chinese laborers. He is chagrined to discover that his victim is carrying no gold. Schuster's strange new life then ends.

Without food and shelter and suffering keenly, he regains his former personality, returns to San Francisco, and resumes his old, staid ways with no one the wiser. This episode in his otherwise emi-

A page from the manuscript for McTeague *(from the 1928 Argonaut Manuscript edition of Norris's works, which included a leaf from the 245-page manuscript in each copy)*

nently respectable life, as it turns out, is "a reversion to type," an atavistic lapse for which he is not deemed personally responsible. As the story ends the narrator relates his recent discovery that Schuster's grandfather was a stage robber who ended his days in San Quentin. Genes will, inexorably, tell; thus did Norris recontextualize a vintage western story line in the post-Darwinian California that he knew.

What was western for Norris included not only Iowa Hill, Angels Camp, and Pachecho Pass but also, to Norris's mind, the most exotic, albeit urban, locale imaginable: San Francisco. Here was the setting for another kind of western literature, free from the trappings of saddles, six-shooters, and red shirts. For example, the hero of "Bandy Callaghan's Girl" does not wear spurs; he rides a streetcar as a conductor. Bandy is intent upon collecting the money owed him by a denizen of San Francisco's Chinatown, the pursuit of whom leads him into an opium den where he discovers a "white slave." He rescues her, assists her in beginning a new life, and falls in love only to discover that suicide is her only means of escape from addiction to heroin. The story was one of Norris's earliest contributions to *The Wave,* published in April 1896 but dated May 1894.

Chinatown drew him again in 1897, and the reason was immediately apparent in the beginning of "The Third Circle" as he focused on this "noisome swamp" and "the strange, dreadful life that wallows down there in the lowest ooze of the place—wallows and grovels there in the mud and in the dark." This story, too, focuses on a case of white slavery, the kidnapping of Harriett Ten Eyck, who is discovered years later, an opium-addicted and alcoholic drudge now named Sadie and the property of Ah Yee. She earns her keep by manufacturing *yen shee* (pelletized scrapings from the bowls of opium pipes) that will be sold in San Quentin. Here and in the many other ethnic and polyglot neighborhoods are discovered sensations of the kind that Deadeye Dick and the Apache Kid never knew.

In his third novel, *Blix* (1899), Norris would treat Chinatown in exactly the opposite manner, positioning his hero and heroine in the midst of its exhilarating—because so foreign—sights, sounds, and smells. Their visit to a restaurant there proves one of the most memorable experiences of their courtship. Indeed, the lyrical *Blix* is Norris's paean not only to that sensorially invigorating neighborhood but also to the seemingly infinite variety of piquant stimuli encountered elsewhere in the city. Echoing in several *Wave* pieces the point he made in the article "Japan Transplanted" (1897), Norris reveled in the fact that *his* West had imported the Far East.

More intriguing, Norris discovered in locales such as Telegraph Hill that the Anglo-Saxon West of the Native Sons was in the midst of radical demographic change. In "Among Cliff-Dwellers" (1897) he describe an African American and a "Chinese slave girl," an Italian woman and the descendant of a Pueblo Indian and a Spaniard, and a Jew and a Chinese American—each racially mixed couple engaging in "a fusing of peoples." "Cosmopolitan San Francisco" (1897) pictured the western American analogue of Charles Darwin's Galapagos Islands, with Norris proving prescient in regard to the variation within the species in that locale during the succeeding century.

In his first novel, which was being serialized as he concluded his tenure with *The Wave* in early 1898, Norris dramatically illustrates his conviction that there was indeed a western difference more profound than dialect and outward appearances. In *Moran of the* Lady Letty: *A Story of Adventure off the California Coast* the shanghaied Ross Wilbur is soon taken out of sight of land and away from the United States into Baja California. Yet the novel provides the bizarrely embellished key to Norris's orientation as a western writer.

The lurid fantasy of *Moran of the* Lady Letty, involving the violence-suffused and sexually titillating initiation of an effeminate San Francisco swell into the mysteries of *real* manhood, is clearly related to literary precedents made available by Rudyard Kipling, Robert Louis Stevenson, Anthony Hope, and Guy Boothsby. Yet the risk to his local reputation as a sophisticate that Norris took when waggishly initiating this flamboyant account of "battle, at least one murder, and several sudden deaths" was not thus lessened. Norris would likely not have proceeded had it not been for the rationale that western American literature provided him. *Moran of the* Lady Letty is rooted in the belief that served as the premise for the majority of "Wild West" thrillers: that patent improbabilities became less unlikely the farther one moves west beyond the Mississippi River. Norris was literally convinced that the inarguably claptrap, hackneyed mechanism by which Wilbur is shanghaied in 1898 was in fact true to life. In San Francisco, at least, anything was possible.

"Things can happen in San Francisco," proclaims Norris in "An Opening for Novelists" seven months before *Moran of the* Lady Letty began its appearance in *The Wave.* Nob Hill, Telegraph Hill, Chinatown, the Barbary Coast, the Mission, Spanish Town, and Fisherman's Wharf—there is "an indefinable air about all these places that is suggestive of stories at once." Norris then advances the theory that accounts for the difference focused upon in western literature as a whole and particularly writing of the kind that he thought capable of exploiting successfully the unique characteristics of San Francisco: "there is perhaps one feature of the city that conduces to this effect, that is its isolation. . . . Isolation produces individuality, originality."

Viewing himself at the time as a short-story writer rather than a novelist, Norris provides a self-definition in "An Opening for Novelists" by explaining the need for a storyteller whose skills are commensurate with the unequaled fictional opportunities afforded by San Francisco. Proclaiming the need for a "California Kipling," he is, of course, describing himself as the man to fill the void. At the time Kipling was perceived by polite readers as a too-graphic purveyor of tales featuring violent behavior, less-than-noble motivations, and coarseness of character hardly providing the inspirational "uplift" expected in Victorian art. Known as an ultra-realist and even attacked as a disciple of naturalist Emile Zola, Kipling was a progressive high-culture warrant—if the 1896 author of "Zola as a Romantic Writer" needed one—to mine in the most unrestrained manner possible the immediately-at-hand resources of his adopted state, its colorful past, and its equally extravagant present.

Wondering who will be equal to the challenge of capturing this special quality of the life before him, he poses the question "Where is the man who shall get at the heart of us, the blood and bones and fiber of us, who shall go a-gunning for stories up and down our streets and into our houses and parlors and lodging houses and saloons and dives and along our wharves . . . ?" As he launches an attack on Gelett Burgess and like triflers of his day who neglected in art the "Life that we want, the vigorous, real thing," the données for several works like *Moran of the* Lady Letty suddenly materialize: "While you are rounding a phrase a sailor has been shanghaied down there along the water front; while you are sustaining a metaphor, another See Yup has been hatcheted yonder in Gamblers' Alley; a man has time to be stabbed while you are composing a villanelle; the crisis of a life has come and gone while you have been niggling with your couplet."

When Ross Wilbur drinks a drugged Manhattan at a Barbary Coast dive and then is dropped through a trapdoor in the floor to a boat that will carry him out to the piratical Captain Kitchell's ship, Norris answered the call to arms that he had trumpeted. By the conclusion of *Moran of the* Lady Letty, Wilbur has countered the eastern effeteness that has infected the better class of San Franciscans; put to the test in mortal combat, he has assumed the identity of the aggressive Anglo-Saxon who won the

Binding for Norris's second novel, set in San Francisco and Death Valley

West. He enjoys an atavistic lapse pictured as considerably more positive in its outcome than Paul Schuster's in "A Reversion to Type."

In late 1897 Norris executed in variant form his 1895 plan for the conclusion of *McTeague*. The scenes set near Colfax, California, then south in the Panamint Mountain Range, and finally in Death Valley are impressive uses of dramatic western settings. For example, of prime importance to cultural historians of the West is the way in which Norris contrasts the West and the East at the beginning of chapter 20 as McTeague is discovered in the Sierras: "The entire region was untamed. In some places east of the Mississippi nature is cosey, intimate, small, and homelike, like a good-natured housewife. In Placer County, California, she is a vast, unconquered brute of the Pliocene epoch, savage, sullen, and magnificently indifferent to man." Still, after chapter 19 Norris seems to be falling back on the tried-and-true materials that had served Harte so well for three decades.

In 1898 he wrote to book reviewer Isaac F. Marcosson proffering thanks for his positive notice of *Moran of the* Lady Letty and indicating that he might not have heard himself echoing Harte in the last chapters of *McTeague:* "I have great faith in the possibilities of San Francisco and the Pacific Coast as offering a field for fiction. Not the fiction of Bret Harte, however, for the country has long since outgrown the 'red shirt' period—the red shirt referring to the typical dress of mid-century miners." Cribbens, McTeague's fellow prospector in the Panamint Mountain Range, is, however, distinctly of the type developed by Harte. As well, the novel's hero of limited mental ability is as pathetically inarticulate and as droll in his antics as Harte's best sourdough figures: "Gold is where you find it" is McTeague's oracular utterance, made in response to Cribbens's more scientific description of mineralogical indicators of where one should dig. Norris is clearly acting as though the vein that Harte struck was not wholly exhausted.

Critics have lately argued, however, that in *McTeague* Norris's intention is parodic rather than emulative. Such a reading appears supported by Norris's late 1897 comic retelling of Harte's "The Outcasts of Poker Flats" in a *Wave* collection of parodies titled "Perverted Tales." But when measuring just how traditionally western Norris sometimes is in his canon, one should give equal attention and weight to his straightforward appropriation of "red shirt" fiction that is the little-noted "Short Stack, Pugilist." Published in *The Wave* in 1897, it is set at the Big Dipper Mine at Iowa Hill that appears in *McTeague* and is a wry delineation of a young miner exactly Hartean in its descriptive particulars and bemused tone.

One of Norris's striking accomplishments in *McTeague* is his description of Polk Street, which provides a microcosmic definition of California as a land of vivid contrasts and startling combinations. While in "A Neglected Epic," another essay collected in *The Responsibilities of the Novelist,* Norris laments that no one had treated the epic figures in the history of the winning of the West—for example, the Alamo heroes William Barrett Travis, Davey Crockett, and Jim Bowie—he was drawn instead to a humble "accommodation street" in San Francisco where the complacent, Neanderthal-like dentist of Irish extraction McTeague finds himself wed to Trina, a slight but energetic German Swiss girl as prone to efficiency as she is to displays of insecurity and acquisitiveness. Their neighborhood is populated by as motley a group of people as is imaginable: a Polish Jew, redheaded no less, seized by a mania for gold; a Mexican American cleaning

woman who is nearly as obsessional; two superannuated lovers of British extraction whose behavior gauges the extremes of English "reserve"; Trina's father, whose rage for order is positively Prussian; and his nephew, Marcus Schouler, ever bristling with hostility and just as determined as his uncle to make life conform to his expectations.

When Marcus leaves San Francisco to become a cowboy in southern California and when McTeague joins the prospector Cribbens, it is immediately clear that the West is Norris's subject. However, the saloon keeper Joe Frenna, harness maker Heise, the weirdly picturesque Cliff House, and Schuetzen Park in Alameda are just as much a part of that reality as the dispossessed "good Indian" named Big Jim whom McTeague meets on his way to Death Valley. When compared to what Norris's modern experience in the West offers, Bowie, Travis, and Crockett seem dull alternatives, promising only a surfeit of fustian declamations and histrionic gesticulation. So far as is known, Norris never actually planned to treat them in fiction.

While he wrote for *The Wave* Norris repeatedly discovered and communicated to his readers that truth is as strange as fiction on the West Coast. For example, "Man-Hunting," an article for the 13 June 1896 issue, has as its subtitle "The Coast Range as a Refuge for Bandits." Take "a three hours' journey to the southeast" of San Francisco, "one of the world-cities," Norris asserts, and "you will find yourself in the heart of a country that has been, and that is even now, a very paradise for outlaws, bandits, and fugitive criminals." The Pachecho Pass of "The Riding of Felipe" is located in this exotic environment. Citing criminal activity fresh to memory such as "the flight of Dunham" and "the Evans-Sontag affair," Norris describes the mountainous terrain south of Monterey as the "old battle grounds" of brigands and lawmen—"old as the days of such 'famous bandits' as Jesus Tejada, Tiburcio Vasquez, Chaves, and Juan Soto."

After brief descriptions of Tejada's difficult capture and Dunham's still-successful retreat into this hinterland, Norris recounts the story of Sheriff Harry Morse's 1871 tracking down of Juan Soto and a protracted gunfight between the two leading to a stirring finale: "one can imagine the looks of [Soto] as he came running down the side of the cañon, a pistol in each hand, his hair in the wind, holding his fire till . . . killing would be a certainty. . . . Morse did not fire until Soto was close upon him, then killed him with a single shot though his brain." Norris's point is that such mayhem—action that realists such as Henry James or William Dean Howells would never represent—was much more the stuff of western reality than might be expected. It was quite possible that the ongoing search for Dunham would have a similar climax. As Norris was wont to declare in other contexts, "life is better than literature" as a source of material for the writer.

The train robbery by the character Dyke, his pursuit, and his capture in *The Octopus* provided Norris with the occasion to use in full the potential of the real-life events that he had recorded and analyzed in "Man-Hunting." When concluding that essay he reflects: "Even the author of *Nick Carter,* or *Old Sleuth,* might shrink from inventing so wonderful a situation." A few years later Norris found, happily, a confirmation of his argument in "Fiction Is Selection" (1897) that the exercise of artistic imagination is little more than selection and arrangement of what one already knows: He discovered that he had to invent little when writing *The Octopus* and needed only to flesh out what his eye-opening experiences as a *Wave* writer had made available. He was convinced that Dyke's frenzied efforts to escape the grasp of the law, the exchanges of gunfire, his ultimate capture in the foothills, and even the unlikely holdup of a train required no special justification as credible events. Thanks to the machinations of the railroad trust that drove the economically ruined Dyke to such behavior, the Wild West of yore easily reemerged in all of its archetypal splendor (or gaudiness) in a unique contemporary setting that was made to order for a writer with romantic proclivities.

In another essay included in *The Responsibilities of the Novelist,* "The Frontier Gone at Last," Norris, eight months after the publication of *The Octopus,* ridicules William Cody and the men he hired to create the illusion of a kind of westernness that had disappeared with the frontier. Yet, while Norris thus anticipated by almost twenty years E. E. Cummings's declaration that "Buffalo Bill's / defunct," he could not resist adding to *The Octopus* an anachronism so patent and yet still so melodramatically alluring as the scene of the shoot-out in Annixter's new barn when Delaney disrupts his former employer's barn-building celebration.

Norris makes Delaney a veritable cliché, the mean hombre. A "good man gone bad," he opens fire at Annixter in the crowded barn, seeking revenge for being unfairly sacked. As is clear from Presley's warning of Annixter, Norris is quite aware that he has overdressed Delaney for the part he is to play when he arrives. Relates Presley, "He's got the buckskin, and he's full of bad whiskey and dagored. You should see him; he's wearing all his cowpunching outfit, hair trousers, sombrero, spurs and all the rest of it, and he has strapped himself to a big revolver." Bullets aplenty fly with the results usually seen in Hollywood treatments of such scenes; miraculously, no innocent bystander is hit. Finally and equally miraculously, given the feckless performance of both gunmen, Annixter uses his last bullet to effect a flesh wound. Delaney drops his empty revolver as his wrist is struck and flees into the night.

Much more credible for modern readers is the climax of the novel, the accidentally initiated gunfight between the ranchers and the sheriff who is accompanied by the railroad thugs intent on seizing the ranchers' properties. It is an economically rendered scene, free from "cowboy" posturing, that grimly ends the conflict central to the main plot in which a corporation rather than a Black Bart is cast as the villain. Justice is not established, though. Rather, an impersonal corporation controlling economic and political life in the valley triumphs over the equally unheroic, equally corrupt agribusinessmen: rancher Magnus Derrick, for example, is possessed by a get-rich-quick and consequences-be-damned point of view. Crushed thus are the scions of the '49ers who ravaged the landscape and much more in their displays of inordinate acquisitiveness during the previous decades.

Norris in *The Octopus* is a realist as well as a romanticist, radically revising the formula one expects from western, or eastern, moral melodramas. All of the principals are flawed–though Annixter, when he dies during the gun battle, is in the process of transcending his base personality traits, becoming a magnanimous hero whom Gary Cooper might have played had Hollywood given *The Octopus* cinematic treatment in the 1940s. Beneath the surface manifestations of what may be termed traditional popular writing about the West, then, Norris was writing in a new vein. He was synthesizing historical detail concerning the actual Mussel Slough confrontation between wheat growers and the Southern Pacific railroad in 1880 with events of the late 1890s and incorporating romantic legend from the period in which Spain controlled California with hard facts about "Robber Barons" who are both urban and rural. He laced the whole with staples from the repertoire of writers such as those lampooned by Stephen Crane, Norris created a magnum opus on the West, the scope of which anticipated that of James Michener's *Centennial* (1974).

One of the obvious reasons that Norris has not loomed larger in the gallery of western authors is that a markedly less noteworthy set of intentions is repeatedly seen in a posthumous publication quite different in nature from *McTeague* and *The Octopus.* One might speculate, upon a first glance at its title,

Scenes on Polk Street: the coffee shop where McTeague ate and his "Dental Parlors" over the post office

that *A Deal in Wheat and Other Stories of the New and Old West* has served as the focal point for many commentaries by western American literature specialists. But this volume, assembled and given its title by brother Charles G. Norris, has not.

When Norris wrote these short stories in 1901–1902, he was a professional author who, after he assumed high national visibility with *The Octopus,* found that he–like Jack London a few years later–could sell virtually anything from his hand. Anxious to earn enough to quit the part-time position he took in 1900 as a manuscript reader for Doubleday, Page and Company in New York City and to reestablish residence in California, he exploited the opportunity with evident haste. And so "A Bargain with Peg-Leg" begins in a promising way at the Big Dipper Mine: "we emerged from the cool, cave-like dampness of the mine and ran out into the wonderful night air of the Sierra foothills." But this quickly gives way to the staleness of a too-colorful millwork dialect and a yarn replete with regional allusions–all of which produce little positive effect since the tale might have been situated in any locale where rogues may be found. "I knew a one-lunger once," begins Bunt McBride, "and the acquaintance was some distressful by reason of its bringing me into strained relations with a cow-rustlin', hair-liftin', only-one-born-in-captivity, man-eatin' brute of a one-legged Greaser which he was named Peg-Leg Smith." Such garrulousness finally eventuates in a "comic" situation: Peg-Leg is told to jump from the fourth floor of a burning hotel into a blanket held by four men; he does; and Bunt then explains the joke, that there was no blanket.

Another anecdote, without doubt originally a paragraph selected to fill white space in a newspa-

per, appears to have been the source for "The Passing of Cock-Eye Blacklock." Bunt is, it turns out, one who has lived through the Old West, becoming fully experienced in gold mining, gambling, and driving cattle from Texas to Dodge City; he had witnessed the emergence of the New West with the disappearance of the buffalo and the advent of barbed wire. Viewing him in an evolutionary context, Norris offers the reader a character who "had seen the rise of a new period, the successive stages of which, singularly enough, tally exactly with the progress of our world-civilization: first the nomad and hunter, then the herder, next and last the husbandman." Such a panoramic and culturally significant view of changing conditions is wasted upon Bunt, though; he, and Norris in this instance, would much rather recount how the late Cock-Eye Blacklock used to fish. He "passed" one day when he tossed a stick of dynamite into the water and his faithful dog retrieved it. The fatal explosion noted, Bunt goes on to demonstrate his familiarity with "The Outcasts of Poker Flat" as he describes the epitaph written for Cock-Eye. It is a variation on Harte's for John Oakhurst.

"A Deal in Wheat," the best-known story, is not concerned with the West except in a tangential way. One also finds that the "West" forced upon four other stories by editor Charles G. Norris is actually the Pacific Ocean, whereon more yarns like Bunt McBride's are spun by equally voluble raconteurs. In fact, only the remaining three tales are truly western works at heart. "The Riding of Felipe," described above, offers one a taste of Spanish-California experience in the romantic style. "A Memorandum of Sudden Death" is set in the Southwest and is the manuscript record of a man whose party is surrounded by Native American warriors and killed one by one. It is, inarguably, as "western" as the illustration by Frederic Remington that accompanies it—but it is also as generic.

The disservice Charles G. Norris rendered his late brother by raising expectations that were too high when they were not false is mitigated by only one of the short stories, "The Wife of Chino." Set at the Big Dipper Mine, it is redolent of the atmosphere of the Sierras at its start, and it focuses on a young mining engineer, Lockwood, becoming more and more susceptible to the charms of Chino Zavalla's wife, Felice, who prefers him to her husband. Circumstances make it possible for Lockwood to kill Chino, who transports gold from the mine to the express station in town: the Reno Kid, a highwayman, is said to be in the vicinity, and Lockwood need only plead mistaken identity if he shoots Chino on the trail in the dark of night. Lockwood instead proves a "thoroughbred."

He resists the temptation, only to shoot Chino by mistake, whereupon Norris takes the opportunity to indulge the racism for which critics have given him a good deal of attention since the early 1960s. Felice assumes that Lockwood has shot her husband on purpose and expresses her appreciation: "now we git married soam day byne-by, eh?" His attraction to her ends at that moment: "All the baseness of her tribe, all the degraded savagery of a degenerate race, all the capabilities for wrong, for sordid treachery, that lay dormant in her, leaped to life at this unguarded moment, and in that new light, that now at last she had herself let in, stood pitilessly revealed, a loathsome thing, hateful as malevolence itself." Thus is pictured the female counterpart of the hot-blooded "greaser" male figure, quick to anger and the use of a knife as seen in "Execution Without Judgment," which appeared in *The Wave* in 1897.

At the same time, though, it should be noted that Chino Zavalla is "absolutely trustworthy, as honest as the daylight, strong physically, coolheaded, discreet"; that he is entrusted regularly with the delivery of gold to the express office at Iowa Hill contradicts the notion of a "degenerate race" and identifies Norris as one of many western writers who simply did not transcend, or logically resolve, conflicting attitudes toward those with Latin "blood." Indeed, André Poncet has even argued in "Anti-Racist Strategies in Frank Norris's Fiction" that Norris uses racial stereotypes—for Jewish and Asian Americans as well—only to undercut them thus and to call into question the too-easy assumption of Anglo-Saxon superiority. The extent to which this is the case in Norris's canon remains de-

batable; what is not is that his attitudes were more complex, or conflicted, than was assumed when Norris-baiting on the question of racism enjoyed its heyday in the 1960s.

"Western Cosmopolitans" is the term that Glen A. Love has used to describe the many characters Norris created to measure the kind of experience—positive and negative—his modern West afforded to those of his generation. Regarding the positive, Travis Bessemer, the heroine of *Blix,* is Norris's most sustained attempt to visualize, explain, and extol what journalists of the time saw as one of the most distinctive products of western, as opposed to eastern, life: the "California Girl." Standing in contrast with her anemic, transcontinental counterparts, sprightly Travis is an urban "New Woman" who at the close of the novel is pursuing a career in medicine. In *The Octopus* Hilma Tree is the rural, more traditional apotheosis of vibrant womanhood, a veritable Ceres not to be confused with the neurotic heroine of *The Pit,* whose hereditary backgrounds are associated with Massachusetts and North Carolina. The challenge for Norris's males is to be worthy of the western woman at her best.

Norris also attempts an examination of the problems of western society that is both scrupulous and sweeping. Neither positively nor negatively did Norris proceed by half measures, and his ambition is best indicated by the Balzacian subtitle that did not appear on the title page of the posthumously published *Vandover and the Brute* (1914): "A Study of Life and Manners in an American City at the End of the Nineteenth Century." This novel dealing with what is awry in the social class of which Norris himself was a member does not focus on a "degenerate race" but on the Anglo-Saxon supposedly in the vanguard of evolutionary progress. It concludes with its hero situated not in the "lowest ooze" of Chinatown but in the "mud and dark" of an otherwise luxurious Anglo-American environment.

As in the case of McTeague, Norris records Vandover's degeneration downward step by downward step, through several well detailed socioeconomic strata. The description of the different levels of society in *Vandover* is the true tour de force of Norris's career because of the more elevated station from which the hero declines before he descends through the highest level achieved by the Polk Street dentist. Honoré de Balzac's aim was his: to measure his society from top to bottom, from the drawing room of Van's fiancée, the virtuous Victorian Turner Ravis; through the tawdry front parlor of the "fast girl" Ida Wade; to the Imperial Café presided over by the prostitute Flossie; and into the cottages rented by working-class people that the Har-

The photograph of Norris published as the frontispiece for
The Pit

vard graduate with a neurological disorder caused by syphilis scours for his meager living.

In both *McTeague* and *Vandover* Norris makes good use of his *Wave* experience as a feature writer focusing on the noteworthy nooks and crannies of San Francisco that give the city its peculiar identity. He believed the *peculiar* was the essential for one writing as a regionalist about the West–or the South or New England. More specifically, Norris, like Owen Wister in *The Virginian* (1902) or John Steinbeck in *Tortilla Flat* (1935), focused closely upon the atypical that he felt was most typical.

When a bowdlerized *Moran of the* Lady Letty was published by Doubleday and McClure Company in September 1898, Norris must have been surprised as well as gladdened to find that his determination to be true to "the vigorous, real thing" was countenanced in the 17 December issue of *Literature* by none less than the Dean of American letters, William Dean Howells. While Howells dubbed *Moran of the* Lady Letty "romanticistic"–his pejorative for novels that only feign realism–he confessed that he read it with "breathlessness" and even "gasped . . . in the crucial moments." Summarizing the outland-

ish plot fairly, and in consequence apologizing for having "an unkind air of mocking it," Howells went on to praise *Moran of the* Lady Letty as a distinctively modern and undeniably American work: "The story gains a certain effectiveness from being so boldly circumstanced in the light of common day, and in a time and place of our own." As importantly for those measuring Norris's place in western American letters, he paid the highest compliment possible for a regionalist to receive, explaining that he appreciated the "curious glimpses of conditions" on the West Coast. Reading the novel Howells was "aware . . . of a San Francisco world . . . interestingly unlike other worlds on either shore of the Atlantic."

Less surprising, perhaps, was Howells's reaction to *McTeague* three months later in the 24 March issue of the same magazine. In his review he began by reflecting on how long American literature had displayed the influence of European writers and related that he had been looking forward to the time at which "we are to invade and control Europe in literature." On that note he turned to Norris's latest novel, declaring that it "ought not to be strange that the impulse in this direction should have come from California. . . . I felt, or fancied I felt, the impulse in Mr. Frank Norris' 'Moran of the Lady Letty,' and now in his 'McTeague' I am so sure of it that I am tempted to claim the prophetic instinct of it." These two novels, both of which are now known for their exaggerated extravagances, were recognized by one of the most temperate and judicious critics of the era for the originality Norris sought to infuse in them as he imaginatively chronicled experience in California. Both had the ring of truth for Howells, and the truth in question was western.

Norris's propensity for attempting grand effects is one of the traditional stumbling blocks for critics who might otherwise have developed a keener appreciation of his accomplishments. Howells, too, admitted reservations about Norris's sometimes too excitable imagination. In "Frank Norris," which appeared in the December 1902 issue of *The North American Review* after Norris's death at thirty-two following an appendix operation, he recalled "a bad moment" in *McTeague* when "the author is overcome by his lingering passion for the romantic, and indulges himself in a passage of rank melodrama." But he went on as well to admit the essential, that "even there he does nothing that denies the reality of his characters, and they are always of a reality so intense that one lives with them in the grotesquely shabby San Francisco street where, but for the final episode, the action passes." About *The Octopus* he wrote that it "will not be suggesting too much for this story to say, that there is a Homeric largeness in the play of passions moving it. They are not autochthons, these Californians of the great Wheat farms, choking in the [hold] of the railroad, but Americans of more than one transplantation; yet there is something rankly earthy and elemental in them which gives them the pathos of transplanted Titans." Seeing *McTeague* and *The Octopus* as Norris's *Odyssey* and *Iliad*, Howells correctly sensed how Norris's epical intentions were adjusted, respectively, to focus on an individual hero mainly in a restricted San Franciscan setting and then on a group of principals in a more expansive regional frame of reference.

Norris never wrote the epic of the Old West that he called for in "A Neglected Epic." But, as Howells sensed when describing him as a western contributor to the nation's literary heritage, Norris did succeed in bringing the West, reinvented literarily in light of actual conditions of the post-frontier era, into focus for turn-of-the-century readers who might enjoy discovering what he had in the region that he adopted as his homeland.

Letters:

Frank Norris: Collected Letters, edited by Jesse S. Crisler (San Francisco: Book Club of California, 1986);

Joseph R. McElrath Jr. and Sal Noto, eds., "An Important Letter in the Career of Frank Norris," *Quarterly News-Letter* (Book Club of California), 55 (Summer 1990): 59–61;

Jesse S. Crisler, ed., "Four New Frank Norris Letters," *Quarterly News-Letter* (Book Club of California), 56 (Summer 1991): 67–75; (Autumn 1991): 98–103.

Bibliographies:

Jesse S. Crisler and Joseph R. McElrath Jr., *Frank Norris: A Reference Guide* (Boston: G. K. Hall, 1975);

Thomas K. Dean and others, "Current Publications: Update," *Frank Norris Studies,* no. 2 (Autumn 1986): 3–4; continued in subsequent issues;

McElrath, *Frank Norris: A Descriptive Bibliography* (Pittsburgh: University of Pittsburgh Press, 1992).

Biographies:

Franklin Walker, *Frank Norris: A Biography* (Garden City, N.Y.: Doubleday, Doran, 1932);

André Poncet, *Frank Norris (1870–1902),* 2 volumes (Paris: Librairie Honoré Champion, 1977).

References:

Denison Haley Clift, "The Artist in Frank Norris," *Pacific Monthly,* 17 (March 1907): 313–322;

Charles L. Crow, "Norris, Crow and the Mussel Slough Tragedy," *California English* (March–April 1990): 20–21, 30–31;

Richard Allan Davison, "*Of Mice and Men* and *McTeague:* Steinbeck, Fitzgerald, and Frank Norris," *Studies in American Fiction,* 17 (Autumn 1989): 219–226;

William B. Dillingham, *Frank Norris: Instinct and Art* (Lincoln: University of Nebraska Press, 1969);

Charles Caldwell Dobie, "The First Californian Authors," *Bookman* (American), 72 (February 1931): 590–596;

David Fine, "Running Out of Space: Vanishing Landscapes in California Novels," *Western American Literature,* 26 (November 1991): 209–218;

Warren French, *Frank Norris* (New York: Twayne, 1962);

French, "Frank Norris (1870–1902)," in *Fifty Western Writers: A Bio-Bibliographical Sourcebook,* edited by Fred Erisman and Richard W. Etulain (Westport, Conn.: Greenwood, 1982), pp. 347–357;

Don Graham, *The Fiction of Frank Norris: The Aesthetic Context* (Columbia: University of Missouri Press, 1978);

Graham, ed., *Critical Essays on Frank Norris* (Boston: G. K. Hall, 1980);

Lucy Lockwood Hazard, *The Frontier in American Literature* (New York: Crowell, 1927);

Barbara Hochman, *The Art of Frank Norris, Storyteller* (Columbia: University of Missouri Press, 1988);

William Dean Howells, "Frank Norris," *North American Review,* 175 (December 1902): 769–778;

William J. Hug, "*McTeague* as Metafiction? Frank Norris' Parodies of Bret Harte and the Dime Novel," *Western American Literature,* 26 (November 1991): 219–228;

Mary Lawlor, "'Life' and 'Literature' in Frank Norris's Cowboy Tales," *Prairie Winds* (Spring–Summer 1986): 34–40;

Benjamin S. Lawson, "The Presence of Joaquin Miller in *The Octopus,*" *Frank Norris Studies,* no. 6 (Autumn 1988): 1–3;

Glen A. Love, "Frank Norris's Western Metropolitans," *Western American Literature,* 11 (March 1976): 3–22; republished in *Critical Essays,* edited by Graham;

Ernest Marchand, *Frank Norris: A Study* (Stanford, Cal.: Stanford University Press, 1942);

Stoddard Martin, *California Writers: Jack London, John Steinbeck, The Tough Guys* (London: Macmillan, 1983), pp. 7–17;

Joseph R. McElrath Jr., *Frank Norris Revisited* (New York: Twayne, 1992);

McElrath and Elizabeth Knight, *Frank Norris: The Critical Reception* (New York: Burt Franklin, 1981);

Irving McKee, "Notable Memorials to Mussel Slough," *Pacific Historical Review,* 17 (February 1948): 19–27;

John R. Milton, *The Novel of the American West* (Lincoln: University of Nebraska Press, 1980);

Donald Pizer, *The Novels of Frank Norris* (Bloomington: Indiana University Press, 1966);

André Poncet, "Anti-Racist Strategies in Frank Norris's Fiction," in *Les Américains et Les Autres,* edited by Serge Ricard (Aix-en-Provence: Publications de l'Université de Provence, 1982), pp. 55–63;

Robert Roripaugh, "The Writer's Sense of Place," *South Dakota Review,* 26 (Winter 1988): 111–120;

Edgeley W. Todd, "The Frontier Epic: Frank Norris and John G. Neihardt," *Western Humanities Review,* 13 (Winter 1959): 40–45;

Don D. Walker, "The Western Naturalism of Frank Norris," *Western American Literature,* 2 (Spring 1967): 14–29;

David Wyatt, *The Fall into Eden: Landscape and Imagination in California* (New York and Cambridge: Cambridge University Press, 1986).

Papers:

The major collection of Frank Norris's papers is at the Bancroft Library, University of California, Berkeley. Manuscripts are also held by the libraries of the State of California, Sacramento; the University of Southern California; Stanford University; Yale University; Northwestern University; Amherst College; Wellesley College; Columbia University; and the University of Virginia.

Bill Nye

(25 August 1850 – 22 February 1896)

David B. Kesterson
University of North Texas

See also the Nye entries in *DLB 11: American Humorists, 1800–1950* and *DLB 23: American Newspaper Journalists, 1873–1900.*

BOOKS: *A Howl in Rome* (Chicago, Milwaukee & Saint Paul, circa 1880);

Bill Nye and Boomerang; or, The Tale of a Meek-Eyed Mule and Some Other Literary Gems (Chicago: Belford, Clarke, 1881);

Forty Liars and Other Lies (Chicago & Saint Louis: Belford, Clarke, 1882);

Baled Hay: A Drier Book Than Walt Whitman's "Leaves o' Grass" (Chicago & New York: Belford, Clarke, 1884);

Boomerang Shots (London & New York: Ward, Lock, 1884);

Hits and Skits (London & New York: Ward, Lock, 1884);

Remarks, by Bill Nye (Chicago: A. E. Davis, 1887); republished as *Bill Nye's Red Book* (Chicago: Thompson & Thomas, 1906);

Bill Nye's Cordwood (Chicago: Rhodes & McClure, 1887);

Bill Nye's Chestnuts Old and New: Latest Gathering (Chicago & New York: Belford, Clarke, 1888);

An Aristocrat in America: Extracts from the Diary of the Right Honorable Lord William Henry Cavendish-Bentinck-Pelham-Clinton-St. Maur-Beauchamp-Devere, K. G. (New York: M. J. Ivers, 1888);

Nye and Riley's Railway Guide, by Nye and James Whitcomb Riley (Chicago, New York & San Francisco: Dearborn, 1888; London: Trübner, 1888); republished as *Nye and Riley's Wit and Humor* (New York: Neely, 1896); republished as *On the "Shoe-String" Limited* (Chicago: Thompson & Thomas, 1905); material by Nye republished as *Bill Nye's Grim Jokes* (Chicago: Conkey, n.d.);

Bill Nye's Thinks (Chicago, New York & San Francisco: Dearborn, 1888);

An Almanac for 1891 (N.p.: Privately printed, 1890);

Bill Nye's History of the United States (Philadelphia: Lippincott, 1894);

Bill Nye

Bill Nye's History of England From the Druids to the Reign of Henry VIII (Philadelphia: Lippincott, 1896);

A Guest at the Ludlow and Other Stories (Indianapolis & Kansas City: Bowen-Merrill, 1897);

The Funny Fellows Grab-Bag, by Nye and others (New York: Ogilvie, 1903).

PLAY PRODUCTIONS: *The Cadi,* New York, Union Square Theater, 21 September 1891;

The Stag Party, New York, Garden Theater, December 1895.

An essayist, journalist, platform lecturer, playwright, and writer of burlesque history, Bill Nye was one of the most important humorists of the second half of the nineteenth century. Although born in the East and raised in the Midwest, he achieved his fame in Laramie, Wyoming, as editor of the *Laramie Boomerang* and as author of books of humorous sketches and essays, many of which exhibit western influence in subject matter and literary techniques. As a humorist and satirist, Nye was ambivalent toward the West, being chauvinistic about his adopted region but also caustically critical of it. As he once commented, "The West is well known as the home of fearless and deadly journalism. It brings out all there is in a man and throws him upon his own resources. It also throws him down stairs if he is not constantly on his guard."

Edgar Wilson Nye was born in Shirley, Maine, the eldest of the three sons of Franklin Nye, a lumberman, and Elizabeth Mitchell Loring Nye, a member of the prominent Loring family of Piscataquis County. The Nye family soon moved to Hudson, Wisconsin. Nye later claimed in jest that he led his parents there by hand when only two years old. His only formal schooling was sixteen weeks at the local academy and two terms in a military school at nearby River Falls. At various times in young adulthood he was a miller, teacher, student at law, and budding journalist for local newspapers. When a position in a metropolitan newspaper in Minneapolis–Saint Paul failed to materialize, Nye left the Midwest and headed west to seek his literary and journalistic fortune, which he found in Laramie, Wyoming. After writing for the *Laramie Sentinel* in 1876 and 1877, where he first used the pen name Bill Nye, he helped to found a rival newspaper, the *Laramie Boomerang,* in 1881 and edited it until 1883. He also served as notary public, justice of the peace, U.S. land commissioner, and Laramie postmaster. In addition he was president of the Forty Liars Club, a gathering of local wits who met to tell stories and engage in lively discussion.

On 7 March 1877 he married Clara Francis Smith of Illinois, and by 1883 he had become the father of two daughters. (Five sons, one of whom died in infancy, were born after the Nyes left the West.) In 1883 ill health forced Nye to seek lower altitudes, and, after a short stay in Greeley, Colorado, he moved his family back to Hudson, Wisconsin. When he left Laramie, he wrote a humorous letter to President Chester A. Arthur announcing his resignation as postmaster. He facetiously informed the president that he was herewith delivering "the great seal and the key to the front door of the office" and added the combination to the safe. His letter con-

cluded with the suggestion that the president should "keep the heart-breaking news" of Nye's retirement from the great powers of Europe "until the dangers of a financial panic are fully past. Then hurl it broadcast with a sickening thud." Nye's wit was ever at play, even during times of adversity.

Nye's experiences in the West shaped his writings for his entire career. *Bill Nye's Chestnuts Old and New* (1888), for example, includes several western episodes (largely reprinted sketches from earlier books); his burlesque *Bill Nye's History of the United States* (1894) is written in an exaggerated western literary style; his autobiographical play *The Cadi* (1891) is about his life in Laramie as postmaster, justice of the peace, and newspaper editor; and even in his last book, the posthumously published *A Guest of the Ludlow and Other Stories* (1897), a few chapters have western settings or points of reference. The four books that derive most fully from Nye's years in the West, however, are *Bill Nye and Boomerang; or, The Tale of a Meek-Eyed Mule* (1881), *Forty Liars and Other Lies* (1882), *Baled Hay* (1884), and *Remarks, by Bill Nye* (1887, republished in 1906 as *Bill Nye's Redbook*).

Only two of these books, *Bill Nye and Boomerang* and *Forty Liars,* were published while Nye lived in the West. *Bill Nye and Boomerang* consists largely of sketches, essays, and short narratives that Nye contributed to the *Denver Tribune* and *Cheyenne Sun* during his early years in Laramie. In *Forty Liars* he collected pieces that he had written for the *Laramie Boomerang.* When Nye left Laramie for Wisconsin in 1883, he took with him clippings from the office file of the weekly *Boomerang,* which, along with some of his pieces for the *Denver Tribune,* form the contents of *Baled Hay. Remarks,* which appeared two years into Nye's career as platform lecturer, includes much material fashioned for the comic lecture circuit but retains considerable topical and narrative material that is western in nature and flair.

In these volumes Nye was fond of discussing the geographical, climatic, agricultural, and ecological characteristics of the West—as well as various aspects of western life and western versus eastern lifestyles and attitudes. The focus on the people of the West lends a vital element of local color to these writings. Nye was especially aware of Native Americans, Mormons, Chinese, outlaws, and western women; but politicians, miners, and other newspaper editors also drew his attention. Nye frequently employs satire, especially parody and burlesque, while using exaggeration in the forms of verbal extravagance, the tall tale, bizarre incidents, and slapstick antics. Occasionally he relies on violent or dan-

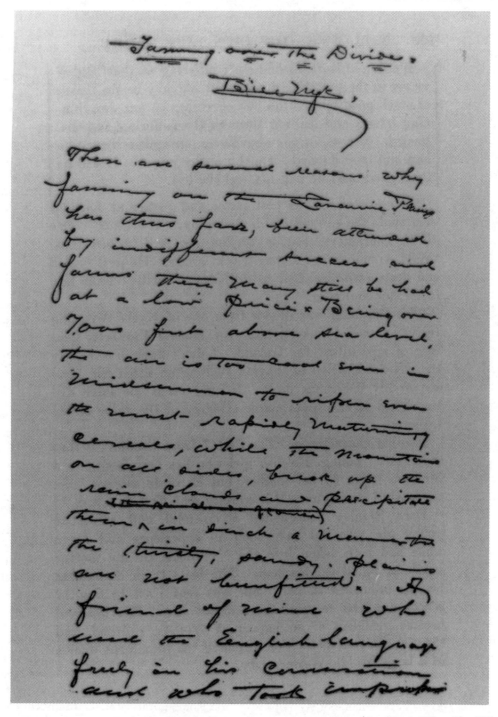

Page from the manuscript for one of Nye's columns about western agriculture (from Frank Wilson Nye, Bill
Nye: His Own Life Story, *1926)*

gerous incidents to convey comic effect, and he also uses picturesque language, anticlimax, understatement, and an occasional pun. Nye's ability to employ both dry wit and outrageous verbal flamboyance varies the tenor of his prose and renders it ever lively and full of surprises.

Since many of the pieces in Nye's first three full-length books were originally newspaper col-

umns, they are short, averaging two to four book pages in length. Other pieces were written especially for the published volumes, and Nye modified many of the newspaper columns by shortening pieces, rewriting portions, and supplying necessary transitions. The selections take the form of sketches, essays, short narrative interludes, anecdotes (often satiric), and occasional poems. Informal, lively, and

ROPING IN AN INVALID.

Illustration from Forty Liars and Other Lies, *a collection of comic essays and sketches inspired by the Rocky Mountain Division of the Independent Order of Forty Liars, a Laramie club to which Nye belonged*

witty in tone, the pieces usually focus on and develop single topics; Nye did not normally digress.

The "Boomerang" in the title *Bill Nye and Boomerang; or, The Tale of a Meek-Eyed Mule, and Some Other Literary Gems*—as well as the name of Nye's Laramie newspaper and a mine in which Nye invested—is his pet mule Boomerang. Nye dedicates the volume to the mule, "whose low, mellow notes are ever sounding in my ears, to whom I owe all that I am as a great man, and whose presence has inspired me ever and anon." The first piece in the volume is a poem to Boomerang, "Apostrophe to an Orphan Mule." The book includes 114 selections, mainly essays, sketches, burlesques, and other satires. More than a third of the pieces focus directly on some aspect of the West, its people, mining, ge-

ography, weather, customs, or other facets of life there. He exulted poetically in the glory of a western sunset ("A Rocky Mountain Sunset") but has reservations about the climate: "Sometimes I wish that Wyoming had more vegetation and less catarrh, more bloom and summer and fragrance and less Christmas and New Year's through the summer" ("The Weather and Some Other Things"). He wrote about planting seeds but was not hopeful of favorable results in a place "where winter lingers in the lap of spring till after the Fourth of July." Cabbage plants, he wrote, have to arise from their beds on a summer day "and run up and down the garden walk to keep their feet from freezing" ("Agriculture at an Altitude of 7500 Feet").

In *Bill Nye and Boomerang,* as in the books to follow, Nye's favorite subject is the people of the West. He could be quite understanding of people and the conditions they face, or he could be surprisingly harsh and callous. One of his favorite subjects was miners and mining. Seven pieces in this book cover the trials and tribulations of the western miner, the difficulties and loneliness of mining, and the exasperation that often accompanies the enterprise. But he could poke fun at the enterprise too, as in "A Miner's Meeting—My Mine—a Mirage on the Plains," in which he playfully wrote of conducting a miners' meeting: "I presided over the meeting to give it an air of terror and gloom. It was very impressive. There was hardly a dry eye in the house as I was led to the chair by two old miners."

In some thirteen selections in *Bill Nye and Boomerang* Nye reveals his blatant prejudices against Native Americans. Like many other white Americans of his time, he thinks little of Indians, especially the Utes, seeing them as an unproductive and ignoble people. Their only redeeming grace to Nye is their oratorical skills, which he often extols. In "Ute Eloquence," for example, Nye gives a version of a speech made by the chieftain Colorow to his followers and white onlookers as the Indians are about to be displaced from their land. Nye comments that "few people actually know the true spirit of Greek and Roman oratory that still lingers about the remnants of this people." It is possible that Nye's kinder treatment of Native Americans in this regard stems from his own keen interest in public speaking, an interest that later led Nye to the lecture circuit.

Nye is not as harsh toward the Chinese who had come to Wyoming to work in mining camps. Although he does engage in some social satire, as in the sketch "You Fou," and employs the dark humor of physical discomfort in "Hong Lee's Grand Benefit at Leadville," he is normally more accepting of the Chinese than of Native Americans. He concludes "William Nye and the Heathen Chinee" (a take-off on Bret Harte's well-known poem) by commenting: "There is a feeling now too prevalent among our American people that the Chinaman should be driven away, but I do not join in the popular cry because I enjoy him too much, and he soothes me and cheers me when all the earth seems filled with woe."

Several selections in *Bill Nye and Boomerang* are characterized by the sort of western humor that Nye employed frequently throughout his career. Nye exhibits his skill in the classic exaggeration of frontier humor in descriptions such as his commentary on an inedible pumpkin pie ("the first genuine cane-bottomed pie, with patent dust damper and nickel-plated movement that we have tasted since we came west") and his account of a rancher examining a frozen steer that is "near enough [to death] to hear the rush of wings, and was just going to register and engage a room in the new Jerusalem when he returned to consciousness." It is often Nye's large doses of signature bizarre phrasing that make his writing so interesting. For example, the title of a sketch such as "The Buckness Wherewith the Buck Beer Bucketh" illustrates Nye's characteristic playing with words and their sounds.

Named after the club Nye presided over in Laramie, *Forty Liars and Other Lies* comprises 119 selections, mostly prose and many on western subjects. The title page quotes George Gordon, Lord Byron: "Praise be all liars and all lies." In the "Overture," or preface, Nye establishes the comic tone of the book by saying facetiously that his first book attained such great heights of success that this second volume is "in response to a clamoring appeal on the part of the American people." (Nye was actually correct about the popularity of his writing. Each of his first three books, in fact, sold more than one hundred thousand copies and went through ten editions.) *Forty Liars* boasts illustrations by Livingston Hopkins.

Two of the essay-sketches in *Forty Liars and Other Lies* are about meetings of the Liars' Club (officially named the Rocky Mountain Division of the Independent Order of Forty Liars) and are among the funniest satiric pieces in the book. In "The Forty Liars" the group selects as the "Most Noble Prevaricator of the Year" Brother Jedediah Holcomb, who boasts that he became a successful capitalist after finding a procession of 13,521 blind hogs on the prairie near Chicago and leading them to the stockyards. "The Forty Liars. The April Meeting" recounts a prevaricator's preposterous story of a man who, alone and starving on the prairie, eats an entire Indian tribe.

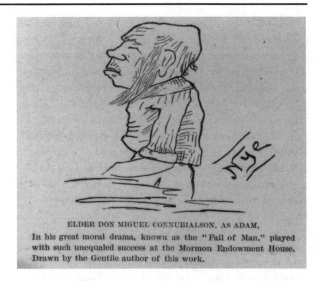

ELDER DON MIGUEL CONNUBIALSON, AS ADAM,
In his great moral drama, known as the "Fall of Man," played with such unequaled success at the Mormon Endowment House. Drawn by the Gentile author of this work.

Illustration by Nye for "Are You A Mormon?" in Baled Hay

Like Nye's first book, *Forty Liars and Other Lies* includes several essays about Native Americans and conditions in the West. As in all Nye's western books, there are also sketches on the Mormons, against whom Nye was also decidedly prejudiced. Nye's later claim in *Remarks, by Bill Nye* that he was "moderately liberal and free upon all religious matters" did not hold true in his views of the Latter-Day Saints. Other western humorists from Artemus Ward to Mark Twain depicted the Mormons in a humorous and critical vein, reflecting the attitudes of many of their contemporaries, but Nye's satire of the sect often resorts to Swiftian invective. He vilifies them in "The Mormons," a sketch about a trainload of Latter-Day Saints passing through Laramie: "Those who passed through yesterday were in a damaged condition. . . . When they got here their trainer took the hose and turned it on the cages to purify the air a little." A similar condemnation is registered in "About the Mormon," in which Nye's chief criticism is over their practice of polygamy: "When a man dies it takes so much gloom to go around among the members of the family." In "An Explanation" he says that there is no green grass on Brigham Young's grave because the voluminous tears of widows and orphans so taint the ground "that a bilious cactus in one corner of the prophet's corral has all it can do to drag out a miserable existence." Similar criticism of the Mormons is levied in "The Morbidly Matrimonial Mormon" and "A Cruel Stab."

Nye's treatment of the Mormons in *Forty Liars and Other Lies* is offset by his more positive, or at least more genuinely humorous, treatments of other aspects of life in the West, from journalism to mining. The book is rich in Nye's dry wit and picturesque speech. In "Patrick Oleson" young Patrick's father, who is convicted of killing Patrick's mother, is "unanimously chosen by a convention of six property-holders of the county to jump from a new pine platform into the sweet subsequently." The hilarious antipastoral "Sleeping With a Rocky Mountain" shows Nye at his cleverest in evoking images. Responding to many people's desire to camp out in the pristine Rocky Mountains and enjoy getting away from civilization, Nye tells of having done it and suffered all the accompanying hardships:

> The everlasting snow-capped mountains, lifting their sunlit summits to the sky, are a pretty good thing, but they look better about thirty-seven and a half miles distant than they do when they are in bed with you, because they have got such cold feet. The little dancing torrent as it canters along to the ocean and bathes the feet of the mountain, is a pretty good thing–in a blue covered book–but when you come to grasp the reality and see that same little streamlet waddle along over the corns and chilblains on the foot of the mountain, and hear it murmur all night so that you can't sleep, the murmuring gets tiresome, and you begin to murmur yourself after a while.

Baled Hay: A Drier Book Than Walt Whitman's "Leaves o' Grass" comprises 138 selections, largely essays, sketches, and satiric narratives but also some forty-one "space fillers": jokes, witticisms, puns, and amusing tidbits of information. Nye dedicated the book to his wife, "Who has courteously and heroically laughed at my feeble and emaciated jokes, even when she did not feel like it; who has again and again started up and agitated successfully the flagging and reluctant applause, who has courageously held my coat through this trying ordeal, and who, even now, as I write this, is in the front yard warning people to keep off the premises until I have another lucid interval." Except for two drawings by Nye himself, the book is illustrated by the well-known illustrator Fred Opper.

Since most of the contents of *Baled Hay* consist of Nye's *Boomerang* columns, they closely resemble the writings in the first two books, except for the clever space fillers. The book again includes essays on subjects such as Native Americans, the Mormons, miners and mines, outlaws, journalism, western topography, and holding public office. Nye's humor, especially his use of hyperbole, is ever present. In "Congratulatory" he describes his service as notary public in Laramie, humorously inflating the status and importance of the position and its duties: "The nation to-day looks to her notaries public for her crowning glory and successful future. In their hands rest the might and the grandeur and the glory which, like a halo, in the years to come, will encircle the brow of Columbia. I feel the responsibility that rests upon me, and I tremble with the mighty weight of weal or woe for a great nation which hangs on my every official act."

Baled Hay also includes examples of Nye's darker, sometimes even sick, humor, which reflects the harsh reality of life in the West. The details can be gruesome. In "Yanked to Eternity" a drunken mining crew descends a mountain on a runaway push car. Attempting to stop the car and save the others, one man leaps off the cart with a rope tethered around him. The other miners are saved, but the rescuer will "never entirely return. He has done so partially, of course, but there are still missing fragments of him, and it looks as though he must have lost his life." In "A Letter from Leadville," describing a narrow railroad tunnel that is twenty-six-hundred feet long and located at the highest railroad point in the United States, Nye wrote that the brakeman makes passengers close their windows when the train goes through this tunnel because the railroad does not like to hire extra help "to go through the tunnel twice a day and wipe the remains of tourists off the walls." Nye often wrote about the outlaws of the West, in ways reminiscent of Mark Twain's accounts of J. A. Slade and other bad men in *Roughing It* (1872). In "His Aged Mother," one of several sketches on Jesse James that appear throughout Nye's works, Nye ponders why there was not an autopsy performed on Jesse's corpse to determine what made him ill-natured. He concludes that Jesse's mother would have felt "wretched and gloomy when she saw her son with his vitals in one market basket, and his vertebrae in another." The morbid, grotesque, and unsavory are vital components of western humor. Nye adopted them and gave them his own grimly comic treatment.

By the time Nye published the fourth of his western books, *Remarks, by Bill Nye* (1887), his life and career had changed considerably. After settling in Wisconsin he had become active as a humorous lecturer and was soon to become a major star on the platform circuit. *Remarks* includes 191 selections, generally longer and more fully developed than the pieces in Nye's first three books. The book also includes more than 150 illustrations by J. H. Smith. Although more than 20 percent of the contents relate to the West, the range of subjects covered illustrates how Nye's interests and knowledge had broadened since he left Wyoming. He had begun to write about history and biography, which he later approached in two burlesque histories of the United States and England. He also discussed platform lecturing, journalism, and a wide assortment of new subjects, including Washington, D.C., foreign countries, and the sport of boxing. His exaggerated wit is subdued and his colorful language is less apparent in *Remarks*. His writing is more catholic and mature, and his essays and sketches are more penetrating, encompassing, and often more serious in nature. He humorously acknowledged the different nature of this volume in his prefatory "Directions," quipping, "The range of subjects treated in this book is wonderful, even to me. It is a library of universal knowledge, and the facts contained in it are different from any other facts now in use." He calls this volume his "greatest and best book. It is the one that will live for weeks after other books have passed away." The volume also includes a brief biographical sketch of Nye, punctuated by humorous quotations from him about various stages of his life.

There are still some essays on Indians, Mormons, and miners and mining in *Remarks,* but there is also more commentary about the culture of the West and more narrative material. Western women were a subject dear to Nye, who acknowledged their contributions to western life and boasted about Wyoming's being the first state in the union to allow female suffrage. In Nye's western books there are several pieces about women and their importance to the growth and maturity of the West. Even the ironic "Women's Wonderful Influence," narrated by the rustic Woodtick Williams, extols the importance of women despite the narrator's limited perceptivity.

In *Remarks* Nye explores the culture and the aura of the West perhaps more fully than in the three earlier books, often contrasting it to eastern culture, which he depicts as overly civilized to the point of effeteness. Sometimes he writes of the danger and cruelty in western culture. For example, in "The Opium Habit" he recounts an incident near Medicine Bow in which a young man is shot by a herdsman on a sheep ranch. The sketch explores how a group of citizens takes the law into their own hands, hanging the killer and then claiming that he committed suicide by overdosing on opium. Nye quips, "Death by opium, it seems, leaves a dark purple ring around the neck. . . . People who die by opium also tie their hands together before they die." Sometimes the savagery of the West is more myth than reality, and Nye wrote essays that attempt to depict the West from a more balanced perspective. For example, in "The Cow-Boy" he exploded the myth of the rough-and-tough cowboy who is not only skilled with firearms but eager to use them: "I've known more cow-boys to injure themselves

Title page, with a caricature of Nye, for his burlesque version of American history

with their own revolvers than to injure anyone else. This is evidently because they were more familiar with the hoe than they are with the Smith & Wesson." Whereas myth has it that the cowboy, "with his abnormal thirst for blood," is born "in a buffalo wallow at the foot of some rock-ribbed mountain," generally he "was born in unostentatious manner on the farm."

In "The Holy Terror," a narrative somewhat resembling Stephen Crane's "The Blue Hotel" (1899), Nye depicts a New Englander who comes west to experience the tough, wild environment he has imagined. He buys himself a revolver and journeys to Cheyenne (which he pronounces "Chieene"), but there he meets with nothing but disappointment. At the railroad station he finds "hacks and 'busses and carriages" to transport people to the hotel, which he finds comfortably furnished and equipped with gas lights. There he is asked to check his gun at the reservation counter. He attends an opera performed by Italian singers. Even the streets are lit with electricity, and the people politely look down on him for the way he is dressed and acts. As the easterner observes, "They seemed to look at me as if I wasn't to blame for it, and as if they felt sorry for me. If I'd had my United States clothes with me, I could have had a good deal of fun in Chi-eene, going to the opera, and the lectures, and the concerts, et cetera." In this narrative, as in many other sketches and essays throughout his western books, Nye attempted to set the record straight about life in the West, and he often disparaged effete easterners who looked on the West condescendingly or with false romantic notions about western life.

Nye also felt that the West was solving many of its social problems more successfully than the East. He believed that the typical openness and directness of westerners led to the improvement of society. That improvement, however, is not without its disadvantages. In "No More Frontier" he wrote about how the advent of the railroad had civilized the West to the detriment of its once pristine state and wholesome pioneer life. The railroad bed, moreover, "is lined with empty beer bottles and peach cans that have outlived their usefulness. No landscape can be picturesque with an empty peach can in the foreground."

Two of the liveliest narratives in *Remarks* are "Twombley's Tale" and "Broncho Sam." "Twombley's Tale," set in Utah's Wasatch Mountains, is a delightful spoof of the romantic tale as well as a tongue-in-cheek tall tale of the West. G. O. P. Twombley, a goatherd, falls down an abandoned mine shaft, where he resolves to remain "until I could decide what was best to be done." Yet, he adds, "I hated to spend the next few weeks in the shaft, for I had not locked up my cabin when I had left it, and I feared that someone might get in while I was absent and play the piano." After a comely young woman also falls down the shaft, the two discuss marriage (though she is already one of several wives of a Mormon). Finally they decide to get out of the shaft and elope, which they do. The anticlimax, understatement, and non sequitur of this narrative are examples of Nye at his best. Deft phrasing and use of humorous techniques are also evident in "Broncho Sam," a sketch reminiscent of Mark Twain's unfortunate experience with the "Genuine Mexican Plug" in *Roughing It*. Nye's narrator so admires the way Broncho Sam Stewart breaks fresh horses that he decides to try one himself. In classic understatement he admits that "it occupied my entire attention to safely ride the cunning little beast, and when he began to ride me I put in a minority report against it." He concludes that having experienced both an earthquake and an Indian outbreak, he would prefer either to being astride "a successful broncho eruption."

For Nye *Remarks* was a transitional book that hearkens back to his experiences in the West and draws from the broader circle of activities in which he had become involved in Wisconsin and on the lecture circuit. It is a rich book, one that can still be enjoyed for its variety of humorous, and serious, approaches to a wide range of subjects.

Nye's rise to fame as a platform lecturer was already in motion when *Remarks* was published. He soon became one of circuit entrepreneur Major James B. Pond's "one-hundred-dollar-a-night men," and toured the United States and Canada. He also made some appearances abroad. In 1887 his renown prompted the *New York World* to offer Nye a role as weekly humor columnist, and Nye and family moved to New York. He wrote a Sunday column as well as continuing to lecture until his death in 1896. He left New York in 1891 and moved his family to the Asheville, North Carolina, area.

Despite his heavy commitments as lecturer and columnist, Nye continued to produce books and even wrote two plays. His play *The Cadi,* which ran on Broadway for 125 performances, is set in Wyoming and New York and features Nye as newspaper editor, postmaster, and justice of the peace. The script has not survived, but comments from reviews reveal that it was the Nye persona and, in part, the western material, that lent the play its special appeal.

Three of the twenty-eight essays in *A Guest at the Ludlow and Other Stories* (1897), which are reprinted from Nye's columns for the *New York World,* can be said to include Nye's last words on the West. In "A Journey Westward" he revisits his "old haunts" in Colorado and Wyoming after an absence of seven years and also goes to Salt Lake City, Utah. Impressed by the extent to which real estate has supplanted mining as the chief profit-making enterprise, he even buys a piece of land in Salt Lake City for the price of one night's lecture receipts. He visits friends in Wyoming, and in Cheyenne both houses of the legislature adjourn for an hour in his honor. He jests that the welcoming speech by one legislator was "almost as good and truthful as an epitaph." In "A Prophet and a Piute" he speaks of buying property in Oakland, California, and then paints a colorful portrait of the Paiute Indian who met him at the train depot in Reno, Nevada, and praised Nye's work, saying he had collected all of Nye's writings in a scrapbook at home. Nye discovers later that the Paiute "was an earnest and hopeful liar" who has neither scrapbook nor house. The final essay, "As a Candidate," is an account of Nye's unsuccessful 1877 campaign for the Wyoming legislature. With the exception of parts of "A Prophet and a Piute"

"Nye Contemplating His Birthplace," illustration by Eugene Zimmerman ("Zim")

the pieces in this book are quite different from the majority of western materials in his early books. They are much more restrained and urbane in their humor, more fully developed, and more reflective on the changes that were occurring in the West in the 1890s. In "A Journey Westward" Nye jokes that three coyotes in Wyoming eye him as if to say, "Why, partner, how you have fleshed up." To which Nye replies, "Go East, young men, and flesh up with the country." No matter how Nye changed after moving east, his western experience always provided an undergirding, an enriched resource to be mined at his will, and he never ceased to take advantage of it.

Nye was so popular during the 1880s and 1890s that pirated editions of his books were published, and after he died in 1896 his publishers continued to publish new and reprinted collections of his writings. Nye's persona—a tall, angular, bald-headed figure—was well known to the public because caricature sketches of him usually appeared in his newspaper columns. It has been reported that Nye sometimes received letters with only the caricature and the words *New York, N.Y.* on the envelope. As early as 1882 Will M. Clemens said that "Bill Nye has, during the past two years, written a larger quantity and a better quality of first-class, genuine humor, than any other funny man in America." Walter Blair fully agreed, saying that Nye was "about the last man in the nineteenth-century humorous school to win popularity."

Always ready with some witty sage comment on any situation, Nye was known as a genial humor-

ist who could laugh at himself as a flawed cog in the imperfect machinery of the world. Yet there was also a darker side to his humor. It could be grim and cynical as Nye pondered the ultimate nature and progression of life, which he termed the "pathway to the grave." He sometimes wrote of life's transiency and the vanity of human endeavors. Dark humor occasionally punctuated his western writings, and his humor could be cruel, even resorting to invective. He could damn the West in one moment, praise it and defend it in another, and express ambivalence toward it in the next. He used humor to get at the hidden meanings of life and coped with its realities through ironic insights.

Bill Nye is obviously no longer a household name. Like that of the rest of the literary comedians, his reputation has suffered decline. As early as 1906, in fact, just ten years after Nye's death, Twain looked back on the literary comedians and declared there were no survivors, proclaiming an anthology of their writings a "cemetery." There has been some resurgence of interest in the literary comedians among scholars since the mid twentieth century, with Walter Blair, Hamlin Hill, and Jesse Bier framing them in new light. Nye's memory has been kept alive in Wyoming, where the current *Laramie Boomerang* occasionally reprints some of Nye's columns. Unfortunately for general readers, however, not only has the style of humor changed, but the forms in which Nye wrote—mainly short sketches, brief essays, and vignettes crafted for newspaper columns or lecture interludes—do not constitute popular reading today. Yet Nye's writings have an ironic, often sardonic point of view that is much in keeping with modern tastes. Since he largely avoided topical political satire and the dated devices of faulty grammar, intentional misspellings, and other verbal tricks, his prose would be more palatable to the contemporary reader than that of many of his contemporaries. The modern reader who delves into Nye's works discovers a writer who, as T. A. Larson has said, produced much that "still transmits to the contemporary reader the whimsy and the idiocy that make people laugh." Moreover, he articulated a perspective of the American West that, despite his prejudices, helped the rest of the nation to understand that fascinating, developing part of the nation.

Letters:

"Letters of Riley and Bill Nye," edited by Edmund H. Eitel, *Harper's,* 138 (March 1919): 473–484;

Letters of Edgar Wilson Nye Now in the University of Wyoming Library, edited by Nixon Orwin Rush (Laramie: University of Wyoming Library, 1950).

Bibliography:

David B. Kesterson, "Edgar Wilson (Bill) Nye," *Bibliography of American Fiction 1866–1918,* edited by James Nagel and Gwen L. Nagel (New York & Oxford: Manly/Facts On File, 1993), pp. 298–300.

Biography:

Frank Wilson Nye, *Bill Nye: His Own Life Story* (New York: Century, 1926).

References:

Jesse Bier, *The Rise and Fall of American Humor* (New York: Holt, Rinehart & Winston, 1968);

Walter Blair, "The Background of Bill Nye in American Humor," dissertation, University of Chicago, 1931;

Blair, *Horse Sense in American Humor* (Chicago: University of Chicago Press, 1942);

Blair, *Native American Humor, 1800–1900* (New York: American Book Company, 1937);

Frank Sumner Burrage, "Bill Nye (1850–1896)," *Annals of Wyoming,* 18 (January 1946): 79–87;

W. E. Chaplin, "Bill Nye," *Frontier,* 22 (March 1931): 223–226;

Chaplin, "Bill Nye in Laramie," in *Second Biennial Report, 1921–1923, State Historian of Wyoming* (Sheridan, Wyo.: Mills, 1923), pp. 142–158;

Chaplin, "Some Wyoming Editors I Have Known," *Annals of Wyoming,* 18 (January 1946): 79–87;

Levette J. Davidson, "'Bill' Nye and the *Denver Tribune,*" *Colorado Magazine,* 4 (January 1927): 13–18;

O. N. Gibson, "Bill Nye," *Annals of Wyoming,* 3 (July 1925): 95–104;

David B. Kesterson, *Bill Nye* (Boston: Twayne, 1981);

Kesterson, *Bill Nye: The Western Writings* (Boise, Idaho: Boise State University, 1976);

Melville D. Landon, *Kings of the Platform and Pulpit* (Chicago: Werner, 1895);

T. A. Larson, ed., *Bill Nye's Western Humor* (Lincoln: University of Nebraska Press, 1968);

Larson, "Laramie's Bill Nye," *The Denver West–1952 Brand Book* (Denver: Westerners, 1953), pp. 34–56;

J. B. Pond, *Eccentricities of Genius* (New York: Dillingham, 1900).

Papers:

The most complete collection of Nye's manuscripts, letters, and documents is the Bill Nye Collection at the University of Wyoming library.

Francis Parkman
(16 September 1823 – 8 November 1893)

Michael J. Mullin
Augustana College

See also the Parkman entries in *DLB 1: The American Renaissance in New England; DLB 30: American Historians, 1607–1865;* and *DLB 183: American Travel Writers: 1776–1864.*

BOOKS: *The California and Oregon Trail: Being Sketches of Prairie and Rocky Mountain Life* (New York & London: Putnam, 1849); revised as *The Oregon Trail* (Boston: Little, Brown, 1872);

History of the Conspiracy of Pontiac, and the War of the North American Tribes against the English Colonies after the Conquest of Canada (2 volumes, London: Bentley, 1851; 1 volume, Boston: Little, Brown / London: Bentley, 1851; revised edition, Boston: Little, Brown, 1868; enlarged, 2 volumes, 1870);

Vassall Morton: A Novel (Boston: Phillips, Sampson, 1856);

Pioneers of France in the New World, part 1 of *France and England in North America. A Series of Historical Narratives . . .* (Boston: Little, Brown, 1865; London: Routledge, 1868; revised and enlarged edition, Boston: Little, Brown, 1886);

The Book of Roses (Boston: Tilton, 1866);

The Jesuits in North America in the Seventeenth Century, part 2 of *France and England in North America . . .* (Boston: Little, Brown, 1867; London: Routledge, 1868);

The Discovery of the Great West, part 3 of *France and England in North America . . .* (Boston: Little, Brown, 1869); revised and enlarged as *La Salle and the Discovery of the Great West* (Boston: Little, Brown, 1879);

The Old Régime in Canada, part 4 of *France and England in North America . . .* (Boston: Little, Brown, 1874; London: Sampson Low, 1875; revised and enlarged, 1894);

Count Frontenac and New France under Louis XIV, part 5 of *France and England in North America . . .* (Boston: Little, Brown, 1877);

Some of the Reasons against Woman Suffrage (N.p., 1883);

Francis Parkman

Montcalm and Wolfe, part 7 of *France and England in North America . . . ,* 2 volumes (Boston: Little, Brown, 1884; London: Macmillan, 1884; revised and enlarged edition, Boston: Little, Brown, 1886);

Our Common Schools (Boston: Citizens' Public School Union, 1890);

A Half-Century of Conflict, part 6 of *France and England in North America . . . ,* 2 volumes (Boston: Little, Brown, 1892; London: Macmillan, 1892);

The Journals of Francis Parkman, 2 volumes, edited by Mason Wade (New York: Harper, 1947).

Collection: *The Works of Francis Parkman,* 20 volumes (Boston: Little, Brown, 1897–1898).

OTHER: William Smith, *Historical Account of Bouquet's Expedition against the Ohio Indians, in 1764,* preface by Parkman (Cincinnati: Clarke, 1868);

"Louis, Count Frontenac," in *Appletons' Cyclopaedia of American Biography,* volume 2, edited by James Grant Wilson and John Fiske (New York: Appleton, 1887), pp. 553–555;

"Marquis de Montcalm," in *Appletons' Cyclopaedia of American Biography,* volume 4, edited by Wilson and Fiske (New York: Appleton, 1889), pp. 363–365;

Mary Hartwell Catherwood, *The Romance of Dollard,* preface by Parkman (New York: Century, 1889);

"Robert Cavalier de la Salle," in *Appletons' Cyclopaedia of American Biography,* volume 3, edited by Wilson and Fiske (New York: Appleton, 1900), pp. 621–622.

SELECTED PERIODICAL PUBLICATIONS–
UNCOLLECTED: "The Scalp-Hunter," *Knickerbocker,* 25 (1845): 297–303;

"The History of the Conspiracy of Pontiac," *North American Review,* 73 (1851): 495–529;

"The Works of James Fenimore Cooper," *North American Review,* 74 (December 1852): 147–161;

"Exploring the Magalloway," *Harper's,* 29 (1864): 735–741;

"The Tale of the Ripe Scholar," *Nation,* 234 (1869): 558–560.

Francis Parkman was the first scholar to take the colonial frontier seriously as a subject, and his multivolume history, *France and England in North America* (1865–1892), shaped the conventions for writing colonial, frontier, and Native American history until World War II. His writing illustrated the continuity between America's attempt to subdue the area west of the Mississippi and England's efforts at taming the American continent east of the Mississippi a century earlier. The ingenuity, toughness, and fortitude of the California migrants Parkman observed were manifested in his characters. The reaction of the peoples of the Plains to the migrants passing through their land had already been played out in Pontiac's Rebellion. Parkman's focus on the environment set the tone for western scholarship in the years to come. Nature forced his characters to adapt, survive, triumph, or fail. His strength as a writer lay in his ability to convey the immediacy of historical events to the reader.

Francis Parkman, son of the Reverend Francis Parkman and Caroline Hall Parkman, was born in Boston in 1823 to a life of privilege. The family's wealth had been accumulated through the business acumen of Samuel Parkman, Francis's paternal grandfather, and this financial security was to provide young Francis Parkman with the independence he needed to pursue a career as an author.

At the age of eight Parkman, who was not a healthy child, was sent by his family to live with his maternal grandfather in Medford, Massachusetts, where his parents hoped the new surroundings would improve his condition. He lived in Medford nearly five years, and there he spent his time exploring the surrounding Middlesex Fells area. These experiences gave him a love of nature and wilderness, and they also nurtured his desire for the active life that distinguishes the heroes of his writings. As a typical protagonist, René-Robert de La Salle Cavelier, is one example of a Parkman hero who is more comfortable in the wilds of America than in the courts of Europe. Parkman's books depict wilderness as "an ecological conditioner of civilized man," and his early experiences at Medford left him dreaming of untouched wildernesses, areas he visited even after he entered Harvard College in 1840.

Francis was not the best of students at Harvard. He failed a mathematics examination because, as he said, shooting his rifle interested him more than studying mathematics. He displayed other such acts of defiance at Harvard, and his actions reveal personal attitudes that are also evident in his writing. He either liked something or did not like it, and his attitudes rarely changed. One subject that interested him was the history of the American colonies, and, according to Edward Wheelwright, while Parkman was attending Harvard, he decided to write his history of "the Old French War."

Jared Sparks and Edward Tyrrell Channing were two Harvard scholars who encouraged young Parkman. Sparks encouraged him to pursue his interest in the colonial struggle between France and England, and Sparks often recommended specific works on the subject. Years later Sparks continued to help by writing to his colleagues abroad and requesting that they help Parkman, his former student, in locating materials to begin his historical researches. Channing, Parkman's other mentor, was a rhetoric professor who helped the young man by building on skills Parkman had begun to develop under William Russell, an earlier teacher. Russell, who had wanted to teach Parkman to write well through imitating good writers, had encouraged Parkman to translate Greek and Latin texts in prose and verse. Channing taught Parkman to go beyond imitation and improved his student's style. Channing's prose, along with Sparks's encouragement and Parkman's later experience in law school, helped Parkman focus his topic, evaluate his evi-

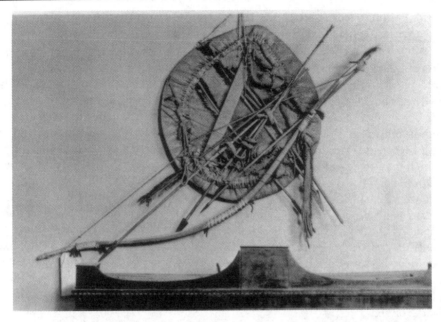

Sioux shield, bow, and arrows, souvenirs of Parkman's Oregon Trail excursion of 1846

dence, and revise his writing until it was coherent and readable. To convey his appreciation Parkman later dedicated his *History of the Conspiracy of Pontiac, and the War of the North American Tribes against the English Colonies after the Conquest of Canada* (1851) to Sparks.

Throughout his life Parkman read and admired the works of George Gordon, Lord Byron; Sir Walter Scott; and James Fenimore Cooper. Encouraged by Cooper's Leatherstocking tales, Parkman later decided to write his own version of the colonial frontier, and he used as models for his Native Americans those of Cooper's works. Parkman's graduation oration at Harvard revealed Cooper's influence, and Parkman also praised Cooper's books in "The Works of James Fenimore Cooper," an article published in the *North American Review* in December 1852. In the first edition of *The California and Oregon Trail: Being Sketches of Prairie and Rocky Mountain Life* (1849) Parkman acknowledges his admiration for Byron and Scott by beginning his chapters with passages from their works.

Parkman spent his summers visiting the American frontier during his years as a student at Harvard, and as he prepared to write his study of the Anglo-French struggle for North America, he continued to take these trips after he graduated in 1844. The most famous of these trips was his Oregon Trail experience in 1846, but even while he was still a student in 1841, he and a companion visited the White Mountains of New Hampshire. One experience on this early trip almost cost him his life when he foolishly climbed a ravine near Crawford Notch. Halfway up he became stuck, and the rocks beneath him began to give way. Keeping his wits, however, he managed to work up the ravine to safety.

Parkman incorporated this episode into "The Scalp-Hunter," a fictional tale he published anonymously in *Knickerbocker Magazine* in 1845. In this story a group of colonial hunters are pursuing a Native American in the White Mountains, and gradually the number of pursuers diminishes until only a lone hunter remains. The situation Parkman had experienced on his 1841 climb provides the climax when the warrior escapes his pursuer by making a daring climb up this same ravine. When Parkman's fictional pursuer becomes stuck, however, the warrior sees the settler fall to his death on the rocks below, and he returns to the body to scalp the dead man.

The hunter in this early story features qualities Parkman later emphasizes in all his heroes: tenacity of purpose and a willingness to pursue an objective despite all odds, even if it means death. "The Scalp-Hunter" marks Parkman's debut as a writer, and it shows his fondness for adventure narratives as well as his willingness to draw on his own experiences in writing. He continued to draw on his personal experience of places in his later historical writings, as is seen in "Exploring the Magalloway," a narrative based on an 1842 trip into the wilderness and published in *Harper's Magazine* in 1864. As articles such as "The Scalp-Hunter" and "Exploring the

Magalloway" reveal, Parkman learned to create his historical pieces by interlacing personal experiences into his narrative, often blending fact and fiction.

During his travels Parkman also kept journals, and in these he recorded firsthand accounts of the places he was to write about. He regularly referred to these journals in writing, and he integrated whole sections from them into his published works. They provided him with records for descriptions of the environment in which the subjects of his pieces later appeared. For example, Howard Doughty writes that a revised account of Parkman's 1841 trip provided the core of Parkman's description "of [Samuel de] Champlain's famous Ottawa voyage" in *Pioneers of France in the New World* (1865). Parkman's Oregon Trail journal provided the foundation of his first full-length work, *The California and Oregon Trail,* the book that established his reputation as a writer about the American frontier.

More travelogue than history, *The California and Oregon Trail* remains Parkman's most popular book. It recounts his trip from Saint Louis to Fort Laramie, Wyoming, and south to Pueblo, Colorado, before his return to the East. Parkman took the trek hoping to spend time among Native Americans, and at a Teton-Dakota camp he got his wish. What gives the book its vitality is the intimacy of Parkman's narrative, for he is not only the narrator but also a participant. Throughout the book he offers judgments about the characters he encounters, judgments most often uncomplimentary toward frontiersmen and women. His seven months on the Oregon Trail marked his last major trip into the American wilderness, for after 1849 health problems and his marriage (to Catherine Scollay Bigelow in 1850) restricted him to making limited excursions and to writing. In letters to friends he lamented having to give up such travels.

After completing *The California and Oregon Trail* Parkman began his study of Pontiac, the Ottawa war chief. His *History of the Conspiracy of Pontiac,* written when Parkman believed that he was dying, was the first historical work that Parkman wrote, and in it one can see the beginning of Parkman's merging of history and literature. *Pontiac* convinced him that the public would read a historically accurate account of the Anglo-French struggle for North America, although Parkman presents the Native American characters more as archetypes than as people: they appear less complex, more naive, more violent, and less thoughtful than twentieth-century scholars know them to have been. These flaws in Parkman's accounts disappeared as he completed his seven-volume series, *France and England in North America.* By

the end of that series his Native Americans appear as multidimensional characters.

While not part of that historical series, *Pontiac* shares many similarities with it. Through providing a study of matched opposites in the characters of Pontiac and Maj. Henry Gladwin, commander of Fort Detroit, in the first three chapters of *Pontiac,* Parkman adopts the framework that he follows in structuring his series by pairing up heroes and villains. Moreover, his writing is best when he can match his hero against an opponent, and this opponent need not be human, as Parkman's presentation of nature reveals in both *Pontiac* and his subsequent series. Pontiac's wilderness home contrasts starkly with urban British civilization. Geography and weather serve Parkman's literary purposes.

After publishing *History of the Conspiracy of Pontiac* he turned to writing fiction in *Vassall Morton: A Novel* (1856), a book that Parkman wrote while he was bedridden and that his wife helped him complete. This novel was not well received, and Parkman later ignored it: he did not include it in various editions of his collected works, and it has become virtually unread and unknown. The significance of *Vassall Morton* lies in how Parkman incorporates his experience and others who participated in that experience into his fictional narrative. Parkman has Morton, the protagonist, climb the same ravine that Parkman had climbed in 1841, that the warrior had climbed in "The Scalp-Hunter," and that Gen. James Wolfe was to climb in *Montcalm and Wolfe* (1884), the seventh of the volumes in *France and England in North America.* In the same way Edith Leslie, the heroine of the story, is modeled on Pamela Prentiss, a young woman whom Parker had met during that same summer vacation and whom he probably had intended to impress by climbing that ravine. Having completed *Vassall Morton,* Parkman finally began to contemplate the first volume of what he called the "Old French War." Before he could begin writing it, however, he had to overcome various mysterious maladies that he called his "enemy."

Throughout most of his adulthood Parkman suffered a series of illnesses—severe headaches, temporary bouts of blindness, water on the knee, indigestion, and occasional intervals of insomnia. His strenuous activities were thought to have caused some of these problems. His eye problems, for example, were blamed on his Oregon Trail experience in 1846. Just as Parkman labored to overcome illnesses, his protagonists strove to defeat the wilderness of America, the native inhabitants of that wilderness, and the European rivals for those colonies. Parkman identified with General Wolfe, whose leadership ultimately brought about the fall of New

France to the British, because Wolfe had been forced to overcome ailments before leading his army to victory. Parkman saw himself struggling to overcome his own "enemy" as he strove to complete his multivolume history.

Parkman suffered two additional sources of grief shortly after *Vassall Morton* was published. The Parkmans had two daughters–Grace (born in 1851) and Katherine (born in 1857)–who lived into adulthood, but their only son, Francis (born in 1854), died in 1857. Parkman's wife then died the following year. Seeking solace for his losses and relief from his own physical suffering, Parkman traveled to France. His health did not improve, but the trip provided him with an opportunity to collect more documents relating to the historical study he planned to undertake.

His language skills and financial independence allowed Parkman not only to perform research wherever his sources took him but also to pay for copying whatever documents he felt were necessary. He was an inveterate collector: Parkman wrote to one editor of a volume on the history of North Adams, Massachusetts, to inform this historian that, although he already had copies of most of the letters that were to appear in this volume, he wished that the editor would "oblige me by putting down my name as a subscriber to the printed volume." Parkman's collection of such documents gave him a strong foundation for writing *France and England in North America*.

His interests in nature did not slacken in times of illness and other suffering. Turning his attention to horticulture, Parkman produced and patented the *Lilium parkmanni* flower, wrote twenty-six articles on a variety of horticultural subjects, and published *The Book of Roses* (1866). His secretary, Charles Haight Farnham, maintained that Parkman's interest in roses grew from his love of nature, and they were the only means "by which his love came in from the wilderness." Parkman was more circumspect. He claimed that horticulture interested him because it was challenging and because roses demanded a "high degree of mental activity."

He brought to gardening the same ethos with which he conducted his historical inquiries. In *The Book of Roses* he discusses the "Culture of the Rose." In his historical contrasts of French and English cultures Parkman often discriminates between roses of "pure blood" and those of "mixed or hybrid origin." His favorite roses are those of the "aristocratic race," and his writing of the protagonists of his books also reflects these same social biases. His heroes are often aristocrats or those from "a good family." In gardening, as in life, he believed that the

Parkman in the early 1850s

members of elite classes are more noteworthy than those of lesser orders. For Parkman, growing roses was like writing history. It demanded selectivity, proper care, knowledge, and talent. Both the writing of history and gardening provided him opportunities to escape the limitations imposed by illness.

As early as 1864 Parkman had been telling correspondents that he was ready to begin writing his history of the French and Indian War, and he expected that the project would take twenty years. Yet because he suffered recurring bouts of illness, it took nearly thirty years, and instead of taking a unified form, his history episodically recounts great events and focuses on heroic people. Critics complain that this episodic form of presenting history in *France and England in North America* makes it lack points of central focus. This criticism is incorrect. One central point concerns the eventual triumph of English colonists over their French counterparts, and a second focus–one that is more implicit than articulated–is in Parkman's presentation of the influence of wilderness and nature in the events of colonial history.

Illness made it impossible for Parkman actively to serve the Union cause during the Civil

War, although his thoughts were clearly on the war when *Pioneers of France in the New World* was published. Otis A. Pease writes that Parkman regretted being unable to participate and wrote of his desire for "a life of action and a death in battle." Such comments may betoken an easy show of courage in a safe, noncombatant environment, but Parkman wrote a series of newspaper articles expressing his hopes for a Union victory and dedicated *Pioneers of France* to the memory of three kinsmen slain in the Union cause.

Pioneers of France establishes the French presence in colonial America. Divided into two parts, it is an important piece of writing on frontier history in which Parkman describes the American wilderness at the time of European colonization. His narrative presents the vastness of the new continent, and he reminds readers how weak and vulnerable the European enterprise was. Wilbur R. Jacobs writes that, in presenting the wilderness as a major force with which colonists had to contend, Parkman shows how the environment "tested the fortitude of the pioneers." In its use of Darwinian language *Pioneers of France* illustrates how "the weak perished and the strong grew stronger" in the American wilderness. Yet this book shows danger to be present everywhere, not just in the wilderness, because to Parkman's pioneers, rival colonizers are even more dangerous enemies than the wilderness is.

The first part of *Pioneers of France* details the failure of the French Huguenots during the sixteenth century to settle in what is now Florida, and in this section of his narrative Parkman reveals his animosity toward Catholicism. For instance, he finds the efforts of the Huguenots to colonize the American wilderness to be ruined by Catholic duplicitly, and he pronounces no organization to have been more responsible for the demise of French Protestantism than the "Black Jesuits" of France. He believed that the Jesuits, who were as interested in governing as in proselytizing, impeded French colonial success because they embraced superstition and mystery, and Parkman saw history as the overcoming of mystery and religion by humans. This hostility for groups such as the French Huguenots permeates all of Parkman's narrative in *France and England in North America*.

By slighting the colonial successes of the Spanish, Parkman also frees himself from having to discuss the frontier experience of the Spanish in later works of this series. In addition, the political institution of monarchy receives Parkman's antipathy in *Pioneers of France* as he suggests that the struggle between France and England in the colonies was avoidable—that Charles I might have saved the colo-

nies 150 years of conflict had he not returned Quebec to the French in 1631 "for a sum equal to about two hundred and forty thousand dollars."

The second part of *Pioneers of France* chronicles Samuel de Champlain's attempt to create a permanent colony in what is now Canada. Focusing on Champlain allows Parkman to present another favorite literary theme: the heroism of an individual who overcomes nature and the efforts of human opponents. To Parkman, Champlain is the first colonizer to envision the potential wealth of the North American frontier, the first to try to create a western empire for France. Other men whom Parkman saw looking westward and sharing Champlain's vision of the American West are Rene-Robert Cavelier de La Salle; Louis de Buade, Count Frontenac; and Robert Rogers.

Champlain's heroism ensured the survival of New France, and his explorations of the North American interior gave French traders an advantage over their English counterparts. In Parkman's view Champlain understands that the new French empire will depend on alliances with, rather than domination of, its Algonquian neighbors. Hence, from the very beginning New France had better relationships with the native inhabitants than the English did. Yet what Champlain struggled to create before his death in 1635 others destroyed through their pettiness, corruption, and imbecility. Parkman believed that the destruction of New France was a consequence of such human weaknesses, and the rest of his histories chronicle this inevitable destruction of French colonial efforts.

Modern scholarship rejects assumptions made by nineteenth-century determinists, particularly about events along the frontier. Parkman found an advantage in making such deterministic assumptions, however, for his strength as a writer was not in analyzing but in describing events. By seeing the destruction of New France as ordained, he could dispense with analysis and do what he did best: describe the people, places, and events of the past. Through his descriptions he re-created the past—or his vision of the past—in a manner few other writers could match. This was particularly apparent in the second installment of his series, *The Jesuits in North America in the Seventeenth Century* (1867).

The Jesuits in North America is the type of history he wrote best. It presents men challenging nature, men pursuing a noneconomic goal at the cost of their lives. Although he disliked Jesuit religious beliefs, he admired the perseverance, endurance, and self-sacrifice of the order. In the character of Father Paul Le Jeune, who became involved in Iroquois-Algonquian wars, Parkman found an opportunity to

Chapter XV
1680

Hardihood of La Salle

The winter Journey, — the deserted Town, — Starved Rock; — Lake Michigan; — The Wilderness; — War Parties; — La Salle's Men give out; — Ominous Ill tidings; — Meeting; — chastisement of the Mutineers

The winter had been a severe one. When La Salle and his five companions reached Peoria Lake, they found it sheeted with ice from shore to shore with ice thick that stopped the progress of their canoes but was too thin to bear the weight of a man. They dragged their light vessels up the bank and into the forest, where the city of Peoria now stands; made two rude sledges, placed the canoes and baggage upon them, and, toiling knee-deep through the saturated snow, dragged them four leagues through the woods, till they reached a point where the motion of the current kept the water partially free from ice open. They were

A page from Parkman's manuscript for LaSalle and the Discovery of the Great West

write about heroic deeds and great events, and Le Jeune's travels allowed Parkman to give breadth to his descriptions of the American wilderness. He vividly relates the hardships Le Jeune and others endured. The "indomitable and irrepressible" intellect and energy of Father Isaac Jogues also captured Parkman's imagination, and as David Levin notes, it was not the piety of these religious figures as much as "their self-sacrifice, their perseverance, and their endurance that compelled his [Parkman's] admiration." Father Jogues's death at the hands of a Mohawk provides a dramatic climax for Parkman's narration, for Jogues encapsulates the strengths and weaknesses of the Jesuits in New France.

The Jesuits continued Champlain's quest to create a French empire in the West, but the Iroquois thwarted this attempt by keeping Frenchmen from penetrating the American interior. Yet in Parkman's view the Iroquois were also destined for failure. While "liberty may thank the Iroquois" for ruining "the trade which was the life blood of New France," Parkman writes, "the contest on this continent between Liberty and Absolutism was never doubtful." Once the English arrived Iroquois extinction was a certainty. The Jesuits' failure to establish a viable empire opened the door "for other actors [to] enter the stage."

While intrepid Jesuits continued to explore the American West and to look for converts, no priest rivaled La Salle, the central figure of *The Discovery of the Great West* (1869), Parkman's next book in the series. This work chronicles the struggles and explorations of La Salle and the Jesuits to push the French frontier into the Great Lakes and Mississippi River regions. La Salle's social standing in France, his apparent unhappiness in society, and his explorations captured Parkman's imagination. La Salle was the "crusader" who guided Europeans "to the possession of her richest heritage," a western empire in opposition to those of people too tied to European traditions and Old World values. Parkman liked La Salle. He identified with La Salle's struggles with the Jesuits and rival traders, and his presentation of La Salle's western vision for New France continues a theme begun in the two earlier histories.

Parkman sees the New France of La Salle as "racked by the discord of conflicting interests and passions." These factions pitted politicians against each other and priests against politicians; rival religious orders challenged each other for supremacy; and fur traders opposed each other. The one thing that these various factions shared was their opposition to La Salle, as each felt threatened by his vision of the West. Parkman portrays La Salle—with his irrepressible will, the "Herculean labors" that he per-

forms, and his tragic flaws that ultimately result in his death—as a hero of a Greek tragedy.

By comparing and contrasting La Salle with Champlain and the Jesuits, Parkman connects *The Discovery of the Great West* to his earlier works in this series and introduces his readers to new characters, such as Count Frontenac, who become central figures of later works in this series. La Salle's ambition was, as Champlain's had been, "to found another France in the West," but La Salle was not a "chivalrous mediaeval" character as Champlain had been. Like the Jesuits, La Salle dreamed of French greatness in the New World, but he had little interest in Indian conversions or in expanding Jesuit influence. Through the efforts of men such as La Salle and Frontenac, Parkman recounts how France created a wilderness empire while the British colonies barely extended inland from the Atlantic Ocean.

From this study of La Salle and his significance in the history of colonial development in North America, Parkman turned his attention to the social history of New France in *The Old Régime in Canada* (1874). Some scholars fault the book for its lack of clarity; others praise *The Old Régime* as a watershed in the series or as a pioneering essay in social history because it analyzes an array of historical subjects. Because the book concentrates on the economic and social dimensions of French colonization, it lacks the unity of Parkman's earlier studies of New France. By addressing such diverse subjects in this work, he freed himself from having to discuss them in later studies and thereby impairing the power of his narrative of historical events.

In *The Old Régime* Parkman articulates his belief that New France was doomed. His task, he informs readers, is to explain "why it failed." He begins by discussing the problems that New France suffered from being directed by the "political and social machine" of the French colonial enterprise, a theme explored at length in the subsequent volumes of the series. By examining the social and institutional context behind the French colonial efforts, he lays the groundwork for presenting the heroic but failed efforts of figures such as Frontenac and Louis-Joseph de Montcalm-Grozon, Marquis de Montcalm, who appear as central characters in his later histories.

Covering the entire history of New France, Parkman divides *The Old Régime* into three sections. Beginning in the 1640s, the first section focuses on "The Feudal Chiefs of Acadia" in presenting a capricious French monarchy and the struggles of Charles Turgis Sainte-Étienne de La Tour and Charles de Menou, Seigneur d'Aulney Charnizay, to re-create feudal France in Acadia. In this section Parkman also demonstrates how the clergy of New England, not just the French Jesuits, undermined early efforts to conquer portions of New France.

The second section explores political relations among Native Americans and other groups in New France. For instance, François Xavier de Laval, the first bishop of Quebec, tried to create a Jesuit state, but as he was implementing "the rights of the church," the French monarchy was rethinking its approach to New France. After 1661 the interest that the French monarchy took in the colony grew as Louis XIV and his ministers looked to New France as a potential source of new wealth. Returning to a theme initiated in *Pioneers of France,* Parkman also attacks the Jesuits of the colony for their interest in mystery, rather than science, and in gaining political power over, as much as salvation for, Native Americans. In *The Old Régime* Parkman's Jesuits become allies of the devil—the Huron tribes—for political advantage, and he argues that the Jesuits permitted their Algonquian allies to torture captured enemies for religious rather than political reasons. Laval is not a holy prelate, as his admirers claim, but an "arbitrary and domineering" man.

What Parkman finds so evil about Laval is his unnaturalness. Parkman presents him trying to dominate nature and men, and one result of such efforts is that French authority becomes centralized under the Jesuits in Canada, so that the Church, more than any other institution, thus "shaped the character and the destinies of the colony." According to Parkman, this domination condemned the efforts of France to succeed in establishing a New France colony. *The Old Régime* suggests that the victory of English Protestantism over French Catholicism was inevitable, and in Parkman's view the Canadian Church became "purer and better" as a result.

The final section of *The Old Régime* details Louis XIV's decision to intervene in New France and the disastrous ramifications of that decision. While his policies weakened the Jesuit influence in Canada, they also produced corrupt trade monopolies and corrupt officials. Parkman shows his nationalistic biases in this segment as he suggests that the benign-neglect policy adopted by England toward its colonies was superior to the royal patronage lavished on New France by Louis XIV. England was destined to defeat France in North America because the political and social machinery of the French regime had corrupted New France: "Freedom," Parkman concludes, "is for those who are fit for it. The rest will lose it, or turn it to corruption."

After examining the social and economic background of events in the history of New France, Park-

man returned to writing episodic history in *Count Frontenac and New France under Louis XIV* (1877). Completing *Count Frontenac* was relatively easy for him. His readers knew the central character from his appearance in *The Discovery of the Great West,* and they knew Parkman's thesis: that royal authority was responsible for the destruction of New France. Parkman saw Frontenac as a visionary, "the most remarkable man who ever represented the crown of France in the New World." Frontenac had overcome crisis and conflict, and he was responsible for conducting the military strategy that France adopted for the remainder of the colonial period—that of trying to encircle British colonists along the eastern seaboard. Parkman's nationalism shows when he blames Frontenac and his policies for the outbreak of war between New England and New France.

The first of five sections that comprise *Count Frontenac* discuss Frontenac's failed first term as governor of New France. The second presents the failures of his successors in the 1680s, and part 3 recounts the return of Frontenac as governor. This narrative details his problems with the Iroquois and the English, whose opposition threatened his western agenda. The fourth part covers events through 1697 and emphasizes Frontenac's conflicts with the Jesuits. The final section concerns the war that Frontenac waged against the Iroquois confederacy and the opening of the West to French settlers. After Frontenac died in 1698, Gov. Louis-Hector Callières, his successor, took advantage of Frontenac's successful conduct of this war and, in 1701, secured a peace settlement with the Five Nations of the Iroquois.

Count Frontenac is important in the study of the American West because it shows the importance of Native American affairs in the westward expansion of European colonists. The war between the French and the Iroquois had begun when those nations, opposing the plans of La Salle and Frontenac for French hegemony in the West, sought to divert the fur trade from New France and toward Albany. According to Parkman, the results of this war destroyed the "power of the Iroquois," and by 1701 New France, stretching from the mouth of the Saint Lawrence River to the Gulf of Mexico, encircled the English colonies by occupying the American interior. Only the British remained to contest French plans for a western empire, and the remaining question was whether the French could hold their possessions.

Robert L. Gale calls *Montcalm and Wolfe* "the crowning achievement" of Parkman's research. In this volume Parkman personifies the English-French rivalry by making Marquis Montcalm and

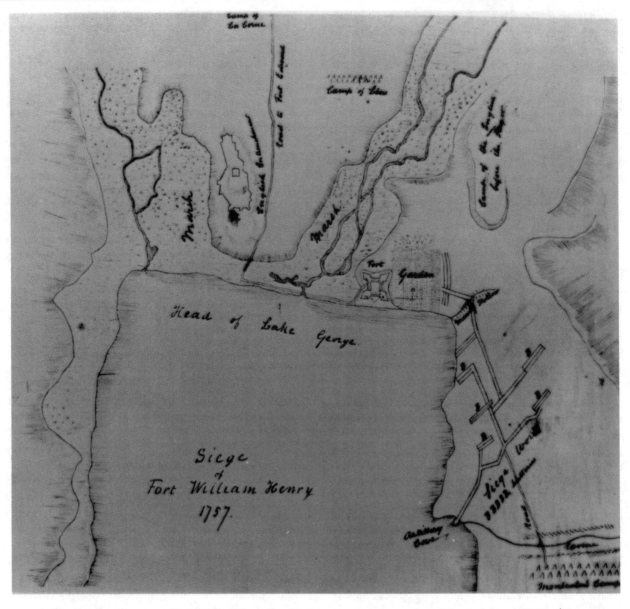

Parkman's map of the siege of Fort William Henry, a printed version of which appears in Montcalm and Wolfe *(Harvard College Library)*

General Wolfe representatives of their respective nations and reaffirms his thesis that the political and social machinery of the French regime doomed its colonial venture in North America. Parkman begins the book with an overview of the two central figures and contrasts the French and English models of colonial control. In Parkman's view Roland-Michel Barrin, Marquis de la Galissonière, governor of New France, made two fateful decisions. First, he decided to maintain and even enlarge the forts linking New France and Louisiana. Second, he imported new colonists for settlement in the West. Because British traders and colonists also had their eyes on

the American interior, these actions aggravated the English and contributed to the Seven Years' War.

Montcalm and Wolfe is organized chronologically around the important people and events from 1748 to 1763, a period in which new villains such as François Bigot, who served as intendant of New France from 1748 to 1759, and new heroes—Montcalm, Wolfe, William Pitt the Elder, Robert Rogers, and George Washington—appeared in France, England, and America. Following a discussion of the Treaty of Paris and the state of European affairs Parkman ends his narrative in 1763 because he believes that "the Seven Years War made England what she is . . . [and] supplied the United States with the indispensable condition of their greatness."

Neither Montcalm nor Wolfe receives the heroic stature that Parkman gives to Champlain, La Salle, or Frontenac in earlier volumes of the series. Parkman finds Montcalm, the devoted servant of Louis XV's tainted regime, to be a tragic figure who was destined for defeat because of the corruption of Bigot and the ineptitude of Pierre de Rigaud, Marquis de Vaudreuil-Cavagnal and the last governor of New France. General Wolfe embodies English ingenuity in his daring plan for capturing Quebec, and his victory opened the West to colonial settlement by the British.

What is important about Parkman's version of the Montcalm-Wolfe struggle is his belief that individual action determines the outcome of events. While the defeat of France is inevitable, the timing of that defeat is unknown, and for Parkman, Wolfe and his army establish the time. In narrating these events Parkman builds suspense by showing readers how internal divisions between the English colonists and the British forces hinder their efforts in this event, how Bigot's undermining of Montcalm hinders the capability that New France has to survive, and how Native Americans—whose allegiances reflect their confusion about the consequences of a British victory—are also divided.

After publishing *Montcalm and Wolfe* Parkman took his time completing the last volume of his series, *A Half-Century of Conflict* (1892). Covering events from 1700 to 1748, it fills the chronological gap between events re-created in *Count Frontenac* and those in *Montcalm and Wolfe*. He begins *A Half-Century of Conflict* with details of Queen Anne's War (1702–1713), a conflict that gave Britain a maritime and colonial advantage over France and Spain. The book concludes with the signing of the Treaty of Aix-la-Chapelle (1748), which ended King George's War but, like that war, failed to resolve the question of which European power was going to develop the American frontier.

A Half-Century of Conflict presents at least three themes. The first is that peace in Europe did not bring peace to the North American frontier: border warfare continued between colonists and Native Americans. A second theme is that European rivalries for the interior of North America continued unabated throughout the eighteenth century. Third, Native American polities were significant in determining the eventual victor in the Anglo-French competition for North American colonies.

The events recounted in *A Half-Century of Conflict* illustrate the perils of frontier life in the eighteenth century, and Parkman's understanding of frontier history highlights the differences between English and French frontier societies. His understanding of the differences suggests that issues separating New France and New England were irreconcilable. One of the two nations had to emerge victorious, with the colonists of that victor replacing the Native Americans as occupiers of the North American continent.

By regularly drawing on his personal experiences in writing his narratives, Parkman attempted to re-create the past for his audience, and these re-creations made his works popular. As for apprehensions that readers might have about the historical veracity of these re-creations infused with insertions of material from Parkman's own experience, he insisted that his works were historically accurate, and he saw no incongruity between reporting and re-creating the past. He based his characters on documentary records, and if he extrapolated into his works the details of weather, personal views, or thoughts he had recorded in his own journal, Parkman regarded all these practices as nonetheless adhering to the documentary evidence. He was breathing life into the documents.

In addition to writing histories Parkman contributed pieces on many social issues of his day. He opposed woman suffrage, for example, because he believed that it contradicted nature and the lessons of history. In *Some of the Reasons against Woman Suffrage* (1883) he argues that history has taught that women were "subservient to men," and he adds that "political or social quackery" was responsible for the woman suffrage movement. He felt that civilization, like wilderness, was subject to natural laws, and his position on female suffrage was that of a conservative who did not like social changes occurring around him. Jacobs writes that Parkman saw himself as a member of "a wise patrician class" providing guidance needed by a changing and increasingly egalitarian United States.

His views of history inform his writing on such contemporary topics, for when Parkman discusses woman suffrage, for instance, themes from *France and England in North America* reappear. He believed that female suffrage would produce a "government of abstractions and generalities" such as that which the French Revolution had brought to power. Just as Parkman saw the French monarchy providing the model of incompetence in the struggle for the New World, he saw the French Revolution providing an example of what happens when the political process is opened. Therefore, the woman suffrage movement in the United States had to be defeated.

Parkman also disapproved of universal education, and, as he wrote in "The Tale of the Ripe

Scholar" (1869) in *The Nation*, he thought that "the diffusion of education and intelligence" was undermining the creation of an intellectual elite. While American education produced many "readers," it did not produce many "thinkers." Educators were satisfied with "sweeping statements, [and] confident assertions" rather than with knowledge. The result was a decline in intellectual ability, and Parkman wanted educators to develop students who could observe, analyze, reason, and comprehend. He wanted educators to develop "a class of persons" who could "hold their ground against charlatanry, and propagate sound and healthy thought throughout the community." Again Parkman drew from his study of history in making his argument. The heroes of his books were men who had held their ground against doubters, naysayers, and promoters of mystery. His antipathy for universal education reflected his attitude toward the America he saw evolving around him.

Although Parkman opposed the historical trends of his time, he did not ignore the works of his contemporaries. He read George Bancroft's volume on La Salle and the Jesuits before writing his own account. Like William Hickling Prescott or Edward Gibbon, Parkman believed that a grand theme involving dynamic personalities was essential to writing good history—and that one wrote good history by making the story informative and interesting. This emphasis on heroism and theme marked Parkman as a writer of history in the Romantic tradition.

Like other Romantic historians Parkman believed that the westward expansion of the nation was inevitable. He believed that the history of humanity was a story of progress and regarded Champlain, La Salle, and Wolfe as admirable agents of progress. Pontiac represents an opponent of progress, and his attack on the English had to fail for two reasons. First, the Native Americans were still influenced by the supernatural. Second, the British and their colonists embodied the advance of civilization westward, and according to Parkman's writings, people who were civilized would overcome those less sophisticated.

From the beginning critics challenged Parkman's historical interpretations. Theodore Parker and Herman Melville criticized *History of the Conspiracy of Pontiac* for its portrayal of Indians and Quakers. Other critics accused Parkman of being antireligious, anti-Catholic, and anti-French. Perhaps the most distressing criticism came from Abbé Henri-Raymond Casgrain, a Canadian friend who charged Parkman with having purposefully ignored sources that challenged the Bostonian's literary re-creations. Parkman denied Casgrain's charge, and in the intro-

ductions to *Count Frontenac* and *Wolfe and Montcalm* Parkman defended his choices of documents and the interpretations he formed from them.

Twentieth-century criticisms of Parkman's work are more numerous. Critics such as W. J. Eccles do not approve of Parkman's aggressive Protestant perspective, and others argue that Parkman did not understand the economic or sociological settings of those periods about which he wrote. His recounting of events such as the buffalo hunt in which he participated while he was on the Oregon Trail attracts the opprobrium of environmental critics, who see typical examples of Americans' wanton destruction of their environment in such actions.

One of the more serious criticisms of Parkman's works is in Mason Wade's argument that Parkman promoted a "great man theory" of history. In fact, Parkman focuses his books, whenever possible, on specific individuals whose actions are of great significance in the history of the American frontier. As Jacobs makes clear, Parkman uses events in the lives of those individuals to illustrate the period rather than to document their lives. For Parkman, biography provides the means to organize his study of the American frontier and thereby to examine the scope of French and English colonial history.

Another serious criticism of Parkman's history writing is that of Francis Jennings, who attacks him for failing to appreciate the Native American peoples he writes about. Parkman readily admitted his distrust of Native American sources, and he presents these characters from personal observation and from the works of nineteenth-century scholars. He sought advice about Native American lives and customs from Lewis Henry Morgan and Henry Rowe Schoolcraft, and Parkman integrated their findings into his writing. His willingness to incorporate Native Americans into his histories marked a drastic departure from traditional scholarly approaches to American colonial history. His books showed that Native Americans afforded legitimate subjects for historical inquiry.

What makes Parkman's writing timeless is his ability to provide readers with sweeping portraits of people and places. He was the first to take settings and events on the American frontier seriously and to present them as central to his historical narrative. Rain on the Oregon Trail, winter in Quebec, pristine forests in western Pennsylvania, and unmapped rivers in the interior provide drama in his histories. These natural forces determine outcomes as much as the actions of people. His writing fuses literature and history, and in this fusion Parkman established the importance of the West in the writing of American history.

Letters:

Letters from Francis Parkman to E. G. Squier, edited by Don C. Seitz (Cedar Rapids, Iowa: Torch, 1911);

Letters of Francis Parkman to Pierre Margry, edited by John Spencer Bassett (Northampton, Mass.: Department of History of Smith College, 1923);

Letters of Francis Parkman, 2 volumes, edited by Wilbur R. Jacobs (Norman: University of Oklahoma Press, 1960).

Biographies:

Charles Haight Farnham, *A Life of Francis Parkman* (Boston: Little, Brown, 1900);

Henry Dwight Sedgwick, *Francis Parkman* (Boston: Houghton, Mifflin, 1904);

Edward Wheelwright, "Memoir of Francis Parkman, LL.D.," *Publications of the Colonial Society of Massachusetts,* in volume 1 (Boston: Colonial Society of Massachusetts, 1905), pp. 304–350;

Joseph Schafer, "Francis Parkman, 1823–1893," *Mississippi Valley Historical Review,* 10 (1924): 351–364;

Mason Wade, *Francis Parkman: Heroic Historian* (New York: Viking, 1942);

Howard Doughty, *Francis Parkman* (New York: Macmillan, 1962);

Wilbur R. Jacobs, *Francis Parkman, Historian as Hero: The Formative Years* (Austin: University of Texas Press, 1991).

References:

W. J. Eccles, "The History of New France According to Francis Parkman," *William and Mary Quarterly,* third series 18 (1961): 163–175;

Robert L. Gale, *Francis Parkman* (New York: Twayne, 1973);

Wilbur R. Jacobs, "Francis Parkman—Naturalist-Environmental Savant," *Pacific Historical Review,* 61 (1992): 341–356;

Francis Jennings, "A Vanishing Indian: Francis Parkman Versus His Sources," *Pennsylvania Magazine of History and Biography,* 87 (1963): 306–323;

David Levin, *History as Romantic Art: Bancroft, Prescott, Motley, and Parkman* (Stanford, Cal.: Stanford University Press, 1959);

Otis A. Pease, *Parkman's History: The Historian as Literary Artist* (New Haven: Yale University Press, 1953).

Papers:

Many of Parkman's manuscripts and papers are held by the Massachusetts Historical Society. Harvard University houses his library and maps, and additional Parkman letters are in the Huntington Manuscripts Collection of the Huntington Library, San Marino, California.

John Wesley Powell

(24 March 1834 – 23 September 1902)

Southern Utah University

BOOKS: *Report of Special Commissioners J. W. Powell and G. W. Ingalls on the Condition of the Ute Indians of Utah; the Paiutes of Utah, Northern Arizona, Southern Nevada, and Southwestern California, the Go-si Utes of Utah and Nevada, the Northwestern Shoshones of Idaho and Utah, and the Western Shoshones of Nevada, and Report Concerning Claims of Settlers in the Mo-A-Pa Valley (Southeastern Nevada)* (Washington, D.C.: U.S. Government Printing Office, 1874);

Exploration of the Colorado River of the West and Its Tributaries in 1869, 1870, 1871 and 1872, Explored Under the Direction of the Secretary of the Smithsonian Institution (Washington, D.C.: U.S. Government Printing Office, 1875);

Report on the Geology of the Eastern Portion of the Uinta Mountains and a Region of the Country Thereto (Washington, D.C.: U.S. Government Printing Office, 1876);

Introduction to the Study of Indian Languages (Washington, D.C.: U.S. Government Printing Office, 1877);

Report on the Lands of the Arid Region of the United States, With a More Detailed Account of the Lands of Utah (Washington, D.C.: U.S. Government Printing Office, 1878);

On the Organization of Scientific Work of the General Government (Washington, D.C.: U.S. Government Printing Office, 1885);

Indian Linguistic Families of America, North of Mexico (Washington, D.C.: U.S. Government Printing Office, 1891);

Canyons of the Colorado (Meadville, Pa.: Flood & Vincent, 1895); republished as *The Exploration of the Colorado River and Its Canyons* (New York: Dover, 1961; London: Constable, 1961);

Truth and Error, or the Science of Intellection (Chicago: Open Court, 1898; London: Kegan Paul, Trench & Trübner, 1898);

Anthropology of the Numa: John Wesley Powell's Manuscripts on the Numic Peoples of Western North America, 1868–1880, edited by Don D. Fowler and

Catherine S. Fowler (Washington, D.C.: Smithsonian Institution Press, 1971).

OTHER: "From Savagery to Barbarism," *Anthropological Society of Washington–Transactions,* 3 (1885): 173–196.

SELECTED PERIODICAL PUBLICATIONS–UNCOLLECTED: "From Barbarism to Civilization," *American Anthropologist,* 1 (April 1888): 97–123;

"The Lesson of Conemaugh," *North American Review,* 149 (August 1889): 150–156;

"Prehistoric Man in America," *Forum,* 8 (February 1890): 638–652;

296

"The Irrigable Lands of the Arid Region," *Century,* 39 (March 1890): 766–776;

"The Non-Irrigable Lands of the Arid Region," *Century,* 39 (April 1890): 915–922;

"Institutions for the Arid Lands," *Century,* 40 (May 1890): 111–116;

"The Study of Indian Languages," *Science,* 17 (February 1891): 71–74;

"Technology, or the Science of Industries," *American Anthropologist,* 1 (April 1899): 319–349;

"Sophiology, or the Science of Activities Designed to Give Instruction," *American Anthropologist,* 3 (January–March 1901): 51–79;

"Classification of the Sciences," *American Anthropologist,* 3 (October–December 1901): 601–605.

Maj. John Wesley Powell was an explorer, writer, geologist, anthropologist, land planner, and bureaucrat. He explored the last blank spot on the map of the United States; wrote one of the great real-life adventure stories in American literature, *Exploration of the Colorado River of the West* (1875); produced significant works in geology, anthropology, and land policy; and directed two federal agencies, the U.S. Geological Survey and the Bureau of Ethnology. His divergent interests resembled one of the braided streambeds in his beloved canyon country, branching out in many directions but ultimately beginning and ending in the same stream.

Powell's parents, Joseph and Mary Powell, immigrated to New York from England in 1830. His father was a Methodist preacher and a tailor. Both parents had some education and high moral principles. Joseph Powell also possessed religious zeal and a restless spirit. Gradually he pushed the family west across New York. At Mount Morris on 24 March 1834 his second son, John Wesley, was born. After eight peripatetic years in New York, the family moved to Jackson, in southern Ohio, where they lived for a short time. Then they settled on a farm in Walworth County, Wisconsin. Powell had some formal schooling in Ohio, but he was mostly self-taught, reading widely in literature, history, science, and philosophy. When he was eighteen, he helped his family move to Illinois, and at roughly the same time he left home and began the first of a series of teaching jobs in Illinois. He also squeezed in a few terms as a college student at Illinois College in Jacksonville, at Illinois Institute in Wheaton (later Wheaton College), and at Oberlin College. During the summers he collected fossils along the Ohio, Mississippi, Illinois, and other midwestern rivers. Powell aspired to be a scientist, and the field knowledge, river skills, and self-confidence he acquired on these trips proved valuable, especially during his 1869 voyage down the Green and Colorado Rivers.

When the Civil War began in 1861, Powell promptly enlisted and within a month rose to the rank of second lieutenant. In fall 1861 he married his first cousin Emma Dean of Detroit and then rushed back to Missouri to find that he had been commissioned a captain in the artillery. At the Battle of Shiloh in April 1862 Powell took a bullet in his right arm, which a military surgeon amputated two inches below the elbow. Although he recovered and was able to return to active duty, Powell suffered pain in the arm the rest of his life.

Powell distinguished himself in the Vicksburg campaign (November 1862–July 1863) and elsewhere under Generals Ulysses S. Grant and William T. Sherman, leaving the army in January 1865 at the rank of major. Returning to Illinois he accepted a science professorship at Illinois Wesleyan University in Bloomington. Powell revolutionized the teaching of science by taking his students on field trips to study plants, animals, and rocks. After two years at Illinois Wesleyan, Powell moved to neighboring Illinois State Normal University. He also became secretary and curator of the Illinois Natural History Society and Museum, where he immediately decided to increase the museum collections and organized a scientific expedition to Colorado. The Powell group, mostly students and teachers, spent the better part of the summer of 1867 collecting rocks, plants, and animals for the museum. By the time Powell returned to Illinois in the fall, he had formulated a plan to explore the plateaus and canyons of the Colorado River, aiming to give special attention to the possibilities of irrigation in this arid region. After just one season in the West, Powell was apparently formulating ideas already about arid-lands agriculture. These ideas eventually culminated in his classic statement of environmental history, *Report on the Lands of the Arid Region of the United States* (1878). On his second expedition to Colorado, in 1868, Powell encountered a band of Ute Indians in the White River Valley of western Colorado. This meeting rekindled an interest in native cultures that he had first developed in southern Ohio. His studies of Native Americans eventually led him to directorship of the Bureau of Ethnology and helped to establish anthropology as a federally funded science.

In early spring 1969 Powell boarded a train from Denver to Chicago, where he designed boats to carry him and his party into "the great unknown." He started his river adventure in Green River, Wyoming, because it lay on the recently completed transcontinental railroad line. When Powell

The Emma Dean Second *on the Colorado River in Marble Canyon. For much of his second Colorado expedition, Powell traveled in the chair bolted to the deck (photograph by John K. Hillers, August 1872; U.S. Geological Survey)*

and his nine men, mostly trappers and mountain men, left Green River in four boats on 24 May 1869, not much was known about the Green and Colorado Rivers he was setting out to explore. Powell had provisions calculated to last ten months, but two weeks later in Lodore Canyon one boat hit a rock. Many provisions and some scientific instruments were lost, increasing tensions among the explorers and necessitating that they move more quickly than they had planned through the canyons. A few months later in the Grand Canyon proper, the party faced some of the worst rapids in North America—as well as relentless rain, which caused a major problem because their ponchos had become shredded and provided little shelter. On 27 August they reached what later became known as Separation Rapid. Frightened by what they considered the worst rapid yet, mentally and physically exhausted by the rigors of the trip, and possibly fed up with Powell's domineering manner, three men left the expedition and hiked out of the canyon. Powell and the remaining men emerged from the Grand Can-

yon unscathed a few days later, but when Powell returned to the area the next year, he learned that the men who had left the party had been murdered on the Shivwits Plateau. At the time their killers were thought to be Shivwits Paiutes who mistook the explorers for miners from south of the river, but at least two twentieth-century scholars have suggested that Mormons killed them, mistaking the three for polygamist-hunting federal agents.

Although little tangible scientific information resulted from the 1869 trip, Powell, as his notes indicate, had taken in the broad geologic outlines of the canyon country. Already he grasped its basic structure: uplift and erosion. Ultimately, Powell's greatest direct contributions to geology were the terms he introduced to describe Colorado Plateau drainage systems in *Report on the Geology of the Eastern Portion of the Uinta Mountains* (1876): "antecedent," "consequent," and "superimposed" river valleys and "base level of erosion." In these and other conceptions Powell laid the foundations of the American school of geomorphology.

In autumn 1869 Powell returned to Illinois a national hero. Since his river exploits had captured the fancy of an eastern public starved for news of western adventuring, Powell embarked on the lecture circuit. While talking about his trip, he was shaping, refining, and expanding the story that would become his best-known book, *Exploration of the Colorado River.*

In 1870, his fame assured, Powell acquired congressional funding for a second expedition. For this trip he hired a crew of mostly fellow teachers and students, a significant step up in professionalism from the first trip. His brother-in-law, Prof. Almon H. Thompson, served as the geographer and second in charge. Another member of the group was Frederick S. Dellenbaugh, a distant relative and talented artist who later became one of the most prominent Colorado River historians and wrote the only published account of the 1871–1872 expedition, *A Canyon Voyage* (1908). John K. Hillers, who signed on in Salt Lake City as a boatman, later became well known as a U.S. Geological Survey photographer, a skill he picked up during the expedition. This trip was one of the most documented in nineteenth-century western exploration: nearly every member of the crew kept a detailed journal. Largely run by Thompson, the expedition not only produced the first map of this previously blank spot, it also discovered the last major river in the United States, the Escalante, and the last mountain range, the Henrys, named after Joseph Henry of the Smithsonian Institution.

In 1873 Powell resigned from his teaching position at Normal and established residence in Washington, D.C., with his wife and two-year-old daughter, Mary Dean. There he began to direct a more or less permanent survey. He also received a special commission with Indian agent G. W. Ingalls to investigate the problems of the Numic Indians—the Ute, Shoshone, Bannock, and Pauite tribes of Utah and eastern Nevada. Their *Report of Special Commissioners J. W. Powell and G. W. Ingalls on the Condition of the Ute Indians* (1874) was the first ethnographic study of the Numa. This research allowed Powell to complete his series of Numic vocabularies, record their mythologies and social institutions, and collect for the Smithsonian artifacts relating to Indian dress, food, arts, warfare, and ceremonies. Since his first encounter with the White River Valley Utes in 1868, his professional interests had been changing from geology to ethnology.

Between intermittent field work in 1873 and 1874 and work in Washington, Powell hired geologists Grove Karl Gilbert and Clarence E. Dutton. As Wallace Stegner wrote in his biography of Powell, during the time these men worked with Powell, the three "were probably the most brilliant geological team in the business." Powell shared his many overarching ideas about canyon-country geology with Gilbert and Dutton, and their combined efforts no doubt produced finer results than whatever study any one of them might have produced without input from his colleagues.

Gilbert's *Geology of the Henry Mountains* (1877) appeared as a Powell Survey monograph and stands as the classic statement on arid-lands erosion and laccoliths. Gilbert also contributed to Powell's *Report on the Lands of the Arid Region,* served as ranking geologist for the U.S. Geological Survey, and was Powell's closest friend. Dutton was something of an aesthete in the style of his Yale classmate and fellow geologist Clarence King. Dutton's *Tertiary History of the Grand Canyon District* (1882) and *Geology of the High Plateaus of Utah* (1880) show him to be not only a brilliant theorist working out theories of erosion and volcanism but also a superb prose stylist. His descriptions of the canyon country are still considered classics of nature writing.

Powell also hired two artists whose work greatly enhanced Powell Survey publications. Thomas Moran became one of the best-known American landscape painters. Not as well known as Moran, but increasingly recognized for his genius in portraying the canyon country, was William H. Holmes, who executed superb, fine-line drawings of the country. Like Powell, Holmes was a polymath. Beginning as a scientific illustrator, he became a geologist, an ethnologist, and a curator at the Field and National Museums. He also headed the Bureau of Ethnology and the National Gallery.

As Thompson and Powell's other men finished their reconnaissance of the Colorado River country in the early 1870s, Powell felt pressure from his supporters, Spencer Baird of the Smithsonian and Representative James A. Garfield, to publish a report of his explorations. In June 1874 he submitted the manuscript for *Exploration of the Colorado River,* and it was published the following year. This classic adventure story gained a large readership even as Powell finished revising the *Report on the Geology of the Eastern Portion of the Uinta Mountains,* published in 1878. Taking up where the second part of *Exploration of the Colorado River* left off, this geological treatise further propounded Powell's theories about uplift and erosion.

The last geological study that Powell published, the Uinta Mountains report meshes with his later work on reclamation and ethnology. His basic philosophy in all his scientific work was fully Darwinian. When he looked at the geology and physiography of the canyon country, he saw the gradual evolution of a landscape, hastened by uniform processes of erosion and uplift. Similarly, when he studied Native Americans, Powell perceived a gradual evolution of these societies from "savagery" to "barbarism" to "civilization." When he studied the problems of developing water in the arid region, he also used Darwin's idea of "adaptation."

Four published versions of Powell's account of the 1869 trip down the Colorado River appeared during his lifetime. Some of the material and illustrations differ greatly from one text to the next. Powell scholars usually refer to the 1875 edition, *Exploration of the Colorado River of the West and Its Tributaries in 1869, 1870, 1871 and 1872, Explored Under the Direction of the Secretary of the Smithsonian Institution.* Part 1 comprises accounts of the 1869 trip from Green River, Wyoming, to the mouth of the Virgin River, of an 1870 journey through present-day Zion National Park across the Arizona Strip to the Uinkaret Plateau, and of Thompson's overland trip to the Dirty Devil River in 1872. Part 2 is "On the Physical Features of the Valley of the Colorado," a serious geologic treatise on the canyon country.

One published account predates the 1875 book: "Major J. W. Powell's Report on His Exploration of the Rio Colorado in 1869" appeared in the second edition (1870) of W. A. Bell's *New Tracks in America.* Another version was published as "Canyons of the Colorado" in the January, February, and March 1875 issues of *Scribner's Monthly.* A fourth article, "An Overland Trip to the Grand Canyon," appeared in the October 1875 issue. The fourth version is *Canyons of the Colorado* (1895), which omits part 2 of the 1875 book and adds other material. Behind these four texts lie at least two journals by Powell, as well as many newspaper reports and oral presentations in the years between 1869 and 1874.

By the time Powell sat down to write *Exploration of the Colorado River* he had hired John C. Pilling, who served as an amanuensis. According to Grove Karl Gilbert, Powell's terse, imagistic, and exciting style is the result of his dictating the book to Pilling. In *Exploration of the Colorado River* Powell took historical liberties with some facts in order to shape his story. For example, he placed many incidents from the 1871–1872 or later expeditions in the story of his 1869 trip. Some Colorado River historians—including Robert B. Stanton, Julius Stone, and Otis Marston—have criticized Powell for transposing information. While Powell opted for art over exact chronology, however, he never distorted scientific fact.

Science, in fact, forms the theme and structure of the narrative; namely, he employs the hero-as-

scientist archetype to frame his story. Powell, the scientist/hero, enters the fabled canyon country to roll back the myths, unravel the secrets of the rocks, and thus reveal the mysteries of the earth's origins. Even though he achieves a victory, it comes at a high price—the deaths of the three men who ignore the calculations of the scientist/hero. Powell's dominant metaphors and aesthetic flow from nineteenth-century romanticism. Yet the details and the methodology of *Exploration of the Colorado River* reflect the new literary realism.

After Powell retired from the U.S. Geological Survey in 1894, he published *Canyons of the Colorado,* apparently to meet public demand for *Exploration of the Colorado River,* long out of print. In *Canyons of the Colorado* the text for the descriptions of the 1869 river trip and the overland trip to the Shivwits Plateau is virtually identical to that of *Exploration of the Colorado River.* But Powell added considerable written and illustrative material to *Canyons of the Colorado,* including a considerably revised version of a December 1875 *Scribner's Monthly* article, "The Ancient Province of Tusayan." The 1895 book also supplied considerably more ethnographic information on the Hopis than was included in the 1875 book, reflecting nearly two decades of ethnographic work by Powell and the Bureau of Ethnology.

For this popular account of his Colorado explorations Powell dropped the geological treatise that formed part 2 of *Exploration of the Colorado River* and opened the book with a ninety-page overview of Colorado Basin physiography and ethnology. Written for the layman, this account still is one of the most comprehensive and illuminating descriptions of the environmental history of the Colorado Plateau. *Canyons of the Colorado* also includes many more illustrations than the previous versions. Powell used more than 250, drawn from virtually every Powell Survey, U.S. Geological Survey, and Bureau of Ethnology publication pertaining to the Colorado Plateau. Finally, he added a ten-page conclusion, "The Grand Canyon," as concise a statement of his feelings for the canyon-country landscape as he ever made. All in all, *Canyons of the Colorado* is distinctly different from *Exploration of the Colorado River.*

In the decade after his first venture west Powell saw the region changing in ways that alarmed him. For every instance of cooperation he found among people such as the Mormons, he found ten examples of greed, exploitation, and environmental ignorance. Beginning in 1867 Powell had oriented his surveys toward Populist, agrarian concerns. The young man who grew up farming in the Midwest envisioned a West where other Americans could do the same. He realized, however, that aridity dictated the terms of western settlement. Yet between 1867 and 1894 he had to fight many myths about western agriculture. His first attempt to debunk them appeared in his *Report on the Lands of the Arid Region* in 1878.

In addition to challenging myths such as the rain-follows-the-plow theory (the erroneous belief that tilling the soil increases rainfall), *Report on the Lands of the Arid Region* proposed a radical new set of rules for western settlement. These proposals were widely ignored until the mid twentieth century, long after much environmental damage had occurred in the West. Powell probably began writing this report in 1874, at the same time he was working on *Exploration of the Colorado River* and *Report on the Geology of the Eastern Portion of the Uinta Mountains*.

Powell wrote most of *Report on the Lands of the Arid Region,* with Gilbert, Dutton, and Thompson adding chapters of their own. Taking up the question of the public lands in the arid region—east of the Sierra Nevada ranges and west of the one hundredth meridian—this report is critical of the Homestead Act of 1862, a well-meaning land-distribution law that encouraged the capitalistic practices of land and water speculation. The report urged a more socialistic system of land and water apportionment. It also sought to debunk the popular perception of the West as a garden, a myth propounded by the railroads, speculators, and western congressmen. It was a challenge to Americans' beliefs in rugged individualism and self-reliance, and finally it disputed the notion that getting rich is an American birthright.

In short, Powell wanted to remake America in the West. When his report appeared as House of Representatives Executive Document 73, many congressmen and western newspapers decried it as socialistic. Most of these detractors probably did not read the report. If most legislators and farmers had done so, they would have found that Powell proposed forming irrigation districts where members provided the labor, laws, and capital for the irrigation works. He called this approach the "colony system" and based it on the thirty-year Mormon experiment in Utah. Under Powell's plan an arid-lands rancher would also participate in a grazing district of shared pastures. An essential principle underlying his irrigation and grazing districts was that the lay of the land should dictate land use and land distribution—a novel idea at that time. Powell knew that a rectangular-grid plan would not work in the West and called for a different agricultural paradigm, supported by new laws and institutions.

Report on the Lands of the Arid Region was far ahead of its time and proved too much for Congress. Powell was calling for restraint and limited settlement in a country that perceived its destiny as God-given and the resources of the continent as infinite. Moreover, he was asking land planners to abandon their geometric thinking and to conceive of land units based on natural systems such as water basins—an idea that resembles the late-twentieth-century notion of bioregions.

Powell's plan also had a few flaws. For example, he misunderstood watershed degradation; he did not appreciate the role of fire in forest ecology; he ignored the importance of hunting to Native American subsistence; and he saw nature in strictly utilitarian terms. Powell certainly looked further ahead than most of his contemporaries, but he was more of a conservationist than a preservationist. Despite its shortcomings *Report on the Lands of the Arid Region* remains an important contribution to American land policy. Many of its ideas ultimately made their way into laws, as well as government policies set by agencies established to protect grazing (the Bureau of Land Management), water (the Bureau of Reclamation), and timber (the U.S. Forest Service). It also laid the foundation for Theodore Roosevelt and Gifford Pinchot's sweeping Progressive conservation reforms in the early 1900s, and it inspired the Soil and Water Conservation Districts established during the New Deal era of the 1930s. *Report on the Lands of the Arid Region* has been called the first environmental-impact statement, and it certainly speaks to Americans of the late twentieth century, even though it could not make itself heard above the roar of its own times.

At the same time Powell was writing *Report on the Lands of the Arid Region,* he took up the fight to consolidate his survey team with three other western surveys, led by Clarence King, Lt. George M. Wheeler, and F. V. Hayden. The survey groups had often met in the field, and sometimes they overlapped each other. Consolidation, therefore, was inevitable. Working behind the scenes, Powell made the consolidation happen; yet his report was not included in the consolidation bill even though it was recommended by the National Academy of Sciences. The Powell Survey, however, became the Smithsonian Institution Bureau of Ethnology, with Powell as the director. Hayden lost out to King for the directorship of the U.S. Geological Survey.

King lasted a little more than a year as director of the U.S. Geological Survey. When he quit in March 1881, after a five-month leave of absence, President James A. Garfield named Powell to replace him. Powell also remained head of the Bureau of Ethnology. Both endeavors brought him considerable praise and power—and made some lesser scientists jealous. Eventually some of them helped

Powell talking to a woman of the Ute tribe in the Uinta Valley of Utah (photograph by John K. Hillers, 1873 or 1874; Smithsonian Institution)

western politicians undo Powell's greatest dream, the Irrigation Survey.

Powell clearly possessed a genius for organization. Both his supporters and his critics commented on his remarkable powers of classification and synthesis. At both the U.S. Geological Survey and the Bureau of Ethnology he chose capable assistants, shared knowledge with them, and then let them work independently. In front of congressional committees he organized his facts and presented them clearly so that even the most unlearned congressman could understand them. According to one contemporary scientist, when Powell appeared before legislators with his charts and maps, "he had so full command of all pertinent facts that his opponents in Congressional committees were often left with nothing but their opposition to stand on."

Between 1881 and 1894 Powell made the U.S. Geological Survey the pride of American science. It became the largest scientific organization of its kind in the world, and the world took notice. European universities bestowed honorary degrees and other awards on Powell. During his tenure the U.S. Geological Survey budget grew from $100,000 to $719,000. Most important, however, were the number and quality of U.S. Geological Survey publications during Powell's years. Powell also formulated the first system of mapping conventions—including symbols, nomenclature, and colors for different rock ages. His system has become the American standard and has influenced European standards as well.

In 1888, after two years of extremely harsh weather in the West, an opportunity arose for Powell to implement many of the land-reform policies he had proposed a decade earlier in *Report on the Lands of the Arid Region*. Western congressmen, led by Sen. William M. Stewart of Nevada, pushed for legislation to inaugurate an irrigation survey. Powell clearly stood as the most knowledgeable and best situated person for the job, so the Irrigation Survey was assigned to him. In the fall of 1888 it appeared that Powell stood on the threshold of revolutionizing Western land law and agriculture, but he soon ran into considerable opposition from Stewart. The Nevada senator wanted the Irrigation Survey to locate dam sites and irrigable lands and then turn them over to private enterprise—laissez-faire capitalism with a little boost from the government. Powell's proposal bordered on socialism: cooperative control of irrigation by those within a particular watershed and government supervision over land and water monopolies. By fall 1889 the two men had become political enemies. When Powell appeared before the House Appropriations Committee in June 1890, Stewart and others reduced the appropriation for the Irrigation Survey from the $720,000 Powell requested to $162,500, effectively killing the Irrigation Survey and Powell's dreams of reforming Western agriculture through scientific planning.

During this fight with Congress, Powell set forth his plans to the public in three articles for *Century* magazine: "The Irrigable Lands of the Arid Region" (March 1890), "The Non-Irrigable Lands of the Arid Region" (April 1890), and "Institutions for the Arid Lands" (May 1890). Elaborating on the water and grazing district concepts first developed in *Report on the Lands of the Arid Region*, he said that government would locate the dam sites and then local cooperative associations in what he called hydrographic basins. It would provide the capital, labor, and rules for establishing and distributing water. His plan, which combined Jeffersonian agrarianism, communalism, and American know-how, also challenged the dominant ideology of the American free-enterprise system and the American myth of rugged individualism. Powell's ideas for the role of federal science ultimately helped to precipitate the modern welfare state that came of age during the Depression of the 1930s. His ideas also helped to move the American government toward a socialistic notion of public lands, especially in regard to natural resources. Yet in 1890 his grand plan was defeated. Powell decided to resign as soon as he could groom a successor. He chose Charles D. Walcott, a distinguished geologist and longtime Geological Survey associate. Powell stepped down in 1894 but maintained his association with the Bureau of Ethnology.

When Powell began practicing anthropology, it was a nascent science, full of amateurs and wild theories. When he left it, the Bureau of Ethnology had given the discipline the reputation of being "serious science." Although many of Powell's own anthropological theories have been discarded, the Bureau of Ethnology he founded, like the U.S. Geological Survey, remains one of the foremost scientific organizations in the world. The discipline of anthropology that Powell began practicing in the winter of 1868 in western Colorado may have lacked a long professional tradition, but it possessed a strong conceptual background in the contemporaneous work of Charles Darwin, Thomas Malthus, Herbert Spencer, and Lewis Henry Morgan. Nineteenth-century anthropology, however, had not yet arrived at the idea of "cultural relativism." Anthropologists measured other cultures against European standards, and by modern standards this kind of thinking appears racist and ethnocentric. Morgan, for example, proposed an elaborate theory of human social evolution from what he called "savagery" through "barbarism" to "civilization." His theory assumed the superiority of white Europeans and the inferiority of so-called savages. Morgan's influence can be seen most clearly in Powell's "From Savagery to Barbarism" (1885) and "From Barbarism to Civilization" (1888). Following Morgan also helped Powell's fieldwork, however, and there Powell made some lasting contributions.

Except for *Report of Special Commissioners J. W. Powell and G. W. Ingalls,* most of Powell's anthropological fieldwork was not published until 1971 when it was collected in *Anthropology of the Numa: John Wesley Powell's Manuscripts on the Numic Peoples of Western North America, 1868–1880*. This collection of myths, customs, songs, vocabularies, place-names, and other data is a substantial contribution to an understanding of the Numic peoples, authenticating much of the material gathered by later anthropologists. Moreover, Powell's collection of material culture on the Numa (deposited in the National Museum of Natural History) is one of the largest and most varied of its kind. His major contribution to Indian studies, however, came in linguistics. He began an important attempt to classify Indian languages, *Introduction to the Study of Indian Languages* (1877). In addition to overseeing many landmark publications of the Bureau of Ethnology, Powell initiated *The Handbook of American Indians* (1907), which began as a dictionary of names and became what is still one of the most indispensable reference works on Native Americans.

During his last years at the Bureau of Ethnology, Powell's interests moved toward formulating a survey of "man's knowledge and philosophy through the span of time from the primitive savage . . . to the modern age of science and technology." That effort, *Truth and Error, or the Science of Intellection* appeared in 1898. This first volume of a projected trilogy is an eccentric attempt at an introduction to the philosophy of science. Reviewers did not praise the book, nor have later readers. Undaunted, Powell began the second part of the trilogy, "Good and Evil," published as a series of papers in the *American Anthropologist* in 1901. The third part of the trilogy, "Pleasure and Pain," never progressed further than one essay and some notes.

In the years between his resignation in 1894 and his death in 1902, Powell spent less and less time running the Bureau of Ethnology. He largely turned over the bureau to W. J. McGee. In 1896 he purchased a house in Brooklin, Maine, and spent long summers there sailing and studying the local Penebscot Indians. In November of 1901, frail and in ill health, Powell suffered a stroke. He recovered by the new year, but the next summer in Maine he suffered another and died soon thereafter.

John Wesley Powell bequeathed to the nation a legacy of fearless exploration, brilliant science, and dedicated public service. With his *Report on the Lands of the Arid Region* he gave America a model for environmental planning, and with his account of his 1869 voyage down the Colorado he left behind one of the great adventure stories in American literature.

Bibliographies:

P. C. Warman, "Catalogue of the Published Writings of John Wesley Powell," *Proceedings of The Washington Academy of Sciences,* 5 (18 July 1903): 131–187;

Lawrence F. Schmeckbier, *Catalog and Index of the Hayden, King, Powell, and Wheeler Surveys,* U.S. Geological Survey Bulletin 222 (Washington, D.C.: U.S. Government Printing Office, 1904).

Biographies:

Mrs. M. D. Lincoln, "John Wesley Powell," *Open Court,* 16 (December 1902): 705–715; 17 (February 1903): 14–25, 86–93;

William Culp Darrah, *Powell of the Colorado* (Princeton: Princeton University Press, 1951);

Wallace Stegner, *Beyond The Hundreth Meridian: John Wesley Powell and the Second Opening of the West* (Boston: Houghton Mifflin, 1954).

References:

Thomas Alexander, *A Clash of Interests* (Provo: Brigham Young University Press, 1977);

Alexander, "John Wesley Powell, The Irrigation Survey and the Inauguration of the Second Phase of Irrigation Development in Utah," *Utah Historical Quarterly,* 37 (1969): 190–206;

Alexander, "The Powell Irrigation Survey and the People of the Mountain West," *Journal of The West,* 7 (January 1968): 48–53;

James M. Aton, *Inventing John Wesley Powell: The Major, His Admirers and Cash-Register Dams in the Colorado River Basin,* Southern Utah State College Distinguished Faculty Lecture No. 9 (Cedar City: Southern Utah State College, 1988);

Aton, *John Wesley Powell* (Boise: Boise State University, 1994);

D. L. Baars, "Major John Wesley Powell, Colorado River Pioneer," *Geology and Natural History of the Grand Canyon Area* (Durango, Col.: Four Corners Geological Society, 1969), pp. 10–18;

Richard A Bartlett, *The Great Surveys of the West* (Norman: University of Oklahoma Press, 1962);

Bartlett, "John Wesley Powell and the Great Surveys," in *The American West: An Appraisal,* edited by Robert G. Ferris (Sante Fe: Museum of New Mexico Press, 1963), pp. 48–67;

W. H. Brewer, "John Wesley Powell," *American Journal of Science,* 14 (1902): 377–382;

John Cooley, ed., *The Great Unknown: The Journals of the Historic First Expedition Down the Colorado River* (Flagstaff: Northland Publishing, 1988);

William Culp Darrah, ed., "The Exploration of the Colorado River in 1869," *Utah Historical Quarterly,* 15 (1947): 1–153;

Frederick Dellenbaugh, *A Canyon Voyage* (New York: Putnam, 1908);

Dellenbaugh, *Romance of the Colorado* (New York: Putnam, 1902);

Don D. Fowler, Robert Euler, and Catherine Fowler, *John Wesley Powell and the Anthropology of the Canyon Country,* U.S. Geological Survey Professional Paper 670 (Washington, D.C.: U.S. Government Printing Office, 1969);

Grove Karl Gilbert, "John Wesley Powell," *Open Court,* 17 (1903): 228–347;

Gilbert and others, "John Wesley Powell," *Science,* 16 (October 1902): 561–567, 781–790;

William H. Goetzmann, *Exploration and Empire* (New York: Norton, 1966);

Herbert E. Gregory, ed., "Diary of Almon Harris Thompson," *Utah Historical Quarterly,* 7 (1939): 1–140;

Wesley P. Larsen, "The Letter or Were the Powell People Really Killed by Indians?," *Canyon Legacy,* 17 (Spring 1993): 12–18;

Otis "Dock" Marston, ed., "The Lost Journal of John Colton Sumner," *Utah Historical Quarterly,* 37 (Spring 1969): 173–189;

Dale L. Morgan, ed., "The Exploration of the Colorado River and High Plateaus of Utah in 1871–72" [includes all journals of the expedition], *Utah Historical Quarterly,* 16,17 (1948–1949): 1–540;

Lindsey Gardner Morris, "John Wesley Powell: Scientist and Educator," *Illinois State University Journal,* 31 (February 1969): 2–47;

Stephen J. Pyne, *Dutton's Point: An Intellectual History of the Grand Canyon* (Grand Canyon, Ariz.: Grand Canyon Natural History Association, 1982);

Pyne, *Grove Karl Gilbert: A Great Engine of Research* (Austin: University of Texas Press, 1980);

Henry Nash Smith, "Clarence King, John Wesley Powell, and The Establishment of The United States Geological Survey," *Mississippi Valley Historical Review,* 34 (June 1947): 37–58;

Smith, *Virgin Land: The American West as Symbol and Myth* (Cambridge, Mass.: Harvard University Press, 1951);

Robert Brewster Stanton, *Colorado River Controversies* (New York: Dodd, Mead, 1932);

Hal G. Stephens and Eugene Shoemaker, *In The Footsteps of John Wesley Powell* (Boulder, Col.: Johnson Books, 1987);

Everett Sterling, "The Powell Irrigation Survey, 1888–1893," *Mississippi Valley Historical Review,* 27 (December 1940): 421–434;

C. D. Walcott, "John Wesley Powell," in *24th Annual Report of the U.S. G. S. 1902–3* (Washington, D.C.: U.S. Government Printing Office, 1903), pp. 271–287;

Walter Prescott Webb, *The Great Plains* (Boston: Ginn, 1931);

Donald Worster, *An Unsettled Land* (Albuquerque: University of New Mexico Press, 1994);

John J. Zernel, "John Wesley Powell: Science and Reform in a Positive Context," dissertation, University of Oregon, 1983.

Papers:

Most of Powell's papers are housed in Washington, D.C., at the National Archives, the Smithsonian Institution, and the Library of Congress. Another valuable collection is located at the Utah State Historical Society in Salt Lake City.

Frederic Remington

(4 October 1861 – 26 December 1909)

Colleen Marie Tremonte
Michigan State University

See also the Remington entry in *DLB 12: American Realists and Naturalists.*

BOOKS: *Pony Tracks* (New York: Harper, 1895);
Crooked Trails (New York: Harper, 1898);
Stories of Peace and War (New York & London: Harper, 1899)—comprises stories from *Pony Tracks* and *Crooked Trails;*
Sundown Leflare (New York & London: Harper, 1899);
Men with the Bark On (New York & London: Harper, 1900);
John Ermine of Yellowstone (New York & London: Macmillan, 1902);
The Way of an Indian (New York: Fox, Duffield, 1906; London: Gay & Bird, 1906);
Frederic Remington's Own West, edited by Harold McCracken (New York: Dial, 1960);
Frederic Remington's Own Outdoors, edited by Douglas Allen (New York: Dial Press, 1964).
Collection: *The Collected Writings of Frederic Remington,* edited by Peggy Samuels and Harold Samuels (Garden City, N.J.: Doubleday, 1979).

SELECTED PERIODICAL PUBLICATIONS—
UNCOLLECTED:
FICTION
"The Affair of the –th of July," *Harper's Weekly,* 39 (2 February 1895): 105–107;
"Joshua Goodenough's Old Letter," *Harper's Monthly,* 93 (November 1897): 879–894;
"Massai's Crooked Trail," *Harper's Monthly,* 94 (January 1898): 240–248;
"When a Document Is Official," *Harper's Monthly,* 95 (September 1899): 608–622.

NONFICTION
"Horses of the Plains," *Century,* 37 (January 1889): 332–343;
"Artist Wanderings among the Cheyennes," *Century,* 37 (April 1889): 536–547;
"A Scout with the Buffalo Soldiers," *Century,* 37 (April 1889): 899–911;

Frederic Remington, circa 1908

"On the Indian Reservations," *Century,* 37 (July 1889): 393–406;
"Chasing a Major General," *Harper's Weekly,* 34 (6 December 1890): 946–947;
"The Art of War and Newspaper Men," *Harper's Weekly,* 34 (6 December 1890): 947;
"With the Fifth Corps," *Harper's Monthly,* 94 (November 1898): 960–978.

Frederic Remington, perhaps best known as a painter, sculptor, and illustrator, ranks as one of the most important chroniclers of the nineteenth-century American West. His depictions of cowboys, frontiersmen, and Indians—many of which appeared in national magazines such as *The Century, Harper's Monthly,* and *Collier's*—his paintings, and his bronzes etched a West of mythic stature that continues to hold sway in late-twentieth-century American popular consciousness. But Remington was also a shaper of words, and the West and western life found in his writings both complement and complicate the visions articulated in his art. Grounded in the romantic notions garnered from reading adventure stories as a youth and in the realities of his own travels through the West in the 1880s and 1890s, Remington's essays, short stories, and novels grapple with change and loss in ways of life and cultures amid a vanishing landscape.

Frederic Sackrider Remington was born on 4 October 1861, in Canton, New York, a village not far from the Saint Lawrence River. His parents, Clara Sackrider Remington and Seth Pierre Remington, were well-respected members of the community with ties to prominent families. Clara was the daughter of a hardware merchant with substantial commercial property in Canton; Seth was the son of a minister in the Universalist Church who had been instrumental in founding Saint Lawrence University. Remington's father was also a political aspirant with strong Republican convictions, as was evident in the weekly newspaper he began editing and publishing in 1865, the *Saint Lawrence* (N.Y.) *Plaindealer*. These same convictions likely prompted him to enlist in the Union Army (the First United States Volunteer Cavalry for the War for the Suppression of the Rebellion—the Civil War) when Frederic was only eight weeks old. While Seth was serving in Virginia and Maryland, with tours of Louisiana, Mississippi, and Arkansas, Frederic and his mother lived with her parents. By the time his father returned to Canton six years later, Remington had constructed an image of him as a war hero, one which helped forge a lasting parental-filial relationship.

In 1870 Seth Remington took a position as collector of United States Customs and moved the family to Ogdensburg, New York. Remington spent the next few years reading adventure stories, fishing and hunting, and occasionally sketching. Structured schooling and academics were not to his liking, and when enrolled at the Vermont Episcopal Institute in Burlington, Vermont, in 1875, Remington was neither prepared for nor suited to the school's strict rules. He fared better at the Highland Military Academy in Worcester, Massachusetts, to which he transferred in 1876. Here, although his responses to the military discipline were only halfhearted, they were also good-natured. His physical appearance—stoutness and strength—and his congeniality distinguished him among his peers and won him many friends. So, too, did his talents for drawing popular caricatures of the officers and teachers and sketches of figures in motion. Gleaned from his earlier readings of the journals of Meriwether Lewis and William Clark, the leatherstocking tales of James Fenimore Cooper, and the contemporary narratives of the West found in popular magazines and books, the figure sketches, though somewhat crude, were original in composition and style, and Remington began to consider seriously the study of art. Against the wishes of his parents, who viewed art as more of a pastime than a career, Remington entered the Yale School of the Fine Arts in 1878. However, he found the art curriculum with its emphasis on classical European art training dull and routine. He regarded his academic studies in much the same way and found Yale football more to his liking and better suited to his physical talents. In 1879, at a height of 5' 9" and a weight of 190 pounds, Remington was a powerful presence on the football field. But in football, too, he seemed to lack commitment. Upon finding his father seriously ill with tuberculosis during the Christmas holiday break, Remington decided against returning to Yale.

The death of his father in February 1880 left Remington at a loss, and he spent the next few years in pursuit of a vocation that had little to do with art or writing. In summer 1881, while waiting to assume an actuarial clerkship secured for him by a family member, Remington bartered for a trip to the Montana territory. He was barely sketching at the time and did not intend for his travels to provide anything more than an adventure or escape. Nonetheless, the two-month trip introduced him to the color, shape, and power of the western landscape in a hitherto unimagined manner. The slaughtered buffalo, Custer's battlefield site, Indians confined and not confined to the reservation—each scene provided an opening for interpretation.

In 1882 two events occasioned a shift in Remington's attitude toward the West and toward his art: he came into his inheritance, which assured him a certain amount of economic autonomy and freedom, and *Harper's Weekly* published one of his sketches in redrawn form. His interest in drawing western figures rekindled, he bought a small ranch, sight unseen, near Peabody, Kansas, with the intention of raising sheep. Again, Remington's initial enthusiasm outstripped his commitment. Not only did the Kansas landscape not match his expectations of westernness, but also the drudgery and routine of raising sheep undermined his romantic notions of ranching. A subsequent drop in the price of wool in 1884 convinced him of the folly of his undertaking; he sold the ranch and immediately moved to Kansas City. Still, the period afforded Remington an oppor-

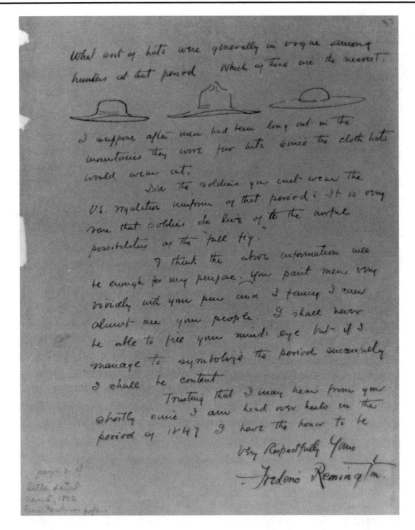

Second page of a 5 January 1892 letter from Remington to Francis Parkman,
regarding illustrations for The Oregon Trail *(Massachusetts Historical Society)*

tunity to gain yet another perspective on the West. During this time he took at least one horseback trip through Indian territory and New Mexico, often sketching in the field. While this excursion did not noticeably alter Remington's romantic boyhood impressions, it did provide a tangible point of reference against which he could juxtapose his earlier and later impressions of the West. The trip also left him with an invaluable cache of sketches.

Upon moving to Kansas City, Remington decided to renew his suit to marry Eva "Missie" Caten, a woman he first had met in August 1879. Since Remington had no prospects of future earnings in 1879 and since Eva's mother was dying, Eva's father had refused a first proposal of marriage. Now he welcomed Remington's offer. Unfortunately, Remington seemed no better directed in his pursuits in Kansas City than in Peabody, and life with him was not what he had led Eva to believe it

would be. Remington was not in the brokerage business, nor was he a member of the social set; rather, he was a silent partner in a saloon, a business Eva found unseemly, even reprehensible. In the summer of 1885, since the saloon was no longer profitable and her husband's attempts to earn money by freelancing were stalled, Eva felt compelled to return to her parents' home in Gloversville, New York. Only after she departed and he was completely broke did Remington begin to sketch and paint in earnest.

Remington spent the remainder of that summer traveling and sketching in southern Arizona, a tempestuous territory where Chief Geronimo had persistently if sporadically led raids against white settlers for the past several years. At the same time, Remington submitted to various eastern magazines sketches drawn during his travels west in 1883. Encouraged by the sale of another illustration to *Harper's Weekly,* Remington convinced Eva to move with him to New York City. Once there, however, he had trouble earning a living as an illustrator. He even sought to supplement his formal art training by attending classes at the Art Students League of New York. It was only when United States and Mexican troops escalated their campaigns against Geronimo that Remington found himself in a fortuitous position: with the general public's interest in the "Apache War" roused, he sold all of the Arizona sketches to *Outing Magazine,* and, more important, seized the moment to promote himself and his art. Dressed in cowboy garb and spinning himself as a mythic personage, he brashly approached Henry Harper with his portfolio and promptly sold two more sketches. With the appearance of "The Apache War: Indian Scouts on Geronimo's Trail" on the cover of *Harper's Weekly* in January 1886, Remington had begun to establish himself as both a popular illustrator and a resident expert on western subjects.

The year 1886 also marked the beginning of Remington's career as a writer. In May *Harper's* decided to send a special artist—a war correspondent of sorts—to report on Geronimo's continued struggles with the army. Remington's background and experiences made him an attractive recruit. Once out west, however, Remington abandoned the chase for Geronimo to focus on the army soldiers, whose lives and character he greatly admired. Not only does the resulting series of illustrations for *Harper's Weekly* on "Soldiering in the Southwest" (August 21) reveal a deep respect for the U.S. Army, so, too, does Remington's journal-travelogue. This collection of descriptions and notes, though uneven and inconsistent, is his first attempt at written reporting.

Curiously, these writings betray a certain tension in Remington's attitudes toward people of different cultures and races that his visual works do not. For example, he writes disparagingly about the Mexican people in the journal, describing "the Greasers" as a "villinous [sic] looking set," yet he does not draw the Mexicans this way. In time, and in his more mature writings, Remington confronts the tension between an artist's objectivity in seeing versus a writer's subjectivity in responding. Entries made during a later trip to Arizona reveal a more complex though still conflictual attitude toward Indians. On the one hand he wrote sympathetically: "The one thing about our aborigines which interests me most is their peculiar method of thought. With all due deference to much scientific investigation which has been lavished upon them, I believe that no white man can ever penetrate the mystery of their mind or explain the reason of their act." Yet he continued to support the army's attempts to subdue

the "Wild Tribes" and publicly endorsed the continuance of the reservation system. This essentially noncritical trust in soldiering and the military sometimes blinded Remington, as seen during a four-day visit to Fort Reno. He neglected an opportunity to investigate for himself the treatment of the Indians during the military depredations in 1864, 1868, and 1876, when he chose not to interview survivors.

By 1888 Remington's commonly accepted expert vision, a conflation of the realistic and the romantic, had secured his standing in the eastern art establishment as well as the general public. In 1888 three of Remington's paintings, including *Return of a Blackfoot War Party,* were hung in the National Academy, and *Harper's Weekly, Outing,* and *Youth's Companion* ran no less than 113 of his illustrations. Of greater consequence to Remington's standing as a writer, *Century* magazine commissioned him to write a series of articles on the Southwest to be published in 1889. Written in a straightforward, reportorial manner rich in detail and description, these illustrated articles are his first efforts at sustained writing. Conscious of his role as a magazine correspondent and chronicler of history, Remington sought to meliorate the expression of the West and westerners found in his earlier journal writings. Fueled by his travels with the Tenth Cavalry in Arizona, "Horses of the Plains" explores the various breeds that had developed in America from Spanish and Arabian strains (Remington considered himself an expert on the horse). The next articles—"A Scout with the Buffalo Soldiers," " On the Indian Reservations," and "Artist Wanderings among the Cheyennes"—report life on the southwestern reservations. Over the next eight years Remington published a total of seven illustrated articles in *Harper's Monthly* and nineteen in *Harper's Weekly.*

Remington's first book, *Pony Tracks,* is a collection taken from more than three dozen pieces written for *Harper's Monthly* and *Harper's Weekly.* Published in April 1895 and dedicated to "the fellows who rode the ponies that made the tracks," the book falls into three general categories: reports of hunting and fishing expeditions, descriptions of ranching in Mexico, and accounts of military life. Structurally, each narrative is set up as an eyewitness report of an event; thematically, each is linked to the others by a sensibility toward the western environment, one that prizes the individual's ability to confront the world about him, one that elevates self-reliance and skill. Whether participating in the hunt, as in "Bear-Chasing in the Rocky Mountains," or facing harsh ranch life, as with "In the Sierra Madre with the Punchers," this dignified individual with specialized knowledge and acquired competency commands re-

Remington in his studio at New Rochelle, New York,
circa 1895

spect and admiration. The same characteristics hold
true for the soldiers who people those narratives
chronicling military life in the United States Army.
Together, the pieces collected in *Pony Tracks* pay
homage to those men who survived, even thrived,
in the harsh and dangerous environment of the
West—men who "possess minds which, though lacking all embellishments, are chaste and simple," and
who know how to deal competently with any problem.

Unfortunately, Remington builds his esteem
for the soldier at the expense of the Indian, whom
he judges to be brutal when responding to the rule
of law that an army imposes. In "The Sioux Outbreak in South Dakota," for example, Remington
draws upon his travels in South Dakota in 1890
when he was assigned to report on the Sioux uprisings that culminated in the Wounded Knee Massacre. As in the Geronimo campaign, however, Remington missed the actual event, having departed a
nearby encampment to return to New York the day
of the massacre: he did not witness the slaughter of
nearly two hundred Sioux, many of them women
and children, by the U.S. Army. Hence, he depicts
the soldier as possessing greater moral character
and physical ability than the Indian. Remington extends his complaint against the Indian character in
"Lieutenant Casey's Last Scout," which disparages
not only those who break the law of the land but
also those who sympathize with them. Here he in-
dicts Washington politicians whose "sentimental
concern for savages" has resulted in the death of a
heroic young officer.

While Remington's portrayal of the Indian
seems consistent in *Pony Tracks,* his writing style is
not. At least one of the pieces, "The Affair of the —th

of July," qualifies as a short story, one that purposefully recasts a historical recounting. The story grew
out of Remington's reports for *Harper's Weekly* on
the 1894 Pullman strikes and riots in Chicago. But
rather than giving a straight report of the action,
Remington, through his narrator and the employment of the epistolary form, manipulates the scene
of the uprising. The story, reported in the form of a
letter from a military aide-de-camp present at the ri-
oting, is a conscious attempt to experiment with narrative structure. On one level it can be read as a
tract against those who threaten civil order (the aide
denounces the strikers as anarchists and praises the
military men sent to enforce the law); thus it is in
keeping with themes of earlier writings. On another
level the epistolary structure reveals a calculated, albeit awkward, employment of technique for effect.
The ending of the story confirms Remington's
awareness that he is using poetic license as the aide
writes: "Of course, my dear friend, all this never
really happened, but it might very easily have happened if the mob had continued to monkey with the
military buzz-saw."

Between 1896 and 1902 Remington perfected
his skills in bronze and also produced a vast number
of paintings and illustrations. His creative impulses
extended to his writing, in which his continued exploration into and purposeful mythologizing of the
West took on a new complexity. Recognizing that
what remained of the West was passing, Remington
sought to infuse his writing with a sense of immediacy and historicity. The resulting narratives, especially those exploring Indian life, are tinged with a
dark romanticism more often found in the writing of
earlier authors such as Nathaniel Hawthorne.

Remington's second book, *Crooked Trails,* published in 1898, was much like *Pony Tracks,* a collection of essays previously published in *Harper* magazines. Unlike *Pony Tracks,* however, this collection is
Remington's first attempt to treat the West in a historical context that remained consciously romantic.
Again he turned to narrative technique in his attempt to articulate the tenuous connection between
past and present. In "Joshua Goodenough's Old Letter," originally published in the November 1897
Harper's Monthly and later collected in *Stories of Peace
and War* (1899) as well as in *Crooked Trails,* Remington employs the same epistolary technique as in
"The Affair of the —th of July," to both better and
worse effect. The protagonist writes to his son from
Albany, New York, in 1789, describing both his life
as a scout with Rogers's Rangers in the 1750s and
his participation in a series of conflicts over the previous forty years. Joshua tells of fighting with the
British against the French at the Battle of Ticon-

deroga in 1758, fighting against the Indians on the frontier, and fighting against the British in the Revolution. Old age has provided him a vantage point, and he tries to convey to his son what he has learned. Echoing the same sentiments Remington expressed earlier toward soldiers and soldiering, Joshua argues that skill and courage are needed to survive in the wilderness, that incompetency in a frontier soldier is costly, and that consistency is a byword for duty. Ironically, the advantage of the story, the ring of authenticity in reproducing a historical document, is also the disadvantage as it is overly detailed and somewhat tedious.

Three other stories in *Crooked Trails* are notable as they reflect Remington's awareness of the past and reveal his revised stance toward Indians in theme, language, and rhetoric. In "Massai's Crooked Trail," although Remington still casts the Apache warrior as an unregenerate savage, he also expresses an uncertain admiration for the Indian's ability to resist his pursuers. In "The Sergeant of the Orphan Trail" the protagonist, Sergeant Carter Johnson, is similarly moved to reassess his attitude toward the Indian. An able, resourceful, and courageous soldier in pursuit of a Cheyenne warrior, Carter responds in a fair manner when unexpectedly confronted with an orphaned child. Remington's new sensibility finds its greatest expression in "The Spirit of Mahongui," an extended exploration of Indian character and culture. Written in the form of a memoir, the story tells the adventures of a French voyageur in Canada who is captured by the Iroquois, adopted into an Indian family, and drawn by a desire to fight with the Indians against the French. In the story-within-the-story, that of a dog's possession by a great warrior's spirit, Remington articulates a growing appreciation for the Indian's relationship with the spirit and with the natural world. In these stories Remington recognizes that his past characterization of the Other was more than a structural weakness in storytelling: it was a thematic weakness that undermined the complexity of his vision of the West.

Just as *Crooked Trails* is steeped in historical consciousness, so, too, is Remington's first full-length novel, *Sundown Leflare*, published in 1899. A transitional work formatted in a manner similar to earlier works (a collection of short stories published originally in *Harper's Monthly*) and consistent in themes, it demonstrates a maturity and coherency not present in his earlier writing. The story line is simple: a first-person narrator, an eastern painter presumed to be Remington, reports a series of conversations he has had with Leflare while traveling through the West. In this work Remington intensi-

fies his mythologizing and romanticizing of the West and of the Indian's way of life to make explicit that the white man's preoccupation with progress and domination are destructive. He juxtaposes the nobility of a vanishing landscape against the nobility of a present one, exploring in depth the problems of Otherness and intercultural relations and the general failure of assimilation.

The first story, "The Great Medicine Horse," opens as usual with the first-person narrator, only now his voice is the last in a line of narrators: Old Paint tells a story which he heard from his father, who, in turn, heard it from his father. Since Old Paint speaks in the Crow language, Leflare must translate the legend for the white man, who records it for the reader. But the listener-writer has difficulty separating "Paint's mysterious musings" from those of Leflare, whom he casually describes as "cross-bred, red and white . . . [not] in sympathy with either strain of his progenitors." The chronicler's dilemma—how to distinguish Sundown's interpretation from Paint's version—foregrounds the difficulties of intercultural communications. It also comments indirectly on Remington's continuing struggle to handle fictional material, for the further he moves from the writing of a verifiable, historical account, the more voices he interjects into the narrative.

"The Great Medicine Horse" is the only piece in *Crooked Trails* written before Remington traveled to Cuba as a correspondent for *Harper's Weekly* during the Spanish-American War in 1898, a particularly disillusioning experience for him. Throughout the 1890s he had desired to participate in some manner in a "European" war, believing it would be a great experience. But his Cuban experience had an impact of inverse proportion: rather than glorifying the greatness of war, the experience gave testament to the horrific and devastating effects of modern technological warfare. The remaining Leflare stories reflect this disillusionment. "How Order No. 6 Went Through," which relates the minor heroics of a young Sundown who braves a blizzard to deliver an order, sets the perspective of an older, experienced Leflare against that of a younger, inexperienced Leflare: the Sundown who *appears* in the action of the story is an Indian scout for General Miles; the Sundown who *narrates* the story is much more experienced in the ways of the white society. The tension lies between the realistic and the romantic: Leflare engages in romantic, even heroic, tasks and deeds, but he undercuts this impression in telling of them. For example, Leflare stresses his own cowardice and common sense, casually revealing that the woman for whom he so bravely fought

White-Owl he later sold to a white man for $300. "Sundown Leflare's Money" tells how Leflare meets an itinerant gambler, makes a considerable amount of money at cards and dice, and is eventually run out of a Montana frontier town when his cheating is discovered. The issue raised for the listener-writer (and the reader) about Leflare's actions is whether to judge those actions as naive, fraudulent, or justifiable. Although Sundown has tried to adapt to the white man's ways in his attitudes, gestures, and even clothing, he remains a victim of the differences between the value systems of Indian and white societies. Leflare himself locates the source of his dilemma in progress: "Back yondair, een what year you call '80—all same time de white man was hang de oddar white man so fas'—she geet be bad. De buffalo . . . was all shoot up. . . . Den come de railroad; after dat bad, all bad." Remington intensifies his critique of a vanishing West and the vagrancies of white society at the expense of the Indian in "Sundown Leflare's Warm Spot." An aging Sundown talks of his various loves and relationships, ending with the story of the white prostitute who abandoned him and their infant son. Implicit in his indictment of the woman is one of white society at large. Leflare misses the irony that the woman's actions nearly mirror his own actions of selling an Indian woman. These conflicting stances find full fruition in "Sundown's Higher Self" in which Leflare reveals his intentions to take his son east and raise him white. Although he may argue the value of the Indian way of life, Leflare recognizes the reality of the white world with which he must contend.

Simply to cast Sundown in the role of mediator would be easy. He moves between the Indian world and the white world, between two cultures, because he knows "about half as much concerning Indians as they did themselves [and] his knowledge of white men was in the same proportion." He is a storyteller responsible for seeing and interpreting the history outside of which and in which he stands. The moral dilemmas, the clash of values, that he faces illustrate the hardships of the Other in the world of the white man without absolving the Other of personal responsibility. Leflare is Ralph Ellison's invisible man made visible, an alien whose present situation is potentially but not ultimately tragic. As Leflare reminisces about the past, Remington increasingly directs attention away from the present: he arranged the stories in reverse chronology so that in the last story Leflare appears as a noble young medicine man. Hence, although his perspective—that of an older man looking back—provides ironic distancing, it ultimately turns back in on itself. The narrative voice undercuts deeds, but the narrative structure

undercuts the narrative voice. The illustrations of the text also undercut Leflare's self-parody. The frontispiece shows Sundown in the present, as a half-breed in white man's clothing, an ill-fitting costume. Throughout the stories the pictures become more stylized and more "Indianized" until, in the last illustrations, Sundown appears in full Indian dress, magnificent in stature.

As a conscious exploration of the failure of white industrialized civilization to assimilate indigenous western peoples, *Sundown Leflare* succeeds. As a publishing venture, however, it failed; it was not widely reviewed or noticed, and it sold poorly. For his next book Remington returned to a proven format, an anthology of previously published essays and articles. Published in 1900, *Men with the Bark On* through its themes marks Remington's continued development as a writer: he accepts that the old West has passed and that the new West that has emerged and is possessed by institutional and technological forces beyond human control. In its epigraph Remington writes: "Men with the bark on die like wild animals, unnaturally, unmourned, and even unthought of mostly." These men and women are both white and Indian, soldier and brave; these men and women are alienated, erased, and subsumed by something greater than "white" society and culture—progress.

After returning from Cuba in 1898 Remington worked enthusiastically, devoting himself to painting, sculpting, and writing. The thrust toward impressionism that had first begun to appear in his paintings after Wounded Knee became stronger and more assertive in all of his work, including his writings. Not surprisingly, Remington is at his most mature, developed, and despairing in his last two novels: *John Ermine of Yellowstone,* published in 1902, and *The Way of an Indian,* serialized in *Cosmopolitan* from 1905 to 1906 and published in book form in 1906. The protagonists of these novels—John Ermine and Fire Eater, respectively—fail to fit the model of the more romantic and heroic if somewhat ironic protagonist such as Sundown Leflare. Rather, the weight and realities of the new West defeat both: at the close of *John Ermine,* the protagonist is dead, shot in the back by a bitter Crow scout; at the close of *The Way of an Indian* the protagonist, carrying the corpse of his infant son, is fleeing the cavalry into the wintry foothills with a broken band of Cheyennes.

Critics have long noted that Remington probably modeled his earliest short stories after the works of Mark Twain, which were likewise written in epistolary or diary form. These early Remington stories, like his essays, were realistic. When he abandoned the epistolary technique and began experimenting with other techniques, such as the frame

SUNDOWN LEFLARE, WASHED AND
DRESSED UP

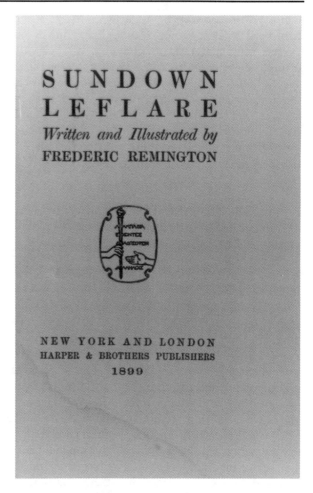

*Frontispiece and title page for Remington's 1899 book, in which an eastern painter listens to the stories of a man he describes as
"crossbred, red and white"*

stories of *Sundown Leflare,* his fiction acquired an impressionistic and somewhat naturalistic shade reminiscent of Stephen Crane's "The Bride Comes to Yellow Sky" (1898) and "The Blue Hotel" (1899). A similar shift had already occurred in Remington's visual artwork, as those paintings completed after 1890 were less realistic than impressionistic and were different in form, color, composition, and conception from earlier ones. In his later writings Remington continued experimenting with narrative voice, structure, and style. Characters in Remington's fictional pieces written in and after 1897 remain recognizable types—cowboys, Indians, troopers, frontiersmen—but are darkly romantic, curiously ironic, and rhetorically self-aware. His characters may seem "fatalistic," and the major tensions in the narratives may fall within the purview of the conflict between protagonist and environment, but the question of who or what transformed whom or what suggests that Remington sought to locate his fiction beyond naturalism and anticipated the descriptions and themes of alienation and displace-

ment found in modernist narratives, such as those of Sherwood Anderson.

The novel *John Ermine,* which held the public's attention for a year before being adapted as a play, appeared the same year as Owen Wister's classic, *The Virginian* (1902), which Remington regarded as contrived and formulaic. In an attempt to situate *John Ermine* in a more identifiable context, Remington chose a period and environment he knew well—the years and general area surrounding the Custer massacre—and drew his characters from among the Indian-fighting army and the Crow Indians who sought to live cooperatively with the whites. He tells the story of White Weasel, a white boy who had been raised by a band of Crow Indians since infancy. When White Weasel becomes an adolescent, Crooked Bear, a deformed white recluse whom the Indians regard as an oracle, takes in the young man. Crooked Bear renames the boy John Ermine and educates him in the ways of the white people—including reading, writing, arithmetic, and moral philosophy. He eventually sends Ermine back to the white world by way of an army outpost where Ermine acts as a scout. Although Ermine is not versed in the manners and mores of the white troops, he performs his duties well and earns the respect of fellow soldiers and the commander. When the unit returns to summer quarters, Ermine meets, rescues, and falls in love with Major Searle's daughter, Katherine. In stereotypic fashion, Katherine admires Ermine's handsomeness and finds his discomfiture in her presence amusing, and in stereotypic fashion Ermine mistakes her gestures and responses, proposes marriage, and is devastated when she rejects him. Thereafter Ermine quickly falls into corrupt white ways, including drinking and playing cards. The narrative culminates in his attempt to shoot his rival for Katherine's affections, his subsequent escape, and his eventual return, which results in his death.

Though a melodrama, *John Ermine* avoids the trap of sentimentality by clearly articulating the contradictions and consequences for a white man who cannot move between worlds, whose displacement and alienation are immutable. Biologically (or racially) white but culturally Indian, Ermine is ill-equipped to live in either world; as he travels between the Indian and white worlds, he finds himself trapped in a cycle, repeatedly outsider, insider, and stranger. His own mixture of red and white sensibilities causes him agonizing internal conflict: he has two names, is referred to as two separate characters, and prays to two gods. Believing he can negotiate a place for himself, Ermine initially asserts, "I have no relations anywhere on the earth, but I have friends." After the shooting, however, he is suspended in limbo: the Crows shun him and he, in turn, abandons Crooked Bear. In the end, Ermine knows he has "one friend left, just one . . . the Night." Ermine believes that whites and Indians are two distinct people, two distinct races, who although they can be brought together, cannot be reconciled. Ermine understands this duality as the root of his alienation and displacement, and in the end he ascribes to the white soldiers' characterization of him as a man with "two hearts: one is red and one is blue; and you feel with the one that best suits you at the time." Ermine's decline, his death, is entropy at its worst.

John Ermine is as interesting for the story it fails to tell as for the one it does, that of Katherine Searles. This novel is not only about irreconcilability of the past and the present, of Indian and white societies, but also about relations—"hostilities"—between men and women. Katherine is attracted to this Indianized white man because of his looks, flowing hair, and broad hands. Ermine's desire for Katherine is similarly physical and sexual: "he wanted her body, he wanted

her mind, and he wanted her soul merged with his." Yet it also betrays the persistent patriarchal fear of women that marked nineteenth-century culture, for "as he looked at her now his mouth grew dry, like a man in mortal fear or mortal agony." Katherine is characterized not only as an object of desire but also as a threat to men in general and Ermine in particular: "She played the batteries of her eyes on the unfortunate soldier and all his [Mr. Butler's] formations went down before them," and her gaze "penetrated Ermine like a charge of buckshot." And just as Ermine easily mistakes Katherine's attentions, the reader easily dismisses her explanation that their "relationship has not been rightly understood."

In *John Ermine* Remington raises the specter of a conventional, generic western only to thwart the reader's expectations. In *The Way of an Indian* he makes no pretense at convention. In this work the protagonist, a full-blooded Indian who encounters white men and women only as enemies, embodies Remington's vision of the shrinking possibilities in the West at its bleakest—no possibilities. The action opens in 1821 with a young Cheyenne named White Otter being initiated into manhood. When he comes back from his fast in the mountains, he brings with him the body of a small bat which he has caught and which he adopts as his "medicine." White Otter is renamed Bat. Shortly afterward he conducts a raid into Crow territory, where he steals two ponies and kills a young man innocently waiting for his lover in a wooded creek bottom. A series of similar exploits follows, during one of which he leads an assault against white traders who defend themselves with dynamite. This incident earns him the name Fire Eater. Convinced that he is invincible, Fire Eater becomes more and more reckless and eventually leads a charge of which he is the only survivor. Shamed, he chooses not to return to his own village but instead joins the Shoshones. Years later he rejoins the Cheyennes, having invented a story that presents him as a reincarnation of himself—a great hero.

Although the action in the novel progresses from chapter to chapter, the characters do not develop or change. At the end of the story Fire Eater is an old man simply waiting for a final "evil." Each of the experiences which should cause him to gain in maturity and knowledge moves him nowhere, and the action of the book is ultimately static. Fire Eater's life may be filled with sundry victories, but it is also marked by cowardice as his individual acts of combat are acts against helpless or unsuspecting victims. He even wins the incident in which he earns his name Fire Eater because the white traders die of thirst. Hence, Remington suggests and reiterates that the renowned victories and the multiple "re-births" Fire Eater experiences are tempered and nonrenewable. The horror—of the history and the way of this particular Indian—is best illustrated in a closing scene in which the chief shows his grandson a dead white soldier. The baby, soon to freeze to death himself, is led to stab the dead corpse: "Pulling his knife from its buckskin sheath, he [Fire Eater] curled the fat hand around its shaft and led him to the white body. . . . He drew up and drove down, doing his best to obey the instructions, but his arc was far too weak to make the knife penetrate." By the end of this novel Fire Eater accepts the futility of resisting historical progress and the white man's time while the reader recognizes the inherent instability in the *idea* of historical progress.

The Way of an Indian was Remington's last fictional work, in part because he may have felt his vision of the West and its inhabitants had reached its logical conclusion, in part because he may have exhausted his ability to put forth a sustained literary effort only to have it rejected by the public at large. Remington had consistently shown a maturing sensibility toward the difficulties of reconciling conflicting images embedded in a national landscape. He recognized the risk of articulating assimilation through historical documentation and the complexities of describing a heroic vision of the Old West at the expense of the Other. When he died of complications from appendicitis on 26 December 1909 at his newly completed home in Ridgefield, Connecticut, Remington had become painfully aware of the limits of literary representation. Nonetheless, his writings provide a critical perspective on the various discourses present in the late nineteenth-century cultural conversation: theories of evolution, practices of assimilation, beliefs in imperialist policies, and attitudes toward the ideas of the past and history. Remington's writings, perhaps even more powerfully and forcefully than his art, provide the late-twentieth-century reader and critic a compass by which to navigate his vision of the West.

Letters:

Frederic Remington—Selected Letters, edited by Allen P. Splete and Marilyn D. Splete (New York: Abbeville Press, 1988).

Biography:

Peggy Samuels and Harold Samuels, *Frederic Remington: A Biography* (Garden City, N.Y.: Doubleday, 1982).

References:

Douglas Allen, *Frederic Remington and the Spanish-American War* (New York: Crown, 1971);

La Verne Anderson, *Frederic Remington: Artist on Horseback* (Champaign, Ill.: Garrard, 1971);

Christine Bold, "How the Western Ends: Fenimore Cooper to Frederic Remington," *Western American Literature,* 17 (August 1982): 117–135;

Fred Erisman, *Frederic Remington* (Boise, Idaho: Boise State University, 1975);

Peter Hassrick, *Frederic Remington* (New York: Abrams, 1973);

Hassrick and Michael Shapiro, editors, *Frederic Remington: The Masterworks* (New York: Abrams, 1988);

Linda Logan, "The Geographical Imagination of Frederic Remington: The Invention of the Cowboy West," *Journal of Historical Geography,* 18 (1992): 75–90;

Harold McCracken, *Frederic Remington: Artist of the Old West* (Philadelphia: Lippincott, 1947);

McCracken, *The Frederic Remington Book: A Pictorial History of the West* (Garden City, N.Y.: Doubleday, 1966);

Ralph N. Miller, "Frederic Remington: Francis Parkman's Illustrator," *Gateway Heritage,* 2 (1981): 38–48;

Alexander Nemerov, *Frederic Remington & Turn-of-the-Century America* (New Haven & London: Yale University Press, 1995);

Ben Marchant Vorpahl, *Frederic Remington and the West: With the Eye of the Mind* (Austin: University of Texas Press, 1978);

Vorpahl, *My Dear Wister: The Frederic Remington–Owen Wister Letters* (Palo Alto, Cal.: American West, 1972);

G. Edward White, *The Eastern Establishment and the Western Experience: The West of Frederic Remington, Theodore Roosevelt, and Owen Wister* (New Haven, Conn.: Yale University Press, 1968).

Papers:

The Kansas State Historical Society in Topeka has notebooks and letters from Remington to his wife; the Owen Wister papers at the Library of Congress include Remington's letters to Owen Wister; the Archives of American Art, Smithsonian Institution, Washington, D.C., has additional papers; the St. Lawrence University Library in Canton, New York, has letters to friends; and the Frederic Remington Art Museum in Ogdensburg, New York, has notebooks, diaries, and letters as well as books from Remington's library, with the artist's notations.

Theodore Roosevelt

(27 October 1858 – 6 January 1919)

David Teague
University of Delaware

See also the Roosevelt entry in *DLB 47: American Historians, 1866–1912*.

BOOKS: *The Summer Birds of the Adirondacks in Franklin County, N.Y.,* by Roosevelt and H. D. Minot (Salem, Mass.: Privately printed, 1877);

Notes on Some of the Birds of Oyster Bay, Long Island (New York: Privately printed, 1879);

The Naval War of 1812; or, The History of the United States Navy during the Last War with Great Britain (New York: Putnam, 1882); republished as *The Naval Operations of the War Between Great Britain and the United States* (London: Low, 1910);

Hunting Trips of a Ranchman (New York & London: Putnam, 1885; London: Kegan Paul, Trench, 1886);

Thomas Hart Benton (Boston: Houghton, Mifflin, 1886);

Essays on Practical Politics (New York & London: Putnam, 1888);

Governeur Morris (Boston & New York: Houghton, Mifflin, 1888);

Ranch Life and the Hunting-Trail (New York: Century, 1888; London: Unwin, 1888);

The Winning of the West; An Account of the Exploration and Settlement of Our Country from the Alleghanies to the Pacific, 4 volumes (New York: Putnam, 1889–1896);

New York (London & New York: Longmans, Green, 1891);

The Wilderness Hunter: An Account of the Big Game of the United States and Its Chase with Horse (New York: Putnam, 1893);

Hero Tales from American History, by Roosevelt and Henry Cabot Lodge (New York: Century, 1895);

American Ideals, and Other Essays, Social and Political (New York & London: Putnam, 1897);

The Rough Riders (New York: Scribners, 1899; London: Kegan Paul, Trench & Trübner, 1899);

Oliver Cromwell (New York: Scribners, 1900; London: Constable, 1900);

Theodore Roosevelt (photograph by Underwood & Underwood)

The Strenuous Life: Essays and Addresses (New York: Century, 1900; London: Richards, 1902);

California Addresses (San Francisco: California Promotion Committee, 1903);

Outdoor Pastimes of an American Hunter (limited edition, New York: Scribners, 1903; New York: Scribners, 1905; London: Longmans, Green, 1905; enlarged, New York: Scribners, 1908);

Addresses and Presidential Messages of Theodore Roosevelt, 1902–1904 (New York & London: Putnam, 1904);

Good Hunting (New York & London: Harper, 1907);

Addresses and Papers, edited by Willis Fletcher Johnson (New York: Sun Dial, 1908);

The Roosevelt Policy: Speeches, Letters and State Papers, Relating to Corporate Wealth and Closely Allied Topics, of Theodore Roosevelt, 2 volumes (New York: Current Literature, 1908); enlarged edition, edited by William Griffith, 3 volumes (New York: Current Literature, 1919);

Outlook Editorials (New York: Outlook, 1909);

Stories of the Great West (New York: Century Company, 1909);

African Game Trails, An Account of the African Wanderings of an American Hunter-Naturalist (New York: Scribners, 1910; London: John Murray, 1910);

African and European Addresses (New York & London: Putnam, 1910);

American Problems (New York: Outlook, 1910);

The New Nationalism (New York: Outlook, 1910);

Realizable Ideals (The Earl Lectures) (San Francisco: Whittaker & Rey-Wiggin, 1912);

Theodore Roosevelt: An Autobiography (New York: Macmillan, 1913);

Progressive Principles: Selections from Addresses Made During the Presidential Campaign of 1912, edited by Elmer H. Youngman (New York: Progressive National Service, 1913);

History as Literature, and Other Essays (New York: Scribners, 1913; London: John Murray, 1914);

Life-Histories of African Game Animals, 2 volumes, by Roosevelt and Edmund Heller (New York: Scribners, 1914; London: John Murray, 1915);

Through the Brazilian Wilderness (New York: Scribners, 1914; London: John Murray, 1915);

America and the World War (New York: Scribners, 1915; London: John Murray, 1915);

A Book-Lover's Holidays in the Open (New York: Scribners, 1916; London: John Murray, 1916);

Fear God and Take Your Own Part (New York: Doran, 1916; London: Hodder & Stoughton, 1916);

Americanism and Preparedness. Speeches, July to November, 1916 (New York: Mail and Express Job Print, 1916);

The Foes of Our Own Household (New York: Doran, 1917);

National Strength and International Duty (Princeton: Princeton University Press, 1917);

The Great Adventure: Present-Day Studies in American Nationalism (New York: Scribners, 1918; London: John Murray, 1919);

Average Americans (New York & London: Putnam, 1919);

Newer Roosevelt Messages: Speeches, Letters and Magazine Articles Dealing with the War, Before and After, and Other Vital Topics, edited by Griffith (New York: Current Literature, 1919);

Roosevelt in the Kansas City Star: War-time Editorials by Theodore Roosevelt (Boston & New York: Houghton Mifflin, 1921);

Campaigns and Controversies (New York: Scribners, 1926);

East of the Sun and West of the Moon, by Roosevelt and Kermit Roosevelt (New York & London: Scribners, 1926);

Literary Essays (New York: Scribners, 1926);

Social Justice and Popular Rule: Essays, Addresses, and Public Statements Relating to the Progressive Movement (New York: Scribners, 1926);

Theodore Roosevelt's Diaries of Boyhood and Youth (New York & London: Scribners, 1926);

Colonial Policies of the United States (Garden City, N.Y.: Doubleday, Doran, 1937);

The Hunting and Exploring Adventures of Theodore Roosevelt, edited by Donald Day (New York: Dial, 1955).

Collections: *The Works of Theodore Roosevelt, Memorial Edition,* 24 volumes, edited by Hermann Hagedorn (New York: Scribners, 1923);

The Works of Theodore Roosevelt, National Edition, 20 volumes (New York: Scribners, 1926).

OTHER: *American Big-Game Hunting,* edited by Roosevelt and George Bird Grinnell (New York: Forest and Stream, 1893);

Hunting in Many Lands, edited by Roosevelt and Grinnell (New York: Forest and Stream, 1895);

Trail and Camp-fire, edited by Roosevelt and Grinnell (New York: Forest and Stream, 1897).

The persona Theodore Roosevelt projected as, among other things, president of the United States, man of letters, Rough Rider, historian, big-game hunter, and conservationist has come to symbolize the temper of his time. The noted historian Albert J. Beveridge observed in the *Theodore Roosevelt Cyclopedia* (1941), edited by Albert Bushnell Hart and Herbert Ronald Ferleger, that "More than any other man of his period, [Roosevelt's] character and his life typified the character and the life of the American people as a whole." Roosevelt brimmed with all the expansiveness, enthusiasm, and progressivism of the nation at the beginning of the twentieth century, as well as with its contradictions, biases, and prejudices. While some modern scholars count some of the most enlightened impulses of the United States toward conservation of natural and

Roosevelt on a roundup, 1885 (photograph by Ingersoll)

human resources as part of Roosevelt's legacy, others point to imperialistic and paternalistic attitudes of the country toward nature, other cultures, and other countries.

Roosevelt was, as his friend John Burroughs observed, "a many-sided man" who united "such versatility, such vitality, such thoroughness, such copiousness" as is rarely seen in one human being. Nearly the entire constellation of Roosevelt's complex persona finds expression in his attitudes toward the American West. In his letters, journals, histories, adventure narratives, and political theory, the West becomes an emblem for the brightest possi-

bilities of U.S. civilization. And in ways of which Roosevelt does not seem to have been aware, it also becomes an emblem for the most destructive, chauvinistic, and racist impulses of the nation. Roosevelt saw the vast West as a natural wonderland innocent of the excesses of civilization, a blank slate on which the history of the nation might be written. Roosevelt would himself write much of that history during his lifetime.

Theodore Roosevelt came from a well-established New York family of Dutch descent. His earliest American ancestor, Klaes Martensen van Rosenvelt, came to Manhattan Island in 1644, only eighteen years after Peter Minuit had "bought" it from its indigenous Canarsee inhabitants for sixty guilders. His great-grandfather James served in the Continental Army during the Revolutionary War and afterward set up a hardware business in New York. His grandfather Cornelius Van Schaack Roosevelt expanded the family fortune greatly; among other business accomplishments, he was one of the founders of the Chemical Bank of New York.

Roosevelt's father, Theodore Roosevelt Sr., worked in the family hardware business and was one of the founders of the Metropolitan Museum of Art and the American Museum of Natural History. His mother, Martha, was from a wealthy Georgia slaveholding family and seems to have possessed the courage of her southern convictions to the extent of flying, on occasion, a Dixie banner outside the Roosevelt home at 33 East Twentieth Street in New York City. Martha Bulloch Roosevelt, however, does not seem to have influenced her son's development to the extent his father did. Nevertheless, the Roosevelt family was by all accounts a warm and close-knit one.

Roosevelt was born on 27 October 1858 squarely into upper-class eastern society, a child whose educational and social opportunities in New York City seemed to stretch almost limitlessly before him. His one obvious limitation was that, like many late-nineteenth-century Americans who would become associated with the history of the West, his health was poor. Young Roosevelt suffered from severe asthma. His condition was so dire that, by many accounts, he barely survived childhood. Although Roosevelt's education, in particular his spelling skills, may have suffered from the spotty schooling he received in childhood because of these health problems, his response to his illness was to develop his powers of concentration, his dedication to the task at hand, and his physical stamina to remarkable levels in his youth and young manhood. In many ways he turned the misfortune of his early ill health to account as he developed lifelong habits of physical exercise that counteracted his infirmity.

One of the consequences of Roosevelt's asthma and his subsequent attachment to outdoor activity seems to have been his early interest in natural history, which he manifested before age ten. This fascination would come to represent a major component of his interest in the West because in his mature years around the turn of the century the West represented some of the last unspoiled "natural" habitat in the country. It was to become a land of treasure for Roosevelt, who in the 1860s began to develop skills as a naturalist, hunter, and outdoorsman.

At age eight Roosevelt began his career as an amateur, though highly accomplished, student of nature. In the window of a Broadway market near his home he noticed a seal recently killed in New York Harbor. The next day he returned with a folding rule, a pencil, and a notebook and measured the seal thoroughly. He wrote a detailed description of it in his notebook, drawing conclusions about the seal's "strength." Eventually, he persuaded both the owner of the market and his parents to allow him to have the skull of the seal, where it later became the first exhibit in "The Roosevelt Museum of Natural History," housed in his bedroom.

At age nine Roosevelt began his first diary. Its initial entry, "August 10th Munday, (1868)," recorded in Barrytown, New York, describes the encounter between "a gentleman . . . of whom I do not know the name" and a brown bear. Starting from his first entry Roosevelt's childhood diaries, which were published in 1926 as *Theodore Roosevelt's Diaries of Boyhood and Youth,* abound in such descriptions of natural phenomena.

Roosevelt's early interest in the field of natural history is clear from his youthful reading. Among the first of the thousands of books to catch his interest was David Livingstone's *Missionary Travels and Researches in South Africa* (1857), published the year before Roosevelt's birth. The child delighted in the descriptions the volume supplied of antelopes, zebras, rhinoceroses, buffalos, lions, and giraffes. He also enjoyed books with titles such as *The Boy Hunters, Afloat in the Forest,* and *Wild Life, or Adventures on the Frontier.*

His later education also contributed a great deal to the literary perspective from which Roosevelt would eventually approach the West. By fourteen he had become a prodigious reader. His lifelong interest in Scandinavian and Germanic cultures dates from his reading of Henry Wadsworth Longfellow's "The Saga of Olaf" and the summer of 1873 that he spent learning German in Dresden. He also became familiar with Charles Darwin's theories of evolution, and he was exposed to Herbert Spencer's theory of Social Darwinism. Before he left home to study natural history at Harvard—where he candidly admits in his autobiography that he learned little he thought useful—he accompanied his family on vacations into the still-rural Hudson Valley and the still-wild Adirondacks; to Egypt and Syria, the animals of which appeared to him exotic indeed; and to Oyster Bay, where his recorded natural history of the region became increasingly precise, systematic, and thorough. He drew on these family excursions for his first two books, both privately printed: *The Summer Birds of the Adirondacks in*

Franklin County, N. Y. (1877), which he wrote with H. D. Minot, and *Notes on Some of the Birds of Oyster Bay, Long Island* (1879).

By the time he entered Harvard in the fall of 1876, Roosevelt was so fascinated with the natural world that his exposure to the rational scientific methods of studying natural history at the university disillusioned him. The method of laboratory study at Harvard, in his eyes, ignored the value of the field naturalist. Instead of studying nature as a vocation, Roosevelt learned during this time to make natural studies his avocation, and one of his principal methods became hunting.

As an undergraduate he took three trips to the Maine wilderness. One of the excursions took place in March 1879 during a time when, according to Roosevelt, the temperature seldom rose above zero. Nevertheless, during this trip he felt immensely comfortable, and his chronic asthma did not affect him. The remission of his physical symptoms during outdoor activity soon became a common and lifelong phenomenon for Roosevelt and later became a large part of the attraction of the West.

From about the time of his graduating twenty-first in a class of 158 from Harvard in 1880 Roosevelt's life seems in many ways to fit into the pattern suggested by the promising circumstances of his birth and youth. In 1878 the death of his father, an event that saddened him deeply, had resulted in his receiving $125,000. He would use this money to start a ranch in North Dakota in the coming years. On 27 October 1880 he married Alice Lee. In the next three years he established a home with her and began a promising, if contentious, political career in New York as a state assemblyman. He built a reputation as a reformer, protector of the public interest, and adversary of political machines and special privileges for business corporations. By 1882, when he was reelected to the New York state assembly by a two-to-one majority, he was one of the leading politicians in the state.

After the 1882 election Roosevelt made an important connection to the West. While speaking at a meeting of the Free Trade Club of New York City on 28 May 1883, he met H. H. Gorringe, a retired naval officer who was a great admirer of his book *The Naval War of 1812: or, The History of the United States Navy during the Last War with Great Britain* (1882). During their conversation Gorringe assured Roosevelt that it was still possible to find buffalo in the valley of the Little Missouri River. Roosevelt, who was fascinated by the idea of shooting such an animal, agreed to make a trip to the Little Missouri with Gorringe before the fall was over. Around his busy political campaign he scheduled a summer hunting trip, for, as he told Gorringe in a remark recorded in Carleton Putnam's *Theodore Roosevelt, the Formative Years, 1858–1886* (1958), "I am fond of politics, but fonder still of big game hunting." There is also evidence that his poor physical health, owing to recurring asthma attacks as well as anxieties associated with his ambitious political career, had begun to take their toll. His trip was to be a respite from life in the East. Roosevelt was committed to the idea of the hunting expedition; when it turned out that Gorringe could not accompany him, he made the journey on his own.

On 8 September 1883 at about three in the morning, Theodore's association with the West began when he stepped off the Northern Pacific train at a small cattle town in the Badlands of North Dakota. As he recounts in *Theodore Roosevelt: An Autobiography* (1913), he stepped almost literally into a land of myth, for in remembering the experience he appeals to the two most prominent western mythmakers of his time, Owen Wister, the author of many western stories and the novel *The Virginian* (1902), and Frederic Remington, the noted sculptor, illustrator, and painter of the West. Roosevelt remembered that "It was still the Wild West in those days, the far West, the West of Owen Wister's stories and Frederic Remington's drawings, the West of the Indian and the buffalo-hunter, the soldier and the cow-puncher."

Roosevelt spent the remainder of the night in the town's only hotel, and the following day he secured hunting-guide services in preparation for his expedition. By most standards this hunting trip in the Dakota Badlands would hardly count as a roaring triumph. Many of the Dakota inhabitants, his guide among them, distrusted Roosevelt's greenhorn looks and were hesitant to do business with him on anything but a cash basis. Bad weather, bad luck, and bad aim marred the hunt. Roosevelt did not bag his buffalo until nearly two weeks into the expedition.

But it was during this trip that Roosevelt first caught a glimpse of what he would later term "the strenuous life," the outdoor life of challenge and hardship that he would forever associate with the West. This strenuous life was an existence that, if it did not kill them, seemed to make American men such as himself stronger. Roosevelt saw himself rise in the opinion of the westerners with whom he hunted and bunked as he faced rain, cold, mud, and hunger out in the Dakota wilderness, and as the westerners' opinions of him rose, so did his opinion of the West. Before he departed from North Dakota for New York, he had left a check in the hands of Bill Merrifield and Sylvane Ferris for the amount of

$14,000, with which they were to buy stock for a ranch to be known as the "Maltese Cross." Henceforward, Roosevelt was not only a New York politician, he was also a westerner.

Events in the East would soon drive him westward under less happy circumstances. On 14 February 1884 his wife died of Bright's disease immediately after the birth of their only child, Alice, and his mother died of typhoid fever on the same day. In his diary for this date Roosevelt entered an *X* and wrote "The light has gone out of my life." Although he returned to Albany within a week after the double funeral and pursued his work with dedication, he no longer thought of himself as an assemblyman. By 30 April he was making plans to return to North Dakota and to remain in the wilderness hunting for "two or three years." As soon as the 1884 Republican National Convention in Chicago concluded, he returned to the Badlands, looking to the landscape for solace.

Roosevelt does seem to have found release from the grief of his family losses and from the pressure of his career in eastern politics. During the years 1884–1892 he divided his time between life in New York and life on his ranch, and his health improved. As a young assemblyman in New York, his appearance, according to Richard Welling in *As the Twig is Bent* (1942), had once prompted New York philanthropist D. Willis James to remark, "To think that the interests of our great city depend on that frail young man." In the 1890s and later, however, much of Roosevelt's reputation as a public figure rested on his remarkable physical stamina.

Punching cattle and hunting brought out his "bully" persona. Roosevelt spent $26,000 more on cattle upon his return to the Badlands and wrote of the "glorious time" he was having in Dakota. One of his first orders of business upon arriving in the Badlands was to secure a buckskin suit. He had himself photographed in the suit and wore it for years on hunting trips before passing it on to one of his sons. Roosevelt thus associated himself with earlier American literary versions of hardy men in the wilderness, for of the buckskin he observed in *Ranch Life and the Hunting-Trail* (1888), "It was the dress in which Daniel Boone was clad when he first passed through the trackless forests of the Alleghenies and penetrated into the heart of Kentucky; it was the dress worn by grim old Davy Crockett when he fell at the Alamo." Although he may have linked his life in the East with grief and death, his life in the West was connected to a vital and still-developing historical tradition of which he saw himself a part.

Roosevelt's experiences in the West colored his outlook on American culture in general, and the literary expression of his association with the region

Roosevelt (right) with his Harvard classmate Charles F. Lummis

is varied. The most direct articulation of his early experiences in North Dakota, however, are readily identifiable: *Hunting Trips of a Ranchman* (1885), *Ranch Life and the Hunting-Trail,* and *The Wilderness Hunter: An Account of the Big Game of the United States and Its Chase with Horse* (1893). The three volumes were so successful that they tempted Roosevelt to make writing his vocation. They represent a refinement of the hunting-narrative genre.

The books are not typical linear accounts of animals sighted and trophies claimed but instead provide a more holistic narrative of the hunting experience. Roosevelt's accounts of the hunt include vivid descriptions of the aesthetic effects of the stark landscapes of the Badlands while also detailing hunting techniques. Reflecting his lifelong affinity for natural history, these books provide carefully written descriptions of wildlife and comprehensive accounts of the lives of big-game animals. His depiction of the bighorn sheep in *Ranch Life and the Hunting-Trail* and his treatment of the grizzly bear in *The Wilderness Hunter* represent marked improvements upon traditional literature of their sort, and these books struck his contemporaries as exciting—"tinglingly alive, masculine," in the words of one critic.

The literary influences upon Roosevelt's early hunting narratives remain uncertain. He names only four of the books he kept at Elkhorn Ranch—Elliott Coues's *Birds of the Northwest* (1874), Col. Richard Dodge's *The Plains of the Great West and Their Inhabitants* (1877), John Dean Caton's *The Antelope and Deer of America* (1877), and T. S. Van Dyke's *Still-Hunters* (1883)—and certainly relied less heavily on literary precedent than on personal experience, a legacy of his childhood and youth spent pursuing nature studies on his own. According to Stuart Edward White in *The Works of Theodore Roosevelt, Memorial Edition* (1923), Roosevelt "preferred to argue from experience rather than authority."

Reviewers of Roosevelt's three hunting books were favorably impressed in general, comparing his work to the writing of earlier influential naturalists such as Isaak Walton's *Compleat Angler* (1653). Roosevelt was also placed alongside famous contemporary nature writers such as Henry David Thoreau and John Burroughs. Especially compelling to his contemporary readers was his skill at natural observation, although George Bird Grinnell discerned in Roosevelt's *Hunting Trips of a Ranchman,* a tendency to take the observations of others, which were sometimes erroneous or incomplete, at face value.

In *Ranch Life and the Hunting-Trail* Roosevelt articulates more fully than in the other two books his growing appreciation for empty western spaces and the strenuous life pursued there by ranchers and hunters. It is not merely a treatment of the Dakota Territory but a volume that explores all the "grazing lands of the West," which Roosevelt in the first lines of the book identifies as "New Mexico, part of Arizona, Colorado, Wyoming, Montana, and the western portion of Texas, Kansas, Nebraska, and Dakota." The book is illustrated by Remington, the preeminent cowboy artist and one of the leading American artists of the time. In these western hunting books Roosevelt caught the imagination of Americans who were beginning to turn their attention toward the western territories.

By the time he composed the final volume of his western hunting trilogy, Roosevelt had lived in the Badlands on and off for ten years. In *The Wilderness Hunter* his observations of plant and animal life are especially acute, owing to his familiarity with the landscape. More remarkable perhaps than his natural history, however, is his developing sociohistorical perspective on the life lived in the West. In his first two volumes his treatment of the region is focused primarily on the appearance of the land itself. In the preface to *The Wilderness Hunter* Roose-

velt examines the role of human beings, U.S. citizens in particular, on the landscape. He describes the "free, self-reliant, adventurous life, with its rugged and stalwart democracy," to be lived out west, and he hypothesizes that "it cultivates that vigorous manliness for the lack of which in a nation, as in an individual, the possession of no other qualities can possibly atone." The wilderness of the New World is seen as a proving ground for early American citizens such as Boone, Crockett, and, by implication, Roosevelt and men like him.

Roosevelt's experience of the West as represented in these three hunting books provides the foundation for much of his more culturally oriented western writing, most notably the four-volume *The Winning of the West; An Account of the Exploration and Settlement of Our Country from the Alleghanies to the Pacific* (1889–1896) and *The Strenuous Life: Essays and Addresses* (1900). It is important to understand that for Roosevelt the landscapes of the West were more than merely empty places on the map of the nation, beautiful playgrounds, recreational areas, or pristine wilderness. Roosevelt and many other influential men of the time such as Remington, Wister, and Frederick Jackson Turner recognized that the West had exerted and would continue to exert a great influence on the direction in which the culture of the United States would develop.

Throughout the 1890s Roosevelt and his peers began to feel something wrong at the heart of American culture, a kind of slowing down of the progress of civilization in the United States, a failure to live up to the ideals and standards they expected the young democracy to meet. Civilization, as Roosevelt made plain in his address on "The Strenuous Life" at the Hamilton Club of Chicago in 1899, made men soft. The "over-civilized man," he held, loses "the great fighting, masterful virtues." To the businessmen of Chicago he proclaimed that "our country calls not for the life of ease but for the life of strenuous endeavor," a life that would, should each of its citizens pursue it, make the nation a great one for centuries to come. This "strenuous life" admonition helps explain the importance of the West in Roosevelt's writing. It was a challenging land where strength and a fighting spirit, the virtues necessary to a successful civilization, were bred.

Roosevelt's sense of the importance of the West to the future of civilization can be traced back as far as his interest in German history as a teenager. He considered Teutonic and Scandinavian peoples to be important historically because of their conquests in earlier European history, and he considered the Teutonic influence to have been an important one upon the emerging England. In the first chapter of *The Winning of the West,* titled "The Spread of the English-Speaking Peoples," he asserts that during "the past three centuries the spread of the Teutonically-inflected English-speaking peoples over the waste spaces of the globe has been not only the most striking feature in the history of the world, but also the event of all others most far-reaching in its effects and importance." Roosevelt represents the course of recent history as culminating in the conquest of the North American continent by white, English speakers. These conquerors, because of their European heritage, appeared to Roosevelt to be members of a more advanced civilization than Native Americans or Mexicans, and they were therefore able to "win" the West by right of might.

Roosevelt writes about the region as a racial proving ground, a place where white Americans justly dominated not only the landscape but also people of other races and nationalities who inhabited it, thus proving their superiority to the other peoples of the world. This is the approach that Roosevelt would later take, for instance, to the Philippines. When Roosevelt read Stephen Crane's Texas short story "A Man and Some Others," in which a party of Mexicans kills an American sheepherder, he wrote Crane a letter congratulating him on the quality of the story but suggesting that in the future Crane might write "another story of the frontiersman and the Mexican Greaser in which the frontiersman shall come out on top; it is more normal that way!"

Roosevelt's chauvinistic response to the settlement of the West was not personal, nor was it unusual for his time. Many Americans were uneasy about the future of civilization, specifically the sort of progressive, Anglo-American, continent-taming civilization of which many U.S. citizens considered themselves a part. In 1890 the Superintendent of the Census had declared that the frontier could not "any longer have a place in the census reports." Part of the fin-de-siècle mood of the 1890s, the prominent historian Roderick Nash has noted in *Wilderness and the American Mind* (1967), involved "the belief . . . that the United States, if not the entire Western World, had seen its greatest moments and was in an incipient state of decline." Another social critic, Tom Lutz, has included "the 'closing' of the continental frontier and the beginnings of an overseas empire" as one of the "social and cultural change[s]" between the years of 1890 and 1910 that contributed to the common turn-of-the-century pathological condition he calls "American Nervousness." When in July 1893 Turner, in his paper "The Significance of the Frontier in American History," asserted before the American Historical Association

that "the advance of American settlement westward explain[ed] American development," Americans seemed to have good reason to fear a decline in the national character.

One way to overcome this apprehension about the future of the United States was to prove the superiority of its most prominent cultural group. Roosevelt was by no means alone in his American jingoism, either in its application to the West or in its application overseas. He attributed the effectiveness of his Rough Rider regiment in the Spanish-American War to the hardening and toughening influence of the West.

There is another, more clearly beneficial manifestation of Roosevelt's attachment to such "American" ideals as the "manhood" and "independence" of life in the West. Because he perceived the untamed West to be central to the national character, Roosevelt made it a top priority to preserve this wilderness. In this way, too, he was very much a product of his time. Nash finds that "[a]s a result of [its] discontent with civilization, which was no less uncomfortable because of its vagueness, *fin-de-siècle* America was ripe for the widespread appeal of the uncivilized." An affection for things natural pervaded the culture. This affection found practical manifestation in the founding of such institutions as the Sierra Club in 1892 and the United States Forest Service in 1905.

Roosevelt was an integral part of the growth of the American conservation movement at the turn of the century. As early as 1887, when he began a long association with George Bird Grinnell, the editor of *Forest and Stream* magazine, Roosevelt had expressed his desire to preserve and protect western lands. In December 1887, as a response to the overhunting of game animals in the West, Roosevelt and Grinnell founded the Boone and Crockett Club. The club, while explicitly concerned with hunting, was involved in a range of issues that would inform Roosevelt's conservationist perspective in the coming years. In particular, the club's constitution emphasizes its interest in the "preservation of large game," especially through legislation, and in the promotion of "inquiry into . . . observations on the habits and natural history of the various wild animals."

The club's practical commitment to its ideals is evident in the formation of its Committee on Parks, a watchdog agency concerned with activities undertaken in national parks. This committee was a response to the failure of Congress to include a law-enforcement provision in the act that created Yellowstone National Park in 1872. By the time the Northern Pacific Railroad had built a line to the park ten years later, the park was still not protected.

Roosevelt and John Muir at Glacier Point, 1903

It soon fell under the control of a syndicate called the Yellowstone Park Improvement Company, which wasted no time in building a sawmill in the park to cut lumber for hotels.

This violation of the spirit of the National Park ideal did not go unnoticed by members of Roosevelt's Boone and Crockett Club, nor did it go unnoticed in Washington. Soon, Sen. George Vest of Missouri and Arnold Hague of the U.S. Geological Survey joined the club, and the group became involved in the successful fight to protect Yellowstone Park from further depredations. By April of 1890 Grinnell proudly wrote the *New York Tribune* to proclaim that Roosevelt was one of Yellowstone's staunchest defenders. Among the most notable achievements of the club was lobbying for the March 1891 bill that created the national forest system, investing the president with the power to set aside forest reservations.

From his association with the Boone and Crockett Club also came the books Roosevelt co-edited with Grinnell, *American Big-Game Hunting* (1893), *Hunting in Many Lands* (1895), and *Trail and Camp-fire* (1897). The books consisted of articles on hunting written by members of the club, and they came to be known as the "Boone and Crockett Club Books." Roosevelt contributed several articles to the series.

From his successful conservation efforts with the Boone and Crockett Club, Roosevelt learned how to combine his political skill, his social convictions, and his love for wild western landscapes. Thus, when an assassin's bullets ended the life of President William McKinley on 14 September 1901, elevating Roosevelt to the office of president, he assumed the position from which he would promulgate one of his most important texts on the West. It was his first annual address to Congress, delivered on 3 December 1901. In his address Roosevelt carefully explained to Congress and to the American public the value of ecologically intact forest land because, as he maintained, "Forests are natural reservoirs." Further, Roosevelt held that contact with these pristine lands would provide "rest, health, and recreation" for "ever-increasing numbers of men and women" in the United States. He also predicted that the arid lands of the West would "enrich every portion of our country, just as the settlement of the Ohio and Mississippi valleys brought prosperity to the Atlantic States." He concluded that the forest reserves should be expanded and "set apart forever, for the use and benefit of our people as a whole and not sacrificed to the shortsighted greed of a few."

This speech, more than any of his other literary endeavors, affected the way Americans would approach the West. Roosevelt's conviction that the arid lands of the West should be "reclaimed" by citizens eager to advance the progress of the United States resulted in the passage of the Reclamation Act of 1902, which led to thousands of acres of western desert land being irrigated and turned to agriculture. For better or worse, Roosevelt's "strenuous life" approach to activity in the West led to feverish labor aimed at changing the arid landscape to a green one. Among other tangible results of the ideas expressed in Roosevelt's western writing is the 280-foot-high Roosevelt Dam on the Salt River of Arizona, a structure that asserts human dominance over a challenging landscape, changing the ecology of Arizona forever. By the time Roosevelt left office in 1909 thousands of acres of desert had "bloomed" under his strenuous reclamation activity.

Roosevelt also placed under government protection almost 150 million acres of forest land, largely in the West, and during his administration five national parks were created, including Crater Lake and Mesa Verde. His feelings about national-park land arose from the sentiments expressed in his western writing, that wild land contributed to the strength and health of individuals as well as the culture in which they lived. As he interpreted the words "for the people" in the United States Constitution, they must "always include the people unborn as well as the people now alive, or the democratic ideal is not realized."

Neither Roosevelt's practical nor his literary association with the West ended with the close of his presidency in 1909. He continued to contribute articles about conservation and hunting to maga-

zines such as *Outlook,* and he maintained close friendships with such literary naturalists as John Muir and John Burroughs. He furthered his pursuit of the "strenuous life" in Africa and South America, thus extending the literary myth of the American "Wild West," of which he was so completely a part, to the far corners of the globe.

In the summer of 1918, the year before his death, Roosevelt continued to take a lively interest in the ecology of the West. Having read an article by his old friend Grinnell describing the plight of starving elk in Yellowstone National Park, Roosevelt responded with indignation and concern in a letter. He predicted that if the government continued, misguidedly in his opinion, to protect the elk from hunters, they would soon "fill the whole United States" and die of starvation. His concern for the health of western ecosystems, especially those that supported big-game animals, remained with him until his death. But Roosevelt's desire to manage and protect the wilderness often seemed to conflict with his enthusiasm for exploiting it. These seemingly contradictory elements of his life and work are likely to remain questions for Roosevelt scholars to ponder well into the future. His contradictions also are those of an American culture he helped shape and will continue to inform the conception of the American West.

Letters:

Theodore Roosevelt's Letters to His Children, edited by Joseph Bucklin Bishop (New York: Scribners, 1919);

Letters from Theodore Roosevelt to Anna Roosevelt Cowles, 1870–1918 (New York & London: Scribners, 1924);

Selections from the Correspondence of Theodore Roosevelt and Henry Cabot Lodge, 2 volumes (New York: Scribners, 1925);

Letters to Kermit from Theodore Roosevelt, 1902–1908, edited by Will Irwin (New York & London: Scribners, 1946);

Letters of Theodore Roosevelt, edited by Elting E. Morison, 8 volumes (Cambridge: Harvard University Press, 1951–1954);

Cowboys and Kings: Three Great Letters by Theodore Roosevelt, edited by Morison (Cambridge: Harvard University Press, 1954).

Biographies:

Lincoln A. Lang, *Ranching with Roosevelt* (Philadelphia & London: Lippincott, 1926);

Henry Pringle, *Theodore Roosevelt: A Biography* (New York: Harcourt, Brace, 1931);

William Henry Harbaugh, *The Life and Times of Theodore Roosevelt,* revised edition (New York: Collier, 1963);

David McCullough, *Mornings on Horseback* (New York: Simon & Schuster, 1981);

Nathan Miller, *Theodore Roosevelt: A Life* (New York: Morrow, 1992).

References:

John Burroughs, *Camping and Tramping with Roosevelt* (Boston: Houghton, Mifflin, 1907);

Paul Russell Cutright, *Theodore Roosevelt: The Making of a Conservationist* (Urbana & Chicago: University of Chicago Press, 1985);

Thomas G. Dyer, *Theodore Roosevelt and the Idea of Race* (Baton Rouge & London: Louisiana State University Press, 1980);

Dewey Grantham, ed., *Theodore Roosevelt* (Englewood Cliffs, N. J.: Prentice-Hall, 1971);

George Bird Grinnell, ed., *Hunting at High Altitudes* (New York: Harper, 1913);

Hermann Hagedorn, *Roosevelt in the Badlands* (Boston: Houghton Mifflin, 1921);

Albert Bushnell Hart and Herbert Ronald Ferleger, eds., *Theodore Roosevelt Cyclopedia* (New York: Roosevelt Memorial Association, 1941);

Tom Lutz, *American Nervousness* (Ithaca: Cornell University Press, 1991);

Edmund Morris, *The Rise of Theodore Roosevelt* (New York: Coward-McCann & Goeghegan, 1979);

George E. Mowry, *The Era of Theodore Roosevelt, 1900–1912* (New York: Harper, 1958);

Roderick Nash, *Wilderness and the American Mind* (New Haven: Yale University Press, 1967);

Aloysius Norton, *Theodore Roosevelt* (Boston: Twayne, 1980);

Carleton Putnam, *Theodore Roosevelt, the Formative Years, 1858–1886* (New York: Scribners, 1958);

Frederick Jackson Turner, "The Significance of the Frontier in American History," in his *The Frontier in American History* (New York: Holt, 1962), pp. 1–38;

Edmund Wagenknecht, *The Seven Worlds of Theodore Roosevelt* (New York: Longmans, Green, 1958);

G. Edward White, *The Eastern Establishment and the Western Experience: The West of Frederic Remington, Theodore Roosevelt, and Owen Wister* (New Haven & London: Yale University Press, 1968);

R. L. Wilson, *Theodore Roosevelt—Outdoorsman* (New York: Winchester Press, 1971);

Owen Wister, *Roosevelt: The Story of a Friendship 1880–1919* (New York: Macmillan, 1930).

Papers:

The main collections of Roosevelt papers are held at the Houghton Library, Harvard University, and at the Library of Congress.

George Frederick Ruxton

(24 July 1821 – 29 August 1848)

Richard H. Cracroft
Brigham Young University

BOOKS: *The Oregon Question, A Glance at the Respective Claims of Great Britain and the United States, To the Territory in Dispute* (London: John Ollivier, 1846);

Adventures in Mexico and the Rocky Mountains (London: John Murray, 1847; New York: Harper, 1848); republished as *In the Old West,* edited by Horace Kephart (New York: Outing Publishing Company, 1915);

Life in the Far West (Edinburgh: Blackwood, 1849; New York: Harper, 1849); revised as *Wildlife in the Rocky Mountains,* edited by Kephart (New York: Outing Publishing Company, 1916);

Ruxton of the Rockies, collected by Clyde Porter and Mae Reed Porter, edited by LeRoy R. Hafen (Norman: University of Oklahoma Press, 1950).

Edition: *Life in the Far West,* edited by LeRoy R. Hafen (Norman: University of Oklahoma Press, 1951).

Although George Frederick Ruxton, a British soldier, hunter, explorer, adventurer, and writer nonpareil, lived only twenty-seven years, he lived bravely and fully and left two remarkable narrative accounts of life in the American West in the years 1846–1847. *Adventures in Mexico and the Rocky Mountains* (1847) and *Life in the Far West* (1849) have enriched the writing of western history, indelibly shaping the literary and historical image of the mountain man and endearing the young adventurer to western scholars and aficionados alike as "Ruxton of the Rocky Mountains."

George Augustus Frederick Ruxton (he generally omitted the "Augustus") was born on 24 July 1821 at Eynsham Hall estate, Oxfordshire, England, the third of six male children born to John and Anna Maria Hay Ruxton. When George was seven years old, the family moved to Broad Oak, near Tunbridge Well, Kent (thirty miles southeast of London). His father died when George was nine years old, and the boy's self-styled "truant and way-

George Frederick Ruxton (portrait by an unknown artist; from Ruxton of the Rockies, *1950)*

ward disposition" and an indulgent mother led him to what he termed "a succession of scrapes and schoolboy atrocities" and an impatience with confinement and humdrum routine that he never outgrew.

Destined for a military career, the barely fourteen-year-old boy entered the Royal Military College of Sandhurst, at Berkshire, in July 1835. Balking at any suggestion of restraint, the youth found his studies "irksome," and his penchant for making forbidden solitary wanderings on the heath near the Royal Military College and for breaking college rules got him expelled from Sandhurst after two troublesome years.

Soon after his expulsion he managed to purchase a commission in the Ceylon Rifles. On learning, however, that his commission would take some time, the irrepressible sixteen-year-old youth was swept up in the war fervor surrounding the outbreak of civil war in Spain. In December 1837 Ruxton joined Gen. Diego León's loyalist Lancers and went to war against the Carlist enemies of Queen Isabella II. The young soldier's fragmentary record of his Spanish war experiences (first published in 1950 in *Ruxton of the Rockies*) reveals his sharp eye for detail, keen ear for English and Spanish vernacular, considerable skill at seeing and ordering events dramatically and imaginatively, and the ability to tell a good tale.

Ruxton was cited for gallantry in the Battle of Belascoin (29 April–1 May 1839) and was awarded the Cross of the First Class of the Military Order of San Fernando, which made him a knight of Spain. Having served the Spanish royalist cause from December 1837 to late spring 1839, Ruxton returned to England in July, a combat veteran, a decorated knight of Spain, an astute observer, an accomplished marksman and hunter, and a fluent speaker of Spanish. He was barely nineteen years old.

Awaiting him in England was his commission in the Ceylon Rifle Corps, and he was immediately gazetted to a lieutenancy. Before joining the Ceylon Rifles, however, he was transferred in September 1839 to the 89th Foot Regiment and remained at Hampshire until August 1840, when he was transferred to Ireland, where he served at several posts. In the spring of 1841 he was sent to join the main body of his company, recently transferred from the West Indies to Canada.

On 8 July 1841 Ensign Ruxton arrived at Amherstburg, Ontario, Canada, a few miles east of Detroit, Michigan. Soon finding his duties in a peacetime army all too humdrum and admitting in his Canadian notebook (published in *Ruxton of the Rockies*) that his love of hunting "had ever been my delight," Ruxton succumbed to his ardor for hunting, fishing, and reading James Fenimore Cooper's Leatherstocking tales. He exulted in his journal: "worked up to the highest pitch by reading the adventures of Natty Bumppo and his friends the Mohegans in the admirable romances of Cooper, I had always wanted to pull a trigger in the woods of America, and now the opportunity had arrived." With Peshwego, his Chippewa guide and friend, and Dash, his hunting dog, Ruxton undertook several hunts in the

wilds of upper Canada, interrupted only by a leave of absence in England, from August 1841 until the end of May 1842. Ruxton served at his post in Montreal until October 1843, when he sold his commission and left the British army.

Before returning to England, Ruxton and Peshwego undertook several additional winter hunts in southeast Ontario. Although fragmentary, his journal from this period is a superb hunting narrative of his 1843–1844 winter wilderness adventures, disclosing his hardy zest in the face of daunting periods of hunger and cold and his exceptional skill as a hunter and woodsman. These notebooks, also published in *Ruxton of the Rockies*, reveal once more his remarkable eye for detail, his uncanny ear for the rhythms of Yankee dialect and Indian pidgin, and his conscious imitation of the feats of Cooper's Natty Bumppo. Like Bumppo, Ruxton delighted in astonishing the Indians and Yankee frontiersmen with feats of marksmanship with his English rifle. Near the conclusion of his last Canada hunt, for example, Ruxton engaged in a shooting match with an overbearing American frontiersman who had mocked the Englishman's prowess and his lightweight double-barreled rifle. The Yankee marksman lost face and his bet as Ruxton hit a shot at 150 yards, "almost in the center of the mark," causing the Yankee's son to splutter:

"Darn me, Father. Stranger's struck it, if he hasn't, right in the soft cut, by Sambo! Well that beats!"

At which his humiliated Yankee father conceded,

"A right smart piece, stranger, that's a fact! You draw a tight bead, you do! Come, let's liquor."

Ruxton returned to England in the spring of 1844, but by late June the itinerant Englishman had again left home, this time on the first of two unsuccessful exploring trips through North and Central Africa. Stymied during his first foray by the outbreak of war in North Africa, Ruxton undertook a second expedition from December 1844 to March 1845, this time to tropical Central Africa. His objective was to become the first Englishman to traverse Africa along the tropical parallel. The three-month expedition, subsequently reported in an article in *Nautical Magazine* (January 1846) and collected in *Ruxton of the Rockies*, was thwarted at every point and nearly ended in the deaths of Ruxton and his companion.

After his return to England, Ruxton undertook a more enticing mission, one to Mexico and the American West, sailing on 2 July 1846 from South-

Ruxton's sketch of his Canadian camp, circa 1841–1843 (from Ruxton of the Rockies, *1950)*

ampton to Vera Cruz, Mexico, and the culminating adventure of his life. In the first narrative that emerged from this remarkable journey, *Adventures in Mexico and the Rocky Mountains* (1847), Ruxton deftly chronicles his eventful journey from the southern coast of Mexico to the Rocky Mountains and eastward along the Santa Fe trail to Saint Louis. Then, still bursting with untold fur-trapper tales and mountain lore gleaned from his four-month rendezvous with end-of-era mountain men in the winter of 1847, Ruxton wrote his classic novel cum history, *Life in the Far West* (1849). Grounded in authentic history and richly detailed anthropology, Ruxton's two exciting narratives continue to be regarded as trustworthy records of historic events in 1846–1847, a memorable "year of decision" in the West, and his depiction of western life, especially of mountain-man lifestyle, occupation, and speech, has come to be regarded as nearly definitive.

Setting out by coach from Vera Cruz on 19 August, Ruxton traveled to Mexico City, where he outfitted himself with two horses and four mules and a *mozo* (attendant)—an untrustworthy Mexican guide who, despite being foiled early on in a clumsy attempt at bushwhacking Ruxton, continued with him to Durango, Mexico. Ruxton's threethousand-mile journey took him from the southern coast of Mexico northwesterly through Durango, Chihuahua, El

Paso, Socorro, Santa Fe, Taos, past the Spanish Peaks (*Wah-to-yah,* "the breasts of the world"), and down the front range of the Rocky Mountains to the Arkansas River and Pueblo. In the spring Ruxton rode the Santa Fe Trail to Fort Leavenworth, whence he embarked by various transports for Saint Louis, New York City, and Liverpool, arriving home in the summer of 1847.

Ruxton memorialized this epic journey in *Adventures in Mexico and the Rocky Mountains,* one of the most important western travel narratives since the journals of Meriwether Lewis and William Clark. If only for the number of harrowing experiences and hairbreadth escapes, *Adventures in Mexico and the Rocky Mountains* must rank in importance with the classic western travel narratives of Washington Irving and Josiah Gregg and with the 1846–1847 trail accounts of Francis Parkman, Susan Shelby Magoffin, and Lewis H. Garrard.

Ruxton rode through brigand-infested Mexico in wartime when every English-speaking stranger, regardless of his nationality, was identified as a *Yanqui* and an enemy. He relates, with admirable control and flashes of humor, frequent brushes with death at the hands of cutthroats, undisciplined soldiers, rebellious Mexicans, Indians on the warpath, spooked horses, forest fires, frozen feet, subzero weather, and mountain blizzards. Ironically, he says nothing about his fall from horseback onto a tent picket and the resulting internal and spinal injuries that contributed to his death a year later.

Ruxton was surrounded by danger. Only a week after he left Taos (where he had been the guest of Sheriff Lee) and Arroyo Hondo (where he had stayed at Turley's Mill), Mexicans killed the Americans at both outposts, including Lee, Turley, and Charles Bent, governor of New Mexico Territory. Early in his trip Ruxton was forced to stab one attacking robber (and did not wait to learn the man's condition); he was badly hurt when thrown from his horse and trampled; he had two brushes with marauding Comanches in the northern Mexican states of Durango and Chihuahua; he was knocked from his mule into the icy water of the Rio Grande and suffered from exposure; and in a snowstorm above Arroyo Hondo he narrowly missed plunging over a five-hundred-foot precipice when his horse, Panchito, suddenly halted and threw himself back on his haunches, saving them both.

After suffering terribly from exposure in crossing the Sangre de Cristo mountains, during which one of his feet was badly frozen, Ruxton arrived at the mountain men's winter settlement at Pueblo on the Arkansas River, probably late in January 1847. He spent the remainder of the winter recuperating from the frozen foot, frostbite, and the fall from horseback. It was, nevertheless, a memorable winter. In company with John Hawkens, Rube Herring, Old Bill Williams, Tom Tobin, Johnny Albert, and other mountain men, Ruxton was in his element. During that winter, wrote Bernard DeVoto in *Across the Wide Missouri* (1947), "Ruxton talked with more mountain men of the great age than anyone else who ever wrote about them." Many of these stories found their way into *Life in the Far West,* Ruxton's paean to the mountain man, but he would include in *Adventures in Mexico and the Rocky Mountains* two anecdotes, "The Legend of the Boiling Fountain," an Indian legend, and his somewhat different version of the story of Hugh Glass (Ruxton names him John), his fight with the grizzly, being abandoned as dead, and his ninety-mile crawl to the fort. In Ruxton's version, when he arrived at the fort, Hugh/John exclaimed to his *companyero,* "Hurraw, Bill, my boy! you thought I was 'gone under' that time, did you? but hand me over my horse and gun, my lad; I ain't dead yet by a dam sight!"

One purpose for Ruxton's journey, other than the desire for adventure that had earlier taken him to Spain, the Canadian woods, and Africa, was, according to Bruce Sutherland, "to conduct geographical and ethnological investigations." This purpose was partially thwarted by the total loss of a kit of papers. As Ruxton explained in his preface to *Adventures in Mexico and the Rocky Mountains,* they were destroyed while he was crossing the Pawnee Fork of the Arkansas River. The waterlogged mule pack—discovered days after the mule's submersion in the river—contained "notes and memoranda of the country I passed through, as well as several valuable and interesting documents and MSS connected with the history of Northern Mexico and its Indian tribes, which I had collected." "On opening the trunk," he lamented, "I found all the papers completely destroyed, and the old manuscripts . . . reduced to a pulpy mass; every scrap of writing being perfectly illegible."

The presence of a former British army officer in a war zone of the Mexican-American War, observing and recording feverish military preparations, has led DeVoto and others to assume an intelligence-gathering purpose for Ruxton's journey. Ruxton contributed to the suspicion that he was a British spy with his cryptic and mysterious statement in the preface: "It is hardly necessary to explain the cause of my visiting Mexico at such an unsettled period; and I fear that circumstances will prevent my gratifying the curiosity of the reader, should he feel any on that point."

In fact, Ruxton was a British agent but not a spy. According to Frederic E. Voelker, Ruxton was representing Her Majesty's government as a commercial agent "in the dual capacity of roving commercial attaché of the British diplomatic service and commercial agent of the Mexican government," a twofold purpose confirmed by Lt. J. W. Abert of the U.S. Army Corps of Topographical Engineers, who read Ruxton's credentials at Valverde and explained Ruxton's mission in his official report to Congress (1848). Carrying British diplomatic credentials and at least $3,000 in cash, Ruxton was to aid in reestablishing war-interrupted international trade along the Santa Fe Trail to assure British traders in the region of the solicitude and protection of their government and also to assure British tradesmen of safe conduct and the good will of the Mexican government.

Still, Ruxton's primary reasons for his journey lay in his unregenerate passion for nature, in seeking the freedom found only in untrammeled wilderness, and in the sheer adventure derived from pitting oneself against a hostile environment and, winning or losing, accepting the consequences. After concluding a long and dangerous solitary hunt in South Park, near Pike's Peak, Ruxton confessed: "I quite regretted the abandonment of my mountain life, solitary as it was . . . ; there was something inexpressibly exhilarating in the sensation of positive freedom from all worldly care."

Adventures in Mexico and the Rocky Mountains is a work of literature made remarkable by a point of view that reveals a keen observer possessed of a rich imagination. As Neal Lambert suggests in his thoughtful literary analysis of Ruxton's work, "The character of Ruxton himself gives [*Adventures in Mexico and the Rocky Mountains*] . . . its unity and wholeness." Ruxton willingly shared his opinions on many issues. While he generally admired Americans, for example, he had little respect for the too-independent American soldier. While being impressed with the beauty of Mexican women, he found Mexican towns "dreary and desolate beyond description," the government "corrupt, impotent," the natives "a cadaverous, stunted race," and the soldiers cowardly, base, and poorly disciplined. Even the dogs are "the most miserable of the *genus cur*," and, he concluded, "I regret to have to say that I cannot remember to have observed one single commendable trait in the character of the Mexican." With mountain men, however, Ruxton seems to have willingly suspended judgment or to have judged by different criteria. Regardless of the rough and reckless nature of the mountaineers' lives, Ruxton, himself a refined gentleman by nature and nurture, found a spiritual and emotional affinity with mountain men and a physical affinity as well.

Indeed, Ruxton had so well adapted himself to life in the Far West that returning to civilization was a challenge. Arriving at the Planters' House hotel in Saint Louis, he slept in a bed

> for the first time for nearly ten months, much to the astonishment of my limbs and body, which, long accustomed to no softer mattress than mother earth, tossed about all night, unable to appreciate the unusual luxury. I found chairs a positive nuisance, and in my own room caught myself in the act more than once of squatting cross-legged on the floor.

He also described the awkwardness of eating with forks, of exchanging moccasins for confining boots, and of resuming the "torture" of civilized fashions. He had come to dress, act, and speak like a mountain man, and at Fort Leavenworth he was delighted to report that "I was appealed to by two . . . dragoons to decide a bet as to whether I was a white man or a redskin."

Ruxton's return to England in August 1847 initiated a period of remarkable literary productivity. By the end of the year Ruxton had published *Adventures in Mexico and the Rocky Mountains.* He also wrote and published a paper, "On the Migration of the Ancient Mexicans, and their Analogy to the ex-

ADVENTURES IN MEXICO

AND

THE ROCKY MOUNTAINS.

By GEORGE F. RUXTON, Esq.,

MEMBER OF THE ROYAL GEOGRAPHICAL SOCIETY, THE ETHNOLOGICAL SOCIETY, ETC. ETC.

LONDON:
JOHN MURRAY, ALBEMARLE STREET.
1847.

Title page for Ruxton's nonfiction account of his 1846–1848 journey from Santa Cruz, Mexico, through the Rocky Mountains, and east to Saint Louis during the Mexican-American War (courtesy of the Lilly Library, Indiana University)

isting Indian tribes of Northern Mexico," and two sketches, "The Texan Ranger" and "The Battle of Buena Vista," all collected in *Ruxton of the Rockies.* During the winter and spring of 1848 he completed *Life in the Far West,* his most ambitious literary effort. This work ran serially in *Blackwood's Edinburgh Magazine* from June to November 1848 and appeared in book form early in 1849, nearly six months after Ruxton's death.

Losing his journey notes and manuscripts freed Ruxton from the tyranny of his itinerary and enabled him to approach the writing of *Life in the Far West* as a work of imagination. Furthermore, telling the story from the point of view of the mountain men allowed Ruxton to set aside his distancing English worldview and permitted him to hang his mountain-man tales on a framework that enabled greater imaginative and formal freedom and unity of focus.

Ruxton clustered his tales of western mountain life about two prototypical mountain men, La Bonté and Killbuck (named after Cooper's Deerslayer), whose lives, suggests fur-trapper historian LeRoy R. Hafen in an appendix to the 1951 edition of *Life in the Far West,* resemble the lives of real mountain men with whom Ruxton associated during the winter and spring of 1847. Ruxton insisted that, while "I have no doubt jumbled the *dramatis personae* one with another, and may have committed anachronisms," all of the stories really happened. "With regard to the incidents of Indian attacks, starvation, cannibalism, &c.," he insisted, "I have invented not one out of my own head. They are all matters of history in the mountains." While the narrative does not purport to be history, Ruxton pointed out to his publishers at *Blackwood's,* neither is it fiction:

> I think it would be well to correct a misapprehension as to the truth or fiction of the paper. It is *no fiction.* There is no incident in it which has not actually occurred, nor one character who is not well known in the Rocky Mountains, with the exception of two [La Bonté and Killbuck] whose names are changed.

According to Hafen, Ruxton, the first author to use the mountain man imaginatively, succeeded in presenting "the most lively, flavorful, and complete picture of the mountain man and his time that has ever been written."

Life in the Far West begins with Killbuck spinning yarns around the campfire. In the "language spoken in the 'far west,'" mountain-man lingo, Killbuck tells the story of Moses "Black" Harris and the "putrified [petrified] forest":

> "I've trapped beaver on Platte and Arkansa, and away up on Missoura and Yaller Stone, I've trapped on Columbia, on Lewis Fork, and Green River; I've trapped . . . on Grand River and the Heely (Gila). I've fout the 'Blackfoot' (and d—d bad injuns they are); I've 'raised the hair' of more *than one* Apach, and made a Rapaho 'come' afore now; I've trapped in heav'n, in airth, and h—, and scalp my old head, . . . I've seen a putrefied forest."

Killbuck is scarcely through with his narration when a band of Arapaho warriors attacks, kills four trappers, and makes off with their mules. La Bonté and Killbuck track the Indians, kill and scalp two of them in a thrilling and gory skirmish, regain their mules, and return to their camp, where they are joined by "a solitary stranger"–presumably Ruxton himself.

Later that night the stranger persuades La Bonté to relate the story of his splendid wayfaring, and the reader follows him via a book-length flashback as he ranges across the West and through sixteen years of rugged adventures. Much of the book is, then, a loosely arranged, episodic recounting, for the benefit of "the stranger" and the reader, of La Bonté's and Killbuck's adventures, interspersed with those of their fellow trappers. This framework enables Ruxton to repeat the tales as he heard them from the lips of John Hawkens, Rube Herring, Bill Williams, and others, while wintering with them in the trappers' fort.

The saga Ruxton tells, as he heard it from these principal actors, is tinged with nostalgia. With the collapse of the market for beaver skins, the beaver trade was over. The last rendezvous had taken place five years earlier; most of the beaver were gone; and the trappers had "gone under," gone home, or gone into farming or business. *Life in the Far West* is a near-epochal, nostalgic celebration of the ever-shrinking primal wilderness and of a lost breed–the mountain men and their formidable Native American adversaries. These "men to match my mountains" become mythic projections of the American Dream and embodiments of American enterprise, individualism, pragmatism, derring-do, and know-how in mythic stories of American heroes engaged in a dramatic life-and-death struggle in a region of unparalleled grandeur–a Never-Never Land and its heroic inhabitants, none of which will never be the same again.

In this epic saga La Bonté becomes the representative man, and his story, as he tells it to the stranger, establishes the heroic journey to the West and manhood as a rite of passage that became the prevailing pattern of western literature in general and of mountain-man fiction in particular. Born in Mississippi, La Bonté is a free spirit who, in Tennessee, falls in love with the lovely Mary Brand (real name: Mary Chase), who returns his love. Enraged by former rival Big Pete's flirtation with Mary, which she innocently invites, La Bonté challenges Pete in a duel and kills him. Though slightly wounded himself, he flees the law and loses Mary. Making his way to Saint Louis, La Bonté takes up with an old mountain man and enters into a fur-trade apprenticeship. The greenhorn rapidly becomes an accomplished mountain man, killing his first buffalo, learning to trap beaver, counting "coup" and "lifting hair" in battle with the Indians, marrying and losing several squaws, and collecting battle scars. With Killbuck, La Bonté experiences terrible privation, "rubs out" many Indians, and watches as his friends, in turn, "go under." He enjoys trapping, freedom, bedding Indian women, the annual rendezvous, hard drinking, and tumultuous fandangos in Taos, during one of which he assists Ned (sometimes "Dick") Wooton in abducting a willing senorita.

Having recounted these feats, which take up much of the book, Ruxton returns the reader to the present—early spring 1847—and a band of trappers seated with the stranger around the campfire. Campfire talk has focused on a nearby party of wintering Mormon pioneers whose wagon trains, with the return of good weather, are again on the move to the Great Basin. Ruxton awkwardly interrupts his narrative to interject a one-sided, unsympathetic but mostly accurate history of the Latter-Day Saints. Through these Mormon pioneers Ruxton re-introduces La Bonté's long-lost Mary Brand to the story. Although none of them has joined the Mormon Church, the Brand family is traveling west in company with the Mormons. On learning that Mary's impatient father has insisted that the family continue the trip alone, in advance of the slower wagon train, and on realizing that Brand is unknowingly leading his family into an Arapaho ambush, La Bonté, Killbuck, and the stranger "bounded like lightning to the rescue." They arrive just in time to save Mary and most of her kin from the scalp knife. Love is promptly rekindled, and Mary and La Bonté soon part with Killbuck and mountain life to marry and return to civilization. In an afterword Ruxton concluded his narrative with the death of Old Bill Williams—a fiction that did not become a reality until the spring of 1849 when Williams—along with Dr. B. J. Kern—was killed by Indians during an attempt to recover equipment left behind during John C. Frémont's disastrous expedition of the previous winter.

In *Life in the Far West* Ruxton not only established the mythic western journey as the standard prototype for western American fiction, but he also demonstrated the literary power of imaginative fiction grounded in authentic history and detail, thus prefiguring the rise of literary realism. Ruxton's finely honed descriptions of geography, weather, Indian camps, and dress, his attention to hunting techniques and the technical details of beaver trapping, and his colorful descriptions of the life, dress, and gear of the Rocky Mountain trapper resound with the authority of his own considerable experience as a hunter, explorer, and adventurer. None has told it better—neither Washington Irving, who covered some of the same ground in *Astoria* (1835) and *The Adventures of Captain Bonneville, U.S.A.* (1836), nor A. B. Guthrie Jr. in *The Big Sky* (1947), which draws heavily on Ruxton's work to follow Boone Caudill's rough journey through the mountain West.

Much of the impact of Ruxton's mountain man on the literature of the fur trade arises from his unparalleled rendering of mountain-man parlance. Whether in Spain, Africa, Mexico, or on the Arkansas River, Ruxton showed a keen ear for the vernacular and the ability to record colorful and idiosyncratic regional idioms and cadences. Indeed, Ruxton's recording of mountain-man patois in *Life in the Far West* has become the standard literary vernacular of the mountain men of western fiction. Vardis Fisher, Harvey Fergusson, Stewart Edward White, Frederick Manfred, and A. B. Guthrie Jr., as well as Lewis H. Garrard in *Wah-to-yah, and the Taos Trail* (1850), all honor Ruxton's keen ear with repeated use of such Ruxton-recorded Rocky Mountain diction as, "half-froze," "waugh," "gone under," "rubbed out," "gone beaver," "don't shine," "meat's meat," "keep [your] eye skinned," "on his own hook," "meat bag" (stomach), and "fofarrow" (decoration, anything unnecessary). Thanks to Ruxton, every fictional trapper worth his "possible sack" calls himself "critter," "coon," "nigger," or "child."

Ruxton's rendering of distinctive mountain-man speech rings authentic not only because it seems to rise so clearly from trapper experience but also because it "mirrors," in the words of Paul S. Lehmberg, "the mountain man's uncivilized and unlettered free existence" and captures "the idea of the spirit of *Life in the Far West* in early nineteenth-century mountain America."

Fortunately for the modern reader, *Life in the Far West* is not written completely in mountain-man speech. Not far into his romance, Ruxton, sensitive to his reader's probable bewilderment, suggested that "perhaps it will be as well, to render La Bonté's mountain language intelligible, to translate it at once into tolerable English," and for the rest of the book he slipped in and out of the patois as seemed natural to him and contextually understandable to the reader.

Twentieth-century authors not only have made Ruxton's recording of mountain-man vernacular the standard for the mountain-man genre, but also, as Richard H. Cracroft has pointed out, continue to borrow content as well. For example, in *Mountain Man* (1962) Vardis Fisher used Ruxton's account of a life-or-death game of "Hands" played by a Burntwood Sioux and a Crow warrior. Ruxton's vivid account of the fandango in Taos no doubt influenced Lewis H. Garrard's trail narrative, *Wah-to-yah, and the Taos Trail*, and in fiction the fandango fracas became a central episode in Mayne Reid's *The Scalp Hunters* (1856), Harvey Fergusson's *Wolf Song* (1927), and Stewart Edward White's *The Long Rifle* (1930). In *Wolf Song* Fergusson also fol-

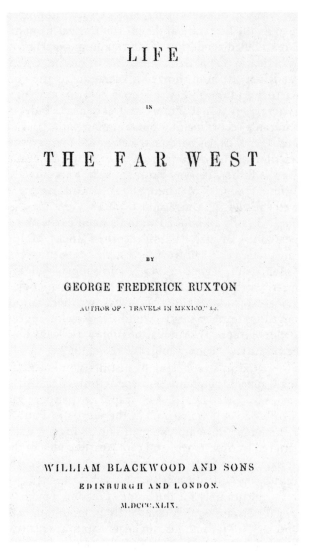

LIFE

IN

THE FAR WEST

BY

GEORGE FREDERICK RUXTON

AUTHOR OF " TRAVELS IN MEXICO," &c.

WILLIAM BLACKWOOD AND SONS
EDINBURGH AND LONDON.
M.DCCC.XLIX.

Title page for Ruxton's fictionalized account of his experiences among fur trappers in the Rocky Mountains (courtesy of the Lilly Library, Indiana University)

"Now, boy, I'll soon be under. Afore many hours. . . . So . . . put your knife in this old niggur's lights and help yourself."

Similarly, in Guthrie's *The Big Sky* (1947), Jim Deakins, wounded and near death, says to his sidekick Boone Caudill,

"I ain't got long. . . . I'll be under come tomorrow or next day. . . . Take your knife, Boone. Get it out."

As J. Golden Taylor asserts in *A Literary History of the American West* (1987), "No novelist could presume to achieve verisimilitude in portraying fictional mountain men without drawing upon Ruxton." Ruxton's *Life in the Far West* continues to be "recognized by students of the fur trade," notes Mae Reed Porter, "as a classic of its kind."

Life in the Far West was Ruxton's final literary effort. While still at work on the book he indicated in a May 1848 letter to a friend:

I have been confined to my room for many days, from the effects of an accident I met with in the Rocky Mountains, having been spilt from the bare back of a mule, and falling on the sharp picket of an Indian lodge on the small of my back. I fear I injured my spine, for I have never felt altogether the thing [his lower spine] since, and . . . the symptoms became rather ugly.

Determined to return to the mountains where he hoped to regain his health, the ailing Ruxton sold royalty rights for *Life in the Far West* to finance his trip, promised his mother that after this trip he would "settle down for good," and wrote a letter to *Blackwood's* explaining in mountain-man vernacular that "human natur can't go on feeding on civilised fixings in this 'big village'; and this child has felt like going West for many a month, being half froze for buffler meat and mountain doins."

In August 1848, while en route to the West, and after visiting his brother Augustus Alexander in Halifax, Nova Scotia, Ruxton chanced to meet an old companion from the Santa Fe Trail, Lewis H. Garrard, in a Buffalo, New York, hotel. In a footnote in his *Wah-to-yah, and the Taos Trail* (1850), Garrard reported that they

had a talk of the old scenes, [Ruxton's] book and other matters, . . . [and of] the Blackwood series of "Life in the Far West.". . . He was then on his way to the mountains—that afternoon he left, but the poor fellow died in St. Louis. He was a true gentleman, and his loss is much to be deplored.

lowed Ruxton's account of Black Harris's fabled visit to the "putrefied forest." There is, however, no better illustration of *Life in the Far West* as a major source for mountain-man fiction than in the wholesale liftings by Frederick Manfred and Guthrie of Ruxton's account of the near-starvation of the snowbound La Bonté and Killbuck in which Killbuck offers his starving comrade "fair-killed" meat from his own body. In Ruxton's *Life in the Far West* a weakened and starving Killbuck whispers to LaBonté:

"Boy," he said, "this old hos feels like goin' under, and that afore long . . . ; boy, put your knife in this old niggur's lights, and help yourself."

Hugh Glass, in Manfred's *Lord Grizzly* (1954), makes the same offer to Jim Bridger:

On 15 August Ruxton reached the Planters' House in Saint Louis, where he had stayed on his previous visit. He soon fell victim to an epidemic of dysentery, which was complicated by the internal and spinal injuries he had suffered the previous year. Despite the attentive care of doctors and the Sisters of Charity, Ruxton grew steadily weaker and died on 29 August 1848. He was twenty-seven years old. Following Episcopalian services, Ruxton was interred in Christ Church Episcopal Cemetery. Since then, Ruxton's remains have been twice reinterred, and there is no record of the present whereabouts of his grave.

George Frederick Ruxton's two enduring narratives do more than record life in the Far West during 1846–1847: they touch a chord in civilized readers that has to do with largely imagined but unexpressed and unnamed yearnings for untrammeled freedom in unspoiled wildernesses—with the fact that civilized humankind is "half-froze for mountain doins." Readers hankering for wilderness, in whatever time or place, will continue to sympathize with Ruxton's confession in *Adventures in Mexico and the Rocky Mountains:*

> I must confess that the very happiest moments of my life have been spent in the wilderness of the Far West; . . . with no friend near me more faithful than my rifle, and no companions more sociable than my good horse and mules, or the attendant cayute which nightly serenades us. . . . Scarcely, however, did I ever wish to change such hours of freedom for all the luxuries of civilized life.

References:

James W. Abert, *Western America in 1846–47: The Original travel diary of Lieutenant J. W. Abert who mapped New Mexico for the United States Army,* edited by John Galvin (San Francisco: John Howell Books, 1966), pp. 66–70;

Crawford R. Buell, Introduction to Ruxton's *Adventures in Mexico and the Rocky Mountains* (Glorieta: Rio Grande Press, 1973);

Buell, Introduction to Ruxton's *Life in the Far West* (Glorieta: Rio Grande Press, 1972);

Storm Colton, "George Augustus Frederick Ruxton," in *A Catalog of the Everett D. Graff Collection of Western Americana* (Chicago: University of Chicago Press, 1968), pp. 544–547;

Richard H. Cracroft, "*The Big Sky:* A. B. Guthrie's Use of Historical Sources," *Western American Literature,* 6 (Fall 1971): 163–176;

Cracroft, "'Half-Froze for Mountain Doins': The Influence and Significance of George F. Ruxton's *Life in the Far West,*" *Western American Literature,* 10 (May 1975): 29–43;

Bernard DeVoto, *Across the Wide Missouri* (Boston: Houghton Mifflin, 1947);

LeRoy R. Hafen, ed., *Mountain Men and the Fur Trade of the Far West,* 10 volumes (Glendale: Arthur H. Clarke, 1966);

Horace Kephart, Introduction to Ruxton's *In the Old West* (New York: Macmillan, 1924), pp. 5–24;

Neal Lambert, *George Frederick Ruxton,* Western Writers Series, no. 15 (Boise, Idaho: Boise State University, 1974);

Paul S. Lehmberg, "Ruxton's *Life in the Far West* as Fiction," *Rendezvous,* 9 (Spring 1976): 11–15;

J. Munro, "Ruxton of the Rocky Mountains," *Good Words,* 34 (August 1893): 547–551;

Lawrence Clark Powell, "The Adventurous Englishman," *Westways,* 65 (November 1973): 19–22, 70–71;

Bruce Sutherland, "George Frederick Ruxton in North America," *Southwest Review,* 30 (Autumn 1944): 86–91;

J. Golden Taylor, "Across the Wide Missouri: The Adventure Narrative from Lewis and Clark to Powell," in *A Literary History of the American West* (Fort Worth: Texas Christian University Press, 1987), pp. 71–99;

Frederick E. Voelker, "Ruxton of the Rocky Mountains," *Missouri Historical Society Bulletin,* 5 (January 1949): 79–90.

Papers:

George Frederick Ruxton's papers are in the Everett D. Graff Western American Collection at the Newberry Library in Chicago.

Charles Sealsfield
(Carl Postl)
(3 March 1793 – 26 May 1864)

Walter Grünzweig
University of Dortmund

See also the Sealsfield entry *DLB 133: Nineteenth-Century German Writers to 1840.*

BOOKS: *Die Vereinigten Staaten von Nordamerika, nach ihrem politischen, religiösen und gesellschaftlichen Verhältnisse betrachtet: Mit einer Reise durch den westlichen Theil von Pennsylvanien, Ohio, Kentucky, Indiana, Illinois, Missuri, Tennessee, das Gebiet Arkansas, Missisippi und Louisiana,* 2 volumes, as C. Sidons (Stuttgart & Tubingen: Cotta, 1827); volume 1 revised and translated anonymously by Sealsfield as *The United States of North America as They Are in Their Political, Religious, and Social Relations* (London: Simpkin & Marshall, 1828); volume 2 revised and translated anonymously by Sealsfield as *The Americans as They Are: Described in a Tour through the Valley of the Mississippi* (London: Hurst, Chance, 1828);
Austria as It Is: or, Sketches of Continental Courts. By an Eye-witness, anonymous (London: Hurst, Chance, 1828);
Tokeah; or, The White Rose, 2 volumes, anonymous (Philadelphia: Carey, Lea & Carey, 1829); revised as *The Indian Chief; or, Tokeah and the White Rose. A Tale of the Indians and the Whites,* 3 volumes, anonymous (Philadelphia: Carey, Lea, & Carey, 1829; London: Newman, 1829); revised, enlarged, and translated anonymously by Sealsfield as *Der Legitime und die Republikaner: Eine Geschichte aus dem letzten amerikanisch-englischen Kriege,* 3 volumes (Zurich: Orell, Füßli, 1833);
Transatlantische Reiseskizzen und Christophorus Bärenhäuter, 2 volumes, anonymous (Zurich: Orell, Füßli, 1834);
Der Virey und die Aristokraten oder Mexiko im Jahre 1812, 3 volumes, anonymous (Zurich: Orell, Füßli, 1835);
Lebensbilder aus beiden Hemisphären: Die große Tour, 2 volumes, anonymous (Zurich: Orell, Füßli, 1835); revised as *Morton oder die große Tour,* 2

Charles Sealsfield

volumes, anonymous (Stuttgart: Metzler, 1844);
Lebensbilder aus beiden Hemisphären, dritter Theil: Ralph Doughby's Esqu. Brautfahrt oder Der transatlantischen Reiseskizzen dritter Theil, anonymous (Zurich: Orell, Füßli, 1835);
Lebensbilder aus beiden Hemisphären, vierter Theil: Pflanzerleben oder Der transatlantischen Reiseskizzen vierter Theil, anonymous (Zurich: Schultheß, 1836);
Lebensbilder aus beiden Hemisphären, fünfter Theil: Die Farbigen oder Der transatlantischen Reiseskizzen fünfter Theil, anonymous (Zurich: Schultheß, 1836);

Lebensbilder aus beiden Hemisphären, sechster Theil: Nathan, der Squatter-Regulator, oder Der erste Amerikaner in Texas. Der transatlantischen Reiseskizzen sechster Theil, anonymous (Zurich: Schultheß, 1837);

Neue Land- und Seebilder: Die Deutsch-amerikanischen Wahlverwandtschaften, 4 volumes, anonymous (Zurich: Schultheß, 1839–1840); translated anonymously as *Rambleton: A Romance of Fashionable Life in New York, during the Great Speculation of 1836* (New York: Winchester, 1844);

Das Cajütenbuch oder Nationale Charakteristiken, 2 volumes (Zurich: Schultheß, 1841); translated by C. F. Mersch as *The Cabin Book; or, Sketches of Life in Texas* (New York: Winchester, 1844); translated by Sarah Powell as *The Cabin Book; or, National Characteristics* (London: Ingram, Cooke, 1852);

Süden und Norden, 3 volumes, anonymous (Stuttgart: Metzler, 1842–1843); translated by Joel T. Headley as *North and South; or, Scenes and Adventures in Mexico* (New York: Winchester, 1844);

Gesammelte Werke, 18 volumes (Stuttgart: Metzler, 1843–1846);

Die Grabesschuld: Nachgelassene Erzählung, edited by Alfred Meissner (Leipzig: Günther, 1873);

Sämtliche Werke, edited by Karl J. R. Arndt and others, 33 volumes projected (Hildesheim & New York: Olms, 1972–).

Editions in English: *Life in the New World; or Sketches of American Society,* translated by Gustavus C. Hebbe and James A. Mackay (New York: Winchester, 1844);

Scenes and Adventures in Central America, selected and translated by Frederick Hardman (Edinburgh & London: Blackwood, 1852);

Frontier Life; or, Scenes and Adventures in the South West, selected and translated by Hardman (Buffalo: Derby, Orton & Miller, 1853);

America: Glorious and Chaotic Land. Charles Sealsfield Discovers the Young United States. An Account of Our Post-Revolutionary Ancestors by a Contemporary, abridged, adapted, and translated by E. L. Jordan (Englewood Cliffs, N.J.: Prentice-Hall, 1969);

The Making of an American: An Adaptation of Memorable Tales by Charles Sealsfield, edited and translated by Ulrich S. Carrington (Dallas: Southern Methodist University Press, 1974).

Charles Sealsfield is not only one of the earliest and most important German/Austrian American writers but also an early western author. Although largely unknown to twentieth-century American readers, his novels are a part of the western tradition in American literature, especially with regard to the "Texas novel." The complexity of his fiction, largely unnoticed for more than a century after his death, has received renewed appreciation from critics since the 1970s. There has been a long-standing scholarly fascination in Sealsfield's biography, which remains a subject of speculation and dispute.

Sealsfield was born as Carl Postl on 3 March 1793 in Poppitz (then part of the Austrian Empire, today Popice, Czech Republic) in rural Southern Moravia. His early familiarity with life in the country may have contributed to his appreciation of landscapes and his skillful use of natural western scenery in his later novels. He was the eldest of eleven children, four of whom died at an early age. His parents, Anton and Juliane Rabl Postl, were vintners and therefore could not provide their children with an education that would enable them to rise above their social class. Thus, for the unusually gifted Carl, the only option for a higher education was to enter upon a clerical career. Both Moravia, where he went to school, and Prague, where he received his theological training, were ethnically mixed, providing Postl with an early understanding of the complexities and the potential of a multicultural society.

Postl took his vows in 1813 and became a priest one year later. After a remarkable career as secretary in the Order of the Holy Cross with the Red Star, he suddenly disappeared in 1823. Investigation by the all-powerful Austrian police led to nothing. Biographers have variously suggested monastic life, politics, the machinations of Freemasons, and sexuality, or the lack thereof, as reasons for Postl's sudden disappearance.

Whether or not he did take the cashbox of the order, as some anecdotal speculations have it, the breaking of his vow amounted to a crime, and Postl felt under constraint to hide his true background for the rest of his life. The revelation that Charles Sealsfield, clergyman, American citizen, purportedly born in Pennsylvania and a longtime resident in Switzerland, had once been Carl Postl became manifest only in the course of the execution of his last will, in which he left his estate in America to two male descendants of the Postl family willing to immigrate to the New World.

Intense biographical inquisitiveness into Sealsfield's life has led to few tangible results. Eduard Castle's extensive biography, while based on studies of the writer's correspondence and other sources, is tainted by a tendency to fill the enormous gaps left by missing documents with narratives taken from Sealsfield's fiction and by an ideology reflecting the Nazi period during which the book was

Advertisements for Sealsfield's works in Spring 1844 issues of
the New World

created. Thus, the many claims made for Sealsfield's subsequent life, including his establishment as a planter and slaveholder in Louisiana; his work for the Napoleon clan in New York, London, Paris, and Switzerland; and especially his connections with international Masonry, remain largely unsubstantiated. Even verified sources are highly questionable: Postl-Sealsfield's carefully and lovingly constructed American roles complicate the interpretation of his correspondence.

The emphasis on biographical research that has proved largely futile has precluded a close investigation of the oeuvre consisting of twelve novels and a body of short prose, much of which cannot be safely attributed to Sealsfield. As Sealsfield had grown up with German and also used this language in the major part of his works, scholarship automatically placed him in a purely German or Austrian literary tradition. The term "German American," which was at times used to characterize his fiction, is pure decoration in most studies, as no attempt is made actually to analyze the American dimensions of his works. This Eurocentric view does not take into account Sealsfield's prolonged stays in the United States and the change of his vision in the course of his experience there. In the late 1960s the first attempts were made to identify Sealsfield's place in the American canon. In the course of the two decades following, a growing body of American-studies research placed Sealsfield in an American context; deconstructive approaches helped to explain Sealsfield's complex fiction as an important antecedent of the modern multicultural tradition in American literature.

Sealsfield's formative first stay in the United States lasted, with one interruption, from 1823 until 1830. He lived variously in Louisiana, Pennsylvania, and New York and may have visited Mexico. During a visit to Europe in 1826 and 1827 Sealsfield worked on his first two works, both nonfiction. Consisting of two parts, his first book, *Die Vereinigten Staaten von Nordamerika, nach ihrem politischen, religiösen und gesellschaftlichen Verhältnisse betrachtet: Mit einer Reise durch den westlichen Theil von Pennsylvanien, Ohio, Kentucky, Indiana, Illinois, Missuri, Tennessee, das Gebiet Arkansas, Mississippi und Louisiana* (1827; translated as *The United States of North America as They Are in Their Political, Religious, and Social Relations* and *The Americans as They Are: Described in a Tour through the Valley of the Mississippi,* 1828), is a politically motivated travelogue presenting the United States from a strongly Jacksonian point of view. This orientation implies a western bias and results in the celebration of the democratic simplicity of life in the West, at that time including Ohio and Kentucky. The ide-

alized frontier, which is so characteristic of Sealsfield's later fiction, does not occur in these initial volumes on the United States. Somewhat in the vein of J. Hector St. John de Crèvecoeur, Sealsfield depicts frontiersmen as savages who, though necessary forerunners of civilization, cannot be accepted into civilized society. His second nonfiction work, *Austria as It Is: or, Sketches of Continental Courts. By an Eye-witness* (1828), is a political polemic against Austrian absolutism.

Sealsfield's first novel, the only one he wrote in English, *Tokeah; or, The White Rose,* was published anonymously in Philadelphia in 1829. Sealsfield examines the conflict of white and Native American cultures on the egalitarian Jacksonian frontier, a subject that had proved popular in James Fenimore Cooper's Leatherstocking tales. German critics, ever enamored of exotic, Rousseauian noble savages, have interpreted this text as a defense of Native Americans, whereas others have pointed out its pronounced Jacksonian point of view. The "General" appears in the novel reveling in his brilliant victory over the British in the War of 1812, and his pronouncements on the Native Americans reflect President Andrew Jackson's policy of Indian removal. Although Indian chief Tokeah leads his tribe to Lake Sabine, in present-day Texas, to protect his people from destruction at the hands of the whites (thereby employing one of the most popular Jacksonian arguments for removal), the logic of the novel clearly indicates that the future of the West would be white.

Sealsfield's careful balance between Native Americans and white Americans indicates that he did not want to take sides but was interested in exploring questions of ethnic hegemony. *Tokeah,* which was published by the same house that brought out *The Last of the Mohicans* (1826), like Cooper's novel deals with the Indians' hopeless struggle for survival. There are also allusions to Cooper's *The Prairie* (1827), which, like *Tokeah,* features a well-meaning democratic squatter as protagonist. The German version of *Tokeah,* titled *Der Legitime und die Republikaner* (The Legitimate and the Republicans, 1833), further strengthens the position of the "republican" squatters vis-à-vis the "legitimate" natives. Large sections of the book reflect the predominant white American attitude toward Native Americans, referred to by Roy Harvey Pearce as "savagism," a mixture of pity and censure.

Sealsfield returned to Europe in 1830, and his subsequent novels were written in Switzerland. His first story of the Southwest was "George Howard's Esq. Brautfahrt" (translated as "The Courtship of George Howard, Esquire," in *Life in the New World;*

or *Sketches of American Society,* 1844), which was included in *Transatlantische Reiseskizzen und Christophorus Bärenhäuter* (Transatlantic Travel Sketches and Christopher Loafer, 1834), but he did not immediately continue in that vein. In *Der Virey und die Aristokraten oder Mexiko im Jahre 1812* (The Viceroy and the Aristocrats; or, Mexico in the Year 1812, 1835) he tells his story against the backdrop of Mexico's political upheavals before its independence. The unfinished novel originally titled *Lebensbilder aus beiden Hemisphären: Die große Tour* (Pictures of Life from Both Hemispheres: The Grand Tour, 1835) follows an American protagonist to Europe and was intended as the first two parts of a series of books presenting both the New and the Old Worlds. The subsequent novels in the series, however, were all set in the Western Hemisphere. When Sealsfield put together his *Gesammelte Werke* (Collected Works, 1843–1846), he retitled *Die große Tour* as a separate work, *Morton oder die große Tour* (Morton or the Grand Tour, 1844), and created a new title for his series, *Lebensbilder aus der westlichen Hemisphäre* (Pictures from Life in the Western Hemisphere). The five novels collected in this series, as well as *Das Cajütenbuch oder Nationale Charakteristiken* (1841; translated as *The Cabin Book; or, Sketches of Life in Texas,* 1844), constitute Sealfield's main claim as an American western writer.

The five-novel cycle is held together by the first-person narrator George Howard, a curious mixture of plantation owner and western pioneer. In *George Howard's Esq. Brautfahrt,* the first part of *Lebensbilder aus der westlichen Hemisphäre,* Howard, a planter's son from the Deep South, moves to the Red River. Although Howard repeatedly uses classic southwestern frontier rhetoric in order to justify his move–throughout the cycle there are allusions to the works of Timothy Flint, William Gilmore Simms, and James Kirke Paulding–his insecurity, fear, and clumsiness render him unfit for the demands of western life. By placing Howard on the western frontier and then revealing his inadequacy to live up to the codes that are part of his rhetoric, Sealsfield created an ironic westerner. The discrepancy between Howard's proud rhetoric and his fear of any action leads Sealsfield's readers to question the validity of the western myth.

One interesting example of the conflict between rhetoric and action is plain in the strong antagonism the Anglo-American newcomers show for the ethnic French inhabitants of Louisiana, an antagonism characteristic of all five parts of the cycle but especially prominent in the first and the second, *Ralph Doughby's Esq. Brautfahrt* (translated as "The Courtship of Ralph Doughby, Esquire," in *Life in the New World*), which was published initially as *Lebensbilder aus beiden Hemisphären, dritter Theil: Ralph Doughby's Esqu. Brautfahrt oder Der transatlantischen Reiseskizzen dritter Theil* (1835). Whereas the Anglo-Americans, especially Howard, chide the French for keeping to their traditions rather than joining the expansionist westward drive of the western pioneers, the unraveling plot actually makes it abundantly clear that Howard (and other Americans) would not have survived without the French. The American ridicule of the French is therefore ridiculous in itself.

Howard is a slaveholder who believes in both western expansion and slavery. Sealsfield scholarship has long and uselessly debated whether the author was for or against slavery. Those scholars who saw the author as writing from a European, antiabsolutist point of view argued that his seemingly positive representation of slavery was an unfortunate error. Other studies, pointing to the Jacksonian context of these novels, recognized affinities to southern ideological models emphasizing the compatibility of American-style democracy and the "peculiar institution." Recent deconstructive criticism, however, ignoring the question of authorial intention and pointing to the instability of the slaveholder, who is both the first-person narrator and the spokesman for the dominant white ideology, has been able to identify powerful subtexts revealing a vibrant, autonomous African American culture within Sealsfield's polyphonic fiction.

In the third and fourth parts of the cycle titled *Pflanzerleben* (translated as "The Life of a Planter" and "Scenes in the South-West" in *Life in the New World*), Howard's slaves stage a small rebellion. The oblivious Howard ignores the hints that a rebellion is in progress and notices little to nothing. Sealsfield models the preparations for this rebellion after *The Confessions of Nat Turner* (1831), a record of the bloodiest slave rebellion of the American South from the point of view of its main instigator. His strategy permits the readers to grasp the organizational skill and the high motivation of the slaves, thus ridiculing Howard's failure to understand the significance of the slaves' actions.

In the fifth and final part of the cycle, *Nathan, der Squatter-Regulator, oder Der erste Amerikaner in Texas* (1837; translated as "The Squatter Chief; or, The First American in Texas" in *Life in the New World*), the narrator is Nathan Strong, whose stories and reminiscences are framed within the story told by Howard. Providing insight into the early Anglo-American settlement of Louisiana before the Louisiana Purchase, the long narrative suggests that the territory could never have been won for the

Page 34.

Illustrations from The Cabin Book; or National Characteristics, *Sarah Powell's translation of Sealsfield's* Das Cajütenbuch oder Nationale Charakteristiken

United States without the work of black slaves; the rugged vegetation and torrid climate would have prevented the "conquest" of that portion of the Southwest. Even though Nathan is a more convincing character than Howard, much in the tradition of Daniel Boone, a close reading of his vigorous narrative reveals contradictions and ironies that also permit a critical view of the western project.

Nathan starts out in Kentucky, but when it becomes too crowded, he moves to Louisiana. There, too, he eventually feels the constraints of civilization as represented by encroaching American institutions and decides to move on to Texas. In the person of Nathan, Sealsfield makes the inherent contradiction of the frontier myth almost explicit. Following his instinct for freedom and independence, Nathan is always drawn to new territories and untouched wilderness. At the same time, however, he is the herald of the civilization he is running from. Thus, he is forever forced to escape from the order he keeps helping to create. Whereas this contradiction is inherent in the western frontier myth at large, Sealsfield is one of the earliest to question it through fiction.

Critics have frequently claimed that Nathan and his western clan are Sealsfield's ideal Americans; indeed, there is much that recommends them as honest and straightforward human beings and patriots. However, Sealsfield uses the contradictions inherent in his characters and their situations as well as the violence and craftiness required to take possession of the land to raise questions about the prevailing ideology of expansion. The celebratory reference to American democracy is a characteristic example of the expansionist rhetoric permeating the narratives of Anglo-Americans:

> It is that alone which has broken through the seven-fold armor of our cold selfishness, armed millions of mechanical hands with a free will, broken down the curtain concealing the western land from the east, and crossed the Alleghenies, never resting until its dominion was established beyond their range—a dominion, equal in extent to the Roman with its imperial lustre, and which has been gained without a drop of blood—not with the sword, but the axe; which in seventy years, will be inhabited by a hundred millions of free citizens—a monster republic, resting its right foot on the shores of the Atlantic, and its left on the Pacific; sustaining millions of freemen, living under the law of Christ, and speaking the language of Shakespere and of Milton!

Even a cursory reading of the passage reveals telling contractions: "mechanical hands with a free will" or the democracy based on freedom referred to as a "monster republic." To a reader outside the South

the fact that a slaveholder fantasizes of a "hundred millions of free citizens" must be particularly ironic, even more so when that same narrator later states that the land could never have been developed without the slaves. Since one of the central chapters of the book, telling of the illegal initial American presence in non-American western territory, is titled "The Bloody Blockhouse," the claim that American empire building is peaceful is shown to be mere rhetoric and propaganda.

Following the completion of the cycle, Sealsfield interrupted his residence in Switzerland by a trip back to the United States, ostensibly to take care of personal and financial affairs. There he experienced the Panic of 1837, which became the background of *Neue Land- und Seebilder: Die Deutschamerikanischen Wahlverwandtschaften* (1839–1840; translated as *Rambleton: A Romance of Fashionable Life in New York, during the Great Speculation of 1836,* 1844), which he published unfinished. Another loosely constructed work in several parts, it takes place in Europe and New York City and in upstate New York, chronicling the futile relationship between a European aristocrat and an American belle.

Sealsfield's most famous novel, *Das Cajütenbuch oder Nationale Charakteristiken,* connects thematically to the novel cycle on the Southwest. It is one of the most sought for items in the American antiquarian book business because it forms a natural part of any collection of early Texana. Along with Timothy Flint's *Francis Berrian* (1826) and Anthony Ganilh's *Mexico. vs. Texas* (1838), its two immediate predecessors which were almost certainly known to Sealsfield, *Das Cajütenbuch* also deals with the battle over national and religious hegemony in the Southwest. The novel appeared at a time when nativist feelings and tensions about an alleged Catholic conspiracy were building in the United States. As Ray Allen Billington, a historian of the nativist movement in the United States and a scholar well acquainted with Sealsfield, puts it in *The Protestant Crusade: 1800–1860* (1952), one of the tasks the nativists had set for themselves was to counter the alleged Catholic policy of encirclement and, especially, to "save the West from the Pope."

Das Cajütenbuch is made up of five loosely connected narratives told at a dinner party of rich southern planters at Natchez around the year 1840, some five years before the annexation of Texas. The first two parts deal with the "liberation" of Texas from Mexico. As in the novel cycle, a young southerner, Edward Morse—probably an allusion to Samuel F. B. Morse, an inventor who was also a central figure in the anti-Catholic movement—moves to the frontier. After discovering that his claims to a tract of land in Texas are not valid, Morse has a conversion experience and eventually becomes a general in the Texan army. This conversion may best be described as a kind of "regeneration" at the western frontier. After losing his way in the Texas prairie and wandering about for days without food and water, he is eventually saved by a robber and murderer, Bob Rock. In Texas, evidently, the worst of criminals can serve as agents of Manifest Destiny. Under the influence of this wilderness experience and especially through Bob Rock's example, Morse has a chance to unlearn his genteel attitude and become a useful servant to the Lone Star Republic.

Following his dramatic rescue, Morse meets with a justice of the peace, an American who is nominally in the service of the Mexicans. This man, a philosopher-politician in the radical enlightenment tradition of Thomas Jefferson, spells out the official ideological definition of Texan frontier spirit: "In the prairie . . . a light starts shining inside you that is different from that in your big cities; after all, your cities are constructed by humans, are polluted by human breath; the prairie, however, is made by God; there, life is given by His pure breath." The regenerated Morse learns that life in the West necessitates a different value system from that in the established states of the East. Indeed, it has been suggested that the function of the neo-Texan's narrative is to remind the established and saturated Natchez planters, who are wary of any political changes, of their obligation to ideals of the American Revolution that have just been reiterated in Texas.

Sealsfield, however, once again provides plenty of evidence to enable his readers to question both the soundness of the American expansionist argument and the western code characterizing his protagonists. The same Jeffersonian justice of the peace who speaks of the American West in terms of reason, enlightenment, and divine guidance cynically introduces a Nietzschean dimension of the law of the strongest:

> it is always the same story, the stronger overcome the weaker, those with more brain outwit those with less. . . . I studied the history of the country of origin we both have in common [the United States] and must admit, for your peace of mind, that I believed in it just as the most pious catholic believes in the Credo.—But when I looked around the world, I stopped believing. . . . Already old Moses knew how to use an electrostatic machine, knew how to produce lightning and thunder, had God appear in every corner—usually, when he was planning some mischief.

Thus, even divine guidance is revealed to be human show and deception.

Sealsfield, though almost at the beginning of the tradition of western literature celebrating manifest destiny, exposes the doctrine as a weapon used to further American interests. When Sealsfield has two of his squatters argue that all the land surrounded by the Mississippi is theirs because Louisiana is composed of Mississippi mud transported from northern territories that are in American possession, the expansionist argument is presented on the level of a tall tale. International law is openly ridiculed and, as in the following passage, declared irrelevant by General Morse:

> I admit that this line of reasoning will not be found correct by Hugo Grotius and Pufendorf, but think what would have become of England, what would have become of the world, if professors of international law had controlled the wheel of history!

The American argument is thus weakened in the eyes of the reader. Sealsfield's novels about the American West expose much of the ideology of westward expansion, seemingly attractive at first, as a series of foul arguments. The other narratives that make up *Das Cajütenbuch* relate to Ireland and the Latin American struggle for independence from Spain. The novel, then, is a "western" with global dimensions, examining both the rhetoric of liberation and the beginnings of modern imperialism.

Although Sealsfield's final novel, *Süden und Norden* (South and North, 1842–1843; translated as *North and South; or, Scenes and Adventures in Mexico*, 1844), is a novel about Mexico, it is directly connected to the expansionist theme of the previous novels. Four American travelers are on an exploratory trip through Mexico pursuing some vague commercial interests. They are joined by an eccentric German researcher who offers frequent comic relief. The American narrator of the novel and his American friends, like Sealsfield, are strongly anti-Catholic and show contempt for Mexico and its culture, but they are fascinated nonetheless. The country and its people keep eluding them—and the readers—for the novel is an intricate and confused conglomerate of dialogues, delirious monologues, and mysterious events. Sealsfield contrives a fantastic Mexico where the American visitors, as well as the reader, are in a state of permanent confusion, panic, and fear.

In the course of the novel the visitors are actually brought to the brink of madness. In a postscript, which is central to an understanding of the work as a whole, the narrator, Hardy, describes the recur-

A letter written by Sealsfield in the year of his death
(Landschaftsmuseum Znaim)

ring periods of temporary insanity to which he is subjected following the Mexican adventure. His fellow travelers are victims of similar problems. This partial insanity is anticipated throughout the novel by periodic feverish dreams and temporary losses of identity and consciousness.

The power and suddenness of the reaction of these young itinerant businessmen to Mexico suggests a profound cultural antagonism caused in part by the undue interest the Americans take in the country. Rather than wanting to acquaint themselves with a different culture, they search it out in order to subjugate and exploit it, an implicitly imperialistic approach to a foreign culture. What seems in *Süden und Norden* to begin as an innocuous journey

results in a cultural confrontation that foreshadows the profound problems of communication between Gringos and Latin Americans or even between members of the developed and the underdeveloped worlds.

Although Sealsfield claimed to have finished another work which he promised to his publisher, nobody ever actually saw it. "Osten und Westen" (East and West) may have failed for the same reason *Neue Land- und Seebilder: Die Deutsch-amerikanischen Wahlverwandtschaften* remained unfinished: the author's inability to make the industrial development of the eastern part of the country, which was "foreign" to him, compatible with his western outlook. Although it is not known why Sealsfield gave up writing some two decades before his death, it may well be that increasing sectional tensions in the United States and the rising inequality there as a result of industrialization led to his inability to create an integrated fictional whole representing America.

Throughout the 1830s and in the early 1840s Sealsfield, whose works appeared anonymously in Germany, enjoyed an enormous reputation as the "Great Unknown"–an allusion to Sir Walter Scott, with whom he was frequently compared. There was an immense interest in America, both by prospective immigrants and by the many ardent devotees of Cooper, who had effectively introduced America as fictional locale and theme into German consciousness. Sealsfield's works were also popular among the leftist liberals of Germany and Austria, who approved of the political message they perceived in his work and at times placed him with the revolutionary "Young German" writers.

Just after he had stopped writing, Sealsfield reached a short-lived fame in the United States as a result of a public-relations scheme. In 1843 the reputable British journal *Blackwood's Edinburgh Magazine* started publishing unauthorized translated excerpts of Sealsfield's novels. The attention devoted to a previously unknown German American author inspired the interest of Jonas Winchester, who, long before the introduction of an international copyright law, specialized in pirated translations and republications of European authors.

Winchester's project, the translation of almost all the works of this "genuinely" American author into English, was accompanied by an unusual and intensive campaign celebrating "Seatsfield" (as he was called as a result of a reading error) as the "greatest American author." This claim about an author previously unknown in the United States resulted in a lively discussion in the American press. Although the most popular American poet of this time, Henry Wadsworth Longfellow, once called Sealsfield "our favorite Seatsfield" (Sealsfield's traces in Longfellow's *Evangeline,* 1847, are well documented), the literary avant-garde pronounced a negative judgment. With bitter scorn Nathaniel Hawthorne and Edgar Allan Poe ridiculed the "Seatsfield" phenomenon as a hoax, designed to undermine the development of an original national American literature.

This negative attitude, while it may also have some aesthetic motivations, was probably mainly due to the competitiveness that characterized the American literary market. American authors were at a great disadvantage because their books, for which royalties had to be paid, were more expensive than pirated editions of European authors or books published in Europe. This was partially compensated for by the American locale and subject matter by means of which American writers managed to interest their own audiences. Now, however, an author writing in German intruded into their own territory. Hawthorne's ironic comment on the "celebrated Seatsfield" in his sketch "A Select Party" attacked Sealsfield from the point of view of literary nationalism. However, his and Poe's comments also testify to Sealsfield's prominence in the United States in and around the year 1844.

Soon thereafter interest in Sealsfield subsided both in the United States and in Europe. He entered the final phase of his life preoccupied with increasing his sizable fortune. The origin and extent of his wealth are unknown; certainly only a small part of it could have come from royalties. He invested much of his money in U.S. railway stocks.

Sealsfield, who remained single throughout his life, spent a second prolonged period in the United States from 1853 to 1858 without any literary consequence. Thereafter he lived in Switzerland until he died in 1864, three years after the onset of the American Civil War. During this final period he became deeply concerned about the future of his adopted country. On his gravestone in Solothurn, Switzerland, Sealsfield referred to himself as "Citizen of the United States of North America," emphasizing the role he had played through his mature life.

Sealsfield remained a frequently republished author in German-speaking countries, although his works never regained the popularity they had at the time of their original publication. A host of politically inclined literary historians descended on him in the course of the decades after his death, each attempting to use him for his or her own purpose. As a representative of German writing in Czechia, he was used by both Nazis and anti-Nazis. In spite of the intercultural structure of much of his writing and his understanding of the difficult position of the Slavic nations in the Habsburg Empire, he was enlisted by the Sudeten Germans, many of whom were expelled from Czechoslovakia after World War II, as a major exponent of the ethnic Germans of the region.

In the United States, Sealsfield retained a modest popularity chiefly among those interested in German literature and among specialists in the Southwest. The fact that he both internalized and critically examined the West early in American literary history makes him a remarkable figure. Future research, especially from a comparatist and intercultural perspective, will doubtless reveal additional and more complex connections between this German American author and early western literature. Such research will aid the revision of the traditionally monocultural approach to the American West into a pluralistic model.

Letters:

Der große Unbekannte: Das Leben von Charles Sealsfield (Karl Postl). Briefe und Aktenstücke, edited by Eduard Castle (Vienna: Werner, 1955).

Bibliographies:

Otto Heller and Theodore H. Leon, *Charles Sealsfield: Bibliography of His Writings Together with a Classified and Annotated Catalogue of Literature Relating to His Work and His Life* (Saint Louis: Washington University, 1939);

Felix Bornemann and Hans Freising, *Sealsfield-Bibliographie 1945–1965* (Stuttgart: Charles-Sealsfield-Gesellschaft, 1966);

Albert Kresse, *Erläuternder Katalog meiner Sealsfield-Sammlung: Stand am 1. September 1960* (Stuttgart: Charles-Sealsfield-Gesellschaft, 1974);

Alexander Ritter, *Sealsfield-Bibliographie 1966–1975: Mit einem Kommentar von Karl J. R. Arndt zum Publikationsstand der "Sämtlichen Werke"* (Stuttgart: Charles-Sealsfield-Gesellschaft, 1976);

Ritter, "Sealsfield-Bibliographie 1976–1986," in *Schriftenreihe der Charles-Sealsfield-Gesellschaft,* volume 1, edited by Ritter and Günter Schnitzler (Stuttgart: Charles-Sealsfield-Gesellschaft, 1987), pp. 50–65.

Biographies:

K. M. Kertbeny, *Erinnerungen an Charles Sealsfield* (Brussels & Leipzig: Ahn, 1864);

Eduard Castle, *Das Geheimnis des Grossen Unbekannten: Charles Sealsfield–Carl Postl. Die Quellenschriften* (Vienna: Wiener Bibliophilen-Gesellschaft, 1943);

Castle, *Der große Unbekannte: Das Leben von Charles Sealsfield* (Karl Postl) (Vienna & Munich: Manutius Presse, 1952); republished as volume 25 of *Sämtliche Werke,* edited by Günter Schnitzler (Hildersheim & New York: Olms, 1993).

References:

Karl J. R. Arndt, "Charles Sealsfield: 'The Greatest American Author,'" in *Proceedings of the American Antiquarian Society for October 1964* (Worcester, Mass., 1965), pp. 248–259;

Arndt, "Sealsfield's Early Reception in England and America," *Germanic Review,* 18 (1943): 176–195;

Nanette M. Ashby, *Charles Sealsfield: "The Greatest American Author." A Study of Literary Piracy and Promotion in the 19th Century* (Stuttgart: Charles-Sealsfield-Gesellschaft, 1980);

Charlotte L. Brancaforte, ed., *The Life and Works of Charles Sealsfield (Karl Postl), 1793–1864* (Madison, Wis.: Max Kade Institute, 1993);

Bernd Fischer, "Baumwolle und Indianer: Zu Charles Sealsfields *Der Legitime und die Republikaner,*" *Yearbook of German-American Studies,* 19 (1984): 85–96;

Fischer, "Form und Geschichtsphilosophie in Charles Sealsfields *Lebensbildern aus der westlichen Hemisphäre,*" *German Studies Review,* 9 (May 1986): 233–255;

Walter Grünzweig, "American Birds of Passage: Westward Expansion in Charles Sealsfield's Fiction," in *Westward Expansion in America (1803–1860),* edited by Wolfgang Binder (Erlangen: Palm & Enke, 1987), pp. 127–139;

Grünzweig, *Charles Sealsfield* (Boise, Idaho: Boise State University Press, 1985);

Grünzweig, *Das demokratische Kanaan: Charles Sealsfields Amerika im Kontext amerikanischer Literatur und Ideologie* (Munich: Fink, 1987);

Grünzweig, "Fatal Attractions: Charles Sealsfield and the Political Implications of a Mexican-American Romance," *Journal of the American Studies Association of Texas,* 20 (1989): 15–26;

Grünzweig, "The Italian Sky in the Republic of Letters: Charles Sealsfield and Timothy Flint as Early Writers of the American West," *Yearbook of German-American Studies,* 17 (1982): 1–20;

Grünzweig and Viviane N'Diaye, "Voodoo im Biedermeier: Charles Sealsfield's *Pflanzerleben* aus afroamerikanischer Sicht," in *Schriftenreihe der Charles-Sealsfield-Gesellschaft* (Stuttgart: Charles-Sealsfield-Gesellschaft, 1989), pp. 147–166;

Otto Heller, "Some Sources of Sealsfield," *Modern Philology,* 7 (1909/1910): 587–592;

Murray G. Hill, "Some of Longfellow's Sources for the Second Part of *Evangeline,*" *PMLA,* 31 (1916): 160–180;

Wulf Koepke, "Charles Sealsfield's Place in Literary History," *South Central Review,* 1 (Spring-Summer 1984): 52–66;

Glen E. Lich, "Sealsfield's Texan: Metaphor, Experience, and History," *Yearbook of German-American Studies,* 22 (1987): 71–79;

Morton Nirenberg, "Review Essay: The Works of Charles Sealsfield," *German Quarterly,* 52 (January 1979): 81–87;

Alexander Ritter, "Charles Sealsfield (1793–1864): German and American Novelist of the Nineteenth Century," *Mississippi Quarterly,* 47 (1994): 633–644;

Ritter, "Charles Sealsfields gesellschaftspolitische Vorstellungen und ihre dichterische Gestaltung als Romanzyklus," *Jahrbuch der deutschen Schillergesellschaft,* 17 (1973): 395–414;

Ritter, "Charles Sealsfield's 'Madonnas of(f) the Trails' im Roman *Das Kajütenbuch.* Oder: Zur epischen Zähmung der Frauen als Stereotype in der amerikanischen Südstaatenepik zwischen 1820 und 1850," *Yearbook of German-American Studies,* 18 (1983): 91–112;

Ritter, *Darstellung und Funktion der Landschaft in den Amerika-Romanen von Charles Sealsfield (Karl Postl): Eine Studie zum Prosa-Roman der deutschen und amerikanischen Literatur in der ersten Hälfte des 19.Jahrhunderts* (Stuttgart: Charles-Sealsfield-Gesellschaft, 1970);

Jeffrey L. Sammons, "Charles Sealsfield: A Case of Non-Canonicity," in *Autoren damals und heute: Literaturgeschichtliche Beispiele veränderter Wirkungshorizonte,* edited by Gerhard P. Knapp (Amsterdam & Atlanta: Rodopi, 1991), pp. 155–172;

Sammons, "Charles Sealsfield: Innovation or Intertextuality?," in *Traditions of Experiment from the Enlightenment to the Present: Essays in Honor of Peter Demetz,* edited by Nancy Kaiser and David E. Wellbery (Ann Arbor: University of Michigan Press, 1992), pp. 127–146;

Sammons, "Charles Sealsfields *Deutsch-amerikanische Wahlverwandtschaften*: Ein Versuch," in *Exotische Welt in populären Lektüren,* edited by Anselm Maler (Tübingen: Niemeyer, 1990), pp. 49–62;

Sammons, "Land of Limited Possibilities: America in the Nineteenth-Century German Novel," *Yale Review,* 68 (1978–1979): 35–52; republished in his *Imagination and History: Selected Papers on Nineteenth-Century German Literature* (New York, Bern, Frankfurt am Main & Paris: Lang, 1988), pp. 217–236;

Wendelin Schmidt-Dengler, "Charles Sealsfield: Das Kajütenbuch (1841)," in *Romane und Erzählungen zwischen Romantik und Realismus: Neue Interpretationen,* edited by Paul Michael Lützeler (Stuttgart: Reclam, 1983), pp. 314–334;

Günter Schnitzler, *Erfahrung und Bild: Die dichterische Wirklichkeit des Charles Sealsfield (Karl Postl)* (Freiburg: Rombach, 1988);

Jerry Schuchalter, *Frontier and Utopia in the Fiction of Charles Sealsfield* (Frankfurt am Main, Bern & New York: Lang, 1986);

Franz Schüppen, *Charles Sealsfield, Karl Postl: Ein österreichischer Erzähler der Biedermeierzeit im Spannungsfeld von Alter und Neuer Welt* (Frankfurt am Main & Bern: Lang, 1981);

Schüppen, ed., *Neue Sealsfield-Studien: Amerika und Europa in der Biedermeierzeit* (Stuttgart: M & P, 1995);

Friedrich Sengle, "Karl Postl, pseud. Charles Sealsfield (1793–1864)," in his *Biedermeierzeit: Deutsche Literatur im Spannungsfeld zwischen Restauration und Revolution 1815–1848,* volume 3: *Die Dichter* (Stuttgart: Metzler, 1980), pp. 752–814;

Reinhard F. Spiess, ed., *Charles Sealsfields Kritik im Spiegel der literarischen Kritik: Eine Sammlung zeitgenössischer Rezensionen* (Stuttgart: Charles-Sealsfield-Gesellschaft, 1977);

Hartmut Steinecke, "Literatur als 'Aufklärungsmittel': Zur Neubestimmung der Werke Charles Sealsfields zwischen Österreich, Deutschland und Amerika," in *Die österreichische Literatur: Ihr Profil im 19.Jahrhundert (1830–1880),* edited by Herbert Zeman (Graz: Akademische Druck- und Verlagsanstalt, 1982), pp. 399–422;

Walter Weiss, "Der Zusammenhang zwischen Amerika-Thematik und Erzählkunst bei Charles Sealsfield (Karl Postl): Ein Beitrag zum Verhältnis von Dichtung und Politik im 19. Jahrhundert," *Literaturwissenschaftliches Jahrbuch der Görres-Gesellschaft,* new series 8 (1967): 95–117; republished in *Deutschlands literarisches Amerikabild: Neuere Forschungen zur Amerikarezeption der deutschen Literatur,* edited by Ritter (Hildesheim & New York: Olms, 1977), pp. 272–294.

Papers:

Most of Sealsfield's manuscripts are lost, possibly destroyed by the author. The Zentralbibliothek Solothurn, Switzerland, has the most complete collection of Sealsfield letters, books, and other materials. A complete list of the holdings can be found in volume twenty-seven of *Sämtliche Werke.*

Charles A. Siringo

(7 February 1855 – 18 October 1928)

Donald A. Barclay
New Mexico State University

BOOKS: *A Texas Cow Boy or, Fifteen Years on the Hurricane Deck of a Spanish Pony* (Chicago: M. Umbdenstock, 1885; expanded edition, Chicago: Siringo & Dobson, 1886);

A Cowboy Detective: A True Story of Twenty-Two Years with a World-Famous Detective Agency (Chicago: W. B. Conkey, 1912);

Two Evil Isms, Pinkertonism and Anarchism (Chicago: Charles A. Siringo, 1915);

A Lone Star Cowboy, Being Fifty Years Experience in the Saddle as Cowboy, Detective and New Mexico Ranger, on Every Cow Trail in the Wooly Old West (Santa Fe, N.M.: Charles A. Siringo, 1919);

The Song Companion of A Lone Star Cowboy: Old Favorite Cow-Camp Songs (Santa Fe, N.M.: Chas. A. Siringo, 1919);

History of "Billy the Kid": The True Life of the Most Daring Young Outlaw of the Age (Santa Fe, N.M.: Chas. A. Siringo, 1920);

Riata and Spurs: The Story of a Lifetime Spent in the Saddle as Cowboy and Detective (Boston & New York: Houghton Mifflin, 1927); revised as *Riata and Spurs: The Story of a Lifetime Spent in the Saddle as Cowboy and Ranger* (Boston & New York: Houghton Mifflin, 1927).

The primary subject of the writings of Charles Angelo Siringo, author, was the life of Charlie Siringo, Texas cowboy and cowboy detective. Because Charlie Siringo participated in events ranging from cattle drives up the Chisholm Trail to epic horseback pursuits of western outlaws to the filming of early western movies, Charles A. Siringo had a wealth of autobiographical material on which he could draw. Although Siringo's unpolished, straightforward writing style will prevent him from ever being numbered among the most literary of western writers, his *A Texas Cow Boy* (1885), the first full-length, published autobiography of a cowboy, assures his place in western American literary history. Siringo is also significant because *A Texas Cow Boy* and his later books on his experiences as cowboy

Charles A. Siringo, circa 1892

and cowboy detective helped to shape the national mythology of the cowboy.

By his own account Siringo enjoyed "my first warm meal on the seventh day of February, 1855, in the county of Matagorda Texas." He was the son of an Italian immigrant father (whose first name is lost to history) and Bridget White Siringo, an Irish immigrant. Siringo's early childhood was marred by the death of his father and the arrival of war at the doorstep of the family home. While Federal and

348

Confederate troops were battling for control of the Texas coast, the bodies of soldiers regularly washed up on the beaches where young Charlie played, and the youngster saw a neighbor mortally wounded when the foolhardy man applied a live coal to an "empty" federal artillery shell. The Federals eventually established a permanent garrison not far from where the Siringos were living, an action that inspired South Texas Confederates to round up and drive inland all local cattle, thereby ensuring that Texas beef would not go to feed Union soldiers. After the war ended, a job helping a neighbor round up and brand the maverick offspring of these cattle gave eleven-year-old Siringo his introduction to the cowboy's life.

In 1868 Siringo followed his remarried mother to Illinois, where, as Siringo described it, "the misery of a boy began." Because Siringo's new stepfather, a Mr. Carrier, was a drunkard who quickly squandered the family's small savings and then disappeared, young Siringo was forced to undertake a series of grueling jobs at starvation wages. Eventually he followed his family to Saint Louis, where—unable to locate his mother and sister—he lived as a street child until landing a job as a bellhop in the Planters' House. Siringo enjoyed a year of relative prosperity in the hotel business until a fistfight with another bellhop ended his tenure at the Planters' House. This incident was not the last time that an outbreak of impetuous temper altered Siringo's destiny.

From Saint Louis, Siringo made his way to New Orleans, where a Mr. and Mrs. Myers, a well-off, elderly couple, adopted the "little Texas hoosier that had strayed off from home and was about to starve." The Myerses tried to give Siringo a good education, but the boy ran away after knifing a schoolmate during a playground fight. Siringo soon returned to the Myerses and school but not before he had stowed away, so he claimed, on board the *Robert E. Lee* and witnessed from her decks the famous race against the *Natchez*. Siringo's second attempt at formal schooling ended much like the first. This time, though, his fight was with a teacher, and following the fight the steamer he stowed away on took him to south Texas, the place where his cowboy career soon began in earnest.

From 1870, the year he ran away from the Myerses and school for good, until he opened his combination cigar store, ice-cream parlor, and oyster house in Caldwell, Oklahoma, in September 1883, Siringo earned his living almost exclusively as a cowboy. He started out working in coastal slaughterhouses that dealt mostly in hides, and by the time he was sixteen he was working longhorns as a full-

fledged cowboy on Able H. "Shanghai" Pierce's Rancho Grande, a huge south Texas cattle operation. This tough brush-country cowboying called for hands who really knew how to ride and rope. Siringo and his companions spent much of their time rounding up nearly wild longhorn cattle that spent their days in dense thickets, venturing onto the small open prairies only at night and in the early morning. When not employed by Pierce, Siringo made his living by breaking wild horses and working in the quasi-legal trades of branding mavericks and skinning dead cattle. Such experiences helped the young man perfect his cowboy skills and toughened him for whatever hardships his future life might bring. In addition to the usual hard work and rough outdoor living, Siringo later wrote that during his early years as a cowboy he was shot through the knee, dragged several hundred yards by a runaway horse, nearly drowned during a hurricane, and bitten on the foot by a rattlesnake. As evidence of his toughness, Siringo claimed he did not miss any work because of the snakebite even though his leg and foot swelled up terribly.

Human beings were not the only creatures to suffer physical pain as a result of the cattle business. Animals suffered too, and Siringo nonchalantly reported the familiar cruelties that come with roping, throwing, and branding cattle as well as those involved in the rough business of breaking wild horses. He also wrote of more unusual sufferings inflicted on animals. Texas cowboys would sometimes tie down unruly "cow brutes" with the beasts' own tails, laming the animals for several days afterward, and they would sew shut the eyes of cattle that were prone to run off into the woods. As Siringo wrote of this operation, "That would bring them to their milk, as they couldn't see timber." All Siringo's writings shows an insensitivity to animal suffering that seems incongruous with the apparent joy he took in his many pet horses and dogs. In one instance, while riding on the prairie Siringo chased a buffalo heifer calf, roped her, managed to throw her after many attempts, then cut her throat with a dull pocket knife because, for perhaps the only time in his adult life, he was without his "Colt's 45 pistol" and Bowie knife. Another time he impetuously shot his loyal dog, Ranger, when he caught the animal harassing a calf. On a boating trip in Alaska, Siringo took a potshot at a whale just to see what a bullet from a Winchester would do to such a large creature. Near the end of his life, after he had to give up his Santa Fe, New Mexico, ranch and move to California, he led his aged pet horse, Patsy, into the woods and put a bullet in the animal's brain rather than risk letting him "fall into cruel hands." While

Siringo during his early years as a cowboy

brating in rough cattle towns such as Dodge City. It was in Dodge City that Siringo was wounded by Bat Masterson, who, acting as a barkeeper and not as a gunfighter, clipped Siringo's head with a well-aimed beer glass instead of the more traditional bullet from a six-shooter.

One of Siringo's trail drives helped establish the LX Ranch on the Texas Panhandle. Siringo put in much of his time as a cowboy at this ranch. Ranch-hand Siringo led the hard but carefree life of a regular waddie, living in bunkhouses and line camps, taking part in roundups, and generally avoiding the responsibilities that come with being a boss. One time when Siringo did not turn down extra responsibility proved to be significant. Asked to lead a party of cowboys to New Mexico to recover Panhandle cattle stolen by Billy the Kid, Siringo accepted, and in November 1880 he set out for New Mexico with a small party of cowboy "warriors" and a chuck wagon. Siringo's orders were to recover all the stolen Panhandle cattle he could find. Catching the thieves was of secondary importance. During the seven months he spent on this errand Siringo served his employers well by collecting evidence against Pat Coghlan (also spelled Coghlin), a powerful New Mexico rancher who had knowingly bought stolen Texas cattle from Billy the Kid. Less to Siringo's credit was the fact that while in New Mexico he gambled away money that belonged to the LX Ranch. Also, when he was given the opportunity to pursue Billy the Kid, Siringo loaned a few of his cowboys to Sheriff Pat Garrett but otherwise stayed out of the search. Siringo's apparent reluctance in this matter is the subject of some debate. He may have been following his orders to put finding the stolen cattle before all else, but it is also clear that Siringo was sympathetic to Billy the Kid, whom he claimed to have met on the LX Ranch in 1878. Both men came from similar hardscrabble, half-orphan backgrounds, and they were so physically similar that Siringo was sometimes mistaken for Billy the Kid. In his book about Siringo, Orlan Sawey goes so far as to argue that a purported photograph of Billy may instead be a photograph of Siringo. Whatever the facts of Siringo's adventures in New Mexico may be, his time there was significant because it provided him with his first taste of detective work, the career that would occupy more than twenty years of his life.

In March 1883, following a six-day courtship, Siringo married fifteen-year-old Mamie Lloyd; by the end of the year he had given up the cowboy life and settled into the role of storekeeper in Caldwell, Oklahoma. It is unclear whether this change was sparked by marriage and maturity or by the realiza-

such actions may shock the modern reader, Siringo's straightforward, unsentimental reporting of them gives a truer picture of a nineteenth-century cowboy's attitude toward animals than the one so often presented in romanticized novels and films.

In 1876 Siringo graduated to trail herding–the big time of the cowboy profession–making his first complete trip "up the trail." He helped to push W. B. Grimes's herd of twenty-five hundred cattle from south Texas to Wichita, Kansas. During this trip Siringo experienced all the events that would become the popular clichés of the trail-drive saga:

> Everything went on lovely with the exception of swimming swollen streams, fighting now and then among ourselves and a stampede every stormy night, until we arrived on the Canadian river in the Indian territory; there we had a little indian scare.

The Indian scare turned out to be no more than the product of nervous imaginations, but the required end-of-the-trail visit to town proved far from imaginary. While celebrating in Wichita, Siringo spent money with wild abandon and limped away from his spree with a piece of buckshot in his leg. Siringo made the trip up the trail several times during his cowboy career, collecting as he went an invaluable stock of trail-herding experiences: long nights standing guard, singing lullabies to nervous cattle, chasing stampedes, searching for water holes, and cele-

tion that the days of the open range were at their end. During his time as a storekeeper Siringo wrote and published *A Texas Cow Boy.*

In the simplest analysis *A Texas Cow Boy* is the straightforward story of an ordinary Texas waddie. Using unpolished, sometimes eccentric prose, Siringo tells the story of his life from his birth to the time he gave up his life as a cowboy. As he tells his story he often jumps from event to event without transition and sometimes skips long periods of his life altogether, a structure that suggests campfire tales more than a carefully crafted work of literature. He is also prone to leaving out important details of the stories he does tell. For example, in *A Texas Cow Boy* he reports that he was shot through the knee while cowboying in south Texas but gives no further details. In *Riata and Spurs* (1927), his later reworking of his cowboy and detective experiences, he adds the information that he was shot because his overzealous mavericking and skinning activities had angered a local cattle baron, and he further informs his readers that it was only the timely arrival of a black cowboy named Lige that kept him from being murdered rather than merely wounded. Both the jumpiness of Siringo's storyteller structure and his frequent omissions of major events and key details set patterns that continued, to greater or lesser degrees, in all of his writing.

Beneath the slapdash surface of *A Texas Cow Boy,* however, there is evidence of a shrewd consciousness at work. For one thing, Siringo exhibits a dry, well-developed sense of humor—one that helped shape the popular notion of what cowboy humor should be. In one instance Siringo tells of his horse Satan, an animal that apparently earned its devilish name: "I tried to sell Satan . . . , but no one would have him as a gift, as they said they would have to get their lives insured before mounting him." This comment is classic cowboy humor because it is self-deprecating (Old Charlie is stuck with an outlaw horse that no one will buy), while at the same time it inflates the status of the teller (Old Charlie rides a horse that other men will not mount without insuring their lives). The first words of *A Texas Cow Boy*—"My excuse for writing this book is money—and lots of it"—are intentionally humorous while again demonstrating Siringo's conscious mind at work. He was aware that people who were not cowboys might buy books about cowboys. Such an awareness of the appeal of the cowboy life to the general public was not likely to be widespread among ordinary working cowboys in the mid 1880s. Similarly, the final joke in *A Texas Cow Boy*—"before you criticize it [*A Texas Cow Boy*] from a literary standpoint, bear in mind that the writer had fits un-

til he was ten years of age, and hasn't fully recovered from the effects"—shows that the author is aware that someone might consider the book to be literature and not simply a collection of autobiographical yarns. Yet another example of the author's self-awareness is his title-page claim that *A Texas Cow Boy* is the work of "An Old Stove Up 'Cow Puncher.'" Since Siringo was barely thirty years old at the time his first book was published, this statement shows that he knew he was creating a literary character and not simply recording the facts of his own life. Finally, he attached to the second edition of *A Texas Cow Boy* (1886) a thirty-page addendum that appears to be a cliché piece of western boosterism. Yet Sawey has observed in a 1972 article "that the entire essay is written with tongue in cheek" by an author who is well aware that the greatest days of the cowboy had already passed.

Although *A Texas Cow Boy* reportedly sold well and Will Rogers would later write in a letter to Siringo that the book "was the Cowboy's Bible when I was growing up," Siringo does not seem to have considered taking up writing full time following the publication of his first book. After giving up his store in Caldwell in 1886, Siringo and his young wife turned up in Chicago just in time for the Haymarket bombing—an incident that turned Siringo into a lifelong opponent of anarchism. Shortly after the bombing, Siringo went to work for the Pinkerton Detective Agency, taking as his first assignment the job of watching the jury during the trial of the Haymarket defendants. He claimed that he became interested in detective work after a blind phrenologist in Caldwell told him he would make a good detective. His previous experience chasing cattle thieves in New Mexico, along with a letter of recommendation from Pat Garrett, helped him obtain his job with the Pinkerton Agency.

Siringo did most of his detective work in the West, where he frequently investigated cases involving rustling, train robbery, mine salting, and, most notoriously, union activism. Although he prided himself on being a good detective, his methods were more akin to spying than true detective work. Typically, he posed as an ordinary cowboy or miner, befriended suspected criminals, and stayed with them until they confided to him enough information to win a conviction. In one case Siringo traveled with a suspect for seven months before the man finally admitted his role in a dynamiting case, and during his time in the Coeur d'Alene mining district in 1891–1892 Siringo so successfully infiltrated the miners' union that he was elected recording secretary of the organization. After federal troops and state militia suppressed the Coeur d'Alene miners,

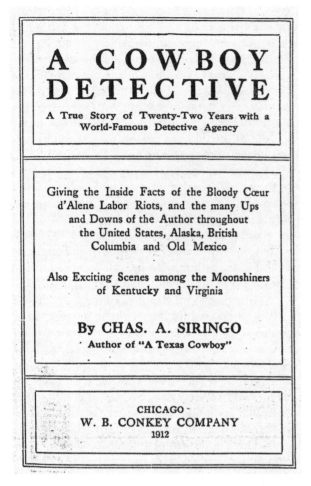

A COWBOY DETECTIVE

A True Story of Twenty-Two Years with a
World-Famous Detective Agency

Giving the Inside Facts of the Bloody Cœur
d'Alene Labor Riots, and the many Ups
and Downs of the Author throughout
the United States, Alaska, British
Columbia and Old Mexico

Also Exciting Scenes among the Moonshiners
of Kentucky and Virginia

By CHAS. A. SIRINGO
Author of "A Texas Cowboy"

CHICAGO
W. B. CONKEY COMPANY
1912

Title page for Siringo's account of his experiences as a Pinkerton agent in Chicago and the West during the years 1886–1907

Siringo's testimony led to the conviction of eighteen union leaders.

In 1907, after more than twenty years as a Pinkerton agent, Siringo went into semiretirement on his homestead ranch near Santa Fe, New Mexico, taking occasional freelance detective jobs and again trying his hand at writing. The first fruit of this period was *A Cowboy Detective* (1912) in which Siringo gave his detective career much the same treatment he gave his cowboy career in his first book. In typical Siringo fashion *A Cowboy Detective* jumps from incident to incident, and the prose reads as if Siringo has rigorously followed the literary philosophy described in his preface: "The author is not a literary man, but has written as he speaks, and it is thought that the simplicity thus resulting will not detract from the substantial merit of the tales, which are recitals of facts and not of fiction."

Siringo's mention of reporting facts instead of fiction is worth noting, coming as it does after his admission just a few sentences before that in *A Cow-*

boy Detective he used "fictitious names in many places." The reason for these substitutions of fiction for fact was the Pinkerton Detective Agency, which argued that by using real names its former employee was giving away agency secrets. A Chicago judge sided with the powerful detective agency, enjoining Siringo from giving away Pinkerton Agency secrets and from using his original title: "Pinkerton's Cowboy Detective, A True Story of Twenty-two Years with Pinkerton's National Detective Agency." Thus in *A Cowboy Detective* the Pinkerton Detective Agency becomes the "Dickenson Detective Agency," Pinkerton superintendent James McParland (a former rank-and-file Pinkerton detective whose testimony led to the hanging of thirteen Molly Maguires) becomes "James McCartney," and the notorious Pinkerton operative and hired killer Tom Horn becomes "Tim Corn."

Such thin disguises fooled no one, but the arrangement mollified the Pinkerton Detective Agency enough to allow Siringo to publish *A Cowboy Detective*. Siringo, however, lost money because of the agency's actions against *A Cowboy Detective*. In 1915, motivated by his hot temper and a desire for revenge, Siringo published the pamphlet *Two Evil Isms, Pinkertonism and Anarchism*. Where *A Cowboy Detective* had been generally friendly toward the "Dickenson Agency," *Two Evil Isms* was a two-fisted attack on the Pinkertons. In the 109-page book, which does not use pseudonyms and says almost nothing about anarchism, Siringo accuses the Pinkerton Agency of a host of crimes, including overbilling clients, bribery, and kidnapping. Just before publication Siringo sent a copy of the manuscript of *Two Evil Isms* to Pinkerton's New York office, including with it a taunting letter that may have been an attempt to blackmail the detective agency. The Pinkerton Agency responded to Siringo's taunt by going to court to stop publication and distribution of *Two Evil Isms*. Armed with a court order, Pinkerton agents seized all unsold copies of the book as well as the plates from which the book had been printed, actions that resulted in a severe financial loss to Siringo. As a crowning insult, the agency nearly managed to get their former employee extradited from New Mexico to Illinois, where he would have had to stand trial on libel and contempt-of-court charges. Had it not been for New Mexico governor William C. McDonald, who refused to extradite his old crony, Siringo almost certainly would have ended up behind bars in Illinois.

The foolhardiness of his actions aside, Siringo's about-face change in attitude toward the Pinkerton Agency shows that his claim to be a simple reporter of "facts not fiction" is a dubious one. Indeed, the strikingly different treatments of the Pinkerton Agency in *A Cowboy Detective* and *Two Evil Isms* bring up the question of just how much truth there is in any of Siringo's writing. Certainly the main facts of his life as he presents them are true: he was a Texas cowboy, and he did work as a detective for the Pinkerton Agency. But what about the many intriguing particulars for which Siringo himself is the only source of information? Did he really befriend Billy the Kid in 1878, or did he fabricate this brush with infamy in order to capitalize on the legendary outlaw's national appeal? Did his pursuit of the outlaw Kid Curry really cover twenty-five thousand miles, much of it on horseback? Did Siringo really remain the honest detective he claimed to have been when, by his own report, accepting kickbacks and framing suspects were standard operating procedures for Pinkerton detectives?

It is certain that Siringo lied, or at least greatly exaggerated, some of the time. But his writing comes across as so honest that most readers, including Siringo scholars, are willing to take the bulk of what he reports at face value. No less a scholar of the West than J. Frank Dobie wrote of Siringo, "His cowboys and gunmen were not of Hollywood and folklore. He was an honest reporter." Part of what made Dobie, and many others, so willing to believe Siringo is his apparent readiness to admit to his own faults—or to admit selected faults. Siringo freely admitted being a fool when it came to gambling, writing often of how he lost his own money (and, on occasion, money that was not his own) at monte and other games of chance. Similarly, he admitted being an easy mark in Chicago, where bootblacks and city sharpers quickly separated the distinctively dressed cowboy from his hard-earned money. Siringo wrote of so many personal shortcomings—failing to win the hand of a sweetheart, abandoning his plans to become a trapper after only two disastrous days of trying, letting his horse get away from him in the middle of a waterless desert—that readers are lulled into believing that any writer who is so forthcoming about himself, who is so reluctant to portray himself as a perfect cowboy hero, must be honest.

Counterbalancing this apparent honesty, though, are those failings of character Siringo chose not to mention. He says almost nothing of his three brief, failed attempts at marriage following the death of his first wife, Mamie, in 1889. (He married Lillie Thomas in 1893, a woman named Grace in 1907, and Ellen Partain in 1913.) Viola Siringo Reid, his daughter by Mamie, gets only brief mention in any of Siringo's books, while William Lee Roy Siringo, his son by Lillie, gets none at all. Significantly, in none of his books does Siringo admit

that he killed another human being despite describing many brushes with violence and making frequent references to his ever-present Colt pistol. In *Charles A. Siringo: A Texas Picaro* (1967) Charles D. Peavey has identified two sources that suggest that Siringo did kill.

Siringo's wavering between honesty and deception is perfectly in character for a man whose life is a study in contradictions. Siringo spent much of his life chasing rustlers; yet as a young cowboy he unabashedly killed other men's cattle for beef and engaged in mavericking activities that were tantamount to rustling. He helped break unions; yet he swore that he sympathized with the men who joined them. He admitted that he regularly drank and caroused with dance-hall girls as part of his detective duties; yet he claimed to be a loving husband to Mamie. Taken all together, the contradictions that make up Siringo's life show that the West itself was not the land of clearly defined right and wrong—of white hats and black hats—that is described by popular history. Perhaps the most striking illustration of this point is the fact that William C. "Outlaw Bill" Moore, the LX Ranch foreman who sent Siringo after the cattle stolen by Billy the Kid, was himself rustling cattle from the LX Ranch. On top of that, Siringo admitted that while pursuing the stolen cattle, "The grub we ate wasn't very expensive as we stole all of our meat, and shared with our honest neighbors who thought it a great sin to kill other people's cattle." Following the *Two Evil Isms* fiasco, Siringo accepted a position as a ranger for the Cattle Sanitary Board of New Mexico. The job, personally arranged by Governor McDonald, was a godsend because Siringo needed the money, loved working on horseback, and was reluctant to accept detective work that would take him out of New Mexico and into states where he still faced the possibility of extradition. Siringo tried writing again while working as a ranger; and in 1918, when the Cattle Sanitary Board ran out of money to pay its rangers, he turned his full attention to writing in hopes that a successful book could pull him out of the financial woes into which he had fallen. Among other debts, Siringo owed money to printing firms and had several times mortgaged Sunny Slope, the Santa Fe area ranch he had homesteaded in 1891.

Having the book printed at a Santa Fe print shop, Siringo published *A Lone Star Cowboy* (1919), a pale reworking of *A Texas Cow Boy,* which had gone out of copyright. In the same year he also published *The Song Companion of A Lone Star Cowboy,* a mediocre collection of cowboy songs. During this same period Siringo claimed to be working on a novel called "Prairie Flower, or Bronco Chiquita." This novel

Cover for the pamphlet Siringo wrote after the Pinkerton Detective Agency went to court to prevent Siringo from using its name and the names of its employees in A Cowboy Detective (courtesy of the Lilly Library, Indiana University)

was never published, however, and apparently no manuscript of it exists. The last product of Siringo's final stay in New Mexico was *History of "Billy the Kid"* (1920), a small paperback that had nothing new to say about the most written-about outlaw in the history of the West. Like the two books that preceded it, *History of "Billy the Kid"* served only to drive Siringo deeper into debt.

In 1922, sick, old, and broke, Siringo left Santa Fe for southern California. He chose this location in part because his daughter, Viola, was living in San Diego, but the area also drew him because it was the movie capital of the world. Siringo was a movie buff and may have had hopes of cashing in on the movie craze by becoming a successful screenwriter. He had once written a fan letter to his favorite actor, western star William S. Hart. Hart had replied with a letter praising Siringo's books—evidence that Siringo helped to shape the movie image of the cowboy. Hart's letter so pleased Siringo that he had it printed on the back of his business cards as an advertisement. Whatever his real motivations for leaving

New Mexico may have been, his health improved soon after he arrived in southern California, and before long he was living in "Siringo's Den," a cabin located behind the home of a Hollywood friend. Siringo often walked the few blocks from his den to the Water Hole Saloon, a hangout for extras in western movies. Siringo became something of a celebrity during the Hollywood phase of his life. He got bits of work as an extra in westerns, was befriended by Hart, Will Rogers, Charles M. Russell, Eugene Manlove Rhodes, Edward L. Doheny, and other local notables interested in the Old West, and got to see himself written up in the *Los Angeles Times, Scribner's,* and *Sunset.* The *Sunset* article, written by Rhodes, describes the seventy-two-year-old Siringo as "Quick to retort; shrewd wit–and a chuckle. Much more than 'a cowboy type.'" Perhaps the most valuable friendship Siringo struck up in Hollywood was with the writer Henry Herbert Knibbs, who managed to get his publisher, Houghton Mifflin, interested in Siringo. Houghton Mifflin rejected "Bad Man Cowboys of the Early West," a manuscript Siringo had worked on in Hollywood, but they expressed interest in a book that would bring together his cowboy detective experiences. The result was *Riata and Spurs,* Siringo's last book and his only book to be published by a major press during his lifetime. The hand of an experienced, professional editor is evident in *Riata and Spurs,* which is written in relatively polished prose with regularized spelling. The plotting is carefully constructed, and details are added to fill out incidents. While it is possible that some of Siringo's colorful language was lost in the editing process, *Riata and Spurs* is probably Siringo's most readable book and the best introduction to Siringo for the contemporary reader, covering as it does the highlights of both *A Texas Cow Boy* and *A Cowboy Detective.*

Riata and Spurs started out to be the crowning success of Siringo's writing career. Gifford Pinchot, former chief of the U.S. Forest Service and a friend from Siringo's Idaho days, wrote the introduction. Will Rogers wrote Siringo a warm letter praising the book, and Houghton Mifflin placed excerpts from this letter in prominent spots on the jacket of the book. On the first day of publication a better-than-expected thirty-five hunded copies were sold, and the initial reviews, including one by J. Frank Dobie in *The Nation* (13 July 1927), were kind to *Riata and Spurs.* Then the Pinkerton Detective Agency stepped in to revive the all-but-forgotten injunction handed down by a Chicago court more than ten years earlier. Houghton Mifflin, eager to bring out a second edition, tried to negotiate, but the Pinkerton Agency insisted that the injunction be followed to the letter.

In the end every section of *Riata and Spurs* that dealt with Siringo's detective experiences was dropped and replaced with material from "Bad Man Cowboys of the Early West." Even the subtitle of the book had to be changed from *The Story of a Lifetime Spent in the Saddle as Cowboy and Detective* to *The Story of a Lifetime Spent in the Saddle as Cowboy and Ranger.* The Pinkerton Agency had won again, this time depriving a sick, impoverished old man of his last chance for a comfortable old age. Because of the changes forced by the Pinkerton Agency, Siringo got no royalties at all from the first edition. He had been hoping to receive a dollar for each copy sold.

The second edition of *Riata and Spurs* eventually sold well enough to turn a profit in spite of all the revisions, but Siringo never saw much money for his work. Following *Riata and Spurs* he tried, unsuccessfully, to interest Houghton Mifflin in "Prairie Flower, or Bronco Chiquita," but the publishing house rejected the manuscript. Siringo also tried his hand at writing for western-story magazines, again without much luck. On 18 October 1928 Charlie Siringo died at his son's home in Altadena, California. He was seventy-three.

Riata and Spurs continued to sell respectably after Siringo's death, and Houghton Mifflin reprinted it in 1931. All of Siringo's major works, including *Two Evil Isms,* have been republished over the years and are available to readers with access to a good-sized public or academic library. Siringo's colorful accounts of his remarkable, era-spanning life have helped to shape the way we think cowboys, both real and fictional, should be.

References:

J. Frank Dobie, "Charlie Siringo, Writer and Man," introduction to *A Texas Cowboy* (New York: Sloane, 1950);

John Hays Hammond, "Strong Men of the Wild West," *Scribner's Magazine,* 77 (February–March 1925): 215–225, 246–256;

Charles D. Peavy, *Charles A. Siringo: A Texas Picaro* (Austin, Tex.: Steck-Vaughn, 1967);

Ben E. Pingenot, *Siringo: The True Story of Charles A. Siringo* (College Station: Texas A&M University Press, 1989);

Eugene Manlove Rhodes, "He'll Make a Hand," *Sunset,* 63 (June 1927): 23, 89–91;

Orlan Sawey, *Charles A. Siringo* (Boston: Twayne, 1981);

Sawey, "Charlie Siringo: Reluctant Propagandist," *Western American Literature,* 7 (Fall 1972): 203–210.

Charles Warren Stoddard
(7 August 1843 – 23 April 1909)

M. E. Grenander
State University of New York at Albany

BOOKS: *Poems* (San Francisco: Anton Roman, 1867; London: Trübner, 1867);

South-Sea Idyls (Boston: James R. Osgood, 1873; republished as *Summer Cruising in the South Seas,* London: Chatto & Windus, 1874; second revised American edition, New York: Scribners, 1892);

Mashallah! A Flight into Egypt (New York: Appleton, 1881);

A Trip to Hawaii (San Francisco: Oceanic Steamship Co., 1885);

A Troubled Heart and How It Was Comforted at Last (Notre Dame, Ind.: J. A. Lyons, 1885);

The Lepers of Molokai (Notre Dame, Indiana: Ave Maria Press, 1886);

Hawaiian Life: Being Lazy Letters from Low Latitudes (Chicago & New York: F. T. Neely, 1894);

The Wonder-Worker of Padua (Notre Dame, Ind.: Ave Maria Press, 1896);

A Cruise Under the Crescent: From Suez to San Marco (Chicago & New York: Rand McNally, 1898);

Over the Rocky Mountains to Alaska (Saint Louis: B. Herder, 1899);

Father Damien: The Martyr of Molokai (San Francisco: Catholic Truth Society, 1901);

In the Footprints of the Padres (San Francisco: A. M. Robertson, 1902; revised edition, San Francisco: A. M. Robertson, 1911);

Exits and Entrances: A Book of Essays and Sketches (Boston: Lothrop, 1903);

For the Pleasure of His Company: An Affair of the Misty City, Thrice Told (San Francisco: A. M. Robertson, 1903);

The Island of Tranquil Delights: A South Sea Idyl and Others (Boston: Herbert B. Turner, 1904; London: Chatto & Windus, 1905);

Apostrophe to the Skylark; The Bells of San Gabriel; Joe of Lahaina; Father Damien Among His Lepers; An Appreciation of Charles Warren Stoddard, by George Wharton James (Los Angeles: Arroyo Guild Press, 1909);

Poems of Charles Warren Stoddard, compiled by Ina Coolbrith and Thomas Walsh (New York: John Lane, 1917);

Charles Warren Stoddard's Diary of a Visit to Molokai in 1884, introduction by Oscar Lewis (San Francisco: Book Club of California, 1933);

Cruising the South Seas: Stories by Charles Warren Stoddard, edited by Winston Leyland (San Francisco: Gay Sunshine Press, 1987).

In 1977 Robert L. Gale published a précis on Charles Warren Stoddard. It is an admirable, brief account of his works and life except for its avoidance of the issue of his homosexuality. Among the critics who noted this omission was Roger Austen, who set about to remedy the lacuna, first in a 1983 article in the *Journal of Homosexuality* and then in a book, *Genteel Pagan: The Double Life of Charles Warren Stoddard* (1991), edited by John W. Crowley after Austen's death. Gay and lesbian studies were newly fashionable in literary criticism, and Austen's article was followed by other studies of Stoddard in the same vein. Unfortunately, however, in recognizing his historical place in the literary development of homosexuality, these writers have not merely overlooked but have even denigrated his genuine artistic achievements. Austen goes to the extreme of downplaying Stoddard's literary value for the sake of emphasizing his homosexuality, stating that on the basis of his writing he does not "warrant a full-length critical biography" and that "many of his books are admittedly second-rate." Such judgments swing too far in the opposite direction from Gale. Stoddard may now be an accepted figure among specialists in gay studies, but he was also a prolific writer whose talent was recognized by such figures as Robert Louis Stevenson, Ambrose Bierce, Mark Twain, and William Dean Howells. Consequently, Gale's emphasis on the literary value of his work needs to be reintroduced and emphasized. Stoddard's sexual proclivities are important in understanding his work, but it is, after all, precisely because of that work that they take on significance.

Charles Warren Stoddard, whose family tree included both Jonathan Edwards and Aaron Burr, was born 7 August 1843 in Rochester, New York. Shy, withdrawn, and apprehensive, he spent his childhood and youth in upstate New York except for two significant years in the rowdy but cosmopolitan and colorful San Francisco of 1855–1856, where his father had found a job with a shipping firm. In 1857, however, he was sent back east with an ailing brother. He settled in with his harshly pious maternal grandparents on a farm in western New York, where he decorated his attic room with oriental objets d'art he had brought back from San Francisco. The bleakness of his life on the farm was relieved, however, by a visit to his paternal grandfather, Dr. Abijah Stoddard, a well-to-do physician and worldly Unitarian. Stoddard was sent to a boarding school where he acquired a succession of friends different in physique from himself, of a type to which he remained drawn all his life.

At the age of fifteen Stoddard, sent for by his father, returned to San Francisco, determined to become a poet. From this point on he regarded northern California as his home, always returning there from the extensive travels he undertook to get material for his articles and books, and finally settling there to die.

San Francisco had grown more sophisticated during his first absence, and by the 1860s literary life there was flourishing. Under the pseudonym "Pip Pepperpod" he began to contribute poems to the *Golden Era*. He also made several unsuccessful efforts to continue his education. His sexual attitudes were generally recognized and accepted by his friends, but most nineteenth-century Americans lacked the terms to define them. Young homosexuals of that era consequently often felt that they were alone in their predilections and thought of themselves in idiosyncratic terms.

Although he was clearly homoerotic in his emotional attachments, Stoddard was no misogynist, and all his life had close women friends. His most enduring female attachment was to a woman near his own age whom he met at this time, fellow poet Ina Coolbrith. In 1863 she and Stoddard, together with Bret Harte, formed a trio of writers known as the "Golden Gate Trinity."

In 1864, plagued by ill health, Stoddard traveled to Hawaii on medical advice. During his six-month stay there he was drawn to a handsome native boy, Kane-Aloha, with whom he apparently had his first affair. This relationship, which he was later to describe in *The Island of Tranquil Delights: A South Sea Idyl and Others* (1904), marked the inception of his interest in the brown-skinned youths he called "barbarians," to whose "instinctual" life his own instincts could respond with delight.

When he returned to San Francisco, however, his conduct was more restrained, and he assumed the role of an effeminate piano-playing dandy, a pose marred only by his increasing tendency to get drunk. Another trait which had manifested itself even in his childhood, and which was to cause him trouble all his life, was his total inability to exercise self-discipline. This failing went far beyond simple laziness. His attempts to conform to a regular schedule invariably brought about a nervous collapse and prevented him, despite his bookishness, from completing any kind of formal schooling. Thus, he never learned to spell, punctuate, control his syntax, or even write legibly. His abortive career as an actor, a vocation

Stoddard as a young man

for which his melodious voice and skill at role-playing made him particularly well suited, also foundered on his failure to conform to the rigid professional demands of the theater. But his talents as a good listener and fondness for the bottle contributed to his popularity with a variety of friends, including Ambrose Bierce, Mark Twain, and, in 1870, Joaquin Miller.

Stoddard had been contributing verses to a new journal, the *Californian,* and in 1867, aided by Harte, he brought out his first book, *Poems.* Published by Anton Roman, sumptuously illustrated, elegantly bound, and stamped in gold, it was, despite its derivative contents, "the first example of fine book making to be produced in California," according to biographer Carl Stroven. The same year, hungering for the sheltering warmth of a forgiving religious institution, Stoddard converted to Catholicism, drawn by its welcoming priests and the elaborate ritual that satisfied aesthetic needs in his temperament.

In 1868 Stoddard's sister, who had married a wealthy Hawaiian planter's son, invited him to visit her, and he sailed once again for Honolulu, this time with a roving commission to write a series of Hawaiian travel letters for the *San Francisco Evening Bulletin.* In July 1869, after eight months in the island kingdom, he returned to San Francisco, writing sketches of the Hawaiian youths he had met for the newly founded *Overland Monthly* as well as a weekly column for the *Golden Era* in which he posed as a languid boulevardier. Then in the spring of 1870 he departed again for the South Seas, sailing for Tahiti (to be described in *The Island of Tranquil Delights*) on a French vessel with a gay crew. Although Stoddard enjoyed his travels, his money ran out, and in less than three months he returned to San Francisco penniless.

By 1870 most of his California friends had left for the East or for England. He himself posed once more as a genteel aesthete and joined the Bohemian Club, which in its early days lived up to its title, not yet having become the wealthy and powerful group it is today. He made another trip to Hawaii in early 1872, returning to San Francisco a few months later. His trips to the Pacific Islands had given him material for his most famous book, *South-Sea Idyls,* published in 1873 by James R. Osgood of Boston through the intercession of Harte and Howells. Stoddard then prepared to sail for Europe, lured by the circle of West Coast expatriates who were already there and financed by a roving commission from the *San Francisco Chronicle.*

Stoddard's transatlantic sojourn from 1873 to 1877 was radically different from his visits to the South Seas. He moved in highly sophisticated circles, and he was meeting San Francisco friends who were already in Europe. The 1870s were a decade when Americans residing in England enjoyed some celebrity, in part because of the romantic appeal the American West held for Britons. Stoddard, one of the most gregarious of the group, joined Twain, Bierce, Miller, and Prentice Mulford. But his lavender elegance was at the opposite end of the spectrum from the Wild West stereotype Miller's roughneck persona was carrying to ridiculous extremes.

Stoddard engaged in more-or-less settled affairs with men his own age who were usually, like himself, recognized artists in one medium or another. But he was taking risks that did not exist in either California or the South Seas. The Americans seem not to have clearly understood the sexual component of the gay orientation. The British, however, did not share the indulgent tolerance of homosexuality that was prevalent in California. In their view it was a crime, as Bierce had discovered to his amazement. When he learned that Stoddard was coming to England, he wrote a letter on 28 August 1873 (now at the Huntington Library) advising that Stoddard should visit him before proceeding in London. But Bierce was in Paris when Stoddard arrived; so he left him another letter on 28 September 1873, warning him: "You will, by the way, be under a microscope here; your lightest word and most careless action noted down, and commented on by men who cannot understand how a person of individuality in thought or conduct can be other than a very bad man." Bierce told Stoddard to "Walk, therefore, circumspectly" and "avoid any appearance of eccentricity."

Shortly after Stoddard's arrival, Mark Twain, who was lecturing in England to great acclaim, hired him in November-December 1873 as a secretary-companion with merely nominal duties. After Twain left London, Stoddard moved in with a group of young men who were probably homosexuals and with whom, as Austen says, he "proceeded to violate all of Bierce's canons for good behavior," although he managed to avoid arrest.

During this period Chatto and Windus published a British edition of *South-Sea Idyls* under the title *Summer Cruising in the South Seas* (1874). Stoddard then visited Miller in Rome and had two audiences with Pope Pius IX. In Italy he moved in brilliant social circles, both secular and ecclesiastical, and published his accounts of life abroad not only in the *San Francisco Chronicle* but also in the *Overland Monthly*.

After his recovery from a broken (and permanently stiff) arm suffered in a horseback-riding accident, he traveled about Italy, settling finally in Venice with Civil War drummer boy and Harvard Phi Beta Kappa Francis Davis Millet, an artist-writer who later perished on the *Titanic*. Stoddard then left Italy, touring Great Britain and western Europe. In the fall of 1875 he wrote from Munich that he had been to hear Richard Wagner's "magnificently produced" operas. Stroven quotes Stoddard's comment that in the eyes of King Ludwig II, Wagner is "little less than an archangel, so he gives him vast sums of money to produce his operas in the best style." During Stoddard's stay in Munich the young California artist Joseph Strong painted his portrait, bearded and dressed as a monk to symbolize his recurring desire to renounce the world for a life devoted to the Church.

Finally, early in 1876, he sailed for the Middle East, subsequently returning to Europe and then to the United States in August 1877. Eventually he was to describe various aspects of his life abroad in *Mashallah! A Flight into Egypt* (1881), *A Cruise Under*

the Crescent: From Suez to San Marco* (1898), and *Exits and Entrances: A Book of Essays and Sketches* (1903).

After a sojourn in the East, Stoddard came back to San Francisco. He was by this time a heavy-set man with an assured manner, bald and bearded, yet still elegant and handsome. He was delightful, witty, and popular, although he and Bierce, who was disenchanted with homosexuality, grew estranged. Stoddard became a friend of Robert Louis Stevenson, whose interest he aroused in the South Sea Islands. Stevenson characterized him in the novel *The Wrecker* (1892) as a "youngish, good-looking, fellow, . . . lively and engaging." Stoddard's apartment, according to Stevenson, was "a museum of strange objects . . . evidences and examples of another earth, another climate, another race, and another (if a ruder) culture." Stevenson reported that in their conversations he "first heard the names—first fell under the spell—of the islands." Even more important for Stevenson was his marriage to a mutual friend of theirs, Mrs. Fanny Osbourne.

In addition to relaxing at the Bohemian Club, Stoddard also engaged in a series of attachments with much younger men, each of whom he referred to as his "Kid." But he was in financial difficulty, and his life seemed aimless. When an unexpected offer came to write editorials for a Honolulu paper, he gladly returned to Hawaii. His life there, however, was equally pointless, enlivened only with a frequently frustrating affair with another "Kid," a three-month visit to San Francisco, and the publication of *Mashallah!* and *A Trip to Hawaii* (1885). Hence he accepted, with some misgivings, an invitation to teach English and American literature at the University of Notre Dame.

His stay at Notre Dame for a year and a half beginning in 1885 was, despite an auspicious beginning, troubled. Although his classes were lively and popular, they were disorganized and undisciplined. Worse, he was smitten by a succession of good-looking young students. The Catholic staff criticized him for his intimacies with them; and, incensed and suffering from malaria, he resigned. He did, however, publish two books during this period: *The Lepers of Molokai* (1886), which describes the heroic priests, including Father Damien, who cared for the sick on that island; and *A Troubled Heart and How It Was Comforted at Last* (1885), an account of his conversion to Catholicism that is regarded as one of his best books. Gale describes *A Troubled Heart* as one chapter in Stoddard's planned autobiography which, if completed, "might well have reached greatness." Stoddard had also taken a summer trip to Alaska with the physical-science instructor at the university

Frontispiece and title page for Stoddard's 1902 book, in which he recalls his youth in northern California

that furnished him material for what was to become *Over the Rocky Mountains to Alaska* (1899).

After leaving Notre Dame, Stoddard moved to Kentucky, staying with the family of the youth with whom he had had his most serious affair, Tom Cleary. Early in 1888 he traveled to New England, at long last meeting Howells. He then made another trip to Europe with a Mrs. Theodore Vail and her son. In Rome in 1889 he met Bishop John J. Keane, who had just been named rector of the newly established Catholic University of America in Washington, D.C. Keane offered him the chair of English literature there, which he accepted. Assured that this post would be more to his liking than the one he had held at Notre Dame, he returned to the Clearys' home to begin work on his lectures.

Stoddard taught at the Catholic University for thirteen years, and a scroll on his tombstone in the Catholic Cemetery in Monterey, California, is inscribed "TO THE MEMORY OF CHARLES WARREN STODDARD, A TOKEN OF AFFEC-

TION, REGARD AND ESTEEM FROM THE FACULTY, AND PUPILS, OF THE CATHOLIC UNIVERSITY OF AMERICA." His early tenure, beginning in 1889, was on the whole successful. He had a suite of rooms on the campus furnished with his exotica; his lectures were successful and occasionally applauded; and in 1892 he published a new edition of *South-Sea Idyls* with high praise from Howells. Socially, he moved among accomplished friends and acquaintances in Washington, including Henry Adams. He traveled extensively during his free time, and an old San Francisco friend, Theodore Dwight, head of the Boston Public Library, introduced him to homosexual circles in Boston. But Stoddard yearned for such contracts in Washington. His students there, already priests, were reserved in their personal contacts with him.

Then Stoddard fell in love with Kenneth O'Connor, a fifteen-year-old tough. Playing the role of a devoted foster father, Stoddard moved from his university quarters into a house in Washington, hired a servant, and settled down in 1895 to what he anticipated would be a life of idyllic happiness. However, O'Connor's drinking and his demands for money broke up the relationship. Strangely, Stoddard's colleagues at Catholic University and his friends in town seemed undisturbed by his relationship with O'Connor. They regarded it as the paternalistic rescue of a wayward youth from an unhappy home.

More serious for Stoddard was the deterioration of his professional life at the Catholic University. Bishop Keane was replaced as rector by Dr. Thomas Conaty, and another faculty member, Maurice Francis Egan, was hired in 1895 to teach English. Nominally outranked by Stoddard, he was much better qualified and began to draw Stoddard's students away. Meanwhile Stoddard, troubled by poor health, was frequently absent from classes and faculty meetings. Although he continued to be regarded with affection by his fellow faculty members, they nevertheless decided to ask for his resignation. When Conaty gave him the news, his reaction was relief at deliverance from duties he had come to regard as onerous. In the summer of 1902 they came to an end. He could, of course, no longer afford to maintain a house of his own and was taken in for an unhappy year by the O'Connor family.

In his literary life during this period Stoddard was a "chronicler of bygone days," as Austen says, summarizing his output as follows: "a new edition of *The Lepers of Molokai* in 1893," a "cheap paperback edition" of *Hawaiian Life, Being Lazy Letters from Low Latitudes* (1894), and a "life of his beloved Saint Anthony," *The Wonder-Worker of Padua* (1896). Austen continues, "*A Cruise Under the Crescent* (1898) recalled his trip to Egypt and the Holy Land. *Over the Rocky Mountains to Alaska* (1899) was based on the summer he spent in the Northwest during his unhappy Notre Dame period. *In the Footprints of the Padres* (1902) contained youthful memories of colorful spots in Northern California."

Gale singles *Footprints* out for special praise, particularly the essay "A Bit of Old China," describing Chinatown in San Francisco. The book as a whole is well organized, beginning with an autobiographical account of Stoddard as a San Francisco teenager and then moving through space and time, facts and fantasies, to conclude with the fictive Paul Clitheroe, who reappears in *For the Pleasure of His Company: An Affair of the Misty City, Thrice Told* (1903). According to Gale, *Footprints* comprises much of Stoddard's best writing, revealing his mastery of "painterly prose" and sure selection of details.

Exits and Entrances, as Austen continues, "interwove personality sketches (of Harte, Twain,

and Stevenson) with picturesque travelogue. *A Troubled Heart* was republished in 1900." The big publishing event in Stoddard's life during this period, however, was the appearance, at long last, of *For the Pleasure of His Company,* the strange novel that Rudyard Kipling had been urging him for years to complete; it finally came out in 1903. Thomas Yingling calls its protagonist, Paul Clitheroe, "arguably the first gay character in American fiction." Stoddard annotated George Wharton James's copy, identifying real-life models for its characters and events. When he discovered that many of the individuals portrayed, including Ina Coolbrith, were less than happy with the way they had been represented, he became embarrassed that he had ever allowed the book to appear in print. But as Austen points out, "the real cause for shame was not that he had written a roman à clef, but that he had written it so badly."

From 1902 on, Stoddard suffered increasingly from bouts of ill health that occasionally necessitated his hospitalization. In the spring of 1903 he left Washington permanently and traveled north, depending on the hospitality of friends for extended periods, including two years in Cambridge, Massachusetts. After recovering from a particularly serious illness he felt rejuvenated, and with commissions for periodical essays, a monthly $50 annuity from a well-to-do friend named Maria Longworth Storer, and the publication in 1904 of *The Island of Tranquil Delights,* he returned to San Francisco, arriving in April 1905. The Bohemian Club honored him at a dinner on 13 April. Although Henry James was also a guest, it was Stoddard who was feted as "the master." Austen raises the possibility that James may have attended under the misapprehension that he was to be the guest of honor.

Stoddard then traveled up and down the coast and stayed with various friends, including Miller, thereby escaping the devastating San Francisco earthquake of 18 April 1906, before he finally settled in Monterey. Meanwhile, he began directing his affections toward fellow writers, notably George Sterling and Jack London. Sterling, referring to a picture of himself with Miller and Stoddard in the February 1906 *Sunset* magazine, noted that they were all drunk, and added that "Stoddard is 'all in,' and becomes maudlin after one drink; also takes on an affectionate manner toward others of his own sex that is open to surmise." Somewhat taken aback when Stoddard addressed him in a poem as a "faun" whose body was a "beaker of wine," Sterling wrote Bierce on 18 September 1907 that "the old devil will wind up by 'compromising' me." The more sophisticated London, however, to whom Stoddard was drawn even more strongly than to Sterling, responded warmly, though mainly by correspondence.

But the fat and elderly Stoddard, who had been a heavy drinker all of his adult life, was growing weaker as his health continued to deteriorate. His heart was giving out under the strain, and it finally failed him on 23 April 1909. Sterling wrote Bierce on 6 July: "I guess the old man was glad to die, for he had hardly a sound organ in his body. What really killed him was alcohol—he couldn't leave it alone and so give his heart a rest; and so his heart finally 'lay down on the job.'" Both Sterling and Miller were pallbearers at his funeral, which Ina Coolbrith attended, "a sibyl of stone" leaning on her stick.

Like the autobiographical Paul Clitheroe in *For the Pleasure of His Company,* whose friends tell him that he has narrowly escaped being a young woman, Stoddard had always had a feminine streak. After he died, Sterling characterized him as "a lonely old man, and the gentlest creature I ever knew—the woman's soul, it may be." A character in Kevin Starr's historical novel *Land's End* described him as "a very tormented man, . . . troubled by drink, art, sexuality, and religion—which come to think of it, are rather noble preoccupations."

The terminology of sexual orientation and even some of the concepts in use today were not current in Stoddard's time. Consequently, words such as *homosexual* and *gay* were not applied to him by his contemporaries, nor was the frequently vicious homophobia of today a factor then. Stoddard may have felt that he was misunderstood and unappreciated. He was not, however, treated with loathing and contempt despite his promiscuity and the fact that his strongest attachments were nearly always with susceptible adolescents. Critical attention was more properly reserved for his work.

Before Stoddard died his landlady burned many of his papers at his behest. But his old friend Coolbrith set about resurrecting his poems from the periodicals in which they had appeared over the years; in 1917, together with Thomas Walsh, she edited and published a selection of them. Of the fifty-five poems in this posthumous volume, only fourteen were reprinted from the forty-seven included in his 1867 *Poems.* Austen mistakenly identifies the co-editor as Father Thomas Walsh, who had been president of Notre Dame when Stoddard taught there. In fact, however, the co-editor was a journalist who, as a youth, had been a great admirer of Stoddard's work. Walsh met Stoddard in 1897 and described him as having been at that time "a

stout man, somewhat past middle age; handsome in a weary, passé way; short of wind and inactive."

It is instructive to compare Stoddard with Henry James. As Austen points out:

> on the surface the two men did, in fact, resemble each other in striking ways. Exactly the same age, they were equally short and stout and balding, and both had remarkable blue eyes—James's were hard, piercing, and omniscient, while Stoddard's were soft, liquid, and beseeching. Above all, each man had the dignity and the stage presence of a personage; each projected the aura of an urbane, courtly, slightly fastidious grand old man of letters.

Furthermore, both were immensely popular, in frequent demand in rather exalted circles as guests for dinner, an evening's entertainment, or overnight visits, occasionally for extended periods. The reason for their popularity is not difficult to recognize: they were witty and entertaining. Why, then, was Stoddard unable to use his cultivated and distinguished contacts in his writing while James was able to transmute them into great art?

The difference lay in their study of their friends and acquaintances, which one is tempted to explain by the arcane Coleridgean concepts of "Fancy" and "Imagination." Stoddard had Fancy; he was an acute observer of superficial details, and he was a master of tropes with a remarkable flair for words. But he lacked the powerful shaping imagination that enabled James to construct complex personalities, both male and female, suggested by the merest hints he picked up from the people among whom he moved. The solipsistic Stoddard went through life wanting to be loved, and his self-regarding attitude permeated his writing. He was never able to grasp the outlines, much less understand the depths, of another human being. Everything he wrote about was refracted through the perspective of his own vision. Yet he was good at describing what he saw and how it affected him, and he was not lazy, although that charge was frequently leveled against him (sometimes, indeed, by himself). Although he had to labor at his own pace and could never tolerate an externally imposed schedule, no one could publish, as he did, more than nine hundred contributions to periodicals, in addition to fifteen books, without having worked hard and long. And if Stoddard was no James, he had a real, if minor, talent.

The best analysis of Stoddard's work is to be found in the brief study by Gale, who points out that Stoddard wandered over the globe, absorbing and describing impressions: green forests, purple mountains, and tropical fish "like prisms with fins" in the South Seas; the graphic horror of a leprous child on whose blackened skin lay "a kind of moss, or mould, gummy and glistening," whose "protruding eyeballs, now shapeless and broken, looked not unlike bursted grapes"; in Beirut, a garden flooded by moonlight "so green it looked as if it had been filtered though an emerald." Stoddard's elegiac descriptions of the Middle East convey, in Gale's words, "the ruined splendor of Egypt's ancient rulers and the hopelessness of its present-day swarming millions"; Stoddard noted that "all [Smyrna's] history is a handful of leaves that are scattered in the winds." In the American West he compared "flame-colored oaks and blood-spotted azaleas" to a "blazing candelabra" and fog to "the ghost of unshed showers—atomized dew"; a "thin ring of silver light" spreads from a fallen leaf in a lake of "stainless crystal."

As Gale says, Stoddard "deserves to be read more widely" for his descriptive powers and his humor. At times his poetry is quite moving, and he was "a stylist capable of rare charm." *Hawaiian Life* is "close to a minor classic," and his "beautiful depictions of life in Old California" and other faraway places should be preserved. It is more than probable that Gale's plea for greater attention to Stoddard is on the verge of being granted. One consequence of the increased scholarly and critical attention to gay and lesbian studies and "queer theory" will undoubtedly be an increasing focus on Stoddard, whose life and work represent a dazzling early example of the problems currently being encountered in this emerging field.

Letters:

Jay B. Hubbell, "George Henry Boker, Paul Hamilton Hayne, and Charles Warren Stoddard: Some Unpublished Letters," *American Literature,* 5 (May 1933): 146–165;

M. E. Grenander, "Ambrose Bierce and Charles Warren Stoddard: Some Unpublished Correspondence," *Huntington Library Quarterly,* 23 (May 1960): 261–292.

Bibliography:

Ray C. Longtin, *Three Writers of the Far West: A Reference Guide* (Boston: G. K. Hall, 1980).

Biographies:

Carl G. Stroven, "A Life of Charles Warren Stoddard," dissertation, Duke University, 1939;

Robert L. Gale, *Charles Warren Stoddard,* Western Writers Series, no. 30 (Boise, Idaho: Boise State University Press, 1977);

Roger Austen, *Genteel Pagan: The Double Life of Charles Warren Stoddard,* edited by John W. Crowley (Amherst: University of Massachusetts Press, 1991).

References:

Roger Austen, *Playing the Game: The Homosexual Novel in America* (New York: Bobbs-Merrill, 1977);

Austen, "Stoddard's Little Tricks in *South Sea Idyls,*" *Journal of Homosexuality,* 8 (Spring/Summer 1983): 73–83;

Mary Bell, "The Essayist of the West—Charles Warren Stoddard," *University of California Magazine,* 2 (November 1896): 272–287;

Pierre Beringer, "Charles Warren Stoddard," *Overland Monthly,* new series 43 (April 1904): 346;

Joseph A. Boone, "Vacation Cruises; or, The Homoerotics of Orientalism," *PMLA,* 110 (January 1995): 89–107.

John W. Crowley, "Howells, Stoddard, and the Illustrations for *Summer Cruising in the South Seas,*" *Gay Studies Newsletter,* 13 (November 1986): 23–25;

Crowley, "Howells, Stoddard, and Male Homosocial Attachment," in his *The Mask of Fiction: Essays on W. D. Howells* (Amherst: University of Massachusetts Press, 1989), pp. 56–82;

M. E. Grenander, "California's Albion: Mark Twain, Ambrose Bierce, Tom Hood, John Camden Hotten, and Andrew Chatto," *Papers of the Bibliographical Society of America,* 72 (Fourth Quarter 1978): 455–475;

Grenander, "A London Letter of Joaquin Miller to Ambrose Bierce," *Yale University Library Gazette,* 46 (October 1971): 109–116;

George Wharton James, "Charles Warren Stoddard," *National Magazine,* 34 (August 1911): 659–672;

James, "Charles Warren Stoddard—An American Appreciation," *Ave Maria,* 68 (22 May 1909): 650–656;

Jonathan Katz, ed., *Gay American History: Lesbians and Gay Men in the U.S.A.* (New York: Crowell, 1976);

Brian McGinty, "Charles Warren Stoddard: The Pleasure of His Company," *California Historical Quarterly,* 52 (Summer 1973): 153–169;

Francis O'Neill, "Stoddard, Psalmist of the South Seas," *Catholic World,* 105 (July 1917): 511–516;

Charles Phillips, "Charles Warren Stoddard," *Overland Monthly,* new series 51 (February 1908): 135–139;

Kevin Starr, *Americans and the California Dream, 1850–1915* (New York: Oxford University Press, 1973);

Starr, *Land's End* (New York: McGraw-Hill, 1979);

Robert Louis Stevenson and Lloyd Osbourne, *The Wrecker* (New York: Scribners, 1892);

Franklin Walker, *San Francisco's Literary Frontier* (New York: Knopf, 1939);

Thomas Walsh, "Notes on Charles Warren Stoddard," *Nation,* 115 (4 October 1922): 340;

Thomas Yingling, untitled review of 1987 editions of *For the Pleasure of His Company* and *Cruising the South Seas, American Literary Realism,* 21 (Spring 1989): 91–93.

Papers:
Stoddard's widely scattered papers are located at the University of San Francisco Library; Bancroft Library, University of California, Berkeley; University of Hawaii at Manoa Library; Bernice P. Bishop Museum, Honolulu, Hawaii; the Huntington Library, San Marino, California; University of Notre Dame Archives; Robert Louis Stevenson House, Monterey, California; Lilly Library, Indiana University; Clifton Waller Barrett Library, University of Virginia; Columbia University Library; Beinecke Library, Yale University; George Arents Research Library, Syracuse University; Brown University Library; Houghton Library, Harvard University; and Stanford University Libraries.

Frederick Jackson Turner
(14 November 1861 – 14 March 1932)

David M. Wrobel
Widener University

See also the Turner entry in *DLB 17: Twentieth-Century American Historians.*

BOOKS: *The Character and Influence of the Indian Trade in Wisconsin,* Johns Hopkins University Studies in Historical and Political Science, ninth series, no. 12–13 (Baltimore: Johns Hopkins Press, 1891);

The Significance of the Frontier in American History (Madison: State Historical Society of Wisconsin, 1894);

Rise of the New West, 1819–1829, volume 14 of *The American Nation: A History,* edited by Albert Bushnell Hart (New York: Harper, 1906);

List of References in History 17: History of the West (Cambridge, Mass.: Harvard University, 1911); republished as *List of References on the History of the West* (Cambridge, Mass.: Harvard University Press, 1913; revised, 1915); revised again by Turner and Frederick Merk (Cambridge, Mass.: Harvard University Press, 1922);

Guide to the Study and Reading of American History, revised and augmented edition, by Turner, Edward Channing, and Hart (Boston & London: Ginn, 1912);

The Frontier in American History (New York: Holt, 1920);

The Significance of Sections in American History (New York: Holt, 1932);

The United States, 1830–1850: The Nation and Its Sections, edited by Avery O. Craven, Merrill H. Crissey, and Max Farrand (New York: Holt, 1935);

The Early Writings of Frederick Jackson Turner (Madison: University of Wisconsin Press, 1938);

Frederick Jackson Turner's Legacy: Unpublished Writings in American History, edited by Wilbur Jacobs (San Marino, Cal.: Huntington Library, 1965);

Frontier and Section: Selected Essays of Frederick Jackson Turner, edited by Ray Allen Billington (Englewood Cliffs, N. J.: Prentice-Hall, 1961);

History, Frontier, and Section: Three Essays by Frederick Jackson Turner, edited by Martin Ridge (Albuquerque: University of New Mexico Press, 1993);

Frederick Jackson Turner, circa 1905

Rereading Frederick Jackson Turner: "The Significance of the Frontier in American History" and Other Essays, edited by John Mack Faragher (New York: Holt, 1994).

OTHER: "Geographical Interpretations of American History," *Journal of Geography,* 4 (January 1905): 34–37.

Frederick Jackson Turner was one of the most influential American western writers of the nineteenth century, and his name has become synonymous with the western frontier. While Owen Wister, Frederic Remington, John Muir, Theodore Roosevelt, Charles Marion Russell, and many other writers and artists were nurturing the public's fascination with the Old West, Turner was placing that region at the center of the American experience. His fame stems most directly from a single conference paper, "The Significance of the Frontier in American History," delivered in 1893. The "frontier thesis," as it is commonly known, transformed the field of American history; indeed, it became the single most influential and controversial essay by an American historian, generating a mountain of critiques and defenses. Its impact was so profound that the theme of frontier settlement became synonymous with western American history and with the history of the nation as a whole. Until the mid twentieth century, generations of Americans viewed the history of their nation through a Turnerian lens. As historian Martin Ridge has astutely noted, Turner's frontier thesis "more than any other piece of historical scholarship, most affected the American's self and institutional perceptions."

Yet irony surrounds the consideration of Turner as a nineteenth-century western writer. For one thing, the bulk of Turner's professional career falls within the twentieth century. In addition, Turner's "West" was the Middle West (more specifically the Old Northwest), not the Far West commonly associated with western imagery and mythology. What is more, Turner, first and foremost, viewed himself as a social scientist, not as a writer. Finally, as many scholars have observed, when it came to actual writing output, Turner was less a writer than a procrastinator, who literally overwhelmed himself with the weight of the evidence he amassed. Luckily for Turner and his family, his primary source of income was not book royalties; had it been, they would have suffered a rather meager existence.

Turner was born in Portage, Wisconsin, on 14 November 1861, the son of Andrew Jackson Turner and Mary Hanford Turner. By the time of Turner's childhood Portage was no longer an isolated frontier outpost; it was a growing town and a county seat. Still, this semirural setting, once a stop on the old fur-trading route, provided young Turner a sense of the frontier environment that had attracted his father to the area in the mid 1850s. By the time Turner was born, his father had become the owner, publisher, and editor of the local weekly paper, the staunchly Republican *Wisconsin State Register*. Andrew Jackson "Jack" Turner later became mayor of Portage, serving four terms. His wife had been a schoolteacher and seems not to have had a major influence on their son's life. All Turner's biographer Ray Allen Billington was able to say about Mary Turner was that "she was wise enough to let her son grow to manhood without any of the oedipal problems common in modern society." Young Turner undoubtedly learned a great deal about local politics from his father, who also introduced him to the great outdoors, where he developed a special love for fishing. Meanwhile, he proved himself an eager student in the public-school system, gaining special renown as an orator. All in all, his boyhood years seem to have been rather pleasant.

In 1878 young Fred Turner went off to begin a preparatory course of studies at the University of Wisconsin in nearby Madison. After completing a successful first year, Turner suffered a painful attack of acute spinal meningitis and did not return to Madison until the spring of 1881. By the fall of 1882 he had found an inspirational force among the faculty, historian William Francis Allen, who sparked Turner's interest in the discipline. When he graduated in 1884, Turner was twenty-two years old, well versed in the classics, a prize-winning orator (in a time when such talents were valued), and an aspiring historian, though not yet certain that the study of the past would mark his future.

After a brief stint as a reporter, Turner returned to the University of Wisconsin in 1885. Professor Allen, overburdened with classroom responsibilities, had been granted a leave and needed someone to teach his classes. Thus, his prize pupil began working as an instructor in history and rhetoric. Turner completed a master's degree at the university in 1888, writing a thesis on "The Influence of the Fur Trade in the Development of Wisconsin." To secure a permanent teaching post at Wisconsin, Turner knew he had to earn the degree that marked the new professionalism and academic specialization of the age, the doctorate. Later that year Turner enrolled in the history doctoral program at the Johns Hopkins University, the foremost graduate institution in the United States.

The young midwesterner went east to Baltimore and at Hopkins was introduced to the "germ theory" of historical development (which found the origin of American institutions in medieval German systems) by Herbert Baxter Adams and to the complexities of political economy by Richard T. Ely. Turner also made the acquaintance of a host of bright young history students including medievalist Charles Homer Haskins and future president Woodrow Wilson. These were years of significant intellectual growth and excitement for Turner, who was surrounded at Hopkins by some of the best and most innovative minds of his age.

Turner and Charles Homer Haskins while they were graduate students at Johns Hopkins University

In 1889 Turner returned to Wisconsin, and on 16 November he married his fiancée of two years, Caroline Mae Sherwood, thus beginning a happy and affectionate partnership that would last a lifetime and produce three children. Then, on 9 December, Turner's mentor, Professor Allen, died. The young graduate student was greatly moved by his professor's death, but the tragedy also brought opportunity. The University of Wisconsin hired Turner as Allen's replacement. He received his doctorate the following year, expanding his master's thesis into a dissertation, which was published as *The Character and Influence of the Indian Trade in Wisconsin* (1891). With his position at Wisconsin secure Turner was ready to begin a new and quite remarkable phase of his career.

Turner's first notable essay was published in the October and November 1891 issues of the *Wisconsin Journal of Education*. "The Significance of History" is an undervalued piece that demonstrates the modern qualities of Turner's historical approach. Noting that "Each age writes the history of the past anew with reference to the conditions uppermost in its own time," Turner, with this recognition of the elusiveness of historical truths, provided an early example of what would two decades later come to be known as the "New History." The young scholar pointed to the importance of studying all social groups rather than just the elites, urging the historian to draw on the advances in the social sciences, including geography, economics, and political science, along with humanities such as theology. He also stressed that the historian needed to be cognizant of both positive and negative developments in U.S. history—history should be more than a mere paean to those past achievements that led to present glories. While recognizing that historical perspective was subject to change, Turner warned against the "partisan . . . treatment of history," which leads the historian to "misinterpret the past for the sake of the present." Aspiring historians of any generation would do well to read "The Significance of History." Yet, unfortunately, neither Turner's most ardent supporters nor his most vocal detractors have paid sufficient attention to this early essay, and their oversight mirrors the lack of interest paid the piece upon its publication. Ridge has noted that had Turner been a more distinguished academic at the time, this essay "would have caused quite a stir in the profession."

The following fall Turner published another important essay that created no great stir in the academic community, but it did help lay the groundwork for his famous frontier thesis. "Problems in American History" appeared in the 4 November 1892 issue of the University of Wisconsin student newspaper, the *Ægis*. Reflecting on the works of East Coast historians, Turner lamented their narrow vision, which was restricted to the Atlantic states and to the germ theory of development. He pointed instead to the colonization of the Great West as the driving force of American history; "the ever retreating frontier of free land," he noted, "is the key to American development." Here Turner sought to direct scholarly attention toward a central problem in American history, and among the other problems he highlighted were the process by which American regions were formed (the "evolution of sections"), the effects of immigration into the country and migration from region to region, "the effect of the Indian on our political institutions," and the "management of the public domain, with the associated topics, internal improvements and railroad building." Even in compiling this ambitious list of topics, Turner demonstrated that there was much more to American history than the East Coast historians, with their intensive yet fundamentally insular analysis of the original thirteen colonies, were suggesting.

Turner concluded the bold piece with a stirring statement that he would repeat almost verbatim in his famous essay the following summer: "What the Mediterranean Sea was to the Greeks, breaking the bond of custom, offering new experiences, calling out new institutions and activities, that the ever retreating Great West has been to the eastern United States directly, and to the nations of Europe more remotely." In "Problems in American History" he also emphasized the theme, common in the Darwinian intellectual climate of the late nineteenth century, of society as an evolving, developing organism. Students interested in the genesis of Turner's famous 1893 paper would do well to read "The Significance of History" and "Problems in American History." These essays also merit attention because, despite the passage of more than a century, they still speak to fundamental problems that American historians must tackle—most notably issues of objectivity and relativism and the migration and interaction of various races and cultures.

With a few uninfluential essays behind him the young professor accepted an invitation to present a paper at the American Historical Association (AHA) meeting in Chicago. The AHA was then a fledgling organization, but the setting was a spectacular one. Chicago was host in 1893 to the World's Fair, or Columbian Exposition, which marked (albeit a year late) the four-hundredth anniversary of Christopher Columbus's arrival in the New World. There is some irony in the fact that Turner's Hopkins professor, the renowned germ theorist Herbert Baxter Adams (secretary of the AHA), had invited him to speak at the meeting, for Turner's paper was driven by its author's reaction against the germ theory. Turner's regional pride

had suffered a little during his Hopkins years. While he had been an outstanding student whose talents won him the attention of his faculty mentors, few historians at Hopkins, or on the East Coast, or for that matter anywhere in the country, paid much serious attention to the area west of the eastern seaboard, the area that had become the chief focus of Turner's attention.

Until that time American historians had followed Adams's lead, viewing the development of American social and political institutions as a direct outgrowth of European influences, specifically, medieval Teutonic germs, literally carried to and transplanted in the "New World." According to this theory, there was nothing intrinsically original about American society. The New World was a mere mirror of its European progenitor. Turner's frontier thesis offered a strikingly different explanation of American development, one that focused on the western interior of the continent—not on the East Coast, where European influences were most marked—and emphasized the nation's uniqueness or exceptionalism. Turner's approach was markedly American, thoroughly nationalistic, even chauvinistic.

In Europe the term *frontier* was traditionally used to describe a stationary boundary (often a geographic barrier, such as a mountain range) between countries. Yet in North America the term suggested the line of westward advance of white settlement (and the retreat of Native American peoples). Thus, as white Americans moved in a westwardly direction, they became part of a transient frontier process, which was how Turner viewed the frontier—not as a fixed boundary but as a process. He proclaimed in his essay, "The existence of an area of free land, its continuous recession, and the advance of American settlement westward, explain American development." He saw the frontier as the source of American democracy, individualism, and nationalism. The frontier provided certain advantages to the American people that no longer existed in Europe, where land was expensive and population was large. The combination of demographic and geographic factors in the United States guaranteed special advantages for the nation's European elements. "So long as free land exists," Turner declared, "the opportunity for a competency exists."

When it came to explaining what the frontier was, Turner—as many critics have noted—was rather elusive. In the space of two paragraphs he described the frontier as "the outer edge of the wave—the meeting point between savagery and civilization," as "the hither edge of free land," and, recounting the Census Bureau definition, as "the margin of settlement which has a density of two or more to the square mile." His contention that "the term [frontier] is an elastic one that does not need sharp definition" has, understandably, infuriated and baffled scholars who wonder how the thing Turner presented as the shaping force of America's character and institutions could possibly belie exact definition. Yet, it is worth noting that the elasticity of Turner's definition of *frontier* has helped make his thesis so influential and has sustained such interest in it for more than a century. Sometimes the most compelling terms are acutely elusive, and *frontier* was such a term, acting on the level of metaphor—for promise and opportunity—as well as descriptor—of physical reality (more specifically, of geographic and demographic circumstances).

Turner contended that, as white American civilization moved westward, the process of social evolution occurred over and over again as each new frontier was reached. In an era marked by the prevalence of Darwinian ideas, there was nothing unusual in emphasizing social development as an evolutionary process. What was unusual was Turner's emphasis on the American environment as a unique shaping force of that process. As Americans came into contact with the wilderness, he contended, they were transformed by that dangerous and challenging frontier environment and its inhabitants. As Turner noted in one of the most famous passages of the essay,

Turner in 1893, the year he wrote "The Significance of the Frontier in American History"

> The wilderness masters the colonist. It finds him a European in dress, industries, tools, modes of travel, and thought. It takes him from the railroad car and puts him in the birch canoe. It strips off the garments of civilization and arrays him in the hunting shirt and the moccasin. . . . Before long . . . he shouts the war cry and takes the scalp in orthodox Indian fashion.

At first the rugged frontier environment proved stronger than the colonist. But then, as the colonist adjusted to his surroundings, he began to transform them and became a different person—a frontiersman—more rugged, self-reliant, intuitive, independent, and individualistic.

Furthermore, Turner explained, as communities began to form in the sparsely populated frontier environment, settlers were directly involved in establishing and running their own systems of government. That direct involvement in local politics fostered democracy, and the availability of land provided every white settler the opportunity for ownership, which in turn helped secure political and economic equality. Also, on the frontier social ancestry counted for little. People were judged according to their individual merits, not their family back-

grounds, helping to produce a distinctive brand of rugged, individualistic frontier democracy. Regarding nationalism, those colonists who ventured out onto the frontier were at the forefront of the nation-building process, extending the boundaries of their country, and thus were likely to be more nationalistic than Americans on the East Coast. As the frontier advanced farther from the East Coast, the influence of Europe was reduced because American merchants began to supply frontier communities. Indeed, Turner suggested that the western frontier was the most American part of America.

On the frontier, Turner added, as waves of new settlers came into contact with the rugged wilderness, they became, quite literally, a new breed of men (Turner said little about women pioneers). The frontier was the place where European immigrants were Americanized and assimilated. The outcome of the process, Turner contended, "is not the old Europe, not simply the development of Germanic germs. . . . The fact is, that here is a new product that is American." In another of the famous passages of the essay Turner added, "In the crucible of the frontier the immigrants were Americanized, liberated and fused into a mixed race, English in neither nationality or characteristics." Here he was providing an early allusion to the idea of America as a "melting pot"—a notion that would become part of the national consciousness in the next decade with the publication in 1909 of Israel Zangwill's play of that name. Furthermore, Turner saw the frontier as the source of distinctly American character traits such as strength, inquisitiveness, practicality, inventiveness, and restlessness. As the frontier moved west and the country became settled, those frontier influences would continue to have a positive effect on the nation as a whole, although Turner was not sure for how long.

According to Turner, these were the benefits of the frontier process. The frontier accounted for just about every benign aspect of the American character and institutions. Contrary to the presumptions of many critics of Turner's frontier thesis, however, its author also pointed to certain negative frontier influences. For example, frontier democracy, "strong in selfishness and individualism, intolerant of administrative experience and education, and pressing individual liberty beyond its proper bounds, has its dangers as well as its benefits." Too much individualism, he added, had hindered the development of a civic spirit, which in turn had led to political corruption. Yet Turner's biggest concern was not the negative effects of the frontier (he viewed it as a largely positive force) but its disappearance.

While certainly a paean to the glories of the frontier past, Turner's frontier thesis was also a lament on the postfrontier present. He began the essay with a quotation from the Census of 1890: "Up to and including 1880 the country had a frontier of settlement, but at present the unsettled area has been so broken into by isolated bodies of settlement that there can hardly be said to be a frontier line." He repeated this point a few pages later and concluded the essay with the declaration that "the frontier has gone, and with its going has closed the first period of American history."

Turner's frontier thesis, while it provided a positive account of America's unique democratic heritage, actually began and ended on an alarmingly pessimistic note, raising new questions about the future. If the frontier had been the wellspring of so many positive features of American life, then it followed that with the passing of the frontier the nation's future looked grim. If the frontier had been the chief force for assimilating immigrants, then how would immigrants be Americanized without it? If the frontier process had fashioned a distinctively restless, energetic, expansionist temperament in the American people, then would new territorial frontiers have to be sought to channel that energy? If the frontier had been the foundation stone of nationalism, then would the American spirit dissipate and national unity crumble once that foundation was removed? If the frontier had sustained and fortified American democracy, then would democracy disappear with the frontier? The frontier had been an antidote to social disease and decay, but now that it was used up, would the nation's immune system deteriorate? While Turner's thesis lauded the nation's frontier past, it also contained an ominous portent of a frontierless future.

American thinkers had actually been pondering the dilemma of a frontierless nation for some time before the publication of Turner's paper in 1894 (in the AHA *Annual Report for 1893,* the *Proceedings* of the State Historical Society of Wisconsin, and later that year as a pamphlet). Indeed, Turner's essay was symptomatic of a broader anxiety about the closing of the American frontier that had been first expressed more than a century earlier by statesmen such as Thomas Jefferson and Benjamin Franklin, who worried that a fully settled United States would inevitably come to suffer the same social disease and decay that afflicted Europe. Similar fears had been expressed periodically throughout the nineteenth century. By the 1880s the argument that free or cheap lands helped preserve democracy and economic opportunity had gained widespread currency, and many American intellectuals were expressing concern that the supply of western lands was running out. Special emphasis was placed on the idea of the frontier as a safety valve for urban discontent. According to this theory, the frontier afforded eastern factory workers the opportunity to make a fresh start in the West, and their departure reduced the labor force in the East, thus keeping wages high and ensuring that the class conflict common in nineteenth-century Europe did not afflict the United States. Turner did not place much emphasis on the safety-valve theory in his 1893 essay. That same year, however, the prominent economist Richard T. Ely (Turner's former teacher) contended that the closing of the frontier safety valve necessitated population control to prevent a social explosion. Also in 1893, Populist leader Ignatius Donnelly declared, "When the valve is closed, swarming mankind every day will increase the danger of explosion."

Wondering how large numbers of new emigrants from southern and eastern Europe could be assimilated without the frontier, some observers proposed restrictive immigration laws to offset its loss. The rapid industrialization and urbanization of the nation—and the class antagonisms and ur-

Turner on a camping trip during the early 1920s

ban squalor that accompanied such modernization—made other observers wonder if the effects of the closed frontier were not already being felt. In the last two decades of the nineteenth century, many prominent observers, including novelist Hamlin Garland, naturalist John Muir, artist Frederic Remington, aspiring historian, politician, and outdoorsman Theodore Roosevelt, Evangelical missionary Josiah Strong, and Social Darwinist William Graham Sumner, expressed in books and magazine articles their anxieties over the passing of the western frontier and the deleterious effects it would have on the American character and institutions.

Indeed, by 1893 the concerns of agrarian America had been manifested in the shape of the Populist Party; the nation had entered its worst economic depression yet (1893–1897); giant corporations were monopolizing sectors of the economy; politicians were more concerned with private gain than the public good; and labor disputes such as the Homestead Strike of 1892 were demonstrating that the United States was not immune to the various problems that afflicted the Old World. A few months after Turner delivered his paper in Chicago, the Pullman Palace Car Com-

pany in that city drastically reduced wages while refusing to reduce rents in its company town. The strike that followed constituted the kind of industrial violence that the American frontier was supposed to prevent; or, when viewed another way, perhaps this violent strike was a manifestation of the social decay that was destined to develop in the United States as it entered the postfrontier age. Whatever the case, the dispatching of two thousand federal troops was required to end the Pullman Strike in July 1894, and the nation was shocked by the entire episode. The sparkling White City—an impressive complex constructed by the City of Chicago to house the 1893 World's Fair—was intended as a testament to technological progress, undeniable evidence of the wonders of modernity. Yet it was clear that progress had its price and modernization had some less laudable consequences. Here was the great dilemma for Turner: he was an ardent advocate of progress, yet he suggested that the nation was purer, more innocent, more enviable in its premodern, frontier stage. The progress he applauded was advancing at the expense of the frontier wilderness that he reckoned to be America's most precious and significant commodity, and the conundrum that faced Turner also faced the nation in the crisis-ridden 1890s.

"The Significance of the American Frontier" serves as a particularly poignant example of the considerable national unease that marked the close of the nineteenth century as the United States made the awkward transition from a simple agrarian society to a complex urban industrial one. Yet, paradoxically, Turner's frontier thesis also provided the young nation with a proud past—an enviable frontier heritage. Established countries have long-standing myths and legends to serve as cultural reference points and molders of national identity. (The Scandinavian legends and British Arthurian tales are good examples.) The United States, however, was demographically the product of already established countries and had to create a distinctly American heritage. The notion of the western frontier as the most American part of America had been circulating since the Revolutionary War era. Turner's essay gave academic legitimacy to a set of assumptions, stretching back a century, about the special value of the American environment. In forging a sense of national self-identity, American geography—according to that national creation myth, the frontier thesis—would prove a stronger force than European demography.

It is this blend of national pride and concern, praise and lament, and triumph and tragedy that makes Turner's frontier thesis so compelling a commentary on American development. His juxtaposition of a beneficent frontier heritage with a foreboding frontierless future remained at the heart of Turner's thinking for much of the rest of his life. He periodically sought solutions to the dilemma his thesis had postulated—how can a democratic spirit nurtured by the frontier prosper, or even persist, in the absence of that frontier? Turner hoped at one point that the state universities would sustain the democratic spirit. Later, in the 1920s, he expressed the fear that a frontierless America might not be able to sustain its growing population, that Americans might sink to a miserable, peasantlike existence, and that it might be better for the country if a "friendly comet" or a "chemist's bomb" brought civilization to an abrupt end.

In the years immediately following his Chicago paper, while he was acutely concerned with the dilemma that his thesis illuminated, Turner was making a name for himself as an energetic teacher-scholar at the University of Wisconsin and enjoying a happy marriage. His intellectual angst was not inconsiderable; yet he was hardly traumatized by the matter. While he was clearly concerned by the pass-

ing of the frontier, it would be wrong to characterize Turner as a nervous, worried thinker at this early stage in his career; rather, he was a rising academic star, growing in confidence and championing an important new theory.

No great wave of interest in Turner's frontier thesis appeared immediately after its delivery. In fact, the actual setting on the evening of 12 July 1893 had been somewhat inauspicious. Turner's paper followed four others, including one on "English Popular Uprisings in the Middle Ages" and another on "Early Lead Mining in Illinois and Wisconsin." The audience was probably quite fatigued by the time the young Wisconsinite took the podium. Turner most likely read his audience well and delivered only an abridged version of the prepared address. The paper that would come to dominate American historiography and play a significant role in shaping national self-perceptions received little reaction at the time and did not appear in print until the following year and even then in publications not read by any sizable portion of the American public.

Yet Turner, never shy when it came to self-publicity, sent copies of the essay to notable historians and newspaper editors and shared his ideas with his growing cadre of loyal students at the university. More essays would follow as Turner sought to popularize the West as a fruitful field for historical research: "The Frontier" (an abridged version of his 1893 essay) in *Johnson's Universal Encyclopedia* (1894); "Western State-Making in the Revolutionary Era" in the first two issues of the AHA journal, the *American Historical Review* (October 1895 and January 1896); and a review essay, "Recent Studies in American History" in *The Atlantic Monthly* (June 1896). Meanwhile, more renowned writers such as Woodrow Wilson and Theodore Roosevelt were popularizing the frontier thesis, and the scholarly world was slowly taking interest. As the close of the century drew nearer, lamentations on the taming of the Wild West, the passing of the Old West, the disappearance of the wilderness, the closing of the frontier, and the loss of agrarian purity and simplicity constituted an integral element of the American cultural milieu. The climate was growing more receptive to Turner's ideas.

Turner first found the larger audience he had been seeking with the publication of "The Problem of the West" as the lead essay in the September 1896 issue of *The Atlantic Monthly*. In an era of sectional tensions, created in part by the Populist (and previous agrarian) protests in the South and West, the title of Turner's essay must have struck a chord with the reading public. Indeed, on 9 July, less than two months before the appearance of the essay, William

Jennings Bryan had delivered his famous "Cross of Gold" speech, securing the Democratic presidential nomination as the candidate of the party's southern and western constituents, who sought currency inflation. On 22 July the Populist Party (also known as the People's Party) endorsed Bryan as well, and the stage was set for a 3 November electoral showdown between Bryan and Republican candidate William McKinley, defender of the gold standard (stable currency) and eastern business interests.

Turner's essay, while not the direct commentary on Populism that *The Atlantic Monthly* editor Walter Hines Page had probably hoped for, nonetheless provided some historical perspective on the topic of sectional discord. The piece opens with a bold declaration: "The problem of the West is nothing less than the problem of American development," and it concludes that the issue "means nothing less than the problem of working out original social ideals and social adjustments for the American nation." Less prolix and in many ways more readable than the ultimately better-known frontier essay of 1893, "The Problem of the West" repeats many of the same themes. Turner presented the western frontier as the wellspring of nationalism, idealism, and a brand of democracy featuring healthy measures of both individual liberty and equality. He added a more explicit sectional or regional twist to the theme of the frontier as a transforming factor. In the frontier thesis he had focused on the European becoming an American in the crucible of the frontier; in "The Problem of the West" he asserts that the "Westernized New England man was no longer the representative of the section that he left. He was less conservative, less provincial, more adaptable and approachable, less rigorous in his Puritan ideals, less a man of culture, more a man of action." He also critiqued the germ theory more directly than he had in 1893: "This new democracy," he declared, "came from no theorist's dreams of the German forest. It came, stark and strong and full of life, from the American forest."

With the East suspicious of the West and its seemingly radical support for inflationary measures, Turner sought in "The Problem of the West" to calm such fears by suggesting that western development would in time bring that region "more into harmony with the East." The problem of the West was the nation's problem, Turner contended, and the passing of the frontier was its primary cause. "The free lands are gone, the continent is crossed," he announced, "and all this push and energy is turning into channels of agitation." The old pioneers who had built up the trans-Mississippi West in the frontier era were now leading the Populist charge

and demanding government intervention to lessen their plight as the nation entered the postfrontier period. The government, Turner concluded, would have to play a role in helping the nation adjust to postfrontier realities.

The newspapers had barely noticed Turner's conference paper in 1893, but in 1896 "The Problem of the West" garnered a good deal of media coverage. Eastern papers reacted unfavorably to the essay, reluctant to accept Turner's bold claims for the West; western publications, not surprisingly, expressed their approval. Sectional discord and the Populist crusade had helped to ensure the timeliness of Turner's ideas. Assured of the efficacy of Turner's work, Page planned a whole series of articles on the nation's regions.

Like so many publishers who eagerly sought manuscripts from Turner as the young historian's reputation grew, Page must have been a little disappointed by the results. Turner completed only one article for the series, "Dominant Forces in Western Life," which appeared in the April 1897 issue. This essay, which was more pedestrian than Turner's earlier *Atlantic* article, focused on the Old Northwest and provided more background on the rise of Populism. Again, the conclusion was an optimistic one: Turner suggested that the Old Northwest, which featured both western and eastern characteristics, could serve somehow as a regional bridge between the New England and Mid-Atlantic states on the one hand and the South and Far West on the other. Media reaction confirmed again for Page that he should solicit more contributions from Turner; but the solicitation would prove to be an acutely painful and ultimately unsatisfactory process. It was five and one-half years before another Turner essay, "Contributions of the West to American Democracy," graced the pages of *The Atlantic Monthly* (January 1903).

During the intervening period Turner developed an acute interest in diplomatic history, which involved him in the time-consuming task of editing collections of correspondence. He continued to publish well-received articles in scholarly journals and gradually built his reputation as one of the foremost historians in the United States. Brimming with confidence and unrealistic self-expectations, Turner brought temporary gratification to many eager publishers, signing contracts for no fewer than nine separate books with five separate companies during the second half of the 1890s. (None of these contracts was fulfilled.)

In the closing year of the nineteenth century tragedy struck the Turner family twice. On 11 February Turner's oldest daughter, Mae Sherwood

Turner at the Huntington Library, circa 1927–1928

Turner, died after contracting diphtheria, and on 22 October his only son, Jackson Allen Turner, died after suffering a ruptured appendix. Turner spent the remaining months of the century in mourning. "When he finally returned to the classroom," Billington noted, "he was only a walking shadow, his spirit gone . . . friends noted that the sparkle was gone from his eyes, the bounce from his step."

While the nineteenth century ended in disaster for Turner, the new century brought increased recognition. Yet somehow Turner's considerable scholarly promise did not translate into the kind of output one might expect from so vibrant an academic mind. Turner's publication record was meager to say the least. Over a career that spanned forty years, he produced only four books. Two of these volumes were published during his lifetime: *Rise of the New West, 1819–1829* (1906) and *The Frontier in American History* (1920), a collection of his previously published essays. Two works appeared posthumously; one of them, *The Significance of Sections in American*

History (1932), which received the Pulitzer Prize, was also composed of previously published essays. The second, *The United States, 1830–1850: The Nation and Its Sections* (1935), had been a source of frustration to Turner for much of his life and had to be completed by others. Turner worked better in the provocative essay format, raising questions for others to consider. He simply did not have the patience or discipline required for the kind of book-length studies that would have provided answers to the questions he raised. Indeed, historian Albert Bushnell Hart, who helped to edit *Rise of the New West* and had placed heavy pressures on Turner to complete the project, reflected on the matter shortly after Turner's death and declared, "It ought to be carved on my tombstone that I was the only man in the world that secured what might be classed an adequate volume from Turner." Yet, as historian Wilfred McClay has noted, paraphrasing Sir Winston Churchill, "never had so many been influenced by one who wrote so little."

As Turner entered the new century he found himself being courted by several prestigious institutions, including the University of Chicago, the University of Pennsylvania, and a few years later Johns Hopkins University, Amherst College, the University of California at Berkeley, and Stanford University, and he developed a talent for wringing increased salaries and benefits from the University of Wisconsin when such offers were made. He was engrossed in two main intellectual tasks: further promotion of his frontier thesis and the development of a "sectional theory" that would occupy him for the rest of his life. The two theories were inextricably linked. In the first decade of the new century, writing in popular magazines and speaking at various forums, including many college graduation ceremonies, Turner drove home his message that the western frontier had been the great shaping force of American character and institutions.

Meanwhile, Turner was shifting his focus to the study of the process by which the various regions, or sections, of the United States had formed. He was contemplating the complex interplay of culture, demography, geography, economics, and politics in shaping distinct sectional entities, and he was considering the interrelationships between these sections and their relation to the nation, drawing comparisons and contrasts with the conglomeration of diverse nation-states that constituted Europe. Turner had exhibited profound interest in the works of geographers and demographers from the beginning of his career, and the sectional thesis had begun, in the most embryonic of forms, as early as his 1892 essay on "Problems in American History." *Rise of the New West, 1819–1829,* which examines the construction of various distinct regions within the nation, employs both the frontier and the sectional themes. Turner also produced several essays on the topic, including "Is Sectionalism in America Dying Away?" (*American Journal of Sociology,* March 1908), "Geographical Influences in American Political History" (*Bulletin of the American Geographical Society,* August 1914), "Sections and Nation" (*Yale Review,* October 1922), and "The Significance of the Section in American History" (*Wisconsin Magazine of History,* March 1925).

Unlike his frontier thesis, Turner's ideas about sections did not spark the imagination of fellow academics and the broader public. As Turner scholars Michael C. Steiner and Wilbur Jacobs have pointed out, the two concepts were inseparable in Turner's mind—the frontier process helped shape the sections of the nation, and the relations between those sections held the key to the postfrontier future. Turner's frontier, Steiner has perceptively

noted, was a "self-destroying process" that provided only "a provisional explanation for American development." Turner spent the bulk of his career, Steiner adds, "searching for a more lasting explanation," and the section, in his mind, provided the answer. Indeed, the Turnerian legacy appears rather ironic when one considers that much of the criticism leveled at the frontier thesis centers on Turner's supposed monocausational approach (the frontier as single shaping force), while the sectional concept was multicausational in design. The simplicity of the frontier thesis helped to guarantee its bewildering endurance, and the complexity of the sectional thesis helped to ensure its relegation into the realm of near oblivion.

Turner found himself in an unusual intellectual tangle for the remainder of his career. He was obligated to continue popularizing the frontier thesis, which had proven to be his ticket to academic stardom, yet he craved similar recognition for his sectional thesis. Sure evidence of Turner's ascendancy among the American historical community came in 1907 when he was elected to the second vice presidency of the American Historical Association, which assured his assumption of the presidency two years later. In 1910 he was finally lured away from Wisconsin to Harvard University. At Harvard his reputation and influence continued to grow in the second decade of the twentieth century. *The Frontier in American History,* which included his famous 1893 essay and his *Atlantic* articles of 1896 and 1897, became the subject of many glowing reviews and enabled Turner to achieve about as much renown as any academic can hope for. Yet his Harvard years, while they brought recognition and prestige, did not bring any great happiness to a man whose disaffection for East Coast gentility had been evident in his first important essays back in the early 1890s.

Four years after the publication of *The Frontier in American History,* Turner, then nearly sixty-three years old, retired from Harvard. In 1927, after a brief and unsatisfactory period in the familiar environs of Madison, Wisconsin (where the frigid winters did nothing to improve his failing health), Turner accepted a position as senior research associate at the Henry E. Huntington Library in San Marino, California, near Pasadena, where he spent his last years, inspired by the major western-history collections of the library but frustrated by periodic bouts of illness and his inability to complete *The Nation and Its Sections.* He died of heart-related problems on 14 March 1932.

The story of Turner's legacy has occupied a span of time roughly as long as his life, and the controversy that surrounds his ideas, most particularly his frontier thesis, has surfaced periodically since and is likely to continue to do so. By the 1920s the influence of the frontier thesis was evident in works on American literature such as Ralph L. Rusk's *The Literature of the Middle Western Frontier* (1925) and Lucy L. Hazard's *The Frontier in American Literature* (1927). Other works, including Frederick Logan Paxson's *History of the American Frontier, 1763–1893* (1924) and Archer Butler Hulbert's *Frontiers: The Genius of American Nationality* (1929), further popularized the frontier thesis. By this time, however, some of the early criticism of the frontier thesis was also beginning to appear. Some historians stressed the influence of factors other than the frontier—such as the city, industrialization, and immigration—on American institutions and character. Social critics such as Waldo Frank, Van Wyck Brooks, John Dewey, and Lewis Mumford argued (as Turner had, though to a much lesser degree, in his 1893 essay) that the frontier was an antisocial force, that unrestrained frontier individualism was dangerous, and that America had failed to develop artistic and literary genius comparable to Europe's because the frontier was an anti-intellectual force.

By the time of Turner's death the frontier thesis was being used to justify government efforts to provide relief during the Great Depression. New Deal spokesmen, including President Franklin D. Roosevelt, argued that the American physical frontier had once acted as a safety valve for the poor and discontented, but with the safety valve of opportunity shut down the government would have to provide direct assistance to the needy. Critics of the New Deal, on the other hand, claimed that there was still a great deal of opportunity left in America, that new frontiers of business enterprise were always open to those who had the necessary individualistic pioneer spirit. Moreover, former president Herbert Hoover declared that the government was killing that self-reliant frontier spirit by providing assistance to people who ought to be taking care of themselves.

Meanwhile, as the frontier theme became an important part of the debates over government policy in the 1930s, scholars mounted a strong assault on the validity of Turner's frontier thesis. Turner's essay, which stresses agrarianism and rugged individualism, seemed to have less relevance for explaining an urban-industrial society in the midst of economic catastrophe and in desperate need of cooperation to survive. Critics raised questions about the hallowed interpretation of American and western development. How could the frontier have created democracy when western settlers established political systems based on those in the East? How

did the frontier nurture individualism when settlers moved in groups for the purpose of building communities and better defending themselves? How could the frontier have promoted nationalism when there was no real evidence that westerners were any more nationalistic than their eastern counterparts? How had the frontier acted as a safety valve for urban discontent when unemployed and poor laborers in the East could not have afforded to relocate to the West? Some reacted negatively to the frontier thesis because it stressed American uniqueness, or exceptionalism, when what the world needed (in light of the rise of fascism in Nazi Germany and in Italy) was an emphasis on the essential unity among peoples, not their national differences.

While Turner's reputation and that of the frontier thesis have periodically risen and fallen in the last half century, since the mid 1960s scholars have been particularly critical of the Turnerian legacy. This criticism centers as much on what the thesis failed to include as it does on the actual content. Turner was, in many ways, an academic innovator, but he was also a product of his time. His thesis chronicled the triumphant march of white European men across the continent. He paid little attention to the role of women on the frontier, and he presented Native Americans as merely an impediment to the advance of the white frontier and a foil for frontiersmen who would adopt the useful aspects of their culture and ignore, discard, or destroy the rest. When Turner characterized the frontier as the "meeting point between savagery and civilization," it was clear whom he thought to be the savages. Turner's explanation for American development fit the mood of an expanding nation that rarely questioned the absolute superiority of white Anglo-Saxons, but such an account has become increasingly less acceptable. Since the 1960s, as scholars have devoted more attention to the history of women, Native Americans, other peoples of color, and the environment, the frontier thesis has increasingly come to be seen as old-fashioned and Eurocentric. Still, in the 1960s and 1970s, Billington provided vigorous defenses of Turner and his legacy and produced a masterful biography, *Frederick Jackson Turner: Historian, Scholar, Teacher* (1973).

Since the mid 1980s Turner's frontier essay has become the target of particularly spirited attacks from a new generation of western historians who view it as a narrow, Eurocentric justification for the conquest of peoples of color and the despoliation of the environment. Perhaps the most influential of these recent assaults on the Turnerian heritage is Patricia Nelson Limerick's *The Legacy of Conquest: The Unbroken Past of the American West* (1987). Limerick argues that Turner's colorful, romantic thesis has obscured the darker realities of the settlement of the West–the exploitation of labor, women, peoples of color, and the environment. Still, it is worth noting that Limerick's most spirited attacks are reserved not for Turner but for the overzealous defenses of the frontier thesis by other scholars. Turner's dedication as a teacher and mentor guaranteed large numbers of enthusiastic followers who defended the frontier thesis far more vigorously than its originator had. Ironically, assaults on the frontier thesis in the late 1980s and early 1990s served once more to revive scholarly interest in Turner and the frontier. The centennial of his frontier thesis in 1993 added to the swelling of interest as many books and scores of articles were published to mark the occasion.

Turner's frontier thesis now has few defenders and no longer serves as the theoretical framework for studies of the American West or national development; yet it still seems to have a hold on the imagination of many Americans. Indeed, the frontier concept has become something of a cliché, but its symbolic power is still strong. The term *new frontiers* is used to promote new products, new technologies, and new ways of thinking and has become common parlance in the United States. Turner's short essay (about thirty pages) has had a remarkable history. Its author has been such a prominent fixture, not just in the comparatively narrow field of American historiography, but in the broader field of American thought and culture, for more than a century because his ideas sparked both the scholarly and (albeit less directly) the public imagination. If there is such an amorphous entity as a national psyche in the United States, then Frederick Jackson Turner, as much as any scholar before or since, struck a chord in it.

Letters:

The Historical World of Frederick Jackson Turner. With Selections from His Correspondence, edited by Wilbur R. Jacobs (New Haven: Yale University Press, 1968);

"Dear Lady": The Letters of Frederick Jackson Turner and Alice Forbes Perkins Hooper, 1910–1932, edited by Ray A. Billington, with the collaboration of Walter Muir Whitehill (San Marino, Cal.: Huntington Library, 1970).

Bibliographies:

Everett E. Edwards, "A Bibliography of the Writings of Frederick Jackson Turner," in *Early Writings of Frederick Jackson Turner* (Madison: University of Wisconsin Press, 1938);

Vernon E. Mattson and William E. Marion, *Frederick Jackson Turner: A Reference Guide* (Boston: G. K. Hall, 1985).

Biography:

Ray Allen Billington, *Frederick Jackson Turner: Historian, Scholar, Teacher* (New York: Oxford University Press, 1973).

References:

Ray Allen Billington, *America's Frontier Heritage* (New York: Holt, Rinehart & Winston, 1966);

Billington, *The Frontier Thesis: Valid Interpretation of American History?* (New York: Holt, Rinehart & Winston, 1966);

Billington, *The Genesis of the Frontier Thesis: A Study in Historical Creativity* (San Marino, Cal.: Huntington Library Press, 1971);

Billington and Wilbur R. Jacobs, "The Frederick Jackson Turner Papers in the Huntington Library," *Arizona and the West,* 2 (Spring 1960): 73–77;

Avery Craven, "F. J. T," in *Marcus W. Jernigan Essays in American Historiography,* edited by William T. Hutchinson (Chicago: University of Chicago Press, 1937), pp. 252–270;

William Cronon, "Revisiting the Vanishing Frontier: The Legacy of Frederick Jackson Turner," *Western Historical Quarterly,* 18 (April 1987): 157–176;

John Mack Faragher, "The Frontier Trail: Rethinking Turner and Reimagining the American West," *American Historical Review,* 98 (February 1993): 106–117;

James R. Grossman, ed., *The Frontier in American Culture: Essays By Richard White and Patricia Nelson Limerick* (Berkeley & Los Angeles: University of California Press, 1994);

Richard Hofstadter, *The Progressive Historians: Turner, Beard, Parrington* (Chicago: University of Chicago Press, 1968);

Wilbur Jacobs, *On Turner's Trail: 100 Years of Writing Western History* (Lawrence: University Press of Kansas, 1994);

Howard R. Lamar, "Frederick Jackson Turner," in *Pastmasters: Some Essays on American Historians,* edited by Marcus Cunliffe and Robin W. Winks (New York: Harper & Row, 1969), pp. 74–109, 419–426;

Patricia Nelson Limerick, "Turnerians All: The Dream of Helpful History in an Intelligible World," *American Historical Review,* 100 (June 1995): 697–716;

Wilfred M. McClay, "A Tent on the Porch," *American Heritage,* 44 (July-August 1993): 88–93;

Fulmer Mood, "The Development of Frederick Jackson Turner as a Historical Thinker," *Publications of the Colonial Society of Massachusetts,* 34 (1937–1942): 283–352;

Gerald Nash, *Creating the West: Historical Interpretations, 1890–1990* (Albuquerque: University of New Mexico Press, 1991);

Martin Ridge, "The Life of an Idea: The Significance of Frederick Jackson Turner's Frontier Thesis," *Montana: The Magazine of Western History,* 41 (Winter 1991): 2–13;

Henry Nash Smith, "The Myth of the Garden and Turner's Frontier Hypothesis," in his *Virgin Land: The American West as Symbol and Myth* (Cambridge, Mass.: Harvard University Press, 1950), pp. 250–260;

Michael C. Steiner, "Frederick Jackson Turner and the New Western History," *Pacific Historical Review,* 64 (November 1995): 479–501;

Steiner, "Frederick Jackson Turner and Western Regionalism," in *Writing Western History: Essays on Major Western Historians,* edited by Richard W. Etulain (Albuquerque: University of New Mexico Press, 1991), pp. 103–135;

Richard W. White, "Frederick Jackson Turner," in *Historians of the American Frontier: A Bio-Bibliographical Sourcebook,* edited by John R. Wunder (Westport, Conn.: Greenwood Press, 1988), pp. 660–681;

David M. Wrobel, *The End of American Exceptionalism: Frontier Anxiety from the Old West to the New Deal* (Lawrence: University Press of Kansas, 1993).

Papers:

Turner's papers, including correspondence, manuscript materials, voluminous notes and clippings, and his book collection, are in the Henry E. Huntington Library, San Marino, California. For information about this collection see Ray Allen Billington and Wilbur Jacobs's "The Frederick Jackson Turner Papers in the Huntington Library" and Billington's biography. Smaller collections of Turner's papers are housed at the Houghton Library at Harvard University, the State Historical Society of Wisconsin, and the Memorial Library at the University of Wisconsin.

John C. Van Dyke

(21 April 1856 – 5 December 1932)

Peter Wild
University of Arizona

BOOKS: *How to Judge of a Picture: Familiar Talks in the Gallery with the Uncritical Lovers of Art* (New York: Hunt & Eaton, 1880);

Books and How to Use Them: Some Hints to Readers and Students (New York: Fords, Howard, & Hulbert, 1883);

Principles of Art (New York: Fords, Howard, & Hulbert, 1887);

Art for Art's Sake: Seven University Lectures on the Technical Beauties of Painting (New York: Scribners, 1893; London: Sampson, 1893);

The Story of the Pine (New York: Author's Club, 1893);

A Text-Book of the History of Painting (New York & London: Longmans, Green, 1894);

Nature for Its Own Sake: First Studies in Natural Appearances (New York: Scribners, 1898; London: Sampson, 1898);

The Desert: Further Studies in Natural Appearances (New York: Scribners, 1901; London: Sampson, 1901); with illustrations from photographs by J. Smeaton Chase (New York: Scribners, 1918); with illustrations from photographs by Chase and notes by Dix Van Dyke (New York: Scribners, 1930);

The Meaning of Pictures: Six Lectures Given for Columbia University at the Metropolitan Museum of Art (New York: Scribners, 1903; London: George Newnes, 1903);

Renaissance Painting in Italy: A Catalogue of Carbon Photographs, with Descriptions (Boston & New York: A. W. Elson, 1904);

The Opal Sea: Continued Studies in Impressions and Appearances (New York: Scribners, 1906; London: T. W. Laurie, 1906);

Studies in Pictures: An Introduction to the Famous Galleries (New York: Scribners, 1907; London: T. W. Laurie, 1907);

The Money God: Chapters of Heresy and Dissent Concerning Business Methods and Mercenary Ideals in American Life (New York: Scribners, 1908);

The New New York: A Commentary on the Place and the People (New York: Macmillan, 1909);

John C. Van Dyke, circa 1930

What Is Art?: Studies in the Technique and Criticism of Painting (New York: Scribners, 1910);

London: Critical Notes on the National Gallery and the Wallace Collection, with a General Introduction and Bibliography for the Series, New Guides to Old Masters, no. 1 (New York: Scribners, 1914);

Paris: Critical Notes on the Louvre, New Guides to Old Masters, no. 2 (New York: Scribners, 1914);

Amsterdam, The Hague, Haarlem: Critical Notes on the Rijks Museum, The Hague Museum, Hals Museum, New Guides to Old Masters, no. 3 (New York: Scribners, 1914);

Brussels, Antwerp: Critical Notes on the Royal Museums of Brussels and Antwerp, New Guides to Old Masters, no. 4 (New York: Scribners, 1914);

Munich, Frankfort, Cassel: Critical Notes on the Old Pinacothek, the Staedel Institute, the Cassel Royal Gallery, New Guides to Old Masters, no. 5 (New York: Scribners, 1914);

Berlin, Dresden: Critical Notes on the Kaiser Friedrich Museum and the Royal Gallery, Dresden, New Guides to Old Masters, no. 6 (New York: Scribners, 1914);

Vienna, Budapest: Critical Notes on the Imperial Gallery and Budapest Museum, New Guides to Old Masters, no. 7 (New York: Scribners, 1914);

St. Petersburg: Critical Notes on the Hermitage, New Guides to Old Masters, no. 8 (New York: Scribners, 1914);

Madrid: Critical Notes on the Prado, New Guides to Old Masters, no. 12 (New York: Scribners, 1914);

The Raritan: Notes on a River and a Family (New Brunswick, N.J.: Privately printed, 1915);

The Mountain: Renewed Studies in Impressions and Appearances (New York: Scribners, 1916);

American Painting and Its Tradition, as Represented by Inness, Wyant, Martin, Homer, La Farge, Whistler, Chase, Alexander, Sargent (New York: Scribners, 1919);

The Grand Canyon of the Colorado: Recurrent Studies in Impressions and Appearances (New York: Scribners, 1920);

The Open Spaces: Incidents of Nights and Days under the Blue Sky (New York: Scribners, 1922);

Rembrandt and His School: A Critical Study of the Master and His Pupils, with a New Assignment of Their Pictures (New York: Scribners, 1923);

Venice, Milan: Critical Notes on the Venice Academy, the Brera Gallery, the Poldi-Pezzoli Museum, New Guides to Old Masters, no. 9 (New York: Scribners, 1924);

Rome: Critical Notes on the Borghese Gallery, the Vatican Gallery, the Stanze and Loggie, the Borgia Apartments, New Guides to Old Masters, no. 11 (New York: Scribners, 1924);

The Meadows: Familiar Studies of the Commonplace (New York: Scribners, 1926);

Florence: Critical Notes on the Galleries of the Uffizi, the Pitti, and the Academy, New Guides to Old Masters, no. 10 (New York: Scribners, 1927);

The Rembrandt Drawings and Etchings: With Critical Reassignments to Pupils and Followers (New York: Scribners, 1927);

In Java, and the Neighboring Islands of the Dutch East Indies (New York & London: Scribners, 1929);

In Egypt: Studies and Sketches along the Nile (New York: Scribners, 1931);

In the West Indies: Sketches and Studies in Tropic Seas and Islands (New York: Scribners, 1932);

The Autobiography of John C. Van Dyke: A Personal Narrative of American Life, 1861–1931, edited by Peter Wild (Salt Lake City: University of Utah Press, 1993).

OTHER: *Modern French Masters: A Series of Biographical and Critical Reviews by American Artists,* edited by Van Dyke (New York: Century, 1896);

Timothy Cole, *Old English Masters, Engraved by Timothy Cole, with Historical Notes by John C. Van Dyke and Comments by the Engraver* (New York: Century, 1902);

Cole, *Old Dutch and Flemish Masters, Engraved by Timothy Cole, with Critical Notes by John C. Van Dyke and Comments by the Engraver* (New York: Century, 1911);

Autobiography of Andrew Carnegie, edited by Van Dyke (Boston & New York: Houghton Mifflin, 1920; London: Constable, 1920).

"All Southwestern book trails lead to *The Desert,*" says Lawrence Clark Powell in *Southwest Classics* (1974). The book to which Powell refers is *The Desert: Further Studies in Natural Appearances,* John C. Van Dyke's acclaimed 1901 volume. Powell's praise echoes that of earlier scholars of the West. In *A Literary History of Southern California* (1950) Franklin Walker lauds Van Dyke as the man who "led the way" in appreciating the arid landscapes of the nation. Powell sums up the generous disposition of previous critics toward the man and his landmark book and concludes that during Van Dyke's visits to the desert he "truly saw it first and said it best."

John Charles Van Dyke was born in a country mansion near New Brunswick, New Jersey. Since the arrival of Thomasse Janse Van Dyke in New Amsterdam in 1652, the Van Dykes and families they married into had produced civic and cultural leaders, including Revolutionary War heroes, a famous mathematician, a well-known poet, and many politicians. Van Dyke's father was a lawyer, a bank president, a congressman, and a member of the New Jersey Supreme Court. By Van Dyke's time, the family enjoyed prosperity and considerable power in Republican Party affairs.

Declining an appointment to West Point, Van Dyke studied law at the Columbia Law School in New York City; he was admitted to the bar in 1877, but he never practiced. He was dazzled by Art for Art's Sake, a new movement sweeping the upper classes, and while still in his twenties he prepared himself to become a major cultural influence of the day. He settled in New Brunswick, near New York,

Van Dyke (right) visiting a ranch in northern Mexico (Special Collections and Archives, Rutgers University Libraries)

with its wealth and powerful art circles, and became a librarian at the New Brunswick Theological Seminary, located on what is still known locally as "Holy Hill." By 1886 he was the library director, and a few years later he held a concurrent position as the first professor of art history at Rutgers College (now University). Despite his teaching and library work, his duties were light. Armed with a growing reputation as an art critic, he delegated many of his everyday duties to others; thus freed, he roamed the world, visiting art museums and establishing friendships with their often wealthy patrons. Plagued by respiratory problems, he also withdrew periodically to the American Southwest, seeking relief provided by its clear, dry air.

Meanwhile, in the 1880s and 1890s Van Dyke was publishing books as well as articles in the taste-setting magazines of the day—treatises on art appreciation, nature writing, and travel that were important to his career. At the time, and up until the advent of World War I, the nation was experiencing its first flush of prosperity from the rapid industrialization following the Civil War. The new captains of industry, with their excess wealth, often patronized the arts; symphony orchestras and art museums began to appear in America. Van Dyke made himself a part of this new cultural effervescence. He traveled

extensively, walking through art museums of London, Paris, and Saint Petersburg, visiting every continent except Antarctica, and becoming friends with notable figures such as Mark Twain, James Abbott McNeill Whistler, and Theodore Roosevelt. His reputation grew when he became an art adviser to steel magnate Andrew Carnegie, the richest man in America. Using such connections, Van Dyke easily became the most successful fund-raiser of his seminary. Over the years, he converted the dour library building, built like a Romanesque church, into a museum with floor tiling from Italy, marble statuary, and new stained-glass windows.

In the midst of such activity it is difficult to imagine that Van Dyke spent much time and energy in the classroom or at his desk as library director. But both Rutgers and the seminary so valued his name that they gladly indulged his desire to travel. The seminary even built a house on campus specifically for him. When not living in it, Van Dyke, by then a member of the new international set, could be found in Champs Elysées hotels, country mansions of railroad presidents, or Carnegie's castle on the moors of Scotland.

But part of that world was unspoiled nature. Van Dyke's upper-class circles saw nature quite differently than do middle-class American tourists, campers, and hikers today. Wealthy Americans, many of whom Van Dyke knew intimately, felt hounded by insoluble social problems. Foreigners by the millions had been coming from southern Europe; crowded into American cities, they created or at least aggravated slum conditions, and with their different ethnic, linguistic, and religious backgrounds they threatened the very fabric of stable society, in the view of the elite. In periodic despair, some members of Van Dyke's social set turned to nature for temporary relief. Unlike fetid city slums, nature was beautiful, predictable, and nonthreatening. So the wealthy often escaped at least to their lavish country estates; Van Dyke himself owned a "cottage" at Onteora in the Catskill Mountains north of New York City. Onteora was an expansive development for the rich, with costly homes and guards at the gate.

Bearing more immediately on the making of Van Dyke's *The Desert,* such attitudes can also be found in the Art for Art's Sake movement popular among the privileged classes. At times the individual approaches of this movement become so nebulous as to defy definition, but one general principle was that the appreciation of beauty was the highest good in life. Thus, art was another escape from an unruly world. Furthermore, Van Dyke, among other adherents, held that the highest beauty was not manmade but dwelt in forms and colors of pristine nature. Accordingly, around the turn of the century when he traveled to the Southwest seeking better health, Van Dyke applied his Art for Art's Sake precepts while writing about the landscape before him in *The Desert.*

In this view, sand dunes were hardly an impediment to a person looking out a Pullman car window but seemed "as graceful as the lines of running water," and "rhythmical and flowing in their forms." Sounding much like advocates of Art for Art's Sake back East, Van Dyke adds that the sands spreading around him are not wastes but are important "simply because they are beautiful in themselves and good to look upon." (Such a statement would have astounded pioneers having to make their way through them.) It follows that all this beauty should be preserved, not for the insensitive masses but for people of refinement to enjoy as they speed by in lavishly appointed railroad cars. Such concepts, which Van Dyke brought to *The Desert,* were hardly new. But his application of them was original since up to that time no book-length work had applied them to the American deserts.

Yet that does not explain the immediate popularity of the volume with the American reading public. *The Desert* happened to be the right book at the right time. In *Wilderness and the American Mind* (1967) Roderick Nash ably traces how the national attitudes toward wild nature changed over the centuries. To ill-equipped Pilgrims huddled at Plymouth, the vast forest about them was a "howling wilderness," an unknown and dangerous place full of wolves, Indians, and even devils. These fears set the paradigm for the nation as it spread ever westward across the continent. As long as nature was wild, unknown, and threatening, settlers feared it; when it was tamed, the forests put to the axe, and Indians killed or shuffled onto reservations, however, a change occurred. The wilderness could then be safely romanticized, and an increasingly industrialized nation could look back nostalgically on its brave pioneer past and the wildness recently lost.

Yet deserts suffered from an unusually bad reputation. Dry, remote, hot, and presenting little but cactus flats and treeless mountains, they were particularly scorned by settlers accustomed to the fields and woodlands of more humid climates. To such people deserts were dangerous places, inhabited by bandits and Apaches. Until a hundred years or so ago, when people thought of such places, they thought of scalped corpses and the bones of unfortunate travelers marking dry waterholes.

Attitudes showed signs of shifting, however, as technological civilization overwhelmed even the seemingly intractable desert. The U.S. Cavalry settled the Apache problem; railroads began crisscrossing the dunes; and machinery to dig deep wells made water more abundant. Also, people with respiratory problems, among them Van Dyke, found health in the desert air. Added to these factors was the romantic urge for wild places in the minds of a recently urbanized public. People at leisure who wanted to experience nature in all her glorious wildness were steered by Van Dyke to a long-ignored region where exoticism triumphed. *The Desert* gave definite voice to amorphous yearnings.

Though popular in Van Dyke's time, *The Desert* was often overshadowed by the larger reputation of his art criticism. Only in more recent times has the book been singled out of the body of his writing and praised both for its immediate influence on readers of travel books and for its more enduring worth. Its preface opens the volume with a call for readers to turn their backs on an overly urbanized culture and follow Van Dyke "beyond the wire fence of civilization to those places . . . where the trail is unbroken and the mountain peak unblazed." The entire preface is a rhetorical masterpiece. Seizing the moral high ground, Van Dyke establishes his authority as guide and mentor and leads his readers out of their workday lives to discover "the beautiful things in this desert world" and the "great truths" of nature.

Reading *The Desert,* armchair travelers back East began to see the desert with new eyes. It is not a drab wasteland but a wonderland, "the most decorative landscape in the world . . . , a dream landscape," where the air is colored. By day a delicate, "lilacblue veiling" hangs above the distant mountains, and by night a huge, "misshapen orange-hued desert moon" rises over the ridges to bathe the flats in a phosphorescent light. In this mysterious land indigo lizards flit across hot sand, and wildcats peer out with eyes "like great mirrors" and with "teeth like points of steel." *The Desert* becomes a visual feast through such vivid description.

As the chapters unfold, the reader begins to understand that *The Desert* is highly organized and substantive, with sections exploring separate topics such as desert birds, cacti, and desert geology. For example, the chapter on mirages describes mountain ranges shrinking weirdly in the distance, then expanding, playing tricks in the superheated air and making a lake of cool water seem to appear. Then Van Dyke explains why it happens, giving a solid little lecture on the illusory effects of bending light rays. He follows the same pattern in other chapters, first offering enticing descriptions and then presenting scientific facts behind them. Thus, he gains authority by combining romance and realism. By the end of the book he has proved himself an ideal tour guide: his followers have been both thrilled and informed.

However, *The Desert* is riddled with errors. Van Dyke lectures that the flower of the southwestern giant cactus is purple. In fact, it is white. He advises his readers not to worry about rattlesnakes, since they are "sluggish." Pioneers knew better. In the world of Van Dyke's book the coyote "seldom runs after things." But in the real world coyotes survive only by running after, catching, and eating rabbits and other fleet prey. One possible explanation for these mistakes is that Van Dyke was more a poet and an art lover than a scientist; buoyed by his enthusiasms, he may have let a few factual errors creep in. The gaffes, however, are so numerous that the reader may well begin to wonder whether Van Dyke ever really traveled as he claimed or whether for some reason his mistakes were deliberate. After all, in his art scholarship, such as his landmark *Rembrandt and His School* (1923), Van Dyke showed that he could be a meticulous scholar and a near fiend for accurate observation. Upon a closer reading of *The Desert* other profound anomalies begin to appear. The "A.M.C." on the dedication page, for example, is not some fellow nature lover who is as pained as Van Dyke says he is at the destruction of wild lands. Undoubtedly A.M.C. is Van Dyke's friend Carnegie, one of the greatest polluters and wreckers of nature in his and Van Dyke's generation. Such discrepancies require further explanation.

Van Dyke the art critic had what amounted to a disdain, perhaps even loathing, for the masses and for anything that smacked of popular culture. Aspiring to higher levels of appreciation, in *Principles of Art* (1887) he condemned the realism in paintings dear to the general public as "the lowest and most contemptible form of art," while in *What Is Art?* (1910) he damned "anything that is of popular interest." Powell makes Van Dyke's position clear enough for all to see when in his *Southwest Classics* he quotes part of a letter from Van Dyke to his publisher about *The Desert.* "It is a whole lot better that the swash which today is being turned out as 'literature,'" he states, adding, "and it will sell too, but not up in the hundreds of thousands. It is not so bad as that. My audience is only a few thousand, thank God." Van Dyke was not alone in holding the public in low esteem. Many of his contemporaries, including Whistler, felt that the stupidity, bad breeding, and lack of education of the public rendered it incapable of grasping true art. To salon habitués, hoaxing the masses was a pleasant pastime.

Why, then, would Van Dyke bother to mention potential sales of a book to his publisher? More dramatically, why would he write using the generalized "you," thereby not only directly addressing the thousands of mass readers he despised but also inviting them along on his desert trek? It is hard to overestimate the inconsistencies and ironies at play in Van Dyke's writings; these are faults and sarcasm that the writer took pleasure in exercising. Although scholars know little about his finances, his frequent trips abroad and his long stays in exclusive hotels catering to the wealthy suggest that he was not dependent on sales of his books for income. Yet despite money and hauteur, he was eager for both handsome royalties and widespread public applause. In his letters to Scribners, he urges his editors to place his books in the marketplace, and he expresses his delight when his royalties mount. With a keen eye for numbers, he discovers an error in a financial statement and quickly demands that his publisher send him the extra $1.65 due him. It would seem to be in character for such a person to take perverse pleasure in flattering the book-buying public by addressing it directly in his preface, throwing into the main text enough popular—if sometimes false—science to attract a wide interest, and at the

The Autobiography of

A Personal

Narrative of

American Life

1861–1931

Edited by

Peter Wild

Foreword by

Philip L. Strong

University of Utah Press
Salt Lake City

Two-page title for Van Dyke's last book, which includes some reminiscences judged to be unreliable

same time slyly disguising the true purpose of his book.

A thoughtful reading of the preface reveals Van Dyke's crafty design at work. As the paragraphs evolve, the "you" referring to all the readers of his book changes until it applies to a specific "you" as indicated by clues such as a reference to a mutual friend and phrases such as "When you are in Rome again" which exclude the average American of the day, for whom a trip to Italy would have been prohibitively expensive. This individual "you" is most likely Carnegie, the person to whom the preface is dedicated. Van Dyke's stratagem unfolds fully on the last page of the preface where he makes clear to one catching on to the literary game he has been playing that the book is addressed not to the public but to an exclusive group: to "you, and the nature-loving public you represent." That is surely code language for Van Dyke's coterie, a handful of wealthy Art for Art's Sake sympathizers. Along with Carnegie himself, many of them profited by destroying vast swaths of nature even as they extolled the beauty surrounding their private summer homes. At any rate, in the mind of the elitist Van Dyke they alone possessed intelligence and artistic

sensitivity sufficient to enable them to understand *The Desert* not as a travel guide so much as a treatise on art.

Van Dyke turned out to be correct in his assumption that most readers would miss his real intent. *The Desert* was popular with the public, but for the wrong reasons; a review in *The Dial* stated that the book, as if it were a guide to a tawdry carnival, "should be in the travelling-bag of every transcontinental tourist by Central and Southwestern routes." Van Dyke must have felt vindicated in his low opinion of the public taste.

Although Van Dyke was a diligent scholar in some of his other works, the deception in *The Desert* established the pattern for much of his other western writing. Presenting all such material as nonfictional, he nevertheless used the West as a playground in which he acted out several complex fantasies at once, besides deriding his mass audience. He was well known as a bookish man with envied positions in two prestigious institutions and a frequenter of elaborate if stuffy private New York clubs. Yet in the West of his books he threw himself into the role of the rugged adventurer quick with a gun and living out derring-do myths of the West. Furthermore, since Van Dyke was often too frail to mount the lecture platform, he may also have been making fun of his robust friend Theodore Roosevelt, who even then was warning fellow Americans that they must lead the "strenuous life" lest they lose forever their pioneer drive. Van Dyke also used the western regions for a more serious purpose, as a setting in which the aesthete could wander, spinning prose into arresting descriptions of pure landscapes.

The fact that Van Dyke succeeded with his fanciful ruses, whatever his motives, is a comment both on the convincing quality of his writing and on the gullibility of most of his readers. Down through the decades not one critic emerged to challenge his sometimes obvious chicanery in print. A fairly straightforward example of Van Dyke's trickery is *The Grand Canyon of the Colorado: Recurrent Studies in Impressions and Appearances* (1920). As with *The Desert,* it enjoyed a wide readership and remains in print today. Albeit focused on a particular place, *The Grand Canyon,* like its predecessor, displays a lush descriptive treatment of a desert landscape. As the writer explores the rarely visited labyrinths of the canyon he looks back up at the serrated rim thousands of feet above him and notes that "the blue sky seems to fit in the flutings like an inlay of lapis lazuli." Descriptions of this sort help make the work satisfyingly romantic, given the drama of its setting.

Yet when he writes that taking food and water along is not necessary because "any athlete or Indian will tell you that you can travel better without them," the reader suspects such a comment. In the rocky furnace of the Grand Canyon, which is nearly waterless except for the river at the distant bottom, water is the hiker's constant concern. To advise traveling without it is madness. Van Dyke seems unaware of the difficulties of hiking in the canyon; more of his descriptions of the canyon fit views reached by easy strolls or by driving along the tourist track out from the elegant El Tovar Hotel, where he once stayed, according to the journals of his friend Edward Everett Ayer.

An example with a different approach is Van Dyke's *The Mountain: Renewed Studies in Impressions and Appearances* (1916). In this treatise in the Art for Art's Sake mode on the aesthetics of mountains around the world, Van Dyke journeys to the Alps, the Carpathians, the Caucasus Mountains, and the Rocky Mountains, comparing and contrasting the appeal of their forms and colors. Here, as in several other works such as *Nature for Its Own Sake: First Studies in Natural Appearance* (1898), the many examples drawn from the Rockies show Van Dyke's fascination with the West, where he often visited friends and relatives. A curious feature of *The Mountain,*

however, is "From Afar," its opening chapter, which is more an adventure tale than an integral part of the text. It is Van Dyke's account of accompanying Sioux Indian buffalo hunters across the plains when he was a boy. Of the innumerable buffalo hunts appearing in western literature, Van Dyke's is one of the most dramatic. He catches the frenzy of riders and horses plunging along in the midst of a stampede. In a quieter tone he depicts the Indians alert one evening for enemies, the "half-naked Sioux silhouetted against the blood-red twilight, each one bunched over his pony's shoulder and peering cat-like into the gathering gloom." The only problem is that, as with many of his accounts of western adventure, Van Dyke probably never experienced what he describes. The chapter shows a talented imagination at work, but once more its author is spinning a colorful fantasy.

Throughout his books Van Dyke is wont to burst into self-righteous rage at man's stupidity, especially regarding the folly of abusing the earth on which he depends for survival. In *The Open Spaces: Incidents of Nights and Days under the Blue Sky* (1922) Van Dyke voices his disgust at automobiles spreading trash across the countryside and thus resembling "the plagues of Egypt." For the most part, however, this book about his adventures in the outdoors is his most relaxed and enjoyable. Here, in advancing years, the professor reminisces about hikes in earlier years—most of them, significantly, in the region that kept drawing him back, the West. *The Open Spaces* charms the reader with aesthetic excitements alternating with physical exploits, thus lending a delightful rhythm to the whole book. Camped on the Mexican border, an ever-watchful Van Dyke outsmarts five menacing bandidos and sends them scurrying away. In contrast, pulling himself up a cliff in the Rockies, he pauses, becomes an aesthetician, and admires a "pale-pink flower on a long thin stem" growing from a crack in the rock wall. Turning humorist, he recalls his hard-riding days as a cowboy in Montana and Wyoming, including the time he supposedly cured a cowpoke's attack of appendicitis out on the range with a dose of castor oil. Van Dyke, who years earlier had had his own appendix removed by a surgeon, knew that castor oil is no cure for appendicitis. Once again such details provide clues that these western thrills and amusing diversions are really tall tales. The frontispiece photograph, titled "The Mohave Desert," presents a giant saguaro cactus against the distant background of a stark mesa; but the fact is that there are no saguaros in the Mojave Desert of California. Moreover, the language and events of *The Open Spaces* sometimes echo those found in books by Van Dyke's elder brother Theodore, a bona fide rancher on the Mojave Desert who wrote accurate outdoor accounts and lived the kind of adventures that the visiting eastern professor undoubtedly envied.

In his closing years Van Dyke's health, which was never very good, worsened. But even then, as he sat down to write his *Autobiography* (1993) and thoughts of death ought to have improved his veracity, he continued to present himself in further self-flattering western fictions. He hews generally to the outlines of his life as he reflects on his friendships and his role in the art world, but when he deals with cowboys, Indians, and desert trekking he produces a hodgepodge of contradictions and facts mixed with fancy. For example, he tries to depict himself learning frontier skills from Sioux Indians in Minnesota, in a town that had a library and a high school. He insists that he shot at wolves on the attack in places where wildlife biologists report that there were no wolves, and he claims to have encountered grizzlies where the bears had probably been exterminated years before. When Van Dyke comes to reflecting on adventures leading to *The Desert* he depicts himself riding well armed into the great unfenced unknown; in truth, roads, fences, and railroads were by this time already crisscrossing that recently tamed desert. But perhaps readers should not fault Van Dyke. According to one interpretation all art is a beautiful lie, an escape from the drudgery of daily reality and into an idealized world. People want to dream, and for this reason over the decades Van Dyke's reading public has believed his fictions and fantasies, and relished his lush prose.

It is to Van Dyke's masterpiece, *The Desert,* that critics and other readers return with most delight, particularly in modern times when interest in the desert has reached an almost faddish intensity. Much of the praise, including that of Walker and Powell, is amply deserved. In terms of literary history and cultural change, few volumes rival the impact of *The Desert* on the West and the way the nation now views the region. Before it was published most people despised the vast stretches of sand and cactus as God's mistake in an otherwise bountiful nation. Van Dyke's classic, the first book celebrating the desert for its beauty, unique landforms, strange plants, and delicate lighting effects, seemed to accomplish the impossible. What had been scorned was now looked upon as a national treasure; what had been avoided by most travelers became a mecca for innumerable tourists. Few books have been so pivotal as that. Rightly deserving his place as the father of an entire genre, Van Dyke led the way for Joseph Wood Krutch, Edward Abbey,

and dozens of others in the growing band of desert writers.

The impact of *The Desert* as a work of literature is understandable. Van Dyke wrote with a power placed in the service of subtlety and with sometimes a lush, overwhelming imagery. In his visual feasts Van Dyke captures the dust storms and lizards of the desert and the awe of ancient, abandoned cities that stood for centuries on the neighboring mountaintops. Few Victorians could resist the sweep of his Wagnerian descriptions. In one passage the traveler remembers:

> I have seen at sunset, looking north from Sonora some twenty miles, the whole tower-shaft of Baboquivari change from blue to topaz and from topaz to glowing red in the course of half an hour. I do not mean edgings or rims or spots of these colors upon the peak, but the whole upper half of the mountain completely changed by them. The red color gave the peak the appearance of hot iron, and when it finally died out the dark dull hue that came after was like that of a clouded garnet.

That description of a southwestern sunset illustrates the grip of *The Desert* on readers through the decades—a grip growing firmer in recent times. Ironically, the burgeoning population of the modern Southwest, responsible for turning the desert into freeways and subdivisions, excessively romanticizes the cactus-studded landscape it is destroying. If in the modern age the desert is fast disappearing, the desert lovers of today can at least behold its former glory in the pages of Van Dyke's masterpiece.

Van Dyke was particularly well equipped to write such a book as *The Desert.* Heightening its popularity was the personality behind it. In addition to possessing literary talent, he was unusually sensitive. He simultaneously praised the desert and was pained at thoughts of abuse he saw coming to it. As he rode in the moonlight past the rocky peaks despised by the rest of the nation, the desert became his mistress and he, as he calls himself, her solitary "lover." In his introduction to a recent reprint of *The Desert* the poet Richard Shelton explores Van Dyke's relationship to the arid lands and expresses appreciation of his attitudes. Common enough today, they were unique for a man of a century ago. While traveling across the desert, Van Dyke "was in love, and the book is a by-product of that love affair."

For all of these reasons *The Desert* remains in print after nearly a hundred years, an admirable feat for any book. The problem is that in their romantic rush and in their devotion to their own enthusiasms, critics have lost sight of both the man and his book. In fact, the book was something of a sham, while the man was rather the reverse of a saint. Far from deflating the most popular desert volume about the Southwest, however, such critical conclusions make the man and his book all the more fascinating, for they have revealed a complex author and his aesthetics, and they have allowed modern readers to explore the cultural milieu responsible for producing such a work.

References:

Edward Everett Ayer, "Second Part of Mr. Ayer's Journal for 1918," manuscript in Special Collections, Newberry Library, Chicago;

Zita Ingham and Peter Wild, "The Preface as Illumination: The Curious (If Not Tricky) Case of John C. Van Dyke's *The Desert,*" *Rhetoric Review*, 9 (1991): 328–339;

Roderick Nash, *Wilderness and the American Mind* (New Haven, Conn.: Yale University Press, 1967);

Lawrence Clark Powell, "John C. Van Dyke," in his *Southwest Classics: The Creative Literature of the Arid Lands* (Los Angeles: Ward Ritchie, 1974), pp. 314–328;

Theodore Roosevelt, "The Strenuous Life," in his *The Strenuous Life: Essays and Addresses* (New York: Century, 1900), pp. 1–21;

Richard Shelton, introduction to *The Desert,* by John C. Van Dyke (Salt Lake City: Peregrine Smith, 1980), pp. xi–xxix;

Franklin Walker, *A Literary History of Southern California* (Berkeley: University of California Press, 1950), pp. 115–117, 185–189, 200;

Peter Wild, "Curmudgeon or Campus Ornament? Focusing the Images of John C. Van Dyke, Librarian/Professor," *New Jersey History,* 108, no. 1–2 (1990): 31–45;

Wild, *Interviews and Notes Regarding John C. Van Dyke,* American Academy of Arts and Letters, New York City / University of Arizona Library, sealed until 2009;

Wild, *John C. Van Dyke:* The Desert (Boise, Idaho: Boise State University, 1988);

Wild, "A New Look at Our Foremost Desert Classic," *North Dakota Quarterly*, 63 (Winter 1996): 116–127;

Wild, "Van Dyke's Little Trick: Catching the Wily Esthetician in a Net of Poetry—Some of It (Probably) His Own," *New Mexico Humanities Review,* 32 (1989): 116–128;

Wild and Neil Carmony, "The Trip Not Taken," *Journal of Arizona History,* 34, no. 1 (Spring 1993): 65–80.

Papers:

Most of Van Dyke's personal papers have disappeared, and what exists is scattered. Correspondence and some related material are housed at the Princeton University Library; Columbia University Library, both in the Rare Book and Manuscript Library and in the Avery Architectural and Fine Arts Library; the American Academy of Arts and Letters, New York City; the Archives of American Art at the Smithsonian Institution; one extremely important letter in the Robert H. Forbes Collection at the Arizona Historical Society, Tucson (Box 12, File 11); the Gardner A. Sage Library, New Brunswick Theological Seminary; the Andrew Carnegie Papers, Library of Congress; the John Hay Papers, Brown University Library; the John Ferguson Weir Papers, Yale University Library; and the Charles F. Lummis Manuscript Collection, Braun Research Library, Southwest Museum, Los Angeles.

Owen Wister

(14 July 1860 – 21 July 1938)

Loren D. Estleman

See also the Wister entries in *DLB 9: American Novelists, 1910–1945* and *DLB 78: American Short-Story Writers, 1880–1910.*

BOOKS: *The Lady of the Lake* (Cambridge, Mass.: Chorus Book, 1881);

The New Swiss Family Robinson: A Tale for Children of All Ages (Cambridge, Mass.: Charles W. Sever, University Bookstore, 1882);

The Dragon of Wantley: His Rise, His Voracity, and His Downfall: A Romance (Philadelphia: Lippincott, 1892);

Red Men and White (New York: Harper, 1896; London: Osgood, McIlvaine, 1896);

Lin McLean (New York & London: Harper, 1898);

The Jimmyjohn Boss and Other Stories (New York & London: Harper, 1900);

Ulysses S. Grant (Boston: Small, Maynard, 1900);

The Virginian: A Horseman of the Plains (New York & London: Macmillan, 1902);

Philosophy 4: A Story of Harvard University (New York & London: Macmillan, 1903);

Musk-ox, Bison, Sheep and Goat, by Wister, Caspar Whitney, and George Bird Grinnell (New York & London: Macmillan, 1904);

A Journey in Search of Christmas (New York & London: Harper, 1904);

Lady Baltimore (New York & London: Macmillan, 1906);

How Doth the Spelling Bee (New York & London: Macmillan, 1907);

Mother (New York: Dodd, Mead, 1907);

The Seven Ages of Washington: A Biography (New York: Macmillan, 1907);

Members of the Family (New York & London: Macmillan, 1915);

Padre Ignacio; or, The Song of Temptation (New York & London: Harper, 1911);

The Pentecost of Calamity (New York & London: Macmillan, 1911);

A Straight Deal; or, The Ancient Grudge (New York & London: Macmillan, 1920);

Owen Wister, 1887

Indispensable Information for Infants; or, Easy Entrance to Education (New York: Macmillan, 1921);

Neighbors Henceforth (New York & London: Macmillan, 1922);

Watch Your Thirst: A Dry Opera in Three Acts (New York: Macmillan, 1923);

When West Was West (New York & London: Macmillan, 1928);

Roosevelt: The Story of a Friendship, 1880–1919 (New York: Macmillan, 1930); republished as *Theodore Roosevelt: The Story of a Friendship, 1880–1919* (London: Macmillan, 1930);

Two Appreciations of John Jay Chapman (New York: Privately printed, 1934).

Collection: *The Writings of Owen Wister,* 11 volumes (New York: Macmillan, 1928).

The importance of Owen Wister to the literature of the American West–and, by extension, to the development of American literature in the twentieth century–cannot be overstated. *The Virginian: A Horseman of the Plains* (1902) lifted the frontier story out of the dime-novel category founded by Ned Buntline and Prentiss Ingraham and placed it securely in the mainstream. With *The Virginian* Wister fashioned both a native language and a national voice, characteristics sorely lacking in previous attempts to establish a literary culture independent from that of Europe. Most if not all of the staples associated with the western genre–fast-draw contests, the Arthurian code, and such immortal lines as "This town ain't big enough for both of us" and "When you call me that–smile!"–first appeared in this groundbreaking novel about one man's championship of justice in the wilderness. Wister's interpretation of the West as a place where few of the civilized concepts of social conduct apply separated his stories from the sensational accounts then popular. More significantly, his awareness of the frontier as something unique in the collective human experience helped to propel his country into a global contest of letters then dominated by Emile Zola and Count Leo Tolstoy.

Nothing in his early life heralded Wister as the founder of an entertainment industry that would launch the careers of artists as disparate as Ernest Haycox, William S. Hart, Willa Cather, and John Wayne. Born in Philadelphia on 14 July 1860 to Owen J. Wister, a physician, and Sarah Butler Wister, a socialite, Owen Wister early displayed talents that seemed to destine him for a career in music. He graduated from Harvard with honors in 1882, then studied musical composition in Paris, where he attracted the attention of Franz Liszt and Richard Wagner, but was forced to return to the United States for reasons of health. Several biographers cite a disagreement between Wister's mother, daughter of the flamboyant actress Fanny Kemble, and his father, a stolid professional man of old Pennsylvanian stock, over whether their son belonged in business or the arts for his subsequent nervous collapse.

If the accounts are true, the argument was a fortunate one. During his rest cure Wister made the first of fifteen visits to Wyoming, discovering there an infatuation with the West that would only strengthen with time. This, despite completion of a three-year course in law at Harvard and admittance to the Pennsylvania bar, would direct the course of his life.

According to his own recollections, Wister experienced his epiphany one evening in 1890 while dining in the aggressively eastern institution, the Philadelphia Club, with his friend Walter Furness. Discussing their mutual interest in the West, the pair concluded that while Theodore Roosevelt had written factually about the West and Frederic Remington had captured its essence upon canvas, the frontier remained bereft of a Rudyard Kipling to tell its story before it passed out of existence.

"Walter," exclaimed Wister suddenly, "I'm going to try it myself!" With that, he claimed, he raced upstairs to the club library and composed before midnight the greater portion of "Hank's Woman" (*Harper's Weekly,* 27 August 1892), his first western story.

The anecdote may be apocryphal. Entries in Wister's own journal indicate he had seriously considered basing fictions upon incidents he observed while hunting in Wyoming the previous spring. In any case, "Hank's Woman" was eventually published, along with a second story, "How Lin McLean Went East" (*Harper's New Monthly Magazine,* December 1892); Harper and Brothers paid him $175 for both.

In 1898 Wister married Mary Channing Wister, a distant cousin. By this time his reputation as a chronicler of the West was well established, bringing him celebrity and official approbation upon the one hand and harsh criticism upon the other for the perceived failure of his writing to "uplift" the reader, much as high-profile artists of nearly a century later would be targeted for ignoring the burning political issues of the day. Some disapproval came from close to home. Sarah Butler Wister upbraided her son for the violent theme of "Hank's Woman," a censure that would hound the genre he created for many years after he had ceased to have anything to do with it.

Three story collections and his biography of Ulysses S. Grant made Wister a public figure by his fortieth year. Publication of *The Virginian* brought him international acclaim and the admiration of a new generation of writers who would re-create American literature in their own image, among them Ernest Hemingway, who knew and revered Wister. The latter's minimalist style and objective approach to narrative are found in Hemingway's seminal works.

The timing could not have been better for the appearance of *The Virginian,* Wister's magnum opus. The popularity in Europe of William "Buffalo Bill" Cody's touring Wild West extravaganza had tapped

Wister as a boy (American Heritage Center, University of Wyoming)

into an enthusiastic world market for border-country derring-do. Roosevelt, a longtime Wister associate (owing as much to their shared eastern aristocratic background as to their affection for the West), was in the White House, which provided a broad arena for support of the "strenuous life." And in 1903, the year following the debut of the book, Thomas A. Edison's fledgling motion-picture company filmed a jerky *Great Train Robbery* with rural New Jersey standing in for the prairie, inaugurating a love affair between Hollywood and the rowdy West that would continue into the turn of the next century. These were the peak years of Manifest Destiny, when pride in American achievement had reached a level not to be equaled until the victory over Japan in 1945. The book sold more than fifty thousand copies in two months.

The role played by Roosevelt in Wister's fortunes invites close scrutiny. Himself a prolific and immensely readable writer, the twenty-sixth president admired his friend's facility with fiction, accompanied him on protracted hunting trips through the plains, and called upon him to help deliver the vote in Philadelphia when Roosevelt made an unsuccessful bid for a third term in 1912–thus inventing the celebrity political endorsement. In his turn, Roosevelt escorted Wister from behind his desk into the national limelight, anticipating the marriage of politics, entertainment, and literature associated five decades later with John F. Kennedy's Camelot.

Ironically, at this time Wister's artistic energies began to decline. Much of his work after *The Virginian* was anticlimactic. In 1903 he adapted the book for the Broadway stage; the play received mixed reviews but success at the box office. (It formed the basis of the screenplay for D. W. Griffith's 1914 motion-picture version of *The Virginian,* the first of four cinematic versions of the by-then-familiar tale.) In 1907, inspired by the example of his presidential friend and incensed by the "bossism" he believed had seized control of the city of his birth, Wister competed with a machine candidate for a post on the Philadelphia city council but was defeated by a margin of nearly five to one. Although embittered by the hostile campaign, he continued to involve himself in politics, stumping for Theodore Roosevelt five years later and risking arrest to speak out against Franklin D. Roosevelt's unlawful attempt to seize control of the Supreme Court in 1937. His own earlier failed bid for office had disillusioned him, however. When Woodrow Wilson defeated Theodore Roosevelt in the 1912 presidential election, Wister remarked to his intimates that he was relieved.

Wister wrote little after World War I, producing only one important work, *Roosevelt: The Story of a Friendship, 1880–1919* (1930). In 1911 Wister's death was falsely reported to the press, affording him the unusual opportunity to read his own obituaries and assess his career through the eyes of the world. (Both Mark Twain and Ernest Hemingway had the same experience, as if death and resurrection were prerequisites to assuming the crown of Great American Novelist.)

Wister succumbed in 1938 to a cerebral hemorrhage at his summer home in North Kingston, Rhode Island, at the age of seventy-eight. Although he had lived to see *The Virginian* filmed twice and reprinted numerous times, including a deluxe edition containing an expanded dedication to Theodore Roosevelt and illustrated by both Frederic Remington and Charles Marion Russell, at the time of Wister's death the western genre was judged by pundits to have been exhausted by his many imitators. The following year John Ford's epic motion picture *Stagecoach* premiered to critical acclaim and packed theaters, inspiring hundreds of big-budget Hollywood westerns over the next four decades and also two remakes. John Wayne's laconic Ringo Kid was acknowledged in most circles to have been based upon Wister's Virginian. A television series employing Wister's title and major characters aired on the NBC network from 1962 to 1971, and as late as the mid 1990s the Western Writers of America, a professional organization, honored writers of signifi-

cant contribution to its genre with a lifetime achievement award named for Wister.

The New Swiss Family Robinson: A Tale for Children of All Ages (1882) merits notice specifically because it is Wister's first published book-length work. A satire about life at Harvard based upon Johann Wyss's popular *The Swiss Family Robinson* (1812–1813), it was collected from a series of articles Wister wrote for the *Harvard Lampoon* during his career as an undergraduate. But in spite of a complimentary letter from Twain, it received little critical attention. Like Hemingway's *The Torrents of Spring* (1926) and John Steinbeck's *Cup of Gold* (1936), *The New Swiss Family Robinson* is an atypical effort, a crucible for the removal of impurities left over from the author's adolescence, during which he played Robert Louis Stevenson's "sedulous ape" to writers of established reputation.

The stories collected in *Red Men and White* (1896) mark Wister's emergence as a western storyteller and are altogether more worthy of dissection than either *The New Swiss Family Robinson* or his sophomore publication, *The Dragon of Wantley: His Rise, His Voracity, and His Downfall: A Romance* (1892). Comprising eight tales previously published in *Harper's Weekly,* this anthology of his early frontier fiction continues to belie the oft-repeated canard that the western is racist and Eurocentric in nature. Uniformly the stories present a thoughtful, balanced view of alien cultures in collision.

Typical of this view is "Little Big Horn Medicine," in which the charlatanism of a war-loving young Sioux medicine man and the ignorance and chauvinism of the American government set the stage for tragedy. "A Pilgrim on the Gila" follows the adventures of a representative cross-section of the national "melting pot" stripped by physical hardship to the bones of its native prejudice. The latter story, the theme of which echoes Guy de Maupassant's "Boule-de-suif" (1880), is a more effective western adaptation of the French tale, which is set during the French Revolution, than either Haycox's much later "The Stage to Lordsburg" or the screenplay based upon it by Dudley Nichols for the film *Stagecoach.*

Although in his preface to the 1907 edition of *Lin McLean* (1898) Wister was mildly boastful about having invented a new structure for the novel by stringing together these stories about a young man's adventures out west into a single cohesive narrative, he overlooked a contribution far greater. In his cocky, wanderlustful hero he created an American type that would dominate literature for a century and influence thinking about the national character worldwide. Fictional protagonists from Heming-

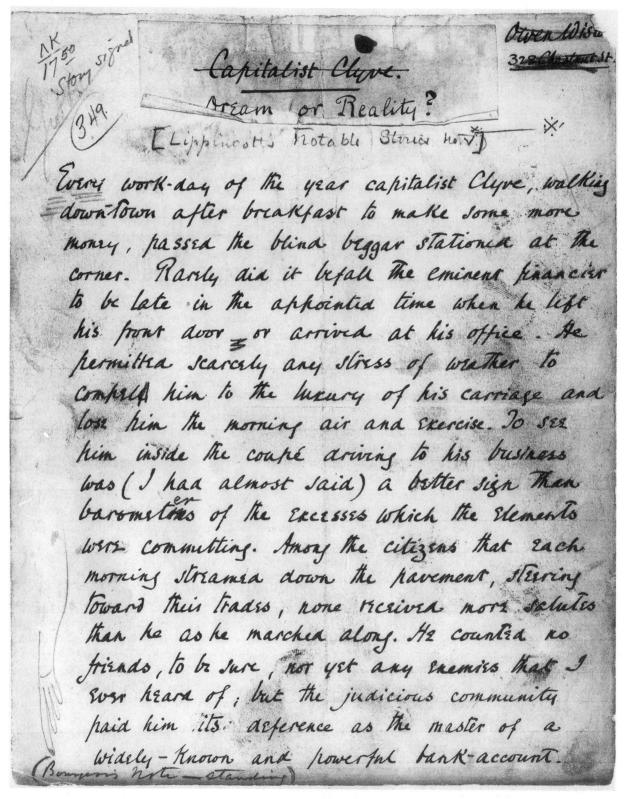

First page from the manuscript for a story that Wister published in the July 1894 issue of Lippincott's Magazine *(Owen Wister Collection [#6327], Clifton Waller Barrett Library, Alderman Library, University of Virginia)*

way's Nick Adams to J. D. Salinger's Holden Caulfield owe much to McLean, and it is difficult to place the popularity of film stars such as Clark Gable, James Dean, and Kevin Costner outside that matrix. Nathaniel Hawthorne's stodgy Puritanism was not capable of such a creation; Herman Melville's Billy Budd would have looked askance at it. The character of McLean had to have come from the frontier, and it could be appreciated only by a canny easterner. McLean's combination of youthful arrogance and schoolboy charm was in its time unique. Today it is inseparable from the American mythology. Seven short years after Wister's death Adolf Hitler's Wehrmacht recognized in their fresh-faced Yankee conquerors a familiar frontier type from American films and fiction dubbed and translated into German. When during the 1980s Soviet premier Leonid Brezhnev denounced President Ronald Reagan's truculence toward the U.S.S.R. as the tactics of a movie cowboy, he was in fact paying tribute to a Wister invention.

Two entries in *The Jimmyjohn Boss and Other Stories* (1900) are of particular interest to students of Wister as he approached his artistic maturity. "Hank's Woman" traces the cultural and religious differences of a miner and his new wife to their tragic outcome in a tough tent camp, and "Padre Ignazio" explores the opposite theme of religion as redemption through the developing friendship between a lonely pastor and a disenchanted drifter. Both stories exhibit an attitude of weary tolerance toward the foibles of an imperfect humanity which, when considered against the backdrop of the Victorian-Edwardian society in which they first appeared, are innovative and startling.

"Hank's Woman" was Wister's first attempt at western fiction. Although he revised it substantially between its initial publication in *Harper's Weekly* and its inclusion in this collection—among other things he interpolated the Virginian, partly to take advantage of the character's popularity—its sense of approaching doom and Wister's use of violence remained unchanged.

Hank, a feisty resident of a mountain mining camp, becomes increasingly disturbed by the Catholicism of his foreign bride, finally to the point of destroying the crucifix in their tent that she worships. Driven to madness by this act and the psychological bullying that leads to it, the woman slays her husband with an axe and, attempting to conceal the murder by pitching his body off a high cliff, falls after it to her death. It is an altogether different exploitation of violence than was commonly found in the dime novels of the period. In those, sanguinary acts were piled one atop another merely for melodra-

matic effect, as demonstrated by this apologia written by Buffalo Bill Cody to his editors:

> I am sorry to lie so outrageously in this yarn. My hero has killed more Indians on one war trail than I have killed in all my life. But I understand this is what is expected of border tales. If you think the revolver and bowie knife are used too freely, you may cut out a fatal shot or stab wherever you think wise.

In Wister's hands the bloody denouement provides the inevitable full stop to the escalating emotional and psychosexual conflict between the principals of the story. Although he was roundly criticized in his own time for his recourse to violence, the acts themselves take place offstage. The dual effect is to distance the narrative from them while increasing their impact, just as Macbeth's murder of King Duncan somewhere in the wings of William Shakespeare's Globe Theater served to make that crime seem even more sordid and harrowing. This technique, employed to similar effect by Flannery O'Connor, William Faulkner, and Shirley Jackson, was to become a Wister hallmark long before any of them used it.

The coda of the story is as important as its climax. Declares Lin McLean: "all this fuss just because a woman believed in God." The Virginian replies: "You have put it down wrong; it's just because a man didn't." As originally published, "Hank's Woman" called for McLean to serve as the conscience of the story, but Wister, sensing the need for a "Greek chorus of an intelligence more subtle," gave these closing words to the Virginian when he revised the story, indicating that he was not just pandering to the public taste by adding a character that had worked itself more thoroughly into the mainstream.

Wister himself was more satisfied with "Padre Ignazio," in which a parish priest exiled to a California mission forsakes at last his homesickness for Europe in the knowledge that he has given comfort to another banished soul. A placid tale, more cerebral than vivid, "Padre Ignazio" was said to have compelled Remington to throw down his brushes in despair of illustrating it. Yet Wister considered it a greater success than "Hank's Woman" for its ability to maintain reader interest through introspection and dialogue rather than through conventional action. As a study in crises of conscience the story belongs less to the genre Wister is credited with having invented than it does to the character-driven school of a later day. His fascination with themes of psychological conflict at a time when Sigmund Freud's theories were unknown to most Americans was rare for its time and was virtually nonexistent in

Wister with his "govt. hoss"

the western fiction of the period. Here and in "Hank's Woman" Wister places behind him the rank sentimentality of his Victorian contemporaries to locate the voice he requires to tell the tale for which he will best be remembered.

The Virginian employs Wister's most effective device, the outsider-narrator observing for the first time a culture as alien to him as it presumably was to most of his readers. Onto its broad stage enter the archetypes that have remained with the genre ever since: the reluctant, laconic hero, admired by his companions, beloved of his woman, and feared by his enemies; the villain as Devil Incarnate; the virginal "schoolmarm," staunchly representative of American womanhood stranded in a wilderness; and the rancher-judge, wisely surveying Odinlike his Valhalla of heroes, sirens, and mischiefmakers. None of the players is a gunman by trade, little blood is shed, and perhaps the most wrenching passage involves a poultry suicide–that of the tragicomic Em'ly. But pioneer that it was, the book established most of the clichés with which Wister's literary heirs are still grappling.

Volumes have been written and academic careers built upon the sweeping changes that took place in the vast arena west of the Mississippi River between 1902 when *The Virginian* appeared and 1907 when it was reissued in a new edition. As the book

went to press Butch Cassidy and the Wild Bunch were still in flight from Pinkerton agents sworn to their death or capture. Jim Younger, released with his brother Cole from a twenty-five-year prison sentence, shot himself to death that autumn in Saint Paul, Minnesota, less than fifty miles from the Northfield bank the botched robbery of which had been his undoing. Wyatt Earp was breeding trotters in California. Tom Horn, Indian scout and "regulator" for the big cattle interests in Wyoming, would hang the following year for the ambush-murder of a sheepman's fourteen-year-old son. Within five years the great ranching combinations would be broken up by federal edict, the open range crisscrossed with barbed wire, and the frontier itself so far removed from the new country that the book, praised initially for its vigorous portrayal of an ongoing phenomenon, was perceived in its new format as a historical novel. Wister's driving fear, that his subject was disappearing behind his scribbling hand, was no chimera.

This was a foreign land indeed, this frontier, though only a week's ride by rail from the home of its anonymous narrator. The abiding philosophy of the frontier–"A man has got to prove himself my equal before I'll consider him one"–as expressed by the Virginian (nameless as well, as if storyteller and storied hero occupy opposite sides of the same coin), vile insults deployed as endearments among close male companions, and in particular Judge Henry's brilliant, rational defense of lynch law in the absence of the statutory kind place Wister's setting on a plane ineffably distant from those modes of behavior referred to as civilized and make it peculiar to the New World.

The market Wister sought required a romantic love interest. Too often this requirement was a liability; because of the ironclad morality of the time much of its popular literature is saccharine and unreadable by today's cynical standards. Wister, however, manipulates the growing attraction between his hero and Molly Wood, the pretty young teacher newly arrived from the East, to hammer home the basic theme of cultures in conflict. This Socratic exchange is an example:

"All men are born equal," he now remarked slowly.

"Yes," she quickly answered, with a combative flash. "Well?"

... "I used to have to learn about the Declaration of Independence. I hated books and truck when I was a kid."

"But you don't any more."

"No. I cert'nly don't. But I used to get kep' in at recess for bein' so dumb. I was 'most always at the tail end of the class. My brother, he'd be head sometimes."

"Little George Taylor is my prize scholar," said Molly.

. . . "Who's last?"

"Poor Bob Carmody. I spend more time on him than on all the rest put together."

"My!" said the Virginian. "Ain't that strange!"

. . . "I don't think I understand you," said Molly, stiffly.

"Well, it is mighty confusin'. George Taylor, he's your best scholar, and poor Bob, he's your worst, and there's lots in the middle–and you tell me we're all born equal!"

Molly could only sit giggling in this trap he had so ingeniously laid for her.

The plot has become standard. Tension among ranchers near Medicine Bow, Wyoming, has been heightened by large-scale cattle rustling, which the Virginian, as the new foreman at Judge Henry's Sunk Creek Ranch, eventually traces to Trampas, one of the cowboys he supervises. Trampas inveigles Shorty, an honest cowhand, into joining the gang. "Trampas has got hold of him," declares the Virginian. The foreman and a posse track down and hang two of the rustlers, one a close friend of the Virginian, but fail to capture Trampas, who has murdered Shorty for his horse. Later, on the eve of the hero's wedding to Molly, the antagonists face off on the main street of Medicine Bow, and the Virginian shoots Trampas down. All of these elements are later lifted and exploited by writers of varying skill (perhaps none so blatantly as when Larry McMurtry appropriates the lynching-of-a-friend scene in his 1985 *Lonesome Dove*), but rarely with Wister's subtlety and restraint: "A wind seemed to blow his sleeve off his arm, and he replied to it, and saw Trampas pitch forward."

Readers accustomed to the Sturm und Drang of the conventional "horse opera" are frequently put off by the seeming aridity of Wister's prose. Despite his own early complaint to his mother, "As for style–what on earth is style? The only thing I know about it is that it's something I haven't got myself," his minimalism was influenced both by his admiration of William Dean Howells, another writer known for his plainness, and by his suspicion of the florid prose of Henry James, whom he was determined not to emulate. More than anything else, this decision to kill Trampas, made in cold blood, is what makes *The Virginian* still readable today–and aggressively still in print–when most of the other novels of the period are gathering dust in their original editions on antiquarians' shelves.

To a great extent, notwithstanding the first appearance of many of the mythic trappings that critics point to as adulterations of history, belief in the West of Wister's works is still prevalent. Events and characters in *The Virginian* are universally recognizable, and Wister's deceptively flat style may be found in the works of non-U.S. writers as diverse as Joseph Conrad and Gabriel Garcia Marquez.

The West that Wister knew, however, like Edith Wharton's New York, had ceased to exist everywhere but in fiction by the close of World War I. While the stories in *Members of the Family* (1915) vibrate with frontier adolescence, the characters in the significantly titled *When West Was West* (1928) are acutely conscious of the changing quality of their surroundings. Emblematic of the theme of *When West Was West* is "At the Sign of the Last Chance," in which the "citizens" of Drybone, once a lusty boomtown but now a weathered husk of boarded-up buildings and streets tangled with tumbleweeds, gather around a poker table to reminisce about the glory days of Drybone. At length, in a ceremonial act of farewell to a vanished way of life, they take down the sign of the Last Chance Hotel and bury it by the side of the creek that gave the town life. Sentimentally in the tale but pragmatically in life, Wister is interring the legend he did so much to create. He never again wrote fiction set in the nineteenth-century American West.

Roosevelt: The Story of a Friendship, written though it was during Wister's decline, is compelling reading even today, which is more than can be said for most of the bloodless biographies produced by the academics of the time. Wister was a storyteller first and a historian second. (Fiction, he once declared, is "the only thing that has always outlasted fact.") Moreover, his is a personal account of a meteoric life, with all the naive enthusiasm of the two men's early association and the disenchantment brought on by Wister's own bitter experience with politics, though restored to proper perspective by time and reflection. As an account of democracy in action, the biography is more seasoned than either *Ulysses S. Grant* (1900) or *The Seven Ages of Washington: A Biography* (1907), both of which Wister had written from the point of view of a political outsider. Many of the passages in *Roosevelt: The Story of a Friendship* apply as well to the post-Watergate, post-Vietnam world as they do to the society of the Square Deal and Prohibition. *Roosevelt: The Story of a Friendship* is among the first of the many sources consulted whenever anyone undertakes to write a new biography of Theodore Roosevelt.

Unlike his numerous imitators–among them the sentimental Zane Grey and heavy-handed Max Brand, tied as they are to their genre by their artistic shortcomings–Wister today occupies a place on the short shelf of American literature between Edith

Wharton and Jack London. His studied view of a native phenomenon from the point of view of an open-minded outsider, his musician's ear and attorney's eye for the authentic and the unusual, and his plain style separate him from the sensationalism of a Buntline and the relentless crowd-pleasing of a Louis L'Amour, while his awareness that the details and the character types he attempted to preserve were vanishing assures him the historical importance of a George Catlin.

As is the case with Stevenson, reverence for Owen Wister has declined from the summit it reached at the time of his death. Historians frown at his use of mythology, and even a recent Wyoming tour guide includes a gentle apology for being forced to cite *The Virginian* among the state's contributions to literature. In many such cases the criticism is inspired less by the book than by the four films and one television series that have been based on it and that failed consistently to capture the philosophy of the book. If the importance of a work is evaluated by the number of people it reaches, *The Virginian* stands among the three or four important books this century has produced. By 1952, fifty years after its first publication, eighteen million copies had been sold, and it had been read by more Americans than any other book. It is included in *Masterplots: Digests of World Literature,* the standard guide in fifteen volumes, alongside Voltaire's *Candide* (1759) and John Milton's *Paradise Lost* (1667). In 1987 the Western Writers of America named Wister to its Hall of Fame, joining James Fenimore Cooper, Edna Ferber, and Mark Twain. "*The Virginian,*" wrote the editors of the ambitious multivolume series on the Old West published by Time-Life Books, "became more than a bestseller. It was the archetype that fixed the myth of the West."

Letters:

Owen Wister Out West: His Journals and Letters, edited by Fanny Kemble Wister (Chicago: University of Chicago Press, 1958).

Bibliographies:

N. Orwin Rush, "Fifty Years of *The Virginian*," *Papers of the Bibliographical Society of America,* 46 (Second Quarter 1952): 99–120;

Dean Sherman, "Owen Wister: An Annotated Bibliography," *Bulletin of Bibliography and Magazine Notes,* 28 (January–March 1971): 7–16;

Sanford F. Marovitz, "Owen Wister: An Annotated Bibliography of Secondary Material," *American Literary Realism 1870–1910,* 7 (Winter 1974): 1–110.

Biographies:

J. Edward White, *The Eastern Establishment and the Western Experience: The West of Frederic Remington, Theodore Roosevelt, and Owen Wister* (New Haven, Conn.: Yale University Press, 1958);

Richard W. Etulain, *Owen Wister* (Boise, Idaho: Boise State College, 1973);

John L. Cobb, *Owen Wister* (Boston: Twayne, 1984);

Darwin Payne, *Owen Wister: Chronicler of the West, Gentleman of the East* (Dallas: Southern Methodist University Press, 1985).

References:

John G. Cawelti, *The Six-Gun Mystique* (Bowling Green, Ohio: Bowling Green University Popular Press, 1970);

Philip Durham and Everett L. Jones, *The Western Story: Fact, Fiction, and Myth* (New York: Harcourt Brace Jovanovich, 1975);

Loren D. Estleman, *The Wister Trace: Classic Novels of the American Frontier* (Ottawa, Ill.: Jameson Books, 1987);

William K. Everson, *A Pictorial History of the Western Film* (Secaucus, N.J.: Citadel Press, 1969);

Paul O'Neil, *The End of the Myth* (Alexandria, Va.: Time-Life Books, 1979);

Henry Blackman Sell and Victor Weybright, *Buffalo Bill and the Wild West* (New York: New American Library of World Literature, 1959);

Keith Wheeler, *The Chroniclers* (Alexandria, Va.: Time-Life Books, 1976);

Will Wright, *Six Guns and Society: A Structural Study of the Western* (Berkeley: University of California Press, 1975).

Papers:

Most of Owen Wister's papers are in the Library of Congress, where his journals, letters, manuscripts, and scrapbooks fill more than a hundred containers. Other papers not in the hands of private collectors are in the libraries of the universities of Virginia and Wyoming, the Houghton Library of Harvard University, the Historical Society of Pennsylvania, the Arizona Pioneers' Historical Society, and the American Academy of Arts and Letters.

Books for Further Reading

Barnett, Louise K. *The Ignoble Savage: American Literary Racism, 1790–1890*. Westport, Conn.: Greenwood Press, 1975.

Betts, Robert B. *In Search of York: The Slave Who Went to the Pacific with Lewis and Clark*. Boulder: Colorado Associated University Press, 1985.

Billington, Ray Allen. *Land of Savagery, Land of Promise: The European Image of the American Frontier in the Nineteenth Century*. New York & London: Norton, 1981.

Bold, Christine. *Selling the Wild West: Popular Western Fiction, 1860 to 1960*. Bloomington: Indiana University Press, 1987.

Bredahl, A. Carl Jr. *New Ground: Western American Narrative and the Literary Canon*. Chapel Hill: University of North Carolina Press, 1989.

Brumble, H. David III. *American Indian Autobiography*. Berkeley: University of California Press, 1988.

Cline, Gloria Griffin. *Exploring the Great Basin*. Norman: University of Oklahoma Press, 1963.

Clough, Wilson O. *The Necessary Earth: Nature and Solitude in American Literature*. Austin: University of Texas Press, 1964.

Davidson, Levett Jay, and Prudence Bostwick, eds. *The Literature of the Rocky Mountain West, 1803–1903*. Caldwell, Idaho: Caxton Printers, 1939.

DeVoto, Bernard. *Across the Wide Missouri*. Boston: Houghton Mifflin, 1947.

DeVoto. *The Year of Decision: 1846*. Boston: Little, Brown, 1943.

Doig, Ivan. *Winter Brothers: A Season at the Edge of America*. New York: Harcourt Brace Jovanovich, 1980.

Durham, Philip, and Everett T. Jones. *The Negro Cowboys*. New York: Dodd, Mead, 1965.

Etulain, Richard W., and N. Jill Howard, eds. *A Bibliographical Guide to the Study of Western American Literature*, second edition. Albuquerque: University of New Mexico Press, 1995.

Fender, Stephen. *Plotting the Golden West: American Literature and the Rhetoric of the California Trail*. Cambridge, U.K.: Cambridge University Press, 1981.

Frink, Maurice, and Casel E. Barthelmess. *Photographs on an Army Mule*. Norman: University of Oklahoma Press, 1965.

Gangewere, Robert J., ed. *The Exploited Eden: Literature on the American Environment*. New York: Harper & Row, 1972.

Goetzmann, William H., and William N. Goetzmann. *The West of the Imagination*. New York: Norton, 1986.

Harvey, Lewis Carter. *"Dear Old Kit": The Historical Christopher Carson with a New Edition of the Carson Memoirs.* Norman: University of Oklahoma Press, 1968.

Jacobs, Elijah L., and Forrest E. Wolverton. *Missouri Writers: A Literary History of Missouri, 1780–1955.* Saint Louis: State Publishing, 1955.

Jones, Howard Mumford. *The Frontier in American Fiction: Four Lectures on the Relationship of Landscape to Literature.* Jerusalem: Magness Press, Hebrew University, 1956.

Kimball, Stanley B. *Historic Sites and Markers along the Mormon and Other Great Western Trails.* Urbana & Chicago: University of Illinois Press, 1988.

Kowalewski, Michael, ed. *Reading the West: New Essays on the Literature of the American West.* Cambridge, U.K.: Cambridge University Press, 1996.

Lamar, Howard R., ed. *The Reader's Encyclopedia of the American West.* New York: Crowell, 1977.

Lee, L. L., and Merrill Lewis. *Women, Women Writers, and the West.* Troy, N.Y.: Whitston, 1979.

Lee, Robert Edson. *From West to East: Studies in the Literature of the American West.* Urbana: University of Illinois Press, 1966.

Lewis, Marvin, ed. *The Mining Frontier: Contemporary Accounts from the American West in the Nineteenth Century.* Norman: University of Oklahoma Press, 1967.

Limerick, Patricia Nelson. *The Legacy of Conquest: The Unbroken Past of the American West.* New York & London: Norton, 1987.

Maguire, James H., ed. *The Literature of Idaho: An Anthology.* Boise: Boise State University, 1986.

Merriam, H. G., ed. *Way Out West: Recollections and Tales.* Norman: University of Oklahoma Press, 1969.

Milner, Clyde A. II, Carol A. O'Connor, and Martha A. Sandweiss, eds. *The Oxford History of the American West.* New York & Oxford: Oxford University Press, 1994.

Milton, John R. *The Novel of the American West.* Lincoln: University of Nebraska Press, 1980.

Mitchell, Lee Clark. *Witness to a Vanishing America: The Nineteenth-Century Response.* Princeton, N.J.: Princeton University Press, 1981.

Morgan, Ted. *A Shovel of Stars: The Making of the American West 1800 to the Present.* New York: Simon & Schuster, 1995.

Nash, Roderick. *Wilderness and the American Mind,* third edition. New Haven, Conn.: Yale University Press, 1982.

Nelson, Herbert B. *The Literary Impulse in Pioneer Oregon.* Corvallis: Oregon State College Press, 1948.

Noble, David W. *The Eternal Adam and the New World Garden: The Central Myth in the American Novel Since 1830.* New York: Braziller, 1968.

O'Connor, Richard. *Iron Wheels and Broken Men: The Railroad Barons and the Plunder of the West.* New York: Putnam, 1973.

Pearce, Roy Harvey. *Savagism and Civilization: A Study of the Indian and the American Mind.* Berkeley: University of California Press, 1968.

Peavy, Linda, and Ursula Smith. *Women in Waiting in the Westward Movement.* Norman & London: University of Oklahoma Press, 1994.

Pike, Zebulon Montgomery. *The Journals of Zebulon Montgomery Pike with Letters and Related Documents,* 2 volumes, edited by Donald Jackson. Norman: University of Oklahoma Press, 1965.

Pilkington, William T. *Imagining Texas: The Literature of the Lone Star State.* Boston: American Press, 1981.

Poulsen, Richard C. *The Landscape of the Mind: Cultural Transformations of the American West.* New York: Lang, 1992.

Powell, Lawrence Clark. *California Classics: The Creative Literature of the Golden State.* Los Angeles: Ward Ritchie Press, 1971.

Reedstrom, E. Lisle. *Scrapbook of the American West.* Caldwell, Idaho: Caxton Printers, 1991.

Savage, William W. Jr. *The Cowboy Hero: His Image in American History & Culture.* Norman: University of Oklahoma Press, 1979.

Slotkin, Richard. *Regeneration through Violence: The Myth of the American Frontier, 1600–1860.* Middleton, Conn.: Wesleyan University Press, 1973.

Smith, Henry Nash. *Virgin Land: The American West as Symbol and Myth.* Cambridge: Harvard University Press, 1950.

Sonnichsen, C. L. *From Hopalong to Hud: Thoughts on Western Fiction.* College Station: Texas A&M University Press, 1978.

Starr, Kevin. *Americans and the California Dream: 1850–1915.* New York: Oxford University Press, 1973.

Stauffer, Helen Winter, and Susan J. Rosowski. *Women and Western American Literature.* Troy, N.Y.: Whitston, 1982.

Stegner, Wallace. *The American West as Living Space.* Ann Arbor: University of Michigan Press, 1987.

Stegner. *Beyond the Hundreth Meridian: John Wesley Powell and the Second Opening of the West.* Boston: Houghton Mifflin, 1954.

Stegner. *The Sound of Mountain Water.* Garden City, N.Y.: Doubleday, 1969.

Steiner, Stan. *The Waning of the West.* New York: St. Martin's Press, 1989.

Stevenson, Elizabeth. *Figures in a Western Landscape: Men and Women of the Northern Rockies.* Baltimore & London: Johns Hopkins University Press, 1994.

Stewart, Frank. *A Natural History of Nature Writing.* Washington, D.C. & Covolo, Cal.: Island Press/Shearwater Books, 1995.

Taylor, J. Golden, Thomas J. Lyon, and others, eds. *A Literary History of the American West.* Fort Worth: Texas Christian University Press, 1987.

Tebbel, John. *Fact and Fiction Problems of the Historical Novelist.* Lansing: Historical Society of Michigan, 1962.

Terrell, John Upton. *Land Grab: The Truth about "The Winning of the West."* New York: Dial, 1972.

Thacker, Robert. *The Great Prairie Fact and the Literary Imagination.* Albuquerque: University of New Mexico Press, 1989.

Van Every, Dale. *The Final Frontier: The American Frontier 1804–1845.* New York: Morrow, 1964.

Walker, Franklin. *A Literary History of Southern California.* Berkeley: University of California Press, 1950.

Walker. *San Francisco's Literary Frontier.* New York: Knopf, 1939.

White, Richard. *"It's Your Misfortune and None of My Own": A History of the American West.* Norman & London: University of Oklahoma Press, 1965.

Wiget, Andrew. *Native American Literature.* Boston: Twayne, 1985.

Woods, Lawrence M. *British Gentlemen in the West: The Era of the Intensely British Cowboy.* New York: Free Press, 1989.

Work, James C., ed. *Prose & Poetry of the American West.* Lincoln & London: University of Nebraska Press, 1990.

Wyatt, David. *The Fall into Eden: Landscape and Imagination in California.* New York: Cambridge University Press, 1986.

Contributors

James M. Aton .... *Southern Utah University*

Donald A. Barclay .... *New Mexico State University*

Lawrence I. Berkove .... *University of Michigan-Dearborn*

Mary Louise Briscoe .... *University of Pittsburgh*

Richard H. Cracroft .... *Brigham Young University*

Charles Duncan .... *Virginia Polytechnic Institute and State University*

Thomas W. Dunlay .... *University of Nebraska–Lincoln*

Loren D. Estleman .... *Whitmore Lake, Michigan*

Robert E. Fleming .... *University of New Mexico*

M. E. Grenander .... *State University of New York*

Walter Grünzweig .... *University of Dortmund*

Hamlin Hill .... *Texas A&M University*

David B. Kesterson .... *University of North Texas*

Wayne R. Kime .... *Fairmont State College*

Benjamin S. Lawson .... *Albany State College*

James H. Maguire .... *Boise State University*

Charlotte S. McClure .... *Georgia State University*

Joseph B. McCullough .... *University of Nevada, Las Vegas*

Joseph R. McElrath Jr. .... *Florida State University*

Joseph R. Millichap .... *Western Kentucky University*

Michael J. Mullin .... *Augustana College*

John D. Nesbitt .... *Eastern Wyoming College*

John P. O'Grady .... *Boise State University*

Abe C. Ravitz .... *California State University, Dominguez Hills*

Andrew Rolle .... *The Huntington Library*

Gary Scharnhorst .... *University of New Mexico*

Christine Hill Smith .... *Longmont, Colorado*

David Teague .... *University of Delaware*

Colleen Marie Tremonte .... *Michigan State University*

John O. West .... *University of Texas at El Paso*

Peter Wild .... *University of Arizona*

David M. Wrobel .... *Widener University*

Cumulative Index

Dictionary of Literary Biography, Volumes 1-186
Dictionary of Literary Biography Yearbook, 1980-1996
Dictionary of Literary Biography Documentary Series, Volumes 1-16

Cumulative Index

DLB before number: *Dictionary of Literary Biography,* Volumes 1-186
Y before number: *Dictionary of Literary Biography Yearbook,* 1980-1996
DS before number: *Dictionary of Literary Biography Documentary Series,* Volumes 1-16

A

B

F

"F. Scott Fitzgerald: St. Paul's Native Son
and Distinguished American Writer":

G

K

Cumulative Index

M

ISBN 0-7876-1682-6

90000